Planning Law and Procedure

Planning Law
and Procedure

Michael Purdue LLB, LLM
Solicitor, Professor of Law, University of Newcastle upon Tyne

Eric Young MA, LLB, Hon MRTPI
Solicitor, Reader in Law, University of Strathclyde

Jeremy Rowan-Robinson MA, LLM
Legal Associate of the RTPI, Solicitor (England and Wales),
Senior Lecturer in Law, University of Aberdeen

Butterworths
London and Edinburgh
1989

United Kingdom	Butterworth & Co (Publishers) Ltd, 88 Kingsway, LONDON WC2B 6AB and 4 Hill Street, EDINBURGH EH2 3JZ
Australia	Butterworths Pty Ltd, SYDNEY, MELBOURNE, BRISBANE, ADELAIDE, PERTH, CANBERRA and HOBART
Canada	BUTTERWORTHS CANADA LTD, TORONTO and VANCOUVER
Ireland	BUTTERWORTH (IRELAND) LTD, DUBLIN
New Zealand	Butterworths of New Zealand Ltd, WELLINGTON and AUCKLAND
Puerto Rico	Equity de Puerto Rico, Inc, HATO REY
Singapore	Malayan Law Journal Pty Ltd, SINGAPORE
USA	Butterworth Legal Publishers, AUSTIN, Texas; BOSTON, Massachusetts; CLEARWATER, Florida (D & S Publishers); ORFORD, New Hampshire (Equity Publishing); ST PAUL, Minnesota; and SEATTLE, Washington

A CIP Catalogue record for this book is availble from the British Library.

ISBN 0 406 10383 6

Based on *Scottish Planning Law and Procedure*
by Eric Young and Jeremy Rowan-Robinson
published in 1985 by William Hodge & Co Ltd, Glasgow
ISBN 0 85279 122 4

Typeset by Latimer Trend & Company Ltd, Plymouth
Printed and bound by Mackays of Chatham

PREFACE

Since the Town and Country Planning Act 1947 was enacted, the law on this important area has increased substantially in size and complexity. The main Act, now the Town and Country Planning Act 1971, has been frequently amended and added to by later Acts, so that it is now grossly in need of consolidation. At the same time there has been a steady stream of subordinate legislation which is of particular importance in this area of law. In the last three years much of the detailed law has been drastically reformed and redrafted. We have seen a new Use Classes Order and a new General Development Order, while new procedures have been laid down for the conduct of appeals. Government advice and policy has been recognised by the courts as having an important status in planning law and the introduction of a new system of Goverment Planning Policy Guides has radically changed the form of this vital material. The courts also play a pivotal role in supervising the decision-making work of the Secretary of State and his planning inspectorate in interpreting and implementing the legislation and in the last five years or so the number of challenges in the courts has drastically increased.

All this makes planning law a formidable subject for the average practitioner to tackle. While there are numerous texts on planning law it is felt that there is a need for a book which is both accessible and comprehensive. These are the objectives of this present book. Its antecedents lie in Eric Young and Jeremy Rowan-Robinson's book *Scottish Planning Law and Procedure* (1985, William Hodge & Co Ltd) which it was felt provided a reasonably straightforward guide through the Scottish law on this subject. Scottish planning law, although based on the same principles, differs considerably as to the detail. This present book, although it follows the structure and incorporates much of the text of the Scottish book, is completey rewritten and revised. We hope that all remaining references to Scottish law and practice are intentional!

The final manuscript was handed over to the publishers in February 1989. Since that date there has been the usual process of statutory amendment and accretion of juditial decisions. We have nevertheless attempted to incorporate the most important of these changes in the text.

Michael Purdue
August 1989

'At 1.00 p.m. Winston Churchill closed his Cabinet folder and lit another cigar. Sir Edward Bridges drew his attention to the fact that there was still one remaining item.

'It was the town and country planning. The determination of those days that we would not go back to the 1930s had inspired Beverage, the Cabinet White Paper on full employment, and also the three basic reports on town and country planning by Uthwatt, Barlow and Scott . . .

'W. S. Morrison had assessed these reports and was presenting his conclusions. Winston was not amused. "Ah, yes", said he "All this stuff about planning and compensation and betterment. Broad vistas and all that. But give to me the eighteenth century alley, where foot-pads lurk, and the harlot plies her trade, and none of this new-fangled planning doctrine."'

—Harold Wilson, *The Governance of Britain* (Weidenfield and Nicolson, 1976)

CONTENTS

TABLE OF STATUTES

References in this Table to *Statutes* are to Halsbury's Statutes of England (Fourth Edition) showing the volume and page at which the annotated text of the Act may be found.

CHRONOLOGICAL TABLE OF STATUTORY INSTRUMENTS

TABLE OF CASES

PAGE

E

PAGE

CHAPTER 1

INTRODUCTION

Planning and its objectives

No explicit statements as to the general objectives which town and country planning should serve are to be found in the planning legislation. The absence of any explicit statement of objectives has inevitably resulted in a good deal of litigation over the years concerning the proper scope of planning. The courts have tended to determine such questions on the basis of the particular circumstances of each case; for the most part they have avoided specific statements about the scope of planning and have contented themselves with generalisations. '[A] planning purpose', said Lord Scarman in *Westminster City Council v Great Portland Estates plc*[1] 'is one which relates to the character of the use of land'; and in *Stringer v Minister of Housing and Local Government*,[2] Cooke J observed that 'any consideration which relates to the use and development of land is capable of being a planning consideration'.

The range of purposes for which statutory planning powers can be employed is, therefore, very wide. Presenting perhaps a somewhat idealised picture, Cherry states[3] that town planning has

'come to represent a means of public control over the development of towns, cities, their hinterlands and regions, and the adaptations of these to the changing conditions of modern life. Negatively it is concerned with the control of abuse and the regulation of those things considered harmful to the community; positively it represents social, economic and environmental policy to achieve certain aims unattainable through the unfettered operation of the private sector. It deals with the problems of urbanisation, not only remedying malfunction, but also creating the conditions for harmonious living ... It deals with the allocation of land for stated purposes; it seeks to relate economic policy to the physical structuring of cities and it aims to enhance living conditions for the community as a whole.'

The role of planning and the range of purposes it ought to serve are, however, matters of almost continual debate. As planning is concerned with means rather than ends this is, perhaps, not surprising. It must, inevitably, change with the times. As Cherry says:[4] 'The activity of town planning, mediated through political processes and operated through a variety of

---

1 [1985] AC 661, [1984] 3 WLR 1035, sub nom *Great Portland Estates plc v Westminster City Council* [1984] 3 All ER 744.
2 [1971] 1 All ER 65, [1970] 1 WLR 1281.
3 Gordon E Cherry, *The Politics of Town Planning* (Longman, 1982).
4 *The Politics of Town Planning.*

institutional arrangements, responds and adapts to different expressions of political values and social preferences which change over time.' By its very nature, therefore, town and country planning cannot stand still; it has to adapt to changing circumstances and its scope has changed very considerably over the years. Planning must, in the words of the Uthwatt Committee,[5] 'advance with the condition of the society which it is designed to serve'.

Though there are probably many who would wish to see planning confined to what has been described as its 'mechanistic land allocation function',[6] there are others who see planning (or at least did so when confidence in planning's role was perhaps higher than it now is) as 'the key discipline in the integrated science of urban governance'[7] and the planner as 'the helmsman steering the city'.[8] In recent times the role, objectives, methods, performance and institutional framework of town and country planning have all come under attack from within and without the planning profession.

In 1986 a report of a committee of inquiry appointed by the Nuffield Foundation into Town and Country Planning remarked that

'The immediate post war consensus on planning objectives—the consensus on which the planning system was founded—has largely disappeared. National objectives have swung to and fro with changes in government, giving varied emphasis to the part to be played in development by the public and private sectors, but with perhaps only one major shift, the return to a free market in land. Policies have changed also in response to changing circumstances and new perceptions. The pace of development, of housing, roads and public infrastructure generally, has also been varied from time to time as a means of regulating the economy.'[9]

Indeed allegations of planning's shortcomings have been many and have been made from very different viewpoints; town planning has, for example, been criticised for its ineffectiveness and the slowness of its procedures, for its failure to seek redistributive goals or social change and its 'predominantly upper class and paternalistic ideology',[10] for the weakness of the development planning system, for the limited provision made for public involvement in the process and for the inadequacies of the public inquiry system. Denman goes as far as to suggest that 'land use planning in the UK has become a process without a purpose'.[11]

The Nuffield Report valiantly tried to set out what the purposes of planning should be and came up with the following list:[12]

1. to monitor and control the input on the environment of present and future uses of land;
2. to anticipate and prevent the perpetration of nuisances;

---

5 *Final Report of the Expert Committee on Compensation and Betterment* (Cmd 6386, 1942).
6 J P W B McAuslan, 'The Plan, the Planners and the Lawyers' [1971] *Public Law* 247.
7 See Patrick McAuslan, *Land, Law and Planning* (Weidenfeld & Nicolson, 1975), p 40.
8 See J B McLoughlin, *Urban and Regional Planning: A Systems Approach* (Faber, 1969).
9 See para 1.71.
10 See J F Simmie, 'Physical Planning and Social Policy' 1971 Jo RTPI 450. See too D L Foley, 'British Town Planning: One Ideology or Three?' (1960) 11 *British Journal of Sociology* 211.
11 D Denman, *Land in a Free Society* (Centre for Policy Studies, 1980).
12 See p 144 of the report.

3. to provide a coherent and consistent framework for the operation of the land market in property and development land;
4. to reconcile conflicting demands for land as they arise from the development plans of private and public agencies;
5. to assist in the promotion of whatever developments public and private are considered desirable by the relevant public authority;
6. to provide the information necessary for the effective discharge of these functions.

These are moderate and sensible objectives but in a sense they only mask the inevitable arguments over the degree and extent of public intervention in the development process. Planning objectives must inevitably reflect political values.

Planning law and procedures

Concerned as it is with regulating relationships between private property and public powers, and because of the significant effects it can have on the property and lives of large numbers of people, the law relating to town and country planning is, as Sir Desmond Heap said in 1948,[13] 'invested with a general importance quite beyond that normally accorded to a specialised subject'.

Though the directions taken by town and country planning may alter in response to different political pressures at different times, planning objectives (whatever they may be at any particular time) cannot generally be achieved without legislation. As society's demands and expectations have risen, so, since town planning first made its appearance on the statute book in 1909, has the volume of legislation on the subject increased very considerably. Over the last forty years in particular, fresh and amending legislation has been a frequent occurrence. To the great mass of primary legislation there must be added a large number of orders, regulations and directions, many of them of considerable practical importance. As Professor J Bennett Miller aptly observed, 'almost any point connected with planning seems inexorably doomed to be drowned in verbiage'.[14]

In addition, account must be taken of the very important contribution which the courts have made to planning law. As Wade has pointed out:[15] 'Of all the administrative controls and services which multiply in the modern state, the one which generates most litigation in the courts is town and country planning.' The great body of case law which has been built upon the statutory foundations of planning is indicative not only of the practical importance of town planning but also of the many difficulties to which the legislation can give rise. The questions with which the courts have had to deal in this field are among the most difficult in the field of judicial review of administrative action. In ensuring that statutory duties and procedures are observed and that the many discretionary powers conferred by the planning legislation are exercised within certain limits, the courts play an important role in shaping the way in which the planning system operates. There are,

---

13 Preface to *An Outline of Planning Law* (Sweet and Maxwell, 1st edition, 1949).
14 (1969) 14 JLSS 146.
15 H W R Wade. *Administrative Law* (Clarendon Press, 6th edition, 1988). p 178.

however, important limitations on judicial control; it is necessarily unsystematic and sporadic and is essentially negative in nature in that it is primarily concerned with the detection and correction of error rather than with the effectiveness or adequacy of the planning process.

A substantial body of principle has also been established through decisions of the ministers and inspectors on appeals raising matters of planning law and procedure. We have therefore felt it appropriate to make reference in the text to appeal decisions dealing with questions which have not yet come before the courts. The views on law and procedure expressed in such decisions are not, of course, authoritative but it can be useful, particularly to those considering appeal to the Secretary of State, to know what departmental views have been expressed on a particular point. Further, the general pattern of the law's development in several of the areas dealt with in this book has, in Grant's words,[16] 'been one of ministerial initiative, followed by judicial confirmation or occasional check or reformulation'.

The legislation and judicial decisions which go to make up the body of planning law have been subjected to a number of criticisms. At a 'technical' level the legislation has been criticised as over-complex and as an unsatisfactory amalgam of very general principles and minute detail, poorly integrated and lacking any overall coherence.[17] Grant points out[18] that comprehending and interpreting the law is a difficult enough task for the professional let alone the layman; the paradox is, as he also says, 'that this is an administrative system which is perhaps more than any other reliant on general public support, yet which in an era of public participation evinces every sign of slipping farther and farther away from popular intelligibility.' To somewhat similar effect, Sir Desmond Heap suggested in the Hamlyn Lectures delivered in 1975[19] that the quantity and complexity of planning law were putting in issue the credibility and acceptability of planning control. Though the courts might be accused of contributing to the technicality of planning law, judges too have commented critically on the degree of complexity into which the law has now come.[20]

Procedures relating to both development planning and development control have frequently been criticised as unnecessarily time-consuming with the result that investment is held up and the local, regional or national economy is damaged. In what has so far amounted to a change in emphasis rather than a radical change of direction or philosophy, government has in recent years sought in a number of ways to make planning procedures less time-consuming. Development planning procedures have, for example, been streamlined and efforts have been made to speed up the making of decisions on applications for planning permission and on planning appeals. Certain minor types of development have been removed from the ambit of planning control altogether.

---

16 Malcolm Grant, *Urban Planning Law* (Sweet and Maxwell, 1982), p 152.
17 See, for example, Malcolm Grant, *Urban Planning Law*, p 36.
18 Ibid.
19 *The Land and the Development; or the Turmoil and the Torment* (Stevens, 1975).
20 See, for example, *Britt v Buckinghamshire County Council* [1964] 1QB 77, [1963] 2 All ER 175, 14 P & CR 318; *Brooks and Burton Ltd v Secretary of State for the Environment* [1978] 1 All ER 733, [1977] 1 WLR 1294, and *Ferris v Secretary of State for the Environment* (1988) 57 P & CR 127, [1988] JPL 777.

At the same time central government's distrust of the nature and efficiency of local government has been reflected in a flow of planning powers away from local planning authorities. Urban Development Corporations have been created as the favoured institutions to regenerate the inner urban areas and there has generally been more Central Government intervention.

The present government have also shown an interest in reducing the discretionary element in the planning process and moving towards what might be described as a zoning system for some areas, a system which combines greater certainty for developers with reduced procedural controls. They have introduced enterprise zones in a number of areas of physical and economic decline; the order made by the Secretary of State designating such an area, *inter alia*, grants planning permission for a particular development or development of any class specified. There has also been introduced the mechanism of simplified planning zones—defined areas in which local planning authorities are able to give general planning permission for specified categories of development. It is too early to say whether these initiatives will result in something more than a change in emphasis in the operation of the planning process.

However, so long as the community appears to wish the planning system to control as much as it now does, it is doubtful whether the complexities of the system and the time taken to reach decisions can be materially reduced. The form of many of the present procedures is dictated in large measure by a desire to ensure that individual rights and interests are protected, that those responsible for decision-making have all relevant information before them and that the activities of various bodies are satisfactorily coordinated. Abrogation of such safeguards would speed up the system but probably would not command general support and might well have an adverse effect on the quality of decisions. And at the same time as government has sought to meet criticisms relating to the over-detailed nature of some planning controls and the slowness of decision-making, it has also been faced with arguments that the system is not effective in protecting the environment and that inadequate provision is made for involving groups and individuals in planning. Legislative action has been taken to meet some such criticisms; new controls designed to safeguard the environment have been introduced—for example, in relation to mineral operations—and the United Kingdom's membership of the European Community has resulted in a new system of environmental statements for large projects.

The vision commonly presented by the courts and by many lawyers is that the law provides an apolitical, neutral framework for the exercise of power and is not itself 'biased' in any way for or against a particular philosophy or ideology. That view has not gone unchallenged. It has been argued that the planning legislation and the courts' interpretation of that legislation embody beliefs and value judgments about power and society and that the values permeating the law have in practice contributed to the current disarray of planning and have had an adverse effect on attempts to find solutions to planning problems.[1]

1 See, in particular, J P W B McAuslan, 'Planning Law's Contribution to the Problems of an Urban Society' (1974) 37 MLR 134. See too McAuslan, 'The Plan, the Planners and the Lawyers' [1971] *Public Law* 247.

The scope of this book

While this book does no more than mention those historical, administrative and political aspects of town and country planning which appear necessary to an understanding of the law, and contains little by way of criticism of the law or its ideological basis, this is not because we considered such matters unimportant or because we think that they should not concern lawyers. Such issues are, however, very well dealt with in other works[2] and we considered that there was a need for a book which sought to provide a reasonably straightforward but comprehensive account of planning law and procedure. The book is concerned with what might be described as 'mainstream' planning law—primarily the law contained in the Town and Country Planning Acts, tne subordinate legislation made under those Acts and the relevant judicial and ministerial decisions. It does not deal with other legislation affecting land use. There is a considerable volume of such other legislation and to deal with it in adequate fashion would require substantial enlargement of an already large and complex text. We do not, for example, discuss the legislation dealing with nature conservation and the promotion of access to the countryside contained in the National Parks and Access to the Countryside Act 1949, the Countryside Act of 1968 and the Wildlife and Countryside Act 1981. Furthermore, there are numerous discrete codes of legislation concerned with the regulation of certain special land uses which are beyond the scope of this book. These include, for example, the Caravan Sites and Control of Development Act 1960 and the Ancient Monuments and Archaeological Areas Act 1979.

Even within the parameters of 'mainstream' planning this book does not deal in equal detail with all aspects of planning law and procedure; it concentrates on those matters which we think to be of practical significance and, in particular, on those areas of the law where litigation has shown that difficulties are liable to arise.

Planning legislation before 1947[3]

By way of an introduction to the present system of planning law and procedure we provide a brief summary of the way in which planning legislation has evolved over the years.

The last century saw the implementation of a series of Health and Housing Acts to deal with the insanitary and congested conditions in the main towns and cities, but it was not until this century that, influenced by the ideas of Ebenezer Howard and others, powers were given to local authorities to control the development of towns and districts in their jurisdiction.

Under the powers conferred by the Housing, Town Planning, & c. Act

---

2 Books which deal with planning law in its political, administrative or ideological context include Patrick McAuslan, *Land, Law and Planning*; N A Roberts, *The Reform of Planning Law* (Macmillan, 1976); Patrick McAuslan, *The Ideologies of Planning Law* (Pergamon Press, 1980); and Malcolm Grant, *Urban Planning Law*.

3 On the history of the planning legislation, see G E Cherry, *The Evolution of British Town Planning* (Leonard Hill Brooks, 1974); J B Cullingworth, *Peacetime History of Environmental Planning, Vols I–IV* (HMSO, 1978–1980); and J A G Griffith, 'The Law of Property (Land)', in M Ginsberg (ed), *Law and Opinion in England in the 20th Century* (Stevens, 1959).

1909[4] local authorities might make town planning schemes for defined areas which were in course of development or which appeared likely to be used for building purposes. The Town and Country Planning Act 1932 extended the scope for planning action by enabling local authorities to make planning schemes for almost any land.

The powers of local authorities under the planning legislation enacted prior to the Second World War were, however, hedged about with such restrictions that it proved extremely difficult, even for those authorities who wished to exercise their planning powers, to take any effective planning action. Planning schemes were only a partial control over development, they were very inflexible and the prospect of having to pay heavy compensation to those who sustained loss in consequence of the making of a planning scheme deterred many authorities from taking action under the legislation.

In the 1930s major land use problems began to emerge. It was clear that the existing planning machinery was quite incapable of dealing satisfactorily with those problems or with the further town planning problems brought about by the Second World War. In the words of Sir Desmond Heap: 'New thinking was called for and the hour produced the thinking';[5] in particular the great trilogy of reports—those of the Barlow Commission[6] and the Scott[7] and Uthwatt[8] Committees.[9] Taken together these reports recommended:

'that planning control should cover the whole country, that there should be a national policy for industrial location and population distribution; also that there should be a central planning authority concerned with: urban redevelopment; reduction of congestion; achieving industrial "balance" within and between regions; examining the potential of garden suburbs, satellite towns and trading estates; research and information about industry, resources and amenities; correlation of local planning schemes in the national interest.'[10]

The legislation which followed, and which sought to give effect to the recommendations contained in these reports, culminated in the Town and Country Planning Act 1947 which repealed most of the earlier planning legislation.

The 1947 Act and after

The town and country planning legislation of 1947 has been described as a 'daring experiment in social control of the environment'.[11] The coming into operation of the 1947 legislation on 1st July 1948 resulted in what Sir Desmond Heap aptly calls 'a brand new beginning in the matter of control over land and its development',[12] as he says: 'Nothing associated with the

4 The 1909 Act was amended by the Housing, Town Planning, & c. Act 1919 and the provisions of both Acts were, with some minor amendments, consolidated in the Town Planning Act 1925.
5 *The Land and the Development; or the Turmoil and the Torment.*
6 *Report of the Royal Commission on the Distribution of the Industrial Population* (Cmd 6153, 1940).
7 *Report of the Committee on Land Utilisation in Rural Areas* (Cmd 6378, 1942).
8 *Interim and Final Reports of the Expert Committee on Compensation and Betterment* (Cmd 6291, 1941; and Cmd 6386, 1942).
9 See too the White Paper, *Control of Land Use* (Cmd 6537, 1944).
10 J B McLoughlin, *Control and Urban Planning* (Faber, 1973).
11 Charles Haar, *Land-Use Planning in a Free Society* (Harvard University Press, 1951).
12 *The Land and the Development; or the Turmoil and the Torment.*

land was ever to be the same again.' It should perhaps be said, however, that although the legislation of 1947 can properly be regarded as the starting point of modern land use planning in Britain, certain of the procedures to be found in the Town and Country Planning Act 1947 (and in the legislation currently in force) may be seen as logical extensions of procedures originally introduced by earlier legislation.[13]

Although still based to a considerable extent on the foundations laid by the Town and Country Planning Act 1947—in particular, the concept of development control within the framework of a development plan is still central to the town planning system—planning legislation has been subject to almost constant amendment in the years since 1947. Some of the recent legislative changes have been mentioned above and the changes of direction which have taken place over the years in the law on compensation and betterment are outlined below. Other important changes made in recent times include the introduction of a new type of development plan, provision for increased public involvement in the making of development plans and in the exercise by local planning authorities of development control powers, the devolution to inquiry inspectors of powers previously exercised by the Secretary of State, the strengthening of controls over buildings of special architectural or historic interest, amendments intended to increase the effectiveness of that part of the legislation concerned with controlling breaches of planning control, and the introduction of fees for planning applications. Thus, although almost all of the legislation on town and country planning was consolidated in the Town and Country Planning Act 1971 that Act has been the subject of numerous amendments.[14]

This process will not stop. A new consolidation Act is long overdue and, more importantly, in 1989, a White Paper was issued on 'The Future of Development Plans' which argued for abolition of structure plans and a general streamlining of the procedures. Legislation is soon expected.

Planning and land values

Mention was made in the previous section of the legislative changes over the years in the law on compensation and betterment. Any summary of the evolution of town and country planning would be incomplete without some mention of the development of the law on compensation and betterment with which it is inter-connected.

The exercise of planning powers can have a very great effect on the open-market value of particular parcels of land. This inevitably raises questions as to how such increases and decreases in land values should be apportioned between the community and individual landowners. For example, ought the community to compensate the owner who is refused planning permission and who is therefore unable to carry out development and cannot realise the

13 The present statutory provisions on planning permission can, for example, be seen to have developed out of the provisions relating to interim development permission introduced by the 1919 Act and extended by the 1932 Act and by the Town and Country Planning (Interim Development) Act 1943.

14 See, in particular, the Land Compensation Act 1973, the Town and Country Amenities Act 1974, the Town and Country Planning (Amendment) Act 1977, the Local Government, Planning and Land Act 1980, the Town and Country Planning (Minerals) Act 1981, the Local Government and Planning (Amendment) Act 1981, the Local Government (Miscellaneous Provisions) Act 1982, the Town and Country Planning Act 1984, the Town and Country Planning (Amendment) Act 1985, and the Housing and Planning Act 1986.

development value of his land? When development value is released by a grant of planning permission, ought the community to take some share in the increased value which the community itself has helped to create?

The attempt which was made by the Acts of 1909 and 1932 to deal with these problems was markedly unsuccessful. Under those Acts local authorities were required to pay compensation to landowners who suffered loss as a result of a planning scheme, but in the words of the White Paper *Land*,[15] 'provisions designed to enable these authorities to receive a share of "betterment"—the increases in value which accrued to landowners from public expenditure and planning control—were largely ineffective.' The result was, as the White Paper said, that 'effective planning was financially impossible'.

The Expert Committee on Compensation and Betterment (the Uthwatt Committee), which reported in 1942,[16] concluded that any attempt to deal with gains and losses of development value as they arose was doomed to failure and that the financial problems inseparable from planning action could only be solved by thoroughgoing reform of the system. Though the planning legislation of 1947 did not implement the detailed recommendations of the Uthwatt Committee, it drew heavily on the Committee's work and attempted to provide a comprehensive solution to the related problems of planning, compensation and betterment. The 1947 Act attempted, in effect, to transfer to the state the development value in all land. This the Act sought to achieve by providing:

(a) that if planning permission was granted for the development of land, a development charge (equal in amount to the increase in the value of the land arising from the grant of permission) was to be paid;
(b) that where planning permission was refused or was granted subject to conditions, compensation would not normally be paid; and
(c) that where land was acquired compulsorily, compensation was to be restricted to 'existing use' value.

Owners of land were to be compensated on a 'once and for all' basis for lost development value.

This complex scheme for the control of land values was designed not only to provide an equitable means of recouping betterment but also to enable planning authorities to exercise their increased planning powers on the basis of the suitability of land for a particular purpose irrespective of the value which the land might have been able to command in a free market. In particular, since land was to be available to planning authorities at existing use value rather than market value, authorities would, it was thought, be better able to make use of the powers conferred upon them by the 1947 Act[17] to take positive action to secure the implementation of their plans.

Whether or not the financial scheme of the 1947 Act could ever have worked satisfactorily is still a matter of dispute but following a change of government in 1951 the scheme was largely dismantled. The effects of the Town and Country Planning Act 1953 and the Town and Country Planning

15 Cmnd 5730, 1974.
16 See Cmd 6386.
17 Under the 1947 Act local planning authorities were given very wide powers of compulsory acquisition.

Act 1954 were to abolish the development charge and thus to restore to landowners the development value in land, and to make very limited provision for the payment of compensation to landowners who suffer loss as a result of adverse planning decisions.[18] Under the Town and Country Planning Act 1959 there was a return to market value as the basis of compensation for land acquired by public bodies.

A second attempt by a Labour government to deal with the problems of land values and positive planning was made in 1967 with the establishment of the Land Commission, a body charged with the twin functions of collecting betterment levy and acquiring land required for the implementation of national, regional and local plans. The Land Commission Act 1967 was repealed following a change of government in 1970 and development gains were left to be dealt with under the general taxation system. There was, however, continuing public concern about high land prices and the large unearned profits being made from land, and in 1973 the Chancellor of the Exchequer announced that the (Conservative) government intended to introduce a new tax on development gains. These proposals were adopted by the Labour government which took office in 1974 and were enacted in the Finance Act 1974.

This rare example of a bi-partisan approach proved short-lived. The White Paper *Land*, published in September 1974, made clear that the Labour government was not merely concerned with recouping betterment but also wished to place in the hands of the community greatly increased power 'to plan positively, to decide where and when particular developments should take place'. The White Paper declared that 'the key to positive planning, and to a successful attack on betterment problems', was acquisition by the community of development land 'at the value of its current use rather than at a value based on speculation as to its possible development'. At the heart, therefore, of the Community Land Act 1975, which implemented most of the White Paper's proposals, were provisions designed (a) to ensure that major development took place only on land which was either in, or had passed through, public ownership and (b) to ensure that the price paid by a public authority for land they purchased did not exceed the land's current use value. That position was, however, to be reached by stages, and before the community land scheme came into full effect the 1975 Act was repealed[19] by a conservative government.

Complementing the community land scheme were provisions contained in the Development Land Tax Act 1976 for a new tax payable on the development value of land realised on disposal of the land or on the commencement of a project of material development. This Act was repealed by the Finance Act 1985 and development gains are now only subject to the standard fiscal measures of income tax, capital gains tax or corporation tax.

The present law

The remainder of this introduction is given over to an outline of the main features of planning law as dealt with in this book.

---

18 See chapters 13 and 14.
19 See the Local Government, Planning and Land Act 1980 and the Community Land Act 1975 (Appointed Day for Repeal) Order 1983.

The administrative framework. Chapter 2 contains a brief discussion of the public authorities involved in town and country planning (primarily the Secretary of State for the Environment and the county and district planning authorities), the allocation of functions between those authorities and aspects of the internal functioning of such authorities. The administration of town and country planning is largely a matter for the appropriate local authorities. However, the duties imposed upon those authorities and their wide discretionary powers are subject to a number of administrative checks; in particular, the Secretary of State possesses important supervisory powers over the activities of local planning authorities and there is a right of appeal to him against local planning authorities' development control decisions. Allegations of maladministration can, in appropriate circumstances, be made to the Parliamentary Commissioner for Administration or to the Commissioners for Local Administration.

National planning policy. There is no obligation upon the Secretary of State to prepare national policy statements on town and country planning. Nonetheless, policy 'guidance' is widely employed by the minister to secure the implementation of national objectives, to ensure some consistency and co-ordination in planning policy and practice and to assist those concerned with the development of land. In chapter 3 we consider the main sources of national policy: legislation, both primary and delegated, planning guidelines and circulars.

Local planning policies. The most formal source of planning policy is the development plan. Under the 1947 Act each local planning authority was under a duty to prepare and submit for the approval of the Secretary of State a development plan setting out the authority's main planning proposals. Development plans drawn up under the 1947 Act have now been superseded by development plans of a very different type. Under the new system broad planning strategy is dealt with in structure plans, while detailed planning policies are set out in local plans. Structure plans require the approval of the Secretary of State but local plans do not normally require ministerial approval. Under the new system members of the public have an opportunity to put forward their views at an early stage in the preparation of both structure and local plans.

In the case of the Greater London Area and metropolitan areas the abolition of the Greater London Council and metropolitan counties in 1985 has brought with it the emergence of another new type of plan, the unitary plan, this is an amalgam of the structure plan and the local plan and is in two parts.

The development plan is intended to provide the policy framework within which local planning authorities consider the exercise of their planning powers. The plan also serves as a guide to landowners, developers and members of the public as to local planning authorities' main policies and proposals for the future use and development of land in their areas. The making and approval of structure, local plans, and unitary plans and the effect of non-statutory policies are considered in chapter 4.

Control of development. Although many modifications have been made by subsequent legislation, the basic framework for the control of development established by the 1947 Act remains largely intact.

Central to development control are statutory provisions defining 'development' and laying down that the carrying out of development will normally require planning permission. 'Development' means the carrying out of building, engineering, mining or other operations, or the making of any material change in the use of land. The meaning of 'development' and the large body of case law that has accumulated around the statutory definition are considered in chapter 5.

If particular proposals fall within the statutory definition of development then, subject to certain exceptions (outlined in chapter 6), planning permission will be required. Planning permission may be granted by a development order made by the Secretary of State; under the general development order currently in force planning permission is automatically granted for a fairly wide range of developments (see chapter 6). In most other cases in which planning permission is required application must be made to the appropriate local planning authority. The need to consider each individual application on its own merits gives the development control system a good deal of flexibility.

The procedures relating to the making of applications for planning permission and related types of application are considered in chapter 7. That chapter also deals with the powers of the Secretary of State to 'call in' planning applications and outlines the matters to be taken into account by a planning authority in determining an application. Of particular importance among the matters to which regard must be had in the determination of an application are the provisions of the development plan and 'any other material considerations'; the law on these matters is considered in chapter 8. Local planning authorities are empowered to grant planning permission subject to 'such conditions as they think fit'; this is a wide power but it is not unlimited and the limits which the courts have placed on the discretion of local planning authorities are considered in chapter 9. Aspects of the law relating to local planning authorities' decisions on applications, including the right of an aggrieved applicant to appeal to the Secretary of State, the effect of planning permission, interpretation of planning permissions and the time limits upon planning permissions are considered, together with other statutory provisions concerned with development control, in chapter 10.

Planning agreements. Local planning authorities are empowered by s 52 of the 1971 Act to enter into agreements with persons having an interest in land for the purpose of restricting or regulating the development or use of the land. Such agreements can in some circumstances offer advantages to both parties and the use being made of s 52 agreements is increasing. Difficult questions arise, however, over the interpretation of s 52. The principal difficulties are considered in chapter 11.

Enforcement of planning control. An essential element in the control of development is the power to take action in respect of unauthorised development—whether carried out without the grant of permission required by the legislation or carried out in breach of a condition attached to a grant of planning permission. Despite a number of legislative changes designed to overcome some of the perceived weaknesses in the enforcement machinery, the law on enforcement remains an area of great complexity. A breach of 'ordinary' planning control does not in itself involve a criminal offence. The

1971 Act confers upon local planning authorities a discretion to serve an enforcement notice requiring a breach of planning control to be remedied. Contravention of the terms of an effective enforcement notice may result in sanctions, including, in some cases, prosecution. Chapter 12 deals with the taking of enforcement action, the time limits within which such action must be taken, the right to appeal against an enforcement notice to the Secretary of State, the opportunities for challenging enforcement notices in the courts, the effects of an enforcement notice and the possible use of injunction as a means of restraining a breach of planning control.

Adverse planning decisions: purchase notices and compensation. Chapters 13 and 14 are primarily concerned with the possible remedies (other than appeal or objection to the Secretary of State) where planning decisions have an adverse effect on the value of land. Compensation is not, in general, payable in respect of a refusal or conditional grant of planning permission. There are, however, exceptions to this general principle. One such exception, considered in chapter 13, is that where an adverse planning decision has been made on an application for the carrying out of 'new development' on land to which there is attached an unexpended balance of established development value, compensation may be payable; in practice very few cases qualify.

If the effect of a planning decision—for example, a refusal of planning permission—is to render the land in question incapable of reasonably beneficial use, the landowner may be able, by serving a purchase notice on the planning authority, to compel the authority to acquire the land. The law relating to purchase notices is considered in chapter 14.

Control of existing use. A right to compensation is quite likely to arise where planning action interferes in some way with existing rights. The general effect of the planning legislation introduced in 1947 was to leave to the landowner the right to continue the existing use of land and although the legislation makes provision for action such as the revocation of planning permission or the prohibition of an existing use of land, since such action derogates from existing rights compensation will normally be payable. The provision which statute makes for the control of the existing use of land is considered in chapter 15.

Positive planning. In its original form the 1947 Act envisaged, as did the Community Land Act 1975, that local planning authorities would often take the initiative in ensuring that land was used in the manner desired by them. Although the 'positive planning' role of planning authorities is now much less significant than has at other times been envisaged, and the major function of planning authorities is now that of regulating private sector proposals, local authorities still possess wide powers to acquire land for planning purposes. Development plans are intended to have a promotional as well as a controlling influence on development; they also seek to co-ordinate the planning and provision of infrastructure required for the development of land. The co-ordinating function of development plans and planning authorities' powers to acquire, dispose of and secure the development of land are outlined in chapter 16. This chapter also briefly describes the new emphasis on the regeneration of the inner cities areas and the new institutions and mechanisms such as urban corporations, enterprise zones, simplified planning zones, and inner city grants which have been created to achieve this purpose.

Planning blight and injurious affection. Where the implementation of public authorities' proposals will necessitate acquisition of land at some time in the future, the marketability of that land is likely to be adversely affected. The planning legislation seeks to alleviate the hardship that can be caused by such planning 'blight'; an owner-occupier of such land can in some circumstances serve on the authority responsible for the proposals a blight notice compelling that authority to acquire the land at an 'unblighted' price. Chapter 17 deals not only with 'blight' in this narrow sense but also outlines the provision made by statute for the payment of compensation in respect of depreciation in the value of neighbouring land caused by the carrying out of schemes of public works.

Special controls. The protection and improvement of the physical environment are, of course, matters to which local planning authorities will have regard in the exercise of their general planning powers, but over and above those general powers there are available to planning authorities certain additional powers, the object of which is, in the main, the protection and improvement of the environment.

Buildings listed by the Secretary of State as being of special architectural or historic interest are subject to stringent controls—unless the consent of the planning authority has first been obtained, it is an offence to demolish any such building or to alter it in any manner which would affect its character. Areas which authorities consider to be of special architectural or historic interest can be designated as conservation areas; special regard will be had to the preservation and enhancement of the character and appearance of a conservation area and the demolition of buildings within such an area is subject to control. Special provision is also made for the control of outdoor advertisements, for the making, on amenity grounds, of tree preservation orders and for the making of orders requiring remedial action to be taken in respect of waste land. Mineral operations can present special environmental problems and the Town and Country Planning (Minerals) Act 1981 makes provision for the exercise of additional controls over such operations. There is also now special control over hazardous substances. Each of these special controls is considered in chapter 18.

Appeal and objection procedures. Inevitably, those adversely affected by the exercise of planning powers, whether it be the refusal of a planning application, the service of an enforcement notice, the making of a discontinuance order or the promotion of a compulsory purchase order, will often feel aggrieved. Grievance procedures are an important component of the planning legislation. Generally they take the form of a right of appeal or objection to the Secretary of State. Appeal and objection procedures are discussed in chapter 19. Attention is focused in particular on the use of written submissions and on the public inquiry for processing appeals and objections and on the substantial body of case law which has grown up around these procedures.

Challenging the validity of plans and decisions. Challenge of the validity of structure and local plans and of many of the more important decisions and orders which can be made under the planning legislation is regulated by ss 242 to 248 of the 1971 Act. Those decisions not specified in those sections are subject to the ordinary supervisory powers of the High Court. The somewhat complex position regarding recourse to the High Court by way of judicial review is considered in chapter 20.

CHAPTER 2

THE ADMINISTRATION OF TOWN AND COUNTRY PLANNING

Introduction

Land use planning is a function of government and it is a necessary part of the introduction to this work to provide an account of the public authorities involved in planning, the allocation of functions between them, and their inter-relationships. The focus in this chapter, however, is primarily legal and we can supply no more than a glimpse of the political and financial aspects which are important for an understanding of the planning process. In the main, we are concerned with those parts of central and local government which possess the principal planning powers.

Also considered in this chapter are the powers possessed by the Parliamentary Commissioner and Local Commission for Administration in relation to complaints of maladministration on the part of central and local government in the exercise of planning powers.

A THE PUBLIC AUTHORITIES INVOLVED IN PLANNING

1 The local planning authorities

When the 1947 Act had been passed there was in England and Wales a rather lop-sided system of local government. In some areas there was only one local authority, the county borough, while in others there were two authorities, the county and the district authority. The 1947 Act vested the new planning functions in the county boroughs and the county councils, while allowing the counties to delegate planning functions to the districts. When in 1969 the Redcliffe-Maud Royal Commission on local government in England reported[1] apart from its basic finding that the small size and resources of local authorities prevented efficient and economic administration, the Commission was particularly concerned about the way local authority boundaries divided off town from country, thus causing fierce conflicts when urban authorities attempted to find suitable sites in neighbouring rural authorities for new housing projects. It was also concerned with the overlapping of services between the various authorities and with regard to planning argued that 'In each area of the country one authority should be responsible for land use planning and the whole field of transportation'.[2] In the light of the recent change to one planning authority in the Greater London and metropolitan areas, those words have a certain resonance.

In the event, of course, the incoming conservative government not only opted for a two-tier system of local government throughout England and

1 Cmnd 4040.
2 Para 244.

Wales, but decided to share out the planning functions between the two tiers. In a two-tier system of local government one tier is not supposed to be subordinate to the other: each tier has its responsibilities and should discharge them independently of the other. However, the way the planning powers were originally shared out made the county council the strategic authority with the power in many cases to ensure that the detailed policies of the districts fitted in with their policies. Thus the county could give directions to the districts as to how a planning application should be determined where the district wished to grant permission. Today the county still has that strategic role but has far less power to impose the policies. The Local Government, Planning and Land Act 1980 has made a clear demarcation between applications which are to be determined by the county, mainly mining and waste disposal, and the remainder which are to be decided by the district. The power of direction has been taken away and has only been replaced by a duty to consult on applications with strategic implications and by a duty to achieve the objectives of the structure plans when determining applications. In the case of the metropolitan areas the change has been much more drastic with the strategic planning authorities being abolished by the Local Government Act 1985. The government's proposals to abolish the structure plans could be leading to the return to the position where there will be only one planning authority for each area. If this is a relatively small authority it must lead to the government itself imposing strategic policies, while there exists no regional planning authority. Roberts, in his book *Reform of Planning Law*, points out that 'No one ever seems entirely pleased with the state of local government or planning, either before reforms or reorganisation are attempted or after' but the present position does have a rather stop gap feel to it. We now set out the present allocation of planning functions to local authorities.

Throughout the 1971 Act references are continually made to the 'local planning authority'. Section 1 defines 'local planning authority' as including in a non-metropolitan county both the district and the county planning authorities which are the councils of the county and the districts respectively. Outside the non-metropolitan areas, the only local planning authority is the council of the metropolitan district or the council of a London borough. This means that, unless otherwise indicated, in the non-metropolitan areas the county and the district have concurrent powers and duties regarding planning functions. However, s 182 and Sch 16 of the Local Government Act 1972 (as amended[3]) allocate particular planning functions exclusively to either the district planning authority or the county planning authority, though there will usually be a general duty of consultation.

In the case of development plans, the survey and the preparation of structure plans is the function of the county planning authority (1972 Act, s 183). Local plans can be prepared by either the county or the district depending on which authority is allocated to prepare the particular plan by the local plan scheme (1971 Act, s 11A) but in practice most local plans are prepared and adopted by the districts.

Development control is now primarily a matter for the districts. The county planning authority has only direct control over 'county matters' which are defined so as only to relate to applications appertaining to the

3 See Local Government, Planning and Land Act 1980 and the Local Government Act 1985.

winning and working of minerals and within England waste disposal (1972 Act, Sch 16, paras 15 and 32). All other applications are determined by the districts though there is a duty to consult the county before determining certain classes of application (1972 Act, Sch 16, paras 15 and 19). Similarly, the functions of serving revocation orders (s 45), discontinuance orders (s 51), enforcement notices (s 87) and stop notices (s 90) only apply to the counties when they appear to that authority to relate to a county matter and otherwise they apply exclusively to the district subject to a duty to consult when the function appears to relate to a county matter (1972 Act, Sch 16, para 24). The function of making simplified planning zones can only be exercised by the district.

The special controls relating to advertisements and listed buildings apply exclusively to the district planning authorities (1972 Act, Sch 16, para 25) and in the case of tree preservation orders the county can only make an order in certain special circumstances (1971 Act, s 60 (1A)).

The special powers relating to minerals are only exercisable by the county planning authority who are termed the 'mineral planning authority' for this purpose (1971 Act, s 1 (2B)).

The new control over hazardous substances is vested in the districts who are termed the hazardous substance authority.

Special arrangements apply to the areas covered by national parks. Section 1(2) provides for the creation of 'joint planning boards' to act as county planning authority or district planning authority for the areas or parts of the areas of two or more county councils or district councils. Two such joint planning boards were set up for the first two National Parks; the Lake District Joint Planning Board and the Peak District Joint Planning Board. The Lake District board is now called the Lake District Special Planning Board as it now falls in the area of only one county council (1972 Act, Sch 17). These two boards are the local planning authorities for their areas. In the other national parks, the functions of preparing plans, development control and most other planning functions are to be carried out by the county planning authority (1972 Act, s 182).

Also, the Local Government, Planning and Land Act 1980, in providing for the new institution of the urban development corporation, enabled the statutory instrument creating the corporation to transfer to the corporation the development control functions and many other planning functions (1980 Act, s 149). This has been done in the case of all the urban development corporations which have been set up except the Cardiff Bay Urban Development Corporation.

Finally the Norfolk and Suffolk Broads Act 1988 has created a new public body called the Broads Authority whose members are appointed by the local authorities whose jurisdiction includes or is close to the Broads, and other interested public bodies. This new body is, with its other functions the sole district planning authority in respect of the area of 'the Broads' as defined in the Act.[4]

Planning functions are normally to be exercised by an authority within their own area only and generally there is no difficulty in defining the geographical limits of an authority's jurisdiction. The question has arisen, however, as to the limits of that jurisdiction on the seashore. In *Argyll and*

4 See s 2 of the Norfolk and Suffolk Broads Act 1988 and Sch 3, pt I.

Bute District Council v Secretary of State for Scotland[5] the Second Division of the Court of Session held that there could be drawn from the Town and Country Planning (Scotland) Act 1972 the inference that planning jurisdiction was restricted to the area above low-water mark of tidal waters and that a planning authority therefore had no control over activities carried out below that mark.

Finally, we should mention parish and community councils which constitute a third tier of local government.

In England the parishes that existed in the rural districts remained in being following the 1974 reorganisation and new parishes can be now be established.[6] There are now round about 10,000 such parishes. In Wales the reorganisation of local government created a similar system of community meetings and community councils.[7] There are about 900 such communities. Their powers are limited but in the planning context they provide an important means of ascertaining local opinion. In particular they have a right to be consulted on planning applications if they make written notification to the district planning authority (1972 Act, Sch 16, para 20).[8]

The internal functioning of local authorities. Turning to the way in which local authorities are organised to go about their business, planning is treated like other functions. The first principle of the internal structuring of local authorities is that it is the full council that is the formal authority and it is in the full council that statutory powers are vested in the first instance. Only in exceptional cases are statutory functions vested in the first instance in persons other than the full council and planning is not such a function.

Although the primary allocation of powers to the full council accords with the principle that the major decisions of the authority should indeed be made in the authority's plenary forum, there would be little practical sense in attempting to compel all day to day decisions to be made there. It is obvious that there is a need for the substantial delegation of decision-making within the organisation and this has been the long-standing tradition. Local government is, in the main, government by committee.

But the power to delegate has to be expressly conferred. The normal presumption is that when Parliament confers powers upon a specific authority or type of authority then it does intend that the named authority should actually exercise the power themselves. If no delegation is authorised then an act or decision by someone claiming to act on the authority's behalf will be invalid and it would seem that such an act or decision may not subsequently be ratified by the authority.[9]

Happily, and not surprisingly, powers of delegation within local authorities are expressly conferred and these overcome most, but not all,[10] of the

5 1976 SC 248, 1977 SLT 33. See C M G Himsworth, 'The Limits of the Planning Realm' [1977] JPL 21; and E Young, 'Seaward Limits of Planning Jurisdiction in Scotland' (1977) 22 JLSS 61.
6 See Local Government Act 1972, s 1.
7 Local Government Act 1972, ss 20 and 28.
8 This entitlement is now to be found in Art 21 of the Town and Country Planning General Development Order 1988.
9 See *Co-operative Retail Services Ltd v Taff-Ely Borough Council* (1979) 39 P & CR 223, CA; affd sub nom *A-G(HM) (Co-operative Retail Services Ltd) v Taff-Ely Borough Council* (1981) 42 P & CR 1.
10 See, in particular, the discussion in chapter 12 on estoppel.

legal difficulties which might otherwise arise in the decision-making process. Section 101 of the Local Government Act 1972 permits a local authority to arrange for the discharge of any of their functions by a committee, sub-committee or officer of the authority, or, indeed by another local authority. The power to delegate to an officer was new.[11] There is still no power to delegate formally to a single member—even the convenor of a committee or of the council itself, and in *R v Secretary of State for the Environment, ex p Hillingdon Borough Council*[12] the Court of Appeal affirmed a decision of Woolf J that an enforcement notice was invalid because it had been issued on the sole authority of the chairman of the planning committee. Woolf J also thought that there would be difficulties in the planning committee retrospectively ratifying the chairman's decision. He however suggested the solution of power being given to an officer to make the decision after having consulted the chairman and in *Fraser v Secretary of State for the Environment and the Royal Borough of Kensington and Chelsea*[13] Nolan J held that it was valid to give the power of decision-making to an officer subject to getting the approval of the chairman. This last decision can be criticised on the grounds that in substance it is giving the chairman a veto and as such is arranging for the decision to be made jointly between the member and the official, something which is not authorised by s 101.

Where formal arrangements are made under s 101 for the decision to be made by a named officer, such as the county secretary and solicitor, it seems that the decision does not actually have to be taken by that officer and that informal arrangements can be made for other officers to make that decision.[14]

The legal effect of an authority's arranging for the discharge of a function by a committee, sub-committee or officer, whether this is achieved in the council's standing orders or by an *ad hoc* decision,[15] is that the committee or individual is empowered to act in place of the authority as a whole. The decision of the committee or individual to whom power has been delegated will be effective when made. Such an arrangement can subsequently be revoked but not retrospectively. Notwithstanding the delegation of functions, s 101 (4) of the 1972 Act specifically reserves to the local authority or committee, as the case may be, the power to exercise the functions concurrently. Arranging for the discharge of their functions by several committees does not affect the continuing overall responsibility of the full council for the whole of their functions.[16]

Apart from the formal retention by the full council of overall responsibility for the authority's functions, there is also commonly a further reflection of the need for some routine coherence in a council's policies. Most authorities have a policy and resources committee, or its equivalent, designed to ensure

---

11 New, that is, as a general power. There had been enacted a limited power to delegate planning powers to officers—see the Town and Country Planning Act 1968, s 64 (re-enacted in the 1971 Act, s 3 but now repealed).

12 [1986] 1 All ER 810, [1986] 1 WLR 192; affd [1986] 2 All ER 273n, [1986] 1 WLR 807n, CA.

13 [1988] JPL 344.

14 See *Cheshire County Council v Secretary of State for the Environment* [1988] JPL 30. Also see *Fitzpatrick v Secretary of State for the Environment and Epping Forest District Council* [1988] JPL 564.

15 *Battelley v Finsbury Borough Council* (1958) 122 JP 169, 56 LGR 165.

16 For discussion of the authorities see HWR Wade, *Administrative Law* (Clarendon Press, Oxford, 6th edn, 1988), chapter 11; and C A Cross, *Principles of Local Government Law* (Sweet and Maxwell, 6th edn, 1981), chapter 4.

the co-ordination of plans and policies. And there may, on the other side, be co-ordination through a management team.

Important rights to access and information about local government decision-making have been provided by the Local Government (Access to Information) Act 1985.[17] Previously the Public Bodies (Admission to Meetings) Act 1960[18] had granted very qualified rights to the public and the press to attend the council and committee meetings of local authorities. The 1985 Act adds eleven new sections (A–K) to s 100 of the Local Government Act 1972. The most significant changes are that the provisions now apply to sub-committees and give 'members of the public' the right to inspect, three days before a meeting, the agenda, connected reports and background papers[19] (1972 Act, ss 100 B, 100 D, 100 E). Also the minutes of meetings and related documents have to be kept open for inspection for several years after the date of the meeting (1972 Act, s 100 C). There are still restrictions on the rights of the public to attend meetings. There is a common law power inherent in the chairman of a statutory body to exclude the public if it is clear that members of the public are intent on causing such disruption that the transaction of business is or would be prevented.[20] This power is expressly retained by both the Public Bodies (Admission to Meetings) Act 1960 and the 1972 Act.[1] In addition the public have to be excluded whenever it is likely that confidential information would be disclosed in breach of an obligation of confidence and the public may be excluded if it is likely that exempt information as defined[2] will be disclosed.

It may also be noted that there is nothing to prevent political parties meeting to determine the policy to be taken on a particular decision before the formal meeting as long as members still genuinely exercise their own discretion when it comes to the formal meeting.[3]

The general pattern of internal organisation of local authorities in planning matters is broadly the same as for other functions. In some respects, of course, planning has its own specialised procedures—its own required processes of consultation, its own timetables, its own ways for the making and communication of decisions and these are discussed in later chapters. but these operate in supplementation of the standard legal and non-legal rules of local government practice.

The main extra-statutory characteristic of local government is that, subject to the possibilities for delegation discussed above, it is government by elected members with the substantial assistance and advice of appointed officials in both decision-making and implementation. The fact of their election means that, in modern times, the great majority of members and their councils and

---

17 See Eyre 'Planning and the Local Government (Access to Information) Act 1985' [1987] JPL 311 for a critique of the Act.

18 Applied by s 100 of the Local Government Act to committee meetings as well as council meetings.

19 These are defined as those documents which in the opinion of the proper officer have been relied upon to a material extent in preparing the report.

20 See *R v Brent Health Authority, ex p Francis* [1985] QB 869, [1985] 1 All ER 74.

1 See ss I (8) and 100 A (8) respectively.

2 This is defined in s 100 I and Sch 12A to the 1972 Act and includes matters such as information about employees or commercial contracts.

3 See *R v Amber Valley District Council, ex p Jackson* [1984] 3 All ER 501, [1985] 1 WLR 298 and *R v Waltham Forest London Borough Council ex p Waltham Forest Ratepayers Action Group* (1987) Times, 31 July.

committees are party politically orientated. Members are elected because of their adherence to a party and most important policy decisions are taken on a party basis. Planning is no exception to this general position although the technical nature of many planning decisions tend to reduce their party political significance. The further result is that the professional expertise of officials becomes more important. It would be completely misleading in practice to view officials as performing a merely advisory role. Inevitably they acquire great power and influence over the decisions made in name by the elected members they serve.

2 *The Secretary of State for the Environment and the Department of the Environment*

Any reader of planning legislation will be aware that the role of the Secretary of State for Environment is one that cannot be ignored. Referred to simply as the 'Secretary of State' because, in law, all holders of that office, whatever their individual title, are deemed to constitute a single Secretary of State and, therefore, legally competent to perform the functions of any, the Secretary of State for the Environment is the chief central government minister responsible for planning. He is responsible to Parliament for his own actions and those of his department and, as a member of the government and Cabinet, he shares collective responsibility for the decisions of government as a whole.

The Department of the Environment was created by the Heath Administration in 1970 and was part of a general trend to the amalgamation of existing ministries into new 'super' departments. Its title reflected the then fashionable concern with the environment and the department combined the Ministry of Housing and Local Government, the Ministry of Transport and the Ministry of Buildings and Public Works.

In the words of the White Paper introducing the changes[4] the aim was to ensure that decisions on housing and transport would be associated with 'responsibility for other major environmental matters, the preservation of amenity, the protection of the coast and countryside, the preservation of historic towns and monuments and the control of air, water and noise pollution.' At that time the impact on the environment of building new roads was extremely controversial and critics doubted whether the change would temper the enthusiasm of the road builder. In the event the fusion proved short-lived and in 1976 a separate Department of Transport was split off from the Department of the Environment, though the work of the two departments is coordinated by joint committees and the decisions on the construction of new roads are taken jointly by the two Secretaries of State.

Apart from town and country planning, the Department of the Environment has overall responsibility for many other matters which include local government, environmental protection, conservation and housing. Although the Secretary of State for the Environment has overall responsibility to Parliament for the work of the department, he has three junior ministers under him, one responsible for local government, one responsible for the water industry and town and country planning and one responsible for housing, environmental protection and the countryside. The department

4 'Re-organisation of Central Government' (Cmnd 4506) at para 31.

itself is split up into six main divisions, one of which has the main responsibility for land use planning and there are also regional offices.

The Minister of Town and Country Planning Act 1943 used to impose a duty on that minister of 'securing consistency and continuity in the forming and execution of a national policy with respect to the use and development of land throughout England and Wales.' This duty was repealed in 1970 when the order setting up the Department of the Environment was made.[5] The Town and Country Planning Act 1971 contains no such general duty, though it of course bestows on the Secretary of State many powers, which 'functions' were transferred by the order to the Secretary of State for Environment. So it is technically correct, as Sir Desmond Heap has pointed out, that in carrying out these functions, the Secretary of State is not expressly obliged to ensure 'consistency and continuity in the forming and execution of a national policy' or indeed to have a national policy to land use policy at all.[6] However, such a duty could be implied; powers should not be exercised arbitrarily, and in practice the Secretary of State and his department do try to impose on local planning authorities general policies and standards. Indeed the department since 1988 has begun issuing a series of planning policy guidance notes on major issues in planning. Like the advice given in circulars and the earlier development control notes, these policies have no statutory authority but are undoubtedly 'material considerations'[7] for the purpose of decision-making in development control.

So the position is one by which the Secretary of State enjoys central government responsibility for the planning process but central purposes are achieved principally through the efforts of local planning authorities acting under the various forms of central supervision. The Secretary of State's statutory powers amount, therefore, to those felt necessary by successive holders of the office to control the activities, in both their substance and procedure, of local authorities. To talk of supervision and control in this context is to risk entering a debate about the relationship (both actual and desirable) between central government and local authorities which extends much more widely than the planning process and certainly more widely than can be appropriately handled here. We are confined principally to questions of law and our concern at this point is with the formal statutory relationship between the Secretary of State and local authorities. In accepting these limitations, it is important to acknowledge nevertheless that the statutory position for the time being does not tell the whole story. It does not, for instance, tell us much about the political considerations that brought about or now sustain that position; it does not tell us about the extent of use or non-use of available powers; nor about the informal processes of communication and pressure operating in both directions between levels of government.

The law is, however, a necessary starting point and we shall find that various forms of statutory intervention by the Secretary of State are of great significance. He has, in the first place, wide powers to promulgate delegated legislation and, amongst these, the power to adjust, through the medium of

5 See the Secretary of State for the Environment Order 1970 made under the Ministers of the Crown (Transfer of Functions) Act 1946.
6 See Switzer and Sir Desmond Heap 'The Duty of the Secretary of State for the Environment' [1984] JPL 72.
7 See ch 8 for a discussion of this term.

use class orders, the meaning of development and thus the types of activity requiring planning permission, to provide for the granting of planning permission by development orders for specified categories of development, and to determine the detailed procedure according to which planning applications are processed, development plans are drawn up and public inquiries conducted. The Secretary of State's general powers in determining appeals against adverse planning decisions, his powers to 'call in' applications from planning authorities for determination by himself, his powers of direction, of approving or disapproving development plans and his powers of mediation between authorities represent very substantial formal control over the planning process as a whole. In his broader relationship with local authorities, it is usually said that the Secretary of State's single power of control that dominates all others is the financial power—that of determining the limits of local capital expenditure and, through his fixing of the annual rate support grant, imposing fairly close limits on revenue expenditure also. During a period in which the official central government approach has been one of relaxing needlessly detailed administrative controls to give local authorities greater 'freedom' but, at the same time, seeking to retain the power to safeguard both national economic and financial policy and national social policies implemented through local government, overall spending limits tied in some cases to a degree of programme approval have provided a useful framework of control. This strategy based on financial controls has less immediate relevance to the planning process as such. Of course, financial factors will frequently determine the rate of progress ultimately made towards the implementation of planning goals—financial constraints, for example, clearly affect an authority's freedom to purchase or develop land. But, since the local authority role in planning has less to do with implementation and much more to do with the co-ordination and licensing of development, it is not surprising that in this area the Secretary of State has to place much greater reliance upon the control achieved through detailed legislative and administrative regulation.

3 Other government departments

In Wales the Secretary of State for Wales and the Welsh Office carry out the planning functions which in England are the remit of the Secretary of State for the Environment and the Department of the Environment. However, the policies tend to be the same and most circulars and policy guidance notes are issued jointly by the Department of the Environment and the Welsh Office. Other government departments such as the Department of Transport have impact on planning matters by initiating development projects. In this respect development by the crown, at least on crown land, does not require planning permission but, as explained in chapter 6, local planning authorities have a non-statutory right to be consulted and any disputes are determined by the Department of the Environment. In other cases Ministers, such as the Secretary of State for Transport or the Minister of Agriculture, Fisheries and Food may have a statutory right to be consulted on a planning application.[8] Also, more recently the Departments of Industry and Employment will be involved in attempts to regenerate the inner city areas (see chapter 16).

8 See Art 18 of the General Development Order and ch 7.

4 *The European Economic Community*

Discussion of the public authorities involved in planning would be incomplete without some mention of the role played by the European Economic Community. Although the Treaty of Rome made no specific mention of the pursuit of environmental objectives, the Community has, nonetheless, involved itself with the promotion of social and environmental policies. The Single European Act has strengthened the remit of the community by adding new articles to the Treaty which relate to the environment and in particular lay down the objective of preserving, protecting and improving the quality of the environment.

Until recently, attention had been focused on such matters as the control of pollution and Community policy has had no direct influence on mainstream planning law. However, the Community has now issued a Directive on environmental assessment. This has resulted in regulations having to be made which substantially affect the process of applying for planning permission (see chapter 7).

B MALADMINISTRATION

So far in this chapter we have been concerned with the public authorities involved in the administration of planning and with the way in which they are organised for the discharge of their functions. Considerable attention is given in this book to the remedies available under statute and at common law to those affected by the discharge of these functions. There are, however, other, 'non-legal', remedies open to a person who feels himself aggrieved, perhaps not so much by a particular planning proposal or decision, but by the way in which that proposal or decision has been arrived at. The cause of this type of grievance is commonly referred to as 'maladministration'. 'What every form of government needs', comments Wade, 'is some regular and smooth-running mechanism for feeding back the reactions of its disgruntled customers, after impartial assessment, and for correcting whatever may have gone wrong.[9] One mechanism which has been established for investigating complaints of maladministration by public authorities in the discharge of their functions is the 'ombudsman'.

Ombudsmen operate at different levels. The office of parliamentary ombudsman, or more correctly, the Parliamentary Commissioner for Administration, was established to investigate complaints of maladministration against government departments, including complaints against the Department of the Environment about the way in which it has discharged its functions under the planning legislation. The office of local ombudsman (the Commissioners for Local Administration) was established to investigate complaints about the way in which local authorities have discharged their functions. Both are concerned principally with the correct functioning of the administrative machine. The remainder of the chapter is given over to a brief description of the way in which the ombudsmen operate.

1 *The Parliamentary Commissioner for Administration*

The office of the Parliamentary Commissioner for Administration was

9 H W R Wade, *Administrative Law*, 6th edn, p 78.

established by the Parliamentary Commissioner Act 1967. The Commissioner is appointed by the Crown and holds office during good behaviour. His function is to investigate complaints by members of the public who claim to have suffered 'injustice in consequence of maladministration' by a government department.[10] A complaint must be made in writing and must be submitted through a member of the House of Commons. The intention is that members should filter out cases which are inappropriate for consideration by the ombudsman; it would seem, however, that members generally prefer to let the ombudsman make the decision about the appropriateness of a complaint. Complaints must generally be lodged within twelve months of the date when the aggrieved person first knew of the matters alleged in the complaint.

A number of matters are specifically excluded from the ombudsman's jurisdiction.[11] Amongst these are contractual and commercial transactions, other than the acquisition of land compulsorily or by agreement and the disposal of surplus land so acquired. Furthermore, the ombudsman may not investigate a case where the person aggrieved has or had a remedy in any court of law, or a right of appeal, reference or review in any statutory or prerogative tribunal[12] unless it would not have been reasonable in the particular circumstances of the case to expect the remedy or right to be invoked.[13] Even where he has decided to investigate it would appear that he should consider discontinuing his investigation if in the course of the investigation he discovers there exists an alternative remedy.[14]

'Maladministration' is not defined in the 1967 Act but it includes what is generally referred to as the 'Crossman catalogue'[15] of bias, neglect, inattention, delay, incompetence, ineptitude and arbitrariness. And although the ombudsman may not question the merits of a decision taken without maladministration by a government department in the exercise of discretionary powers[16]—for example, a decision on an appeal against a refusal of planning permission—this has not prevented him from questioning discretionary decisions which are thoroughly bad on their merits. As Wade observes 'bad decisions are bad administration and bad administration is maladministration'.[17] However, case law concerning the local ombudsman would indicate that maladministration relates to the manner in which decisions are made and has nothing to do with the nature or quality of the decision itself. So the ombudsman should not question a policy decision as to how discretion should be exercised.[18] Also a finding of maladministration can

---

10   1967 Act s 5(1).
11   1967 Act, s 5(3) and Sch 3.
12   1967 Act, s 5(2).
13   For example, where the law is in doubt.
14   See *R v Comr for Local Administration, ex p Croydon London Borough Council* [1989] 1 All ER 1033.
15   H C Deb, Vol 734, Col 51 (18th October, 1966); and see note 18 below.
16   1967 Act, s 12(3).
17   H W R Wade, *Administrative Law*, 6th edn, p 88.
18   See *R v Local Comr for Administration for the North and East Area of England, ex p Bradford Metropolitan City Council* [1979] QB 287, [1979] 2 All ER 881 and *R v Local Comr for Administration, for the South, the West, the West Midlands, Leicestershire, Lincolnshire and Cambridge, ex p Eastleigh Borough Council* [1988] QB 855, [1988] 3 WLR 113, sub nom *R v Comr for Local Administration, ex p Eastleigh Borough Council* [1988] 3 All ER 151, CA.

only be made if injustice has been suffered through the maladministration and it would seem it is not enough that the ombudsman thought it likely or possible that injustice might have been caused by the maladministration.[19]

The ombudsman has a discretion whether to investigate a complaint. Any investigation is conducted in private and, subject to limited exceptions, the ombudsman may call for information and papers from any person.

The report of his investigation is submitted to the government department in question, and to the member through whom the case was referred. Although the ombudsman has no sanction to support any recommendation in his report, he has in practice been very successful in securing a remedy for complaints where maladministration has been found to cause injustice. In one case investigated by the Commissioner, for example, neighbours who had made objection to proposed development were not informed by the Minister of Housing and Local Government that an appeal relating to the proposals was to be dealt with by written representations and were given no opportunity to state their case; the ministry refused at first to revoke the planning permission granted for the development but re-opened the matter after the Parliamentary Commissioner had found maladministration in the ministry's handling of the appeal.[20]

Although the office of Parliamentary Commissioner has become well-established, the number of investigations into planning matters in England and Wales has not been substantial.

2 *The Commission for Local Administration*

The Commission for Local Administration, the local ombudsman, is of more recent creation. It came into existence at the same time as local government reorganisation in 1974. It was established by Pt III of the Local Government Act 1974 and there are in fact two Commissions, one for England (consisting of three Commissioners covering three regions in England) and one for Wales (consisting of one Commissioner). The Commissioners are Crown appointments and they hold office during good behaviour.[1] A commissioner is secure in his office until he either voluntarily resigns, or is removed for incapacity or misbehaviour, or reaches the retiring age of 65. His task is to investigate complaints from members of the public who claim to have sustained injustice in consequence of maladministration in connection with action taken by local authorities in the exercise of their administrative functions. A complaint has to be in writing and had to be forwarded to the ombudsman by a member of the council against whom the complaint is made unless the ombudsman is satisfied that a councillor has refused to forward a complaint, when he may take it direct. However, the Local Government Act 1988 has removed this requirement and complaints can now be made direct to the local commissioner.[2] A complaint must normally be made within 12

---

19 See *Eastleigh* decision above.
20 Case 473/67.
1 On these and subsequent aspects of the Commissioner's appointment, powers and procedures see the 1974 Act, Pt III and Sch 4 and 5.
2 It had been argued for a long time that automatic direct access to the ombudsman should be provided. See JUSTICE, *The Local Ombudsman: A Review of the First Five Years* (1980). (This also provides useful discussion of other jurisdictional and procedural aspects of the ombudsman's work.) The Commissioner himself had advocated direct access. See eg Annual Reports for years ended March 1983 and March 1984 (HMSO).

months of the date of the complainant's first knowledge of the matters alleged in the complaint. The ombudsman must not investigate a complaint unless satisfied that the authority have been informed of it and given a reasonable opportunity to respond.[3]

There are other restrictions upon the ombudsman's general power to investigate, only some of which bear upon the field of planning. He cannot investigate action taken in respect of personnel matters (including appointments, pay and discipline) nor action which in his opinion affects all or most of the inhabitants of the area of the authority concerned. This last restriction prevents investigation of matters extending beyond the ambit of individual complaint such as the fixing of the rate. On the other hand, complaints need not come from single individuals. They may be made by groups of people or by companies. Parish councils have complained to the ombudsman. Local authorities themselves, nationalised industries and quangos are barred.

The investigation conducted by the ombudsman, and by investigating officers on his behalf, is private. He has the power, enforceable by the High Court if necessary, to require the attendance of witnesses and production of documents. Following his investigation, the ombudsman reports upon it to the complainant, councillor and authority. Within two weeks of receiving the report, the authority must give public notice (including newspaper advertisement) of its availability for inspection.

If the report is one in which the ombudsman has made no finding of injustice in consequence of maladministration, the authority need take no further action. If such an injustice is reported (and, if it is, it will normally be accompanied by a recommendation as to its removal), then the authority must consider the report and notify the ombudsman of the action they have taken or propose to take. Failing such notification or if the ombudsman is not satisfied with action taken or proposed, he may issue a further report explaining his dissatisfaction and the authority must once again consider this second report and notify the ombudsman of the action they have taken or propose to take. That further report must also be given publicity and it is there that the ombudsman's formal powers stop. Like the Parliamentary Commissioner, he has no power to order a remedy for injustice found. He may recommend a remedy and reinforce that recommendation in a further report but that, at present, is the limit. He does not even have the powerful support available to his Parliamentary counterpart in the shape of Parliament itself, the Commons Select Committee and the procedures for ensuring ministerial accountability. This vulnerability of the local ombudsman to being ignored by the authorities he criticises has encouraged some commentators and indeed the Commissioner himself to advocate the legal enforceability of his findings.[4] However, it is worth noting that in *R v Local Comr for Administration for the South, ex p Eastleigh Borough Council*[5] Lord Donaldson MR stated that: 'The Parliamentary intention was that reports by ombudsmen should be loyally accepted by the local authorities concerned.'

3 In addition to this statutory prerequisite to formal investigation, there have been introduced 'revised operating procedures' under which authorities are given notice by the ombudsman of complaints against them. This can lead to a speedy resolution—whether in favour of the complainant or not—without the need for formal investigation.
4 See Annual Report, 1984, pp 4–5.
5 [1988] QB 855, [1988] 3 WLR 113, sub nom *R v Comr for Local Administration, ex p Eastleigh Borough Council* [1988] 3 All ER 151, CA.

Thus suggesting that a finding of maladministration could not be ignored and that some response was required.

It is not a simple matter to assess the actual impact of the local ombudsman upon the planning system during the decade of his operation. In particular, it is difficult to judge how far decisions on particular complaints affect general decision-making processes either within the authority concerned or more widely. The statistical returns in the commissioner's annual reports show that for the years 1981 to 1985 roughly about a third of the complaints received and formal investigations conducted by the ombudsman concerned planning. This puts planning joint top in the league table of complaints alongside housing. Further research carried out by the Centre for Criminological and Socio-legal Studies at the University of Sheffield[6] indicate that the ombudsman was being used as a means of appeal by disgruntled third parties. Complaints of maladministration may include complaints by planning objectors that they have been inadequately informed or consulted about applications; complaints that misleading statements have been made; complaints about delay; and complaints of inconsistency in handling allegedly similar planning applications. Of course, not all complaints framed in these terms have been upheld on their particular facts and commissioners have been loath to interfere with decisions made within the scope of the discretion of planning authorities.

It is also clear that there is a considerable overlap between the concept of maladministration and the grounds on which planning decisions can be challenged in the courts.[7] However the ombudsman will not normally expect a complainant to use the legal remedy of going to the High Court because of the high costs involved. The advantages of the ombudsman over the courts is that apart from the cost of going to court (the ombudsman is free), both the methods of investigation and the eventual settlement are more flexible and often more effective. In particular, complaints have resulted in large cash settlements. On the other hand the findings of the ombudsman do not automatically result in a remedy. He has no statutory power to force local authorities to make settlements, though in the vast majority of cases authorities do produce remedies satisfactory at least to the ombudsman. The finding by the ombudsman is itself challengeable in the courts by way of judicial review if he has exceeded jurisdiction or otherwise erred in law[8] and it can be a ground for challenge that the ombudsman had failed to consider whether judical review itself was the more approriate remedy.[9]

The Local Government and Housing Bill proposes strengthening the powers of the local ombudsman to obtain redress by requiring the local authority to publicise his findings where they do not comply with the recommendations.

6 See 'Mary Seneviratne and Sarah Cracknell', *Complaints Procedures in Local Government by Norman Lewis* (1987).
7 See Crawford 'Where Judges Fear to Tread' [1982] JPL 619 and Macpherson 'Local Ombudsman or the Courts?' [1987] JPL 92. See guidelines drawn up by the Commission for Local Administration in 1979.
8 See *R v Local Comr for Administration, for South, ex p Eastleigh Borough Council* [1988] QB 855, [1988] 3 WLR 113, sub nom *R v Comr for Local Administration, ex p Eastleigh Borough Council* [1988] 3 All ER 151, CA.
9 See *R v Com for Local Administration, ex p Croydon London Borough Council* [1989] 1 All ER 1033.

CHAPTER 3

NATIONAL PLANNING POLICY

Planning legislation subjects proposals for the development of land to a comprehensive system of control. The way in which the control is applied in a given case is a matter, in the first instance, for the discretion of the planning authority and, in the event of appeal, for the Secretary of State. These characteristics of comprehensiveness and discretion make the preparation of policy guidelines desirable so as to secure a measure of consistency in the application of control in day to day practice and to ensure some coordination between the different levels—local and national—at which the system operates. It would seem to be equally desirable that those concerned with the development of land, whether as promoters or as 'third parties', should be able to obtain guidance on the policies which underlie the exercise of control.

Part II of the 1971 Act accordingly imposes an obligation upon local planning authorities to prepare policy statements dealing with the development and use of land in their areas (see chapter 4). These statements are prepared in the form of structure and local plans. Whilst the Secretary of State exercises some control over the content of these plans, local planning authorities are left with considerable freedom to develop policies appropriate to the circumstances of their areas and to implement these through the operation of the development control process and through other planning powers.

There is no corresponding obligation upon the Secretary of State to prepare national policy statements on land use and in the past he has tended to refrain from doing so except where a clear indication of the 'national interest' was seen to be required. Nevertheless, he has quite frequently issued what might be termed 'operational advice' on aspects of the planning process, often in the form of circulars related to changes in legislation. However, for reasons which are considered below, during the last ten years there has been a significant increase in the amount of land use policy guidance; the flow of operational advice has continued at much the same level.

Our principal concern in this chapter is with sources of national planning policy. However, in practical terms a discussion about sources of policy cannot be entirely divorced from consideration of the way in which policy is formulated, communicated and implemented. In view of the varied and unstructured way in which national policy may emerge some general observations on these matters would seem to be appropriate.

Policy does not suddenly emerge complete and intact. It tends to arise over a period of time due to both internal and external demands and events.[1]

---

1 See Jenkins 'Policy Analysis: A Political and Organisational Perspective' (1978) and Harrington 'Explaining State Policy-making: a Critique of some recent Dualist Models' International Journal of Urban and Regional Planning, vol 7, pp 202–18 (1983).

National policy may, for example, emerge incrementally as the sum of a series of decisions on individual proposals for development. National policy, commented the Outer Circle Policy Unit, is 'secreted in the interstices of individual decisions and evolves over time as a consequence of the decisions that are taken and carried out'.[2] It is, for example, difficult to find that there was ever a major assessment of the thermal reactor programme, yet the sum of the decisions on the individual nuclear power stations amounts to a major national programme. In a similar way, the present government's policy on the emphasis to be given to the allocation of an adequate supply of land for private house building has evolved in an incremental fashion.

Inevitably, proposals for development which raise national implications will come forward from time to time in what might be described as a policy vacuum. The proposals to build a third London Airport at Stansted and a nuclear power station at Sizewell are good examples. Both raised important policy issues and considerable time was devoted at the subsequent public inquiries to argument over where the 'national interest' lay. In such cases, the inquiry becomes a part of the policy formulation exercise and the eventual decision is an important indicator of national policy.[3]

Those involved in planning practice will wish to know where to look for guidance on national planning policy, however formulated. Policy, particularly on land use issues, may well be communicated to practitioners in a single statement. The planning policy guidelines are a good example of this. On the other hand, where land use policy emerges in incremental fashion, the best way to obtain information may be to examine past decisions on development plans and planning appeals.

Operational policy on a specific aspect of the planning process is generally communicated through a combination of legislation, primary or delegated, and circular. The new policy of having simplified planning zones has been effected by new primary legislation (the Housing and Planning Act 1986), regulations made under that legislation and circulars explaining and advising on the new system.

Until recently, the operation of the planning process was not a matter which divided the main political parties.[4] There was a tendency to adopt what might be described as an *ad hoc* approach to operational policy. Changes were made in piecemeal fashion to specific parts of the process as occasion required. However, the present government appears to have fairly definite ideas about what is required of the planning system as a whole and has been carrying through a programme of change to translate these ideas into practice. The importance of speeding up decision-making processes and relaxing unnecessary controls has been stressed. To this end, legislation, both primary and delegated, has been introduced to speed up the development plan process and to relax some of the rigour of development control. The legislation has been supported by a number of circulars explaining and enlarging upon the provisions and stressing the importance of clear policy guidance and of swift and sound decision-taking. The cumulative effect has,

2 The Outer Circle Policy Unit in association with JUSTICE and the Council for Science and Society, *The Big Public Inquiry* (1979).
3 For examination of the way government policy was treated at the Sizewell B inquiry, see O'Riordan, Kemp and Purdue 'Sizewell B: An anatomy of the Inquiry' Ch 6.
4 With the important exception of the compensation/betterment question which is discussed in ch 1.

therefore, been a decided shift in operational policy under the present administration in the direction of a reduced burden of planning control.

Where policy has been formulated at the national level, the Secretary of State has at his disposal, as is indicated in chapter 2, a number of devices for ensuring the implementation of the policy at the local level. He has indicated that development plans should take into account national policies[5] and he has wide powers to refuse or modify structure plan policies which do not adequately reflect these considerations;[6] and he may call in local plans for approval[7] or even direct that a local plan be made, repealed or altered.[8] As regards development control, he can call in applications for his own decision and has directed that he must be notified of certain categories of applications which the local planning authorities do not propose to refuse.[9] Furthermore, he is the ultimate arbiter on matters of planning policy in the event of an appeal by an applicant from an adverse decision by a planning authority.

Whilst, therefore, planning authorities in practice exercise considerable freedom in the day to day operation of the planning process, there is no doubt that the Secretary of State is well equipped to ensure that day to day practice accords with national policies. Furthermore, there is no doubt that national policy now exerts a greater influence on day to day practice than it did ten years ago.

The remainder of this chapter is given over to a more detailed examination of the main sources of national planning policy—legislation, circulars, planning policy guidance and development control policy notes and other ministerial pronouncements—and to a consideration of the weight which they carry in practice.

1 *Legislation*

Policy decisions, particularly on the operation of the planning process, may well be implemented through legislation. Access to such legislation, primary or delegated, should present little difficulty to those concerned with the development of land or, at least, to their legal advisers. Section 287 of the 1971 Act provides that nearly all delegated legislation on planning matters is to be made by way of statutory instrument; it is therefore subject to the publication requirements of s 2 of the Statutory Instruments Act 1946. Although the publication requirements extend only to general statutory instruments (ie those having application throughout England and Wales), a list of local instruments—for example, orders designating enterprise zones—appears in the official bound volumes of statutory instruments published annually by HMSO. The Department of the Environment will supply on request a list of current general Acts and statutory instruments relevant to planning (together with the current circulars and memoranda). The list is updated periodically.

5 See Circular 22/1984, 'Structure and Local Plans'; para 2 (1) (b) of the memorandum.
6 Town and Country Planning Act 1971, s 9.
7 Town and Country Planning Act 1971, s 14 A, as substituted by the Housing and Planning Act 1986.
8 Town and Country Planning Act 1971, s 11B, as substituted by the Housing and Planning Act 1986.
9 Town and County Planning Act 1971, s 35, and Town and Country Planning (Development Plans) (England) Direction 1981, para 4 (see Annex D to Circular 2/81) and the Town and Country Planning (Development Plans) (Wales) Direction 1981, para 4.

Although most planning legislation is concerned with the rules governing the operation of the process, it should be noted that special development orders[10] and orders designating enterprise zones[11] (both are types of delegated legislation) implement policy decisions to grant planning permission for a particular development or particular classes of development in a defined area.

In June 1981 the Secretary of State for the Environment issued a consultative document suggesting the possibility of a much wider use of special development orders. Such orders, it was suggested, might be used to grant planning permission for specified categories of development—for example, industrial and residential development in accord with local plans and the intensification or extension of development in areas already developed with uses acceptable to the relevant planning authority. The object of using special development orders in this way would be to provide developers with the prospect of speed and certainty of decision with a minimum of red tape. The consultative document was the subject of a considerable volume of criticism from local authority associations and others involved in planning on the grounds that it would remove control of individual proposals from the local level and preclude public consultation. In the meantime, however, the Housing and Planning Act 1986 has created the mechanism of simplified planning zones, which enable local authorities to give general planning permission for specified categories of development in defined parts of their areas (see chapter 17).

Access to directions made under statutes or statutory instruments may well be more difficult for those concerned with the development of land. For example, Art 3 of the Town and Country Planning General Development Order 1988 grants planning permission for the classes of development listed in Sch 2. Art 4 provides that the Secretary of State or a local planning authority may direct that the permission granted by Art 3 shall not apply to the development or classes of development specified. Such a direction is a form of sub-delegated legislation. Other powers to issue directions are scattered throughout the general development order.

For those interested in the effect of directions one difficulty relates to publication. Directions issued, for example, by planning authorities under Art 4 of the general development order will have local application and in some cases will be communicated direct to the affected parties. Directions made by the Secretary of State will often have more general application. For example, s 277 A(4) of the 1971 Act empowers the Secretary of State to direct that certain descriptions of buildings in conservation areas do not require conservation area consent to be demolished. The difficulty is that this direction is not published in any formal way and it is not mentioned in the list of Departmental Circulars and Memoranda, Acts and Statutory Instruments. It is tucked away, together with several other directions, in Circular 8/ 87 'Historic Buildings and Conservation Areas'. However, these circulars are published and volume 4 of the *Encyclopaedia of Planning* does usefully list the Ministerial directions made under the town and country planning legislation. Perhaps more importantly such directions do not have to be brought to the attention of Parliament.

10 Made under s 24 of the Town and Country Planning Act 1971.
11 Made under s 179 of and Sch 32 to the Local Government, Planning and Land Act 1980.

2   *Circulars*

Circulars are widely used by the Secretary of State in the planning process. They serve two main purposes. First of all, they draw the attention of planning authorities to new legislation, both primary and delegated, and explain its operation. Secondly, they give advice on policy.

Quite often both purposes will be accomplished in the same circular. Circular 11/1984, for example, introduced the new advertisement control regulations and also indicated the considerations which should guide the control of advertisements in the interests of amenity and public safety.

In drawing local authorities' attention to new legislation circulars not only explain the law but offer advice on the interpretation of the law. For example Circular 8/87 'Historic Buildings and Conservation Areas—Policy and Procedures' advised that the repainting of the façade of a listed building did not constitute works of alteration that would require listed building consent. Such advice cannot have the force of law and in *Windsor and Maidenhead Royal Borough Council v Secretary of State for the Environment*[12] Mann J held that such works do require listed building consent if they affect the character of the building.[13] The position is of course different if the Secretary of State is empowered to make directions and a direction is made by way of a circular: as in Circular 8/87 as mentioned earlier. Even though advice in a circular may not have the force of law, it may nevertheless be susceptible to judicial review.

In *R v Worthing Borough Council, ex p Burch*[14] Mann J quashed an opinion given by the Secretary of State on the grounds that it was based on an unlawful procedure set out in a circular, and in other contexts it has been accepted that the courts can grant declarations as to whether new statutory guidance is incorrect in law.[15] However, normally the issue as to whether statements in circulars are correct in law will arise indirectly when statutory powers are exercised on the basis of such statements.

Although circulars do not have the force of law, there is no doubt that they exert a very considerable influence upon the day to day operation of the planning system. There are three reasons for saying this. First of all, as Lord Wilberforce commented in *Coleshill and District Investment Co Ltd v Minister of Housing and Local Government*[16] on a circular dealing, *inter alia*, with the meaning of 'development', the circular had 'acquired vitality and strength when, through the years, it passed as it certainly did, into planning practice and textbooks, [and] was acted upon, as it certainly was, in planning decisions.' Secondly, the Secretary of State, through his appellate role in the

12   (1987) 86 LGR 402 [1988] JPL 410. Now see circular 18/88.
13   See also *Lewisham Metropolitan Borough and Town Clerk v Roberts* [1949] 2 KB 608, [1949] 1 All ER 815; and *dicta* of Lord Wilberforce in *Coleshill and District Investment Co Ltd v Minister of Housing and Local Government* [1969] 1 WLR 746 at 765; and Lord Scarman in *Newbury District Council v Secretary of State for the Environment* [1981] AC 578 at 621. Contrast *Blackpool Corpn v Locker* [1948] 1 KB 349, [1948] 1 All ER 85, CA; and *Patchett v Leathem* (1948) 65 TLR 69. And see, generally, S M Nott and P H Morgan, 'The Significance of Department of the Environment Circulars in the Planning Process' [1984] JPL 623.
14   (1983) 50 P & CR 53, [1984] JPL 261.
15   See *Royal College of Nursing of United Kingdom v Department of Health and Social Security* [1981] 1 All ER 545 and *Gillick v West Norfolk and Wisbech Area Health Authority* [1986] AC 112, [1985] 3 All ER 402, HL.
16   [1969] 1 WLR 746 at 765.

development control process, is in a strong position to ensure that policy advice given in circulars is implemented. Thirdly, planning authorities are required to have regard to all 'material considerations' when determining a planning application[17] and it would appear that relevant ministerial policies set out in departmental circulars are 'material considerations' and must be taken into account.[18] The courts have not, of course, gone so far as to say that the advice in a circular must be followed, since that would remove the planning authority's discretion altogether and in *R v Camden London Borough Council, ex p Comyn Ching & Co (London) Ltd*[19], Woolf J held in the context of compulsory purchase under the Housing Acts, that, as long as a local authority took into account circulars: 'it is entitled to take the view "we will put the matter before the Minister and try to persuade him to confirm the orders notwithstanding those statements of policy" '. Also in *Gransden & Co Ltd v Secretary of State for the Environment*[20] Woolf J emphasised the limitations of a circular by pointing out that circulars could not make a matter which was otherwise material an irrelevant consideration. Thus circulars can give guidance as to the weight to be given to material considerations but cannot determine what is or is not a material considera- tion as a matter of law.[1] Nevertheless, the requirement to take such policy statements into account must in practice be an important limitation on the exercise of discretion. The overall effect is that policies in circulars are in many cases every bit as influential as formal legislative rules.

No procedures are prescribed for the preparation and issuing of a circular. However, prior consultation commonly takes place with local authority associations and in recent years the Department have made a practice of issuing some circulars in draft form for consultation with a wider group of bodies, including professional associations and other pressure groups.[2] Circulars on planning matters are usually issued jointly by the Department of the Environment and the Welsh Office, though sometimes the Welsh Office issues separate circulars of its own. These circulars are published and numbered and so are generally available from HMSO.[3] This removes some of the early criticisms but the system is still rather confusing and ill-organised. It is often some time until out-of-date circulars are cancelled and there is no easy way to find out what advice or guidance is available except to leaf through the contents page of the *Encyclopaedia of Planning* which includes the most important circulars.

Although many circulars are directed at relatively narrow and technical areas of planning practice, nevertheless, the general way in which the principal legislation is framed allows circulars to be used to accomplish considerable changes of emphasis in the planning process. For example, in introducing Department of the Environment Circular 22/80, 'Development

---

17 Town and Country Planning Act 1971, s 29.
18 See p 204 below.
19 (1983) 47 P & CR 417, [1984] JPL 661; see also *Gransden & Co Ltd v Secretary of State* (1985) 54 P & CR 86, [1986] JPL 519.
20 (1985) P & CR 86, [1986] JPL 519.
 1 See also May L J in *ELS Wholesale (Wolverhampton) Ltd v Secretary of State for Environment* (1987) 56 P & CR 69, [1987] JPL 844.
 2 This consultation can result in important changes of mind as in the case of the draft circular on 'Agricultural Land' published in 1987.
 3 In this book any reference to a circular is to the Department of Environment number unless otherwise indicated.

Control', Tom King, then Minister for Local Government, said: 'I regard this circular as a most important advance in the evolution of the British planning system. Hitherto, there has been too much emphasis on restraint and restriction. From now on, we intend to ensure that positive attitudes prevail.'[4] The significant point is that this 'important advice' was made without recourse to legislation.

3 *Development control notes and planning policy guidance notes*

Since 1969, the Department of the Environment has published development control policy notes. These notes give general advice on particular matters relating to development control such as caravan sites, petrol stations and hotels. Most of these notes were issued in 1969 and are now rather dated. They have now been augmented by a new series of planning policy guidance notes (PPGs) which were first issued in 1988. There are now thirteen of these planning policy notes plus five separate minerals policy guidance notes. The PPGs range from general policy and principles to very specific issues such as telecommunications. Both sets of notes differ from circulars in that they tend to concentrate on giving guidance on policy matters rather than providing detailed explanation of the legislation. The planning policy guidance notes are an important innovation in that they are an attempt at a more comprehensive and systematic statement of government policy. In this regard they are similar to the Scottish national planning guidelines which are issued by the Scottish Office. However, the Scottish guidelines on policy differ in that in some cases they actually designate zones where particular categories of development should be encouraged or discouraged. Furthermore the guidelines set out to define the land-based resources or potential sites for development which are considered to be of national significance. The PPGs do not do this and PPG 6 on 'Major Retail Development' states specifically that: 'The Government has no intention of identifying specific locations suitable for major retail developments or for different types of retailing.' The introduction of the PPGs has resulted in many of the old development control policy notes and circulars being withdrawn. However, unless stated these notes and circulars remain extant for the time being. This could cause confusion where a circular or note covers the same area but uses different language.

The PPGs are published and are available for sale at HMSO. In these publications it is stated that 'The Secretaries of State and their Inspectors will have regard to this guidance in dealing with appeals and called-in applications' and they undoubtedly, like circulars, constitute 'material considerations' and as such must in law be regarded where relevant. In *Penwith District Council v Secretary of State for the Environment*[5] Woolf J quoted a decision of an Inspector where his decision letter had made no mention of a very relevant development control policy note. Woolf J stated:

'It was his view that the Inspector should, if indeed he had taken the circular into account, have indicated why it was that he felt that this was a case in which he should depart from the general prohibition.'

4 Department of Environment Press Notice No 507, 1st December 1980.
5 [1986] 1 EGLR 193, [1986] JPL 432.

The same principles must apply to PPGs.

4 *Other sources of government policy*

Policy may need changing or clarifying. In such a case this may be done by parliamentary statement or even a ministerial speech outside Parliament. A good example is when on 11th May 1987 the Secretary of State, in response to a written question, stated that the advice in circular 15/84 on the calculation of housing supply should be applied flexibly and not in a doctrinaire or legislative manner. Parliamentary statements are published in Hansard and are therefore publicly available. As such they must have the same status as circulars and policy notes and must be regarded. Ministerial speeches are more problematic. In *Dimsdale Development (South East) Ltd v Secretary of State for the Environment*[6] MacPherson J reluctantly took note of an after dinner speech made by Patrick Jenkin, the then Secretary of State for the Environment. It turned out that the speech was not relevant to the planning decision but the judge doubted whether such manifestations should be used in argument, though he did take the speech into account. We would submit that it would be wrong to treat such 'off the cuff' speeches as material considerations as they may not be properly reported and are not an appropriate vehicle for the dissemination of government policy. More formal set piece speeches accompanied by press releases could be different. In a letter to the Journal of Planning and Environment Law,[7] Malcolm Grant pointed out that a minister had made a speech to the Planning Inspectors at their annual meeting giving advice on the status of development plans but at the same time stating that it was not policy and would not be published by HMSO. This speech has now been published both in the *Encyclopaedia of Planning* and in the Chief Planning Inspector's Report, which is published by HMSO. Grant posed the question 'is it now policy?' The chief planning officer, at that time E B Haran, responded that:

'It should also be noted that any public expression by a Minister on a policy matter is to be regarded as an authoritative expression of policy, either new or existing as the case may be and could no doubt be prayed in aid in a planning case if it were relevant. But it is obviously desirable for the effective functioning of the system that expressions of planning policy should be readily available to all through HMSO.'[8]

The reference to HMSO arose because the minister had quoted a previous chief planning officer's statement that 'policy is what can be bought at HMSO.'[9] As Miss Haran indicates it is not so much publication by HMSO that is crucial but the intention to lay down policy and its availability to the general public.

The position of ministerial decisions is also uncertain. Ministers unlike inspectors can lay down government policy when issuing a decision.[10]

6 [1985] 275 Estates Gazette 58, [1986] JPL 276.
7 [1988] JPL 322.
8 [1988] JPL 538.
9 See Journal of Planning Law Occasional Paper No 1, CF Allen 'The Inspector's Criterion'.
10 See *L Sears Blok v Secretary of State for the Environment and London Borough of Southwark* [1982] JPL 248.

However in *Wycombe District Council v Secretary of State for the Environ-ment*[11] Graham Eyre QC sitting as a deputy judge emphasised that an appeal decision should not be the occasion to give general guidance on the application of policy. He went on to state that:

> 'The appropriate place for statements of policy was the development plan, subject, of course, to such statements of policy as emerged from Central Government in what were essentially non-statutory documents such as the circulars but to which regard clearly had to be had.'

Ministerial decisions are undoubtedly an inappropriate occasion to issue general policy statements as they are not widely available. Nevertheless policy can emerge from a series of individual decisions and, until *Wycombe*, there was nothing to suggest that policy could not be laid down in a ministerial decision, however inappropriate. Indeed Graham Eyre QC him-self accepted in *Wycombe* that there was no reason why in a decision, the Secretary of State should not restate or refer to a matter of policy or indicate the importance that was attached to it. That is in substance laying down policy.

11 (1987) 57 P & CR 177, [1988] JPL 111.

CHAPTER 4

LOCAL AND REGIONAL PLANNING POLICY

A INTRODUCTION

In chapter 3 we discussed planning policy at the national level. However, planning policy is made not only at national level but locally as well; local authorities are policy-making bodies and so far as individual citizens or prospective developers are concerned, local authorities' planning policies may well be of greater significance than those of central government. As with central government, local authority policies emerge in a variety of ways and take many forms. In contrast to central government, however, local authorities are required to produce explicit policy statements on certain matters. One of the most important such duties is the obligation upon authorities to produce development plans.

The Planning Advisory Group described the development plan as the 'key feature' of the planning system.[1] Since 1947 local planning authorities have been under an obligation to prepare and publish a development plan for their area. Such a plan sets out policies for the use of land in the years ahead. It also sets out proposals for public sector investment—for example, programmes for the provision of major infrastructure works—which are intended to contribute towards the implementation of the plan.[2]

By effectively nationalising the right to develop land, and thus subjecting all future proposals for development to control by the planning authority, the Town and Country Planning Act 1947 made it theoretically possible for local planning authorities to plan the future use of land in their areas. 'The objects of Town and Country Planning', said Lewis Silkin, the Minister of Town and Country Planning, when introducing the 1947 legislation, '... are to secure a proper balance between the competing demands for land, so that all the land of the country is used in the best interests of the people.'[3] Development plans were, and still are, intended to play a central role in securing this 'balance'.

However, as Grant points out, 'the plan may influence, but it cannot control events'.[4] There are two reasons for saying this. The first is that, short of undertaking an extensive programme of land acquisition and development, the planning authority cannot compel investment in accordance with the provisions of their plan. The choice whether to invest remains in large measure with private developers. All that the planning authority can do is resist, through the development control process, proposals which are not in

1 *The Future of Development Plans* (HMSO, 1965).
2 See ch 16.
3 H C Deb, Vol 432, Col 947 (29th January 1947).
4 Malcolm Grant, *Urban Planning Law* (Sweet and Maxwell, 1982), p 77.

conformity with their plans. This suggests that if policies for the use of land in the years ahead are to be capable of realisation, the planning authority must have due regard to the needs of the market when preparing the development plan.

The second reason for suggesting that the development plan cannot control events is that it is not binding upon the local planning authority[5] or the Secretary of State. And it cannot be used as a sort of rubber stamp with which to process planning applications.[6] This contrasts with the municipal zoning ordinances which are the basis of much of the land use planning system in the United States.[7] The hallmark of the development control process in the United Kingdom is its discretionary nature. Each application for permission to develop land must be considered individually. 'It is a fundamental rule for the exercise of discretionary power', says Wade, 'that discretion must be brought to bear on every case: each one must be considered on its own merits and decided as the public interest requires at the time.[8] The development plan will clearly carry weight in the decision but, subject to certain safeguards,[9] the planning authority may depart from the policies in their plan if they consider that circumstances justify such a decision. This might happen, for example, where a development plan is out of date. In that event it has not been uncommon to find planning authorities looking to other, non-statutory, policy statements prepared by them for guidance. These are considered in more detail below.

Although the development plan cannot control events, it will, subject to what is said above, undoubtedly exert a considerable influence upon them. Developers will take the plan into account when planning investment; and local planning authorities and the Secretary of State are required to have regard to the appropriate development plan in exercising their development control functions[10]—for example, in determining a planning application or deciding what to do about a breach of planning control. 'Individual planning decisions', said Dobry 'should not be made in a vacuum. If decisions are to be correct, fair and above all, consistent, they must be made within a clear and consistently applied framework;'[11] the development plan is intended to provide such a framework. There is a similar statutory requirement to have regard to the development plan when considering whether land should be compulsorily purchased for planning purposes[12] and when making various other sorts of planning decisions. It is in this somewhat indirect manner, therefore, that development plans contribute towards the attainment of the 'proper balance' of which Lewis Silkin spoke.

5 See *Simpson v Edinburgh Corpn* 1960 SC 313, 1961 SLT 17 and *Enfield London Borough Council v Secretary of State for the Environment* (1974) 233 Estates Gazette 53, [1975] JPL 155.
6 See *Stringer v Minister of Housing and Local Government* [1971] 1 All ER 65, [1970] 1 WLR 1281; and *Myton Ltd v Minister of Housing and Local Government* (1963) 61 LGR 556, 16 P & CR 240. And see p 200 below.
7 However, such zoning ordinances can have their own flexibility; see Michael Purdue 'The Flexibility of North American Zoning as an Instrument of Land Use Planning' [1986] JPL 84.
8 H W R Wade, *Administrative Law* (Clarendon Press, Oxford, 6th edn, 1988), p 370.
9 See p 187 below.
10 See, for example, 1971 Act, ss 29(1) and 87(1).
11 *Review of the Development Control System: Final Report* (HMSO, 1975), para 2.64.
12 1971 Act, s 112(1A).

In view of their influential role in the planning process, it is important that development plans should be realistic. The procedures by which the policies in the plans are determined and the format in which they are presented will clearly have a material bearing on this. Important changes have been made in both procedures and format in recent years.

'Old style' development plans and their shortcomings

Under the 1947 Act[13] it was the duty of every local planning authority to submit for the approval of the Secretary of State a development plan indicating the manner in which the authority proposed that land in their area should be used (whether by the carrying out thereon of development or otherwise) and the stages by which any such development should be carried out. Each such 'old style' development plan had to include a written statement, summarising the authority's proposals, and a basic map defining the sites of proposed roads, public buildings, open spaces and so on, and allocating or 'zoning' areas of land for particular purposes.

In the early 1960s development plans made under the 1947 legislation were subjected to increasing criticism. Because of the great amount of detail they contained, plans tended to be inflexible, and although planning authorities were under an obligation to review their development plans at five-yearly intervals, and could, if they wished, put forward amendments at any time, it proved extremely difficult to keep plans up to date and forward-looking. The approval of the Secretary of State was required before the original plan or any amendment could come into operation and there thus came before the minister not only major policy issues but also a mass of detail. The need to examine so much detail and the obligation to afford all objectors the opportunity of a hearing (generally at a public inquiry) meant that a considerable period could elapse before ministerial approval was granted. 'Old style' plans were frequently criticised for the narrowness of their approach—it was said that they were little more than land use allocation maps, that they often paid insufficient attention to economic realities and investment priorities, and that they were not sufficiently concerned with the fundamental question of whether the physical environment was being properly shaped to meet evolving social and economic needs. The procedure for making 'old style' plans was also criticised as affording insufficient opportunity for public involvement at the formative stage of the plan.

As a result of these and other criticisms, provision was made by the Town and Country Planning Act 1968[14] for a completely new system of development planning designed to overcome the problems of the past.

The new system

Under the new system the development strategy for the country area is dealt with separately from detailed local planning policies for each district area. There are to be two tiers of plans, structure plans and local plans;[15] the

13 The provisions of the 1947 Act relating to the making and amendment of 'old style' development plans were re-enacted in Sch 5 to the 1971 Act.
14 See now Pt II of the 1971 Act, as amended.
15 The form of the 'new style' development plan owes much to the recommendations made by the Ministers' Planning Advisory Group in *The Future of Development Plans* (HMSO 1965).

development plan for any area will eventually consist of the provisions of any structure plan relating to the area and the provisions of any relevant local plan.

The structure plan consists, in essence, of a written statement and a key diagram (but not a map). The purpose of a structure plan is to set out the broad policy framework for an area; it is not to be concerned with detailed proposals for the use of particular parcels of land in the area. With its freedom from detail it was hoped that the structure plan would allow strategic issues to be settled more quickly than was possible in the past. Structure plans are prepared by county planning authorities and require ministerial approval.

Detailed planning policies and proposals are set out in local plans. A local plan consists of a map and a written statement. Local plans are normally prepared and adopted by district planning authorities; only exceptionally will a local plan require to be approved by the Secretary of State. A local plan has to conform generally to the provisions of any approved structure plan relating to the area.

It was hoped that the new development planning system would avoid the delays of the past and that by making it possible for plans to take effect more quickly, the new procedures would help to reduce uncertainty and blight and would make it easier for authorities to keep plans up to date. It was also hoped that the new plans would prove more responsive to public opinion than were 'old style' development plans. The extent to which these hopes are being realised is considered below.

The new system was brought into effect gradually in different areas of England and Wales in order to avoid too many plans being submitted at once and to ensure that the system was only brought into force in areas which had at that time sufficient resources and skilled staff. The new structure plans took a long time to prepare and to approve; the last one was approved in 1985, seventeen years after the 1968 Act was passed. In addition the provision of local plans has been sporadic and piecemeal. It has been calculated that it will be 1993 before half the population of England and Wales outside London will be covered by an adopted local plan.

The abolition of the Greater London Council and the metropolitan counties has also resulted in the creation of yet another type of development plan, the unitary plan, for those areas. This plan is to be prepared by the London Boroughs and the district councils and is an amalgamation of the structure plan and the local plan into one document.

The position is complicated by the fact that for many areas the 'old style' development plans remain in force and until the new unitary plans are adopted, the structure and local plans, which have been approved and adopted, still apply. Before dealing with the new system it is therefore still necessary to consider certain aspects of 'old style' plans and to outline the rather complex arrangements for transition to the new systems. The transitional provisions for unitary plans are outlined later in the chapter.

B OLD STYLE DEVELOPMENT PLANS AND TRANSITION TO THE NEW SYSTEM

As is mentioned above, in a number of contexts statute directs that regard must be had to 'the provisions of the development plan'. For the purposes of the relevant legislation there can, as respects any particular piece of land, only be one development plan in operation at any particular time. During the transition to the new system the component parts of the development plan for an area will, however, vary from time to time.

The 'old style' development plan for an area continues in force and is to be treated as being, or as being comprised in, the development plan for that area until it is either revoked by the Secretary of State or is replaced by an appropriate local plan.[16] It seems likely that in some areas 'old style' development plans will continue in force for some time to come and it is therefore necessary to give a brief account of the documents which make up an 'old style' plan.

Form and content of 'old style' development plan

An 'old style' development plan includes 'such maps and such descriptive matter as may be necessary to illustrate the proposals in question with such degree of particularity as may be appropriate to different parts of the district'; in particular, such a plan may define the sites of proposed roads, public or other buildings and works, airfields, parks, pleasure grounds, nature reserves and other open spaces, or allocate areas of land for use for agricultural, residential, industrial or other purposes of any class specified in the plan (1971 Act, Sch 5, para 1(3)).

A development plan may define as an area of comprehensive development any area which, in the opinion of the planning authority, should be developed or redeveloped as a whole for any one or more of the following purposes:

(a) for the purpose of dealing satisfactorily with extensive war damage or conditions of bad lay-out or obsolete development; or
(b) for the purpose of providing for the relocation of population or industry or the replacement of open space in the course of the development or redevelopment of any other area; or
(c) for any other purpose specified in the plan (Sch 5, para 1(4)).

The Town and Country Planning (Development Plans) Regulations 1965 provided that a development plan was to consist of a written statement and a basic map and such other map or maps as might be appropriate (reg 4). The written statement had to include, *inter alia*, a summary of the main proposals of the development plan and an indication of the stages by which the proposals were to be carried out (reg 14). Regulations 5 and 6 of, and Sch 1 to, the 1965 regulations made provision as to the form and content of the obligatory basic map. Any land defined as an area of comprehensive development had to be shown on a comprehensive development area map (reg 8). A development plan could include a programme map showing the stages by which any proposed development should be carried out; however, such a map ceased to be obligatory in 1965 (see reg 14(2)).

A development plan is to have effect as if there were incorporated in it the provisions of certain ministerial orders and schemes relating to roads and new towns (1971 Act, Sch 5, para 5).

The 1947 Act provided that a development plan might designate land as subject to compulsory acquisition and such land could be compulsorily

16 See Sch 7 to the 1971 Act, paras 5A to C.

acquired. The statutory provisions relating to such designation were repealed by the 1968 Act: but new powers to compulsorily purchase land for planning purposes were created (now see Chapter 16).

Amendment of 'old style' development plan

The provisions of the 1947 Act relating to the making and amendment of 'old style' development plans were re-enacted in Sch 5 to the 1971 Act. Under para 3 of that Schedule local planning authorities[17] were able to submit for the approval of the Secretary of State proposals for alterations or amendments to 'old style' development plans; it was, however, provided that the consent of the Secretary of State had to be obtained before any such proposals for amendment of an 'old style' development plan could be submitted to the minister for his consideration (1971 Act, Sch 7, para 1). After the coming into operation of Part II of the 1971 Act (dealing with the making of 'new style' plans) the Secretary of State took the view that any fresh development planning proposals should normally be incorporated in a 'new style' plan rather than in an amendment to an 'old style' development plan; and the Secretary of State was therefore prepared to sanction the submission of proposals for amendment of an 'old style' plan only if the need for development planning action was urgent and strictly localised. In any case now that structure plans have been approved for the whole of England and Wales Sch 5 has been repealed. This means that there can be no further amendment of the 'old style' development plan relating to that area—the 'old style' plan was in effect 'frozen' until replaced by a 'new style' plan.

Replacement of 'old style' development plan

The mere repeal of Sch 5 to the 1971 Act does not mean that the 'old style' development plan for that area thereupon ceased to have effect—the development plan which was in force before the repeal of Sch 5 is to continue in force and is to be treated for the purposes of the planning legislation and of the Land Compensation Act 1961 as being comprised in, or as being, the development plan for the area (1971 Act, Sch 7, para 2).

Nor does the 'old style' plan cease to have effect on the coming into operation of a structure plan made under the new system; in the absence of a local plan for an area, the approved structure plan and the 'old style' development plan will together make up the development plan for that area (see 1971 Act, Sch 7, para 3). In any case of conflict the provisions of the structure plan will for most purposes prevail over those of the 'old style' plan.[18]

Only an appropriate local plan made under the new system can take the place of an 'old style' plan. On the adoption or approval of a local plan for any area, so much of any 'old style' plan as relates to the same area is to cease to have effect unless the Secretary of State, after consulting the planning authority, makes an order directing that all or any of the provisions of the

---

17 Ie, county and district planning authorities.
18 See 1971 Act, Sch 7, para 3. For the purposes of the Land Compensation Act 1961, however, a landowner is entitled, in effect, to the benefit of those assumptions, whether derived from the structure plan or from the 'old style' plan, which are more favourable to his claim (see Sch 7, para 5).

'old style' plan should continue in force (1971 Act, Sch 7, paras 5A–C[19]) such an order would presumably be made on the adoption or approval of a local plan which dealt, for example, with only one or two particular types of development and which was therefore only a partial replacement for the 'old style' plan. The Secretary of State also has power to make an order revoking, in whole or in part, the 'old style' plan for any area (see 1971 Act, Sch 7, paras 6 and 7). In *R v Secretary of State for the Environment, ex p Great Grimsby Borough Council*[20] Russell J held that where the Secretary of State, on the adoption of a local plan, had failed to make an order saving an 'old style' plan, it was possible for the Secretary of State to make a new order reviving the old style plan.

When, in the manner outlined above, the 'old style' development plan has ceased to have effect in any area, the development plan for that area will consist of the provisions of any approved structure plan relating to the area and the provisions of any local plan applicable to the area (see below).

The Secretary of State is under a duty to maintain and keep up to date a register showing when and where Part II of the Act came into operation and this also indicates the local planning authorities' intention to compile new development plans under the Act and when this process will commence (see 1971 Act, s 21 (7A)). As Morgan and Nott have pointed out such indications are of considerable importance as the intention to replace the 'old style' plans with new local plans is in itself a material consideration.[1] This information is also in the register kept by the local planning authorities: see below.

C THE NEW SYSTEM

The legislation on the new type of development plan, originally contained in the Town and Country Planning Act 1968, is now in Pt II of the 1971 Act as amended in a number of important respects by the Town and Country Planning (Amendment) Act 1972, the Local Government Act 1972, the Local Government Planning and Land Act 1980, the Local Government (Miscellaneous Provisions) Act 1982 and the Housing and Planning Act 1986. The legislation relating to the new system of development planning makes provision for the preparation of structure plans and local plans.

Once the 'old style' development plan for an area has ceased to have effect, the development plan for that area will consist of:

(a) the provisions of any structure plan relating to the area, together with the Secretary of State's notice of approval of the plan;

(b) any alterations to the structure plan, together with the Secretary of State's notices of approval thereof;

(c) any provisions of a local plan applicable to the area, together with a copy of the local planning authority's resolution of adoption or, as the case may be, the Secretary of State's notice of approval of the local plan; and

(d) any alterations to that local plan, together with a copy of the local planning authority's resolutions of adoption or, as the case may be, the Secretary of State's notices of approval thereof (see 1971 Act, s 20).

19 Inserted by the Local Government, Planning and Land Act 1980, Sch 14, paras 14, 15.
20 [1986] JPL 910.
1 Morgan and Nott 'Development Control: Policy into Practice' (1988, Butterworths) ch 4, p 130.

Detailed provision as to the form and content of structure and local plans and as to the procedure for their preparation and approval or adoption is made by the Town and Country Planning (Structure and Local Plans) Regulations 1982 (the 1982 regulations). The regulations require both county and district planning authorities to maintain an up-to-date register and index map of structure and local plans affecting their area (see reg 39).

The two parts of the 'new style' development plan, the structure plan and the local plan or plans, are now considered in turn.

1 STRUCTURE PLANS

Section 7(1) of the 1971 Act requires the local planning authority (which is the county planning authority[2]) to prepare and submit to the Secretary of State for approval a structure plan for their area. The Act itself does not set out the functions of the structure plan but circular 22/84 now sets out three main functions. These are to provide a strategic framework for development control, to apply national and regional policies in terms of land use policies and to ensure a framework for local plans. Now that structure plans have been approved for the whole of England and Wales, the rules about preparation are less relevant but still apply with necessary modifications to the alteration or repeal and replacement of structure plans.

(a) *Survey*

The policy framework in the structure plan must be justified by the results of a survey (1971 Act, s 7(4)) and the first action taken by a county planning authority proposing to prepare a structure plan was to institute a survey of their area.

Each county planning authority had, in so far as they had not already done so, to institute a survey of their area examining the matters which might be expected to affect the development of their area or the planning of its development. Surveys have now been carried out by all the county planning authorities but there is a continuing obligation to keep all such matters under review (1971 Act, s 6(1)). The range of matters to be so examined and kept under review is wide; matters to be covered include:

(a) the principal physical and economic characteristics of the area (including the principal purposes for which land is used) and, so far as relevant, those of any neighbouring areas;
(b) the size, composition and distribution of the population of the area (whether resident or otherwise);
(c) the communications, transport system and traffic of the area and, so far as relevant, of any neighbouring areas;
(d) any other considerations which may be expected to affect any of the foregoing matters;
(e) such other matters as may be prescribed by regulations, or direction by the Secretary of State and
(f) any changes already projected in any of the foregoing matters and the effect which those changes are likely to have on the development of the area or the planning of such development (1971 Act, s 6(3)).

2 See the Local Government Act 1972, s 183.

County planning authorities used to be required to submit a report of survey to the Secretary of State along with the structure plan, but this requirement has been dropped by the Local Government, Planning and Land Act 1980. Also notwithstanding the range of matters to be examined, authorities were discouraged from producing large survey reports.[3]

Although the survey provides the basis for preparation of the structure plan, the survey report does not form part of the plan and is not subject to ministerial approval.

(b) *Preparation of structure plan*

Having completed the survey, the county planning authority would analyse the information obtained with a view to preparing the structure plan.

The legislation provides that a structure plan may, instead of consisting of a single document, consist of a series of plans relating to different parts of the authority's area—a form of development planning by instalments—and may, with the approval of the Secretary of State, relate to part only of an authority's area (1971 Act, s 7(7)). There was also provision for the preparation of joint structure plans but this has since been repealed (1971 Act, s 10 A[4]). In addition, the old 1974 regulations provided for urban structure plans for parts of the area which were already urbanised (reg 8(1)). In practice structure plans were only prepared by a single county planning authority for their whole area except where the county had inherited part area plans. The 1982 regulations make no provision for further urban structure plans and where the county structure plan is to be repealed or replaced, it must include proposals for the repeal of any urban structure plan (reg 46).

The procedure for preparing or altering a structure plan is very much in the hands of the county planning authority. However, during the preparatory stage the authority are required to carry out certain consultations and to take steps to give publicity to the matters which they propose to include in the plan.

Before finally determining the content, the county must consult[5] all district planning authorities whose areas or any parts thereof are in the area to which the proposals for alteration or replacement relate and take those views into consideration after affording the districts a reasonable opportunity to express their views (reg 6). Circular 22/84 also asks the counties to consult other public bodies who may be affected by the proposals (para 2.28).

Before authorities have become firmly committed to particular policies and proposals, they must provide an opportunity for members of the public to put forward their views on the structure plan. Before finally determining the content of a structure plan, the county planning authority must take such steps as will in their opinion secure:

---

3 See circular 23/81, para 2.8. This circular was cancelled by circular 22/84 which makes no reference to the survey except to state that the county may if they think fit institute a fresh survey but should avoid unnecessary work; see para 2.3.
4 Repealed by the Local Government Act 1972, s 72 and Sch 30.
5 As to what is involved in a duty to 'consult' another body see *Easter Ross Land Use Committee v Secretary of State for Scotland* 1970 SC 182, 1970 SLT 317 (which arose out of an amendment to an 'old style' development plan). See also Colin T Reid, 'A Planning Authority's Duty to Consult' 1982 SPLP 4.

(a) that adequate publicity is given to the matters which the authority propose to include in the structure plan and to the proposed contents of the explanatory memorandum;

(b) that persons who may be expected to want to make representations on the matters proposed to be included in the plan and to the proposed contents of the explanatory memorandum, are given an adequate opportunity to make representations, and are made aware of this right.

The authority must allow a period of at least six weeks for the making of representations and must consider any representations made within this period (1971 Act, s 8(1), and reg 5).

This requirement to involve the public in the structure plan process is commonly referred as the 'participation exercise' although this is not a term which is used in the legislation. The term was much in vogue around the time that the legislation for the 'new style' of development plan was introduced. During the debate in 1968 on the second reading of the Town and Country Planning Bill, for example, the Minister of Housing and Local Government, Anthony Greenwood, said: 'Above all, I am determined that there shall be more real public participation in planning. I want people to have a much better chance of being involved in the planning of the area they live in and of influencing it. Planning is for people and about their activities, not just about areas.'[6]

The somewhat vague terms of the legislation would not seem to do justice to this vision of the development planning process. As McAuslan comments 'the statutes providing for [participation] are so open-ended and vague that it is difficult to see that any duty has been laid on local authorities at all.'[7] The explanation is twofold. First of all, in *People and Planning* (1969) the Committee on Public Participation in Planning recommended that participation should not be a formalised or rigid process but should be flexible enough to meet all types of local need. To allow for flexibility the statutory requirements were kept to a minimum and it was left to individual authorities to decide upon the methods of promoting participation best suited to the requirements of particular areas. The Secretary of State is, however, required, before he considers a structure plan, to satisfy himself that the purposes of the statutory provisions on public involvement have been adequately achieved (see p 53 below).

Secondly, notwithstanding the use of the word 'participation' in official advice and guidance, it was clearly intended that responsibility for the content of the plan should remain with the county planning authority. The aim of the exercise is, as Grant says, 'to extend the opportunity for the exercise of influence by citizens, not to achieve any transfer of power'.[8] It is presumably for this reason that s 8 of the 1971 Act talks about 'publicity' and 'representations' and not about 'participation'. It is also significant that the legislation does not require the county to give reasons why representations have been rejected.

6 H C Deb, vol 757, Col 1362 (31st January 1968).
7 P McAuslan, *The Ideologies of Planning Law* (Pergamon Press, 1980), p 11.
8 *Urban Planning Law*, p 101. For a detailed discussion of the theory and practice of participation see N Boaden, M Goldsmith, W Hampton and P Stringer, 'Planning and Participation in Practice: A Study of Public Participation in Structure Planning' in *Progress in Planning*, D Diamond and J B McLoughlin, eds, 1981.

The very general terms in which the legislation is framed has permitted some back-tracking in the official guidance on the scope of the publicity and consultation exercise. In particular Circular 22/84 cautions against doing any more than the statutory requirements and states that further publicity work 'should only be undertaken where the authority are satisfied that further work is clearly justified,' (para 2.21). The reason for this change of heart would seem to be a desire to speed up the plan making process, and perhaps also a feeling that public consultation has most to contribute to local plans.

(c) *The form and content of a structure plan*

Having consulted the specified bodies and having afforded the public an opportunity to make representations, the authority can proceed to complete their preparation of the structure plan.

Concerned as it is with broad policy, not with the detailed use of particular parcels of land, a structure plan is quite different in form from the 'old style' development plan.

Section 7(1A) of the 1971 Act provides that a structure plan shall consist of a written statement which is to be illustrated by such diagram or diagrams as may be prescribed. In fact reg 8 of the 1982 regulations only provides for one key diagram, but this itself can contain or be accompanied by insets showing further detail as long as the key diagram just contains the boundary of the inset and the policy and general proposals are shown only on the inset and not in the main body of the key diagram. The key diagram is expressly stated to be part of the structure plan (1971 Act, s 7(1A) (6)) but it is unclear whether the same applies to any insets which accompany the key diagram. As such insets are helping to explain the policy and proposals in the written statement, this would suggest that they are part of the plan. In the event of any contradiction in a structure plan, between the written statement and the key diagram or inset, the provisions of the written statement are to prevail (reg 43).

In line with the recommendations of the PAG Report, reg 8(3) provides that neither the key diagram nor an inset shall be on a map base. The 1971 Act used to state that as well as diagrams the structure plan could contain 'illustrations and descriptive matter.' The proposals put forward by the PAG were attacked by one planner on the grounds that:

'... the illustrative material is quite simply pictorial; picture documents, simply cartoons; mere broad elementary illustrations; mere blobs of colour placed on sheets of paper completely innocent of all precise information as to the towns to which they refer.'[9]

In fact most structure plans are fairly restrained in their use of illustrative material and are informative but in any case 'illustrative material' as opposed to diagrams cannot now be contained in the structure plan itself and is relegated to the explanatory memorandum (1971 Act, s 7(6A)). This is probably due not to the above criticism but as part of the separation of reasons from the policies themselves.

The explanatory memorandum is now the document for the giving of the reasons for the policies and proposals in the structure plan. Originally the

9 See Thomas Sharp 'Planning planning' (1966) Journal of Town Planning Institute 209.

written statement itself had to contain 'a reasoned justification of the policy and general proposals formulated therein.'[10] The Secretary of State in approving structure plans would distinguish between the policies and general proposals and the reasoned justification by putting the policies and proposal in capital letters. The importance of the change, introduced by the Local Government, Planning and Land Act 1980, is that while the reasoned justification was part of the structure plan, the explanatory memorandum is not. This was so held in *Severn Trent Water Authority v Secretary of State for the Environment and South Staffordshire District Council*[11] but David Widdicombe sitting as a deputy judge went on to hold that the explanatory memorandum was nevertheless a material consideration and as such to be regarded as well as the structure plan. However, as it is not part of the plan, it is not formally approved by the Secretary of State and so it could be that the Secretary of State approves of a policy without approving of the county's reasons for submitting that policy.

Many structure plans have been submitted and approved in the old pre-1980 Act form, though, in the case of plans approved after the 1980 Act, the approval will have been limited to the policies and general proposals and the rest of the material treated as if it were the explanatory memorandum. Circular 22/84 in this regard states that:

'Plans should be brought into line with the new system when for other reasons, it becomes necessary to prepare proposals for alteration. It is sufficient to include in proposals for alteration an alteration to remove from the approved written statement the reasoned justification and all other material not distinguished as policies and general proposals. Following the approval of alterations which include the removal of the reasoned justification from the approved pre-1980 written statement, explanatory material for all the policies and general proposals of the approved plan as altered should be included in a separate explanatory memorandum.' (para 2.19)

As to the content of the written statement s 7(1A) provides that the written statement will:

'(a) formulate the authority's policy and general proposals in respect of the development and other use of land in their area (including measures for improvement of the physical environment and the management of traffic).'[12]

The distinction between policies and proposals could indicate that the statement should contain not only the authority's views and attitudes towards private sector developments but also their own programmed development. The only judicial consideration of these words has been in the

---

10 Reg 9(3) of the 1974 Regulations.
11 [1989] JPL 21.
12 In *Westminster City Council v Great Portland Estates plc* [1985] AC661, [1984] 3 WLR 1035 the House of Lords held that the broadly similar provision dealing with the content of local plans in the Town and Country Planning Act 1971 was to be construed as imposing on the planning authority an obligation to include in their plan *all* proposals which they may have for the development and use of land (see p 64 below).

case of *Edwin H Bradley & Sons Ltd v Secretary of State for the Environment*[13] where Glidewell J, after quoting s 7(1A) and the then relevant regulations stated:

'I apprehend that since the early 1970s the staffs of county planning departments have been concerned to distinguish between statements of policy or proposals which can properly be regarded as "general" and thus appropriate to the structure plan and those proposals which are so specific, particularly in defining the land to which they relate, that they should not be included in the structure plan but await the preparation of the local plan, which is intended to be detailed and specific. It is not necessary for me to consider this question, because all learned counsel are agreed that the relevant policies in this structure plan can properly be said to be "general" and thus included in the structure plan. But I have little doubt that uncertainty about where the line between general and specific proposals should be drawn has led to the problems in this case.'

This was because the policy at issue defined with some precision where further residential development should take place and there has been a tendency for structure plans to be more detailed than was probably intended. However, as Glidewell J indicates, a policy would have to be extremely detailed for it to be outside the remit of the structure plan as a matter of law and, in any case, it can be pointed out that the adjective in "general" only strictly qualifies the proposals and not the policies in the written statement.

These are the only express requirements as to what should be put in the written statement. There is provision for the Secretary of State to prescribe other matters by direction but no such directions have been made (1971 Act, s 7(1A)(b)). However, the 1971 Act does lay down that in formulating their policy and general proposals the county shall secure that the policies and proposals are justified by the results of the survey (1971 Act, s 7(4)) and that regard is had to:

(a) current policies for the economic planning and development of the region as a whole; and
(b) the resources likely to be available; and
(c) to such other matters as the Secretary of State may direct them to take into account.

As well as ensuring that the policies are realistic, this wording suggests an important distinction between the policies to go into the written statement and other matters which justify or relate to those policies. This distinction is reinforced by s 7(6A) which requires the explanatory memorandum to summarise the reasons which justify each and every policy and to state their relationship to expected development and other use of land in neighbouring areas. The explanatory memorandum is to contain such other matters as may be prescribed and reg 9 of the 1982 regulations lays down that the memorandum shall contain such indications as the county planning authority may think appropriate of the regard they had to:

(a) current national and regional policies;

13 (1983) 47 P & CR 374, 264 Estates Gazette 926, [1982] JPL 43.

(b) social considerations; and
(c) the resources likely to be available for carrying out the policy and general proposals.

The old 1974 regulations used to contain a much longer list of matters to which policy was required to relate. The change in the content of the matters is not in itself important: most would in any case be proper planning considerations. The important change is the insistence that social considerations are to go into the explanatory memorandum and not the written statement itself. The reason is undoubtedly that the first structure plans tended to include policies that did not directly relate to the use and development of land and there was also a confusion as to what was the policy and what was the reasoned justification. The reaction of the Secretary of State was often to delete the policy or to make it clear that it was a reasoned justification by putting the policy proper in capital letters followed by the reasons and explanation.[14] Circular 22/84 emphasises the need to keep to the distinction between land use policies and reasons by stating:

'Non land use matters, for example, financial support, consultation arrangements and proposed methods of implementation should not be included as policies or proposals in structure or local plans. These should however be included in the explanatory memorandum or reasoned justification where they are relevant to a full understanding of a plan's policies or proposals or provide a context for them.' (para 4.2)

This distinction does flow from the wording of the Act. A policy of taking into account the need for the disabled is not a *land use policy* but it can be a *reason* for requiring access for the disabled in all building design and can be part of a general objective of a fairer and better society. What is less clear is whether it is necessary to make such an absolute distinction. In practice it is often hard to disentangle objectives, policies and their justification. This is shown by the *Severn–Trent* decision, where David Widdicombe QC, having found that the inspector had incorrectly treated a statement in the explanatory memorandum as part of the structure plan, went on to hold that the inspector was entitled to rely on that statement and the mistake had not affected the outcome.

The more important issue is the kind of reasons or objectives which are capable in law of justifying a particular land use policy or proposal. It would seem that the policies must serve a planning purpose but the reference to social and economic considerations in the Act and regulations would indicate that such planning considerations are wide in scope.[15]

In *Westminster City Council v Great Portland Estates plc*,[16] for example, the House of Lords held that a local plan policy directed at safeguarding industrial uses having important linkages with central London activities served a genuine planning purpose. Although the policy incidentally protected certain existing users, its object was to safeguard certain industrial

14 See Jowell and Noble 'Structure Plans as Instruments of Social and Economic Policy' (1981) JPL 466 and Jowell and Noble 'Planning as Social Engineering: Notes on the First English Structure Plans' Urban Law and Policy 1980, 293.
15 For a discussion of the scope of planning purposes see ch 8.
16 [1985] AC 661, [1984] 3 WLR 1035.

activities considered important to the diverse character, vitality and functioning of Westminster. The policy was, said Lord Scarman, 'a powerful piece of
positive thinking within a planning context'. Nevertheless a land use policy
based on political or moral reasons could be outside the scope of the Act and
ultra vires.

There is no fixed end date for a structure plan, as the idea is that they
should evolve flexibly but circular 22/84 states that policies should look 10
years ahead (para 4.5). Monitoring of a plan should indicate the need for
alteration of different parts of the plan at different times.

(d) *Action areas*

A structure plan used to have to 'indicate' any part of the area covered by the
plan which the county planning authority had selected for comprehensive
treatment, to begin within five years of the approval of the structure plan by
the Secretary of State, by means of development, redevelopment or improvement or by a combination of those methods; such an area is termed an 'action
area'[17] (1971 Act, s 7(5); reg 8). A local plan (an 'action area plan') then had
to be prepared for any action area designated in the structure plan (see p 62
below). This provision has been repealed and an action area can be prepared
as a local plan without there being any prior notation in the structure plan.

(e) *Submission to Secretary of State*

When, under s 7(1) of the 1971 Act, a county planning authority submits the
structure plan accompanied by the explanatory memorandum to the Secretary of State, they must also submit to the minister a brief account of the
steps they have taken to satisfy the requirements of s 8(1) of the 1971 Act as
to public consultation (above) and of the consultations they have had with
other bodies (1971 Act, s 8(3); 1982 regulations, reg 15).

No later than the date of submission of these documents to the minister the
authority must make copies of the submitted documents available for public
inspection (see 1971 Act, s 8(2); 1982 regulations, reg 36); copies must also be
made available for sale (reg 38). Each copy of the plan is to be accompanied
by a statement of the period within which objections may be made to the
Secretary of State; that period is six weeks from the date when notice of the
submission is first published (1971 Act, s 8(2); 1982 regulations, reg 16). The
authority must give notice by advertisement that the structure plan has been
submitted and is available for inspection (see 1982 regulations, reg 16 and
Schedule); that notice is to indicate the manner in which and the period
within which objections may be made to the Secretary of State (see 1982
regulations, reg 16 and Schedule).

(f) *Consideration by Secretary of State: (1) adequacy of public consultation*

Circular 22/84 suggests that the account of the steps taken by the planning
authority to consult the public, which must accompany the structure plan
when it is submitted for approval, should be as clear and as brief as possible
(para 2.33). It should demonstrate how representations were considered and
what decision resulted. As indicated above, a copy of the statement is to be
made available for public inspection.

17 Now repealed by the Local Government, Planning and Land Act 1980.

Before considering any structure plan submitted for his approval, the Secretary of State must satisfy himself that the purposes of paragraphs (a) to (c) of s 8(1) of the 1971 Act (requirements as to public consultation—see p 48 above) have been adequately achieved by the steps the authority have taken. It would seem that this provision was inserted in the legislation to avoid the possibility of application for judicial review of the planning authority's action at a late stage in the preparation of the plan.[17] In satisfying himself as to adequacy of the participation exercise, the minister will clearly be influenced to a very large extent by the document setting out the planning authority's account of the steps they have taken. Circular 22/84 gives no guidance on the question of adequacy. Instead, as mentioned above, it sets out what is stated to be a standard procedure for publicity and consultation.

If the Secretary of State is not satisfied with the steps the authority have taken, he will return the plan, directing the authority to take such further action as he specifies and thereafter to re-submit the plan with such modifications as they consider appropriate[18] (1971 Act, s 8(4)). No such direction has been issued to date.

(g) *Consideration by Secretary of State: (2) objections and examination in public*

When the period for submitting objections has expired the Secretary of State will proceed to consider the structure plan. In considering the plan the minister may take into account any matters he considers relevant, whether or not they were taken into account in the submitted plan (1971 Act, s 9(2)).

Unless the Secretary of State decided, as he was entitled to do, that he would reject the structure plan without even going as far as considering objections, then, before determining whether or not to approve the plan, the minister had to:[19]

(a) consider any objections to the plan,[20] and
(b) cause a person or persons, appointed by him for the purpose, to hold such an examination in public of such matters affecting his consideration of the plan as he believes ought to be so examined (1971 Act, s 9(3)(b)).

However, in the case of proposals for the alteration or repeal and replacement of a structure plan (which now are the only cases that can arise) the Secretary of State does not have to cause an examination in public to be held if it appears to him that no matters which require an examination in public arise from either the proposals or the replacement structure plan (1971 Act, s 10(8)).

This power to decide not to hold an examination in public was introduced by the Local Government, Planning and Land Act 1980. It clearly makes sense that the expense and delay of holding an examination in public should not be incurred in respect of a proposal to alter a structure plan to which no

17 *Official Report*, Standing Committee G, Session 1967–1968, Vol IX, Col 119 (22nd February 1968).
18 As to procedure to be followed in such a case see 1971 Act, s 8(5)–(7); and 1982 regulations, regs 17 and 18.
19 1971 Act, s 9(3) (substituted by the Town and Country Planning (Amendment) Act 1972).
20 The Secretary of State can, however, disregard objections relating to certain types of development authorised by or under the Highways Act 1980 and the New Towns legislation (see 1971 Act, s 16, as amended by s 343 of, and Sch 24 to, the Highways Act 1980).

one objects. It is more surprising that, at least in theory, an examination in public does not have to be held in the case of a complete replacement of a structure plan. Even where an examination in public is held, the Secretary of State is able to concentrate the public proceedings on those strategic issues (whether or not they happen to be the subject of objection) which he considers merit examination. Though the minister has a duty to consider all objections to an alteration or replacement, he is not obliged to afford an objector (or any other person or body) an opportunity of a hearing; only those persons and bodies invited to do so by the Secretary of State (or by the person or persons appointed to hold the examination) will be able to take part in the examination in public (1971 Act, s 9(5)), if such an examination is to be held. In the selection of participants (who need not have made objections or representations) the criterion will be the effectiveness of the contribution which, from their knowledge or the views they have expressed, they can be expected to make to the discussion of the matters to be examined.

The Secretary of State did not make regulations with respect to the procedure to be followed at the public examination of a structure plan but instead issued a Code of Practice.[1] This is for guidance only and has no statutory force.

The Code provides that the Secretary of State will provide the names of the chairman and the other members of the panel appointed to conduct the examination. The chairman is independent and usually a planning QC or a retired senior civil servant. There are normally two other members of the panel, one a planning inspector and the other with recent experience of government office in the region. The Secretary of State will also publish a list of the matters to be examined and of those persons or bodies invited to take part. The county planning authority responsible for the structure plan will always be invited. Matters which need to be examined are likely to arise, it seems, from doubts about the validity of forecasts or other justification for the plan; from clashes between the plan and national or regional policies, or the policies of neighbouring county planning authorities or district planning authorities within the county; from any conflicts between the various general proposals in the plan; or from issues involving substantial controversy which have not been resolved. Publication of the list provides an opportunity for comment on the selection of the issues and the participants prior to the examination. A final list will then be published and participants may be invited to provide, in advance of the examination, a statement specifically directed to the matter or matters for examination with which they are concerned. The chairman has the power to invite additional bodies or persons to participate if it appears to him or to them desirable. This power can be exercised before or during the examination (1971 Act, s 9(5)).

The Code describes the examination in public as essentially a probing discussion. It is inquisitorial rather than adversarial in character. Its conduct is in the hands of the chairman. The aim is to create an appropriate atmosphere for intensive discussion and to get away from the formalities of the traditional public inquiry. The chairman and any other members of the panel will take an active part in the examination; an important feature of their role is to ensure that relevant points of view are explored.

---

1 See Code of Practice for the Examination in Public of Structure Plans, published first in 1973 and amended in 1978 and 1984.

Where a matter to be discussed involves the interest of a government department, that department will be invited to send a representative to the examination. He will be there primarily to explain his minister's views about the policies and proposals in the plan and to give appropriate information.

Normally such government witnesses are not expected to give their views on the merits of government policies, see chapter 19.

On the conclusion of the examination the chairman will prepare and submit his report to the Secretary of State. This will not contain a detailed account of the arguments advanced by participants but should provide a balanced assessment of the issues discussed and will normally include recommendations.

If, after the examination, new information becomes available which is of such importance that it leads the minister to a decision he would not otherwise have taken, the Code states that this information will normally be published and an opportunity provided for written comment. In exceptional cases the Secretary of State could re-open the examination.

The examination in public constitutes a statutory inquiry for the purposes of s 1(1)(c) of the Tribunals and Inquiries Act 1971 but not for any other purpose of that Act (1971 Act, s 9(6)). This means that the procedures are subject to the supervision of the Council on Tribunals.

Concern has, not surprisingly, been expressed about the extent of the Secretary of State's powers in relation to the examination in public. He not only decides whether an examination is to take place, he also selects the chairman and any other members of the panel to conduct the examination, he decides upon the issues to be considered and (subject to the power of the chairman) he selects the persons or bodies to take part in the examination. As the Council on Tribunals feared,[2] the examination has the appearance of an entirely administrative process under the control of the Secretary of State.[3] If this all seems rather arbitrary, the reason given is that the procedure is primarily designed to inform the minister on key issues and not to provide a forum for the hearing of objections. 'The primary purpose of the examination in public', states the Code of Practice, 'is to provide the Secretary of State with the information and arguments he needs, in addition to the material submitted with a structure plan and the objections and representations made on it, to enable him to reach a decision on the plan.' The interests of the objector are intended to be safeguarded by the requirement imposed on the Secretary of State to consider any objections to the plan before reaching a decision (1971 Act, s 9(3)).

It may be noted that when the legislative framework for the 'new style' development plan was first introduced in 1967 in the Town and Country Planning Bill, assurances were given in Parliament that the traditional right to be heard in support of an objection to the plan would be retained. Provision was accordingly made in the 1968 Act for the holding of public inquiries into objections to finalised structure plans. However, the government's experience in the late 1960s and early 1970s with the Greater London Development Plan (GLDP) made it think again about the procedure for

---

2 See *Annual Report for 1971–72*, paras 27–32.
3 In *Edwin H Bradley & Sons Ltd v Secretary of State for the Environment* (1983) 47 P & CR 374 Glidewell J said: 'this procedure is not in the nature of a judicial or quasi-judicial hearing between parties . . .'

testing the merits of structure plans. Although there were similarities, the GLDP was not, in fact, a structure plan—it was an 'old style' development plan. Consequently, it contained a considerable amount of detail. This factor, coupled with the emphasis then being given to participation in the development plan process, resulted in some 28,000 objections, all of which were entitled to be supported at a public inquiry. The resulting inquiry sat for two and a half years. As a direct result of this, the government decided to substitute for the public inquiry and the right to be heard in support of objections to a structure plan the examination in public. 'It is essential', says the Code of Practice, 'to reach decisions on structure plans much more quickly than was customary on "old style" development plans.'

It seems that in practice the examination in public has occupied less time than the traditional public inquiry. Nonetheless, experience suggests that the procedure is not free from problems. First of all, in the absence of cross-examination, the effectiveness of the investigation depends on the extent to which the chairman is prepared to probe issues. The exercise has on occasions been described as superficial. 'It has proved a common complaint', says Grant, 'that using discussion rather than questioning as the basic procedure has led to superficiality of treatment of the issues, that participants have been too readily able to avoid being drawn on the legitimate arguments raised by other participants, and have been able to hide behind technical jargon and unexamined assumptions.[4] Secondly, the onus on the chairman to ensure that a probing discussion takes place can result in apparent conflict with the requirement that he should be seen to be impartial.[5] Thirdly, the process has largely failed to involve the public. Few individuals have been selected to take part in the discussion and the public benches have often been empty; whether this is the fault of the examination in public or of the abstract nature of the structure plan is difficult to say. Fourthly, the plan is presented as a coherent whole. The singling out of issues for investigation makes it difficult to break down this coherence so as to allow an effective probing of the individual issues.[6] Finally, and largely as a consequence of the fourth point, it has been argued that the investigation might be more effective if it were to take place earlier in the process, ie, before the planning authority have determined what policies and proposals to include in the plan. This would allow consideration of alternative strategies.[7]

(h) *Final stages*

After considering a proposal relating to a structure plan submitted (or re-submitted) to him, the Secretary of State may approve the plan in whole or in part, and with or without modifications[8] or reservations, or may reject it (1971 Act, s 9(1)). The Secretary of State must give such statement as he considers appropriate of the reasons for his decision (1971 Act, s 9(8)), and

---

4 *Urban Planning Law*, p 108.
5 L Bridges and C Vielba, *Structure Plan Examinations in Public: A Descriptive Analysis* (Institute of Judicial Administration, University of Birmingham, 1976).
6 L Bridges and C Vielba, above.
7 L Bridges and C Vielba, above.
8 It has been held in another context that modification cannot cover a wholesale rejection and replacement; see *Wigan Borough Council v Secretary of State for Energy and National Coal Board* [1979] JPL 610.

although such reasons may be short[9] they must nonetheless satisfy the test laid down by Megaw J in *Re Poyser and Mills Arbitration*.[10] The reasons that are set out must be reasons which will not only be intelligible, but which deal with the substantial points that have been raised.

Where the Secretary of State proposes to modify the proposals in any material respect, he must notify the county planning authority who must advertise the proposed modification and serve notice of the proposed modification on such persons as the Secretary of State directs; the Secretary of State must then consider any objections to the proposed modifications[11] (see 1982 regulations, reg 21).

The Secretary of State's decision on the plan will be notified to the county planning authority in writing and the authority will give public notice by advertisement and will serve individual notice on any persons who have requested to be notified of the decision and on any other persons as the Secretary of State directs (1982 regulations, reg 22). Copies of an operative structure plan together with the reasoned decision letter (which will form part of the plan) must be available for public inspection and copies of the plan must be placed on sale as soon as possible but in the case of alterations the printing can wait until the structure plan is next reprinted (1982 regulations, reg 38). The power of reservation means that the Secretary of State can approve only part of the proposals and reserve approval of the rest. The consequence of a reservation seems to be that the policies remain unapproved but not repealed. The Secretary of State will then normally issue a direction under s 10(1) requiring the submission by a specified date of proposals to replace those which are the subject of the reservation (circular 22/84, para 2.42). The alternative to a reservation is to approve part and to delete the other part.

(i) *Operation and validity of structure plan*

A structure plan takes effect on the date appointed for the purpose in the Secretary of State's notice of approval (1971 Act, s 18(4)). The validity of a structure plan may be challenged in the Court of Session within the period specified in s 244 of the 1971 Act (see chapter 20) but is not otherwise to be questioned in any legal proceedings whatsoever (see 1971 Act, s 242[12]). So far there have only been two reported challenges to a structure plan.[13]

(j) *Alteration or Repeal or Replacement of Structure Plans*

If the structure plan is to serve its purpose it must be kept up to date. The county planning authority are required to keep under review the matters

9   *Edwin H Bradley & Sons Ltd v Secretary of State for the Environment* (1983) 47 P & CR 374; and *Westminster City Council v Great Portland Estates plc* [1985] AC 661, [1984] 3 WLR 1035.
10   [1964] 2 QB 467, [1963] 1 All ER 612.
11   There is no right to object to reservations contained in the notice of approval of a structure plan.
12   The effect of this provision was considered in *Westminster City Council v Secretary of State for the Environment and City Commercial Real Estates Investments Ltd* [1984] JPL 27, where it was held that the validating of a policy could not be challenged in legal proceedings but the *vires* could be raised on a planning appeal by the Secretary of State.
13   See *Edwin H Bradley & Sons Ltd v Secretary of State for the Environment* (1983) 47 P & CR 374 and *Barnham Ltd v Secretary of State for the Environment* (1985) 52 P & CR 10, [1985] JPL 861).

which may be expected to affect the development of that area or the planning of its development (1971 Act, s 6(1)). By monitoring the relationship of the plan to actual changes in the environment, development pressures and political priorities, the authority should obtain information to enable them to judge whether an alteration to the plan is required.

A county planning authority may at any time submit to the Secretary of State proposals for alterations to a structure plan and must submit such proposals if directed to do so by the Secretary of State (1971 Act, s 10(1)).[14] Such proposals may include proposals for the repeal and replacement of a structure plan (1971 Act, s 10(2)). A submission for repeal and replacement must be accompanied by the submission of the replacement structure plan (1971 Act, s 10(3)).

A county planning authority with a single structure plan may repeal and replace it with a different plan and an authority with two or more structure plans operative in their area may replace these with a single plan.

As stated earlier, the procedures for preparation and approval of alterations and replacements are generally the same as applied to the original structure plans (1971 Act, s 10A). As with the structure plans submitted after 1980, proposals to alter or replace plans must be accompanied by an explanatory memorandum justifying the proposals (1971 Act, s 10(4)). This memorandum has the same form and content as that required to accompany the original post 1980 plans (1971 Act, s 10(5) and (6)). The main difference in the procedure for the preparation and approval of alterations and replacements is that there is no longer an absolute requirement to hold an examination in public (1971 Act, s 10(8)).

Circular 22/84 has advised that alterations are likely to be appropriate where:

'(a) the main policies in the approved plan have a short time horizon and at least partial rolling forward of the plan is necessary (paragraph 4.5) or where further policies and proposals are required to deal with unforeseen development problems;

(b) the assumptions or forecasts on which policies in the approved plan were based have proved wrong and this is invalidating the policies, or internal inconsistencies have become apparent, and there is thus a clearly unsatisfactory basis for local plans; or

(c) there has been a significant change in policy within the county planning authority or by central Government, or major difficulties have arisen in the preparation of local plans and this has become a source of conflict.'

and goes on to add:

'In addition there may be a case where proposals for alteration are prepared in response to a direction by the Secretary of State, or to comments made by him when approving a structure plan or proposals for alteration (paragraph 2.41).' (para 2.5)

Repeal and replacements are said only to be normally justified where:

14 The authority may, whenever they think fit, institute a fresh survey of their area (1971 Act, s 6(2)).

'(a) substantial alterations are required to more than one approved plan within the same county; or

(b) the alterations which it is proposed to make to a single approved plan are so fundamental and touch upon so many policy areas that it would be easier to prepare and process a new plan.' (para 2.7)

Alterations can include the removal from old structure plans of the reasoned justification but circular 22/84 advises that this should not be the sole reason for submitting an alteration. On the approval of an alteration the Secretary of State cannot alter a previous explanatory memorandum and any changes have to be made by the county planning authority. Similarly the Secretary of State cannot change other parts of the plan when approving an alteration but he can draw attention in the notice of approval to any parts which are no longer relevant.

A proposal to alter or replace a structure plan creates difficulties when there is in progress the making, alteration or replacement of a local plan as a local plan should generally conform to the structure plan (see below). There are therefore special provisions aimed at ensuring that the structure plan proposals do not delay the adoption of local plans (1971 Act, s 15A(1)). At the same time the approval of an alteration or a replacement structure plan requires that the county planning authority consider whether existing local plans still conform (1971 Act, s 15A(4)).

(k) *Register*

From the time when copies of a structure plan are made available for inspection under s 8(2) of the 1971 Act, particulars of any action taken in connection with the plan must be entered in the register of structure and local plans which county and district planning authorities are required to maintain under reg 39 of the 1982 regulations.

2 LOCAL PLANS[15]

The second tier of the new style development plan comprises the local plan or plans. The structure plan for any area will set out the overall strategy; the local plan interprets that strategy in local site-specific policies and proposals and also includes matters of purely local significance. The two levels of the plan are interdependent. When preparing a local plan, the planning authority must ensure that their proposals conform generally to the structure plan (1971 Act, s 11(4)). The Act contains complex procedures aimed at ensuring that this principle of conformity is adhered to as structure plans are altered and local plans are made or altered (these procedures are described below). However, once it is accepted that a local plan generally conforms to the structure plan, if there is any question of conflict between the provisions of the two plans, the local plan shall be taken to prevail for all purposes (1977 Act, s 15B).

Circular 22/84 states that local plans have four main functions. They are:

(a) to develop the policies and general proposals of the structure plan and relate them to precise areas of land defined on the proposals map;

15 See generally P Healey, *Local Plans in British Land Use Planning* (Pergamon, 1983).

(b) to provide a detailed basis for development control;
(c) to provide a detailed basis for coordinating and directing development and other use of land both public and private; and
(d) to bring local planning issues before the public.

(a) *The need and responsibility for the preparation and adoption of local plans*

There is no legal obligation to prepare and adopt local plans for any area. The 1971 Act used to impose a duty on the local planning authority, to whom it fell to prepare a local plan, to consider and keep under review the desirability of preparing local plans and, if they did consider it desirable, then they were under an obligation to prepare a plan.[16] Now it is left to the 'local plan scheme', which is prepared by the county planning authority to determine what local plans will be made, altered, repealed or replaced in the county area (1971 Act, s 11A). The requirement to have a programme of local plan-making, would suggest that at least one local plan should be prepared but otherwise the question of what local plans should be prepared is left initially to the discretion of the county planning authority, in consultation with the districts. However, the Secretary of State has the powers to require local plan-making. The districts have a right to make representations to the Secretary of State where they are dissatisfied with a local plan scheme and the Secretary of State can then amend the scheme (1971 Act, s 11A(6)). This could possibly be used to amend a scheme so as to require the making of a particular local plan, though it could be argued that the power of amendment could not be expanded to requiring an additional local plan. More realistically s 11B[17] empowers the Secretary of State to direct that a local planning authority should make, alter, repeal or replace a local plan, and such a direction can specify the nature of the local plan or alteration required. Where a direction is made, the county planning authority must make appropriate amendments to the 'local plan scheme'.

It used to be made clear in the Act itself that prima facie local plans were to be prepared by the district planning authorities.[18] This presumption is no longer to be found in the legislation and it is left to the 'local plan scheme', to be drawn up by the county planning authority, to determine which 'local planning authority', the county or the district, should be responsible for a particular local plan (1971 Act, s 11A(2)(c)). However, the districts are required to keep under review the need for and adequacy of local plans for their area and may make recommendations to the county for incorporation in the local plan scheme (1971 Act, s 11A(3)). Further, the Department of the Environment has always made clear that most local plans should be prepared by district planning authorities and that the county planning authority will in general prepare local plans only where they have a primary responsibility, for example for minerals or where a plan formulates proposals for a number of districts (circular 24/87, para 4).

16 1971 Act, s 11(2). This has been replaced by a different s 11 substituted by the Housing and Planning Act 1986.
17 This section was substituted by the Housing and Planning Act 1986 and is a redrafting of similar powers which applied previously.
18 See s 10C of the 1971 Act, replaced by s 41 of the Housing and Planning Act 1986 and substituted by s 11A.

The local plan scheme is therefore a very important document as it determines both whether a local plan will be prepared or altered and by which authority. The county planning authority is required to make and maintain a local plan scheme, setting out a programme for the making, alteration, repeal or replacement of local plans for areas in the county, except for those in a national park (1971 Act, s 11A(1)). The scheme must as regards each local plan for which it provides:

(a) specify the title, nature and scope of each plan;
(b) specify in words or with a map the boundaries of the area to which each local plan is to apply;
(c) designate the local planning authority responsible for each plan; and
(d) where appropriate, indicate the relationship between local plans (1971 Act, s 11A(2)).

A copy of the scheme must be sent to the Secretary of State and the district planning authority who, if they are dissatisfied with a scheme, can make representations to the Secretary of State who can then amend the scheme (1971 Act, s 11A(5) and (6)). Local plans can only be made, altered, repealed or replaced as authorised by the scheme but the county planning authority are to keep the scheme under review and from time to time amend it (1971 Act, s 11A(4) and (7)). The Secretary of State has asked that the schemes should be made available for public inspection.

As local plan-making is optional, many areas are not and will not be covered by local plans. In circular 22/84 it is stated that local plans may not be needed in areas where there is little pressure for development and no need to encourage development or to stimulate growth. However, in many areas local planning authorities have opted for non-statutory plans as an alternative to statutory local plans. The legal status of such non-statutory plans will be considered below but there are signs that the Department of Environment is unhappy about the extent of the use of such plans.[19] At present, adopted local plans only cover about 20% of the non-metropolitan counties of England and Wales.

(b) *Types of local plan*

Section 11(2) provides that different local plans may be prepared for different purposes for the same area but the 1971 Act does not prescribe the different types of local plan that can be prepared except to state that plans can be prepared for 'action areas'. The 1982 regulations do however prescribe the names that are to be given to certain types of plans. There used to be three distinct names: district plans, subject plans and action area plans,[20] but the 1982 regulations now only provide for two names, subject plans and action area plans (1982 regulations, reg 11). However, it is clear from circular 22/84 that district plans are to live on under the name of general plans or just local plans (see para 3.14). According to circular 22/84 a general or district local plan is a plan covering the whole or any part of the area covered by a structure plan and may contain proposals relating to as many or as few subjects as are considered appropriate. The regulations used to require a district plan to be a 'comprehensive consideration of matters affecting

19 See circular 22/84, para 1.15 and recent speeches by Ministers.
20 See Town and Country Planning (Structure and Local Plans) Regulations 1974, reg 15.

development and other use of land in the area to which it relates[1] and circular 22/84 advises that one comprehensive plan is to be preferred to a multiplicity of plans within the same area. 'Subject plan' is a plan based 'on the consideration of a particular description or descriptions of development or other use of land' in the area to which it relates and is to be given the name of that subject followed by the term 'local plan' (1982 regulations, reg 11). An example would be 'Minerals Local Plan' or a 'Green Belt Local Plan'. An 'Action Area Plan' is the local plan for an 'action area' which by s 11(5) is an area 'selected for the commencement during a prescribed period of comprehensive treatment by development, redevelopment or improvement of the whole or part of the area selected, or partly by one method and partly by another'. This comprehensive treatment can be by public authorities or private enterprise but must be intended to take place over a comparatively short time, at present prescribed as 10 years from the date of the deposit of the plan (1982 regulations, reg 14). It will now depend on the wording of the 'local plan scheme' whether an action area plan is to be prepared. Action areas formerly had to be identified in the structure plan and where identified there was an obligation to prepare an action area plan. This obligation was removed by the Local Government, Planning and Land Act 1980 but the obligation still applied where the structure plan had been approved by the Secretary of State before the passing of the 1980 Act (1980 Act, s 89 and Sch 14, para 8(2)).

(c) *Form and content of local plan*

The content of a local plan will depend to a considerable extent on the purposes of that particular plan. Every local plan must, however, satisfy certain basic requirements.

Section 11(1) of the 1971 Act provides that a local plan is to consist of:

(a) a written statement and is to formulate in such detail as the authority think appropriate their proposals[2] for the development and other use of land in that part of their district and for any description of development or other use of land (including in either case such measures as the authority think fit for the improvement of the physical environment and the management of traffic).
(b) a map showing those proposals; and
(c) such diagrams, illustrations or other descriptive material as the authority think appropriate to explain or illustrate the proposals.

The proposals in the written statement are to be set out so as to be readily distinguishable from the rest of its contents which are to include a reasoned justification of the proposals (1982 regulations, reg 11). Unlike the structure plan there is no separate explanatory memorandum and the reasoned justification forms part of the local plan.[3]

1 See above.
2 It is not thought that there is any significance in the omission of the word 'policies' from s 11(1)(a). In *Westminster City Council v Great Portland Estates plc* [1985] AC 661, [1984] 3 WLR 1035 Lord Scarman appeared to interpret 'proposals' as meaning 'proposals of policy'. It could be that the structure plan is the place for policies and the proposals in the local plan are the detailed implementation of such policies.
3 In *Westminster City Council v Secretary of State for the Environment and City Commercial Real Estates Investments Ltd* [1984] JPL 27, it was used to construe the policies in a local plan.

The map is called a 'proposals map' and has to be prepared on an ordnance survey base and show the scale of the map and an explanation of the notation used (1982 regulations, reg 13). It seems that the proposals map should not be diagrammatic (see circular 22/84, para 3.26) and can contain or be accompanied by more detailed 'insets' on a larger scale (1982 regulations, reg 13(2)).

In *Westminster City Council v Great Portland Estates plc*[4] similar provisions relating to the Greater London Area were interpreted by the House of Lords as imposing a duty on the planning authority to include in their local plan *all* proposals which they might have for the development and use of land. In that case the City of Westminster Local Plan stated that the authority's offices policy would be to guide office development to locations within a 'central activities zone'; outside that zone office development would not normally be appropriate. The plan went on to say that the exceptional circumstances in which office development might be permitted outside the zone would be dealt with in non-statutory guidance to be prepared following adoption of the local plan. The respondents, who were substantial landowners in the City of Westminster, challenged the validity of the offices policy in the plan on the ground, *inter alia*, that by relying upon non-statutory guidelines, the authority had failed to comply with the statutory requirement that the local plan should contain their proposals for the development and use of land.

Lord Scarman, giving judgment for their Lordships, accepted that development plans are not inflexible blueprints and that a planning authority, in exercising their planning functions, could have regard to other material considerations and that such considerations might, for example, include exceptional hardship to individuals or other special circumstances justifying a departure from proposals in the plan. Generally, there was no obligation to refer to such considerations in the plan. However, where, as in this case, such exceptions or special circumstances amounted to policies (in this case they were labelled by the authority in the plan as non-statutory policies), the authority were failing in their statutory duty by excluding them from the plan. The effect of excluding from the plan their proposals in respect of office development outside the central activities zone was to deprive persons such as the respondents from raising objections and securing a public inquiry into such objections. The paragraphs in the local plan dealing with the offices policy were accordingly quashed.[5]

Section 11(1) of the 1971 Act provides that the level of detail in which proposals are to be formulated in the plan is a matter for the planning authority. However, it may not be easy for an authority to distinguish between proposals which, following *Great Portland Estates*, must be included in the plan and matters of detail relating to proposals which may appropriately be left for consideration at the planning application stage. In *Sand and Gravel Association Ltd v Buckinghamshire County Council*,[6] for example, a county planning authority defined 'preferred areas' for future mineral

4 [1985] AC 661, [1984] 3 WLR 1035.
5 However, see *Simplex GE (Holdings) Ltd v Secretary of State for the Environment* (1988) 57 P & CR 306, [1988] JPL 809, CA where the argument was rejected that a policy, which stated that a study would be carried out to find out uses compatible to a site's green belt status, was invalid.
6 [1984] JPL 798.

working in a minerals subject plan. The extent of these preferred areas was obtained by excluding particular areas such as 'areas of attractive landscape' which had already been drawn up and which were incorporated into the minerals subject plan. In defining these areas the authority, it was alleged, applied subjective tests and did not permit representations from interested parties. The result was that a person interested in land outside the preferred areas could not establish why his land had been excluded, nor could he ascertain whether the tests had been correctly applied. Furthermore, the opportunity to raise these issues at the local plan inquiry was, it was said, refused by the inspector who limited his consideration to the preferred areas. McNeill J upheld an application to quash the 'preferred areas' policy in the plan; in his view the subjective tests were more appropriate in the circumstances for consideration at the planning application stage. The result of the authority's action in the case was effectively to exclude an opportunity for challenge of the application of the subjective tests. The authority had, therefore, acted unreasonably in the *Wednesbury*[7] sense in the exercise of their powers. Although a local plan does not bind the planning authority when determining a planning application, a developer's chances, observed McNeill J, of obtaining planning permission for a proposal which was not in accordance with the provisions of the development plan were limited in the extreme. McNeill J's decision was, however, overturned by the Court of Appeal.[8] The Court of Appeal held that by concentrating on the misleading terminology of 'subjective' and 'objective' McNeill J had slipped into the error of substituting his view for that of the inspector and the planning authority. Purchas L J said: 'Where planning criteria are concerned, the distinction between subjectivity and objectivity is in almost all cases a false distinction.' 'Overwhelming' evidence was required before the authority's policy could be rejected as unreasonable in the sense of the *Wednesbury* principle; here there was no such overwhelming evidence.

The above cases show the difficulties facing the courts in having to review the exercise of wide and vaguely worded provisions. So far as any clear principles can be extracted it would seem:

(a) if a local plan is being prepared, policies on a subject covered by the plan should not be deliberately excluded by being relegated to a non-statutory form; but that
(b) proposals in a local plan can be defined by reference to designations existing outside the plan itself even if these designations are derived by subjective criteria.

The local plan written statement used to have to include the matters set out in reg 17 of the Town and Country Planning (Structure and Local Plans), Regulations 1974. These were set out in Sch 2, Pt II, and were similar to the present provisions as to the considerations that should be regarded in drawing up structure plans; see above. The 1982 regulations do not set out any matters which have to be put in the written statement but a district planning authority, in discharging their functions, relating to local plans, must have regard to the survey carried out by the county under s 6 and the

---

7 *Associated Provincial Picture Houses Ltd v Wednesbury Corpn* [1948] 1 KB 223, [1947] 2 All ER 680.
8 [1985] JPL 634.

matters set out in sub ss (1)–(3) as they apply to their area (1971 Act, s 11(6)). The local planning authority in preparing a local plan must also take into account the fact that land in their area has been designated an Enterprise Zone (1971 Act, s 11(7)).

Local plans should of course conform generally to the structure plan but there are also rules about possible contradictions concerning the local plans themselves. In the event of a contradiction between the written statement and any other document forming part of the local plan, the written statement is to prevail (1982 regulations, reg 44). Where there is a contradiction between local plans for the same area, ie overlapping plans, the provisions of the more recently adopted or approved shall prevail (1982 regulations, reg 45).

(d) *Preparation of local plans*

The procedure for preparing a local plan is, to a large extent, in the hands of the local planning authority. However, before determining the content of the plan, the authority must undertake a participation exercise. The provisions governing this are almost identical to those which apply to the preparation of a structure plan. The authority must take such steps as will in their opinion secure that adequate publicity is given to the matters they propose to include in the plan and that persons who may be expected to want to make representations on the matters proposed to be included in the plan are made aware of their right to do so; a period of at least six weeks must be allowed for the making of representations to the authority and the authority must consider any representations received within the specified period (1971 Act, s 12(1), 1982 regulations, reg 5). Whichever local planning authority, the county or the district, is responsible for preparing the local plan, must consult the other with respect to their proposals and, having given that authority a reasonable opportunity to express their views, must take those views into consideration (1971 Act, s 12(3)). Circular 22/84 also asks the authority preparing the local plan to consult, as a matter of course, any government department that would be concerned with the proposals (see para 3.40). In *Rand v Secretary of State for the Environment and Chiltern District Council*[9] the argument that the authority preparing the plan have to consult individual land owners, who might be affected, was strongly rejected. Graham Eyre QC sitting as deputy judge, stated: 'There is no obligation whatsoever on the part of an authority preparing a plan to notify individual landowners whatever the nature of the policy which might relate to their land.'

The rules on publicity and public participation are very similar to those governing structure plan preparation but the Housing and Planning Act 1986 has introduced an important departure. Section 12A provides a short procedure to be used for the alteration, repeal or replacement of a local plan where the plan-making authority considers that the issues involved are not of sufficient importance to warrant the full procedure set out in s 12. This enables the authority to cut out the first stage of publicising the matters they propose to include in the plan and to go direct to the stage of putting the draft plan on deposit for inspection and objection (1971 Act, s 12A). They must however advertise the fact that the documents are available for

9 [1988] JPL 830.

inspection and invite the making of representations or observations (1971 Act, s 12A(4)).

Where s 12 or s 12A applies, copies of the proposals must be sent to the Secretary of State (and the other local planning authority) and must be accompanied by a statement as to what steps have been taken to comply with the respective statutory duties to publicise and consult (1971 Act, s 12B(1) and (2)). As with structure plans, the Secretary of State has then got the power to require further steps to be taken if he is not satisfied with the steps already taken (1971 Act, s 12B(3)).

(e) *Action following preparation of local plan*

As indicated, a county or district planning authority who have prepared a local plan must send a copy of the plan to the district or county planning authority as the case may require (1971 Act, ss 12(4)(c) and 12A(2)(c)). This means, for example, that a district planning authority should send a certified copy of the plan to the relevant county planning authority and that a county planning authority should send a certified copy to the district councils to whose areas the proposals relate.

The local planning authority must make copies of the local plan available for inspection at their offices and advertise in the prescribed form that the plan has been prepared and deposited (see 1971 Act, s 12(4)(a), 1982 regulations, reg 25). The notice must specify the manner in which and the period (6 weeks after the date of first publication of the notice) within which objections to the plan can be made (see 1971 Act, s 12(5); 1982 regulations, reg 25, and Schedule). To be valid, an objection must be in writing, must state the matters to which it relates and must be received by the planning authority within the specified period[10] (see 1982 regulations, reg 25 and Schedule).

Not later than the date on which they first give notice of the preparation of a local plan, the local planning authority must send one duplicate and two certified copies of the plan to Secretary of State; the authority are also to submit (1) a brief account of the steps they have taken to comply with the requirements as to public consultation (above); and (2) a brief account of the consultations they have had with other persons (see 1971 Act, s 12B(1)(a) and 1982 regulations, reg 24).

(f) *Consideration of objections*

Unless the Secretary of State has exercised his 'call in' powers (below), the consideration of objections is a matter for the local planning authority (1971 Act, s 14(1)). For the purpose of considering objections the authority may, and shall, in the case of objections made in accordance with the regulations, cause a public local inquiry or other hearing to be held[11] unless all the persons who have made objections in the prescribed way, indicate in writing that they do not wish to appear (1971 Act, S13 (1) and (2)).

Where objectors are content to waive their right to a public inquiry, circular 22/84 suggests that objectors should be given an opportunity to supplement their written representations. In the case where no public inquiry or other hearing is held, the local planning authority are required to prepare

10 A model notice of objection is set out in Annex F to circular 22/84.
11 The Tribunals and Inquiries Act 1971 applies to a local inquiry or other hearing into objections to a local plan (see 1971 Act, s 13(1)).

a statement of their decision with regard to each objection giving reasons (1982 regulations, reg 30). The reference to 'other hearing' means that the local planning authority does not *have* to hold a local inquiry and there is the possibility of holding a more informal hearing but no such hearings have been held.

The Act makes provision for the person holding the public inquiry to be appointed by the local planning authority but no rules have been made under this provision and it is clear that in all cases, the Secretary of State will appoint an inspector to conduct the local inquiry (1971 Act, ss 13(3) and (4)). Rules governing the procedures at inquiries and hearings held in connection with local plans have not been made; the Secretary of State has instead issued a Code of Practice.[12] However, sub-ss (2) and (3) of s 250 of the Local Government Act 1972 apply to an inquiry held under s 13 and so the inspector has the power to summon and examine witnesses (1971 Act, s 13(5)).

The Code provides that, subject to the fundamental principles of openness, fairness[13] and impartiality, the main emphasis of the procedure at a local plan inquiry should be on informality. The objective is not any kind of judicial arbitration between opposing parties but a joint attempt, in discussion, to arrive at decisions on future land use which will reflect the overall public interest.[14] The order of proceedings will be for the person conducting the inquiry, the inspector, to determine. Generally he will try to group together objections which have substantial common ground. He will ask each objector to make an opening statement and to call any witnesses; these witnesses may be questioned by the planning authority. The planning authority will then make a statement in reply and may call witnesses; these in turn may be questioned by the objectors. The objectors will be given an opportunity to make a final statement before the inquiry proceeds to consideration of the next objection or group of objections.

Where an objector wishes to suggest one or more alternative sites or areas for the application of particular policies and proposals, these should be notified to the inspector and the local planning authority in advance of the inquiry. There will, however, be limits upon the degree to which alternatives can be explored. The code used to state that alternative proposals put by objectors will be considered at the inquiry only to the extent necessary to enable the inspector to determine whether he could recommend modifications.[15] If the local planning authority decide, after the inquiry, to pursue any alternatives put forward, these will need to be advertised as proposed modifications to the plan and an opportunity allowed for objection.

12 See s 2 of the booklet 'Local Plans: Public Local Inquiries—A guide to procedure 1984.'
13 In *R v Wakefield Metropolitan District Council, ex p Asquith* [1986] JPL 440, Woolf J upheld a procedure by which the objections to the common policy element of three local plans was examined at one inquiry and then three separate inquiries were held into the objections to the detailed proposals.
14 Problems encountered in such inquiries are considered in M J Bruton, G Crispin and P M Fidler, 'Local Plans: Public Local Inquiries' [1980] JPL 374 and in R E Hellox and S W Biart 'Local Plan & Inquiries—A Case Study' [1982] JPL 17.
15 The nature of the duty of an inspector to entertain evidence on alternative sites was considered by the Court of Appeal in *Buckinghamshire County Council v Hall Aggregates (Thames Valley) Ltd and Sand and Gravel Association Ltd* [1985] JPL 634, CA (overturning the decision of McNeill J reported at [1984] JPL 798). The Court of Appeal appeared to accept that the Code is correct and that any alternative must be put forward in the context of the published policies. This restriction no longer appears in the code; see para 2.5.

Government departments may be represented at the inquiry but any departmental witness may normally be questioned on matters of fact or expert opinion only and not on the merits of government policy. The inspector will always make an inspection of the area covered by the local plan.

After the inquiry, the inspector will prepare a report for submission to the planning authority. This will summarise the arguments advanced, either in writing or by the parties at the inquiry, in respect of each objection or group of objections and it will set out his recommendations. The duty to act fairly would apply to the post inquiry procedure and so, although this is not spelt out in the code, the local planning authority would be under a legal duty to consult the relevant objectors if they disagreed with the inspector's recommendations because they had discovered fresh evidence. Also local plan inquiries are subject to the council on Tribunals' jurisdiction and so complaints about the procedures at such inquiries can be made to the council (1971 Act, s 13(6)).

Where a public local inquiry or other hearing has been held, the planning authority who prepared the plan must, as part of their consideration of objections, consider the report of the person who held the inquiry or hearing and must decide, in the light of that report and each recommendation contained therein, whether or not to take any action as respects the plan; the authority must prepare a statement of their decision, giving reasons therefor[16] (1982 regulations, reg 29(1)). That statement is to be made publicly available along with the report of the person who held the inquiry or hearing (regs 29(2)–30(2)). A failure to provide a statement will not automatically invalidate the decision to adopt the plan. In *Simplex GE (Holdings) Ltd v Secretary of State for the Environment*[17] the local planning authority disagreed with the inspector's recommendation that a site should be excluded from the green belt but did not provide a statement of their reasons. The Court of Appeal upheld a decision by Otton J not to quash the policy on the grounds that the failure had not affected the decision to adopt.

Where no local inquiry or other hearing is held for the purpose of considering objections to the local plan, the planning authority must prepare a statement of their decision on each objection together with reasons (reg 30). The local planning authority may modify the plan to take account of any objections or any other considerations that appear to them to be material (1971 Act, s 14(2)). As originally drafted the local planning authority could only make modifications in response to formal objections but the Local Government Planning and Land Act 1980 changed the wording so that they can now respond to *all* objections and may also modify the plan as circumstances change. If the authority propose to modify the plan they must give notice of their intention and afford a further opportunity for objections. They must consider any further objections, and they may decide that another local inquiry is necessary to consider these objections. However, the local planning authority is only required to hold another inquiry where so directed by the Secretary of State (1982 regulations; reg 31(1)(d)). The Housing and Planning Act 1986 has introduced a new power by which the Secretary of

---

16 These reasons may be briefly stated (*Westminster City Council v Great Portland Estates plc* [1985] AC 661, [1984] 3 WLR 1035), but must be proper, adequate and intelligible (*Re Poyser and Mills' Arbitration* [1964] 2 QB 467, [1963] 1 All ER 612, and *Great Portland Estates*).
17 [1963] 1 All ER 612 [1988] JPL (1988) 57 P & CR 306, [1988] JPL 809 CA.

State can make a direction requiring modifications of a particular nature in which case the authority have to carry out the normal modification procedures and then report back to the Secretary of State (1971 Act, ss 14(4) and (5)).

Research has shown that there is some dissatisfaction with a process which allows the planning authority to sit in judgment on their own plan[18] And in *R v Hammersmith and Fulham London Borough Council, ex p People Before Profit Ltd*[19] Comyn J was critical of the statutory procedures. He said that as the law stood objectors to a local plan may have 'very little real say at all' and that the planning authority were 'in effect judge and jury in their own cause'. He was 'slightly perturbed' to think that the finding of a public inquiry could, as in this case, be so favourable to objectors and yet the authority could dismiss the objections 'virtually out of hand', but it was clear that the authority had the law on their side 'to an extent that may make individuals incredulous'. However, a survey of the outcome of a number of local plan inquiries suggests that, notwithstanding that planning authorities are 'judges in their own cause', objectors have been reasonably successful in securing modifications to policies and proposals in local plans.[20]

(g) *Adoption of local plan*

Before adopting a local plan the local planning authority must advertise their intention to adopt the plan and must serve notice on objectors (see 1982 regulations, reg 32). They must also send to the Secretary of State a certificate that the required notices have been published and served and may not proceed to adopt the plan until 28 days have elapsed since the date the certificate was sent. The main safeguard against the local planning authority abusing their power to adopt in conflict with the recommendations of the inspector is the Secretary of State's power to call in the plan under s 14A and he has power to direct the authority not to adopt the plan until he notifies them that he has decided not to call it in under s 14A(1) of the 1971 Act (see reg 32(3)).

If the Secretary of State does not intervene, the local planning authority may, after the expiry of the 28 day period, adopt the plan, either as originally prepared or as modified to take account of objections or of any considerations which appear to them to be material (1971 Act, s 14(2)). When the authority resolve to adopt or abandon a local plan they must give notice as required by reg 33 of the 1982 regulations. Two certified copies of any plan adopted by an authority must be sent to the Secretary of State (see reg 33(2)).

(h) *Intervention by Secretary of State*

A local plan will normally be adopted by the local planning authority who prepared it. The Secretary of State may, however, direct that a local plan is to be submitted to him for approval (1971 Act, s 14A(1)); the minister can intervene in this way at any time before the plan has been formally adopted by the local planning authority. Circular 22/1984 states that the Secretary of

18 See M J Bruton, G Crispin, P M Fidler and E A Hill, 'Local Plans P.L.I.s in Practice' *The Planner*, January/February 1982, p 16.
19 (1981) 80 LGR 322, 45 P & CR 364.
20 T Burton, 'Local Plan Inquiries' 1982 SPLP 8.

State will seek to be involved in the preparation of local plans only where issues of national importance are involved or where the plan gives rise to substantial controversy (para 3.82). However, where the Minister of Agriculture, Fisheries and Food has made an objection to the plan and the local planning authority do not propose to modify the plan, then the Secretary of State must call in the matter unless he is satisfied that the Minister no longer objects to the proposal (1971 Act, ss 14(6) and 14A(3)).

Where a local plan is called in by the Secretary of State, he must consider the objections and give the person who made the objections a hearing except where the objections have already been considered or a local inquiry or other hearing has already been held. In *R v Secretary of State for the Environment, ex p London Borough of Southwark*[1] it was held in a case concerning similar provisions relating to Greater London, that there is no duty to consult the local planning authority before calling in its plan. Where a local plan has been called in, the Secretary of State may after considering the proposals, either approve it (in whole or part, and with and without modifications) or reject it (1971 Act, s 14B). In the case of new modifications, unless the Secretary of State is satisfied that they are not material, then a process of advertising and hearing objections must be followed (1982 regulations, regs 34(3) and (4)). Otherwise the Secretary of State can in considering the submitted plan consult or not consult as he thinks fit[2] (1971 Act, s 14B(4)).

(i) *Operation and validity of local plan*

A local plan will come into operation on the date appointed for the purpose in the relevant resolution of adoption or notice of approval (1971 Act, s 18(4)). The validity of a local plan may be challenged by way of application to the High Court within the period specified in s 244 of the 1971 Act (see chapter 20) but is not otherwise to be questioned in any legal proceedings whatsoever[3] (1971 Act, s 242).

Local plans have been successfully impugned on at least two occasions. In *Westminster City Council v Great Portland Estates plc*[4] part of a local plan was quashed by the House of Lords on the ground that the planning authority had failed to comply with the statutory duty to include all proposals for the development and use of land in their local plan. In *Fourth Investments Ltd v Bury Metropolitan Borough Council*[5] McCullough J granted an application to quash part of a local plan allocating land to the local green belt on the ground that the inspector who conducted an inquiry into objections to the plan had failed to make any assessment of the likely requirement for housing land in the area as a whole over the whole of the plan period and that as a result he could not reasonably have reached a conclusion as to whether the applicants' land should be included in the green belt. In *Sand and Gravel Association Ltd v Buckinghamshire County Council*

1 (1987) 54 P & CR 226, [1987] JPL 587.
2 See the *London Borough of Southwark* case above, where it was held there was no duty to consult the local planning authority before a decision to reject their plan was made.
3 Once the time limit is up, it may not only be too late to challenge the validity of the plan as such but also too late to challenge the validity of the policies therein in their application to the determination of a planning application—see *Westminster City Council v Secretary of State for the Environment and City Commercial Real Estates Investments Ltd* [1984] JPL 27.
4 [1985] AC 661, [1984] 3 WLR 1035.
5 [1985] JPL 185.

(see p 64 above) parts of a local plan were quashed by McNeill J on the ground that the planning authority had acted unreasonably in drawing up the plan but as mentioned above, that decision was, however, overturned by the Court of Appeal.[6]

The court under s 244 can quash the whole or part of the plan either generally or only in so far as it affects any property of the applicant. However, in the *Sand and Gravel Association* decision Purchas L J pointed out that the effect of the order quashing part of the plan was in substance to amend or rewrite the plan and that, if the application had succeeded, the proper order would have been to quash the whole plan. So the option of quashing part will only apply where the particular policy can be easily severed from the rest.

(j) *Action following adoption or approval of local plan*

When the local planning authority finally adopt the plan, they must give notice by advertisement and inform those who have been asked to be notified. At the same time, two certified copies of the plan must be sent to the Secretary of State (1982 regulations, reg 33). There is a similar obligation on the Secretary of State when he approves a plan (reg 34(5)).

(k) *Alteration, repeal or replacement of local plans*

As with the making of local plans, the alteration, repeal or replacement of local plans once made, is governed by the wording of the local plan scheme. This is because s 11A(7)(a) empowers the preparation of proposals for the alteration etc 'only where authorised to do so by the local plan.'[7] Circular 22/84 states that:

> 'There is no requirement that proposals for the alteration, repeal or replacement of a local plan should be included in the development plan scheme before a local planning authority may proceed . . .' (para 3.89)

but this was written before the drafting changes brought in by the Housing and Planning Act 1986. It must now be the case that where the district authority that adopted the plan, wishes to have it changed, they must first secure changes to that effect in the 'local plan scheme' by making recommendations to the county planning authority.

In the case of local plans which have been approved by the Secretary of State under his call-in powers, the consent of the Secretary of State is further required before proposals for changes to that local plan can be made (1971 Act, s 11A (7)(b)). The Secretary of State has also got the power to force changes by requiring the alteration, repeal or replacement of any local plan by making a direction to a local planning authority (1971 Act, s 11B).

The procedures for altering, repealing or replacing local plans are generally the same as for making of the plans in the first place and the new drafting makes this clear by laying down common sections for the making of local plans *and* their alteration, repeal or replacement, which are all given the common description of 'proposals'. The only difference is that, as described,

6 [1985] JPL 634.
7 This limitation does not apply to plans relating to national parks.

s 12A provides a special short procedure for minor alterations, repeals or replacements.

(i) *Register*

The register, which both county and districts are required to prepare and keep up to date under reg 39, must contain brief particulars of the local plans for their respective areas including proposals for the alteration, repeal or replacement of those plans. The boundaries of the plans should be shown on an index map.

3 CONFORMITY BETWEEN STRUCTURE PLANS AND LOCAL PLANS

As one of the main functions of the local plans is to develop the policies and general proposals of the structure plans, it should follow that local plans should not be in conflict with the structure plan for their area. When the 1968 Act introduced the new system, it was laid down that one planning authority would prepare both types of plan and so the likelihood of conflicts occurring was small. This situation radically changed in 1974, when the reorganisation of local government by the Local Government Act 1972 meant that in most cases the structure plan would be the responsibility of the county planning authority and the districts would prepare and adopt the local plans. Where the two local planning authorities were of different political views, the potential for conflicting policies became very real. The legislation always required that local plan proposals should conform generally to the structure plan but this is not sufficient in itself to ensure such conformity. Then the Local Government, Planning and Land Act 1980 made the status of the structure plan less secure by stating that where there was conflict between the provisions of a structure and local plan 'the provisions of the local plan shall be taken to prevail for all purposes.'[8] This makes it essential to secure conformity *before* the provisions of the local plan have legal effect. To this end procedures of ever-increasing complexity have been devised. An attempt to explain these procedures now follows.

(a) *Procedures where approved structure plan policies remain unchanged*

Now that structure plans for the whole of England and Wales have been approved, the problem of adopting local plans in advance of structure plans has gone.[9] Therefore, as long as the structure plan policies remain fixed, the procedures for ensuring that any local plans, which are made or altered, are in general conformity with the approved structure plan are relatively straightforward.

First s 11(4) requires that 'The proposals in a local plan shall be in general conformity with the structure plan' and so the local planning authority preparing the local plan should try to ensure conformity from the very start of the preparation process. The second safeguard is that, where it is the district planning authority who have prepared the proposals, they cannot

8 Now to be found in s 15B(1) of the 1971 Act.
9 There used to be special procedures for adopting local plans in advance; see old s 15A of the 1971 Act.

proceed to the stage of putting documents on deposit for public inspection (the stage when objections can be made, see page 67 above) without first obtaining 'a certificate that the proposals conform generally to the structure plan' (1971, s 15(1)). It is up to the district to request such a certificate from the county planning authority but if it appears to the county that the proposals do not conform in any respect, they must refer the question to the Secretary of State, who may in any case reserve the question of conformity to his own determination (s 15(2) to (4)). Where the Secretary of State is seized with the question he may:

 (i) direct the county planning authority to issue a certificate;
 (ii) issue a certificate; or
(iii) direct the district planning authority to revise their proposals so that it will conform generally (1971 Act, s 15(5)).

The power to modify the proposals means that modifications could be proposed that do not generally conform to the structure plan. There is no provision for certification of the modifications and the main safeguards are that the authority should not adopt any proposals which do not conform generally to the structure plan (1971 Act, s 14(3)) and the Secretary of State's power to call in the proposals (s 14A).

(b) *Procedures where structure plan policies are changed or are proposed to be changed*

Where a local plan has been adopted, a change in the structure plan policies may mean that the local plan no longer conforms generally to the new policies. To deal with this contingency, on the approval of proposals to alter or replace a structure plan, the county planning authority must consider whether the local plans for the area affected still conform generally to the new structure plan policies (1971 Act, s 15A(4)). The county then must draw up a list of local plans which in their opinion do or do not conform generally. This list must be sent within one month of the date of approval of the new structure plan policies to the Secretary of State and the district planning authorities who are responsible for the relevant local plans (s 15A(5)). The consequence of a local plan being put on the non-conforming list is that, in the case of conflict between the structure plan and the local plan, the local plan does not prevail as is normally the case (1971 Act, ss 15B(1) and (2)). So the local plan remains part of the development plan and it is perhaps significant that the Act does not expressly state that in the case of a conflict between the structure plan and a non-conforming local plan, the structure plan is to prevail but it is likely that the intention is that in such circumstances, the structure plan is to be the dominant document.

Unlike the case where the county refuses to issue a certificate of conformity, the district has no right to dispute the opinion of the county by referring the matter to the Secretary of State. Equally there is no statutory duty on the district to put forward proposals to bring the local plan back into line, but circular 22/84 does advise that 'delay should be avoided because it may create problems in the exercise of development control' (see para 3.88). In any case the Secretary of State can make directions requiring a local plan to be altered or replaced (1971 Act, s 11B).

It may happen that changes are being proposed to structure plan policies at the same time as a local plan is being prepared or alterations proposed. It would be absurd if the local plan policies had to conform generally with outdated structure plan policies which are about to be replaced. The Act tackles this problem by authorising the Secretary of State to direct that it must be assumed that the proposed changes to the structure plan have been approved. Such a direction can only be made after proposals for the alteration or replacement of a structure plan have been prepared and submitted to the Secretary of State and an application asking for such a direction has been made by the authority putting forward the local plan proposals (1971 Act, s 15A(1)). The result is that the preparation and adoption of local plan policies take place on the assumption that the proposed changes to the structure plan have been approved. This means that the local plan policies can be adopted *before* the structure plan changes are approved. However, a direction ceases to have effect should the Secretary of State decide to reject the proposed changes to the structure plan (s 15A(2)). Also the assumption must adapt as modifications to the county's proposal are proposed to the county by the Secretary of State under s 9(1), (s 15A(1)). Nevertheless, the procedure does mean that it may happen that after the local plan is adopted, the changes to the structure plan are approved in a form that means that the local plan no longer conforms generally. In such a case the procedures described above would ensure that the local plan did not prevail over the structure plan.

4 NON-STATUTORY POLICY STATEMENTS

In their report[10] in 1965 the Planning Advisory Group observed that the result of out of date development plans was an increasing reliance by planning authorities on non-statutory policy statements to deal with emerging planning problems. These statements were not subject to the normal machinery for development plan amendments of publicity, objection and inquiry and could, therefore, be speedily prepared and implemented.

The validity of decisions made in reliance upon this sort of non-statutory policy statement has been accepted by the courts in the past.[11] In *Clyde & Co v Secretary of State for the Environment*[12] Sir David Cairns observed in the Court of Appeal that he could see 'no reason why either the local planning authority or the Secretary of State should have to look for considerations of policy only to the development plan'. *Myton Ltd v Minister of Housing and Local Government*[13] arose as a result of a recommendation by the Minister of Housing and Local Government in MHLG Circular 42/55 that planning authorities should consider the establishment of green belts. The circular suggested the preparation and submission to the minister of a sketch plan setting out the proposed boundaries of the green belt, the intention being that the sketch plan would in due course be converted into a formal amendment to the development plan. The circular recommended that, after submission of the sketch plan, there should be a general presumption against development

---

10 *The Future of Development Plans.*
11 But see now the decision of the House of Lords in *Westminster City Council v Great Portland Estates plc* [1985] AC 661, [1984] 3 WLR 1035 (below).
12 [1977] 3 All ER 1123, [1977] 1 WLR 926.
13 (1963) 61 LGR 556, 16 P & CR 240.

in the area. Following the preparation and submission of such a sketch plan, a local planning authority refused planning permission for residential development of land within a proposed green belt on the basis of the general presumption. A subsequent appeal to the minister was dismissed. The applicant appealed to the High Court and argued, *inter alia*, that the ground for the dismissal of the appeal was, in effect, a decision by the minister to include the land in the green belt without the safeguards of objection and inquiry; as a result he would be seriously prejudiced by the blighting of his land. Widgery J concluded, however, that the applicant's appeal had been dismissed because the land was, for the time being, included in a sketch plan indicating a proposed green belt, and that, in the circumstances, and pending the full inquiry which would follow before the sketch plan became an amendment to the development plan, it was undesirable that the land should be developed. The applicant would suffer no substantial prejudice as a full opportunity for objection and inquiry would be given before any green belt was formally designated and his land permanently blighted. More recently in *J A Pye (Oxford) Estates v Secretary of State for the Environment and Wychavon District Council*[14] McCowen J did not question the acceptance by counsel that a non-statutory village plan was a material consideration.

With the advent of the 'new style' development plans and given, in particular, the wide range of matters with which local plans can deal, the Department of the Environment discourages authorities from preparing non-statutory policy statements. For example, circular 22/84 states that:

'Any plan containing proposals for the development and other use of land which is not included in the development plan scheme as a local plan, or as proposals for the alteration of a local plan, and which has not been subject to any of the stages in the statutory procedures ... can have little weight for development control purposes. It cannot be treated as an emerging plan. Where there is a need to devote resources to the preparation of proposals for the use of land; these should be settled in the statutory plan.' (para 1.13)

However, the circular goes on to accept that there is

'... a continuing role for planning guidance which supplements the policies and proposals contained in structure and local plans. This may include, for example, practice notes for development control requirements, development briefs and detailed or sketch layouts for such developments as housing and local space.' (para 1.14)

Such planning guidance may be taken into account by the Secretary of State as a material consideration (para 1.15).

Some support for the distinction made by circular 22/84 between non-statutory policy statements and supplementary development guidance would seem to be derived from the decision of the House of Lords in *Westminster City Council v Great Portland Estates plc*.[15] In that case the City of Westminster District Plan sought to discourage office development outside a

14 [1987] JPL 363.
15 [1985] AC 661, [1984] 3 WLR 1035. Contrast *Covent Garden Community Association Ltd v Greater London Council* [1981] JPL 183 (failure to propose alteration of local plan not unreasonable).

'central activities zone'. The plan stated that the exceptional circumstances in which office development might be permitted outside the zone were best dealt with by non-statutory guidance to be prepared following adoption of the plan. This part of the plan was successfully challenged on the ground that the planning authority had failed to comply with the statutory requirement that a local plan 'shall formulate in such detail as the authority think appropriate the authority's proposals for the development and use of land in that part of their area'. If a planning authority have policy proposals for the development and use of land, they are failing in their statutory duty, declared Lord Scarman, if they choose to exclude them from the plan. However, Lord Scarman seemed to accept that a distinction could be made between matters of policy which must go into the local plan and matters of detail which could be left out.

While the decision in *Great Portland Estates* imposes some limit on the use that can be made of non-statutory policy statements, it is not a limit that can easily be defined. While the local planning authority have a discretion as to the level of detail to be contained in a plan, it may not be easy to say in any particular case whether circumstances are such that proposals are matters of policy to be contained in the plan or matters of detail which may properly be left to be dealt with in extra-statutory guidelines. Neither is it clear what effect reliance upon a non-statutory policy statement (as opposed to supplementary development guidance) will have upon the *vires* of a planning decision. The legal consequences of the litigation in the *Great Portland Estates* decision was that the policies in the local plan, on the prohibition of office development subject to exceptions, were deleted. However, Lord Scarman did not go into the issue of whether such policies could still be relied on in determining a planning application or whether the local planning authority could be required to put non-statutory guidance into the statutory local plan. The implications of *Great Portland Estates* were considered by Purchas L J in *Simplex GE (Holdings) Ltd v Secretary of State for the Environment*[16] where it was alleged that a policy in a local plan was ultra vires as having confirmed a site as within the green belt designation. The plan indicated that the council intended to commission a study of those uses for which the site could be put, consistent with its green belt policies. Purchas L J distinguished *Great Portland Estates* on the grounds that that use concerned a deviation from the overall restriction rather than as in *Simplex* an implementation of the established policy. This reasoning is hard to follow. In both cases the non-statutory guidance is spelling out the circumstances in which development will be allowed. However, it may be that in *Simplex* the guidance was more properly 'supplementary' in that it was fleshing out what the established policy in the plan meant in practice.

Until 'new style' development plans are brought into full operation, local planning authorities are likely to attach considerable weight to the policies in their draft local plans. In *R v City of London Corpn, ex p Allan*[17] Woolf J held that policies in a draft local plan were material considerations which a planning authority should take into account in an appropriate case when determining a planning application.[18] However, although such emerging

16 [1988] JPL 809.
17 (1980) 79 LGR 223.
18 See too p 202 below.

plans are technically non-statutory until all the procedures have been followed and the local plan adopted, the Secretary of State has accepted that proposals for the alteration, repeal or replacement of structure and local plans may be taken into account as a material consideration for development control purposes while going through the statutory procedures leading to approval or adoption. The weight to be afforded to such a plan, or to such proposals will increase as successive stages are reached in the statutory procedures (see Circular 22/84, para 1.12).

Even when the 'new style' plans come into full operation, it seems doubtful whether planning authorities will readily relinquish the use of non-statutory policy statements. There is evidence to suggest that, despite discouragement from the Secretary of State, planning authorities in England and Wales are continuing to make widespread use of a variety of such statements.[19] It would seem that the great majority of such statements do not threaten the integrity of development plan policies; they operate as a supplement to these policies. Their advantage lies in their flexibility of form, content and procedure. Their disadvantage lies in the uncertainty about the weight that will be given to them on appeal.[20] It is fair to say, nonetheless, that in practice such policy statements exert a considerable influence on day to day development control decisions.

If the Secretary of State wished to stop a local planning authority from relying on non-statutory policies, apart from refusing to back such policies up on appeal, he could always use his power under s 11B to direct the local planning authority to make a local plan and to put the non-statutory policies into that plan.

D UNITARY PLANS: GREATER LONDON AND THE METROPOLITAN AREAS

Development plans for Greater London

The system of development plans for the Greater London area took on a slightly different form from that of the rest of England and Wales. Old style development plans had been prepared under the system of local government that operated before the creation of the Greater London Council and the London Boroughs by the London Government Act 1963. These plans together formed 'the initial development plan for Greater London'.[21] A new plan was then prepared for the whole of Greater London called 'Greater London Development Plan'. This, in many respects, was the prototype of the structure plan and is held to be a structure plan by the 1971 Act.[1] Provision

19 See, for example, M J Bruton and D J Nicholson, 'Non-Statutory Local Plans and Supplementary Planning Guidance' [1983] JPL 432; M J Bruton and D J Nicholson. 'The Use of Non-Statutory Local Planning Instruments in Development Control and Section 36 Appeals' [1984] JPL 552 and 663; M J Bruton and D J Nicholson 'Supplementary Planning Guidance and Local Plans' [1985] JPL 837 and District Planning Officers Society, *The Local Plan System: The Need for Radical Change* (1982).

20 While the Secretary of State may take account of informal policies, he may equally take account of informal steps by a planning authority not to follow such policies—see *Philglow Ltd v Secretary of State for the Environment and the London Borough of Hillingdon* [1984] JPL 111.

21 See s 25(2) of the London Government Act 1963.

 1 See Sch 4, para 5(1) to the 1971 Act.

was also made for the preparation of local plans by the London Boroughs if they thought fit[2] and the Greater London Council was only responsible for preparing action area plans where the Greater London Development Plan indicated that it was for the Greater London Council to prepare the plan.[3] There was no provision for development plan schemes but the Local Government, Planning and Land Act 1980 imposed a system of certification to ensure that local plans generally conformed to the Greater London Development Plan.[4] Otherwise the rules (set out in Sch 4 to the 1971 Act) governing the preparation of local plans by the London Boroughs were generally the same as applied outside the Greater London area.

The development plan for any London Borough therefore consists of the local development plan together with the Greater London Development Plan except that where a local plan is not operative the initial development plan still applies.[5]

Unitary plans

The abolition of the Greater London Council and the metropolitan counties also resulted in the creation of a new system of unitary plans for those areas. Unitary plans are made up of two parts; part I covers general policies and part II contains the more detailed development control policies and proposals. In this regard the unitary plan is a combination of the structure and local plans into one plan.

These new provisions, which are set out in Sch 1 to the Local Government Act 1985, did not come into operation on the abolition of the Greater London Council and the metropolitan counties on 1st April 1986. Commencement orders made by the Secretary of State are needed before the Act comes into force and the Act will be brought into force at different times for different areas.[6] A commencement order has been made for the West Midlands Metropolitan County with the exception of Dudley Metropolitan District which is still in the process of preparing and adopting a local plan.[7] In the meantime the Greater London development plan and the approved structure plan for each metropolitan area will continue in force until it is replaced by an operating unitary plan.[8] Similarly any local plan or old development plan (including the initial development plan for Greater London) in force at the date of abolition, continues in force until a unitary plan for that area comes into operation.[9] The London boroughs and the metropolitan district councils can continue to prepare and adopt local plans and make proposals for their alteration until a commencement order is made and the provisions of Pt II of the 1971 Act still apply to such proposals with the exception of the provisions relating to development plan schemes and certificates of general conformity.[10] However, there are no powers to update

---

2 See Sch 4, para 8(3) to the 1971 Act.
3 See Sch 4, para 8(1) to the 1971 Act.
4 See Sch 14, para 13(c) to the Local Government, Planning and Land Act 1980.
5 See Sch 5, para 8(5) to the 1971 Act.
6 See s 4(1) of the Local Government Act 1985.
7 The Unitary Development Plans (West Midlands) (Appointed Day) Order 1988.
8 See Sch 1, para 18 to the 1985 Act. There is also provision for the revoking of a structure plan by the Secretary of State where he approves part of the Unitary Plan.
9 Ibid.
10 See Sch 1, para 20 to the 1985 Act.

the structure plan policies. Any local plan, in force at the time when a unitary plan is being prepared, must be incorporated in Pt II of the new unitary plan.

The rules as to the content, preparation and adoption of unitary plans are generally based on those for structure and local plans but there are important differences. The following pages outline the main innovations.

Strategic guidance

The obvious weakness of the new system of the unitary plans is that unlike the structure plan they cover a much smaller area. Thus 32 unitary plans will be prepared for the Greater London area and will eventually replace the one Greater London Development Plan. There is obviously a danger that the 32 plans will not produce a comprehensive strategy for the problems of Greater London and may indeed conflict one with another. The same problem applies to a lesser extent with the various unitary plans which will be produced for the metropolitan counties. The 1985 Act deals with this potential lack of a coherent strategic policy by requiring the authority formulating the general policies in part I of the unitary plan to have regard 'to any strategic guidance given by the Secretary of State to assist them in the preparation of the plan.'[11] Further, the Town and Country Planning (Unitary Development Plans) Regulations 1988 (the 1988 regulations) require the reasoned justification of the general policies in part I to include a statement of the regard that has been had to any strategic guidance given by the Secretary of State (1988 regulations, reg 8). Circular 3/88 states that this guidance will 'cover land use matters which need to be dealt with on a wider geographical basis than a single district.' Earlier, circular 30/85 had set out the procedures by which this guidance is to be prepared. This provides for consultation and publication in draft before the guidance is formally published and issued. In the case of the Greater London Area, the Local Government Act 1985 provides for the creation of a Joint Planning Committee for Greater London. This committee has to be set up by the local planning authorities in Greater London and the committee's functions are generally to advise and inform on matters of common interest relating to the planning and development of Greater London.[12] The Act does not directly state that the committee's views are to be regarded by individual local planning authorities in preparing the unitary plans but circular 30/85 commits the department to consulting the committee 'about the arrangements for preparing strategic guidance including its scope and content,' (see para 5.3). In this regard, the committee, as soon as it was established, was asked to identify those planning and development matters they considered would require a strategic approach.

The words 'have regard' indicate that the local planning authorities in preparing unitary plans do not have to slavishly follow the strategic guidance but the Secretary of State could no doubt use his power to call-in a plan which was not consistent with his strategic guidance.[13] He could then modify the plan.[14]

11 See Sch 1, para 2(4)(a).
12 S 5 of the Local Government Act 1985.
13 See Sch 1, para 7 to the 1985 Act and para 4.10 of circular 3/88.
14 See Sch 1, para 8 to the 1985 Act.

Format

Part I of a unitary plan like a structure plan consists of a written statement but unlike the structure plan there is to be no key diagram. Any diagrams will be in part II (1985 Act, Sch 1, para 2(2)). There is also no requirement for an explanatory memorandum. Instead, part II of the plan must contain a reasoned justification of the general policies in part I as well as the proposals in part II (1985 Act, Sch 1, para 2(2)(b)). So the reasons for policies form part of the unitary plan but are to be found in part II of that plan.

Preparation and adoption procedures

The rules about publicity in connection with the preparation of unitary plans are generally the same as for structure and local plans except that the short procedure available for alterations applies both to alterations to part I and part II (1985 Act, Sch 1, para 10A), while it cannot be used for alterations to structure plans. This short procedure is not available for the preparation of the first unitary plans even where an authority is including adopted local plans in part II.

The local planning authority can adopt the whole of a unitary plan and so part I of the plan (unlike the case with structure plans) does not have to be approved by the Secretary of State. However, as indicated, the Secretary of State always has the power to either direct that a proposed plan should be modified or call-in the whole or part of the plan (1985 Act, Sch 1, paras 6A and 7). Before adopting a unitary plan, the local planning authority are required to arrange for a public local inquiry or other hearing to be held for the purpose of considering any duly made objections unless all the objectors indicate that they do not wish to appear (1985 Act, Sch 1, para 6). It is only in the case of the Secretary of State, having called-in part I of the unitary plan, that an examination in public may be held rather than a local inquiry, unlike the case with the first structure plans where an examination in public had to be held rather than a local inquiry (1985 Act, Sch 1, para 9). A plan must be called-in if the Minister of Agriculture Fisheries and Food objects and this objection cannot be resolved (1985 Act, Sch 1, para 7(2)).

Questions of conformity

The proposals in part II of a unitary plan have to be in general conformity with part I (1985 Act, Sch 1, para 2(5)) but there is no need for a system of certificates of conformity as there is one plan prepared by one authority. The Act does not lay down any other rules for cases of conflict and so presumably part I will prevail over part II.

Types of unitary plans

Two or more local planning authorities may prepare and adopt a joint unitary plan for the same metropolitan area (1985 Act, Sch 1, para 12). Otherwise it seems that unlike the case with local plans there will only be one unitary plan which will generally cover the whole of the local planning authority's area. There is no provision for different unitary plans for other areas. In the case of action areas, part II of a unitary plan may designate any part of the local planning authority's area as an action area intended for comprehensive treatment by development, redevelopment or improvement and the nature of the treatment should be indicated in the plan (1985 Act, Sch 1, para 2(6)).

E REGIONAL POLICIES

There exists no statutory system of regional planning though s 7(4)(a) requires the county planning authority in preparing their structure plan policies to have regard: 'to the current policies with respect to the economic planning and development of the region as a whole.' Between 1965 and 1979, there existed non-statutory Regional Economic Planning Councils and boards which helped draw up strategic policies for the regions. With the abolition of the regional economic planning councils in 1979 by the incoming conservative administration, some regional strategic guidance has emerged in the form of letters from the Secretary of State for the Environment and circular 22/84 states that 'Further guidance for other regions may be issued as and when necessary' (para 4.7). This guidance has mainly centred on the London and south east region and has usually been made in response to proposals made by the London and South East Regional Planning Conference (SERPLAN). This conference consists of the local planning authorities for that region and it has produced various 'Regional Statements' for south east England. These statements have resulted in further guidance from the Secretary of State for the Environment. So regional planning policies for the south east have emerged as result of this dialogue between the conference and the Secretary of State. The various statements and guidance are now to be found in the *Encyclopaedia of Planning*.

Strategic planning guidance for the west midlands and the Greater London area has also been given by the Secretary of State under the Local Government Act 1985.[15] As stated above, this Act requires the district councils and the London boroughs to have regard to this guidance in drawing up unitary plans.

It seems likely that this system of strategic guidance being issued by the government, which then provides the context for the preparation of development plans, will be extended to the rest of England and Wales. This idea has been put forward by the White Paper 'The Future of Development Plans' which is now considered.

F THE FUTURE OF DEVELOPMENT PLANS

In September 1986, the Department of the Environment published a consultative paper 'The Future of Development Plans'. This paper was critical of both the content of structure plans (they are said to be too detailed or inappropriate) and of the complexity and delay in the preparing and the approval or adoption of plans.[16] The solutions proposed by the government borrow heavily from the scheme of unitary plans being introduced in Greater London and the metropolitan counties. Structure plans as such are to be abolished and replaced by 'statements of county policies' which would be

---

15 Para 2(4)(a) of Sch 1 to the Local Government Act 1985.
16 For a rebuttal of some of these criticisms, see M J Bruton and D J Nicholson 'A Future for Development Plans?' [1987] JPL 687.

prepared in the context of national and regional policies emanating from the Secretary of State. These statements would not form part of the structure plan. District plans would normally be prepared and adopted as now by the district planning authorities but would cover the whole area of the district. These plans would have to be in general conformity with county policies but there would be no system of certification. The procedures for preparing these plans would be streamlined with the public participation and objection stages being amalgamated and the public being consulted earlier in the process.

Slow progress has been made since the consultation paper was issued, but in January 1989 a White Paper 'Future of Development Plans'[17] was published. This proposes legislative changes on the lines of the consultative paper. The main difference between the consultative paper and the White Paper is that as well as the district development plan, there will be a separate minerals development plan prepared by each county council.

The proposed changes reflect the government's concern with the present patchy coverage by local plans and the need for clear up-to-date local plans as a sound basis for the determination of planning authorities. So, in a sense the system has turned a full circle with a return of development plans as precise and down-to-earth guidance on development control.

17 Cmnd 569.

CHAPTER 5

DEVELOPMENT

Introduction

The system of regulatory planning revolves around the definition of 'development' in s 22 of the Town and Country Planning Act 1971. If particular proposals do not constitute 'development', as defined in the 1971 Act, planning permission will not be required for the carrying out of those proposals. If, on the other hand, the proposals fall within the statutory definition, planning permission will almost invariably be necessary.[1] It is not always easy to say whether proposed action comes within the statutory definition of development. As was said by Lord Wilberforce in *Coleshill and District Investment Co Ltd v Minister of Housing and Local Government*.[2] '"Development" is a key word in the planners' vocabulary but it is one whose meaning has evolved and is still evolving. It is impossible to ascribe to it any certain dictionary meaning, and difficult to analyse it accurately from the statutory definition.'

Subject to the provision which s 22 of the 1971 Act makes in relation to specified operations and changes of use (see p 120 below), 'development' means 'the carrying out of building, engineering, mining or other operations in, on, over or under land[3] or the making of any material change in the use of any buildings or other land' (s 22(1)). Although particular activities on land may well involve both 'operations' and a 'material change in the use' of the land, the general scheme of the legislation is, as the Court of Appeal held in *Parkes v Secretary of State for the Environment*,[4] to distinguish between the two concepts. In that case Lord Denning MR stated that 'operations' comprise activities which result in some physical alteration of land, an alteration which has some degree of permanence in relation to the land itself, whereas 'use' refers to activities which are done in, alongside or on the land, but which do not interfere with the actual physical characteristics of the land. The Court of Appeal held in *Parkes* that the sorting, storing and processing of scrap metal was a use of land and not an operation.

Section 290 of the 1971 Act specifically provides that 'use' does not include the use of land for the carrying out of any building or other operations thereon; the fact that one has permission to use land for a certain purpose does not mean that one is entitled to carry out building or other operations

1 For exceptions, see ch 6 below.
2 [1969] 2 All ER 525, [1969] 1 WLR 746.
3 'Land' is defined in s 290 of the 1971 Act as including any building (as defined by s 290); it also includes land covered with water. In *Argyll and Bute District Council v Secretry of State for Scotland* 1976 SC 248, 1977 SLT 33 the Second Division of the Court of Session held that the term 'land' as used in the Town and Country Planning (Scotland) Act 1972 does not comprehend the seabed below low water mark.
4 [1979] 1 All ER 211, [1978] 1 WLR 1308; see too *Cheshire County Council v Woodward* [1962] 2 QB 126, [1962] 1 All ER 517, per Lord Parker CJ.

for that purpose.[5] It is perhaps curious that although s 290 states that 'use' is not to include building or other operations, there is no mention of engineering or mining operations. In *Parkes* (above) the Court of Appeal left open the question whether these sorts of operations could in some circumstances also constitute a 'use' of land[6] and in *West Bowers Farm Products v Essex County Council*[7] Lord Donaldson MR stated that the same activity might constitute both an operation and a change of use. However, in most circumstances the designation of an activity as coming within one leg of the definition will preclude it also coming within the other leg. The distinction between 'operations' and 'use' is important for a number of purposes, especially in connection with the enforcement of planning control (see chapter 12).

The open texture of the statutory definition has meant that a good deal of case law has grown up around the word 'development'. In particular, since the statute provides no specific guidance as to when a change of use is to be regarded as 'material', the courts have been compelled, in order to achieve some degree of certainty and consistency in the application of the legislation, to supplement the statute in a number of important ways. Concepts such as the planning unit, abandonment of use and extinguishment of use provide a legal framework within which the question whether particular proposals amount to development can be considered.

By and large, however, the courts have confined themselves to laying down broad guidelines; it has in the main been left to planning authorities themselves to determine, as a matter of fact rather than as a matter of law, whether particular proposals amount to development. It should, therefore, be emphasised that many decisions on 'development' turn to a very considerable extent on their own particular facts and do not necessarily lend themselves to generalisations. In *Coleshill* (above) Lord Morris of Borth-y-Gest suggested that the 'true path of enquiry' in any particular case first involves ascertaining exactly what it is that it is desired to do, or exactly what it is that has been done, and then ascertaining whether or not that comes within the statutory definition of development. In *Coleshill* the House of Lords refused to consider in the abstract the question whether the demolition of a building involves development; whether or not works which might be described as 'demolition' constitute development depends on the facts of the particular case and it is only when the projected or completed operation or change of use is fully and clearly described that the statutory definition can be applied.

A OPERATIONS

In terms of the 'operations' limb of the statutory definition, the carrying out of 'building, engineering, mining or other operations in, on, over or under land' amounts to development.

---

5 See *Sunbury-on-Thames UDC v Mann* (1958) 56 LGR 235, 9 P & CR 309. See too *Western Fish Products Ltd v Penwith District Council* [1981] 2 All ER 204.
6 See too *Murfitt v Secretary of State for the Environment and East Cambridgeshire District Council* (1980) 40 P & CR 254, [1980] JPL 598 (in which it seems to have been accepted that the placing of hardcore on a site was such an integral part of the use of the site for vehicle parking that it should not be treated separately). See also the decisions on tipping of material on land mentioned at p 90 below.
7 (1985) 50 P & CR 368, [1985] JPL 857.

Some works may be too trifling to be regarded as 'operations' and may be disregarded for planning purposes.[8]

Decisions often simply state that an activity is 'operational' development without specifying which kind of operational development. Nevertheless, the four types of operational development do have differing, if overlapping, characteristics.

(a) *Building operations*

'Building operations' include 'rebuilding operations, structural alterations of or additions to buildings, and other operations normally undertaken by a person carrying on business as a builder',[9] while 'building' includes 'any structure or erection, and any part of a building, as so defined, but does not include plant or machinery comprised in a building' (s 290).

It can be difficult to determine whether a particular object (to use a neutral term) is a 'building' and whether, therefore its erection or installation or alteration amounts to development. In *Barvis Ltd v Secretary of State for the Environment*[10] the appellants owned a tower crane which they used on contract sites. Having no immediate use for it on a contract site, they erected and used the crane at their depot. The crane stood eighty-nine feet high and ran on rails fixed in concrete. Its dismantling and re-erection was a specialist operation which took several days and cost about £2,000. It was the appellants' declared intention to use the crane on contract sites when business needs dictated but they could give no positive indication as to when it was likely to be moved from the depot. The Secretary of State concluded that the erection of the crane constituted an 'operation' within the statutory definition of development. In dismissing an appeal against the minister's decision, Bridge LJ placed emphasis on whether the acts resulted in a 'building' within the definition in the Act and said, 'if it was, then I should want a great deal of persuading that the creation of it had not amounted to a building or other operation.' He then expressed the view that in determining whether an object or installation was a 'structure or erection', assistance was to be derived from a passage in *Cardiff Rating Authority and Cardiff Assessment Committee v Guest Keen Baldwin's Iron and Steel Co Ltd*.[11] in which it was suggested that the following factors might be relevant: Is the object in question of substantial size? Is it something that either had been or normally would be built or constructed on site as opposed to being brought on to the site ready made? Has it some degree of permanence[12] in that it would normally remain *in situ* and only be removed by a process amounting to pulling down or taking to pieces? Is it physically attached to the land? The

---

8 See for example [1977] JPL 122, [1978] JPL 395 and [1985] JPL 210. See too the remarks of Lord Pearson in *Coleshill* (above). Contrast *United Refineries v Essex County Council* (1976) 241 Estates Gazette 389, [1978] JPL 110; *Malvern Hills District Council v Secretary of State for the Environment* (1983) 81 LGR 13, 46 P & CR 58 and appeal decisions noted in [1979] JPL 125 and [1982] JPL 800.

9 See *United Refineries Ltd v Essex County Council* [1978] JPL 110 (stripping of topsoil a building operation) and in *Windsor and Maidenhead Royal Borough Council v Secretary of State for the Environment* (1987) 86 LGR 402, [1988] JPL 410, Mann J held that the painting or repainting of a building came within the definition of building operations; but such works are permitted development under the General Development Order.

10 (1971) 22 P & CR 710.

11 [1949] 1 KB 385, [1949] 1 All ER 27.

12 See, for example, [1978] JPL 487.

court emphasised, however, that size is not necessarily conclusive, nor is the fact that 'by some feat of engineering or navigation it is brought to the hereditament in one piece', and the fact that an object has a limited degree of mobility or that it is not physically attached to the land does not necessarily prevent it being a 'structure or erection'.

Of the three main factors identified of size, permanence and attachment, permanence is the most important and difficult to pin down. An impression of permanence can be derived from objective factors such as size or attachment. More problematically it can depend on the intentions of the owners or occupiers. In *Scott v Secretary of State and Bracknell District Council*[13] David Widdicombe QC, sitting as a deputy judge, upheld a decision of the minister that the placing of a portable office amounted to operational development. The minister and his inspector (with whom the minister ageed) placed importance on the absence of any firm proposal to move or transfer the office and on the fact that it had remained in one place since being brought on the site. Widdicombe did not go into this issue specifically, but he did state that the minister had not taken into account any irrelevant factors in coming to his decision. However, it would seem wrong that the question of whether a building operation has taken place should depend on the occupier's intentions. It would also raise problems as to exactly when the operational development took place. In *Buckinghamshire County Council v Callingham*[14] the Court of Appeal held that a model village and toy railway came within the definition of 'building'. On the other hand, the Divisional Court held in *James v Brecon County Council*[15] that the minister had not erred in deciding that the installation of a battery of six fairground swing-boats capable of being removed as a whole by six men or of being dismantled in an hour, did not constitute development, whether or not the swing-boats were fixed to the land. In *Cheshire County Council v Woodward*[16] the court held that the minister was entitled to find that the placing on land of a wheeled coal hopper and conveyor some sixteen to twenty feet in height did not constitute development, even though, having regard to the nature of the particular site, it would have been difficult to move either piece of equipment. The parking of a caravan on land has generally been treated as a 'use' of land rather than an operation.[17]

There are numerous ministerial decisions as to what amounts to building operations. Most of these turn on their particular facts but they give some guidance. It has been held that a free-standing carport to which small wheels had been attached so as to make it mobile was a building,[18] that the erection of a timber building, bolted together and resting on concrete padstones, was a building operation,[19] and that the installation of vending machines secured

13 [1983] JPL 108.
14 [1952] 2 QB 515, [1952] 1 All ER 1166.
15 (1963) 15 P & CR 20.
16 [1962] 2 QB 126, [1962] 1 All ER 517. See, however, the comments made upon this case in *Barvis* (above).
17 See *Guildford RDC v Penny* [1959] 2 QB 112, [1959] 2 All ER 111; *Britt v Bukinghamshire County Council* (1962) 60 LGR 430, 14 P & CR 332; *Bulletin of Selected Appeal Decisions*, IX/8; and IX/18; and [1982] JPL 267; see, however, *Wealden District Council v Secretary of State for the Environment and Innocent* [1983] JPL 234; [1964] JPL 495; and J Alder, *Development Control*, p 46.
18 [1967] JPL 552; see too [1963] JPL 198; and [1965] JPL 687.
19 [1968] JPL 352; see too [1975] JPL 368; [1977] JPL 47; and [1978] JPL 571.

to the ground by bolts amounted to an operation for the purposes of the planning legislation.[20]

Though the expression 'building operations' clearly embraces a wide range of activities, its scope is limited to some extent by s 22 (2)(a) of the 1971 Act, which provides that 'the carrying out of works for the maintenance, improvement or other alteration of any building, being works which affect only the interior of the building or which do not materially affect the external appearance of the building' is not to constitute development.[1] Works for the alteration of a building by providing additional space therein below ground are not, however, within this exception[2] (see s 22 (2)(a)); such works as the carrying out of excavations in order to create a basement or to lower the floor level of a building are therefore likely to constitute development.

The line between works of maintenance, improvement or other alteration of a building (which do not constitute development) and rebuilding works (which will involve development even though the external appearance of the building is not to be altered) can be difficult to draw. Where, for example, it was discovered in the course of repairing a building that structural defects were more serious than had initially been realised, with the result that additional work had to be undertaken until there remained of the original building nothing but the front façade and the main side walls, the minister, though he accepted that the original intention was to carry out maintenance work only, and that the external appearance of the building had not been materially altered, took the view that the original building had ceased to exist and that the operations which had been carried out were works in connection with the erection of a new building and therefore involved development.[3]

Whether particular works materially affect the external appearance of a building is a question of fact. Such operations as altering an existing window or cutting a window in an otherwise blank wall have been treated as having a material effect on a building's appearance.[4] In *Kensington and Chelsea Royal London Borough Council v C G Hotels*[5] it was held that the placing of floodlights on a building had not materially affected the appearance of the building: and even if the floodlighting materially affected the appearance of the building at night, that result was brought about by the running of electricity through the apparatus (which could not amount to development). When considering whether particular works will materially affect the external appearance of a building, it would seem that it is with the appearance of the building at the time of the decision that comparison must be made and not with its appearance at some earlier time.[6]

As mentioned above, the definition of 'building' includes any part of a

20 *Bulletin of Selected Appeal Decisions*, 2nd Series, 11/40.
1 As to the enlargement, improvement or other alteration of dwellinghouses, see too p 154 below.
2 Unless the works were begun before 5th December 1968.
3 [1968] JPL 414. See too *Street v Essex County Council* (1965) 193 Estates Gazette 537; *Hewlett v Secretary of State for the Environment and Brentwood District Council* [1981] JPL 187; *Bulletin of Selected Appeal Decisions*, 2nd Series, III/65, [1966] JPL 601, [1967] JPL 351, [1970] JPL 165, [1971] JPL 230, [1972] JPL 345, [1974] JPL 162 and 555, [1977] JPL 608, and [1980] JPL 422. See too p 155 below.
4 See [1969] JPL 151; [1979] JPL 326, and [1984] JPL 258. Contrast appeal decision noted in *Selected Enforcement and Allied Appeals*, p 34.
5 (1980) 41 P & CR 40.
6 See [1979] JPL 117.

building. The appellants in *Coleshill and District Investment Co Ltd v Minister of Housing and Local Government*[7] had acquired disused explosives stores and magazines; these buildings were surrounded by blast walls against which had been heaped protective banks of rubble and soil. Without obtaining planning permission the appellants removed the embankments, with the result that the unsightly blast walls were exposed. They proposed also to remove the blast walls. The minister concluded that the blast walls and embankments were an integral part of each building and that the removal of the blast walls would, as an alteration which would materially affect the external appearance of the buildings, constitute building operations. The House of Lords held that there was no error of law in treating the walls and embankments, though physically discontiguous from the buildings they surrounded, as integral parts of the buildings.[8] Lord Pearson declared that 'the character of the whole structure in each case as a purpose-built magazine is an important reason for treating it as a single unit (*unum quid* in the convenient Scottish phrase)'.

In *Glasgow District Council v Secretary of State for Scotland*[9] the Lord Justice-Clerk (Lord Wheatley) and Lord Dunpark were prepared to hold that the partial demolition of a building was a building operation as involving a material alteration in the building's external appearance.

(b) *Engineering operations*

The expression 'engineering operations' is not defined in the 1971 Act but in *Fayrewood Fish Farms Ltd v Secretary of State for the Environment and Hampshire*[10] Mr David Widdicombe QC sitting as a deputy High Court judge, said that the term should be given its ordinary meaning of operations of a kind usually undertaken by, or calling for the skills of, an engineer.[11] Engineering operations can therefore embrace activities ranging from bridge-building to the installation of a fuel storage tank.[12] In *Coleshill* (above) Lord Pearson accepted that while some works may be too small to be 'dignified with the title of an engineering operation', the removal, by excavator and lorry, of large soil and rubble embankments was of sufficient magnitude to constitute an engineering operation.

In *South Oxfordshire District Council v Secretary of State for the Environment*[13] McCullough J in construing Class VI of the General Development Order 1977 determined that engineering operations could result in the creation of a structure or an erection which would be a building; thus suggesting that engineering operations can also amount to building operations. In that case it was accepted that the construction of a reservoir was an engineering operation.

Among the activities which have been treated as involving engineering operations are the drilling of exploratory bore holes,[14] turf-stripping,[15] the

7 [1969] 2 All ER 525, [1969] 1 WLR 746.
8 As to the meaning of 'part of a building' see too *Cooper v Bailey* (1956) 6 P & CR 261.
9 1980 SC 150, 1982 SLT 28, See p 92 below.
10 [1984] JPL 267.
11 See too *Hamilton District Council v Alexander Moffat and Son (Demolition) Ltd* (p 92 below).
12 See [1972] JPL 216.
13 (1985) 52 P & CR 1, [1986] JPL 435.
14 See [1975] JPL 609.
15 See [1981] JPL 829.

laying of tarmac,[16] and the formation of a hardstanding for vehicles.[17] Although the deposit of refuse on land is declared to involve a material change in the use of that land (see p 139 below), the deposit of material on land will in some circumstances involve engineering or other operations.[18]

The 1971 Act specifically provides that engineering operations include 'the formation or laying out of means of access to roads'; 'means of access' is defined as including 'any means of access, whether private or public, for vehicles or for foot passengers, and includes a road' (s 290(1)).[19] Works for the maintenance or improvement of a road, carried out by a local highway authority on land within the boundaries of the road, do not constitute development (s 22(2)(b)), nor do works (including the breaking open of any road or other land) carried out by a local authority or statutory undertakers for the purpose of inspection, repair or renewal of sewers, pipes, cables or other apparatus (s 22(2)(c)).

(c) *Mining operations*[20]

The 1971 Act does not define mining operations but states that the word 'minerals' includes 'all minerals and substances in or under land of a kind ordinarily worked for removal by underground or surface working' (s 290). Such substances as sand, gravel and peat would thus seem to be included in the definition. 'Mining operations' will include the extraction of minerals by surface working or quarrying.

As a result of an amendment to the 1971 Act made by the Town and Country Planning (Minerals) Act 1981, mining operations include:

(a) the removal of material of any description:
    (i) from a mineral-working deposit;
    (ii) from a deposit of pulverised fuel ash or other furnace ash or clinker; or
    (iii) from a deposit of iron, steel or other metallic slags; and
(b) the extraction of minerals from a disused railway embankment.[1]

In *Thomas David (Porthcawl) Ltd v Penybont RDC*[2] the Court of Appeal held that in mining operations each cut by the bulldozer constitutes a separate act of development (see p 321 below).

(d) *'Other operations'*

It is not altogether clear what operations are covered by this phrase. It has been suggested that the expression should be construed *eiusdem generis* with building, engineering and mining operations. In *Ross v Aberdeen County*

16 See [1982] JPL 800.
17 See [1974] JPL 159.
18 See *Northavon District Council v Secretary of State for the Environment* (1980) 40 P & CR 332, [1981] JPL 114; and appeal decisions noted in [1982] JPL 263, [1983] JPL 561; and *Selected Enforcement and Allied Appeals*, p 50. Contrast, however, appeal decisions noted in [1978] JPL 494, [1979] JPL 495, [1980] JPL 348, [1981] JPL 135, and [1983] JPL 618. See too C M Brand and D W Williams, 'Tipping on Land' [1984] JPL 158.
19 As to what amounts to the formation or laying out of a means of access, see [1970] JPL 543, [1972] JPL 109, [1977] JPL 121, and [1981] JPL 380.
20 Mineral operations are subject to a special regime of control—see ch 18 below.
 1 1971 Act, s 22(3A) (added by s 1(1) of the Town and Country Planning (Minerals) Act 1981). This provision came into force on 19th May 1986.
 2 [1972] 3 All ER 1092, [1972] 1 WLR 1526.

Council[3] the Sheriff said, however, that in his view these operations did not constitute a *genus*. In *Coleshill and District Investment Co Ltd v Minister of Housing and Local Government*[4] it was argued that building, engineering and mining were all positive or constructional operations and that 'other operations' could not therefore include demolition, an operation of a destructive character; Lord Guest said that he was 'unable to detect a positive or constructional *genus*' since mining operations are not constructional.[5] Lord Morris of Borth-y-Gest considered, however, that 'the word "other" must denote operations which could be spoken of in the context of or in association with or as being in the nature of or as having relation to building operations or engineering operations or mining operations'.

It may be that 'other operations' include excavation and levelling works (so far as not included in mining or engineering operations). In some circumstances the deposit of materials (other than refuse) may come within this category.[6] It has also been held that the fitting of a protective grille over a shop window amounted to development as 'other operations'. The inspector concluded that the meaning of 'other operations' depended upon its context and that the reference to the term in the definition of 'building operations' in s 290 did not mean that it only had the meaning associated with building operations.[7]

(e) *Demolition*

In *Control of Demolition*[8] Mr George Dobry QC declared: 'Most lawyers would agree that no clear guidance can be derived from the . . . authorities as to when demolition does or does not amount to development . . .' The Dobry Report recommended that the position should be clarified by legislation and that the definition of 'development' should be amended to include total or partial demolition of a building. No action was taken on this recommendation.

Shortly after the 1947 Act came into operation, the view was expressed by the Minister of Town and Country Planning that demolition did not of itself constitute development and did not therefore require planning permission.[9] Similarly, in *Howell v Sunbury-on-Thames UDC*[10] Marshall J, stated: 'To describe the clearing of a site of all buildings and no more as "developing a site" is to do violence to the accepted meaning of the word "development".'

In the *Coleshill* case,[11] however, Lord Morris said that although it may well be that 'some operations which could conveniently be called demolition' would not come within the statutory definition of development, the question whether 'demolition' constitutes development, 'neat and arresting as the question so expressed may seem to be', is not sufficiently precise. 'It is', he said, 'unnecessary and may be misleading to give the work or operation some

3 1955 SLT (Sh Ct) 65.
4 [1969] 2 All ER 525, [1969] 1 WLR 746.
5 See, however, the comments of Lord Robertson in *Glasgow District Council v Secretary of State for Scotland* 1980 SC 150, 1982 SLT 28 (see p 92 below).
6 See, for example, [1982] JPL 741; and see p 92 below.
7 See [1985] JPL 129. It has also been held that the fixing of blinds or canopies can amount to 'other operations'; see [1986] JPL and [1986] JPL 540.
8 HMSO 1974.
9 See Circular 9/1949, now cancelled.
10 (1963) 15 P & CR 26.
11 See p 89 above.

single labelling word and then try to apply the definition to that word.' In *Coleshill* the House of Lords held unanimously that the minister had not erred in law in deciding that the removal of rubble embankments surrounding ammunition stores constituted an engineering operation and that the proposed removal of blast walls surrounding the stores would amount to a structural alteration of the buildings and would therefore involve a building operation.

The question whether the demolition of the top three storeys of a five-storey building involved development was raised in *Glasgow District Council v Secretary of State for Scotland*.[12] The Lord Justice-Clerk (Lord Wheatley) and Lord Dunpark were prepared to accept that the works which had been carried out, involving as they did a material alteration in the external appearance of the building, came within the statutory definition of development. Their Lordships were not prepared to accept the argument that the existence of specific statutory provisions prohibiting the demolition of listed buildings[13] indicated that the demolition of an unlisted building was not to be treated as development. Both the Lord Justice-Clerk and Lord Dunpark left open the question whether the total demolition of a building involves development, Lord Dunpark saying that it was arguable that the total removal of a building could not reasonably be described as a structural alteration.

Lord Robertson rejected the planning authority's argument as expressed in its widest form—that all and any demolition of a building, or part of a building, *ipso facto* involves development. He said: 'Had Parliament intended demolition to be included in "development" as defined . . ., it would have been simple to say so. The emphasis is on developments producing results of a constructive, identifiable character.'[14] Lord Robertson thought it significant that Parliament had considered it necessary to deal specifically with the demolition of listed buildings.

In the rather special circumstances of the *Glasgow District* case the court found that planning permission was not required (see p 225 below).

In *Hamilton District Council v Alexander Moffat & Son (Demolition) Ltd*[15] the Sheriff (I A Macmillan) held, after considering the *Coleshill* and *Glasgow District* cases, that the demolition of a railway viaduct was an engineering operation. The Sheriff's decision appears to have been strongly influenced by the skilled and specialised nature of the proposed works.

The demolition of a building may well form part of a building operation or lead to the making of a material change in the use of the land upon which the building stood.[16] In *Iddenden v Secretary of State for the Environment*[17] the Court of Appeal took the view, however, that where nissen huts had been demolished and a new building erected on the site, all without planning permission, the demolition and the building operations were in planning law separate operations, although, as Lord Denning said: 'No doubt the pulling down of the old and the erection of the new was all one combined operation

12 1980 SC 150, 1982 SLT 28.
13 See chapter 18 below.
14 See *Coleshill* (above), per Lord Willberforce.
15 Sheriff Court, Hamilton (16 February 1984, unreported) but see 1984 SPLP 76). See too appeal decision noted in [1983] JPL 616.
16 See *LCC v Marks and Spencer Ltd* [1953] AC 535, [1953] 1 All ER 1095.
17 [1972] 3 All ER 722, [1972] 1 WLR 1433.

by the workmen.' The Court held that although the erection of the new building was a breach of planning control, the pulling down of the old buildings did not constitute development and therefore did not amount to a breach of planning control.

B MATERIAL CHANGE OF USE

Introduction

It is not every change in the use of a building or land that constitutes development; only when a change of use is 'material' does development occur. The 1971 Act makes specific provision in relation to certain changes of use (see pp 120–141 below), but contains no general guidance as to the circumstances in which a change of use is to be regarded as material. Whether or not a particular change of use is such as to constitute development is very largely a matter of fact and degree (see, in particular, p 101 below); a number of general principles have, however, developed over the years and these provide something in the nature of a framework within which that question is to be considered.

For planning purposes a distinction must, at the outset, be drawn between the primary or predominant use or uses of land and any uses which are merely ancillary to the primary use or uses. In considering whether or not a proposed change of use would be 'material' it is with the primary use of the land that any proposed change of use must be compared. On the other hand a use is not ancillary or incidental to another use just because it is subsidiary in size or importance. Thus in *Lydcare Ltd v Secretary of State for the Environment and Westminster City Council*[18] the Court of Appeal accepted that the viewing of films was not ancillary or incidental to a shop use and so the premises had to be treated from a planning point of view as having a mixed use.

The operation of this principle is to be seen in the decision of the Second Division of the Court of Session in *Alexandra Transport Co v Secretary of State for Scotland.*[19] In that case land had been used as a quarry under a planning consent which contained a condition that all waste material was to be backfilled into the quarry workings. The land having been sold, the question arose whether use of the quarry as a tip for refuse brought in from outside amounted to a material change of use. The appellants argued that planning permission had been granted, albeit subject to conditions, for the deposit of waste materials on the land, that the only change in the situation was in the type of waste materials, which were being deposited, and that that change did not amount to a material change of use. The court held, however, that a material change of use had occurred. Lord Milligan pointed out that the deposit of quarry refuse had to be treated as an ancillary use of the land; the primary use had been use for quarrying purposes. The primary use of the land, not the ancillary use, determined the character of the use and thus when

---

18 (1984) 83 LGR 33, [1984] JPL 809.
19 (1973) 27 P & CR 352, 1974 SLT 81; see too *G Percy Trentham Ltd v Gloucestershire County Council* [1966] 1 All ER 701, [1966] 1 WLR 506; *Shephard v Buckinghamshire County Council* (1967) 18 P & CR 419; *Williams v Minister of Housing and Local Government* (1967) 18 P & CR 514; *Brazil (Concrete) Ltd v Amersham RDC* (1967) 18 P & CR 396; and *L R Jillings v Secretary of State for the Environment* [1984] JPL 32.

the land ceased to be used as a quarry and became a 'dump' a material change of use took place.

The fact that, for change of use purposes the law focuses upon the primary use of land and has little concern with ancillary uses, has a number of important consequences. These are considered below.

(a) *The planning unit*

(i) *General.* In terms of the 1971 Act, development occurs when there is a material change in the use of 'any buildings or other land', but the statute provides no guidance as to the 'buildings or other land' which it may be appropriate to consider in any particular case. When considering whether or not a material change of use has taken place or whether particular proposals will amount to a material change of use, the first logical step therefore is to identify the 'planning unit', ie the area of land to be looked at in considering the materiality or otherwise of the particular change of use.

The main importance of identifying the planning unit correctly is that the answer to the question 'Has a material change of use occurred?' may depend upon the area selected for consideration.[20] In *Williams v Minister of Housing and Local Government*,[1] for example, the owner of a nursery garden who had for several years sold the produce of the garden from a timber building situated on the land began also to sell produce not grown on the land. The planning authority took enforcement action, alleging development by use of the building as a retail shop. Taking the nursery garden together with the building as the appropriate planning unit, the minister upheld the enforcement notice; the primary use of that unit was use for agricultural purposes (including, but only as ancillary to that primary use, sale of the agricultural produce of the unit), but once 'imported' produce was brought on to the land for purposes of sale a change in the character of use occurred—there was then, in effect, use as a general greengrocer's shop. The Divisional Court held that the minister had not erred in treating the whole premises as the proper planning unit. The importance of selecting the right planning unit was emphasised by Widgery J, who pointed out that if the unit for consideration had been the building in isolation, it might well have been contended that since it had been used all along for sale by retail, no material change of use had occurred.

To give another example, in *Kensington and Chelsea Royal Borough v Secretary of State for the Environment and Mia Carla Ltd*,[2] an allegation that a material change had occurred in using a garden as a restaurant foundered because the inspector determined that the correct planning unit was the garden plus the ground floor and basement of a building. These premises were used as a restaurant and so there was no material change in using the garden as ancillary to the restaurant.

These two examples show that in determining whether a change is material

---

20 In *Thomas David (Porthcawl) Ltd v Penybont RDC* [1972] 3 All ER 1092, [1972] 1 WLR 1526 the concept of the planning unit was employed by the Court of Appeal in connection with *operational* development (see p 321 below). See too *Welsh Aggregates Ltd v Secretary of State for the Environment and Clwyd County Council* [1983] JPL 50. The term 'planning unit' has acquired an additional, and rather different, meaning in connection with the extinguishment of existing use rights—see p 111 below.
1 (1967) 18 P & CR 514.
2 [1981] JPL 50.

you must focus on the situation as it was before the change; that is you consider the significance of the change in the context of the planning unit before the change. The change itself will often create a new planning unit which will then be the context in which to judge the materiality of any further changes.

(ii) *Identification of the planning unit.* Prior to the decision in *Burdle v Secretary of State for the Environment*[3] the phrase 'planning unit' was quite frequently employed but the criteria for identifying the unit were not at all clear.[4] In *Jennings Motors Ltd v Secretary of State for the Environment*[5] the Court of Appeal approved what was described as the 'extremely helpful general test' contained in the judgment of Bridge J in *Burdle*. The threefold guide set out by Bridge J in that case can be reconciled with most of the earlier decisions on the subject[6] and has been frequently applied and cited by the courts and ministers.[7]

In *Burdle* Bridge J, while not, he said, 'presuming to propound exhaustive tests apt to cover every situation', considered that it might be helpful to sketch out certain broad criteria appropriate to the determination of the planning unit.[8]

First, he said, whenever it is possible to recognise a single main purpose of the occupier's use of his land (whether or not there are secondary activities which are ancillary to that main purpose) the planning unit is the whole unit of occupation. That proposition emerged clearly, said Bridge J, from the decision of the Court of Appeal in *G Percy Trentham Ltd v Gloucestershire County Council*.[9]

As a working rule, therefore, one starts off with the presumption that the unit of occupation is the appropriate planning unit. That presumption will only be displaced if some smaller unit can be discerned (below). In general, the 'unit of occupation' is the area occupied[10] as a single holding by an individual occupier or by joint occupiers.[11] The notion of occupation is clearly governed by the person, firm or company which is doing the occupation. This can lead to problems where a company or a business occupies a large area or areas of land. Before land can be treated as

3 [1972] 3 All ER 240, [1972] 1 WLR 1207.
4 For detailed discussion of the earlier decisions see W Parkes, 'Determination of the Planning Unit' [1972] JPL 605; SNL Palk, 'The Planning Unit' (1973) 37 Conv 154; and Neil Hawke, 'Recognising the Planning Unit' [1974] JPL 399. On later developments see E Young, 'The Planning Unit: Judicial Creativity in a Statutory Context' (1983) 28 JLSS 339 and 371.
5 [1982] QB 541, [1982] 1 All ER 471, CA.
6 See, for example, *Bendles Motors Ltd v Bristol Corpn* [1963] 1 All ER 578, [1963] 1 WLR 247; *G Percy Trentham Ltd v Gloucestershire County Council* [1966] 1 All ER 701, [1966] 1 WLR 506; *Brazil (Concrete) Ltd v Amersham RDC* (1967) 65 LGR 365, 18 P & CR 396; *Williams v Minister of Housing and Local Government* (1967) 18 P & CR 514, and *Brooks v Gloucestershire County Council* (1967) 66 LGR 386, 19 P & CR 90.
7 In *Duffy v Secretary of State for the Environment* (1981) 259 Estates Gazette 1081, [1981] JPL 811 Glidewell J described Bridge J's judgment as the 'classic exposition' of the law on the subject.
8 The other members of the Divisional Court agreed with Bridge J's judgment.
9 [1966] 1 All ER 701, [1966] 1 WLR 506 (considered below).
10 The question of ownership of the land appears not to be relevant to identification of the unit.
11 See *Johnson v Secretary of State for the Environment* (1974) 73 LGR 22, 28 P & CR 424, per Lord Widgery CJ. See, however, *Kwik Save Discount Group v Secretary of State for Wales* (1978) 77 LGR 217, 37 P & CR 170 (below). For a recent decision showing that several plots in different ownership can amount to one planning unit, see *Rawlins v Secretary of State for the Environment* [1989] JPL 439.

comprising a single unit of occupation, that land must, it seems, be capable of being regarded as a single holding or entity.[12] Although a single planning unit can clearly extend over a group of buildings[13] or several parcels of land, a significant degree of physical separation may be a major factor leading to the conclusion that particular buildings or pieces of land do not form a single planning unit, even though those buildings or pieces of land are occupied by a single occupier for related purposes. In *Duffy v Secretary of State for the Environment*[14] Glidewell J accepted the inquiry inspector's view that buildings lying on opposite sides of a major road and 150 yards from each other did not form part of the same planning unit, even though the buildings were apparently used together for hotel purposes. Similarly in *Fuller v Secretary of State for the Environment*[15] Stuart-Smith J rejected the argument that where several farms were run as one 'agricultural unit', that was the only unit or area of land to be considered. The planning unit might frequently coincide with the agricultural unit as defined in s 207 and the General Development Order but not necessarily so. In this regard physical separation was an important factor but not the only one.[16]

Secondly, where the occupier carries on a variety of activities on the unit of occupation and it is not possible to say that one activity is ancillary to another (as in the case of a 'composite use' where the component activities are not confined within separate and physically distinct areas of land), the entire unit of occupation will again be the planning unit.

Thirdly, however, where within a single unit of occupation two or more physically separate and distinct areas are occupied for substantially different and unrelated purposes, each area used for a different main purpose (together with its incidental and ancillary activities) ought to be considered as a separate planning unit. On Bridge J's criteria, therefore, it is only if some unit smaller than the unit of 'occupation' can be recognised as the site of activities which amount in substance to a separate use both physically and functionally that the unit of occupation is displaced by the unit of 'activity' as the appropriate planning unit.

Bridge J added:

'To decide which of these three categories apply to the circumstances of any particular case at any given time may be difficult . . . There may indeed be an almost imperceptible change from one category to another. Thus, for example, activities . . . once properly regarded as incidental to another use or as part of a composite use may be so intensified in scale and physically concentrated in a recognisably separate area that they produce a new planning unit the use of which is materially changed.'

Put another way, in approaching the question of what is the correct planning unit, the following factors must be taken into account: (1) the area

12 On incorporation of one piece of land with another see *TLG Building Materials v Secretary of State for the Environment* (1980) 41 P & CR 243, [1981] JPL 513.
13 See, for example, *Vickers-Armstrong v Central Land Board* (1957) 9 P & CR 33.
14 (1981) 259 Estates Gazette 1081, [1981] JPL 811. See too appeal decision noted in [1973] JPL 386.
15 [1987] 2 EG LR 189, [1987] JPL 854.
16 Glidewell LJ refused leave to appeal against this decision, holding that both the question of the size of the agricultural unit and the correct planning unit were matters of fact and degree; see (1988) 1 EG 55.

occupied by an identifiable person, firm or company; (2) the actual physical layout; (3) the relationship and physical allocation of the activities taking place on the land. As with the question of whether development has occurred it seems that there is no exact hierarchy between these factors.

Also it would seem that so long as the right criteria are applied, the choice of the planning unit is for the planning authority or the Secretary of State to make as a matter of fact and degree in the circumstances of the particular case,[17] provided that the criteria are not applied unreasonably by the planning authority or the minister, the courts will not intervene.

(iii) *Application of principles.* The presumption in favour of the unit of occupation as the appropriate planning unit appears to be a strong one, and Bridge J's 'working rule' has been employed in many of the cases where a question as to the correct planning unit has arisen.[18] Sometimes this will be of advantage to the 'developer'[19] sometimes not.[20] The presumption in favour of the unit of occupation is particularly strong in the case of dwellinghouses. In *Wood v Secretary of State for the Environment*[1] (in which it was held that the minister had been wrong to treat as a separate planning unit a conservatory attached to a farmhouse and used for retail sales) the view was expressed by Lord Widgery CJ that 'it can rarely if ever be right to dissect a single dwellinghouse and to regard one room in isolation as being an appropriate planning unit . . .'

The broad significance of correct identification of the planning unit has been mentioned above but some examples of the operation of Bridge J's three criteria and some of the consequences of the application of those criteria should perhaps be mentioned here. It may be noted, however, that these consequences might well be complicated by the terms of a specific planning permission relating to the land in question.

1. *Single main use.* In terms of the first of Bridge J's guidelines, where several activities are carried on upon the unit of occupation but it is possible to recognise one of those activities as the primary use of the land and the others as ancillary thereto, it is, of course, the primary use which determines the use of the unit as a whole for planning purposes and the materiality of any change of use must be considered in the context of that primary use.[2]

The facts of *Johnston v Secretary of State for the Environment*[3] provide a good illustration of the operation of this principle. In that case premises

---

17 See for example, *Johnston v Secretary of State for the Environment* (1974) 73 LGR 22, 28 P & CR 424; and *Camden London Borough v Secretary of State for the Environment* (1978) 252 Estates Gazette 275, [1979] JPL 311. However, in one or two earlier cases the courts appear to have treated identification of the unit as a matter of law—see, for example, *G Percy Trentham Ltd v Gloucestershire County Council* [1966] 1 All ER 701, [1966] 1 WLR 506.

18 See, for example, *Burdle* (above); *Wood v Secretary of State for the Environment* [1973] 2 All ER 404, [1973] 1 WLR 707; *Johnston v Secretary of State for the Environment* (1974) 73 LGR 22, 28 P & CR 424; *Wakelin v Secretary of State for the Environment* (1978) 77 LGR 101; and *Hilliard v Secretary of State for the Environment* (1978) 37 P & CR 129; and appeal decisions noted in [1976] JPL 117 and 120, [1977] JPL 188, 195 and 611, [1978] JPL 54 and 784, [1980] JPL 693, [1981] JPL 382, and [1982] JPL 115 and 534.

19 See, for example, *Burdle and Wood* (above).

20 See, for example, *Williams* (above).

1 Above: see too *Brooks v Gloucestershire County Council* (1967) 66 LGR 386, 19 P & CR 90.

2 See, for example, appeal decisions noted in [1979] JPL 54, and [1981] JPL 382.

3 (1974) 73 LGR 22, 28 P & CR 424.

consisting of forty-four garages were originally used for the garaging of taxis belonging to the landowner. Over the years the garages came to be let singly or in groups to different persons. Some of the garages came to be used for vehicle repairs as opposed to garaging *simpliciter*. The appellants contended that the planning authority and the minister should have treated the entire group of forty-four garages as the planning unit. In that case one would have had to consider the materiality of the change in the use of a few of the garages in the context of the whole group; thus regarded, it is conceivable that the change of use might not have been considered a material one. The Divisional Court held that the Secretary of State's conclusion that each garage or small group of garages separately occupied was a separate planning unit could not be criticised. In these circumstances the minister had been entitled to find in relation to the appropriate planning unit that a material change of use had occurred.

Looked at in the context of the primary use of the planning unit, various sorts of change in the activities carried on upon the unit will not involve a material change of use. Uses ancillary to the main use can, for example, be given up or changed, new ancillary uses may be introduced and ancillary uses may be absorbed by the main use (see p 115 below).

2. *Mixed use*. Bridge J's second category would seem to embrace all those cases where several distinct activities are carried on upon the unit of occupation but the different activities are not confined within physically separate areas.[4] This he describes as a composite use but it might be better described as a mixed use.

If a case falls into this category it may well not be a material change of use to change the location of the various uses within the unit, so long as the 'mix' of uses does not change materially.[5]

3. *Dual use*. As regards the third of Bridge J's criteria, it may well be difficult to know when 'physically separate and distinct areas' within a single unit of occupation are occupied for 'substantially different and unrelated purposes' and when, therefore, such areas should be treated as separate planning units, the 'unit of activity' —ie the area upon which a particular activity is carried on—being in this situation preferred to the unit of occupation. Again this is largely a question of fact.[6]

An example of a case which was treated as falling into this category is *David W Barling Ltd v Secretary of State for the Environment*.[7] In this case an area of land had been used for the storage of building materials in connection with the building on another part of the site of two houses for the occupiers of the whole site. After completion of the houses the storage use continued in

4 See, for example, appeal decisions noted in [1973] JPL 261 and [1977] JPL 195.
5 See the comments of Lord Widgery CJ in *de Mulder v Secretary of State for the Environment* [1974] QB 792 [1974] 1 All ER 776 and in *Hilliard v Secretary of State for the Environment* (1977) 34 P & CR 193. See too *Bromsgrove District Council v Secretary of State for the Environment* [1977] JPL 797. And see p 115 below.
6 See *Camden London Borough v Secretary of State for the Environment* (1978) 252 Estates Gazette 275 [1979] JPL 31, per Lord Widgery CJ.
7 [1980] JPL 594. See too *Vyner & Son v Secretary of State for the Environment* (1977) 243 Estates Gazette 597, [1977] JPL 795; *Warnock v Secretary of State for the Environment and Dover District Council* [1980] JPL 690; and appeal decisions noted in [1970] JPL 43, and [1973] JPL 386. Also see recent decision of *Essex Water Co v Secretary of State for the Environment* [1989] EGC 20 which shows that two uses may be separate primary uses even though both related to a much larger undertaking.

connection with the running of a general building business and at that time the area used for storage was fenced off from the houses. The Divisional Court accepted the Secretary of State's conclusion that when it was fenced off the storage area became a separate planning unit with an independent use for commercial purposes.

In *Barling* physical division of the land by fencing would seem to have been relevant. Absence of such division will not, however, tell decisively in favour of a single planning unit. Where part of an old, and apparently largely disused, orchard possessed existing use rights as a caravan site, the Divisional Court held that although the orchard was not physically divided in any way, the caravan site was severable from the remainder of the orchard, and the introduction of caravans on the rest of the orchard constituted a change from agricultural use.[8] On the other hand, in *East Barnet UDC v British Transport Commission*[9] the Divisional Court took the view that an area of land which had not been used for many years should, 'as a matter of common sense', be treated as an unused part of a larger planning unit rather than as a separate unit in its own right, with the result that there was no material change of use when the unused parcel came to be used for the same purpose as the rest of the unit.

(iv) *Sub-division and merger of planning units.* It seems clear from Bridge J's judgment in *Burdle* that certain sorts of change in occupation or activity will result in the creation of a new planning unit.[10] This may happen (1) if two or more planning units are merged,[11] (2) if a planning unit is sub-divided into areas in separate occupation,[12] or (3) if a unit is divided into distinct geographical areas devoted to unrelated uses.[13] In the last case a material change of use will inevitably occur. However, the creation of a new planning unit by methods (1) and (2) will not in themselves result in a material change of use, though the changes that were involved in such a merger or subdivision may amount to a material change, if they have planning consequences.

Where, for example, a part of shop premises has been used for office purposes ancillary to the main (shop) use of the planning unit, and the planning unit is then sub-divided with the result that the office part of the premises comes into separate and independent occupation, a material change of use will occur; there has been a change from shop to office use. Until recently, however, there was no suggestion that the sub-division of a planning unit or the amalgamation of two units *automatically* resulted in a material change of use. Where, for example, premises formerly used as one shop come to be used as two shops in separate occupation, comparison of the use of either of the new units with the use of the former unit would suggest that no material change of use has occurred.

---

8 *Williams-Denton v Watford RDC* (1963) 61 LGR 423, 15 P & CR 11; see too *Brookes v Flintshire County Council* (1956) 54 LGR 355, 6 P & CR 140; and *R v Axbridge RDC, ex p Wormald* [1964] 1 All ER 571, [1964] 1 WLR 442.
9 [1962] 2 QB 484, [1961] 3 All ER 878. Contrast appeal decision noted in [1979] JPL 247.
10 The possibility that a 'new planning unit' may be created by the erection of a building etc, is considered separately below.
11 See, for example, *TLG Building Materials v Secretary of State for the Environment* (1980) 41 P & CR 243, [1981] JPL 513.
12 See, for example, *G Percy Trentham Ltd* (discussed below).
13 See, for example, *David W Barling Ltd* (above). As was the case in *Barling* this may happen where an ancillary use loses its ancillary status.

However, in *Wakelin v Secretary of State for the Environment*[14] the Court of Appeal accepted that the selling off for separate occupation of a large house and lodge forming part of a single planning unit would involve a material change of use. Lord Denning MR declared: 'if you divide a large house and grounds into two units ... that is a material change of use'. In *Winton v Secretary of State for the Environment*[15] Woolf J, said that *Wakelin* undoubtedly broke new ground; he did not, however, accept that Lord Denning was expressing a general view that the sub-division of a planning unit in itself amounted to a material change of use. Distinguishing *Wakelin*, Woolf J held that if the division of a single planning unit into two separate units has no planning consequences, then it does not amount to development. However, he refused to upset the Secretary of State's conclusion that, as a question of fact and degree, the division in the particular case did amount to a material change of use.

In *Johnston v Secretary of State for the Environment*[16] Lord Widgery CJ pointed out that there was at that time no reported case in which the appropriate planning unit had been held to comprise areas of land in different occupation. However, in *Kwik Save Discount Group v Secretary of State for Wales*[17] the Divisional Court held that areas in different occupation *could* form a single planning unit. In this case the occupiers of a garage complex obtained planning permission to change the use of a workshop to a retail showroom. The appellants acquired the workshop and proceeded to use it as a retail supermarket, claiming that with the severance of the workshop from the remainder of the site so far as activities and control were concerned, a new planning unit had come into existence, a planning unit which could be used for any form of retail sales.

The Divisional Court did not think one could create a new planning unit out of a complex of buildings such as these, which were supplementary to one another, simply by selecting one of the buildings and conveying it to an owner or occupier different from the owner or occupier of the rest of the site. The planning unit remained the same throughout, notwithstanding the severance. Lord Widgery stated that planning units were 'not primarily matters of title but of activity'. The planning authority were therefore entitled to restrain the supermarket use as being a material change from the garage use. The Divisional Court's decision in *Kwik Save* was upheld by the Court of Appeal, but on different grounds.[18] The Court of Appeal did not find the question of the planning unit important or helpful in deciding the case.

The reasoning of Lord Widgery in *Kwik Save* is not very convincing. While *Duffy* shows that the presumption that the planning unit is the unit of occupation can be rebutted by the physical layout of site, it will rarely be that two occupiers can reside in one planning unit, especially if their activities are not related. So a change in occupation will usually result in a change in the planning unit and so a new owner can, to use the words of Lord Widgery 'by his own say so whip the workshop out of the planning unit ... and convert it into a new planning unit' as long as there is a change in occupation and not

14 (1978) 77 LGR 101, 46 P & CR 214.
15 (1982) 46 P & CR 205. See too appeal decision noted in [1984] JPL 892.
16 (1974) 73 LGR 22, 28 P & CR 424.
17 (1978) 77 LGR 217, 37 P & CR 170. Also now see *Rawlins v Secretary of State for the Environment* [1989] JPL 439.
18 (1980) 79 LGR 310, 42 P & CR 166.

just a change in title. Also, the Divisional Court's decision seems to run counter to the Court of Appeal's reasoning in *G Percy Trentham Ltd v Gloucestershire County Council*[19] in which the severance of part of a farm was treated as creating a new planning unit. The decision in *Trentham* also shows that the result in *Kwik Save* would have been the same if the areas of separate occupation had been treated as separate planning units.

In *Trentham* the appellants, building and civil engineering contractors, purchased a farmhouse, yard and farm buildings which, prior to the purchase, had formed part of a 75 acre farm. Without obtaining planning permission the appellants proceeded to use some of the farm buildings, which had been used to house agricultural vehicles and machinery and to store corn and hay, for the storage of building materials, plant and equipment. It was argued for the appellants that the use of the buildings both before and after the sale was use as a warehouse or repository and that there had therefore been no material change of use. The Court of Appeal held that the former use was not use as a 'repository' but that in any event, taking as the proper planning unit the whole area purchased, the previous use of the land was for agricultural purposes and that there had been a change from an agricultural use as farm buildings to a store for other purposes. The storage use prior to the appellants' purchase of the land was merely ancillary to the dominant agricultural use and even though the particular use of the particular buildings remained use for storage, the dominant use had changed materially.

It might be suggested that the Divisional Court's approach in *Kwik Save* introduces an unnecessary complication into the law on the planning unit.

(b) *'Material' change*

The use in s 22(1) of the word 'material' to qualify 'change in the use of any buildings or other land' makes clear that no slight or trivial change of use, having regard to the use of the whole planning unit, will amount to development. Some changes of use may be too insubstantial or too brief to be regarded as having any planning significance.[20]

It may sometimes be fairly obvious that a particular change of use is, or would be, material—for example a change from use as a dwelling-house to use as a shop—but in some cases it can be very difficult to determine whether a particular change of use is a material one.[1] Is there, for example, a material change of use if a house formerly occupied all the year round by a single family comes to be used for holiday letting to a succession of families?[2]

The courts will not generally interfere with the decision of a planning authority or the Secretary of State on the issue of the materiality of a particular change unless the decision is one that no reasonable authority or

---

19 [1966] 1 All ER 701, [1966] 1 WLR 506.
20 See, for example, *Kwik Save Discount Group v Secretary of State for the Environment* (1980) 79 LGR 310, 42 P & CR 166 (offering of five cars for sale for a period of about one month in a building with a floor space of about 20,000 square feet). See too *Paul v Ayrshire County Council* 1964 SC 116, 1964 SLT 207, per Lord Justice-Clerk Grant, [1963] JPL 692, [1969] JPL 99, [1971] JPL 583, [1972] JPL 341, and [1974] JPL 300 and 733.
1 When considering whether a proposed change of use will be material, the proposed use must be compared with the last operative use of the land; regard cannot properly be had to a use for which planning permission has been granted but which has not been commenced—see ministerial decision noted in [1975] JPL 616.
2 See, for example, *Blackpool Borough Council v Secretary of State for the Environment* (1980) 40 P & CR 104, [1980] JPL 527.

minister, properly advised as to the law, could have reached. Thus, while a court may, for example, concern itself with the question whether a particular type of change of use is capable of amounting to development[3] or whether irrelevant factors have been taken into account by the Secretary of State in reaching his decision,[4] it has frequently been said that whether a particular change is material is very largely a matter of fact and degree[5] and the court will not intervene where the law has been properly applied, even if on the facts the court itself might have been inclined to reach a different conclusion.[6] In *Bendles Motors Ltd v Bristol Corpn,*[7] for example, the minister concluded that the placing of a vending machine on the forecourt of a garage involved a material change in the use of the premises. The minister having correctly considered the materiality of the change in relation to the use of the planning unit as a whole, the Divisional Court could not say that his decision was wrong, though they themselves might have been inclined to treat the introduction of the machine as *de minimis.*

So much is the matter one of fact and degree that it is very difficult to formulate any helpful general principles as to when a change of use is material. An early circular[8] declared that:

'A change in kind [of use] will always be material—e g from house to shop or from shop to factory. A change in the *degree* of an existing use may be "material" but only if it is very marked. For example, the fact that lodgers are taken privately in a family dwellinghouse would not in the Secretary of State's view constitute a material change of use in itself so long as the use of the house remains substantially that of a private residence.[9] On the other hand, the change from a private residence with lodgers to a declared guest house, boarding-house or private hotel would be "material".'

The concept of a change in 'kind' of use as contrasted with a change in the degree of an existing use may sometimes prove to be a useful initial approach and it has frequently been said that the question to be asked in considering whether or not a proposed change of use is a material one is whether the character of the existing use of land will be substantially altered by the proposed change. The easier it is to typify the present use of land as being of a different 'kind' or 'character' to the proposed use, the more likely it is that a

---

3 See, for example, *Birmingham Corpn v Minister of Housing and Local Government* [1964] 1 QB 178, [1963] 3 All ER 668, and *Lewis v Secretary of State for the Environment* (1971) 70 LGR 291, 23 P & CR 125.

4 See, for example, *Lewis* (above); *Snook v Secretary of State for the Environment* (1975) 33 P & CR 1; and *Winmill v Secretary of State for the Environment and Royal Borough of Kingston-upon-Thames* [1982] JPL 445.

5 See, for example, *Marshall v Nottingham City Corpn* [1960] 1 All ER 659, [1960] 1 WLR 707; *East Barnet UDC v British Transport Commission* [1962] 2 QB 484, [1961] 3 All ER 878; *Bendles Motors Ltd v Bristol Corpn* [1963] 1 All ER 578, [1963] 1 WLR 247; *Gray v Oxfordshire County Council* (1963) 15 P & CR 1; *Howell v Sunbury-on-Thames UDC* (1963) 15 P & CR 26; and *Braddon v Secretary of State for the Environment and Dacorum District Council* [1977] JPL 450.

6 See, however, *Emma Hotels Ltd v Secretary of State for the Environment* (1980) 41 P & CR 255, CA.

7 [1963] 1 All ER 578, [1963] 1 WLR 247.

8 Circular 69/47.

9 See, however, appeal decision noted in [1983] JPL 824 (use of two bedrooms of four-bedroomed house for overnight accommodation for paying guests held to involve a material change of use).

change from the former to the latter is material. A change, for example, from shop to office use will clearly be a material one.

However, for the purpose of gauging the materiality of a change of use, the identification of a change in the 'kind' or 'character' of use can pose very considerable difficulties, especially where the uses under consideration have some features in common. Uses of land can be typified with varying degrees of particularity—for example, a general word like 'hostel' embraces a number of different types of accommodation[10]—and the problem with making an abstract comparison of 'kinds' of use is to know the level of generality at which the uses in question should be categorised. As Lord Parker CJ put it in *East Barnet UDC v British Transport Commission*,[11] the difficulty is to know whether, for the purpose of comparing one use with another, it is right to consider what he called the 'general purpose' to which land is put or whether one should 'descend to the particular' and consider whether the particular purpose is different. He said:

'To take an example, is the purpose for which a shop is occupied the purpose of a retail shop quite generally, or is it the narrower purpose of being used as a retail shop for the sale of a particular commodity? If the former is correct, than a change in the nature of the article sold would not be development; if the latter, it would.'

The *East Barnet* case demonstrates that where the kind of use, the general purpose, to which land is put remains the same, but there is, in Lord Parker's words,[12] 'a change from 'one particular purpose to another particular purpose'—where, for example, land continues to be used for storage purposes but the commodity stored is changed—it may be right to conclude that the change of use is not a material one. In the *East Barnet* case[13] land had previously been used by the British Transport Commission as a coal storage depot, all of the coal being transported to and from the depot by rail. The land came to be used by a motor manufacturing company as a transit depot for the storage and handling of motor vehicles, virtually all of which were transported by rail. The Divisional Court held that the magistrates had been entitled to find that no material change of use had taken place.[14] In *Lewis v Secretary of State for the Environment*[15] the Divisional Court held that the minister had erred in law in treating as material a change in the use of premises from use for maintenance and repair of vehicles belonging to a

10 See *Commercial and Residential Property Development Co Ltd v Secretary of State for the Environment* (1981) 80 LGR 443, per Glidewell J.
11 [1962] 2 QB 484, [1961] 3 All ER 878.
12 *Devonshire County Council v Horton* (1962) 61 LGR 60, 14 P & CR 444.
13 Above. See too *Marshall v Nottingham City Corpn* [1960] 1 All ER 659, [1960] 1 WLR 707 (change from manufacture and sale of wooden buildings to sale of caravans not material); *Devonshire County Council v Allens Caravans (Estates) Ltd* (1962) 61 LGR 57, 14 P & CR 440; and *Devonshire County Council v Horton* (1962) 61 LGR 60, 14 P & CR 444 (change from use of land for camping in tents to use as a caravan site not material); and *Blackpool Borough Council v Secretary of State for the Environment* (1980) 40 P & CR 104, [1980] JPL 527 (holiday letting of dwelling to succession of families not material). See [1980] JPL 342, and [1981] JPL 612 (use of dwelling for holiday lettings not a material change).
14 One might, however, contrast the appeal decision noted in [1976] JPL 248 (change from storage of coal to storage of cars held a material change of use). See too [1978] JPL 343.
15 (1971) 23 P & CR 125; see too *Snook v Secretary of State for the Environment* (1975) 33 P & CR 1; and *Philip Farrington Properties Ltd v Secretary of State for the Environment* (1983) 265 Estates Gazette 47, [1982] JPL 638.

particular company to use for maintenance and repair of vehicles belonging to the public at large; the use throughout having, in the court's view, remained the same, the change could not be material.[16]

On the other hand, even though the 'general purpose' remains the same, a change of use within that general purpose *can* be material. Various sorts of use can, for example, be described at a general level as 'residential' but it is clear that a change within that broad category of use may be material. In *Birmingham Corpn v Minister of Housing and Local Government*[17] houses formerly in single-family occupation came to be used as houses let in lodgings to a number of different occupants. The minister decided that since the houses had remained in residential use throughout, the change in the type of occupancy could not as a matter of law be material. The Divisional Court held that the minister had erred in law. Merely because the uses in question could be described as residential did not debar the minister from considering whether, as a matter of fact and degree, a material change of use had occurred.

A change in the use of premises from use as a single-family private residence to use for multiple paying occupation[18] can amount to a material change of use;[19] and the courts have held the minister entitled to find that a material change of use occurred where there was a change from student hostel to residential hotel;[20] where there was a change from bed-sitting accommodation to hotel;[1] where there was a change from single-family occupation of a house to use as accommodation for hotel staff;[2] where there was a change from guest house to residential accommodation;[3] and where there was a change from one type of social club to another.[4] It would seem that in appropriate circumstances a change from use as a private dwelling-house to use for short holiday lettings could amount to a material change of use,[5] as could a change from a short-stay hostel to a long-stay hostel.[6]

16 However, as Lord Widgery pointed out in *Jones v Secretary of State for the Environment* (1974) 28 P & CR 362, there are circumstances in which a material change of use can occur even though the type of activity on the land has been constant throughout; there may, for example, be a material change where an existing use is intensified (see p 107 below) or where a use which was previously ancillary to another use has become the primary use of the land (see p 117 below).

17 [1964] 1 QB 178, [1963] 3 All ER 668. See too *Borg v Khan* (1965) 63 LGR 309, 17 P & CR 144.

18 On the meaning of 'multiple occupation' see *Duffy v Pilling* (1977) 75 LGR 159, 33 P & CR 85; *Lipson v Secretary of State for the Environment* (1976) 75 LGR 361, 33 P & CR 95; *Winmill v Secretary of State for the Environment and Royal Borough of Kingston-upon-Thames* [1982] JPL 445; *Breachberry Ltd v Secretary of State for the Environment and Shepway District Council* [1985] JPL 180; and appeal decision noted in [1979] JPL 123.

19 See, for example, ministerial decisions noted in [1965] JPL 47 and 144, [1976] JPL 55, [1977] JPL 535, [1984] JPL 822. Contrast [1978] JPL 270 and 578.

20 *Mornford Investments v Minister of Housing and Local Government* [1970] 2 All ER 253.

1 *Mayflower Cambridge Ltd v Secretary of State for the Environment* (1975) 73 LGR 517, 30 P & CR 28.

2 *Clarke v Minister of Housing and Local Government* (1966) 64 LGR 346, 18 P & CR 82.

3 *Breachberry Ltd v Secretary of State for the Environment and Shepway District Council* [1985] JPL 180.

4 *Burkmar v Secretary of State for the Environment* (1984) 271 Estates Gazette 377.

5 See the comments of Jupp J in *Blackpool Borough Council v Secretary of State for the Environment* (1980) 40 P & CR 104 (although in that case the court upheld the minister's decision that no material change of use had occurred).

6 See *Commercial and Residential Property Development Co v Secretary of State for the Environment* (1981) 80 LGR 443, per Glidewell J.

Other examples of changes within the same broad category of use being treated as material might be cited. The courts have, for example, held the minister entitled to find that a change from use for lock-up garages to use for the storage and maintenance of a coach fleet was material;[7] that a change from selling eggs at the farm door to selling eggs by means of a roadside vending machine was a material change;[8] and that a change from plant nursery to garden centre was material.[9]

Decisions such as those mentioned above appear to indicate that abstract comparisons of the character of uses of land may not be very helpful in considering whether a particular change of use is material. It is often more useful to ask whether, as between two uses exhibiting some similarities, the change from one to the other will have consequences which are material or relevant in planning terms.[10] There is a good deal of judicial support for such an approach.[11] In *Devonshire County Council v Allens Caravans (Estates) Ltd*,[12] for example, Lord Parker CJ said: 'The materiality to be considered is a materiality from a planning point of view and, in particular, the question of amenities.' Planning is concerned about the consequences that the change will have upon the area. In this way planning is concerned with the future. However, in circular 67/49 it was stated that 'The Minister is advised that in considering whether a change is a material change, comparison with the previous use of the land or building in question is the governing factor and the effect of the proposal on a surrounding neighbourhood is not relevant to the issue'. Further, in *Cynon Valley Borough Council v Secretary of State for Wales*[13], in another context, the Court of Appeal emphasised that in the concept of material change it is the change *from* use A to use B which is important. However, it now seems clear that in comparing use A with use B the effect which a particular change will have on a locality will often be important.[14] Matters such as increased noise,[15] changes in the volume of traffic or other activity or on-site sales generated by a new use,[16] increased

---

7 *Gray v Oxfordshire County Council* (1963) 15 P & CR 1.

8 *Hidderley v Warwickshire County Council* (1963) 61 LGR 266, 14 P & CR 134.

9 *T A Miller v Minister of Housing and Local Government* (1967) 66 LGR 285, 19 P & CR 263.

10 One is not, of course, considering in this context the *desirability* of the particular change of use.

11 See dicta in *Marshall v Nottingham City Corpn* [1960] 1 All ER 659, [1960] 1 WLR 707; *East Barnet UDC v British Transport Commission* [1962] 2 QB 484, [1961] 3 All ER 878; *Devonshire County Council v Allens Caravans (Estates) Ltd* (1962) 61 LGR 57, 14 P & CR 440; *Wilson v West Sussex County Council* [1963] 2 QB 764, [1963] 1 All ER 751; *Williams v Minister of Housing and Local Government* (1967) 18 P & CR 514; *Commercial and Residential Property Development Co v Secretary of State for the Environment* (1981) 80 LGR 443; and *Burkmar v Secretary of State for the Environment* (1984) 271 Estates Gazette 377. See too appeal decisions noted in [1980] JPL 282; and [1981] JPL 612.

12 Above.

13 (1986) 85 LGR 36, [1986] JPL 760.

14 See, for example, appeal decisions noted in [1971] JPL 72, [1980] JPL 282 and 476, [1981] JPL 612, and [1982] JPL 199.

15 See *Ross v Aberdeen County Council* 1955 SLT (Sh Ct) 65; and appeal decisions noted in [1971] JPL 172, [1972] JPL 219, and [1979] JPL 633. See too *Gray v Oxfordshire County Council* (1963) 15 P & CR 1.

16 See, for example, *Chrysanthou v Secretary of State for the Environment and London Borough of Haringey* [1976] JPL 371, per Lord Widgery CJ; *Snook v Secretary of State for the Environment* (1975) 33 P & CR 1, per Bridge J.

demands on public services[17] and provision of services and residents' length of stay in residential accommodation[18] may all be relevant.

Considerations which are not relevant to planning must, of course, be disregarded. The House of Lords has held in *Westminster City Council v British Waterways Board*[19] that 'it would be of no relevance to the use of the premises to inquire for what purpose the vehicles parked there were to be used when they left their base.'[20] Their Lordships therefore concluded that although the premises were now used as a street cleaning depot this was only one of a substantial range of uses which could properly be carried on without involving a change of use. The House of Lords also held in that case and in *Great Portland Estates v Westminster City Council*[1] (both cases were handed down on the same day) that generally planning was not concerned with the circumstances of a particular occupier. Thus, it has been held that the identity of the person carrying on an activity,[2] a change in the ownership or source of supply[3] or means of subsequent disposal[4] of articles dealt with on the premises in question, and the degree of control exercised over parts of the premises by the individual occupiers of residential premises[5] are not relevant for this purpose.

Yet, in *London Residuary Body v Secretary of State for the Environment*[6] Stephen Brown J accepted that while such matters might be irrelevant in themselves, they could be illuminating of the character of the activities undertaken on the land. Thus, the use of County Hall by the Greater London Council was held to be not an office use but 'use for the exercise of local government statutory functions'. Nevertheless, in general motives or intentions of the occupier should not be relevant and the focus should be the actual activities on the relevant planning unit which are proposed or which have been carried out. Yet it does seem that a material change of use can be inferred from the nature of physical operations; see p 141.

17 See *Guildford RDC v Penny* [1959] 2 QB 112, [1959] 2 All ER 111, per Lord Evershed MR.
18 See *Commercial and Residential Property Development Co v Secretary of State for the Environment* (1981) 80 LGR 443; *Winmill v Secretary of State for the Environment* and *Royal Borough of Kingston-on-Thames* [1982] JPL 445; and *Breachberry v Secretary of State for the Environment and Shepway District Council* [1985] JPL 180.
19 [1985] AC 676, [1984] 3 All ER 737.
20 Per Lord Bridge of Harwich at 684.
 1 [1984] 3 All ER 744, sub nom *Westminster City Council v Great Portland Estates plc* [1985] AC 661.
 2 See *Lewis v Secretary of State for the Environment* (1971) 23 P & CR 125; *East Barnet UDC v British Transport Commission* [1962] 2 QB 484, [1961] 3 All ER 878; *Snook v Secretary of State for the Environment* (1975) 33 P & CR 1; *Shephard v Buckinghamshire County Council* (1966) 64 LGR 422, 18 P & CR 419; *Rael-Brook v Minister of Housing and Local Government* [1967] 2 QB 65, [1967] 1 All ER 262, and appeal decisions noted in [1967] JPL 173, [1971] JPL 653, and [1981] JPL 375.
 3 See *Lewis v Secretary of State for the Environment* (1971) 23 P & CR 125; see too *Marshall v Nottingham City Corpn* [1960] 1 All ER 659, [1960] 1 WLR 707, and appeal decision noted in [1973] JPL 654. However, as Lord Widgery pointed out in *Chrysanthou v Secretary of State for the Environment and London Borough of Haringey* [1976] JPL 371, cases such as *Williams v Minister of Housing and Local Government* (1967) 18 P & CR 514 show that there can be a material change of use if a change in the ownership or source of supply of the articles dealt with is such as to greatly increase the volume of traffic, business or activity on the land. See too *Jones v Secretary of State for the Environment* (1974) 28 P & CR 362.
 4 See *Snook v Secretary of State for the Environment* (1975) 33 P & CR 1.
 5 See *Winmill v Secretary of State for the Environment and Royal Borough of Kingston-upon-Thames* [1982] JPL 445.
 6 [1988] JPL 637.

As to what are 'planning considerations' in *Wilson v West Sussex County Council*[7] Diplock LJ, in obiter dicta, stated that the development plan and the declared policy of the planning authority would be relevant. However, this is doubtful as it could mean that what was a material change would vary from area to area according to the policy and the decision itself was mainly concerned with the issue of whether the change in the occupation of the dwelling was covered by the planning permission.

(c) *Intensification of use*

Intensification of an existing use of land can have significant town planning consequences and may, if marked, amount to a material change in the use of the land.

In this connection the word 'intensification', according to Widgery J, 'is normally used to describe the situation which arises where an area of land is used throughout the relevant time for the same purpose but the intensity of the activity varies; a field may have been used for car-breaking at all material times, but for only three cars at one time and for thirty-three on another occasion.'[8] In *Kensington and Chelsea Royal Borough v Secretary of State for the Environment and Mia Carla Ltd*[9] Donaldson LJ said that the word 'intensification' had to be used with very considerable circumspection; in this context 'intensification' meant a change to something different. According to Lord Donaldson 'if the planners were incapable of formulating what was the use after "intensification" and what was the use before "intensification" then there had been no material change of use.' This would suggest that, where the variations in intensity do not justify a new label or description of what is going on, then a material change cannot have taken place. However, Lord Donaldson's remarks were obiter and he did not refer to the earlier case law which suggests that 'simply more of the same' can amount to a material change of use. Otherwise the question is whether the intensification is so great as to affect what Lord Evershed MR called 'a definable character of the land and its use'.[10] We would therefore suggest that an intensification of use can only amount to a material change of use if it is in some way significant from a planning viewpoint.[11]

In *Guildford RDC v Penny*[12] the Court of Appeal indicated (though it was not necessary to decide the point) that in appropriate circumstances increase or intensification of use was capable of constituting development and in *James v Secretary of State for Wales*[13] it was held that an increase from one to

---

7 [1963] 2 QB 764, [1963] 1 All ER 751.
8 *Brooks v Gloucestershire County Council* (1967) 66 LGR 386, 19 P & CR 90.
9 [1981] JPL 50.
10 *Guildford RDC v Penny* [1959] 2 QB 112, [1959] 2 All ER 111, and see also *Lilo Blum v Secretary for the Environment and London Borough of Richmond upon Thames Council* [1987] JPL 278, where Simon Brown J accepted that where intensification affected the definable character of the land and its use, it could give rise to a material change of use.
11 See, for example, appeal decision noted in [1982] JPL 534.
12 Above: see too *dicta* in *East Barnet UDC v British Transport Commission* [1962] 2 QB 484, [1961] 3 All ER 878; *Marshall v Nottingham City Corpn* [1960] 1 All ER 659, [1960] 1 WLR 707; and *de Mulder v Secretary of State for the Environment* [1974] QB 792, [1974] 1 All ER 776.
13 [1966] 1 WLR 135 (revsd in the House of Lords on other grounds: [1968] AC 409, [1966] 3 All ER 964.

four in the number of caravans on a site could be a material change of use. In another case[14] Lord Denning MR said: 'I doubt very much whether the occupier could increase from twenty-four to seventy-eight [caravans] without permission. An increase in intensity of that order may well amount to a material change of use.'

In *Peake v Secretary of State for Wales*[15] the appellant had, as a part-time but profitable hobby, used his private garage for the repair and maintenance of vehicles; after being declared redundant in his employment in 1968 he carried on the business of vehicle maintenance at the garage on a full-time basis. The Divisional Court held that although the change from part-time to full-time activity could not of itself amount to a material change of use, the Secretary of State had been entitled to find that a material change of use had occurred by intensification in 1968.[16] In *Brooks and Burton v Secretary of State for the Environment*[17] the Court of Appeal held that there was ample evidence to support the Secretary of State's conclusion that there had been a material change of use by intensification where the manufacture of concrete blocks had increased from under 300,000 blocks per annum to about 1,200,000 blocks per annum. (It was, however, held that the change of use did not involve development since both uses fell within the same use class in the Use Classes Order.[18])

It may be difficult to judge in any particular case whether as a matter of fact and degree there has been such a change in the degree of an existing use as to constitute a material change of use. Where, for example, the number of lorries parked on a site was increased from one or two to about forty, the minister decided that a material change of use had taken place.[19] On the other hand, an increase in the number of vehicles parked from 6 to 25 was held by the minister not to be a material change.[20]

(d) *When does a change of use occur?*

In *Caledonian Terminal Investments Ltd v Edinburgh Corpn*[1] a majority of the Second Division of the Court of Session took the view that where planning permission has been granted for a change in the use of land, the change of use does not take place until the land is actually put to the new use.[2] To similar effect, the minister has expressed the view that where a new building is erected, either with or without planning permission, it has no use for the purposes of the planning legislation until it is actually used.[3] However, in

14 *Esdell Caravan Parks Ltd v Hemel Hempstead RDC* [1966] 1 QB 895.
15 (1971) 70 LGR 98, 22 P & CR 889; see too *Dyble v Minister of Housing and Local Government* (1966) 197 Estates Gazette 457; and *Hipsey v Secretary of State for the Environment and Thurrock Borough Council* [1984] JPL 806.
16 See also ministerial decision noted in [1974] JPL 490.
17 [1978] 1 All ER 733, [1977] 1 WLR 1294.
18 See p 124 below.
19 [1960] JPL 807. Other examples of intensification of a use being found to amount to a material change of use are to be found in [1970] JPL 717, [1974] JPL 100 and 733, and [1977] JPL 123.
20 [1963] JPL 349. See too [1964] JPL 363, [1970] JPL 653, [1972] JPL 270, [1973] JPL 264, [1974] JPL 101, [1978] JPL 270 and 395, [1980] JPL 771, and [1982] JPL 534.
1 1970 SC 271, 1970 SLT 362 (see p 127 below).
2 S 290(5)(c) of the 1971 Act, which deals with the 'initiation' of development, is not relevant in this context—see *Burn v Secretary of State for the Environment* (1971) 219 Estates Gazette 586; *Impey v Secretary of State for the Environment* (1980) 47 P & CR 157n; and *Backer v Secretary of State for the Environment* (1982) 47 P & CR 149.
3 See [1975] JPL 616.

Impey v Secretary of State for the Environment[4] Donaldson LJ expressed the view that a change of use can take place before premises have actually been put to a new use, saying that in a case where premises had been converted for residential use and put on the market as available for letting, it was plain that there had on these facts been a change of use. We would submit that although the physical state of a building may be closely linked to a change in the use of that building there is much to commend the approach adopted in *Caledonian Terminal Investments*; an intention to make a change in the use of premises is very different from an actual change of use. It would seem that in law a material change takes place at a particular moment or at least a particular period of time. Where the material change builds up gradually over a long period—for example, where an existing use is intensified; in such a case difficult questions of fact can arise as to precisely when the material change (and therefore development) occurred.[5]

(e) *Discontinuance and abandonment of use*

The mere suspension of a use does not of itself amount to a material change in the use of land. As Ashworth J, said in *Hartley v Minister of Housing and Local Government*:[6] 'If land is put to more than one use, usually referred to as a composite use, the cessation of one of the uses does not of itself constitute development.'[7] (If, however, as in *Wipperman and Buckingham v London Borough of Barking*[8] one of the component uses is allowed to absorb the site to the exclusion of another use, there can be a material change of use.)

Where the use of land has been suspended and is thereafter resumed without there having been any intervening different use, then *prima facie* the resumption does not constitute development.[9] In this way the law recognises the concept of a notional use; that is land will be taken to be in use for a particular purpose even if for periods of time, because of illness or for some other reason, no activity is going on. However, in *Hartley v Minister of Housing and Local Government*[10] Lord Denning MR said: 'When a man ceases to use a site for a particular purpose, and lets it remain unused for a considerable time, then the proper inference may be that he has abandoned the former use.' Once a use has been abandoned, the landowner cannot, said Lord Denning, 'start to use the site again, unless he gets planning permission; and this is so even though the new use is the same as the previous one'[11] In *Hartley's* case the Court of Appeal held, affirming the decision of the Divisional Court, that there were sufficient grounds to support the minister's finding that the previous use of a site for car sales, suspended between 1961 and 1965, had been abandoned and that the resumption of that use

---

4 (1980) 47 P & CR 157n. See too *Backer v Secretary of State for the Environment* (1982) 47 P & CR 149.
5 See ch 12 at p 314 for the problems of drafting an enforcement notice in such circumstances.
6 [1969] 2 QB 46, [1969] 1 All ER 309.
7 See *Philglow v Secretary of State for the Environment and the London Borough of Hillingdon* (1984) 51 P & CR 1, 270 Estates Gazette 1192, CA.
8 (1965) 130 JP 103, 64 LGR 97 (see p 120 below).
9 See *Hartley v Minister of Housing and Local Government* [1969] 2 QB 46 per Ashworth J.
10 [1970] 1 QB 413, [1969] 3 All ER 1658.
11 In *Pioneer Aggregates (UK) Ltd v Secretary of State for the Environment* [1985] AC 132, [1984] 2 All ER 358 (see p 270 below) the House of Lords held that a planning permission could not be abandoned, but cast no doubt on the concept of abandonment of existing use rights.

amounted, as a change from 'non-use' to a positive use, to a material change of use.[12]

It may be difficult to determine whether a use has merely been temporarily suspended or whether it has been abandoned. In *Hartley's* case Widgery LJ treated the occupier's intention not to resume a use as an important indicator of abandonment, whereas Lord Denning appeared to favour the more objective test of whether a reasonable man would conclude from all the circumstances that a use had been abandoned.

However, in considering whether or not a use has been abandoned, the intention (inferred or actual) with which the use was ended would appear to be an important factor.[13] An intention to abandon a use might be inferred from the taking of some action inconsistent with retention of the right to resume that use—the removal, for example, of petrol pumps and the taking of action to render petrol storage tanks useless may indicate a clear intention to abandon the use of the land in question as a petrol filling station.[14] If, after suspension of a particular use, land has been put to some different use, that fact may be relevant as indicating an intention to abandon the original use.[15] Where, however, a change has been made from one use to another without any intervening period of non-use, there is no place for the concept of abandonment.[16] In practice this will not be important as if use A changes to use X and then back again to use A, the reversion back to use A will be a material change of use even if technically the change to X is not to be considered as abandonment.[17] The making of a planning application for a different use of the land may provide some indication of the landowner's intentions[18] but is clearly not conclusive evidence of an intention to abandon a use.[19] Where there is a conflict between the evidence of the actual intention of the occupier and the intention to be inferred from the conduct and behaviour of the occupier, the circumstantial evidence may prevail. As McNeill J put it in *Nicholls v Secretary of State for the Environment*[20] 'Indeed, in any particular case it may be that whatever the owner or occupier has said about his intentions at the material time he may be contradicted by facts and

12 See too *Miller-Mead v Minister of Housing and Local Government* [1963] 2 QB 196, [1963] 1 All ER 459; *T A Miller v Minister of Housing and Local Government* (1967) 66 LGR 285, 19 P & CR 263; *Draco v Oxfordshire County Council* (1972) 224 Estates Gazette 1037; *Ratcliffe v Secretary of State for the Environment* (1975) 235 Estates Gazette 901; *Nicholls v Secretary of State for the Environment* [1981] JPL 890; and *Trustees of the Castell-y-Mynach Estate v Secretary of State for Wales and Taff Ely Borough Council* [1985] JPL 40.

13 See, for example, *Gredley (Investment Developments) Co Ltd v London Borough of Newham* (1973) 26 P & CR 400; and *Wheatfield Inns (Belfast) Ltd v Croft Inns Ltd* [1978] NI 83; see too appeal decisions noted in [1973] JPL 48, [1980] JPL 759, [1982] JPL 119, 194 and 801, and [1983] JPL 129 and 375.

14 [1972] JPL 577 (upheld in *Draco* (above)). See too [1971] JPL 457, and [1977] JPL 326.

15 See *Grillo v Minister of Housing and Local Government* (1968) 208 Estates Gazette 1201; *Maddern v Secretary of State for the Environment and Thurrock Borough Council* [1980] JPL 676; *Balco Transport Services v Secretary of State for the Environment* (1983) 45 P & CR 216, [1969] JPL 707, and [1984] JPL 451.

16 See *Young v Secretary of State for the Environment* (1983) 47 P & CR 165 (this point was not considered in the House of Lords: [1983] 2 AC 662). See too *Balco Transport Services Ltd v Secretary of State for the Environment* (1983) 45 P & CR 216, and appeal decision noted in [1982] JPL 798.

17 But see ch 6, p 145 as to the rights of reversion which are provided by s 23. In applying such rights of reversion it seems the concept of abandonment does not apply; see *Fairchild v Secretary of State for the Environment and Eastleigh Borough Council* [1988] JPL 472.

18 See appeal decision noted in [1981] JPL 914.

19 [1971] JPL 244.

20 [1981] JPL 890.

circumstances so that his intention can be rejected.' So evidence of actual intention is only one of the factors to be considered.

The length of the period of discontinuance of a use will usually be relevant but even a long period may not be conclusive evidence of an intention to abandon the use.[1] The physical condition of the land or any building may also be a relevant factor. In one appeal, for example, the ruinous state of a cottage was one of the factors which led the Secretary of State to conclude that the residential use of the premises had been abandoned.[2]

In *Grover's Executors v Rickmansworth UDC*[3] the Lands Tribunal held that the fact that the use of land had been brought to an end and the land offered for sale with vacant possession did not show an intention to abandon the use; such action was consistent with a desire to obtain a more favourable price for the land.[4] Nor did the service of a purchase notice provide a conclusive indication of intention to abandon the use. It seems that in the case of dwellinghouses, abandonment will not usually be inferred simply from non-use and more positive actions such as reconstruction will be required. The state of repair of the building and whether it is habitable will be important.

Where abandonment applies, subject to any rights of reversion found in s 23 (see p 146 below), resumption of the previous use will require permission even where that use was in existence on or before 1st July 1948.[4a]

(f) *Seasonal or periodic uses*

Where land is put to a seasonal or periodic use—where, for example, land is used as a fairground in the summer months or where it is used as a racecourse for only a few days each year—and is not used for any other purpose for the remainder of the year, the cessation and resumption each year do not amount to a material change of use.[5]

In *Webber v Minister of Housing and Local Government*[6] the Court of Appeal held (disapproving *dicta* in earlier cases) that where land had been used over a period of years for agriculture in the winter and for camping in the summer, the seasonal change from camping to agriculture or vice versa did not involve a material change of use for the purposes of the planning legislation; the 'normal use' of the land from year to year was for two purposes and so long as that normal use continued from year to year there was no material change of use.

(g) *Extinguishment of use*

In *Petticoat Lane Rentals Ltd v Secretary of State for the Environment*[7]

---

1 See, for example, *Fyson v Buckinghamshire County Council* [1958] 2 All ER 286n, [1958] 1 WLR 634, and appeal decisions noted in [1982] JPL 794, [1983] JPL 129, and [1984] JPL 207.
2 See [1981] JPL 914. See too appeal decisions noted in [1978] JPL 651, and [1979] JPL 551.
3 (1959) 10 P & CR 417.
4 See *Trustees of the Castell-y-Mynach Estate v Secretary of State for Wales and Taff Ely Borough Council* [1985] JPL 40 which sets out the various factors. Also see Watkin 'Development upon the Resumption of the Abandoned Use' [1980] JPL 226 and Bourne 'Dwelling Houses—Rebuild or Permitted Development' [1981] JPL 567.
4a See *White v Secretary of State for the Environment* [1989] JPL 692, CA.
5 See *Hawes v Thornton Cleveleys UDC* (1965) 63 LGR 213, 17 P & CR 22 but compare *South Bucks District Council v Secretary of State for the Environment* [1989] JPL 351: each change to Sunday market a material change of use.
6 [1967] 3 All ER 981, [1968] 1 WLR 29. See too [1981] JPL 449.
7 [1971] 2 All ER 793, [1971] 2 WLR 1112

Widgery LJ said that the 'question of how far existing planning rights can be lost by the occupier obtaining and implementing an inconsistent planning permission has not as yet been fully developed in the authorities'. That is probably still the case but the opinions of the House of Lords in *Newbury District Council v Secretary of State for the Environment*[8] and the decision of the Court of Appeal in *Jennings Motors Ltd v Secretary of State for the Environment*[9] shed a good deal of light on how this question should be approached. Although it is clear, as Lord Scarman said in one case,[10] that 'existing use rights are hardy beasts with a great capacity for survival', in the *Newbury* case the House of Lords agreed that if the carrying out of development on land resulted in the creation of a 'new planning unit' or the beginning of a 'new chapter of planning history', the consequence was that existing use rights attaching to the land in question were extinguished.[11] The main question to be considered, therefore, is what are the circumstances in which a 'new planning unit' is created or a 'new chapter in the planning history' of a site begun. In this regard the use of the term 'new planning unit' is confusing as it has a specialist meaning; see page 94 above. It is to be hoped that the term 'new chapter in the planning history' will in future prevail.[12]

The early decisions. The earliest decision on this matter is *Prossor v Minister of Housing and Local Government*.[13] In that case planning permission had been obtained for the rebuilding of a petrol filling station subject to a condition that no retail sales other than of motor accessories should take place on the site. The appellant displayed on the site second-hand cars for sale, claiming that there was attached to the land an existing use right for the display and sale of cars. Though it was held that he had not been able to establish this claim, the Divisional Court also held that the appellant was bound by the condition attached to the planning permission. Lord Parker CJ stated:

'by adopting the permission granted ... the appellant's predecessor ... gave up any possible existing use rights in that regard which he may have had. The planning history of this site, as it were, seems to me to begin afresh ... with the grant of this permission, a permission which was taken up and used.'

One phase of the planning history had been brought to an end and another had started.

In *Leighton and Newman Car Sales Ltd v Secretary of State for the Environment*[14] the Court of Appeal held, on facts very similar to those in *Prossor*, that premises which had been rebuilt under a planning permission constituted a completely new and different planning unit to which the previous use of the original premises was irrelevant.

8 [1981] AC 578, [1980] 1 All ER 731.
9 [1982] QB 541 [1983] 1 All ER 471.
10 *Pioneer Aggregates (UK) Ltd v Secretary of State for the Environment* [1985] AC 132, [1984] 2 All ER 358.
11 Existing use rights can also be lost by the implementation of a planning permission imposing conditions on the future use of the land (see p 238 below).
12 On this, see views of *Divisional Court in South Staffordshire District Council v Secretary of State for the Environment and Bickford* [1987] JPL 635.
13 (1968) 67 LGR 109.
14 (1976) 32 P & CR 1. See too *J Toomey Motors Ltd v Basildon District Council* [1982] JPL 775, CA.

In *Petticoat Lane Rentals v Secretary of State for the Environment*[15] planning permission was granted for the erection of a building on a cleared site which had previously been used as an open-air market. The open ground floor of the building was to be used for car parking and loading. The planning permission expressly provided that this ground floor area might be used for market trading on Sundays but said nothing about such trading on weekdays. After the permission had been implemented the ground floor area was used for market trading on weekdays as well as on Sundays. The Divisional Court held that where a clear area of ground is developed by the erection of a building over the whole of the land, the previous planning unit ceases to exist; the land as such is merged in the new building and a new planning unit with no planning history results. Any existing rights attaching to the previous planning unit are automatically extinguished and any use not authorised by the planning permission can be restrained. As the planning permission in this case did not authorise use for market trading on weekdays, that use was a breach of planning control. A majority of the court reserved for future consideration what the position would be if the whole of the land was not redeveloped by being covered by a building; that matter is considered below.

As mentioned above, judges have sometimes spoken, in the context of the extinguishment of existing use rights, of the creation of a 'new planning unit', sometimes of a 'new chapter in planning history' being started. Any difference between the terms is, it seems, largely a matter of semantics.[16] The important point is that both phrases are used to describe the situation where, as in the *Prossor, Leighton and Newman* and *Petticoat Lane Rental* cases, a change in the physical nature of premises or in their planning status is so radical as to give rise to the inference that any prior use is being given up and a new planning history begun. In effect, the slate is wiped clean. In *Jennings Motors Ltd v Secretary of State for the Environment*[17] the Court of Appeal held that it was in every case a question of fact and degree whether an alteration in the physical nature of a site or in its planning status was so radical as to lead to the extinguishment of existing use rights.

In many ways the concept of extinguishment is similar to that of abandonment with the difference that intention is of far less importance. Indeed as in the *Petticoat Lane* decision a use may be extinguished even where the occupiers attempted to carry on the use.

When are rights extinguished? In *Aston v Secretary of State for the Environment*[18] the Divisional Court had to consider the position where a new building did not cover the whole of the site in question. Lord Widgery expressed the view that whenever a new building was erected, that part of the

15 [1971] 2 All ER 793, [1971] 2 WLR 1112.
16 See the judgments of the majority of the Court of Appeal in *Jennings Motors* (above); see too the opinions of Lord Scarman and Lord Lane in *Newbury* (above). In extinguishment cases the term 'planning unit' is being employed in a primarily temporal sense, rather than in the primarily 'territorial' sense considered above (see pp 92–101). The use of the same term in these rather different senses might be thought unfortunate but in *Jennings Motors* the majority of the Court of Appeal considered that the expression 'new planning unit' was hallowed by usage and should be retained to include the concept of a break in the planning history of a site. Lord Denning thought otherwise; and see *South Staffordshire District Council v Secretary of State for the Environment and Bickford* [1987] JPL 635.
17 [1982] QB 541, [1982] 1 All ER 471.
18 (1973) 43 P & CR 331.

land covered by the new building was merged with it and a new planning unit was thereby created. 'One starts', he said, 'with a new planning unit that has no permitted planning uses except those derived from the planning permission, if any, and from section 33(2) of the Act of 1971 which allows such a building . . . to be used for the purpose for which it was designed.' If, as was the case in *Aston*, the building was erected without planning permission, it had, the Divisional Court agreed, no permitted use at all.

However, in *Jennings Motors* the Court of Appeal held that the mere erection of a new building does not automatically create a new planning unit. It is merely one of the factors to be taken into account in considering whether, in Oliver LJ's words, 'there has taken place in relation to the particular land under consideration a change of so radical a nature as to constitute a "break in the planning history" or a "new planning unit"'. The principle enunciated by Lord Widgery in *Aston* was therefore too widely expressed. However, the majority of the Court of Appeal considered there was no ground for thinking *Aston* to have been wrongly decided on its facts. In *Aston* the new building replaced an earlier building, destroyed eight years previously, that had covered less than half the available area. The new building covered 90 per cent of the available area. There had therefore been a very substantial change in the physical nature of the site.

In *Jennings Motors* the Secretary of State, in deciding an enforcement appeal, had taken the view that the unauthorised erection of a building occupying about 6 per cent of the area of a particular site automatically resulted in the creation of a new planning unit, and therefore of a building which had no permitted use.[19] The Court of Appeal held that the Secretary of State had misdirected himself in law; it was a question of fact and degree whether the change in question was so radical as to lead to the extinguishment of existing use rights.[20] Where the erection of a new building does not effect such a radical change as to result in the loss of existing use rights, those use rights will continue to attach to the site inside the new building.

Equally, the erection or enlargement of a building on one part of a site, will not necessarily extinguish established user rights on another part. In *South Staffordshire District Council v Secretary of State for the Environment and Bickford*[1] the court held that the rights were only lost if the development was inconsistent with the established use.

Physical operations are more likely to lead to the application of the doctrine of extinguishment of use than a mere change in the use of land,[2] but the view was expressed by the House of Lords in the *Newbury* case and by the majority of the Court of Appeal in *Jennings Motors* that a change in the planning status of a site, such as its sub-division into smaller units or its incorporation into a larger planning unit, may lead to the inference that a new chapter in planning history has been started. It might be suggested that

19 The planning authority could, of course, have taken enforcement action in respect of the unauthorised building operation but chose instead to serve an enforcement notice alleging that a material change in the use of the site had taken place.
20 See too *Joyce Shopfitters Ltd v Secretary of State for the Environment* (1975) 237 Estates Gazette 576, [1976] JPL 236; *Hilliard v Secretary of State for the Environment* (1978) 37 P & CR 129; and Oliver LJ's comment on those cases in *Jennings Motors*.
1 [1987] JPL 635.
2 See, however, *J Toomey Motors Ltd v Basildon District Council* (1982) 264 Estates Gazette 141, [1982] JPL 775, CA.

the same principle will apply to the demolition of a building.[3]

In *Petticoat Lane* the building was erected pursuant to grant of planning permission, while in *Grey and Jenning Motors* no permission had been granted. The importance of the grant of planning permission as leading to a new planning chapter is unclear. It has been held that the obtaining and implementation of a planning permission will not by itself prevent the reliance on existing use rights;[4] though if the permission is the subject of a planning condition restricting user rights, the purported implementation of the permission will probably cause the condition to bite.[5] However in *Newbury District Council v Secretary of State for the Environment*[6] both Viscount Dilhorne and Lord Scarman seemed to place importance on the grant of planning permission as helping to lead to a new chapter in the planning history of the site and so it may help to show a break has occurred.[7] Yet it is worth noting that in the *South Staffordshire* case (above) the imposition of a condition restricting the established use was held not in itself to terminate the use, unless it was enforced.

(h) *Multiple uses*

Primary and ancillary uses. Where several activities are carried on within a single 'planning unit' it may be possible to recognise a single primary purpose to which the land is put and to which the other uses of the land are ancillary or incidental. In such a case it is the primary purpose which determines the use of the unit as a whole.[8] This principle was well illustrated by Lord Denning MR in *Brazil (Concrete) Ltd v Amersham RDC*[9] His Lordship said:

'Take for instance, Harrods Store. The unit is the whole building. The greater part is used for selling goods; but some parts are used for ancillary purposes, such as for offices and for packing articles for dispatch. The character of the whole is determined by its primary use as a shop. It is within Class I of the Use Classes Order. The ancillary use of part as an office does not bring it within Class II: and the ancillary use of part for packing does not make it a light industrial building within Class III.'

The terms 'primary' and 'ancillary' are not to be found in the Act but it has become an established concept in the case law.[10] The term 'incidental' is employed in the Act as in 'incidental to the enjoyment' in s 22(2)(d) and the Use Classes Order uses the phrase 'ordinarily incidental' in Art 3(3). This has been the cause of some confusion. In *Lydcare v Secretary of State for the Environment and Westminster City Council*[11] the Court of Appeal made clear that a use can be subordinate in size to the primary use and yet not be ancillary to that use. Thus the use of cubicles for viewing films in a sex shop

---

3 See *Joyce Shopfitters Ltd v Basildon District Council* (1975) 237 Estates Gazette 576, [1976] JPL 236.
4 *Mounsdon v Weymouth and Melcombe Regis Corpn* [1960] 1 QB 645, [1960] 1 All ER 538.
5 See *Kerrier District Council v Secretary of State for the Environment and Brewer* (1980) 41 P & CR 284, [1981] JPL 193.
6 [1981] AC 578, [1980] 1 All ER 731.
7 Ibid at 739 and 754.
8 See p 93 above.
9 (1967) 65 LGR 365, 18 P & CR 396.
10 See for example *Trio Thames Ltd v Secretary of State for the Environment and Reading Borough Council* [1984] JPL 183.
11 (1984) 83 LGR 33, 49 P & CR 186, [1984] JPL 809.

was not ancillary to the main retail use. The terms, ancillary and incidental are usually regarded as interchangeable[12] but it is unclear how far the qualification 'ordinarily' used in art 3(3) also applies in determining whether as a matter of general principle a use is incidental to another primary use. In *Wealdon v Secretary of State for the Environment*[13] Ralph Gibson LJ assumed, but did not decide, that in approaching the question of whether land was used for the purpose of agriculture 'the degree of connection, between the land use in question and the primary agricultural use was accurately expressed by the phrase 'ordinarily incidental.' This could be important as a use might in practice be ancillary or incidental but not be 'ordinarily' so.[14] Finally it could be argued that 'incidental' has a slightly different meaning from 'ancillary' in that 'incidental' means something which cannot be separated from the primary use, while 'ancillary' means something related to the primary use.

Rights to change within unit. Where part of a single planning unit has been put to a use different from, but ancillary to, the primary use of the unit, it would seem that no development will be involved in using that part for the main use or for another use ancillary to the main use. Where, for example, it was proposed to use as offices a caretaker's flat in an office block, the proposed change was held not to involve development.[15] And where the primary use of a site was boat-building and repair, the minister quashed an enforcement notice which alleged that a change in the use of part of the site from car parking to boat sales constituted a breach of planning control; both these uses were ancillary to the primary use and in giving his decision the minister stated: 'It is not considered that the change of use of the appeal land from one purpose ancillary to the business use of the premises to another ancillary use of the premises can be said to involve a material change of use which would constitute development requiring a grant of planning permission.[16]

In like manner, the introduction upon land of a new use which is merely ancillary to the primary use of the planning unit will not amount to a material change of use. In *Restormel Borough Council v Secretary of State for the Environment and Rabey*,[17] for example, a caravan was stationed in the grounds of a hotel. The caravan was to provide sleeping accommodation for two waitresses in the summer season but was not capable of being used as a self-contained living unit. Forbes J upheld the inspector's conclusion that the use was ancillary to that of the hotel and did not therefore involve development. Forbes J said that 'It was inappropriate when a caravan was stationed on land for a particular purpose to look at the stationing of the caravan separately and say that that was something which was development requiring planning permission because it made a change of use.' This was

12 See *G Percy Trentham v Gloucestershire County Council* [1966] 1 All ER 701, [1966] 1 WLR 506, Diplock at 513, and *Wealden District Council v Secretary of State for the Environment and Day* [1988] JPL 268, CA.
13 [1988] JPL 268, CA.
14 However note that in *Wallington v Secretary of State for Wales*, (20 February 1989, unreported) it was held that in deciding whether an activity was incidental it was right to look to what people normally do.
15 [1975] JPL 685. See too appeal decisions noted in [1977] JPL 464, [1978] JPL 578, [1979] JPL 784; and [1982] JPL 534.
16 [1972] JPL 37. See too [1979] JPL 54.
17 [1982] JPL 785.

followed in *Wealden v Secretary of State for the Environment and Day*[18] where it was held that the stationing of a caravan for feed preparation and shelter was ordinarily incidental to the primary agricultural use. It was held that the fact that the stationing of the caravan might have an impact on visual amenities did not make it a material change of use.

So long as it remains ancillary to the main use, the scale of an ancillary use may be varied without there being any material change in the use of the planning unit but if an ancillary use develops to such an extent as to become the main use of the unit or to become a separate use in its own right, it may be that the right conclusion on the facts is that a material change of use has occurred. In *Jones v Secretary of State for the Environment*,[19] for example, it was held that the minister was entitled to find that a material change of use had occurred when the use of premises for the purpose of a road haulage business with ancillary manufacture of trailers was changed to the manufacture of trailers for outside sale. The activity formerly carried on as ancillary to the primary use had itself become 'level to the standard of a primary use'.

The right to use land for some ancillary purpose will, of course, be lost when the primary use ceases.

When is a use ancillary? The question whether a particular use is ancillary to another use or is itself a separate and distinct use will not always admit of an easy answer; factors such as the character and intensity of the uses in question, the proportion of the planning unit devoted to each activity and the degree to which one of the uses is dependent on another would appear to be relevant.[20]

In *Philip Farrington Properties Ltd v Secretary of State for the Environment*,[1] Sir Douglas Frank QC held that there was no material to support an inspector's conclusion that the garage and repair of vehicles (belonging to the main business) was ancillary to the main business of the occupier, where the two activities had been run independently.

A flat situated over a shop might, for example, be regarded as being used for a purpose ancillary to the shop if the occupier of the flat carried out duties connected with the shop, so that his living on the premises facilitated the operation of the shop; a different conclusion would probably be appropriate in a case where it would make little difference to the operation of the shop if the occupant of the flat lived elsewhere.[2] Where two-thirds of the output of a bakery was sold from a shop in the same building, the minister held the bakery use to be ancillary to the shop use.[3] but where, on the other hand, a bakery in a yard behind a shop supplied not only that shop but also several other shops, the minister concluded that the bakery was a light industrial use

---

18 [1988] JPL 268, CA.
19 (1974) 28 P & CR 362. See too *Frith v Minister of Housing and Local Government* (1969) 210 Estates Gazette 213; *Snook v Secretary of State for the Environment* (1975) 33 P & CR 1, *Chrysanthou v Secretary of State for the Environment and London Borough of Haringey* [1976] JPL 371; *Pollock v Secretary of State for the Environment and Greenwich London Borough* (1979) 40 P & CR 94; *L R Jillings v Secretary of State for the Environment and the Broads Authority* [1984] JPL 32; and appeal decisions noted in [1973] JPL 666, [1974] JPL 614, [1975] JPL 687, [1976] JPL 196, [1977] JPL 190, [1983] JPL 400.
20 See for example [1976] JPL 328, [1980] JPL 58 and [1984] JPL 826.
1 (1983) 265 Estates Gazette 47, [1982] JPL 638.
2 See *Vyner & Son v Secretary of State for the Environment* (1977) 243 Estates Gazette 597, [1977] JPL 795.
3 *Bulletin of Selected Appeal Decisions*, XIII/24.

in its own right.[4] In this context, factors such as the identity of the occupiers and the origins of the goods which are not relevant to the question of whether the change is material, can be relevant to the question of whether one use is ancillary to another. However, the intentions or purposes of the particular occupier cannot be conclusive. In *Wealden v Secretary of State for the Environment*[5] Ralph Gibson LJ stated '... that the question whether a particular additional use was ancillary to or included within the primary use of the planning unit was to be determined according to all the evidence, in addition to evidence of what was being done on the land and the assessment of the relationship of the activity to the primary use.'

In *Emma Hotels Ltd v Secretary of State for the Environment*[6] the Secretary of State had taken the view that the use of part of a private hotel as a non-residents' bar was not an incident of the hotel use but a separate use in its own right. The minister had regard to the scale of use of the bar by non-residents, the manner in which the bar was operated and advertised, its distinctive character and appearance and the fact that it could be readily isolated physically from the remainder of the premises. The Divisional Court held, however, that the matters relied on by the Secretary of State were insufficient to justify his conclusion that the non-residents' bar was not an incident of the hotel use.

In contrast in *Lydcare v Secretary of State for the Environment and Westminster City Council*[7] the Court of Appeal held that the viewing of films was neither ordinarily incidental or ancillary to the use as a shop.

The question whether one use is ancillary to another can arise in a great variety of contexts. Although the decision in each case will depend very much on the facts and circumstances of that particular case, a few examples may be of interest.

The minister has held, for example, that tyre fitting and wheel balancing were ancillary to the use of premises for the retail sale of tyres;[8] that the use of the basement of a hotel as a night club was ancillary to the hotel use;[9] that the residential use of a flat above a bank was ancillary to the bank use;[10] that servicing of vehicles and the carrying out of minor repairs was incidental to the sale of vehicles;[11] that the stationing of several caravans on a site was incidental to the main use of the land as a holiday camp,[12] and that the use of a shop forecourt for parking was incidental to the shop use.[13]

On the other hand, it has been held that the storage and sale of furniture in a church building, though for the benefit of the church and other charities, was not ancillary to the church use,[14] that the use of a school for social functions was not incidental to the overall use of the planning unit for

---

4 *Bulletin of Selected Appeal Decisions*, XIII/25. See too *Chrysanthou v Secretary of State for the Environment* [1976] JPL 371.
5 See above.
6 (1980) 41 P & CR 255, and see [1979] JPL 390.
7 (1984) 83 LGR 33, 49 P & CR 186.
8 *Selected Enforcement and Allied Appeals*, p 33.
9 [1978] JPL 869.
10 [1978] JPL 333.
11 [1974] JPL 41.
12 [1980] JPL 126.
13 See, for example [1956] JPL 74, [1959] JPL 812, [1972] JPL 474 and [1984] JPL 889.
14 [1978] JPL 126.

educational purposes;[15] that the sale of petrol was not ancillary to the use of premises for car sales and repairs;[16] that the sale of food and household goods was not ancillary to use as a petrol filling station;[17] that use of part of a farm for the keeping of cattle in transit was not ancillary to the agricultural use of the land;[18] that the installation of eight amusement machines was not ancillary to use of premises as an ice-cream parlour;[19] and that although some recreational and/or amusement element may be fairly introduced into the premises of any club the introduction of seven pool tables and three video machines taking up half the space of a boxing club resulted in the change to part boxing club and part pool-room and amusement centre use.[20]

The retail sale from an agricultural holding of the produce of that holding is normally accepted as being a use ancillary to the use of the land for agriculture,[1] but 'the adaptation for sale of that produce on the holding is not regarded as ancillary to the use of the land for agriculture, and neither is the sale of the produce from the holding after processing elsewhere'.[2] From *Hussain v Secretary of State for the Environment*[3] it seems that in deciding whether an activity is ordinarily incidental the special requirements of particular localities, particular areas and particular customers are not relevant. Thus the facts that a shop serves a Moslem community and that the keeping and slaughtering of chickens is ordinarily incidental to a shop in such a community, do not make that use ordinarily incidental.

Dwellings. It may be that the use, beyond the merely trivial, of even a small part of a private residence for the carrying on of commercial or industrial activities can be regarded as involving a material change in the use of the premises,[4] the use for commercial or industrial purposes involves a completely different kind of use, a use which cannot normally be regarded as ancillary or incidental to the main use of the premises as a dwelling-house.[5] Use of the living room of a private house on three evenings per week for the receipt of taxi bookings by telephone and for the radio control of fifteen taxis (none of which normally called at the house) was, for example, held by the

15 [1978] JPL 51.
16 See *Ben Jay Auto Sales v Minister of Housing and Local Government* (1964), 62 LGR 360, 16 P & CR 50.
17 [1975] JPL 687.
18 See *Warnock v Secretary of State for the Environment and Dover District Council* [1980] JPL 690.
19 [1983] JPL 499.
20 (1983) JPL 623.
 1 See, for example, *Haigh v Secretary of State for the Environment and Kirklees Borough Council* [1983] JPL 40; and appeal decision noted in [1974] JPL 165. A retail sales use will only be ancillary to an agricultural use of land if most of the produce sold is grown on the land—see, for example, ministerial decision noted in [1973] JPL 386.
 2 [1974] JPL 165, and [1977] JPL 740. See too *Bromley London Borough v George Hoeltschi & Son Ltd and Secretary of State for the Environment* (1977) 244 Estates Gazette 49, [1978] JPL 45.
 3 (1971) 23 P & CR 330.
 4 See, for example, ministerial decisions noted in [1968] JPL 485, [1971] JPL 287, [1972] JPL 339, and [1974] JPL 554. Contrast decisions noted in [1963] JPL 677, and [1971] JPL 529.
 5 In an early circular (circular 67/1949) the Secretary of State said that he would not regard it as a material change of use for a professional man such as a doctor or dentist to use one or two rooms in his private dwelling for consultation purposes, so long as that use remained ancillary to the main residential use. However it has been held that the use of part of a house as a consulting room can amount to a material change depending on the extent and scale of the use; see [1984] JPL 599 and [1985] JPL 339.

minister to involve a material change in the use of the premises.[6] Section 22(2)(d) of the 1971 Act specifically provides that use of the curtilage of a dwellinghouse for any purpose incidental to the enjoyment of the dwellinghouse as such does not involve development (see p 121 below).

It is hard to extract a clear line from the ministerial decisions as they all tend to turn on their particular facts. Development Control Policy Note No 2 on 'Development in Residential Areas' concluded

'[It] must depend on the facts of each case, but it may be a matter of degree. For example, if a householder conducted a part time business from his house involving only the occasional use of one room and a telephone, permission might not be required. But if part of a house was exclusively used for business purposes and numbers of people called at the house in connection with the business, it would probably constitute a material change and would need permission.'

Mixed or multiple use—other aspects. Where two or more separate uses are carried on within a single planning unit, the mere cessation of one of the component activities does not in itself amount to a material change of use but if one of the component activities is increased to the exclusion of the other uses, there may be a material change of use.[7]

In *Philglow Ltd v Secretary of State for the Environment and the London Borough of Hillingdon*[8] Stephenson LJ explained that for the principle in *Wipperman* to apply, the component use which continued when the other ceased did not have to necessarily absorb the entire site as the headnote suggested, it was sufficient that it had intensified to a sufficient extent that as a matter of fact and degree a material change of use had taken place. For such a determination there must at least be evidence of some increase in the remaining use; mere cessation of one of the uses was not enough.

What might appear to be separate uses of land may have to be treated for planning purposes as a single use. This possibility is illustrated by the decision in *Re St Winifred's, Kenley.*[9] In that case premises used partly as offices and partly as laboratories were held to have a single use as an industrial research establishment, which use involved elements of laboratory work and of office work but was distinct from use as either laboratories or offices alone; 'what one has here', said Pennycuick J, 'is a single use involving widely disparate activities'.

---

6 [1971] JPL 533; see too *Cook v Secretary of State for Wales* (1971) 220 Estates Gazette 1433.
7 See *Wipperman and Buckingham v London Borough of Barking* (1965) 130 JP 103, 64 LGR 97; *Brooks v Gloucestershire County Council* (1967) 66 LGR 386, 19 P & CR 90; *Emma Hotels v Secretary of State for the Environment* [1979] JPL 390, per Bridge LJ; and *Cook v Secretary of State for the Environment and Penwith District Council* [1982] JPL 644; and appeal decisions noted in [1974] JPL 677, [1978] JPL 871, and [1981] JPL 449. In *Bromsgrove District Council v Secretary of State for the Environment* [1977] JPL 797 Forbes J seems to have regarded the *Wipperman* decision as depending on intensification of use. However, the principle in *Wipperman* seems rather different.
8 (1984) 51 P & CR 1, [1985] JPL 318.
9 (1969) 67 LGR 491, 20 P & CR 583. See too appeal decisions noted in [1980] JPL 693, and [1982] JPL 115.

C USES SPECIFICALLY DECLARED NOT TO INVOLVE DEVELOPMENT

Section 22(2) of the 1971 Act has the effect of excluding from the definition of development certain changes of use. Since 'use' does not include the use of land for the carrying out of any building or other operations thereon (s 290), such operations are not excepted apart from the specific operations covered by s 22(2); see pp 88 and 90 above.

1 *Use of curtilage of dwellinghouse*

The use of any buildings or other land within the curtilage of a dwellinghouse for any purpose incidental to the enjoyment of the dwellinghouse as such does not involve development (s 22(2)(d)).[10]

The word 'curtilage' is not defined in the 1971 Act but in *Sinclair-Lockhart's Trustees v Central Land Board*[11] Lord Mackintosh declared that:

'ground which is used for the comfortable enjoyment of a house or other building may be regarded in law as being within the curtilage of that house or building and thereby as an integral part of the same, although it has not been marked off or enclosed in any way. It is enough that it serves the purposes of the house or building in some necessary or reasonably useful way.'

Thus it has recently been held that the curtilage of a farmhouse only covered the land immediately surrounding and associated with the dwelling and not other agricultural land.[12]

Difficulties arise when land outside the curtilage of a dwellinghouse is incorporated into the curtilage and put to uses incidental to the dwellinghouse, as when agricultural land is incorporated into a garden. In *Sampson's Executors v Nottinghamshire County Council*[13] Lord Goddard said obiter that if agricultural land were brought within the curtilage of a dwellinghouse so that it became part of the dwellinghouse, an alteration would have been made in the use of the land. In contrast in the Scots decision of *Paul v Ayrshire County Council*[14] the Second Division of the Court of Session held that the enclosure of land into a garden and its subsequent use as a garden came within the equivalent Scots provision. The issue is whether an unauthorised material change of use can, by changing the extent of the curtilage, authorise itself retrospectively. It is submitted that *Sampson's* case is to be preferred and that where the change amounts to development as a material change of use it will not be protected by s 22(2)(d).

This view is supported by the recent decision in *Asghar v Secretary of State*

---

10 Since it is now clear that the use of land for a purpose which is merely ancillary or incidental to the main use of that land does not involve development (see above), it may be that this specific provision is unnecessary.

11 1951 SC 258, 1951 SLT 121. See too *Re St John's Church, Bishop's Hatfield* [1967] P 113, [1966] 2 All ER 403; *Methuen-Campbell v Walters* [1979] QB 525, [1979] 1 All ER 606 *A G ex rel Sutcliffe v Calderdale Borough Council* (1982) 46 P & CR 399, [1983] JPL 310 and appeal decision noted in [1983] JPL 68.

12 [1986] JPL 455.

13 [1949] 2 KB 439, [1949] 1 All ER 1051.

14 1964 SC 116, 1964 SLT 207.

for the Environment and Harrogate Borough Council[15] where it seems to have been accepted that the incorporation of land into the curtilage of a dwellinghouse and its use in connection with the dwellinghouse was a material change of use. As the change was unlawful it was held that Class 1 of the General Development Order 1977 did not authorise the construction of a tennis court.

The word 'dwellinghouse' is also not defined in the Act or in related delegated legislation.

In *Gravesham Borough Council v Secretary of State for the Environment*[16] McCullough J held that the question whether or not a particular building is a dwellinghouse is one of fact but that a distinctive characteristic of a dwellinghouse is its ability to afford the facilities required for day to day private domestic existence. He also held that the actual use to which the building was put was not conclusive though it was a factor and that a building did not cease to be a dwellinghouse if it was empty at times or was occupied by different owners from time to time as in a time-sharing scheme. Previously the minister had taken the view that a house or a bungalow used exclusively for letting to holiday-makers throughout the year would not be a dwellinghouse[17] but this is now more doubtful in the light of *Gravesham*.

A ruinous house or one which is not fit for human habitation will also not qualify as a dwellinghouse[18] but McCullough J in *Gravesham* accepted that a house which could not be occupied because it was flooded or was undergoing extensive repair could still be a dwellinghouse.

Whether or not a particular use is for a purpose 'incidental to the enjoyment of the dwellinghouse as such' is generally a question of fact and degree. Use of land within the curtilage of a dwellinghouse for parking a private car or for storing a private caravan will come within s 22(2)(d),[19] whereas the parking of commercial vehicles may well fall outside it.[20] Where a building or caravan situated within the curtilage of a house is used or is capable of use as a separate residential unit it will not normally be possible to treat that use as being for a purpose incidental to the enjoyment of the dwellinghouse as such.[1] Where, however, such a building or caravan is merely used to provide additional sleeping or living accommodation for persons who also make some substantial use of the dwellinghouse, the position may well be different[2] The use of land or buildings within the curtilage of a dwellinghouse for the purposes of a hobby or spare-time activity will normally come within the exception but may cease to do so if the hobby or activity grows into a purely commercial use or comes to be carried

15 [1988] JPL 476 and see also [1979] JPL 189.
16 (1982) 47 P & CR 142, [1983] JPL 307. See too *Scurlock v Secretary of State for Wales* (1976) 33 P & CR 202; and appeal decision noted in [1976] JPL 326.
17 [1974] JPL 241.
18 In *Trustees of the Earl of Lichfield Estate v Secretary of State for the Environment and Stafford Borough Council* [1985] JPL 251, McNeill J seemed to approve the Secretary of State's view that 'there must at all times remain on the land a structure sufficiently intact as to reasonably support the description of a dwellinghouse and not merely the ruins of a dwelling.' See also [1978] JPL 794 and [1978] JPL 806. These were all cases concerning Class 1 of the classes of permitted development in the General Development Order 1977.
19 See, for example, [1976] JPL 586.
20 See too [1971] JPL 646, [1974] JPL 610 and 672, [1976] JPL 529, [1977] JPL 397, [1978] JPL 789, and [1980] JPL 209.
1 See, for example [1965] JPL 319, and [1971] JPL 187.
2 See, for example, [1970] JPL 233, and [1976] JPL 586.

on on a very substantial scale.³ For example the keeping and breeding of dogs as a hobby will normally be incidental⁴ but it has been held that the keeping of 45 dogs, 27 of which were kept for breeding purposes was not incidental as it was an operation on a commercial scale whether or not a profit was made.⁵

2 Use for agriculture or forestry

The use of any land⁶ for the purposes of agriculture or forestry (including afforestation) and the use for any of those purposes of any building occupied together with land so used is not to be taken to involve development (s 22(2)(e)). Whatever the previous use of land, a change to use for the purposes of agriculture or forestry does not, therefore, constitute development.

In *Hidderley v Warwickshire County Council*⁷ it was held that the installation of an egg-vending machine was not a use of the land 'for the purposes of agriculture' so as to bring it within the statutory exception, Lord Parker CJ saying that the expression 'for the purposes of agriculture' clearly refers to 'the productive processes' of agriculture.

The word 'agriculture' is given a wide definition by s 290 of the 1971 Act. That definition encompasses 'the breeding and keeping of livestock (including any creature kept for the production of food, wool, skins or fur, or for the purpose of its use in the farming of land)'. In *Belmont Farm Ltd v Minister of Housing and Local Government*⁸ the Divisional Court held that, taking account of the words in brackets, the phrase 'breeding and keeping of livestock' had to be restrictively construed and did not cover the breeding and training of horses for show-jumping. However, the statutory definition of 'agriculture' also includes 'the use of land as grazing land' and in *Sykes v Secretary of State for the Environment*⁹ it was held that these words should be given their natural meaning and that the use of land for the grazing of horses came within the definition of agriculture. However, in that case Donaldson LJ emphasised that where land was being used for both agricultural and non-agricultural uses it was a question of fact which was the predominant use. He stated that 'what an inspector in these circumstances had to decide was: what was the purpose, and he stressed the word "the", for which the land was being used?' So, if land is being used predominantly for exercising and keeping ponies for recreational purposes this will not be an agricultural use even if incidentally the ponies graze off the grass growing in the field.¹⁰

It has been held that the use of land for allotments falls within the

3 See, for example [1971] JPL 642, [1972] JPL 339, [1976] JPL 588, [1977] JPL 116 and 192 [1978] JPL 200, [1980] JPL 472, and [1984] JPL 288 and 291.
4 [1977] JPL 192 and [1982] JPL 60.
5 [1985] JPL 201. Now also see *Wallington v Secretary of State for Wales* (20 February 1989, unreported).
6 'Land' includes buildings (see 1971 Act, s 290) and accordingly the use of a building for an agricultural purpose is not development and does not require planning permission if the agricultural use is in no way dependent upon the land on which the building stands—*North Warwickshire Borough Council v Secretary of State for the Environment* (1983) 50 P & CR 47, (1984) JPL 435.
7 (1963) 61 LGR 266, 14 P & CR 134.
8 (1962) 60 LGR 319, 13 P & CR 417. See too *Minister of Agriculture, Fisheries and Food v Appleton* [1970] 1 QB 221 [1969] 3 All ER 105.
9 [1981] 1 All ER 954, [1981] 1 WLR 1092, 42 P & CR 19. Contrast appeal decision noted in [1984] JPL 527.
10 See also [1985] JPL 198 and [1985] JPL 731.

definition of 'agriculture'[11] but that the use of land for the keeping of animals in transit does not.[12] The statutory definition of 'agriculture' is wide enough to include fox-farming,[13] and fish-farming[14] but not the keeping and boarding of dogs.[15]

In *Gill v Secretary of State for the Environment*[16] Glidewell J thought that 'the slaughtering wholesale, that was to say in any large numbers, of animals kept on land for the purposes of producing skins or fur was not within the definition of agriculture in section 290' though the occasional killing of animals kept on a farm could be ancillary to normal farming activity. In *Northavon District Council v Secretary of State for the Environment*[17] it was held that the depositing of materials on agricultural land for the purpose of improving the land did not involve a material change in the use of the land.

3 *Use Classes Order*

Section 22(2)(f) of the 1971 Act provides that in the case of buildings or other land used for a purpose of any class specified in an order made by the Secretary of State under this section, the use of the building or other land or, of any part thereof, for any purpose of the same class is not to involve development.

The purpose is therefore to exempt from the need for planning permission certain changes of use which presumably otherwise would be development as a material change of use. The first Town and Country Planning (Use Classes) Order was made on 8th May 1948 under the 1947 Act and since then replacement orders have been made in 1963, 1972 and in 1987. The 1987 order, which followed a report by a subgroup of the Property Advisory Group (published on 2nd December 1985), modernised and recast the classes and, in line with the Conservative government's policy of de-regulation (see White Paper 'Lifting the Burden'[18]), substantially increased the scope of the classes, so freeing more changes from the need for planning permission.

(a) *The way the order works*

To what land does it apply? Article 3(1) of the Town and Country Planning (Use Classes) Order 1987 (the 1987 order) provides that ' where a building or other land is used for a purpose of any class specified in the Schedule, the use of that building or that other land for any other purpose of the same class shall not be development of the land.' In *Winton v Secretary of State for the Environment*[19] it was held that a similar wording meant that a change to a use within the same class was not covered when it was only *part* of the building which was being used for that use and previously the whole of the building had been occupied as one unit. This effectively meant that a sub-division of

11 *Crowborough Parish Council v Secretary of State for the Environment* (1980) 43 P & CR 229 [1981] JPL 281. However, the activity will not come with s 22(2)(e) if a recreational or leisure use is one of the primary components; see *Pittman v Secretary of State for the Environment and Canterbury County Council* [1988] JPL 391.
12 *Warnock v Secretary of State for the Environment and Dover District Council* [1980] JPL 690.
13 See *Gill v Secretary of State for the Environment* [1985] JPL 710.
14 See [1980] JPL 480.
15 See [1970] JPL 156, and [1980] JPL 420.
16 Ibid.
17 (1980) 40 P & CR 332, [1981] JPL 114.
18 Cmnd 9571.
19 (1982) 46 P & CR 205; see Andrew Gilbert, 'Subdivision and the Planning Unit' [1985] JPL 181.

one planning unit into two or more separate units could not come within the Use Classes Order. Since then the Housing and Planning Act 1986[20] has amended s 22(2)(f) so that the change in the use of any *part* of a building or other land is covered by the order, provided it remains within the same class of use that the whole of the building or other land had been put to before the change. Thus a large building could now be sub-divided up into small units without the need for planning permission as long as the use of each new unit remained within the class of the previous use of the whole building. Of course if part of a building were to be used for a use not within the original use class into which the whole of the building had been put, it might not be covered by order. Also in the case of the sub-division of dwellinghouses, art 4 of the 1987 order makes clear that the separate use of part of a dwellinghouse is not covered by the order. The use as two or more dwellinghouses of any building previously used as a single dwellinghouse is deemed to be development (see s 22(3)(a) and p 139 below).

Article 3(2) then states that references in para 4 to a building shall 'include references to land occupied with the building and used for the same purpose'. This means that the order can apply not only to open land and to buildings but also to a site which is comprised of a mixture of the two. Thus in *Brooks and Burton Ltd v Secretary of State for the Environment*[1] the Court of Appeal held that land did not have to be ancillary to the building to be 'occupied with the building' and that it was enough that the land had been used for the same purpose as the building. Thus quite large areas of open land could be included as one unit with a building.

Uses which are sui generis. The various use classes orders have never attempted to encompass all human activities in the classes and therefore many uses are classified as 'sui generis' as they do not come within any of the classes.[2] In this regard in *Tessier v Secretary of State for the Environment*[3] Lord Widgery CJ said that it was desirable not to stretch the Use Classes Order 'to embrace activities which do not clearly fall within it'; in his Lordship's view it was 'no bad thing that unusual activities should be treated as sui generis for this purpose'. However in *Forkhurst v Secretary of State for the Environment*[4] Hodgson J stated that although *Tessier* was undoubtedly authority for the proposition that there can be uses which do not fall within any use class, he did not agree with Lord Widgery's view that the order should be interpreted narrowly. In Hodgson J's view there was no warrant in the legislation for either restricting or stretching the order, and it could not be said to be either a good thing or a bad thing to treat unusual uses as sui generis.

The 1987 order itself makes clear that certain uses are sui generis. Article 3(6) specifies that no class includes:

20 See s 49, Sch 11, para 1.
 1 [1978] 1 All ER 733, [1977] 1 WLR 1294.
 2 For examples under the 1973 order see *Brazil (Concrete) Ltd v Amersham RDC* (1967) 65 LGR 365, 18 P & CR 396 (builder's yard—see too [1974] JPL 239, [1975] JPL 614, [1978] JPL 343. See too *Re St Winifred's, Kenley* (1969) 67 LGR 491, 20 P & CR 583 (industrial research establishment); *Mornford Investments v Minister of Housing and Local Government* [1970] 2 All ER 253 (students' hostel); *Farm Facilities Ltd v Secretary of State for the Environment and South Oxfordshire District Council* [1981] JPL 42 (motor hire business).
 3 (1975) 31 P & CR 161.
 4 (1982) 46 P & CR 89, [1982] JPL 448.

(a) theatres
(b) amusement arcades or centres, or fun fairs
(c) coin-operated launderettes and any premises where goods are received to be cleaned direct from the public
(d) petrol stations
(e) taxi-businesses
(f) scrap-yards, storage or distribution of minerals or breaking of motor vehicles.

A change of use is not 'material' merely because it involves a change from a use falling within one use class to a use which happens to fall within another or because it involves a change to or from a sui generis use to a use falling within a use class. This was made clear in *Rann v Secretary of State for the Environment*.[5] In that decision, Sir Douglas Frank QC sitting as a Deputy Judge, stated that the purpose of the order was to put changes of use outside the ambit of the Act and not vice versa. However, in *London Residuary Body v Secretary of State for the Environment*[6] Stephen Brown J, having found that the use of County Hall by the Greater London Council was not an office use and so outside Class B1 went on to find that the proposed change to office use would be materially different. He concluded that:

'Given that it is necessarily implicit in the Use Classes Order itself that a change from one office use to another may well involve a material change of use . . ., it is surely inconceivable in a case such as this that the Inspector and Secretary of State, having found difference in the character of the use sufficiently significant to preclude the categorisation of the present use as offices could conclude other than a change to office use would indeed be material.'

Stephen Brown J also accepted that in the particular case it was sensible first to determine whether the change would be covered by the order and then to consider if it would be material, as the decision on the order effectively determined both issues. Also as Malcolm Grant points out in his annotations to the 1987 order in the Encyclopaedia, it seems that the courts have been closely guided by the Use Classes Order in their interpretation of what does or does not constitute a material change of use.[7] It is submitted that the correct position is that the Use Classes Order is evidence of the differentiation that can be made between various activities, which differentiation may, but by no means automatically, indicate that certain changes are material. For example some financial services may fall within Class A2 of the 1987 order because they are provided principally to visiting members of the public but it is doubtful whether a material change would take place simply because reorganisation of the way the service is provided took it out of Class A2 into Class B1.

Ancillary or incidental uses and intensification. Article 3(3) of the 1987 order lays down that a use which is included in and ordinarily incidental to any use in a class specified in the Schedule is not excluded from the use to which it is

5 (1979) 40 P & CR 113.
6 [1988] JPL 637.
7 See para 3B-387.

incidental merely because it is specified in the Schedule as a separate use. This is essentially the same as the principle which the courts have applied to the concept of material change of use whereby uses which are ancillary to a primary use are subsumed in that primary use[8] (see above). However, in *Scrivener v Minister of Housing and Local Government*[9] the Divisional Court held that the use of the word 'ordinarily' in this provision makes clear that any ancillary use imported by this article must be incidental to the class of use in general and not merely to a particular example of that class; for example, when applying art 3(3) to Class I of the 1972 order—use as a shop for any purpose—the ancillary use must be ordinarily incidental to the activities carried on in shops generally and not merely to the requirements of a particular trade in a particular shop.[10]

On the other hand, as long as the use remains within the same class, intensification of the use will not require permission even if otherwise it would amount to such a change in character as to be material. Thus in *Brooks and Burton Ltd v Secretary of State for the Environment*[11] the Court of Appeal accepted that the Secretary of State had not erred in law in holding that a material change by intensification had occurred but nevertheless held that as long as the use kept within the same class it was entitled to the benefit of s 22(2)(f).

Finally art 3(4) of the 1987 order specifically allows for a combination of separate classes to be treated as one class and for a certain amount of intensification of those particular classes.[12]

When does the order apply? For advantage to be taken of the order, you require a use which comes within a particular class to be in existence. So a grant of planning permission to institute a particular use, does not in itself authorise a change to another use within the same class. It is necessary first to institute the authorised use and then to take advantage of the order by changing to another use within the same class.

Further in *Kwik Save Discount Group v Secretary of State for Wales*[13] the Court of Appeal held that minimal uses were to be disregarded. What is minimal is a question of fact and degree and in that case it was held that the Secretary of State was entitled to hold that the 'offering of five cars for sale for a period of about one month in a building with a floor space of about 20,000 square feet amounted to no more than a token use of appeal premises as a shop for the sale of motor vehicles, so minimal as to be of no planning significance.'

Once a use is established, it would presumably not matter that the use had ceased at the time of the change to the new use within the same class, though

8 See *Brazil (Concrete) Ltd v Amersham RDC* (1967) 65 LGR 365, 18 P & CR 396; *G Percy Trentham Ltd v Gloucestershire County Council* [1966] 1 All ER 701, [1966] 1 WLR 506; *Shephard v Buckinghamshire County Council* (1966) 64 LGR 422, 18 P & CR 419; *Jillings v Secretary of State for the Environment and the Broads Authority* [1984] JPL 32.
9 (1966) 64 LGR 251, 18 P & CR 357.
10 See *Hussain v Secretary of State for the Environment* (1971) 23 P & CR 330 (slaughtering of poultry on the premises not ordinarily incidental to shop use); and *Lydcare Ltd v Secretary of State for the Environment and Westminster City Council* (1983) 47 P & CR 336; upheld by the Court of Appeal; (1984) 83 LGR 33, 49 P & CR 186, [1984] JPL 809 (showing of films in shop).
11 [1978] 1 All ER 733, [1977] 1 WLR 1294.
12 A similar provision was to be found in art 3(2) of the 1972 order.
13 (1980) 79 LGR 310, [1981] JPL 198.

the principles of abandonment could prevent exploitation of the order. What is not clear is whether the established use must be a lawful use, as s 22(2)(f) does not expressly state that the original use has to be lawful. It would however seem absurd that a legal right to change to a new type of use within a particular class could be obtained by instituting an unlawful material change of use and avoiding the issue of an enforcement notice. The answer may be that even if the last change is not development by virtue of s 22(2)(f), the local planning authority could still take enforcement action with regard to the first material change as long as it was not now immune. But this would only work if you could treat the change within a class as continuing the original material change of use; otherwise the answer to the enforcement notice would be that the unauthorised use had been discontinued. Another approach would be to write in the word lawful into s 22(2)(f) and the courts have done this with respect to the classes of permitted development in the General Development Order 1977[14] but this creates the further complication that the courts have treated unauthorised but immune uses as unlawful[15] and so it might not be possible to take advantage of the Use Classes Order when the established use had been unlawfully commenced prior to 1964.[16]

Conditions restricting the Use Classes Order. In *City of London Corpn v Secretary of State for the Environment*[17] the Divisional Court upheld a condition which prohibited the use of the premises within a named class. Such conditions are therefore valid if they are imposed for sound planning reasons, fairly and reasonably relate to the proposed development and are not totally unreasonable.[18] The development would have to be implemented for the condition to bite and be enforceable[19] and it seems that such a condition cannot be implied and must be imposed in unequivocal terms.[20]

While such conditions are intra vires, it must be noted that as a question of policy the Secretary of State considers such conditions as unreasonable 'unless there was clear evidence that the uses excluded would have serious adverse effects on the environment or on amenity, not susceptible to other control'; see circular 13/87 at para 12.[20a] The circular goes on to state that where conditions are imposed, they should be drafted so as to prohibit a change to a particular unacceptable use or uses, rather than in terms which require future approval of any change of use at all. So local planning authorities who fail to follow this guidance, risk having conditions struck down or redrafted on appeal.

---

14   See *Young v Secretary of State for the Environment* [1983] 2 AC 662, [1983] 2 All ER 1105 and *Asghar v Secretary of State for the Environment and Harrogate Borough Council* [1988] JPL 476.
15   See *Young v Secretary of State for the Environment*, above.
16   See p 325.
17   (1972) 71 LGR 28, 23 P & CR 169. Also see *Caledonian Terminal Investments Ltd v Edinburgh Corpn* 1970 SC 271, 1970 SLT 362.
18   See ch 9 for the law on planning conditions generally.
19   See *East Barnet UDC v British Transport Commission* [1962] 2 QB 484, [1961] 3 All ER 878.
20   Per Sir Douglas Frank QC in *Carpet Decor (Guildford) Ltd v Secretary of State for the Environment* (1981) 261 Estates Gazette 56, [1981] JPL 806.
20a But see *Camden London Borough Council v Secretary of State for the Environment* [1989] JPL 613 where it was held that a condition could be properly imposed restricting the operation of Class B1 to ensure diversity of employment.

A limitation in the description of the development which is being granted does not take effect as a condition and therefore as long as the initial development keeps within the description, it does not limit the terms of the development.[1]

The decision as to whether an activity is inside or outside the Use Classes Order. The Use Classes Order may not be easy to apply in practice; it can, for example, be difficult to decide if on the facts of the case a particular use is an industrial use[2] and, if it is, into which use class it falls. In *Forkhurst v Secretary of State for the Environment*[3] Hodgson J stated that 'The activity either came within the use specified or did not, and he did not think there was any scope for the measurement of the problem in terms of fact and degree. Once the use had been identified it was not a question of fact and degree whether it came within a given use class.'

Yet in *LTSS Print and Supply Services Ltd v London Borough of Hackney*[4] the Court of Appeal held that the word 'warehouse' as used in the Use Classes Order was an ordinary English word and its meaning was not a matter of law. Then in other decisions the courts have laid down the meaning of terms in the Order.[5] So the position probably varies depending on the particular class, but on the whole it is submitted that Hodgson J is wrong and that provided the Secretary of State does not misdirect himself in law, his determination as to whether an activity comes within a use class is a question of fact and degree which should not be upset by the courts unless it is totally unreasonable.

Hazardous substances. Previously the wording of the classes meant that changes in the methods of a use which resulted in the presence of hazardous substances would not require planning permission, if the activity remained within the same class.

The Town and Country Planning (Use Classes) (Amendment) Order 1983 had the effect of excluding from all of the specified classes any use of a building or land which involves the presence on the site of notifiable quantity of a hazardous substance. The change meant that in substance uses involving the presence on the site of hazardous substances are a class in themselves. Of course a change to such a situation will only require permission if it is judged to be material but as planning is concerned with safety matters this is likely to be the case.

This is now set out in art 3(5) of the 1987 order and 'hazardous substance and notifiable quantity' have the meanings assigned to those terms by the Notification of Installations Handling Hazardous Substances Regulation

---

1 For an explanation of the effect of limitations on use of dwellinghouses see Midgley 'The Dwelling-house Use Class' [1987] JPL 620.
2 See, for example, *Tessier* (above) (use of premises as a sculptor's workshop not an industrial use for the purposes of the UCO even though industrial machinery used in the making of sculptures).
3 See above.
4 [1976] QB 663, [1976] 1 All ER 311.
5 See for example *Newbury District Council v Secretary of State for the Environment* [1979] 1 All ER 243, [1978] 1 WLR 1241 on the meaning of 'repository' in Class VIII of the Use Classes Order 1972.

1982.[6] There is to be a special licensing system for uses involving hazardous substances (see Chapter 18 below).

(b) *The classes*

Even though the 1987 order has replaced the 1972 order, the classes set out in the Schedule to the 1972 order, will be important for some time to come as it will be necessary to know whether changes which took place before 1st June 1987 (the date the 1987 order came into effect) were authorised. In addition the 1972 order will have been incorporated into grants of planning permission, leases and the like.

1972 order classes

The Schedule to the the 1972 order set out eighteen classes. There follows a summary of the most important.

Class I relates to use as a shop for any purpose except as (i) a shop for the sale of hot food,[7] (ii) a tripe shop; (iii) a shop for the sale of pet animals; (iv) a cats-meat shop; and (v) a shop for the sale of motor vehicles.[8] 'Shop' is defined as 'a building used for the carrying on of any retail trade or retail business wherein the primary purpose is the selling of goods by retail'[9] but also includes a building used for the purposes of a hairdresser, undertaker, travel agency, ticket agency or post office or for the reception of goods to be washed, cleaned or repaired.[10] It does not include a building used as a fun fair, amusement arcade, pin-table saloon, garage, launderette, petrol filling station, office, betting office, hotel, restaurant,[11] snack bar or cafe, or premises licensed for the sale of excisable liquor for consumption on the premises (art 2(2)).[12] By virtue of the provisions of s 22(2)(f) and the order the use as two shops of premises previously used as a single shop will not involve development.[13]

Class II relates to use as an office for any purpose. 'Office' includes a bank and premises occupied by an estate agency, building society or employment agency or (for office purposes only) for the purpose of car hire or driving instruction; it does not, however, include a post office or betting office (art 2(2)).[14]

6 See art 2 of the 1987 order.
7 In *Glasgow City District Council v Secretary of State for Scotland* 1985 SLT 19 Lord Grieve said that it was clear that all shops which sell hot food are not necessarily 'shops for the sale of hot food' for this purpose.
8 Development consisting of a change of use from a hot food shop, pet shop or betting office to use as any type of shop other than hot foot shop, pet shop or betting shop was permitted by the General Development Order.
9 On the application of this phrase see *Lydcare Ltd v Secretary of State for the Environment and Westminster City Council* (1983) 47 P & CR 336; upheld by the Court of Appeal; (1984) 83 LGR 33, [1984] JPL 809.
10 Use of a dry-cleaning unit will take premises outside the definition of 'shop'—see [1981] JPL 439.
11 A change from use as a restaurant to use for any purpose within Class I, was permitted by the GDO.
12 On the meaning of 'shop' see too *Horwitz v Rowson* [1960] 2 All ER 881, [1960] 1 WLR 803; and *Tandridge District Council v Secretary of State for the Environment and Nutley Print (Reigate) Ltd* [1983] JPL 667.
13 See *Bulletin of Selected Appeal Decisions* IX/10; and [1979] JPL 705.
14 On the meaning of 'office' see too *Shephard v Buckinghamshire County Council* (1966) 64 LGR 422, 18 P & CR 419; *Re St Winifred Kenley* (1969) 64 LGR 491, 20 P & CR 583; and appeal decision noted in [1980] JPL 346.

Classes III to IX dealt with industrial uses.[15] Class III related to use as a light industrial building for any purpose, and Class IV to use as a general industrial building for any purpose, while Classes V to IX, Special Industrial Groups A to E, grouped together certain industrial uses[16] which may be particularly objectionable because of smell, noise, fumes, etc. 'Industrial building' is defined in art 2(2) of the order as a building used for the carrying on, in the course of trade or business other than agriculture, of any process for or incidental to specified purposes including the making, altering, repairing, adapting for sale or breaking up of any article or the getting, dressing or treatment of minerals. In *Rael-Brook Ltd v Minister of Housing and Local Government*[17] the Divisional Court held that neither the making of profit nor any commercial activity is essential before a process may be said to be carried on 'in the course of trade or business' for the purpose of the definition of 'industrial building', and that a cooking centre for school meals run by a local authority came within that definition.

A 'light industrial building' meant an industrial building (not being a special industrial building) in which the processes carried on or the machinery installed are such as could be carried on or installed in any residential area without detriment to the amenity of that area[18] by reason of noise, vibration, smell, fumes, smoke, soot, ash, dust or grit; a 'special industrial building' is an industrial building used for one or more of the purposes specified in Classes V–IX; and a 'general industrial building' means an industrial building other than a light or special industrial building (art 2(2)). In *Scrivener v Minister of Housing and Local Government*[19] Widgery J (delivering the judgment of the Divisional Court) said:

'To decide into which of these three main categories an industrial building falls involves a process of elimination. It must first be considered whether the building is a special industrial building; if not, whether it is a light industrial building; and if the answer is in the negative in each case the building falls into the residual category of a general industrial building ... [I]n our opinion the division of industrial buildings into "light", "general" and "special" is done with a view to classifying them according to the

---

15 For decisions concerning particular industrial uses see *Brain and Drive Yourself Hire Co (London) v LCC* (1957) 9 P & CR 113 (LT) (garage use treated as within Class III); *George Cohen 600 Group Ltd v Minister of Housing and Local Government* [1961] 2 All ER 682, [1961] 1 WLR 944; (whether recovery of scrap metal in Class IV); *Scrivener v Minister of Housing and Local Government* (1966) 18 P & CR 357 (whether cellulose spraying took industrial use into Class VIII); *Walter Chadburn & Son v Leeds Corpn* (1969) 20 P & CR 241 (whether use in Class IV or Special Industrial Group D); *Forkhurst v Secretary of State for the Environment* (1982) 46 P & CR 89 (Class IV).

16 In contrast to Classes III and IV, not limited to activities within a building. See, however, art 2(3) of the order.

17 [1967] 2 QB 65, [1967] 1 All ER 262. But see too *Tessier v Secretary of State for the Environment* (1975) 31 P & CR 161 (use of premises by sculptor not an industrial use); and ministerial decision noted in *Selected Enforcement and Allied Appeals*, p 29.

18 Whether or not detriment is caused to the amenity of the particular area in which the building is situated is irrelevant—see *W T Lamb Properties Ltd v Secretary of State for the Environment and Crawley Borough Council* [1983] JPL 303; and appeal decision noted in [1975] JPL 552.

19 (1966) 18 P & CR 357. See too *Essex County Council v Secretary of State for the Environment* (1973) 229 Estates Gazette 1733; and *Brooks and Burton v Secretary of State for the Environment* [1978] 1 All ER 733, [1977] 1 WLR 1294.

extent to which they may cause nuisance or inconvenience in the neigh-bourhood and thus according to the degree of care required in their siting.[20] In this connection it is not the ultimate purpose of the use which matters but the processes employed on the premises, and the definition of a light industrial building clearly underlines this. We do not think that the intention of this Order can be achieved unless the nature of the "process" is given the same significance when distinguishing general and special industrial buildings as it is when distinguishing general and light industrial buildings . . . [W]e are satisfied that when construing the word "purposes" in Class VIII one must not confine it to the single or overall purposes of the occupier's use of the building but must treat it as referring also to the processes employed.'

Article 3(2) of the order provided that where a group of contiguous or adjacent buildings used as parts of a single undertaking includes buildings used for purposes falling within two or more of Classes III to IX, those particular two or more classes may, in relation to that group of buildings, be treated as a single class for the purposes of the order, provided that the area occupied in that group of buildings by either general or special industrial buildings is not substantially increased thereby. This provision therefore permitted the interchange of industrial uses between the various buildings and in an appropriate case an increase in the area occupied by light industrial buildings at the expense of general or special industrial use.[1]

Each of the other use classes, Classes X to XVII, grouped together a number of similar uses. Class X, for example, related to use as a boarding or guest house or a hotel providing sleeping accommodation (except where licensed for the sale of excisable liquor other than to non-residents or persons consuming meals on the premises),[2] while Class XIII related to use as a home or institution providing for the boarding, care and maintenance of children, old people or persons under disability, a convalescent home, a nursing home, a sanatorium or a hospital.[3]

THE 1987 CLASSES

CLASS A—USES GENERALLY FOUND IN SHOPPING AREAS

The old definition of a shop in the 1972 order was, to use the words of the Planning Advisory Group Report, 'a complex arrangement of inclusions, exclusions and exceptions' which in addition contained the very vague category of 'any other purpose appropriate to a shopping area'. In fact the consequence of the wording was to require planning permission from a change from a standard shop to many uses which might well be considered entirely appropriate to a shopping area such as launderettes and cafes. While the definition of an office similarly meant that premises offering professional

20 For an example of the application of this principle see [1975] JPL 484.
1 See too the provisions of the General Development Order (p 150 below).
2 In *Mornford Investments v Minister of Housing and Local Government* [1970] 2 All ER 253 it was held that a students' hostel was not within this class. See too the comments of Glidewell J in *Commercial and Residential Property Development Co v Secretary of State for the Environment* (1981) 80 LGR 443.
3 On the interpretation of this class, see *Rann v Secretary of State for the Environment* (1979) 40 P & CR 113.

services to the visiting public such as building societies were treated as outside the definition. The majority of the subgroup of the Planning Advisory Group recommended the radical change of creating one broad class which would include 'all uses of premises to provide goods and services of a retail nature to the public visiting the premises'; see para 6.10 of the report. In the event the government opted for the more cautious approach of creating three separate classes within one broad group; shops, professional and financial services and food and drink. The result is that local planning authorities retain control over changes from one class to another within the broad group except where a change is permitted by the General Development Order (see chapter 6, page 159). Nevertheless the inclusion of the three classes within this broad heading and the increasing rights to change around within it, underlines the trend toward increasing flexibility towards shopping areas.

A1 Shops

'Use for all or any of the following purposes:

(a) for the retail sale of goods other than hot food
(b) as a post office
(c) for the sale of tickets or as a travel agency
(d) for the sale of sandwiches or other cold food for consumption off the premises
(e) for hairdressing
(f) for the direction of funerals
(g) for the display of goods for sale
(h) for the hiring out of domestic or personal goods or articles
(i) for the reception of goods to be washed, cleaned or repaired,

where the sale, display or service is to visiting members of the public.'

The new definition of a 'shop' use is more precise and succinct than the old. By omitting the reference to 'any other purpose appropriate to a shopping area', it is clear that only the particular activities listed in Class A1 are deemed to be a shop. The only general qualification is that all the sales, displays or services must be to visiting members of the public. However, by virtue of art 3(3) any sales etc to non-visiting members of the public, which were included or incidental, would be subsumed and would therefore not take the activity out of the class of shop.

On the other hand, certain activities which might otherwise come within the definition of a shop are still excluded. Thus art 3(6) excludes the use of the sale of fuel for motor vehicles and the sale and display for the sale of motor vehicles.

Sale of hot food is still specifically excluded but the sale of sandwiches and other cold food for consumption off the premises is now specifically included. This means that sandwich bars are included and in a ministerial decision it has been held that it is the primary purpose that has to be considered and so 'a sandwich bar does not cease to be in the shops class merely because it also sells hot drinks or if a few customers eat on the premises'.[4] The sale of 'drinks', hot or otherwise, is not expressly referred to in Class A1 but could come within the 'retail sale of goods'. However, where the use is primarily for

4 [1988] JPL 137.

the sale of drinks to be consumed on the premises, the use will come within Class A3.

A2 Financial and professional services

'Use for the provision of:

(a) financial services, or
(b) professional services (other than health or medical services), or
(c) any other services (including use as a betting office) which it is appropriate to provide in a shopping area,

where the services are provided principally to visiting members of the public.'

Here the crucial factors are the fact that 'services are provided principally to visiting numbers of the public' and that 'the services are appropriate to provide in a shopping area.' It in effect creates a new class of specialised services to the visiting public but in practice it will be very hard to distinguish this class from many 'office' uses which come within Class B2 because they are not provided *principally* to visiting members of the public.[4a] The inclusion of 'any other services which it is appropriate to provide in a shopping area' not only increases the vagueness of this class but implies that 'financial and professional services' are normally appropriate to provide in a shopping area. So although a change from a shop to a building society will still require planning permission, the 1987 order accepts that both are appropriate to a shopping area.

A3 Food and drink

'Use for the sale of food or drink for consumption on the premises or of hot food for consumption off the premises.'

This covers activities such as restaurants, 'take-away' food establishments, wine bars, snack bars and public houses. Its main impact is that a change from a restaurant to a fish and chip shop does not require permission. In this regard, even before the creation of Class A3, the introduction of some carry out or take away element might be ancillary to a restaurant use.[5]

Part 3 of the General Development Order 1988 permits a change from class A3 to class A1.[6] Thus a fish and chip shop can change to an antique shop but a change back is not authorised by pt 3.[7]

CLASS B—BUSINESS, INDUSTRIAL AND STORAGE

B1 Business

'Use for all or any of the following purposes:

(a) as an office other than a use within class A2 (financial and professional services),
(b) for research and development of products or processes, or

---

4a See ministerial decision reported at 1988 3 PAD 73.
5 See *City of Aberdeen District Council v Secretary of State for Scotland* [1987] JPL 292.
6 As well as other changes, see ch 6, p 159.
7 But see s 23(8) and *Cynon Valley Borough Council v Secretary of State for Wales* (1986) 85 LGR 36, [1986] JPL 760; see p 146.

(c) for any industrial process,

being a use which can be carried out in any residential area without detriment to the amenity of that area by reason of noise, vibration, smell, fumes, smoke, soot, ash, dust or grit.'

This class is designed to cater for the so-called 'high technology' uses which often involve a shifting balance of activity between office and light industrial use. It allows a change in the mix of activities to take place without there being a need to secure planning permission. The crucial test of limitation is that the use must remain environmentally acceptable to a residential area. In this regard the test is similar but not identical to that used in the 1972 order with respect to light industrial. An important difference is the substitution of the single word 'use' for 'the processes carried on or the machinery installed'. It may therefore be that a 'use' could not be carried on in a residential area not because of the noise caused by the process or machinery but because of the noise generated by the traffic generating from the premises. In this respect, the new class is perhaps narrower than the old light industrial class.

In *W T Lamb Properties Ltd and Crawley Borough Council v Secretary of State for the Environment*,[8] when faced with the similar test for the old Class III, McCullough J held that one had to first assess the noise or whatever emanating from the premises (not the noise on the premises) and then ask the hypothetical questions of 'whether there would or might be detriment to the amenity of any residential area in which the processes were carried on.' So it is irrelevant that the actual area in which the use is carried on is already heavily polluted or is not a residential area. The incorporation of the term 'can be carried out' would seem to suggest that a use may come within or outside B1 depending on the resources taken to minimise the pollution. In this regard it must be the actual use which will be relevant and not what is hypothetically possible.

As to the meaning of the term 'office', in ministerial decisions it has been given the Oxford English Dictionary definition of a place where the transaction of business of any department of a large concern is conducted.[9] Further in *Shephard v Buckinghamshire County Council*[10] Goff J held that because premises had been used as an administrative unit by the United States Air Force, it had been used as an office. However, in *London Residuary Body v Secretary of State for the Environment*[11] Simon Brown J upheld a s 53 determination that the use of County Hall by the Greater London Council was not an office use but was a use for 'the exercise of local government statutory functions' and as such sui generis. He concluded that he had 'no doubt that the singular features of County Hall, and in particular of the main building, both as to its physical construction and yet more particularly as to its precise use, were well able to justify the conclusion that the complex had a London governmental use.' The facts of the case suggest that a distinction may be made between buildings which are used by local authorities for their public and ceremonial activities and buildings which are used by local authorities for purely conventional office uses.

8 [1983] JPL 303.
9 [1980] JPL 346 and [1985] JPL 127.
10 (1966) 18 P & CR 419.
11 [1988] JPL 637. The Court of Appeal has since held that the Secretary of State misdirected himself but nevertheless agreed that the use of County Hall was sui generis and not within class B1; see [1989] EGCS 116.

B2 to B7 General industrial and special industrial uses

These classes have remained unchanged from the 1972 order. B2, the general industrial use, is defined as any industrial process other than one falling within Class B1 or within Classes B3 to B7. The planning advisory subgroup found the definition of general industrial to be satisfactory but they considered the special classes to be in need of modernising and amalgamation. It was also thought that consideration should be given to grading the degree of nuisance and environmental pollution caused by these special classes, so that if the classes were placed in order beginning with the least harmful and ending with the most, it would be possible to allow a change of use without planning permission from one class to another preceding class. A technical review is at present being undertaken and a consultation paper has been published.

B8 Storage or distribution:'Use for storage or as a distribution centre'

This is essentially the old 1972 Class X use of 'wholesale warehouse or repository for any purpose'. The main change is that the class is now defined by reference to the use of land rather than by the type of building. This makes clear that the use can be conducted on open land as well as in buildings. This is an important extension of the class and could lead to some difficulties of interpretation. For example in *Moran v Secretary of State for the Environment* [12] it was argued that 'long-term off-airport car parking' came within the old Class X. This did not have to be decided but McCullough J did remark that two very different uses could each be properly described as storage. So long-term car-parking, but probably not short-term car-parking, might come within Class B8.

Another difficulty is whether storage with a view to sales comes within Class B8. Circular 13/87 states that retail warehouses, where the main purpose is the sale of goods direct to visiting members of the public, will generally fall within the shops class, however much floor space is used for storage. The same would probably not apply to wholesale warehouses where there was selling in bulk to retailers or manufacturers. This kind of use could well be covered by the term 'distribution centre.' [13] Part 3 of the General Development Order 1988 permits change to B8 from any other use within B1 (business) or B2 (general industrial).

CLASS C—RESIDENTIAL

As the case law shows, the term residential can cover a wide variety of uses; from the standard use of a building as the dwellinghouse for a single family to hotels, hostels and homes for the elderly. The 1987 order utilises the existence or non-existence of 'care' to distinguish between institutions and other residential arrangements. A distinction is also drawn between a dwellinghouse use and a more specialised hotel or hostel use. However, rather confusingly this dwellinghouse use also covers a type of residential use which would otherwise come within the class of a residential institution; the small 'home' for the elderly where the residents live as a household.

12 [1988] JPL 24.
13 See in this regard *R v Secretary of State for the Environment and Cambridge City Council, ex p Hadjiouanon* [1988] JPL 497 where the term 'wholesale warehouses' was found not to include selling goods to the general public in larger quantity than is usual in a retail shop.

C1 Hotels and hostels

'Use as a hotel, boarding or guest house or as a hostel where, in each case, no significant element of care is provided.'

This is based on the 1972 order Class XI with the addition of hostels. This is an important extension as it seems otherwise changes from hotels to hostels or even from short-stay hostels to long-stay hostels might be material.[14]

C2 Residential institutions

'Use for the provision of residential accommodation and care to people in need of care (other than a use within Class C3 (dwellinghouse)).
Use as a hospital or nursing home.
Use as a residential school, college or training centre.'

This combines the old Classes XII and XIV so a residential school, college or training centre can change to an old people's home or an institution for the care of the mentally handicapped.

Article 2 defines 'care' to mean 'personal care for people in need of such care by reason of old age disablement, past or present dependence on alcohol or drugs or past or present mental disorder' and in this class 'care' includes 'the personal care of children and medical care and treatment'.

C3 Dwellinghouses

'Use as a dwellinghouse (whether or not as a sole or main residence)—

(a) by a single person or by people living together as a family or
(b) by not more than 6 residents living together as a single household (including a household where care is provided for residents).'

This is an entirely new class and is drawn narrowly. The planning advisory subgroup had recommended that a new residential use class should be created which would include as well as residence as a dwellinghouse other uses by residents which were compatible with the residential use. The 1987 order avoids grasping this particular nettle and therefore only those business uses which are included in and ordinarily incidental to use as a dwellinghouse will come within this class (see art 3(3) and page 121 above). In this regard circular 13/87 comments that 'The new Order does not alter the current position: planning permission for working at home is not usually needed where the use of part of a dwellinghouse for business purposes does not change the overall character of its use as a residence.' (see para 28).

While the courts have held that a change from use as a residence by a single-family to multiple-paying occupation can be a material change of use,[15] it appears clear that the more the multiple occupation resembles the

14 See *Thrasyvoulou v Secretary of State for the Environment* [1988] QB 809, [1988] 3 All ER 781, [1988] JPL 1689 and *Mornford Investments Ltd v Minister of Housing and Local Government* [1970] 2 All ER 253, 21 P & CR 609 and *Commercial and Residential Development Co Ltd v Secretary of State for the Environment* (1981) 80 LGR 443.
15 *Birmingham Corpn v Minister of Housing and Local Government and Habib Ullah* [1964] 1 QB 178 , [1963] 3 All ER 668 and see ministerial decision noted at [1979] JPL 123; also *Duffy v Pilling* (1977) 75 LGR 159, 33 P & CR 85 and *Lipson v Secretary of State for the Environment* (1976) 75 LGR 361, 33 P & CR 95.

single occupation by one family, the less likely that a material change will have occurred; even if the persons are not related. Class C3 does little more than remove any doubts about this principle by equating 'people living together as a family' and 'not more than 6 residents living together as a single household'. More important is the inclusion in this last category of residents for whom care is provided—though again it may not be a material change of use anyway for a family to take in on a paying basis a small number of handicapped or elderly persons. The drafting of this class presumes that the concept of the single household is easily indentifiable, which is doubtful. However, it probably denotes that the residents live as one group sharing household tasks and expenses with some measure of independence.[16a] In this respect circular 13/87 submits that 'In the case of small residential care homes or nursing homes, staff and residents will probably not live as a single household and the use will therefore fall into the residential institution class, regardless of the size of the home.'

CLASS D—NON-RESIDENTIAL

D1 Non-residential institutions

'Any use not including a residential use:

(a) for the provision of any medical or health services except the use of premises attached to the residence of the consultant or practitioner,
(b) as a creche, day nursery or day centre,
(c) for the provision of education,
(d) for the display of works of art (otherwise than for sale or hire),
(e) as a museum,
(f) as a public library or public reading room,
(g) as a public hall or exhibition hall,
(h) for, or in connection with, public worship or religious instruction.'

This covers the former 1972 order Classes XII, XV and XVI.

D2 Assembly and leisure

'Use as:

(a) a cinema,
(b) a concert hall,
(c) a bingo hall or casino,
(d) a dance hall,
(e) a swimming bath, skating rink, gymnasium or area for other indoor or outdoor sports or recreations, not involving motorised vehicles or firearms.'

This incorporates former 1972 order Classes XVII and XVIII except that it has been extended to include bingo halls and most indoor and outdoor sports. Theatres are not included and 'Turkish or other vapour or foam baths' are not expressly included but could come under 'area for indoor recreations'.

16 See ministerial decision [1987] JPL 727.
16a See ministerial decision reported at [1988] 3 PAD 326, for a case concerning what is a household.

D USES SPECIFICALLY DECLARED TO INVOLVE DEVELOPMENT

Three specific changes of use are declared by the 1971 Act to involve a material change in the use of the land.

1 *Use of dwellinghouse as two or more separate dwellings*

The 1971 Act declares 'for the avoidance of doubt' that the use as two or more separate dwellinghouses of any building previously used as a single dwellinghouse[17] involves a material change in the use of the building and of any part thereof which is so used (s 22(3)(a)).[18]

For the purposes of this provision multiple occupation of a dwellinghouse is not enough (though multiple occupation may so alter the character of the use of a house previously occupied as a single-family dwelling as to amount to a material change of use).[19] In *Ealing Corpn v Ryan*[20] it was submitted on behalf of the planning authority that if people were found to be living separately in a building then there were bound to be separate dwellings. The Divisional Court rejected that proposition, Ashworth J saying that 'a house may well be occupied by two or more persons, who are to all intents and purposes living separately, without that house being thereby used as separate dwellings. In other words persons may live separately under one roof without occupying separate dwellings.' Whether or not there is use as two or more separate dwellinghouses will often be a question of fact and degree; in the *Ealing* case Ashworth J, suggested that such factors as the existence or absence of any form of physical reconstruction and the extent to which the allegedly separate dwellings are self-contained and independent of other parts of the same property might be relevant. It seems doubtful whether principles enunciated in cases under the Rent Acts are of any assistance where the question of separate dwellings arises under the planning legislation.[1]

Section 22 (3)(a) is only concerned with dwellinghouses and with change to use as two or more separate dwellinghouses; the minister has determined in one case that a change of use from two flats to use as a single dwellinghouse did not constitute development.[2] In *Camden London Borough Council v Peaktop Properties (Hampstead) Ltd*[3] the Court of Appeal held that s 22(3)(a) of the Town and Country Planning Act 1971 had no application where it was proposed to add an extra storey to a block of flats; the proposals did not involve creating two dwellings out of one.

2 *Deposit of refuse on site already used for that purpose*

Section 22(3)(b) of the 1971 Act provides that 'the deposit of refuse or waste

---

17 As to what constitutes a 'dwellinghouse' see p 121 above.
18 See too *Wakelin v Secretary of State for the Environment* (1978) 77 LGR 101 (p 100 above).
19 See p 104 above.
20 [1965] 2 QB 486, [1965] 1 All ER 137, [1965] 2 WLR 223.
 1 See *Ealing Corpn* (above); and *Birmingham Corpn v Minister of Housing and Local Government and Habib Ullah* [1964] 1 QB 178, [1963] 3 All ER 668, [1963] 3 WLR 937.
 2 *Bulletin of Selected Appeal Decisions*, IX/15; see too [1982] JPL 119.
 3 (1983) 82 LGR 101.

materials[4] on land involves a material change in the use thereof, notwith-standing that the land is comprised in a site already used for that purpose, if either the superficial area of the deposit is thereby extended, or the height of the deposit is thereby extended and exceeds the level of the land adjoining the site.'

Thus, despite the fact that land is comprised in a site already used for the deposit of refuse or waste materials, further deposits on that land will in the specified circumstances involve a material change in the use of the land.[5] It would seem that if refuse is deposited on land such as a former quarry which has already been used for tipping, then so long as the refuse does not extend above the level of the adjoining land or cover more than the area of the quarry, no material change of use will be involved.[6]

The meaning of the phrase 'already used', as employed in this subsection, was considered in *Macdonald v Glasgow Corpn*.[7] In that case the proprietor of an area of land which had been used since 1955 for the deposit of waste materials appealed against an enforcement notice, contending, *inter alia*, that planning permission was not required because at the date of his purchasing the land in 1958 the land was 'already used' for the purpose of depositing waste materials within the meaning of the statute. The Sheriff-Principal held that planning permission was required for the continued use of the land for the deposit of waste materials since the words 'already used' referred to use prior to the coming into operation of the 1947 Act. It was also contended for the appellant that the whole area of the site could be raised by the deposit of waste materials to the level of the highest points of any adjoining land; though it was not necessary to decide this point, the Sheriff-Principal 'inclined to the view that the proper levels to be applied ... are the varying contours of the immediately adjoining lands'.

In *Bilboe v Secretary of State for the Environment*[8] the Court of Appeal held that s 22(3)(b) showed that tipping for the purpose of disposing of waste material was to be regarded as a use of land and not an operation.[9] Nevertheless tipping for some other purpose can amount to operational development either instead of or as well as a material change of use.[10] Section 22(3)(b) only applies where waste materials are tipped for the purpose of disposing of them and not to tipping which amounts to operational develop-ment.[11] Of more practical importance it has been held by the Minister that no

---

4 Whether material is refuse or waste is a matter of fact. The minister has treated subsoil as coming within the statutory provision—see [1981] JPL 911. Also see [1988] JPL 663.

5 See *Alexandra Transport Co Ltd v Secretary of State for Scotland* (1973) 27 P & CR 352, 1974 SLT 81 in which the Court of Session considered the corresponding provision of the 1947 Act (from which, however, certain apparently otiose words were omitted on consolidation in the 1971 Act). It is probably the case that a material change of use occurs on each occasion when waste material is deposited on the site in such a way as to extend the superficial area or height of the deposit—see *Bilboe* (above); and appeal decision noted in [1981] JPL 907.

6 See *Ratcliffe v Secretary of State for the Environment* (1975) 235 Estates Gazette 901.

7 1960 SLT (Sh Ct) 21.

8 (1980) 78 LGR 357, 39 P & CR 495.

9 See too *Roberts v Vale Royal District Council* (1977) 78 LGR 368, 39 P & CR 514 and *R v Derbyshire County Council, ex p North East Derbyshire District Council* (1979) 77 LGR 389.

10 See *Northavon District Council v Secretary of State for the Environment* (1980) 40 P & CR 332 and *West Bowers Farm Products v Essex County Council* (1985) 50 P & CR 368, [1985] JPL 857 (see p 85 below).

11 [1976] JPL 655.

distinction can be drawn between solid and liquid waste and that "refuse or waste materials" includes liquid waste.[12] In the case of liquid waste it will however often be hard to apply s 22(3)(b) as the levels of the waste will be hard to identify.[13]

3 *Display of advertisements*

Use for the display of advertisements of any external part of a building not normally used for that purpose is to be treated as involving a material change in the use of that part of the building (s 22(4)). Where, however, the display of advertisements in accordance with regulations made under the Act[14] involves development, planning permission for that development is deemed to be granted by virtue of s 63 of the 1971 Act and no application for planning permission under Pt III of the Act is necessary.

E APPLICATION TO DETERMINE WHETHER PLANNING PERMISSION REQUIRED

From what has been said above it will be seen that it may well be difficult to decide whether proposed operations or a proposed change of use will constitute development. Under the 1971 Act the planning authority may be asked to determine whether particular proposals amount to development. If any person who proposes to carry out any operations on land, or to make any change in the use of land, wishes to have it determined whether the carrying out of those operations, or the making of that change, would constitute or involve development of the land, he may, either as part of an application for planning permission or independently of any such application, apply to the planning authority to determine that question (s 53(1)). If the authority consider that the proposals will involve development they must then determine whether an application for planning permission in respect thereof is required under Pt III of the 1971 Act, having regard to the provisions of the development order[15] and of any enterprise zone scheme or simplified planning zone[16] (1971 Act, s 53(1)[17]).

The procedure to be followed in making application for such a determination is similar to that laid down in connection with an application for planning permission (see chapter 9) and is set out in art 9(2) of the General Development Order. It is there provided that an application is to be in writing, is to contain a description of the operations or change of use proposed, together with certain other prescribed particulars, and is to be accompanied by a plan sufficient to identify the land to which the application relates. The Town and Country Planning Act 1984 provides (s 1) that for the purpose of enabling Crown land to be disposed of with the benefit of a

12 [1980] JPL 771.
13 [1980] JPL 771.
14 The Town and Country Planning (Control of Advertisements) Regulations 1984 are dealt with in ch 18 below.
15 Planning permission is automatically granted for certain types of development by the GDO. (see p 150 below).
16 An order designating an enterprise zone or simplified planning zone will operate as a grant of planning permission for specified types of development (see ch 16 below).
17 As amended by the Local Government, Planning and Land Act 1980, Sch 32, para 18(3) and the Housing and Planning Act 1986, s 25 and Sch 6, Pt II para 3.

determination under s 53, application for such a determination may be made by the government department or other Crown body responsible for the land or by someone authorised by the appropriate authority[18] (see p 147 below). The planning authority are to keep a register of applications for determinations under s 53 (see 1971 Act, s 34(2) and 53(2), and GDO art 27(4)).

It seems clear that a determination under s 53 cannot be made retrospectively and that an application cannot competently be made in respect of operations or a change of use already carried out.[19] The Secretary of State has no power under s 53 to decide upon the validity of a planning permission,[20] nor is he able under this provision to interpret a specific grant of planning permission.[1]

In *Moran v Secretary of State for the Environment and Mid-Sussex County Council*[2] McCullough J held that the existence of an established user certificate under s 94 was irrelevent in considering a s 53 application. There were two stages in a s 53 application. First, the proposed use had to be compared with the existing use and with nothing else. McCullough J submitted that at this stage one was not concerned with the lawfulness of that change but whether it was material and it was not the established use certificate with which the proposed use was to be compared. The second stage was when, if it was determined that the proposed use did involve development, it was asked whether planning permission was required having regard to the provisions of the development order. Again McCullough J stated that at this stage the question was not whether permission was required having regard to the established use certificate, but only whether the change was covered by the development order.

Where a planning authority or one of its officers has expressed the view that particular proposals will not involve development, such an expression of view will in certain limited circumstances be binding upon the authority even though the statutory formalities relating to application for and making of a determination have not been observed. The leading cases on the application of the doctrine of estoppel in a town planning context are considered in greater detail in Ch 12, but it would seem to be the case that an effective determination can be made even though a formal application for such a determination has not been submitted.

In *Wells v Minister of Housing and Local Government*[3] the Court of Appeal held (Russell LJ dissenting[4]) that where, following the making of an application for planning permission, the planning authority's surveyor wrote to the applicants stating that the works in question were permitted development and that the authority did not propose to consider the application, that

18 Certain provisions of the 1971 Act are modified for this purpose by the Town and Country Planning (Crown Land Applications) Regulations 1984.
19 See ministerial decisions noted in [1980] JPL 342 and [1983] JPL 493.
20 *Edgwarebury Park Investments v Minister of Housing and Local Government* [1963] 2 QB 408, [1963] 1 All ER 124.
 1 See *East Suffolk County Council v Secretary of State for the Environment* (1972) 70 LGR 595 and appeal decision noted in [1982] JPL 115.
 2 [1988] JPL 24.
 3 [1967] 2 All ER 1041, [1967] 1 WLR 1000; applied in *English Speaking Union of the Commonwealth v City of Westminster Council* (1973) 26 P & CR 575. See too *Property Investment Holdings Ltd v Secretary of State for the Environment* [1984] JPL 587.
 4 In *Western Fish Products Ltd v Penwith District Council* [1981] 2 All ER 204 the Court of Appeal stated that they found Russell LJ's judgment 'very powerful'.

letter amounted to a valid determination under the planning legislation—
there had either been a waiver by the planning authority of any formal
application for a determination or the application for planning permission
contained an implied invitation to the authority to make such a determination if they thought fit. The Court of Appeal also held, however, that only
a positive statement by the planning authority can constitute a valid
determination and that the deletion, on a printed by-law consent notification, of a sentence warning against acting on the faith of the bye-law
approval without obtaining planning permission could not be regarded as a
determination under the planning legislation that planning permission was
not required.

In *Western Fish Products Ltd v Penwith District Council*[5] the Court of
Appeal expressed the view (obiter) that the legislation contemplates a
considerable degree of formality in applications and determinations as to
whether planning permission is required and that while an application for
planning permission impliedly contains an invitation to determine that
permission is not required,[6] and accordingly in such a case a formal written
application for a determination is not necessary, that exception should not be
extended beyond cases in which there has been an application for planning
permission.[7]

In *Glasgow District Council v Secretary of State for Scotland*[8] planning
permission for certain proposals had been refused by the planning authority.
On appeal, the Secretary of State concluded that the works in question did
not involve development. It was argued for the planning authority that in the
absence of an application for a s 51 (the Scots equivalent of s 53) determination, the Secretary of State had no power to make such a decision. For the
Secretary of State it was argued, citing *Wells* (above), that an application for
planning permission contains an implied invitation to make a determination
that planning permission is not required. Though it was not necessary for the
Second Division to decide this point, both Lord Dunpark and Lord
Robertson set out their reasons for rejecting the planning authority's
argument. Their Lordships found it unnecessary to rely on *Wells*. Lord
Dunpark did not think that s 51 could be applied to the facts of this case;
there was no application under s 51 and he did not think the Secretary of
State's decision fell to be construed in the sense of a s 51 determination—it
was a decision in an appeal against refusal of planning permission. Lord
Robertson said that s 51 was conceived for the benefit of developers and
applicants for planning permission. It did not limit the powers of the
planning authority or the Secretary of State. He was unable to see any reason
why the wide discretion conferred on the Secretary of State on appeal against
the decision of a planning authority—see p 267 below should be limited by
refusing him power to decide that an application for planning permission was
unnecessary. Similarly in *Property Investments Holdings Ltd v Secretary of
State for the Environment*[9] it was held that on an appeal against a refusal of

---

5 [1981] 2 All ER 204.
6 See *Property Investment Holdings Ltd v Secretary of State for the Environment* [1984] JPL
587.
7 It might be suggested that this represents a very narrow view of the *ratio* in *Wells*. In *English
Speaking Union* (above) the doctrine in *Wells* was applied to a mere exchange of letters.
8 1980 SC 150, 1982 SLT 28.
9 [1984] JPL 587.

planning permission it was open to the Secretary of State to take up the implied invitation in the planning application to declare that planning permission was not required.[10] However, neither the local planning authority nor the Secretary of State are bound to take up this invitation and can treat the application on its merits without going into the question of whether planning permission is in fact necessary.

There is a right of appeal to the Secretary of State against a determination made by a planning authority; appeal can also be made on the failure of a planning authority to give notice of their determination within the prescribed period (see s 53(2)). The Secretary of State can 'call in' for decision by himself an application for a determination (s 53(2)).

Either the applicant or the local planning authority, if dissatisfied with a decision of the Secretary of State under s 53, may appeal to the High Court or require the minister to state a case for the opinion of the High Court (s 247).[11]

The 1971 Act is silent as to the precise effect of a determination under s 53. It would seem that a determination that development is not involved is as good as a grant of planning permission and is, in the words of Lord Denning, 'irrevocable by the planning authority just as is a planning permission'.[12] In *English Speaking Union of the Commonwealth v City of Westminster Council*[13] a determination had been made by the planning authority to the effect that in terms of the Use Classes Order a proposed change of use would not involve development; it was held that this determination was not invalidated by a change made in the relevant provision of the Use Classes Order before the development was carried out. 'The determination', said Pennycuick VC, 'established the right of the plaintiff once and for all and, as held in the *Wells* case, was as good as planning permission.'[14]

---

10 Problems then arise as to whether s 247 can be used to challenge such a determination by the Secretary of State.
11 There would seem to be nothing to prevent a developer seeking a declaration that particular proposals do not require planning permission; see *Pyx Granite Co v Minister of Housing and Local Government* [1960] AC 260, [1959] 3 All ER 1.
12 *Wells v Minister of Housing and Local Government* (above).
13 (1973) 26 P & CR 575.
14 For persuasive criticism of this decision see [1974] JPL 141 (W A Leach).

CHAPTER 6
DEVELOPMENT NOT REQUIRING
SUBMISSION OF A PLANNING APPLICATION

Certain exceptional categories of development, set out in s 23 of the 1971 Act, are declared not to require planning permission. Nor does development by the Crown require such permission; at least on Crown land[1]. Otherwise, planning permission is required for the carrying out of any development of land (1971 Act, s 23(1)).[2] However, an express grant of planning permission by the planning authority may not be necessary in order to allow development to proceed; in certain circumstances planning permission for development is deemed to be granted and in other circumstances permission is granted by development order. These cases are considered in this chapter.

A DEVELOPMENT NOT REQUIRING PLANNING PERMISSION

Section 23 of 1971 Act

Section 23 of the 1971 Act makes a number of exceptions to the general rule that planning permission is required for the development of land.[3] The more important of these exceptional cases are as follows:

(*a*) Where on the appointed day (1st July 1948) land was normally used for one purpose and was also used on occasions,[4] whether at regular intervals or not, for another purpose, then provided that the land was used for that other purpose on at least one similar occasion between the appointed day and the beginning of 1968, planning permission is not required in respect of the use of the land for that other purpose on similar occasions (s 23(3)(b).

(*b*) Where planning permission to develop land has been granted for a limited period, planning permission is not required for the resumption, at the end of that period, of the use of the land for the purpose for which it was normally used before the permission was granted, provided that the 'normal use' was not begun in contravention of Pt II of the 1947 Act or Pt III of the 1971 Act (s 23(5), (6), (10)).

In *Smith v Secretary of State for the Environment*[5] Woolf J held that, in order to take advantage of sub-s (5), the land had in fact to be developed in accordance with a limited period permission. Once such a permission had been implemented, you could resume the normal use as long as the resumption took place at the end of the period that the land was used for the

---

1 See *Lord Advocate v Strathclyde Regional Council* 1988 SLT 546 [1989] JPL 198.
2 Except for development carried out on or before the appointed day of 1st July 1948; Sch 24, para 12. To the 1971 Act.
3 See Michael Purdue, 'The Right to Revert to Earlier Uses of Land' [1984] JPL 6.
4 On the meaning of the expression 'on occasions' as used in this context see *Smyth v Minister of Housing and Local Government* (1966) 18 P & CR 351.
5 (1982) 47 P & CR 194.

purpose permitted by the limited permission. It did not matter if the limited use ceased before it was required to cease; though Woolf J did indicate that a right to revert could be lost where a long period elapsed after the date that the limited permission expired. Finally, he held that where there was a series of limited permissions you could revert back through the series to the first normal use which was lawful; though lawful in this regard did not include a use which had begun in contravention of Pt III of the Act but had since become immune from enforcement.

(c) Where planning permission has been granted subject to limitations by a development order, planning permission is not required to resume the normal use of the land, provided that such a 'normal use' was not begun in contravention of Pt II of the 1947 Act or Pt III of the 1971 Act (s 23(8)(10)).

In *Cynon Valley Borough Council v Secretary of State for Wales*[6] the Court of Appeal gave a wide interpretation to the phrase 'subject to limitations' by holding that it covers any limitations set out in the description of the development being authorised. So sub-s (8) was held to apply to the change from a hot food shop to an ordinary shop authorised by Class III of the 1977 GDO and would presumably apply to other changes of use so authorised. In *Cynon*, a change back to a fish and chip shop was covered by sub-s (8) after a short use as an antique shop. This has important implications for the Use Classes Order as Part 3 of the development order is intended only to allow changes to a use class which is more acceptable in environmental terms. The effect of the *Cynon* case is to authorise a change back and thus undermines the objective. However, s 23(8) only authorises a reversion back to the 'normal use' and so should not apply where the change under Part 3 was instituted some time ago.

(d) Where an enforcement notice has been served in respect of any development of land, planning permission is not required for the use of that land for the purpose for which, in accordance with the provisions of Pt III of the 1971 Act, it could lawfully have been used if that development had not been carried out (s 23(9)). A 'lawful use' for this purpose is one begun with the benefit of a valid planning permission or, alternatively, one begun before 1st July 1948 and not since abandoned or replaced by another use (other than another use begun with the benefit of a planning permission for a limited period or begun in breach of planning control and in respect of which enforcement action has been taken).[7] A use begun in contravention of Pt III of the 1971 Act does not constitute a 'lawful' use for the purposes of this sub-s, even though that use has acquired immunity from enforcement action: if therefore a use which was instituted in breach of planning control but which has acquired immunity from enforcement action is discontinued in favour of a fresh use involving development, and enforcement action is taken in respect of that new use, the occupier will have no right to revert to the former use.[8] An occupier of land can revert to a previous lawful use only if that use immediately preceded the use enforced against; if the immediately

6 (1986) 85 LGR 36, [1986] JPL 760.
7 See *LTSS Print and Supply Services Ltd v London Borough of Hackney* [1976] QB 663, [1976] 1 All ER 311.
8 *Young v Secretary of State for the Environment* [1983] 2 AC 662, [1983] 2 All ER 1105; *LTSS Print and Supply Services Ltd* (above). See too Nigel P Gravells, 'Reversion to Previous Land Use Following Enforcement Proceedings' [1984] Conv 339.

preceding use is unlawful he cannot go back to earlier uses until he reaches the last lawful use.[9]

However, in *Fairchild v Secretary of State for the Environment and Eastleigh Borough Council*[10] it was accepted that if the preceding use was originally lawful, it did not matter that the preceding use had in the meantime ceased and the land had lain unused before the material change the subject of the enforcement notice. In other words it cannot be argued that the preceding lawful use had been abandoned. This interpretation of s 23(9) seems doubtful as reversion only applies to a use to which the land could lawfully have been put at the time of the unauthorised use. If a use has been abandoned its resumption at that time would have been unlawful.

Development by Crown

Crown land is in large measure exempt from the provisions of the planning legislation. 'The reason it is exempt', said Lord Denning MR in *Ministry of Agriculture, Fisheries and Food v Jenkins*,[11] 'is not by virtue of any provision in the Act itself, but by reason of the general principle that the Crown is not bound by an Act unless it is expressly or impliedly included'. According to circular 18/84 this exemption extends to Health Authorities and the Metropolitan Police. However, certain exceptions to the general principle are made by ss 266 to 268 of the 1971 Act and by the Town and Country Planning Act 1984.

'Crown land' is defined in s 266(7) of the 1971 Act as land in which there is a Crown interest, that is, an interest belonging to Her Majesty in right of the Crown, or belonging to a government department, or held in trust for Her Majesty for the purposes of a government department. The 1971 Act provides that certain planning powers may be exercised in relation to such land. It is provided, for example, that a development plan may include proposals relating to the use of Crown land; that a building which is for the time being Crown land may be 'listed' as a building of special architectural or historic interest; and that certain provisions of the 1971 Act, in particular the provisions of Pt III of the Act, relating to general planning control, are to apply to Crown land to the extent of any interest therein which is for the time being held otherwise than by or on behalf of the Crown[12] (s 266(1)(b)).

Not only does the Crown not need to obtain planning permission for development on Crown land, until the coming into operation of the 1984 Act government departments and other Crown bodies were unable to apply for planning permission or other consents under Pts III and IV of the 1971 Act. This could give rise to problems in connection with the disposal of Crown land and the 1984 Act provides for the making of applications for planning permission (see p 181 below), listed building consent, consent to demolish an

9 *Young v Secretary of State for the Environment* (above) (overruling on this point *Balco Transport Services Ltd v Secretary of State for the Environment* (1983) 45 P & CR 216). See too *Denham Developments Ltd v Secretary of State for the Environment* (1983) 47 P & CR 598.
10 [1988] JPL 472.
11 [1963] 2 QB 317, [1963] 2 All ER 147, but see *Lord Advocate v Strathclyde Regional Council* 1988 SLT 546, [1989] JPL 198.
12 S 4(1) of the 1984 Act resolves possible doubts as to the categories of persons possessing an interest in Crown land by providing that a person who is entitled to occupy Crown land by virtue of a written contract is to be treated as having an interest in the land.

unlisted building in a conservation area, or a determination under s 53 of the 1971 Act in anticipation of disposal of such land. The 1984 Act also permits the making of tree preservation orders in anticipation of disposal of Crown land and makes provision for the enforcement of planning control in respect of development carried out on Crown land by trespassers (see p 322 below).

Parts III and IV of the 1971 Act are not applied to Crown land in which no interest is held otherwise than by or on behalf of the Crown, with the result that the Crown does not require planning permission (or other consents) under those Parts of the Act. However, circular 18/84 specifies certain non-statutory procedures to be followed in the consideration of the planning aspects of proposals for development by government departments and other bodies entitled to Crown exemption from the provisions of the planning legislation.

Where a government department or other Crown body propose to carry out development of a type which would, if carried out by a private developer, require a specific grant of planning permission, the department or body will consult the appropriate planning authority.[13] Even where consultation on that basis would not be necessary departments will notify the planning authority of development proposals which are likely to be of special concern to the authority or to the public—for example, where there could be a very substantial effect on the character of a conservation area.

The developing department will send to the planning authority a Notice of Proposed Development; the authority are to treat this Notice in the same way as they would an application for planning permission and will, *inter alia*, undertake the usual consultations. Although development proposals by government departments are not subject to statutory publicity requirements, it is intended that they should be given as much publicity as if the Notice of Proposed Development were an application for planning permission (see p 184 below). After taking account of the views of any bodies they have consulted and of any comments received in response to the publicity given, the planning authority should, within two months, send the developing department their views on the proposed development, stating whether they find it acceptable and if so, on what conditions (if any), or whether they find it unacceptable. Similarly, proposals which would constitute a departure from the development plan should be dealt with like applications for planning permission for similar development in accordance with the Development Plans Directive 1981 (see p 187 below).

Where the planning authority object to the Notice of Proposed Development or to any detailed proposal submitted after a Notice of Proposed Development in outline, or where there is any unresolved disagreement, the developing department will, if they wish to proceed, notify the Department of the Environment. In all cases where there have been objections the planning authority, the developing department and other interested parties will be given an opportunity to express their views. The circular states that it is expected that the written representations method will be suitable for most cases. However, in some cases it may be desirable to hold a non-statutory public inquiry.

13 The circular states, however, that the consultation procedure cannot fully apply to proposals involving national security.

The local planning authorities are recommended to keep a non-statutory addendum to the planning register in respect of Notices of Proposed Development.

Since the Crown is not subject to planning control, any use of land instituted by the Crown, even if intended to be only temporary, can be continued indefinitely by a third party such as a purchaser of the land or the owner of land of which the Crown is a lessee.[14] Section 5 of the Town and Country Planning Act 1984 provides machinery by which the local planning authority may achieve a greater degree of control in such circumstances. The local planning authority may enter into an agreement with the appropriate government department when a material change of use is made or is intended to be made by the Crown. The effect of such an agreement is that if the land ceases to be used by the Crown for the purpose specified in the agreement, the use instituted by the Crown is to be treated as having been authorised by a planning permission granted subject to a condition requiring its discontinuance on the date the Crown ceases to use the land. The result is that planning permission will normally be needed for continuance of the use by someone other than the Crown. The provisions of s 23(5) of the 1971 Act (above) will, however, apply and will authorise the resumption of the use to which the land was normally put prior to the commencement of the use which is the subject of the agreement.

It has formerly been assumed that the Crown's exemption from the provisions of the Town and Country Planning legislation applied generally. However, it now seems that it only applies to Crown land. In *Lord Advocate v Strathclyde Regional Council*[15] contractors on behalf of the Secretary of State for Defence placed obstructions on and built a temporary fence on part of a road belonging to Strathclyde Regional Council. Dumbarton District Council, as planning authority, served upon the contractors an enforcement notice alleging a breach of planning control. A stop notice was also served. The Inner House of the Court of Session held that the relevant sections of the Town and Country Planning (Scotland) Act 1972 bound the Crown as the Crown had no rights of property or interest in the land on which the development had been instituted. All three of their Lordships were unanimous that the principle had been expressed too broadly in *Ministry of Agriculture and Fisheries v Jenkins* and that the Crown is bound by Acts of Parliament (despite the lack of express words or by implication) where the Act is not divesting the Crown of a privilege or a prerogative. Lord Grieve stated:

'In my opinion it would be monstrous if a department of the Crown which did not claim to be acting in pursuance of the Royal Prerogative, was in a position to disregard the provisions of Acts of Parliament to which all other persons were subject in respect of property to which the Crown had no right or title, and indeed in which it had no interest.'

14 See also *Newbury District Council v Secretary of State for the Environment* (1977) 75 LGR 608, [1977] JPL 373 per Goff J.
15 1988 SLT 546, [1989] JPL 198.

B PLANNING PERMISSION DEEMED TO BE GRANTED

In certain circumstances planning permission for development is deemed to be granted. Among the more important such cases are the following:

(a) Where an advertisement is displayed in accordance with the Town and Country Planning (Control of Advertisements) Regulations 1989,[16] planning permission is deemed to be granted for development involved in such display (1971 Act, s 63).

(b) Where the sanction of a government department is required by virtue of any enactment in respect of development to be carried out by a local authority or statutory undertakers,[17] that department may, on granting such sanction, direct that planning permission for the development shall be deemed to be granted[18] (1971 Act, s 40).

(c) Where a local planning authority require planning permission for development in their own area, and that development is not 'permitted development' in terms of the General Development Order (below) or development for which permission is deemed to have been granted under s 40 of the 1971 Act (above), they must follow the procedure set out in the Town and Country Planning General Regulations 1976.

   The regulations, which are outlined at p 274 below, provide that in specified circumstances the Secretary of State is deemed to have granted planning permission for the development in question.

C PERMISSION GRANTED BY DEVELOPMENT ORDER

Where it is proposed to carry out development requiring planning permission, application to the planning authority for such permission is not always necessary: the proposed development may be authorised by a development order made by the Secretary of State. A development order may grant planning permission for development specified in the order or for development of any class so specified (1971 Act, s 24(2)(a)). Such an order may be made either as a general order, applicable (subject to such exceptions as may be specified therein) to all land but which may make different provisions with respect to different descriptions of land, or as a special order, applicable only to such land, or descriptions of land, as specified therein (s 24(3)). (Planning permission granted by a development order may be granted unconditionally or subject to such conditions or limitations as may be specified in the order (s 24(4)).)

The present wording was introduced by the Housing and Planning Act 1986 and enables development orders to make different provisions for different descriptions of land. The previous wording meant that special orders had to be used to vary the application of the General Development Order to special areas of land such as National Parks or Conservation areas.

---

16 See ch 18.
17 Planning permission for certain types of development carried out by local authorities and statutory undertakers is granted by the General Development Order (below).
18 The Secretary of State for Energy is, for example, authorised to grant 'deemed' planning permission for power stations under the Electric Lighting Act 1909 and the Electricity Act 1957.

The result was that every time the General Order was changed there had to be parallel changes to the special orders. Also, as special orders could only apply to the land specified in them and not to descriptions of types of land, the orders had to be constantly updated as new areas of land were designated. The changes have enabled all the various orders to be consolidated into a single new order.

The General Development Order: permitted development

The general development order presently in force is the Town and Country Planning General Development Order 1988 ('the GDO'). This came into force on 5th December 1988 and replaces the 1977 Order as amended. At the same time the 1988 GDO revoked all the special development orders relating to national parks, areas of outstanding natural beauty and conservation areas. Except where its application is limited by a special development order, the GDO is applicable to all land in England and Wales (GDO, art 2(1)).

Under art 3(1) of the GDO planning permission is granted for a total of 76 classes of development specified in the Second Schedule to the GDO and such development may be undertaken without permission of any local planning authority or of the Secretary of State.

It is provided, however, that nothing in art 3 of, or the second Schedule to, the GDO, is to operate so as to permit any development contrary to a condition imposed in any planning permission granted or deemed to be granted otherwise than by the order (GDO, art 3(4)). In granting permission for a dwelling-house, for example, the planning authority might impose a condition to the effect that, notwithstanding any provision of the GDO, no garage is to be erected within the curtilage of the house except with the authority's consent; that condition will override the general permission granted by the GDO for the erection of such a garage and the authority can thus retain control over such matters as the external appearance and siting of any such garage. In *East Barnet UDC v British Transport Commission*[19] Lord Parker took the view that art 3 was referring only to conditions applying at the time the first general development order was issued but although the matter has not been definitively settled by the courts, it seems plain that such a condition would be valid as long it passed the standard tests for the legality of conditions.[20] In circular 22/88 in the context of art 4 directions it is stated that 'The permitted development rights in Schedule 2 to the GDO have been endorsed by Parliament and they should consequently not be withdrawn locally without compelling reasons.' This would suggest that similarly the department would seek sound reasons for the imposition of such conditions and might otherwise overturn them on appeal.

19 [1962] 2 QB 484, [1961] 3 All ER 878.
20 Lord Parker's views which were obiter have been overtaken by the reasoning in *City of London Corpn v Secretary of State for the Environment* (1971) 23 P & CR 169 (see p 128 above) and *Kingston-Upon-Thames Royal Borough Council v Secretary of State for the Environment* [1974] 1 All ER 193, [1973] 1 WLR 1549 (*see* p 239 below). See too the comments of the Lord President (Lord Emslie) in *British Airports Authority v Secretary of State for Scotland* 1979 SC 200, 1979 SLT 197, of Sir Douglas Frank in *Carpet Decor (Guildford) Ltd v Secretary of State for the Environment* [1981] JPL 806, and Forbes J in *Dawson v Secretary of State for the Environment and London Borough of Barnet* [1983] JPL 544. Finally, in *Gill v Secretary of State for the Environment* [1985] JPL 710, it was accepted without argument that General Development Order rights could in appropriate circumstances be overridden by conditions.

Permission granted by the GDO is subject to any relevant exception, limitation or condition specified in Sch 2 (GDO, art 3(2)), The courts have already held with respect to the previous GDO that where a limitation is exceeded—as for example, by the extension of a house by an amount exceeding that permitted by the GDO—the whole development, and not just the excess, is unauthorised.[1] This is made even more clear by the way the present classes are worded as the classes set out descriptions of 'Development not permitted.' Such descriptions presumably cover both limitations and exceptions. The difference between a limitation and an exception is not made plain and this could be important for the operation of s 23(8); see p 146 above.

There is a condition imposed on all permitted development restricting 'hazardous activity' as defined and it is also provided that the GDO is not to permit any development which involves, or is likely to involve, the laying or construction of a notifiable pipeline or the presence of a notifiable quantity of a hazardous substance or, where a hazardous substance is already on the land in a notifiable quantity, development which would, or is likely to, lead to a more than three-fold increase in the amount present (GDO arts 3(7) (8) (9) and 10).[2] The Housing and Planning Act 1986 provides for a separate system of control over hazardous substances and new regulations under that Act are being prepared. When these regulations come into force the hazardous substances provisions of art 3(7) will be amended (see circular 22/88, para 31 and ch 18 below).

The order also provides that, apart from development permitted by pts 9, 11 and 13, it does not authorise any development which requires or involves the formation, laying out or material widening of a means of access to an existing highway which is a trunk or classified road, or creates an obstruction to the views of persons using any highway used by vehicular traffic, so as to be likely to cause danger to such persons (art 3(5)). This is expressed as a limitation rather than as a condition and so the whole development would be unauthorised if this restriction is broken. It may also be noted that the way the last provision is worded makes it difficult to know if a development is or is not authorised.

The 1988 order expressly stated that references to 'the use of land for a specified purpose' does not include references to the use of land without planning permission or in contravention of previous planning control (art 1(4)). This was a new provision and would appear to be intended to make clear that the right to change uses set out in pt 3 of Sch 2 does not apply when the base use is unlawful.[3] The new provision as drafted excluded uses which were implemented without planning permission but were nevertheless lawful either because the use does not require permission, as with agricultural uses, or because it was instituted before 1st July 1948. The Town and Country Planning General Development (Amendment) Order 1989 has remedied this

---

1 See, for example, *Garland v Minister of Housing and Local Government* (1968) 67 LGR 77, 20 P & CR 93; *Rochdale Metropolitan Borough Council v Simmonds* (1980) 40 P & CR 432; and *Ewen Developments Ltd v Secretary of State for the Environment and North Norfolk District Council* [1980] JPL 404.
2 As to the measuring of 'notifiable pipeline' and hazardous substance, see art 1(1) of the GDO.
3 This was already the view taken by the courts; see *Young v Secretary of State for the Environment* (1983) 81 LGR 389, CA.

mistake by substituting the reference to 'the use of land without planning permission', by 'used in contravention of Part III of the Act'.

Certain of the classes of 'permitted development' relate to relatively minor sorts of development while others relate to development by public authorities and statutory undertakers, apparently on the assumption that such developments require less scrutiny than the proposals of private developers.[4] The classes of 'permitted development' are mainly expressed in terms of the type of development rather than of its impact on the environment and have been criticised on the ground that they disregard some of the potential planning problems attendant on the changes thus permitted.[5] There are mentioned below those classes of permitted development which appear to be of most general interest.

Part 1 Development within the curtilage[6] of a dwellinghouse

Part 1 is divided up into eight classes, A to H, which all concern operations relating to dwellinghouses. 'Dwellinghouse' is defined to exclude flats.[7] It appears that pt 1 can only apply in relation to premises which are used solely as a dwellinghouse and that it cannot apply to premises with a dual use—for example, for residential and business purposes.[8]

In *Sainty v Minister of Housing and Local Government*[9] the Divisional Court approved the minister's decision that the class 'must refer to a dwellinghouse which is in existence when the operations mentioned in the class are being carried out'. If, therefore, there is no building capable of use, if need be after repair, for ordinary residential purposes,[10] or if the use of a building as a dwellinghouse has been abandoned,[11] the class will not apply. Whether a particular building is a dwellinghouse is largely a question of fact;[12] however, the factors which may be of assistance in answering that question were considered in *Gravesham Borough Council v Secretary of State for the Environment*.[13]

The order does not make clear whether the dwellinghouse must have been erected under a planning permission for the rights under the various classes to apply. Unlike the case with uses, the definition article does not state that references to operations in the order do not include operations carried out in contravention of Part III of the Act or of previous planning control. The failure to do this would indicate that, once it is too late to take enforcement action against an unauthorised dwellinghouse because of the four-year rule, then the full permitted rights under pt 1 apply to such a dwellinghouse.

---

4 See J B McLoughlin *Control and Urban Planning* (Faber & Faber 1973) ch 2.
5 See for example McLoughlin's *Control and Urban Planning* (above).
6 The meaning of curtilage is considered at p 121 above.
7 It does not include a building containing one or more flats or a flat contained within such a building and flat is defined as a 'separate and self-contained premises which is divided horizontally from some other part of the building' (art 1(1)).
8 See *Scurlock v Secretary of State for Wales* (1976) 33P & CR 202, 238 Estates Gazette 47 and appeal decision noted in [1981] JPL 441.
9 (1964) 62 LGR 179, 15 P & CR 432.
10 See, for example, appeal decisions noted in [1977] JPL 258, [1982] JPL 806, and [1984] JPL 282.
11 See, for example, [1979] JPL 117.
12 As to the meaning of 'dwellinghouse' see above, p 122.
13 (1982) 47 P & CR 142, [1983] JPL 307.

Class A   Enlargement improvement or other alteration of a dwellinghouse

The order makes clear that development is not permitted if:

(a) the cubic content of the resulting building would exceed the cubic content of the original dwellinghouse by more than

    (i) in the case of a terraced house[14] or land within a national park, an area of outstanding beauty, an area designated as a conservation area, an area specified for the purposes of s 41(3) of the Wildlife and Countryside Act 1981 or the Broads (art 1(5) land), by 50 cubic metres or 10% whichever is the greater;

    (ii) in any other case, by more than 115 cubic metres or 15% whichever is the greater, subject in either case to a maximum of 115 cubic metres:

    (The order states that the cubic content is ascertained by external measurement);[15]

(b) the part of the building enlarged, improved or altered would exceed in height the highest part of the roof of the original dwelling;

(c) the part of the building enlarged, improved or altered would be nearer to any highway which bounds the curtilage of the dwellinghouse than—

    (i) the part of the original dwellinghouse nearest to that highway;
    or
    (ii) 20 metres,
    whichever is nearest to the highway;

(d) the part of the building enlarged, improved or altered would be within two metres of the boundary of the curtilage of the dwellinghouse and would exceed four metres in height;[16]

(e) the total area of ground covered by buildings within the curtilage (other than the original dwellinghouse) would exceed 50% of the total area of the curtilage (excluding the ground area of the original dwellinghouse);

(f) it would consist of or include installation, alteration or replacement of a satellite antenna;

(g) it would consist of or include the erection of a building within the curtilage of a listed building; or

(h) it would consist of or include an alteration to any part of the roof.

The term 'original' dwellinghouse which is crucial to the class, means either 'the dwellinghouse as existing on 1st July 1948 or in the case of a building built on or after 1st July 1948, as so built.'

The wording in the 1988 order is substantially different from that in the old 1977 order. As well as simplification, several important changes of substance have been made. First, the new wording permits extensions to those parts of a dwellinghouse which face a highway where the extension is not within 20 metres of a highway or where it is no nearer to the highway than the original building (class A(c)). Previously no extensions could project beyond the forwardmost part of any wall fronted on a highway. This created problems as to what amounted to the forwardmost part[17] and what was the line of the

14 Defined by art 1(1) of the GDO.
15 Art 1(1) and see [1983] JPL 67.
16 The wording of paras A1(b) to (d) was amended by the Town and Country Planning General Development (Amendment) Order 1989.
17 In *City of Bradford Metropolitan District Council v Secretary of State for the Environment* (1977) 76 LGR 454, 35 P & CR 387 the court held that the Secretary of State had not erred in holding that a window sill was part of the wall for this purpose.

wall.[18] Second, it is made plain that any extension which takes place within two metres of a boundary and involves development more than four metres above ground level is not permitted. This reverses the effect of *Wandsworth London Borough Council and Khan v Secretary of State for the Environment*[19] where David Widdicombe QC, sitting as a deputy judge, had interpreted the previous wording as allowing extensions more than four metres high when the starting point of the original building was more than four metres high. Third, the relationship between extensions as distinct from outbuildings is rationalised. Outbuildings for the purposes incidental to a dwellinghouse have always been permitted under a separate class; now see class E of Pt 1. The definition of class A provides that the erection of certain types of buildings must be treated as if they were an extension of the dwellinghouse for all purposes of the order. The result is that for such buildings to be permitted they have to come within class A and, once erected, count in calculating the cubic capacity which has been used up. The outbuildings so treated are those whose cubic content exceeds 10 cubic metres and are within the curtilage of the dwellinghouse and within five metres of that dwellinghouse. In the case of dwellinghouses in art 1(5) land (ie land in national parks etc), all outbuildings over 10 cubic metres are included. In addition where a dwellinghouse would be extended to within five metres of an existing building within the same curtilage, the cubic content of that building will also count in calculating the overall cubic content of the extension (class A 3). Fourth, in the case of dwellinghouses in art 1(5) land, cladding of the exterior of the building with stone, artificial stone, timber, plastic or tiles, is not permitted (class A 2). Finally, no buildings can be erected within the curtilage of a listed building.[20]

Since works which do not materially affect the external appearance of a building do not constitute development[1] permission under class A will only be relevant where there is to be an alteration in a building's external appearance.

It can sometimes be difficult to determine whether particular works fall within class A.[2] It does not cover the complete rebuilding of a dwellinghouse; in *Sainty v Minister of Housing and Local Government*[3] the minister's conclusion that 'After a dwellinghouse is demolished that building is no longer capable of being enlarged, improved or altered and is therefore unable to benefit from the general permission contained in the Order' was upheld by the Divisional Court.[4] However, it will not always be easy to draw the line between 'improvement' or 'alteration' (which comes within class A) and

18 In *North West Leicestershire District Council v Secretary of State for the Environment* (1983) 46 P & CR 154 it was held that where a building was built in the form of a L, the L could be treated as one wall and the wall did not have to take a straight line.
19 (1987) 56 P & CR 393, [1988] JPL 483.
20 Such an erection does not require listed building consent; see *Cotswold District Council v Secretary of State for the Environment* (1984) 51 P & CR 139, [1985] JPL 407.
1 1971 Act s 22 (2)(a) (see p 88 above).
2 See, for example, appeal decisions noted in [1969] JPL 92, [1970] JPL 165, [1974] JPL 373, and [1978] JPL 640.
3 (1964) 62 LGR 179, 15 P & CR 432.
4 See too *C W Larkin v Basildon District Council* (1980) 256 Estates Gazette 381, [1980] JPL 407, and appeal decisions noted in [1974] JPL 162 and 555, [1975] JPL 418, [1976] JPL 249 and [1978] JPL 49. Contrast [1979] JPL 332 (appeal decison).

'rebuilding' (which does not).[5] And, as was pointed out by Lord Parker CJ in *Sainty* (above), 'it may well be that it is possible to arrive at what in effect is a new erection by stages, each stage of which can be said to be an improvement.'

Any earlier extension carried out counts against the limits set out in class A, whether or not permitted under the order or by an express grant of permission (Pt 1 I). So you cannot keep on enlarging enlargements. At one time the wording meant that enlargements carried out under express permission did not count and could be ignored but in *Dawson v Secretary of State for the Environment and London Borough of Barnet*[6] Forbes J held that the new wording introduced by the 1981 amendment order made clear that any enlargements counted whether carried out under express permission or without permission at all. Of course once enlargement under class A has been carried out, there is nothing to prevent permission being granted for an enlargement beyond the tolerances in class A. Further it might be possible, having obtained express permission, first to use up the rights under the GDO and then implement the express permission, but it could be strongly argued that in such a case the express permission would be incapable of implementation as it only permitted enlargement of the dwellinghouse *as it existed* at the time of the grant.[7]

In *Wood v Secretary of State for the Environment*[8] it was held that where an addition is made to a building under the GDO permission, that addition takes upon itself the characteristics of the original building in all respects and that accordingly the permitted uses of a conservatory were the same as the permitted uses of the house to which the conservatory had been added as 'permitted development' under the GDO. This means that while normally the extension can only be used for a dwellinghouse use, it could as in *Wood* be used for some other use such as the sale of goods if this was part of the existing use of the dwellinghouse.

Class B and C   Additions or alterations to roofs

Alterations to roofs are excluded from class A of Pt 1 and so are dealt with separately in classes B and C. Class B deals with alterations of roofs which involve enlarging the roof. Roof extensions are only authorised if they don't exceed the highest part of the existing roof or extend beyond the plane of any existing roof slope which fronts any highway. The latter restriction could result in problems of working out which part of the roof fronts a highway.[9] They are also subject to volume limitations—40 cubic metres for terraced houses and 50 cubic metres for other dwellinghouses. Also the same restrictions on exceeding the cubic content of the original dwellinghouse as apply to class A extensions apply to roof extensions and roof extensions count when calculating an extension under class A. No roof extensions are permitted in national parks, areas of outstanding beauty, conservation areas and the Broads (class B 1 (e)).

---

5 See F J B Bourne, 'Dwellinghouses—Rebuild or Permitted Development' [1981] JPL 567 and appeal decisions cited in that article.
6 [1983] JPL 544.
7 See *Pilkington v Secretary of State for the Environment* [1974] 1 All ER 283, [1973] 1 WLR 1527.
8 [1973] 2 All ER 404. [1973] 1 WLR 707.
9 See *North West Leicestershire District Council v Secretary of State for the Environment* (1983) 46 P & CR 154, [1982] JPL 777.

Class C also deals with roof alterations not involving enlargement, which are allowed subject to the shape of the roof not being materially altered. This would permit the replacement of a roof or the insertion of a roof light.

Class D porches

There are limited rights to erect or construct porches outside any external door of a dwellinghouse.

Class E Outbuildings and other facilities incidental to the enjoyment of the dwellinghouse

This class authorises the permission within the curtilage of a dwellinghouse of any building or enclosure[10] or swimming or other pool required for a purpose incidental to the enjoyment of the dwellinghouse. The reference to purposes incidental to the enjoyment of the dwellinghouse (which term was employed in the old class 1.3 in the 1977 order) has always been taken to exclude the erection of buildings to be used for normal living accommodation. Thus the erection of a building to be used as a cocktail bar, a bedroom, bathroom and study would not be purposes incidental to the enjoyment of the dwelling-house but a swimming pool with playroom, sauna, shower, changing and filter room would be so incidental.[11]

Class E does not expressly state that any building has to be physically separate from the main dwellinghouse to be in the class. However, physical separation is an important factor and where the building is built onto and has access to the dwellinghouse, this will be strong evidence that it comes within class A and not class E of Pt 1.[12] Also the new wording in class E specifically excludes developments if 'it relates to a dwelling or a satellite antenna'. 'Relates' is a very vague term and if applied literally could undermine the whole purpose of the class; 'purposes incidental to the enjoyment of the dwellinghouse' could be said to relate to a dwelling. Presumably it indicates that the development should not connect with or be part of the main dwellinghouse and the main residential uses taking place in that dwellinghouse.

Ministerial decisions had already held that swimming pools came within the meaning of buildings or enclosure required for purposes incidental to a dwellinghouse[13] but the 1988 order removes any doubt by specifically including 'swimming or other pool'. As in the old wording 'the keeping of poultry, bees, pet animals, birds or other livestock for the domestic needs or personal enjoyment of the occupants of the dwellinghouse' is expressly included in purposes incidental to the enjoyment of the dwellinghouse (class E 2).

There are the usual restrictions on the size and positioning of development under class E of Pt 1. In particular any part of the development must not be any nearer any highway that bounds the curtilage than the original dwellinghouse unless it is more than 20 metres from that highway (class E 1 (b)). This is in line with the changes to class A and means that development under class E can be effected between the original dwellinghouse and the highway

10 A boundary wall is not an 'enclosure': see [1973] JPL 320.
11 See ministerial decision noted in [1983] JPL 683. In *Emin v Secretary of State for the Environment* [1989] EGCS 16 it was held that archery could be an incidental use and that although the size of the building was a relevant factor it was wrong to ignore all other factors in favour of physical size.
12 See appeal decision noted in [1987] JPL 733 but compare appeal decision noted at [1986] JPL 447 where access could not be reached from within the dwellinghouse.
13 [1986] JPL 306

as long as the development is not within 20 metres of that highway. The building to be provided must not exceed 10 cubic metres in content where any part would be within 5 metres of the dwellinghouse (class E 1 (c)). The height must not exceed four metres in the case of a building with a ridged roof or in any other case three metres (class E 1 (d)). The total ground area covered must not exceed 50% of the total area of the curtilage of the dwellinghouse excluding the ground area of the original dwellinghouse itself (class E 1 (e)). Finally in national parks, areas of outstanding beauty, conservation areas, the Broads or land within the curtilage of listed buildings, the erection of buildings with a cubic content of more than 10 cubic metres is excluded.

Class F Hard surfaces

The provision of a hard surface for any purpose incidental to the enjoyment of the dwellinghouse is authorised within the curtilage. Previously only hardstanding for vehicles was permitted. The present wording extends to other purposes such as the provision of a patio.

Class G Oil storage tanks

Oil storage tanks for domestic heating are authorised within the curtilage of the dwellinghouse subject to certain restrictions on size, height and position (class G 1).

Class H Satellite antenna

The installation, alteration or replacement of one satellite antenna[14] is permitted on a dwellinghouse or within the curtilage of a dwellinghouse subject to restrictions on size and height (class H 1).

Part 2 Minor operations

Part 2 comprises three classes.

Class A permits the erection or construction of gates, fences, walls or other means of enclosure not exceeding one metre in height from ground level where adjacent to a highway used by vehicular traffic or two metres in height in any other case. The 1977 order employed the term 'abutting on a highway' and in *Simmonds v Secretary of State for the Environment and Rochdale Metropolitan District Council*[15] Forbes refused to upset a finding that a fence 'abutted' a highway even though it was between 0.55 and 0.70 metres back from an existing stone wall which lay on the boundary between the curtilage and the highway. The new wording removes any doubt that the erection does not have to touch the highway and it will be a question of fact and degree for the Secretary of State to determine what is and what is not 'adjacent'.

The maintenance, improvement or other alteration of gates etc is also permitted but the present wording provides that the resulting development must not exceed the height of the original or the permitted heights on new constructions, whichever is the greater.

Developments within the curtilage of, or to a gate etc surrounding, a listed building is not permitted.

---

14 Defined by art 1(1) as 'apparatus designed for transmitting microwave radio energy to satellites or receiving it from them'.

15 [1981] JPL 509. Also see *R (on the prosecution of Lewisham Borough Council) v South Eastern Rly Co* (1910) 74 JP 137, 8 LGR 401 and appeal decisions noted in [1969] JPL 526, [1976] JPL 190, [1981] JPL 70, [1982] JPL 129, [1984] JPL 295 and [1985] JPL 501.

The meaning of 'gate, fence, wall or means of enclosure' was considered in *Prengate Properties Ltd v Secretary of State for the Environment*[16] where it was held that the building of a wall is not authorised unless it has some function of enclosure.[17] However, Lord Widgery CJ said that a wall which enclosed did not cease to come within the class just because it carried out some other function such as retaining soil.

Class B authorises the creation of a means of access on to a highway which is not a trunk road or a classified road where that is required in connection with development permitted by any other class in the order except class A of Pt 2. This access could be provided for a farm building permitted under Pt 6.

Class C grants permission for the painting or colouring of the exterior of any building or works otherwise than for the purpose of advertising, announcement or direction.

Part 3 Changes of use

This class utilises the Use Classes Order 1987 to allow certain changes from one class to another. The rationale is that all those changes so permitted are changes *up* in the sense that the use changed to is considered to be less problematic in planning terms than the original use and there is no provision for a right to change back.

However, as pointed out on p 146 above the decision in *Cynon Valley Borough Council v Secretary of State for Wales*[18] may have provided a means of changing back by way of s 23(8) when the change is temporary.

The changes now authorised (which are set out in classes A to D of Pt 3) are:

Change Permitted—

By GDO Class	From UCO Class	To UCO Class
A	A3 (food and drink)	A1 (shops)
A	Sale of motor vehicles	A1 (shops)
B(a)	B2 (general industrial)	B1 (business)
B(a)	B8 (storage and distribution)	B1 (business)*
B(b)	B1 (business)	B8 (storage and distribution)*
B(b)	B2 (general industrial)	B8 (storage and distribution)*
C	A3 (food and drink) Premises within A2	A2 (financial and professional)
D	(professional and financial) with display window at ground floor level.	A1 (shops)

*not permitted where change of use relates to more than 235 square metres of floor space in the building.

This represents a substantial lessening of control as, prior to the 1988 order, changes from A3 (food and drinks) to A2 (professional and financial

---

16 (1973) 71 LGR 373, 25 P & CR 311.
17 But see also *Ewen Developments Ltd v Secretary of State for the Environment and North Norfolk District Council* [1980] JPL 404 where Lord Widgery CJ refused to upset the conclusion of an inspector that earth embankments were not 'means of enclosure' even though they went in a round circle and produced an enclosure.
18 (1986) 85 LGR 36, [1986] JPL 760, CA.

services) and from A2 to A1 (shops) were not permitted. The restriction on the amount of space that could be changed on a change from B2 (general business) to B1 (business) has been dropped.

In *Young v Secretary of State for the Environment*[19] it was held that the base use has to be lawful for a change under this type of class to be authorised. This qualification has been put beyond dispute by the new definition in the 1988 order that use of land does not include a use of land in contravention of Part III of the Act or of previous planning control (art 1(4)).

A new concept of the flexible planning permission is introduced by class E of Pt 3. This applies where an express grant of permission, following an application made after 5th December 1988, has authorised two types of use. It will now be possible to implement one of those uses and then to change from that use to the other use. This change is not authorised unless it takes place within 10 years of the express grant of permission and of course the first use would have had to have been implemented within five years of the grant otherwise the permission would have lapsed under s 41 of the 1971 Act. From the wording of class E of Pt 3 only one change is authorised, so it would not be possible to make another change to a different use specified in the permission or to change back to the original use implemented. However there would seem to be nothing in the wording to prevent a grant of planning permission specifying three or more uses and giving the developer a choice as to whether to change from use A to use B or C or D.

Part 4 Temporary buildings and uses

Class A permits the erection of temporary buildings, moveable structures, works, plant or machinery in connection with and for the duration of all operations (except mining operations) for which permission has been granted or deemed to be granted.[1] This permission is subject to conditions requiring removal and reinstatement once the operations have been carried out.

Class B permits the use of land (other than a building or the curtilage of a building) for any purpose except as a caravan site[2] on not more than 28 days in total in any calendar year and the erection on the land of any moveable structure for the purposes of that use. In the case of the holding of markets, motor car and motor cycle racing (including trials of speed and practising) the use can only be carried out on a total of 14 days in any calendar year.

The benefit of this permission is not available to a person intending to use a site on a permanent basis—eg as a permanent market once every fortnight or so. A permanent use of land and a temporary casual use for up to 14 or 28 days in any year are quite different things; the main test would seem to be the subjective one of the developer's intention.[3] In a case where substantial works

19 (1983) 47 P & CR 165, CA.
1 The meaning of an earlier but similar provision was considered in *Sunbury-on-Thames UDC v Mann* (1958) 56 LGR 235, 9 P & CR 309 and *Brown v Hayes and Harlington UDC* (1963) 62 LGR 66.
2 Temporary use as a caravan site is dealt with in Pt 18.
3 See *Miller-Mead v Minister of Housing and Local Government* [1963] 2 QB 196, [1963] 1 All ER 459 and *Tidswell v Secretary of State for the Environment and Thurrock Borough Council* [1976] 34 P & CR 152. Also see *South Bucks District Council v Secretary of State for the Environment* [1989] JPL 351.

of a permanent nature were necessary before land could be used for car racing and it was intended that the racing should be a permanent feature with a planned programme of up to twenty-eight meetings a year, the minister concluded that such a use could not be said to be of a temporary nature and held that the general permission granted by the GDO was not available.[4]

The main changes introduced by the 1988 order were the reduction in the number of the days land can be used for clay pigeon shooting from 28 to 14 (now reversed by the 1989 Amendment Order) and the clarification of what is meant by motor car and motor cycle racing.

Part 5 Caravan sites

This contains two classes, formerly classes XXII and XXIII of the 1977 order.

Class A permits the use of land other than a building as a caravan site in certain cases where a site licence is not required under the Caravan Sites and Control of Development Act 1960.[5]

Class B grants permission for development required by the conditions of a site licence issued under the Caravan Sites and Control of Development Act 1960 and in force.

Part 6 Agricultural buildings and operations

This is the most controversial of all the permitted developments and its interpretation has been a source of constant appeals to the Minister and litigation in the courts. The wording in the 1977 order was repeatedly amended and the present wording represents a substantial recasting.

For both class A and C of Pt 6, the land on which the development is carried out must be 'agricultural land'. This is defined as 'land, which before development permitted by this Part is carried out, is land in use for agriculture and which is so used for the purposes of a trade or business and excludes any dwellinghouse or garden.' This is a new definition and it overrules judicial decisions which held that a house and a garden could be used for agriculture.[6] In *Jones v Stockport Metropolitan Borough Council*[7] the Court of Appeal held that there must be an existing agricultural use and a prospective use is not sufficient. This was in relation to the wording in the 1977 order but the same would apply to the present wording. 'Agriculture' used to be defined by reference to the Agriculture Act 1947 but there is now no express definition of agriculture in the 1988 order and so the definition of agriculture in the 1971 Act would apply.[8] The need for the land to be used 'for the purposes of a trade or business' applied in the 1977 order and in *South Oxfordshire District Council v East*,[9] Simon Brown J held that factors, such as whether the occupier had a full-time job elsewhere and whether the accounts showed a loss, were relevant but not conclusive. However, in

---

4 'Selected Enforcement and Allied Appeals' p 27 and [1976] JPL 113.
5 These are set out in para 2 to 10 of Sch 1 to that Act but in relation to para 10 do not include use for winter quarters. These are in the main temporary and minor uses.
6 See *Hancock v Secretary of State for the Environment* (1988) 57 P & CR 140, [1989] JPL 99, CA; *Tyack v Secretary of State for the Environment and Cotswold District Council* (1988) 57 P & CR 140, [1989] JPL 99, CA.
7 (1983) 50 P & CR 299, [1984] JPL 274.
8 See s 290(1) and p 123 above.
9 (1987) 56 P & CR 112, [1987] JPL 868.

Mackay v Secretary of State for the Environment[10] Bernard Marder QC, sitting as a deputy judge, held that the fact that a farming enterprise resulted in very little profit was not to the point in determining whether it was a trade or business: we would suggest that the two cases are compatible on their particular facts. It is undoubtedly true that trades and businesses can be carried out at a loss but nevertheless the profitability of an enterprise can be evidence as to whether the main purpose is business or recreation.

In *East* Simon Brown J also concluded that land did not not have to be exclusively used for agriculture to be 'agricultural land' and could be used for a mixed purpose of agriculture and some other use.

Part 6 is divided into 3 classes. We now address each in turn.

Class A   Building and engineering operations

This permits the carrying out on agricultural land comprised in an agricultural unit of building, or excavation or engineering operations reasonably necessary for the purposes of agriculture within that unit. These rights are subject to several important restrictions but first it is necessary to consider the scope of what is being permitted.

The 1977 order (and its predecessors) had used the word 'requisite' rather than 'reasonably necessary' but it would seem that the courts had already accepted that 'reasonably necessary or reasonably required' was what was meant by requisite.[11] So the change, while making the class more comprehensible has not really altered the substantive sense. In *Jones v Stockport Metropolitan Borough Council*[12] the Court of Appeal accepted that there was no basis for implying a limitation, that the use of the building must be ancillary to the use of the parts of the land which the building is not covering, or that the use of the building must be in some way dependent on the use of the rest of the land. This means, as Purchas LJ accepted, that as in the case of intensive horticulture or intensive breeding all or most of the activity would be in the building erected.[13] The wording in the 1988 order would not seem to have altered this. What the new wording makes clear is that what is reasonably necessary is to be determined by reference to the whole 'agricultural unit' and not just the 'agricultural land' on which the building is being erected. However, this would not prevent a building being necessary for an agricultural unit, where all the activity was focused in the building itself, as long as that activity was agricultural.

In this regard it is important to note that 'agricultural unit' is defined as 'agricultural land which is occupied as a unit for the purpose of farming and includes dwellings which are either occupied by farmworkers or are occupied

---

10 [1989] JPL 590.
11 See *Jones v Stockport Metropolitan District Council* (1983) 50 P & CR 299, [1984] JPL 274 and *Mackay v Secretary of State for the Environment* [1989] JPL 590.
12 (1983) 50 P & CR 299, 269 Estates Gazette 408.
13 See, for example, the appeal decisions reported in [1977] JPL 47, [1981] JPL 604, and [1982] JPL 126 and 584; and see J H Dolman 'Agricultural Permitted Development—Intensive Livestock Units' [1981] JPL 795; F J B Bourne, 'Class VI Again' [1982] JPL 423; and F J B Bourne, 'Class VI—Yet Again' [1983] JPL 156. Also see ministerial decisions reported in [1986] JPL 231. There it was held that in determining whether a building was reasonably necessary or reasonably required for the purposes of agriculture 'the only matters to be considered are those which stem from the inter-relationship between the land and the building and that wider issues are excluded'.

by the farmer for the purpose of farming' (class A3(2)). An agricultural unit can therefore comprise many thousands of acres split up into different physical parcels. In *Fuller v Secretary of State for the Environment*[14] Stuart Smith J rejected the argument that the 'agricultural unit' had to be equated with the planning unit and held that an 'agricultural unit' could comprise several separate planning units because of geographical features.[15] This could be important as, for example, a building for the storage of grain for the whole agricultural unit could come within class A as 'reasonably necessary' for the 'purposes of agriculture within that unit'. Yet if the question were to be looked at in terms of the smaller planning units the grain storage might be judged to be an independent storage use and so a material change of use from agriculture to storage.[16]

In judging whether a building is reasonably necessary, it has been held that the size of the building is not relevant but that it is relevant that the form or design of the building makes it not reasonably capable of being used for agricultural purposes.[17] However, in that case it was accepted that the building was necessary for the poultry-keeping operation and it was the disparity between the size of the building and the size of the holding which was held not to be relevant. It is submitted that size would be relevant where the building was far larger than was necessary for the proposed purpose.

In the case of excavation and engineering operations the main problem has been in relation to the filling in of farming land with waste material. This could be viewed as reasonably necessary to make the land fit for agriculture or as being carried out for a non-agricultural purpose. In *MacPherson v Secretary of State for Scotland*[18] the Court of Session held that in determining whether the works were reasonably necessary the developer's opinion as to whether particular works were 'requisite' for agriculture may carry little or no weight; the test is an objective one. In *MacPherson* it had been contended on appeal to the Secretary of State that a proposal to tip approximately 1.5 million cubic metres of demolition material on a twenty acre site, and thus to fill a glen to an average depth of twenty metres, was requisite for agricultural purposes in that it would ultimately provide a higher quality of grazing land. Lord Cameron (with whom Lords Grieve and Wylie agreed) held that in determining the appeal the reporter had applied his mind to the right question—whether these engineering operations were reasonably necessary for the use of the land for agriculture—and that in concluding that the operations did not fall within the ambit of class VI (1) the reporter had properly taken account of the scale of the operation, the time over which it would extend, and the absence of any explanation of the need for such a depth of infilling.

In *Northavon District Council v Secretary of State for the Environment*[19] Donaldson LJ upheld a decision that drainage works came within class VI

---

14 (1987) 56 P & CR 84, [1987] JPL 854.
15 Ch 5, p 96.
16 If the building were taken to be permitted under class A of Pt 6, it might have the user rights for the purpose for which it is designed; see s 33(2), unless it was taken that class A only permitted the building to be used for agricultural purposes in which case the storage used would be unauthorised.
17 *Mackay v Secretary of State for the Environment* [1989] JPL 590.
18 1985 SLT 134.
19 (1980) 40 P & CR 332.

even though the works involved the disposal of a considerable amount of builder's rubble. He, however, went on to state that to come within the Class it would have to be shown that the object of the exercise was genuinely to improve the quality of the land and not to make money out of providing a last resting place for rubbish.[20]

As the *Northavon* case itself reveals, the two questions as to whether works constitute 'engineering operations' and whether these operations are then requisite for the use of the land for agriculture, are often blurred together. However, even if the minister is satisfied that the works are requisite for agriculture, it may well be that works do not constitute engineering operations and are 'other operations'. As 'other operations' were not referred to in class VI this meant that operations that fell short of building or engineering operations were excluded.[1] However, the 1988 order extends permission to excavations which could cover certain operations, which fall short of being engineering operations. Development was also excluded from the class where the construction of a reservoir, although reasonably necessary for agricultural purposes, involved considerable mining which could not be said to be ancillary to the engineering operation of the construction of the reservoir.[2] Again the employment of the word 'excavation' in the 1988 order will probably authorise the construction of a reservoir which involves substantial excavation of material. In practice the planning problems which arose from the deposit and excavation of materials have been eliminated by the requirement (imposed in 1986 but incorporated in the 1988 order) that development is only authorised if no waste materials[3] are brought onto the land from elsewhere and the minerals extracted are not moved off the land.

As stated previously, the permitted development rights are hedged around with restrictions and conditions. The most important are summarised below.

The development is not permitted if the development would be carried out on agricultural land of less than 0.4 hectare in acre. With regard to the 1977 order the Court of Appeal has held that in calculating the 0.4 hectare, the farmhouse and garden could be taken into account as long as it was used for agricultural purposes and was not separated from the rest of the land by some distinguishing feature, such as a made up public road.[4] The wording in the 1988 order now makes plain that 'agricultural land' does not include the farmhouse and its garden. Further, in calculating the 0.4 hectare two separate parcels cannot be added together (class A 3 (1) (a)). The word parcel is not defined in the order but circular 22/88 indicates that land separated by a road could be treated as two parcels. In *Hancock v Secretary of State for the*

---

20 In a number of appeals the minister has held that the tipping of materials on land did not amount to an engineering operation and was therefore outside the scope of this class—see, for example, [1978] JPL 494, [1980] JPL 348, [1981] JPL 135, [1983] JPL 618 and [1985] JPL 131. Contrast, however, *Fayrewood Fish Farms Ltd v Secretary of State for the Environment and Hampshire* [1984] JPL 267; and appeal decisions noted in [1979] JPL 118, [1982] JPL 263, and [1983] JPL 561.
1 See, for example, ministerial decision noted at [1981] JPL 135.
2 See *West Bowers Farm Products v Essex County Council* (1985) 50 P & CR 368, [1985] JPL 857 and *South Oxfordshire District Council v Secretary of State for the Environment* (1985) 52 P & CR 1, [1986] JPL 435.
3 In the ministerial decision noted at [1988] JPL 663 clay soil brought in to improve the agricultural quality of land was held not to be 'waste material', but compare another ministerial decision noted at [1989] JPL 379, where it was held that surplus material excavated by builders was 'waste material' even though it was principally soil.
4 See *Hancock v Secretary of State for the Environment* (1988) 57 P & CR 140, [1989] JPL 99, CA.

Environment[5] Glidewell LJ coined the phrase 'primary area' which he described as 'an area of land with boundaries defined in some reasonably clear way'. By boundaries he meant physical barriers, not lines on a map. This would seem to be the equivalent of a parcel of land. The consequence is that buildings and engineering works cannot be carried out on tiny small-holdings, allotments or small pieces of agricultural land.

The erection, extension or alteration of dwellinghouses is excluded and the buildings, structures and works must be designed for the purposes of agriculture (class A 1 (b) and (c)). With respect to the latter point, it is not uncommon for buildings which look remarkably like dwellings to be intended for agricultural purposes. In *Belmont Farm Ltd v Minister of Housing and Local Government*[6] it was held that a building 'designed' for the purposes of agriculture meant one so designed 'in the sense of its physical appearance and layout': on that test an aircraft hangar was not a building designed for agricultural purposes.

In *Harding v Secretary of State for the Environment and Bridgnorth District Council*[7] the *Belmont* approach was followed in distinction to *Wilson v West Sussex County Council*[8] where in the context of s 33(2) 'designed' was equated with 'intended' rather than 'architectural design suitable for a particular use'. David Widdicombe QC, giving the judgment said that:

'The purpose of class VI was to permit agricultural buildings which will be put up in the countryside and the purpose was to secure that buildings in the countryside shall look like farm buildings and not like dwellinghouses or aircraft hangars or something else. There was a reason why the draftsman had used the word "designed" in class VI.'

In that case an extension to a dwellinghouse which was identical in appearance to the dwellinghouse had been held not to be designed for agricultural purposes, even though it was purportedly intended as a milking parlour for cows.[9] The buildings, structure or works created must generally (the restriction does not apply to fences[10]) not cover more than 465 square metres, if within three kilometres of the perimeter of an aerodrome, not exceed three metres in height or in any other case, 12 metres or be within 25 metres of the metalled portion of a trunk or classified road.

An important restriction introduced by the 1988 order excludes the construction of livestock units and associated structures such as slurry tanks and lagoons when erected within 400 metres of the curtilage of 'protected buildings' (class A 1 (j)). 'Protected buildings' are defined as any permanent buildings, normally occupied by people, which would cover dwellings, schools, hospitals and offices. However, buildings within the agricultural unit (which can include farm dwellings) and special industrial buildings covered by classes B3-B7 of the UCO are excluded (class A 3 (2)). It would be

---

5 Ibid.
6 (1962) 60 LGR 319, 13 P & CR 417.
7 [1984] JPL 503.
8 [1963] 2 QB 764, [1963] 1 All ER 751, (1964) 14 P & CR 301.
9 See also *Mackay v Secretary of State for the Environment* [1989] JPL 590, appeal decisions noted in [1978] JPL 867, [1981] JPL 129, and [1982] JPL 55.
10 But it does apply to earthworks used for accommodating livestock.

relatively easy to get round this restriction by constructing some other kind of agricultural building and then converting it later to livestock use. However, there is a condition imposed on class A which prohibits the use of any resulting building, structure, excavation or works for the accommodation of livestock or the storage of slurry or sewage sludge within five years, if the development is within 400 metres of the curtilage of a protected building.

Other conditions, as related, prevent waste being brought onto the land or minerals being taken off and there are special conditions relating to national parks and specified areas of land (art 1(6) land) which conditions give the local planning authority the power to determine the siting, design and external appearance of agricultural buildings permitted and the siting and construction of private ways under class A.

Class B Winning and working of minerals

The winning and working of minerals is permitted on land held or occupied for the purposes of agriculture where the minerals are reasonably necessary for agricultural purposes. This is expressly provided to include fertilising land and the maintenance, improvement or alteration of agricultural buildings, structures or works. There is a restriction on excavation within 25 metres of the metalled portion of a trunk or classified road and the movement of minerals off the agricultural unit.

Class C Fish farming

This provision was originally introduced in 1986 and was necessary because of the restriction in class A on removing minerals from the land. It seems that some fish farmers might not have sufficient land to store minerals extracted in the course of creating new fish ponds. The production of fish for food is an agricultural use of land[11] and the construction of a fish pond can amount to an excavation or engineering operation.[12] Class C authorises the construction of fish ponds and other engineering operations on land not exceeding two hectares for any business of fish farming or shellfish farming which has been registered under an order made under s 7 of the Diseases of Fish Act 1983. Circular 3/86 explains how the system of registration works. No operations can be carried out within 25 metres of the metalled portion of a trunk or classified road. Where the operations involve the winning and working of minerals, no excavation may exceed a depth of 2.5 metres and the area of excavation, taken with any other excavations carried out on the land within two years, must not exceed 0.2 hectares.

Development which comes within class C is excluded from class A but class A could allow the construction of fish ponds where the site was larger than two hectares or where for some other reason class C did not apply.

Part 7 Forestry buildings and works

This part is similar to Pt 6 and authorises building operations and other operations which are reasonably necessary for the purposes of forestry including afforestation. The 1988 order, as well as replacing 'requisite' with

---

11 See appeal decision noted at [1980] JPL 480.
12 See *Fayrewood Fish Farms v Secretary of State for the Environment and Hampshire* [1984] JPL 267.

'reasonably necessary', makes clear that development rights, while they extend to 'other operations' do not include engineering or mining operations. However, specifically included are the formation, alteration or maintenance of private ways and operations to obtain the materials for such works. This will cover works which would normally be considered to be engineering or mining operations (see chapter 5).

The permitted development is subject to the standard restrictions and, as with Pt 6, in the case of art 1(6) land (national parks and other specified areas), there are special conditions (class A 2).

Part 8 Industrial and warehouse development

Under this Part permission is granted for the carrying out of specified types of development to industrial buildings,[13] land and warehouses. This includes (subject to certain limitations) extension or alteration of buildings,[14] installation of machinery,[15] sewers, mains, pipes, cables or other apparatus and private ways, and the deposit of waste materials.

The present wording makes clear that with regard both to warehousing and industrial premises, parking and turning areas should not be reduced as a result of development. It is also made clear that the creation of a hardstanding is permitted development. Development at a mine,[16] and the deposit of waste resulting from the winning and working of minerals is now excluded from this class. Development by mineral undertakers and waste at a mine are dealt with in Pts 19 and 21.

Part 19 Development ancillary to mining operations

Class A grants permission for a limited range of development to be carried out without the prior approval of the mineral planning authority. The development may only be carried out on 'land used as a mine' and development at underground mines will be restricted to the approved site as defined in para D 1. The development must be for purposes in connection with the winning and working of minerals brought to the surface at the mine or for treatment, storage or removal of such minerals. There are a number of other limitations including constraints on height and floorspace.

Class B grants permission for a wider range of development subject to the prior approval of the mineral planning authority. Under this class development may be carried out on land used as a mine and on ancillary mining land

---

13 An industrial building means a building used for the carrying out of an industrial process (which is in turn defined in art 1(1)) and includes docks, harbours or quays but not buildings on land in or adjacent to and occupied together with a mine. Industrial land is similarly defined.

14 So long as the height of the 'original building' is not exceeded, the cubic content is not exceeded by more than 25% or the aggregate floor space by more than 1,000 square metres, and the operations do not materially affect the external appearance of the premises. As to the meaning of 'original building' see p 154 above—and appeal decisions noted in [1982] JPL 457; and [1984] JPL 199. In the case of national parks, areas of outstanding natural beauty, conservation areas and the Broads the cubic content must not be exceeded by 10%.

15 See in this regard *South Glamorgan County Council v Hobbs (Quarries) Ltd* (1980) 253 Estates Gazette 1014 as to the problem of the relationship between the old classes VIII and XIX (2).

16 'Mine' and mining operations are defined in art 1(1). Note *English Clays Lovering Pochin Ltd v Plymouth Corpn* [1973] 2 All ER 730, [1973] 1 WLR 1346; affd [1974] 2 All ER 239, [1974] 1 WLR 742 as to the meaning of the former term 'mineral undertaker' used in class XIX.

except at underground mines where it is again restricted to the approved site. Because the prior approval of the authority is required, there are fewer restrictions on the development and permission extends to development in connection with the preparation for sale, consumption or utilisation of the minerals brought to the surface at the mine.

Both classes A and B are subject to conditions that, unless otherwise agreed by the mineral planning authority, the development should be removed within 24 months of the end of mining operations and that the land should be restored to its condition before the development took place.

Class C introduces a permission to enable maintenance or safety works to be carried out at a mine or disused mine subject to the prior approval of the mineral planning authority. There is no restriction on the permitted site for such development. Development may be carried out without the prior approval of the mineral planning authority if the conditions set out in paragraph C2 are satisfied.

Development by British Coal Corporation is dealt with in Pt 20.

Part 27 Use by members of certain recreational organisations

This Part permits the use of land, but not of buildings or land within the curtilage of a dwellinghouse, by organisations holding certificates of exemption under s 269 of the Public Health Act 1936. At present these organisations are the Boys' Brigade, Scout Association, Girl Guides, Salvation Army, Church Lads' Brigade, National Council of the YMCA, Army Cadet Forces Association, Caravan Club, Camping and Caravan Club and London Union of Youth Clubs. The use permitted is for the purposes of recreation or instruction and the erection or placing of tents on the land for the purposes of that use.

Directions restricting permitted development

Either the Secretary of State or a local planning authority may, by a direction under art 4 of the GDO direct that permission granted by art 3 of the GDO is not to apply (a) to all or any development specified in Sch 2 to the GDO (other than class B of Pt 22 or class C of Pt 23); or (b) to any particular development falling within Sch 2.

The making and effects of such a direction are considered in chapter 15, but it may be noted here that circular 22/88 (introducing the 1988 GDO) includes an appendix on art 4 directions. This, appendix D, points out that permitted development rights have been endorsed by Parliament and they should not be withdrawn locally without compelling reasons.

Special development orders

The Secretary of State is empowered by s 24 of the 1971 Act to make special development orders, applicable only to such land as is specified in the order. In *Essex County Council v Minister of Housing and Local Government*[17] it was held that in making a special development order the minister acts in a purely administrative capacity and is not, therefore, obliged to hear objections before making the order.[18]

17 (1967) 66 LGR 23 18 P & CR 531.
18 However, now see *Council of Civil Service Unions v Minister for the Civil Service* [1985] AC 374, [1984] 3 All ER 935 which would suggest that circumstances could give rise to a right to be consulted.

Special development orders have been made for various purposes. They have been used to vary the effect of the GDO with regard to particularly sensitive areas. Thus there were special orders relating to national parks, areas of outstanding natural beauty and conservation areas where the classes of permitted development were more tightly drawn. However, the amendment of s 24 by the Housing and Planning Act 1986[19] enabled the 1988 GDO to be drawn up in such a way as to incorporate these specially sensitive areas.

More controversially, occasionally special orders have been used to grant permission for specific developments and in this way have removed the opportunity for a local public inquiry.[1] Finally, special orders have been used to grant permission for development in the areas of new town development corporations and urban development corporations, provided the development accords with a scheme of development which has been approved by the Secretary of State.[2]

D DESIGNATION OF ENTERPRISE ZONES AND SIMPLIFIED PLANNING ZONES

Certain categories of development may be granted planning permission by way of an order designating an enterprise zone or a simplified planning zone (see p 272 below).

19 See s 49 and Sch 11, para 2 (1).
1 See the orders relating to Windscale, Vauxhall Cross and the potential sites for the disposal of radioactive waste.
2 See s 7(1) of the New Towns Act 1981 and s 148(2) of the Local Government, Planning and Land Act 1980.

CHAPTER 7

CONTROL OF DEVELOPMENT 1: PLANNING APPLICATIONS

Introduction

Unless granted in one of the ways mentioned above, planning permission must be obtained from the local planning authority (or the Secretary of State) before any particular development of land can be carried out (1971 Act s 23(1)). It is this case by case consideration of development proposals that gives the British planning system its flexibility.

Development control—the day to day control exercised by planning authorities over the development of land—is that part of the local planning system with which the individual citizen, whether as landowner, developer or affected neighbour, is most likely to come in contact. Development control is also, as McAuslan says,[1] 'the major area for legal expertise in the planning process'. 'The law', continues McAuslan, 'may be said to be concerned with three things here: (i) it sets out a procedure to be followed for the seeking of, and the giving of decisions on, planning permissions; (ii) it sets out the limits within which planning controls operate and is therefore inevitably involved in making decisions on whether these limits have been overstepped; and (iii) it provides mechanisms and remedies for legal challenges to the process if people feel aggrieved with it.'

However, as McAuslan cautions, just because the role of the law is important here, one should guard against assuming that it is all-important. Matters such as the detailed operation of development control in practice, the variety in local authority practice, and questions about the objectives and impact of development control are important but are beyond the scope of this work.[2] However, although this and the following three chapters are mainly concerned with statutory procedures and the controls exercised by the courts over the decision-making activities of local planning authorities, it is worthy of mention that in recent years there has been a growth of general interest in and criticism of the role of development control. As one commentator put it:[3] 'Indeed, from being the Cinderella of the [town planning] profession, development control has become a fully paid up ugly sister in the eyes of many of its critics.' Criticisms flow around the extent of the control, the delays caused by the control and the lack of public participation in the decision-making. Not all of these criticisms can be reconciled. More consultation must hamper efforts to eliminate delays, while

---

1 Patrick McAuslan, *Land, Law and Planning* (Weidenfeld and Nicolson, 1975), p 350.
2 For consideration of such matters see, for example. J B McLoughlin, *Control and Urban Planning* (Faber, 1973); J Underwood. *Development Control: A Review of Research and Current Issues* (Pergamon Press, 1981); and M L Harrison, 'Development Control: the Influence of Political, Legal and Ideological Factors' (1972) 43 T P Rev 254.
3 H W E Davies, 'The Relevance of Development Control' (1980) 51 T P Rev 7.

a diminution in the activities which require permission or a streamlining of the procedures can lead to a cutting out of third party rights. In recent years, the emphasis has been on deregulation and speed. The White Paper 'Building Businesses, Not Barriers',[4] published in May 1986, argued that:

'Wherever possible development should be encouraged, recognising that there is always a presumption in its favour, unless that development would cause demonstrable harm to interests of acknowledged importance. The planning system should also be simplified and made more efficient. This does not mean that it will be dismantled. It will be maintained and strengthened where careful control is warranted.' (para 5.2 of the White Paper)

From the point of view of the courts, the most difficult question is the legal consequences of a failure to comply with a statutory procedure. It now seems that the courts will not try to distinguish between mandatory and directory procedures but will apply a more flexible approach. In *R v Lambeth London Borough Council ex p Sharp*,[5] Croom-Johnson L J stated:

'When the provisions of such regulations were contravened, almost invariably it was unhelpful to consider what were the consequences of non-compliance with the regulations by classifying them as containing mandatory or directory provisions, or as containing a condition precedent, or as containing a provision which rendered a decision void or voidable, or by considering whether they contain a provision which goes to jurisdiction. What had to be considered was: what was the particular provision designed to achieve? If, as here, it was designed to give the public an opportunity to make objections to what was proposed, then the court was bound to attach considerable importance to any failure to comply with the requirements.'

Application for planning permission

Although a person proposing to carry out development may well have had preliminary discussions with the local planning authority about his proposals (and circular 28/1983 draws local authorities' attention to the need for early informal discussions with applicants and their agents), it is the formal application for planning permission that sets the statutory machinery of development control in motion.

An application may be made for planning permission simpliciter (ie full permission) or for outline permission; the former will include details of the proposed development[6] whereas, in a case where it is desired to obtain a decision in principle on a proposal to carry out building operations, an application for outline permission, which need only be accompanied by a site plan, may be made (below). In either case the principle of the development is placed in issue.

4 Cmnd 9794.
5 (1984) 50 P & CR 284, [1986] JPL 201.
6 However, even though full details have been submitted, the local planning authority may, of their own initiative, impose a condition requiring that the authority's subsequent approval be obtained in regard to specified matters (see p 181 below).

An application for planning permission is to be made to the local planning authority in whose area the development is to take place. This will normally be the district planning authority but where the application appears to relate to a county matter, a copy should be sent to the county planning authority.[7] Of course in the Greater London and metropolitan areas, all planning applications are determined by the districts and the London Boroughs; see chapter 2. The procedure for applying for planning permission is now set out in separate regulations. This used to be set out in the GDO but it seems s 25 requires free standing regulations and these are now to be found in the Town and Country Planning (Applications) Regulations 1988 (the 1988 regulations). Application is to be made on a form issued by and obtainable from the local planning authority and is to include the particulars required by that form: the application is to be accompanied by a plan sufficient to identify the land to which it relates and by such other plans and drawings as are necessary to describe the proposed development, together with such additional number of copies (not exceeding three) of the form and plans as may be required by the local planning authority (reg 3(1) of the 1988 regulations).

The local planning authority may direct the applicant to supply further information and may require the production of evidence to verify any information required (reg 4 of the 1988 regulations).

Where development for which planning permission was granted has not yet commenced and the time limit within which development must be begun or within which an application for approval of reserved matters must be submitted (see p 261 below) has not yet expired, a fresh application for planning permission for that development may be made without submission of the detail required in the initial application (reg 3(3)). All that is required is that the application be made in writing and provide sufficient information to enable the authority to identify the previous grant of permission.

Application for planning permission may be made in respect of buildings or works constructed or carried out, or a use of land instituted, before the date of the application, whether the buildings or works were constructed or carried out, or the use instituted, without planning permission or in accordance with planning permission granted for a limited period (1971 Act, s 32(1)(a) and (2)). Application may also be made to retain buildings or works or continue the use of land without complying with a condition subject to which a previous permission was granted (1971 Act, s 32(1)(b)). The Housing and Planning Act 1986 has also created a new s 31A which provides for applications to revoke conditions attached to a planning permission.[8] On such an application the local planning authority can only consider the desirability of the condition but the authority has the power to impose different conditions as well as upholding or revoking the condition. This means that instead of appealing against a condition an applicant will be able instead to make a s 31A application; the advantage being that the applicant will not risk losing the permission altogether as could happen with an appeal. Section 31A does not apply to permissions which have expired and presumably the s 32(1)(b) procedure will still apply exclusively to permissions which have been implemented but where the applicant wants a condition removed. The 1988 regulations provide for applications made under s 32(1)(b) and

7 See Local Government Act 1972, Sch 16, para 15(3A).
8 See s 49 and para 4 of Sch 11 to the 1986 Act.

s 31A to be made in writing rather than by completing a form as with renewals.

In *Britannia (Cheltenham) Ltd v Secretary of State for the Environment*[9] Sir Douglas Frank thought it competent for the applicants and the local planning authority to agree to a variation of an application at any time up to determination of the application. However, in *Bernard Wheatcroft Ltd v Secretary of State for the Environment*[10] (see p 254 below) Forbes J stressed the importance of not depriving those who should have been consulted on an application of the opportunity to comment, and in view of the statutory provisions on publicity for and consultations on applications it is suggested that it would not be proper, after these steps have been taken, for an application to be amended so as to make it substantially different from that submitted; in such circumstances a completely fresh application would seem to be appropriate.

Application for outline planning permission

By making application for outline planning permission it may be possible for an intending developer to ascertain, without spending time and money upon the preparation of detailed plans, whether the local planning authority are prepared to give approval in principle to the carrying out of operations on a particular site.

'Outline planning permission' means a planning permission for the erection of a building which is granted subject to a condition (in addition to any other conditions which may be imposed) requiring subsequent approval to be obtained from the local planning authority with respect to one or more 'reserved matters' (below) of which details have not been given in the application (GDO art 1(2)). This means that outline application cannot be made for a use of land or for any other operations apart from building operations.[11] It might however be possible to grant the equivalent of an outline permission by imposing an express condition, that reserved details are to be approved later, on a detailed application, as long as it complied with the requirement in the 1988 regulations for plans and drawings to be submitted which are necessary to describe the proposed development.

As s 42(1) of the 1971 Act provides for applications for outline planning permission to be dealt with in a development order, the provision for the grant of outline permission has not been transferred to the separate Applications Regulations and is to be found in art 7 of the 1988 GDO. However, reg 3(2) of the 1988 regulations establishes that an application for outline permission need not give details of reserved matters. Otherwise, as with a full application, an application for outline permission is to be made on a form issued by the local planning authority, must describe the development to which it relates and must be accompanied by a site plan; the application may contain such further information as the applicant desires to submit.

Matters in respect of which details have been included in an application for outline permission cannot, it seems, be treated as 'reserved matters'; if therefore, an applicant wishes to give some purely illustrative indication of

---

9 [1978] JPL 554. See too *Centre Hotels (Cranston) Ltd v Secretary of State for the Environment and London Borough of Hammersmith and Fulham Council* [1982] JPL 108.
10 (1980) 43 P & CR 233.
11 See *Glacier Metal Co Ltd v London Borough of Hillingdon* (1975) 239 Estates Gazette 573 and *Wivenhoe Port Ltd v Colchester Borough Council* [1985] JPL 396, CA.

how the development might ultimately be carried out, the fact that these details do not form part of the application should be made clear. Where the local planning authority are not prepared to approve of some matter of which details have been submitted, they may impose a condition requiring their subsequent approval of that matter, not as a 'reserved matter' under the GDO, but as an ordinary planning condition.[12] The subsequent approval would not be for approval of 'reserved matters' but for any 'consent, agreement or approval ... required by a condition imposed on a grant of planning permission' (see p 181 below).

If the local planning authority are of the opinion that they ought not to consider a particular application for outline permission separately from the consideration of any one or more 'reserved matters' they may inform the applicant that they are unable to entertain the application unless further details on such matters as they may specify are submitted (GDO, art 7(2)). The applicant is entitled to appeal to the Secretary of State against such a decision (GDO, art 26(2)(C).

Every outline planning permission is subject to a condition that application for approval of reserved matters must be made within a specified time limit (see p 261 below).

Application for approval of reserved matters

An application for approval of reserved matters is not an application for planning permission: it is, in Lord Wheatley's words, 'just a step in the process of applying for planning permission and is part and parcel of the application for planning permission.'[13] An application for approval of reserved matters need not therefore be accompanied by a certificate under s 27 of the 1971 Act[14] (see p 182 below).

'Reserved matters' are any matters in respect of which details have not been given in an outline application and which concern the siting, design, or external appearance of any building to which the outline permission relates, or the means of access to such a building, or the landscaping[15] of the site in respect of which the application was made (GDO, art 1(2)).

The courts have not, in general, adopted a strict approach towards applications for approval or reserved matters.[16]

In *Inverclyde District Council v Inverkip Building Co Ltd*[17] outline planning permission was granted for housing development subject to a condition that further approval was to be obtained with respect to the density of the proposed development; the means of drainage and disposal of sewage; the landscaping[18] and treatment of boundary walls and fences; and the reservation of a specified area for such educational, social, commercial and

12 See, for example, *Sutton London Borough Council v Secretary of State for the Environment* (1975) 73 LGR 349, 29 P & CR 350.
13 *Inverclyde District Council v Secretary of State for Scotland* 1980 SC 363, 1981 SLT 26.
14 *R v Bradford-on-Avon UDC, ex p Boulton* [1964] 2 All ER 492, [1964] 1 WLR 1136.
15 'Landscaping' is defined in art 1(2) of the GDO.
16 See, for example, *Cardiff Corpn v Secretary of State for Wales* (1971) 22 P & CR 718 (an application which purported to be for full planning permission in respect of a development for which outline permission had previously been granted could be treated as a valid application for approval of reserved matters).
17 1983 SLT 563.
18 'Landscaping' was not included in the definition of reserved matters in the GDO of 1950 (as amended) which was in operation at the time the permission was granted.

recreational development as the planning authority might approve. The planning authority sought reduction (ie quashing) of the outline permission on the ground that it was *ultra vires* to reserve these matters for subsequent approval as they did not fall within the definition of 'reserved matters'. The Second Division of the Court of Session held that whether a particular condition fell to be treated as a condition relating to a reserved matter depended on the circumstances of the individual case, and that on a broad common-sense approach and having regard to the nature of the development, the matters specified in the condition at issue in this case, apart from the reservation of the specified area, were 'reserved matters' within the meaning of the GDO;[19] in particular, 'density' concerned siting, design and external appearance and could affect means of access; drainage and disposal of sewage concerned siting and to some extent design; and landscaping and treatment of boundary walls and fences concerned siting and design.

On the other hand in *Grampian Regional Council v Secretary of State for Scotland*[20] it was doubted whether an anticipated traffic problem at a road junction about one and a half kilometres from the application site was a matter which could be reserved as concerning 'means of access' in terms of the GDO.

An application for approval of reserved matters must be within the ambit of the outline planning permission,[1] must not depart from it in a material way (though an application for something outside the scope of the outline permission need not invalidate the application—see below), and must be in accordance with the conditions annexed to the outline permission.[2] However, in *Inverclyde District Council v Secretary of State for Scotland*[3] in which the original application for approval of details fell outside the scope of the outline permission, the Second Division of the Court of Session saw no reason why the application could not be amended to bring it into line with the outline permission. Also in *R v Hammersmith and Fulham London Borough Council ex p Greater London Council*[4] the Court of Appeal held that an application for reserved matters could omit one of the uses specified for a building as long as the application was still within the ambit of the outline permission. As Glidewell L J pointed out, where the application for approval of detail showed some additional uses, it would usually be outside the outline permission but not when it was a use which was omitted, especially if, as in that case, the omitted use was a planning disadvantage and not required by the local planning authority.

Application for approval of reserved matters is to be in writing, is to give particulars sufficient to identify the outline planning permission in relation to which it is made, and is to include such particulars and be accompanied by

19 The Lord Ordinary (Lord McDonald) took a rather different view—see *Inverclyde District Council v Inverkip Building Co Ltd* 1981 SC 401, 1982 SLT 401.
20 1983 SLT 526.
 1 It can relate to more than one outline permission—see *Lobb v Secretary of State for the Environment and South Wight Borough Council* [1984] JPL 336.
 2 See *Inverclyde District Council v Secretary of State for Scotland* 1980 SC 363, 1981 SLT 26 (Second Division) and 1982 SLT 200, HL; *Heron Corpn Ltd v Manchester City Council* [1978] 3 All ER 1240, [1978] 1 WLR 937 and *R v Castle Point District Council, ex p Brooks* [1985] JPL 473.
 3 Above.
 4 (1985) 51 P & CR 120, [1986] JPL 528.

such plans and drawings as the authority consider necessary to enable them to deal with the application (GDO, art 8). In *Inverclyde District Council v Secretary of State for Scotland*[5] the House of Lords held that the requirements as to the particulars to be submitted with the application were directory only, so that a failure to comply did not invalidate an application. Lord Keith stated that there was no reason why further particulars should not be allowed to be proferred at a later stage and argued that this was 'not a field in which technical rules would be appropriate, there being no contested lis between opposing parties.'

There would seem to be no reason why application for approval of reserved matters should not be made by stages[6] or relate to part only of the site covered by the outline permission.[7] The local planning authority might, however, refuse approval of a 'piecemeal' application on the ground that they considered that the various reserved matters should not be dealt with separately. There is no reason in law why, where there has been a grant of approval of reserved matters, those reserved matters should not be revised or varied by a further submission of reserved matters under the same outline permission.[8] In *Inverclyde District Council v Secretary of State for Scotland* (above) the House of Lords held that although an application for approval of all reserved matters has to be made within the statutory time limit (see p 26 below), there was no good reason why amendment of an application for approval of reserved matters should not be permitted at any stage, even outside the time limit, provided it was still within the ambit of the outline permission.

An application for planning permission and an application for approval of reserved matters may be contained in the same document. In *Inverclyde District Council v Secretary of State for Scotland* (above) application was made in 1976 for 'any permission' required under the Planning Acts for the erection of houses on an area for which outline permission had been granted in 1974. The 1974 permission showed an area reserved for 'educational, social, commercial and recreational development'. The 1976 application showed the proposed housing development extending over this reserved area. The House of Lords held that in so far as the application related to the reserved area, it was to be regarded as a fresh application for planning permission for that area.

In *Etheridge v Secretary of State for the Environment*[9] Woolf J held that a full planning permission for houses on part of a site for which outline permission had previously been granted for housing served also as approval of details reserved in the original permission.

Assessment of environmental effects

The concept of requiring, in advance of the decision to go ahead with a major project, that there be an assessment of its potential impact on the

5 1982 SLT 200: and see comment in 1982 SPLP 47
6 See *R v Secretary of State for the Environment, ex p Percy Bilton Industrial Properties Ltd* (1975) 74 LGR 244, 31 P & CR 154.
7 See *Inverclyde District Council v Secretary of State for Scotland* 1980 SC 363, 1981 SLT 26 (Court of Session), 1982 SLT 200, HL.
8 See *Heron Corpn Ltd v Manchester City Council* [1978] 3 All ER 1240, [1978] 1 WLR 937.
9 (1983) 48 P & CR 35; see too *Cardiff Corpn v Secretary of State for Wales* (1971) 22 P & CR 718.

environment, is one that has been adopted for some time in the United States.[10] Such an assessment has always been possible under the town and country planning legislation. Environmental consequences are clearly 'material' considerations[11] and their consideration plays an important part at planning inquiries. However, until the intervention of the European Community, there existed no specific requirement for the developer to provide information on the environmental effects and for the local planning authority to assess that information. European Community Directive 85/337 on 'the assessment of the effects of certain public and private projects of the environment' requires such a process.[12] A Directive is a form of European Community legislation which is binding on the member states as to the ends to be achieved but which leaves it to individual member states to implement those ends by way of their own national laws. This is in contrast to regulations which under art 189 of the Treaty of Rome are 'directly applicable' and so do not require or indeed allow the intervention of national laws. Directive 85/337 gave member states until 3rd July 1988 to adapt their legislation or administrative procedures to achieve the ends set out and in England and Wales. This has been mainly achieved through the Town and Country Planning (Assessment of Environmental Effects) Regulations 1988 which came into force on 15th July 1988.[13] Before examining these regulations it is worth noting that not only can action be taken by the European Commission against a member state in the European Court of Justice if the national laws do not meet the requirements of a directive[14] but the European Court itself has held that directives may be capable of being enforced in national courts directly by individuals against their government.[15]

Applications which require the consideration of environmental information. The directive provides that in the case of certain specified projects (set out in Appendix 1 to the directive) information about their environmental effects must be provided by the developer and taken into account by the 'competent authority'. While in the case of the projects set out in Appendix II, they are only required to be made subject to an assessment where member states consider that they are likely to have significant effects on the environment by virtue, *inter alia* of their nature, size or location (arts 2 and 4). It is now clear that this does not give the member states a *policy choice* as to whether the projects contained in Appendix II should be subject to environment assessment but rather the directive leaves it to the *judgement* of the member state as to whether a project is likely to have significant effect on the environment. To this end, art 4(2) does allow member states to establish criteria and/or thresholds by which to determine which projects in Appendix II require

---

10 See the National Environmental Policy Act 1969 and most states have similar legislation.
11 See p 206 below.
12 For an analysis of the Directive, see Nigel Haigh 'Environmental Assessment—The EC Directive' [1987] JPL 4.
13 Also note the changes made to the General Development Order by the Town and Country Planning General Development (Amendment) Order 1988.
14 Art 169 of the Treaty of Rome.
15 See *Van Duyn v Home Office (No 2)* 41/74 [1975] Ch 358, [1975] 3 All ER 190, [1975] 1 CMLR 1, ECJ.

assessment but it seems that at present the Department of the Environment accepts that it is not possible to denote criteria or thresholds which will provide a simple test. Therefore the regulations follow the approach taken by the directive and in Schs 1 and 2 substantially repeat the lists to be found in Appendices I and II of the directive.

Schedule 1 contains nine descriptions of development. These are developments such as power stations, airports and industrial processes with obviously significant environmental effects. Schedule 2 contains 13 descriptions of development and includes such things as pig rearing institutions,[16] the extraction of coal and natural gas, the processing of metals, cement manufacture, yacht marinas, holiday villages, industrial estate development and even urban development.

An application for planning permission for the carrying out of development of any description mentioned in Sch 1 must be the subject of environmental consideration but an application for the carrying out of development of any description mentioned in Sch 2 is only to be the subject of environmental consideration if it would be likely to have significant effects on the environment by virtue of factors such as its nature, size or location *and* the Secretary of State has not made a direction under reg 3 exempting a particular development from the regulations.[17]

The crucial issue is therefore how it is determined that a project comes within Sch 2. This is considered next.

How it is determined whether an application will be a Schedule 1 or 2 application. In the final analysis it is a matter of fact and degree for the Secretary of State to determine whether an application comes within either Sch 1 or 2 but the issue can be decided in a variety of ways and at various stages.

First, the applicant can determine the matter himself by submitting an environmental statement[18] (reg 4(4)(i)) or by making a written statement agreeing or conceding that the submission of an environmental statement is required (reg 4(4)(iii)). Where the would-be developer is unsure as to whether the proposed development would be a Sch 1 or Sch 2 application, he can request a pre-application opinion from the local planning authority who would deal with the application. This procedure is provided for in reg 5 and leads to the second stage.

Second, the matter can be settled by the local planning authority. Where the applicant has asked the authority for an opinion under reg 5 or the authority have received an application for planning permission, the local planning authority can settle the matter by notifying an applicant within three weeks of receiving an application, that they consider that the submission of an environmental statement is required, in which case they must give their full reasons in writing clearly and precisely (regs 5(4) and 9(1)). The developer can then challenge this decision by asking for a direction from the Secretary of State. In the case of a request for a pre-application opinion, a failure to apply for a direction means that the project is taken to require an

---

16 Such projects may of course not require planning permission; see p 123 below.
17 See reg 4(i) and the definitions of Sch 1 and 2 applications contained in reg 2.
18 As defined in reg 2 (1) and Sch 3.

environmental statement (regs 4(4)(ii) and 5(6)(a)). Strangely the regulations prescribe no period in which an application for a direction has to be made.

In the case of an application where the local planning authority have determined that an environmental statement is required, the applicant has three weeks either to accept the local planning authority's view or apply to the Secretary of State for a direction on the matter (reg 9(2)). If the applicant does nothing the permission is deemed to be refused and there is no right of appeal to the Secretary of State (reg 9(3)).

Third, the Secretary of State can determine the issue. This can apply when the Secretary of State or his inspector is seized of the question of whether to grant planning permission, as in the case of an application referred to him under s 35 or in the case of an appeal under s 36. In both cases if the application involved had not been accompanied by an environmental statement and he considers that the application is a Sch 1 or Sch 2 application, he shall within three weeks notify the applicant/appellant that the submission of an environmental statement is required (regs 10 and 11). Otherwise the Secretary of State in effect performs a quasi-judicial or appellate role by settling a dispute between the applicant and the local planning authority as to whether an environmental statement is required. As indicated, this applies when the local planning authority has determined that such a statement is needed either as a pre-application opinion under reg 5 or as a notification in response to an application under reg 9. In each case application can be made to the Secretary of State for a direction on the matter (regs 5(6) and 9(2)). By virtue of reg 2(2) a direction by the Secretary of State that in his opinion the proposed development would be likely, or would not be likely, to have significant effects on the environment shall determine whether the application is or is not a Sch 2 application and so whether an environmental statement is required.

Finally it should be noted that art 14(2) of the General Development Order 1988 gives the Secretary of State the power to make directions exempting a particular proposed development from the regulations or determining that a particular proposed development is or is not development that requires the consideration of environmental information. Alternatively the Secretary of State can make a direction prescribing that development of a certain class is development which requires the consideration of environmental information.

The environmental statement, and the environmental information: their significance. The environmental statement is defined by way of Sch 3(1) as comprising 'a document or series of documents providing for the purpose of assessing the likely impact upon the environment of the development proposed to be carried out, the information specified in paragraph 2.' This information, referred to in the Schedule as 'the specified information', covers a description of the development, the data necessary to identify and assess the main effects on the environment and a description of the likely effects on human beings, flora, fauna, soil, water, air, climate, landscape (including the interaction of all the above), material assets and the cultural heritage. Paragraph 3 of the Schedule then provides that further information may be included, by way of explanation or amplification, on certain specified matters.

Where an application is determined to be a Sch 1 or 2 application, but it is not accompanied by an environmental statement, the applicant must be notified that such an environmental statement is required. The regulations then make plain that in the case of failure to submit such a statement, the application or appeal must be refused (regs 9(4), 10(4), and 11(3) and (7)).

In order to facilitate the preparation of environmental statements, there are provisions by which certain public bodies can be required to assist in their preparation (regs 8 and 22).

The term 'environmental information', as defined by reg 2, is broader than the term 'environmental statement' as it includes in addition any representations made by bodies and other persons about the likely environmental effects of the proposed development. In this regard, it must be noted that regs 12 and 13 provide for public notice to be given of all applications where an environmental statement is submitted and regs 14 and 15 require the bodies set out in reg 8(5) to be consulted. In this way, a bank of information on and an assessment of the environmental effects is built up where the application comes within the scope of the regulation. The crucial provision is then reg 4(2) which lays down that:

'the local planning authority or the Secretary of State or an inspector shall not grant planning permission pursuant to an application to which this regulation applies unless they have first taken the environmental information into consideration.'

This is similar to the requirement in s 29(1) to 'have regard' to the development plan and any other material considerations; (see chapter 8, p 199 below) and probably has a similar legal effect. The difficulty in the case of local planning authorities' decisions to grant permission will be ascertaining how such information has been considered as there is no duty to give reasons for a grant of planning permission and the regulations do not require the local planning authority to give directly their assessment of the environmental consequences. In the case of a decision at Secretary of State level, the position will be different as there is a general duty to give reasons and the decision letter or inspector's report should contain an assessment of the environmental information collated (see chapter 19).

The Department of the Environment's views. The Department of the Environment have issued circular 15/88 on 'Environmental Assessment'. Apart from explaining the new regulations, this circular provides important information as to the government's thinking on the subject. It is made clear that the Secretary of State takes the view that only a small number of projects, which fall within the descriptions in Sch 2, will require environmental assessment as being likely to have significant effects on the environment. The circular states that:

'In general terms the Secretary of State's view is that environmental assessment will be needed for Schedule 2 projects in three main types of use:
  (i) for major projects which are of more than local importance;
 (ii) occasionally for projects on a smaller scale which are proposed for particularly sensitive or vulnerable locations;
(iii) in a smaller number of cases, for projects with unusually complex and potentially adverse environmental effects, where expert and detailed analysis of those effects would be desirable and would be

relevant to the issue of principle as to whether or not the development should be permitted.' (para 20.)

Criteria and thresholds are also set out in Annex 2 to the circular, which offer a broad indication of the type or scale of project which may be a candidate for assessment. Thus under 'Agriculture' it is stated that 'New pig rearing installations will not generally require Environmental Assessment: however, those designed to house more than 400 sows or 5,000 fattening pigs may require Environmental Assessment.' The circular emphasises that these criteria and thresholds are only indicative and that the fundamental test to be applied in each case is the likelihood of significant environmental effects. So projects which exceed these thresholds will not in every case require assessment; conversely, there can be no automatic presumption that projects falling below these thresholds will never give rise to significant effects. It is always a matter of judgment in the particular circumstances (see para 31).

Application for planning permission in anticipation of disposal of Crown land

Until the coming into operation of the Town and Country Planning Act 1984 government departments and other Crown bodies were unable to apply for planning permission when they wished to dispose of Crown land (see p 147 above). Prior to the 1984 Act two procedural devices were employed to overcome this difficulty. First, there was a procedure under which an informal opinion as to acceptable uses of Crown land could be sought from the local planning authority or, in cases of disagreement, from the Secretary of State. However, in *R v Worthing Borough Council, ex p Burch*[19] it was held that the giving of such an opinion by the Secretary of State was an unlawful fetter on the discretion of the local planning authority. Secondly, a third party might be asked to submit a planning application in respect of the land; however, in 1983 the government was advised that the planning legislation precluded the making of such an application.

Under the 1984 Act an application for planning permission may be made by the appropriate authority (the government department owning or managing the land or the Crown Estate Commissioners) or by any person authorised by that authority (s 1(1), (2)). Where such an application is made, the statutory provisions relating to the making and determination of a planning application are to apply as if the land were not Crown land (s 1(2)), subject to the modifications made by the Town and Country Planning (Crown Land Applications) Regulations 1984.[19a] The 1984 Act provides that a grant of planning permission is to apply only to development carried out after the land has ceased to be Crown land or to development carried out by virtue of a private interest in the land (s 1(3)). Section 1(8) retrospectively validates any permission which may have been granted in respect of Crown land in which there was no other interest.

Application for consent, agreement or approval

The planning legislation recognises[20] that a local planning authority may attach to a grant of planning permission a condition, distinct from a

---

19 (1983) 50 P & CR 53, [1984] JPL 261.

19a These regulations preclude the imposition of a condition relating to Crown land which is not part of the application; see reg 3 and *Ealing London Borough Council v Secretary of State for the Environment* [1989] JPL 673.

20 See 1971 Act, s 36(1)(b) (inserted by the Local Government, Planning and Land Act 1980, Sch 15, para 4(2)).

condition requiring the subsequent approval of 'reserved matters', requiring the subsequent consent, agreement or approval of the local planning authority to be obtained for a specified aspect of a proposed development.[1] The local planning authority might, for example, require that before a permitted use is commenced, provision for the abatement of noise should be made in accordance with a scheme approved by the authority. An application for such consent, agreement or approval is not a planning application and does not attract a fee.

Variation of planning permission

After planning permission has been granted for a development the developer may wish to make some minor alteration to the approved proposal.

Apart from ss 31A and 32 (see below, p 172), there is no provision for the submission of an application varying a grant of permission. So a new application will have to be submitted, though the planning fees might not have to be paid.[2] However, in *Lever Finance Ltd v Westminster (City) London Borough Council*[3] Lord Denning MR suggested that a planning officer could authorise immaterial variations and in *Kerrier District Council v Secretary of State for the Environment and Brewer*[4] the Divisional Court accepted that a planning permission could be varied without a fresh application provided it was not material. It was left open whether if the variation was material the council had to insist on the correct form of application; but the court seemed to take the view that an application in the proper form would not always have to be made for a variation or amendment to be valid.

Notification of application for planning permission to owners and agricultural tenants

An applicant for planning permission need not have any legal interest in the land to which the application relates,[5] though he might need to have a genuine hope of acquiring an interest, nor does he require the consent of the owner; but if the applicant is not the owner of the land, he will have to give notice of the making of the planning application to the owner. Notice of the making of an application must in every case be given to any agricultural tenant of the land.

Section 27(1) of the 1971 Act[6] provides that a local planning authority shall not entertain an application for planning permission unless it is accompanied by one of the four certificates specified in that sub-section. Unless the applicant can certify that at the beginning of the period of twenty-one days ending with the date of the application, no person other than the

1 See *Sutton London Borough Council v Secretary of State for the Environment* (1975) 73 LGR 349, 29 P & CR 350; *Roberts v Vale Royal District Council* (1977) 78 LGR 368, 39 P & CR 514; and *Bilboe v Secretary of State for the Environment* [1979] JPL 100; revsd (1980) 78 LGR 357, 39 P & CR 495, CA.
2 See reg 7(1) of the Town and Country Planning (Fees for Applications and Deemed Applications) Regulations 1989.
3 [1971] 1 QB 222, [1970] 3 All ER 496, CA.
4 (1980) 41 P & CR 284, [1981] JPL 193.
5 See *Hanily v Minister of Housing and Local Government* [1952] 2 QB 444 [1952] 1 All ER 1293, per Parker J.
6 As amended by the Local Government, Planning and Land Act 1980.

applicant himself was the owner[7] of any of the land to which the application relates, he must certify that he has given notice of the application to all persons who, at the beginning of the period of 21 days ending with the date of the application, were owners of any of the land to which the application relates; if, after taking reasonable steps, the applicant has been unable to ascertain the names and addresses of some or all of the owners, he must so certify and must also certify that notice of the application has been published in a local newspaper (s 27(1), (2)).

Owners of mineral rights in land are to be notified of an application for the winning and working of minerals in the same way as owners of the land (see p 519 below). In the case of applications for underground mining the requirements as to notification are modified to take account of the difficulty that may be encountered in ascertaining the names and addresses of all owners (see p 520 below).

Any certificate issued for the purposes of s 27 must contain either a statement to the effect that none of the land to which the application relates constitutes or forms part of an agricultural holding[8] or a statement that the applicant has given the requisite notice to any agricultural tenant (s 27(3)).

Any notice or certificate issued for the purposes of s 27 is to be in the form set out in Sch 5 to the GDO (GDO, art 12). Any person who knowingly or recklessly issues a false certificate is guilty of an offence (s 27(5)).

An owner or agricultural tenant has a period of at least 21 days within which he may make representations on the application to the local planning authority. The authority may not decide the application before the expiry of that period (s 27(4)).

As mentioned above, the local planning authority are not to entertain an application for planning permission unless it is accompanied by a certificate under s 27. It would seem that failure to furnish any certificate in the correct form could deprive the local planning authority of jurisdiction to deal with the application.[9] It used to be thought that a factual error or falsehood in the certificate did not give any grounds for holding a subsequent determination to be invalid.[10] However in *Main v Swansea City Council*[11] the Court of Appeal held that an incorrect certificate could lead to any subsequent permission being quashed. In that case, the application had been accompanied by a certificate that notice had been given to the owners of the land when some of the land was owned by an unknown person and no attempt had been made to notify that person. The court held that this would be sufficient to enable the court to strike down the subsequent grant in the case of a prompt application by the owner who had not been notified or even on a much later application by such an owner. However, the court held that such an error did

---

7 For the purposes of s 27 'owner' includes a lessee under a lease with not less than seven years to run (s 27(7), as amended by the Local Government, Planning and Land Act 1980, s 9).
8 As defined in the Agricultural Holdings Act 1948 (see 1971 Act, s 27(7)). The grant of planning permission may result in loss of the security of tenure which an agricultural tenant enjoys under the Agricultural Holdings Acts.
9 See appeal decisions noted in [1966] JPL 492 and [1973] JPL 612.
10 See *R v Bradford-on-Avon UDC, ex p Boulton* [1964] 2 All ER 492, [1964] 1 WLR 1136.
11 (1984) 49 P & CR 26. See also *R v Secretary of State for the Environment, ex p Kent* [1988] JPL 706 where it was argued on the basis of *Main* that a decision was invalid because the certificate was defective as the owner's agent was named rather than the actual owner. No complaint was made by the owner and Pill J said that the purpose of the section was to protect the owners and it was not open for a neighbour to rely on the defect.

not make the grant a complete nullity and the court refused to quash on the application of a non-owner because of the long delay. This means that the applicants must be careful to fill in the certificates correctly otherwise a mistake may lead to a neighbour or a residents' association challenging any grant of permission, but it would seem that, as s 27 is aimed at protecting particular individuals, only those individuals will normally be able to get a grant quashed on judicial review.

Publicity for application

The planning legislation of 1947 proceeded on the basis that an application for planning permission concerned only the applicant and the local planning authority. Although the legislation required an application for planning permission to be recorded in the register of planning applications (see p 261 below), and in that way every application was, in a sense, a matter of public knowledge, there was no obligation on the applicant or the local planning authority to give any public notice of the application or to notify neighbours or other 'third parties'.

The absence of any machinery for involving the public in development control was defended on grounds of principle as well as of administrative convenience. Planning, it was said, was concerned to ensure that development was controlled in the public interest; it was not the function of planning to seek to protect the private interests of members of the public against the activities of others. On the other hand, as Cooke J argued in *Stringer v Minister of Housing and Local Government*,[12]

'The public interest may require that the interests of individual occupiers should be considered. The protection of interests of individual occupiers is one aspect and an important one, of the public interest as a whole.'

The government have always resisted the enactment of a right for neighbours to be notified individually of all prospective development but have accepted that 'opinion should be enabled to declare itself before any approval is given to proposals of wide concern or substantial impact on the environment'; see circular 71/73. The present position is that in the case of certain special categories of development, there is a statutory requirement for publicity, but otherwise it is left to the discretion of the local planning authority. Circular 71/73 has now been cancelled and Appendix B of circular 22/882 gives advice on when publicity should be given and sets out a table on the kinds of proposals and the action recommended (see p 188 below). The position is different in Scotland where there is a statutory requirement to notify all close neighbours.

Developments by government departments do not have to be published but circular 18/84 on crown land does state that the intention is that generally publicity should be provided at the same level.

Where an administrative practice has grown up of consulting certain persons, it might be argued that such persons had a 'legitimate expectation' of being consulted and that a failure to consult would make any subsequent

12 [1971] 1 All ER 65, [1970] 1 WLR 1281.

decision invalid. The extent to which the courts will imply such a duty of consultation or notification is discussed later in this chapter; see p 196 below.

(i) 'Bad neighbour' developments

Section 26 requires the applicant for certain designated types of development both to place advertisements in a local newspaper and to attempt to put up a site notice. Designation is done by way of a development order and has so far been restricted to developments which may have a significant and possibly adverse effect on amenity and are often referred to as 'bad neighbour' developments. The following classes of development are specified for this purpose in art 11 of the General Development Order 1988:

(a) the construction of buildings for use as public conveniences;
(b) the construction of buildings or other operations or the use of land for the disposal of waste materials or the use of land as a scrap yard;
(c) the winning or working of minerals or the use of land for mineral working deposits;
(d) the construction of buildings or other operations or the use of land for retaining, treating or disposing of sewage, trade waste or sludge (other than the laying of sewers, the construction of pumphouses in a line of sewers or the construction of septic tanks and cesspools serving single dwellinghouses, single buildings or single caravans in which not more than ten people will normally reside, work or congregate, and works ancillary thereto);
(e) the construction of buildings to a height exceeding 20 metres;
(f) the construction of buildings or the use of land for the purposes of a slaughterhouse or knacker's yard or for killing or plucking poultry;
(g) the construction of buildings or the use of land for the purposes of a casino, a funfair or a bingo hall, a theatre, a cinema, a music hall, a dance hall, a skating rink, a sportshall, a swimming bath or gymnasium (not forming part of a school, college or university), or a Turkish or other vapour or foam bath;
(h) the construction of buildings or the use of land as a zoo or for the business of boarding or breeding cats or dogs;
(i) the construction of buildings or the use of land for motor car or motorcycle racing, including trials of speed;
(j) the construction of a stadium;
(k) the use of land as a cemetery or crematorium.

In this regard it has been held by the minister that the terms 'amusement arcade' and 'funfair' are not synonymous and that therefore an application for an amusement arcade, which did not contain roundabouts, dodgem cars or shooting machines, did not come within art 8.[13] On the other hand, a planning application for the stationing of caravans was held to come within it as it was clear that if the development was allowed it would involve foul drainage by septic tank or cesspool;[14] but an application for the creation of artificial lakes for fish production with a stockpile of excavated material was

13 [1979] JPL 56.
14 [1983] JPL 138

held not to be 'use of land for the disposal of refuse or waste materials' as alluvial material could not be considered waste.[15]

As with s 27, s 26 does not expressly require newspaper advertisements and site notices, rather it lays down that an application shall not be entertained by the local planning authority unless it is accompanied by certain documents. As to advertisements the application must be accompanied by a copy of a notice in specific form which the applicant must certify has been published in a named newspaper on a specified date (s 26(2)(a) and GDO, art 11(2)).[16] In the case of the site notice, there must be a certificate which states that a notice in the prescribed form has been posted on the land the subject of the application (s 26(2) and (3)). Such a notice must be firmly affixed to some object on the land and be easily visible and legible to members of the public without their going onto the land. Alternatively there can be a certificate stating that the applicant has been unable to post a notice because he had not the right to enter the land even though he took reasonable steps (steps which must be specified in the certificate) to obtain such rights (s 26(2)(b)(ii)).

The notices referred to in the certificates must inform of a place where the application and accompanying documents can be inspected at reasonable hours (s26(6)). The objective is to enable members of the local community to make representations and the application cannot be determined before the end of a period of 21 days from the date on which the notices were either published or posted (s 26(7)).

It has been held that a failure to supply the relevant notices and certificates will invalidate the application and that any determination will be a nullity.[17] In the light of *Main v Swansea City Council* (see p 183 above), this may be too rigid but correspondingly a factual error in the certificate could give grounds for the courts quashing any decision, even if there was apparent compliance on the face of the application. A challenge could be mounted by a neighbour and from *R v London Borough of Lambeth Council, ex p Sharp,*[18] it might not be necessary for that person to show that he himself had been prejudiced.

As with s 27 it is an offence knowingly or recklessly to issue a false or misleading certificate (s 26(8)).

Section 26 does not apply to developments by or on land of local planning authorities.[19]

(ii) *Applications affecting conservation areas*

Under s 28 of the 1971 Act, it is the responsibility of the local planning authority to publicise any application for planning permission in respect of development which would, in the opinion of the authority, (a) affect the character or appearance of a conservation area or (b) affect the setting of a listed building. In such a case the planning authority must publish notice of the application in a local newspaper and, for not less than 7 days, display a

---

15 [1983] JPL 147.
16 As to the extent of this obligation see *Wilson v Secretary of State for the Environment* [1974] 1 All ER 428, [1973] 1 WLR 1083 and *McMeechan v Secretary of State for the Environment* [1974] 232 Estates Gazette 201, CA.
17 [1963] JPL 138.
18 [1987] JPL 440 per Woolf L J at 443–444.
19 *J J Steeples v Derbyshire County Council* [1984] 3 All ER 468, [1985] 1 WLR 256.

notice on or near the land. A period of at least 21 days is allowed for representations on such an application (s 28(3)).

In England, the local planning authorities must also send a copy of the notice to the Historic Buildings and Monuments Commission but there is provision for the Secretary of State to exempt a local planning authority from this obligation (s 28(2A) and (2B)). Formal notice has been given by the Secretary of State that the Commission does not have to be informed about applications affecting the setting of Grade II (unstarred) listed buildings (except in Greater London) or conservation areas where the development is below a specified size.[20]

While non-compliance with s 28 could invalidate any subsequent determination, the subjective wording of the section would suggest that the local planning authority's decision, that s 28 did not apply, could not be easily challenged. In *R v London Borough Lambeth Council, ex p Sharp*[1] the Court of Appeal upheld a decision of Croom-Johnson L J quashing a resolution of Lambeth Council to develop an athletics track in a conservation area. However, this concerned an application which the council had decided would affect the conservation area and in any case involved a failure to comply not with s 28 but with a similar provision in reg 4(2) of the Town and Country Planning General Regulations 1976 which govern development proposals of local planning authorities. Nevertheless this decision would suggest that a clear breach of s 28 would provide grounds for the court to quash any subsequent decision.

(iii) *Applications departing from the development plan*

The Town and Country Planning (Development Plans) (England) Direction 1981 (para 3) provides that, before granting permission for development which does not accord with the provisions of the development plan, the application must have been advertised in a local newspaper and a period of 21 days allowed for representations (see p 201 below).

In *R v St Edmundsbury Borough Council ex p Investors in Industry Commercial Properties Ltd*[2] Stocker J held that para 3 of the direction was not mandatory. However in *R v Doncaster Metropolitan District Council, ex p British Railways Board*[3] Schiemann J quashed a decision for, *inter alia*, a failure to comply with para 3. The better view would seem to be that a plain and serious breach of the direction will give grounds for judicial review where there has been a chance of prejudice.[4]

(iv) *Developments by local planning authorities*

Where a local planning authority require planning permission for development which they propose to carry out, they must give notice of their intention to develop in a local newspaper, indicating where plans of the development may be inspected and allowing a period of 21 days for representations to be made to the authority (see p 274 below).

20 See circular 8/87, para 28.
 1 [1987] JPL 440.
 2 [1985] 3 All ER 234, [1985] 1 WLR 1168.
 3 [1987] JPL 444.
 4 But see Court of Appeal decision in *Co-operative Retail Services Ltd v Taff Ely Borough Council* (1979) 39 P & CR 223.

(v) *Applications where environmental statement is submitted*

Regulation 12 of the Town and Country Planning (Assessment of Environmental Effects) Regulations 1988 applies s 26 to applications which are accompanied by an environmental statement (see p 177 above) and reg 13 similarly requires publicity where an environmental statement follows on an application.

(vi) *Publicity at the discretion of the local planning authority*

Circular 22/88 sets out in Appendix B occasions when the local planning authority may wish to consider publicising applications. It is suggested that this can be done by the site notices, notification of neighbours, newspaper advertisements or the display of applications in public places.

Fees for applications and deemed applications

Under s 87 of the Local Government, Planning and Land Act 1980 the Secretary of State is empowered to make regulations prescribing fees for planning applications[4a]. The government's aim in introducing fees was simply to offset some of the costs of administering development control. Prior to the introduction of fees it was said that it was the government's intention that the scheme would be simple; however, the regulations currently in force, the Town and Country Planning (Fees for Applications and Deemed Applications) Regulations 1989 as amended are fairly complex.[5]

Fees are payable in respect of applications for planning permission; applications for approval of reserved matters; applications for consent to display advertisements; and deemed applications arising from enforcement appeals and established use certificate appeals. Fees are not payable in respect of other types of application. The level of fees is related broadly to the scale of the development in question. The scale of fees is contained in Part II of Sch 1 to the fees regulations.[6]

The regulations exempt certain categories of application from the requirement to pay a fee. The exempted classes include applications for certain alterations to a dwellinghouse which is the residence of a disabled person; applications for alterations to provide access for disabled persons to buildings to which the public have access; applications which are required to be made only because of the withdrawal of 'deemed' permission under the GDO by means of an art 4 direction (see p 410) or by way of a condition attached to a planning permission; and applications for the erection of agricultural buildings (other than dwellinghouses) (see regs 4 and 5). Equally, fees are not payable where permission would not normally be needed because of the application of the Use Classes Order, but is necessary because of the requirements of a condition imposed on a permission granted, or deemed to have been granted (see reg 6).

Where an application is withdrawn or permission is refused by the planning authority or by the Secretary of State, the applicant may submit, without payment of a fee, one further application for development of the same character or description on the same site (reg 8); in such a case the

---

4a In *R v Richmond upon Thames London Borough Council (1989)* Times 7 February, Popplewell J upheld the London Borough of Richmonds' practice of charging a fee for pre-application consultations.

5 Helpful guidance is to be found in circular 19/1985.

6 Experience since the introduction of fees in 1981 suggests, however, that the fees may well be subject to increase at regular intervals, and the Schedule has had to be regularly updated.

revised application must be made within 12 months of the withdrawal or the refusal of permission. A similar exemption is made in respect of applications for planning permission where permission for development of the same character or descriptions has already been granted (reg 7).

Reduced fees are payable in respect of duplicate applications made within 28 days of each other;[7] applications for development crossing local authority boundaries; applications containing alternative schemes for the development of the same land; applications made by community councils; applications by non-profit-making clubs or sporting or recreational organisations relating to playing fields for their own use; applications to continue an existing use or retain an existing building without complying with a condition requiring cessation of the use or removal of the building; applications for the removal of a condition; and certain 'reserved matters' applications (see Sch 1; Pt 1 to the regs.)

The statutory period for determination of an application does not begin to run until the appropriate fee has been paid (GDO art 23(3)(c)). The fees regulations do not prescribe a procedure for the resolution of disputes about the amount of the fee payable in any particular case. However, the dispute can be resolved by the applicant appealing against the non-determination of an application within the prescribed period; the Secretary of State will have to take a view on the correct fee as this will affect his jurisdiction to determine the appeal. Alternatively, an applicant can apply for judical review as in *West Bowers Farm Products v Essex County Council*.[8] There the applicants were arguing that no fees were payable because of reg 5. They unsuccessfully claimed a declaration that reg 5 applied and an order of mandamus requiring the local planning authority to consider and determine the planning application notwithstanding it was not accompanied by a fee.

Examination and acknowledgement of application by planning authority

On receipt of an application for planning permission or for approval of reserved matters and the fee (if any) required to be paid, the local planning authority are to send the applicant an acknowledgement (GDO, art 10 and Sch 3). Article 10 of the GDO makes clear that an application is not to be taken to have been received until any certificate required by s 27 has been received and any fee payable in respect of the application has been paid. Where, after sending an acknowledgement of an application to the applicant, the local planning authority form the opinion that the application may be invalid by reason of failure to comply with the requirements of reg 3 of the 1988 regs or articles 8 or 9 of the GDO or with any other statutory requirement, they must as soon as possible inform the applicant of that fact (GDO, art 10(4)).

Reference of application to the Secretary of State

Under s 35 of the 1971 Act[9] the Secretary of State has power to direct that an application for planning permission or for approval of reserved matters or

---

7 Applicants sometimes submit duplicate applications in order that they can appeal on one in the event of failure on the part of the local planning authority to determine the application within the prescribed period, while still negotiating with the local planning authority on the other application.
8 (1985) 50 P & CR 368, [1985] JPL 857, CA.
9 As amended by the Town and Country Planning (Minerals) Act 1981, Sch 1. para 2, and the Housing and Planning Act 1986, Sch (1), para 17.

for any consent, agreement or approval required by a condition attached to a grant of planning permission should be referred to him instead of being dealt with by the local planning authority. Where an application is thus 'called in' by the Secretary of State, the local planning authority must inform the applicant of that fact, of any reasons given by the Secretary of State for issuing the direction, of the applicant's right to a hearing and that the Secretary of State's decision is final (art 22 of the GDO).

If either the local planning authority or the applicant so desire, the Secretary of State must afford to each of them an opportunity of appearing before and being heard by a person appointed by the minister for the purpose; such a hearing will normally take the form of a public local inquiry. A decision made by the Secretary of State on an application for planning permission referred to him under s 35 can be challenged in the High Court on the grounds specified in s 245 of the 1971 Act (see chapter 20).

These provisions were discussed in the case of *Davies v Secretary of State for Wales*.[10] There the local planning authority had failed to inform the applicant. Sir Douglas Frank QC held that the failure was not a matter which could be the subject of an appeal under s 245; presumably on the ground that only procedural breaches by the Secretary of State himself provide a basis for challenge. Further, he felt that the purpose was to ensure that the applicant knew of his rights to require a hearing and so where a hearing was provided, as in *Davies*, there was no prejudice.

The legislation makes no provision for the making by any person or body of a formal request that the Secretary of State call in an application. In *R v Secretary of State for the Environment, ex p Newprop*[11] a decision of the Secretary of State not to call in an application because he considered it to be of purely local concern was unsuccessfully challenged. Forbes J said that the Secretary of State's discretion was 'wholly at large' and was in essence a purely administrative decision. Therefore his decision could only be challenged if it was wildly perverse, though he did accept that if the Secretary of State gave a wrong reason for his decision then the court could interfere on the ground that he had misdirected himself in law. On the facts of the case Forbes J held that the Secretary of State had not fettered his discretion unlawfully by adopting a policy that applications for planning permission would only be called in if planning issues of more than local importance were involved.[12]

However, in *Rhys Williams v Secretary of State for Wales*[13] the court of Appeal accepted that the discretion to call-in could be reviewed on the basis of what Eveleigh LJ termed as 'the broad *Wednesbury* principles'. This would be less strict than Forbes J's 'wildly perverse' and would be 'whether in all the circumstances . . . the only reasonable course was for the Minister to call in the . . . application'. The application of the *Wednesbury* principles might also, contrary to Forbes J, allow the court to quash a determination if it was based on irrelevant considerations or if the Minister had failed to take into account relevant considerations. Moreover, in *Lakin Ltd v Secretary of State for*

---

10 (1976) 33 P & CR 330.
11 [1983] JPL 386.
12 See circular 2/81 at para 15.
13 [1985] JPL 29.

Scotland,[14] the Second Division of the Court of Session held that a decision not to call in an application could be challenged on grounds of procedural impropriety. In this case the Secretary of State for Scotland had decided not to call in an application for a superstore which the regional council were minded to grant, when an appeal against a refusal to permit a superstore on another site was pending before the Secretary of State. It was common ground that once permission was granted for one site in the area, this precluded the granting of permission on another site for a superstore. The court accepted that the Secretary of State could have determined not to call in the application because it did not raise issues of sufficient importance but that the Secretary of State was wrong to consider the respective merits of the two sites at the level of the decision whether to call-in as this effectively pre-empted the outstanding appeal.

The main means by which the Secretary of State's attention is drawn to applications before they are determined by local planning authorities is under para 4 of the Town and Country Planning (Development Plans) (England) Direction 1981.[15] Under this provision local planning authorities are required to bring to the Secretary of State's attention any proposal which would materially conflict with or prejudice the implementation of any of the policies or general proposals of the structure plan in force in the area or with a fundamental provision of the old development plan so far as it is in force or any provision of a local plan introduced by way of modification by the Secretary of State. Within London different criteria are prescribed by the Town and Country Planning (Development Plans) (Greater London) Direction 1986.

Paragraph 4 of the 1981 direction was considered by the High Court in *R v Carlisle City Council, ex p Cumbrian Co-operative Society Ltd.*[16] This concerned a resolution by the local planning authority to seek permission under the Town and Country Planning General Regulations 1976 but the 1981 Direction applied by virtue of reg 4(4). It was conceded that there had been a breach of para 4 of the direction but Macpherson J concluded that the provisions were only directory and not a condition precedent. However, the more recent decision of the Court of Appeal in *R v London Borough of Lambeth Council ex p Sharp*[17] casts doubt on such an approach.

Consultations on applications

Article 18 of the GDO provides that a local planning authority must, before granting planning permission (either conditionally or unconditionally) for specified types of development, consult with specified bodies or persons. The specified types of development are set out in a table in art 18 which is now reproduced on pp 192–94.

The main change introduced by the 1988 GDO is that the local highway authority's power of direction has been replaced by a right to be consulted in respect of development affecting a classified or proposed road. The 1977 order also requested local planning authorities to consult the Minister of Agriculture, Fisheries and Food, and in Wales, the Secretary of State for

14 1988 SLT 780, [1989] JPL 339.
15 There is a separate directive for Wales.
16 [1985] 2 EGLR 193, [1986] JPL 206.
17 (1986) 55 P & CR 232, [1987] JPL 440.

TABLE

Para	Description of Development	Consultee
(a)	Development likely to affect land in Greater London or in a metropolitan county	The local planning authority concerned
(b)	Development likely to affect land in a non-metropolitan county, other than land in a National Park	The district planning authority concerned
(c)	Development likely to affect land in a National Park	The county planning authority concerned
(d)	Development involving the manufacture, processing, keeping or use of a hazardous substance in such circumstances that there will at any one time be, or is likely to be, a notifiable quantity of such substance in, on, over or under any land	The Health and Safety Executive
(e)	Development likely to result in a material increase in the volume or a material change in the character of traffic— (i) entering or leaving a trunk road; or	In England, the Secretary of State for Transport, in Wales the Secretary of State for Wales
	(ii) using a level crossing over a railway	The British Railways Board or other railway undertakers likely to be affected, and in England, the Secretary of State for Transport and, in Wales, the Secretary of State for Wales
(f)	Development likely to result in a material increase in the volume or a material change in the character of traffic entering or leaving a classified or proposed road	The local highway authority concerned

	Development	Consultee
(g)	Development likely to prejudice the improvement or construction of a classified or proposed road	The local highway authority concerned
(h)	Development involving the formation, laying out or alteration of any means of access to a highway (other than a trunk road)	The local highway authority concerned
(i)	Development which involves the provision of a building or pipeline in an area of coal working notified by the British Coal Corporation to the local planning authority	The British Coal Corporation
(j)	Development involving or including mining operations	The water authority concerned
(k)	Development involving or including the winning and working of coal by opencast methods	The Secretary of State for Energy
(l)	Development within three kilometres of Windsor Castle, Windsor Great Park, or Windsor Home Park, or within 800 metres of any other royal palace or park, which might affect the amenities (including security) of that palace or park	The Secretary of State for the Environment
(m)	Development of land in Greater London involving the demolition, in whole or part, or the material alteration of a listed building	The Historic Buildings and Monuments Commission
(n)	Development likely to affect the site of a scheduled ancient monument	In England, The Historic Buildings and Monuments Commission, in Wales, the Secretary of State for Wales
(o)	Development involving the carrying out of works or operations in the bed of or on the banks of a river or stream	The water authority concerned
(p)	Development for the purpose of refining or storing mineral oils and their derivatives	The water authority concerned
(q)	Development involving the use of land for the deposit of refuse or waste	The water authority concerned

Para	Description of Development	Consultee
(r)	Development relating to the retention, treatment or disposal of sewage, trade-waste, slurry or sludge (other than the laying of sewers, the construction of pumphouses in a line of sewers, the construction of septic tanks and cesspools serving single dwellinghouses or single caravans or single buildings in which not more than ten people will normally reside, work or congregate, and works ancillary thereto)	The water authority concerned
(s)	Development relating to the use of land as a cemetery	The water authority concerned
(t)	Development in an area of special scientific interest of which notification has been given or has effect as if given to the local planning authority by the Nature Conservancy Council in accordance with section 28 of the Wildlife and Countryside Act 1981	The Nature Conservancy Council
(u)	Development involving any land on which there is a theatre as defined in the Theatres Trust Act 1976	The Theatres Trust
(v)	Development which is not for agricultural purposes and is not in accordance with the provisions of a development plan and involves— (i) the loss of not less than 20 hectares of grades 1, 2 or 3a agricultural land which is for the time being used (or was last used) for agricultural purposes; or (ii) the loss of less than 20 hectares of grades 1, 2 or 3a agricultural land which is for the time being used (or was last used) for agricultural purposes, in circumstances in which the development is likely to lead to a further loss of agricultural land amounting cumulatively to 20 hectares or more	In England, the Minister of Agriculture, Fisheries and Food and in Wales, the Secretary of State for Wales
(w)	Development within 250 metres of land which— (i) is or has, at any time in the 30 years before the relevant application, been used for the deposit of refuse or waste; and (ii) has been notified to the local planning authority by the waste disposal authority for the purposes of this provision	The waste disposal authority concerned.

Wales, on all proposed developments involving the loss of more than four hectares of agricultural land which did not accord with the provisions of the development plan. Consultation is now only for proposals involving the loss of 20 hectares or more of grade 1, 2 or 3a land or involving less than 20 hectares if the loss is likely to lead to further losses amounting cumulatively to 20 hectares or more.[18] A new requirement has also been introduced to ensure that water authorities are consulted on development proposals near landfill sites which are likely to emit methane gas. The onus, however, is on the waste disposal authority to identify such sites and to notify them to the local planning authority. There is also now an express duty to consult the British Railways Board and there have been other changes to the scope of development on which other bodies must be consulted.

Article 18 makes clear that whether an application requires consultation is a matter of opinion for the local planning authority and such a judgment could only be overturned in the courts if it was totally unreasonable or misdirected. A failure to consult, when required, would entitle the consultee to apply to have any grant of permission quashed in the High Court, and the Court of Appeal's decision in *Main v Swansea City Council*[19] suggests that other interested persons might also be able to mount a challenge in the right circumstances. Consultation requires the consultee to be given notice of the application, unless the applicant has already served a copy on that person or authority, and the application shall not be determined until at least 14 days after the consultee received notice of the application (art 18(4) of the GDO). Where any representations are received from the consultee they must be taken into account by the local planning authority in determining the application (art 18(5) of the GDO).

A Code of Practice on Consultation was published in 1980 by the National Development Control Forum where on a non-statutory basis a maximum consultation period of 28 days was agreed. It is open to bodies which have to be consulted under the GDO to waive their consultation rights in relation to particular categories of development or for particular geographical areas where they think consultation on individual applications unnecessary.

As with publicity, local planning authorities have been requested to consult in regard to particular proposals. Circular 22/88 usefully includes in Appendix C a list of this non-statutory consultation and the relevant circulars. We discuss later the possible legal consequences of a practice of consultation.

The Secretary of State also has the power to give directions to a local planning authority requiring consultation with any person or body named in the direction, in any case or class of case specified in the direction (art 18(3) of the GDO).[20]

Under para 20 of Sch 18 to the Local Government Act 1972 parish councils and, in Wales, community councils must be informed of all

---

18 See circular 16/87 'Development involving Agricultural Land.'
19 (1984) 49 P & CR 26.
20 See for example the Town and Country Planning (Aerodromes) Direction 1981 which is contained in circular 39/81 which requires consultation with the Civil Aviation Authority or the Ministry of Defence in the case of applications for the development of land forming the site of or in the neighbourhood of aerodromes in respect of which a map has been issued safeguarding the aerodrome.

applications in their area if they apply in writing to the district planning authority or in a metropolitan county to the local planning authority.

Article 21(1) of the GDO then requires the parish or community council to notify the local planning authority by whom the application is to be determined, as soon as practicable, whether they propose to make any representations and to deliver such representations to that authority within 14 days of being notified. Article 21(4) then makes clear that any such representations must be taken into account by the local planning authority. As set out in chapter 2, in non-metropolitan areas planning applications and other related applications which concern 'county matters' are determined by the county planning authority, while all other applications are determined by the district planning authority. Where the district planning authority are required by para 19 of Sch 16 to the Local Government Act 1972 to consult the county, an application for planning permission must not be determined until the expiry of at least 14 days after the county receive notice of the application (art 19 of the GDO). In the case of applications to be determined by the county, the relevant district planning authority must be given at least 14 days in which to make recommendations as to how the application should be determined and the county shall take that recommendation into account (art 20 of the GDO).

Publicity and consultation over and above the stated requirements

The Secretary of State has on several occasions asked local planning authorities to consult certain bodies in connection with particular types of application.[1] In addition, local planning authorities may, of their own initiative or following a request, consult other bodies such as amenity groups and residents' associations.[2] Indeed consultation over and above the statutory requirements has become part of the standard practice of development control decision-making. In this regard in *R v Sheffield City Council, ex p Mansfield*[3] Lord Widgery CJ refused to hold that there was any general obligation to consult where this was not required by statute. Since then the House of Lords decision in *Council of Civil Service Unions v Minister of the Civil Services*[4] would suggest that a practice of consultation might give rise to a 'legitimate expectation' to be consulted. A failure to consult in such circumstances might mean that the courts would invalidate a decision as being unfair. Certainly in *R v Torfaen Borough Council (amended to Monmouth District Council) ex p Jones*,[5] Woolf J held that local planning authorities were under a legal duty to process applications fairly and he quashed a grant of permission where objectors had been deprived of a chance of commenting on amended plans against their previous expectations. However, in *R v Secretary of State for the Environment, ex p Kent*[6] Pill J

1 See circulars 71/73 and 22/88.
2 Even if the applicant is made aware or becomes aware of representations there is no statutory obligation to disclose the contents of such representations or of the names of the people making them and it has been suggested that it is proper for the authority not to do so without consent—see [1981] JPL 622 and [1984] JPL 696; and see letter in 1983 SPLP 26. However failure to at least inform the applicant of the nature of the representations could lead to the decision being invalid on grounds of unfairness.
3 (1978) 77 LGR 126, 37 P & CR 1.
4 [1985] AC 374, [1984] 3 All ER 935.
5 [1986] JPL 686.
6 [1988] JPL 706; upheld on appeal on other grounds see 1989 Times, 12 May.

refused to hold that the practice of notifying persons likely to be affected by developments had created a requirement or duty to notify local residents. He concluded that: 'Had Parliament intended such a general requirement one would have expected to find it specified in the statute along with other requirements which had been included.'

On the other hand, while the courts have refused to imply a general requirement to consult, special individual circumstances may give rise to a duty to provide an opportunity for representation. This happened in the decision of *R v Great Yarmouth Borough Council, ex p Botton Bros Arcades Ltd,*[7] where an application was made to convert a seafront hotel into an amusement arcade. As it was not a section 26 application, it was not advertised on site or in a local newspaper and as a result other traders who owned amusement arcades did not know about the application. The policy background would have indicated that the application would have been refused but the planning committee, on allowing the architect for the applicant to address them, decided provisionally to grant the permission. On learning of this the rival traders requested in writing that the council should defer a decision to enable them to state their objections fully. The council refused to defer and granted permission. Otton J quashed the decision on an application for judicial review. He made clear that although the council by granting permission was departing from its declared policy, there was no duty to inform potential objectors or to hear them before determining the application. Yet Otton J went on to hold that the unique combination of circumstances required that the objectors had the opportunity to make representations. Again in *Wilson v Secretary of State for the Environment*[8] David Widdicombe QC held that, where at the application stage third parties had been notified, it was a breach of the duty to act fairly if they were not informed at the appeal stage. Finally it may be noted that in *R v Secretary of State for the Environment, ex p Kent*[9] Pill J accepted that if there had been a requirement or duty to notify individuals, it should apply, at the appeal stage as well as the application stage.

It is hard to draw a clear distinction between the various cases, but it would seem that a duty to notify or consult over and above the statutory provisions will only arise when a particular relationship has already been established toward a particular person or set of persons (as in *Torfaen*) or the circumstances are particularly unique (as in *Botton Bros*).

DIRECTIONS BY THE SECRETARY OF STATE

Article 14 of the 1988 GDO gives the Secretary of State a general power to give directions which restrict the grant of permission by a local planning authority. This must mean that the Secretary of State can direct that a permission be refused or conditions imposed but not that permission be granted. Such a direction can be made in respect of a particular development or a class of development and can have effect indefinitely or for a specific

---

7 (1987) 56 P & CR 99, [1988] JPL 18, see also *R v Torfaen Borough Council (amended to Monmouth District Council), ex p Jomes* [1986] JPL 686.
8 [1988] JPL 540.
9 See above.

period. It would not appear that any directions have been made under this provision. As stated earlier there is also a specific power to make directions relating to the need for environmental information (GDO art 14(2) and above, p 178).

There are also special provisions relating to development affecting certain existing and proposed highways which are the responsibility of the Department of Transport or the Welsh Office. The relevant local planning authority[10] is required to notify the Department of Transport or the Welsh Office (as appropriate) where the proposed development:

(a) involves new or altered access to trunk roads on which speeds of more than 40 mph are permitted (GDO art 15(1)(a)).
(b) involves new or altered access to motorways (GDO, art 15(1)(a)); or
(c) is within 67 metres (or any other distance prescribed) of the centre line of either a proposed trunk road or motorway or any highway which either Department proposes to improve or construct (GDO, art 15(1)(b)).[11]

The legal consequence is that the local planning authority cannot determine the application until either:

(a) a direction is made under art 14;
(b) a notification is received that no such direction will be made; or
(c) 28 days (or any longer period agreed in writing) has elapsed from the date of notification without a direction being made (GDO, art 15(2)).

This would suggest that any determination in breach of art 15(2) would be *ultra vires* as made without jurisdiction. However, a simple failure to notify does not automatically invalidate a determination of the planning application. In *Main v Swansea City Council*[12] the Court of Appeal rejected an application by a third party to quash a grant where notification had not been made. The court accepted that, where the local planning authority had not merely failed to comply with a statutory requirement directly imposed on them but had also acted in breach of an express prohibition, an interested party as well as the Secretary of State could have the determination held to be invalid by the court. Had an interested party, on learning of the failure, promptly applied to the court, it would have been no answer to say that only the Secretary of State was entitled to apply. Nevertheless the Court of Appeal refused the application because of the delay in applying and because it was clear that the highway aspects of the development had been dealt with by way of a condition which was in accordance with the known requirements of the Secretary of State. This illustrates once again that the legal consequences of a procedural failure nearly always depend on the particular circumstances.

---

10 This is defined by art 15(4) as the district planning authority or the urban development corporation or in the Greater London Area or a metropolitan county, the local planning authority.
11 See Planning Policy Guidance Note 13, Appendix A as to how the procedures work.
12 (1984) 49 P & CR 266.

CHAPTER 8

CONTROL OF DEVELOPMENT 2: THE DEVELOPMENT PLAN AND OTHER MATERIAL CONSIDERATIONS

Determining an application: matters to be taken into account

In determining an application for planning permission the local planning authority must have regard to a number of matters specifically prescribed by the legislation. The principal such matters are:

(1) the provisions of the development plan so far as material to the application (1971 Act, s 29(1));

(2) any other material considerations (1971 Act, s 29(1));

(3) any representations made to the local planning authority within the prescribed period (see p 182 above) by an owner of land or an agricultural tenant who has received notification in terms of s 27 of the 1971 Act (1971 Act, s 29(3));

(4) any representations made to the local planning authority within the prescribed period (see p 184 above) in response to 'neighbour notification' or press advertisement of an application under s 26 of the 1971 Act and art 11 of the GDO (see p 185 above) (1971 Act, s 29(2));

(5) any representations made to the local planning authority within the prescribed period (see p 186 above) in respect of development to which s 28 of the 1971 Act applies (development affecting a conservation area of the setting of a listed building) (1971 Act, s 29(4));

(6) any representations made to the local planning authority within the prescribed period (see p 195 above) in response to consultations carried out under art 18 of the GDO (GDO art 18(5)); and

(7) any representations received by the local planning authority within the prescribed period (see p 187 below) in respect of an application to which the Town and Country Planning (Development Plans) Direction 1981 applies.

Of the matters listed above, the provisions of the development plan and any other material considerations raise particular problems which are discussed below.

Development plans and development control

An important function of a development plan[1] is to provide guidelines for development control. It does not therefore, like many zoning systems,

---

1 Whatever combination of structure, local and 'old style' plans the particular development plan consists of for the time being, see ch 4, p 45.

directly authorise or forbid developments on particular sites.[2] Also, the administrative law principle, that a recipient of a statutory discretion must not fetter that discretion by devising rules in advance which pre-determine the use of that discretion,[3] prevents the local planning authorities from binding themselves to set policies. The statutory development plan is specifically referred to by s 29, but the Act by using the term 'have regard' and by referring to other material considerations that can be taken into account indicates that the plan cannot dictate the answer to an application.

This was first made clear by the courts in the Scots decision of *Simpson v Edinburgh Corpn*.[4] Edinburgh University obtained planning permission for the construction of modern university buildings in George Square, Edinburgh, which required the demolition of two sides of the square and the destruction of its characteristic Georgian appearance. The grant of permission was challenged by the owner of a dwelling in George Square as being contrary to the provisions of the development plan and therefore *ultra vires*. The Lord Ordinary, Lord Guest, said:

'It was argued for the pursuer that this section [now s 26 of the Town and Country Planning (Scotland) Act 1972] required the planning authority to adhere strictly to the development plan. I do not so read this section. "To have regard to" does not, in my view, mean "slavishly to adhere to". It requires the planning authority to consider the development plan, but it does not oblige them to follow it.'

Lord Guest added that if the requirement to have regard to the plan was to be regarded as requiring strict adherence to the plan then the addition of the words requiring the authority to have regard to 'any other material considerations' could mean that the authority might be faced with the impossible task of reconciling the two. Lord Guest said: 'In my opinion, the meaning of [s 26(1)] is plain. The planning authority are to consider all the material considerations, of which the development plan is one.'

This reasoning was applied by the Divisional Court in the case of *Enfield London Borough Council v Secretary of State for the Environment*[5] where a grant of permission by the Secretary of State on appeal was upheld even though it departed from the policies in the original development plan.[5a]

However, a decision on a planning application will be open to challenge in the courts if it can be shown that the local planning authority (or the Secretary of State on appeal) failed to have regard to a relevant policy in the

---

2 But see Michael Purdue 'The Flexibility of North American Zoning as an Instrument of Land Use Planning' [1986] JPL 84 for an account of the way the zoning system in North America has evolved.

3 *Stringer v Minister of Housing and Local Government* [1971] 1 All ER 65, [1970] 1 WLR 1281. See too *H Lavender & Son Ltd v Minister of Housing and Local Government* [1970] 3 All ER 871, [1970] 1 WLR 1231; and *Link Homes Ltd v Secretary of State for the Environment* [1976] JPL 430.

4 1960 SC 313; 1961 SLT 17.

5 (1974) 233 Estates Gazette 53, [1975] JPL 155.

5a But note that with regard to listed buildings and conservation areas the 1971 Act appears to impose a higher standard; see S56(3) and S277(A) and chapter 18.

development plan.[6] Further, a local planning authority (or the Secretary of State) will be treated as having failed in their duty to have regard to the development plan if they misinterpret the provisions of the plan which they are purporting to apply.[7] Sir Douglas Frank expressed the position to be:

'. . . when he [the Secretary of State] expresses himself to be deciding a case under a stated policy, it must follow that if he decides the case other than in accordance with that policy he misdirects himself.'

Finally, if the decision-maker is going to depart from a policy in the plan, clear reasons should be given.[8] Special problems apply when the policies in the development plan change between a public inquiry and the actual decision and that change is not brought to the attention of the inspector or the Secretary of State. In *Wokingham District Council v Secretary of State for the Environment*[8a] Malcolm Spence QC sitting as a deputy judge, held that an inspector, but not presumably the Secretary of State, cannot be faulted for not having regard to such changes if they were not referred to him. The legitimacy of the development control system would be undermined if the development plan could be lightly set aside. Where permission is refused, the main safeguard is the applicant's right of appeal to the Secretary of State, but this course presumes that the minister or his inspector will uphold the plan. In the case where the local planning authority is minded to grant permission the various Development Plan Directions ensure that departures from the plan will be advertised and, in the case of applications which fundamentally conflict, the Secretary of State will be given the opportunity of calling-in the application under s 35 (see chapter 7, p 189).

The Local Government Planning and Land Act 1980 has also attempted to up-grade the status of the structure plan as a strategic planning instrument by requiring the local planning authority in exercising their functions under s 29 'to seek the achievement of the general objectives of the structure plan'

6 See *Holmes v Secretary of State for the Environment* [1983] JPL 476; and *Richmond-upon-Thames London Borough Council v Secretary of State for the Environment* [1984] JPL 24. In *R v Sevenoaks District Council, ex p Terry* [1985] 3 All ER 226, [1984] JPL 420 Glidewell J found that a local planning authority had failed to take account of a policy contained in a structure plan but exercised his discretion not to quash the authority's decision on the ground that they would have reached the same decision even if the relevant policy had been considered.
7 See *Niarchos (London) Ltd v Secretary of State for the Environment* (1977) 76 LGR 480, 35 P & CR 259; *Pyrford Properties Ltd v Secretary of State for the Environment* (1977) 36 P & CR 28; *Molddene Ltd v Secretary of State for the Environment* (1978) 248 Estates Gazette 43, [1979] JPL 177; *Bell and Colvill Ltd v Secretary of State for the Environment and Guildford Borough Council* [1980] JPL 823; *J A Pye (Oxford) Estates Ltd v Secretary of State for the Environment* (1981) 261 Estates Gazette 368; *Tromans v Secretary of State for the Environment and Wyre Forest District Council* [1983] JPL 474; *Westminster Renslade Ltd v Secretary of State for the Environment* (1983) 48 P & CR 255; *Federated Estates Ltd v Secretary of State for the Environment* [1983] JPL 812; *Westminster City Council v Secretary of State for the Environment* [1984] JPL 27, and *Chelmsford Borough Council v Secretary of State for the Environment* [1986] JPL 112.
8 See *Gransden & Co Ltd v Secretary of State for the Environment* (1985) 54 P & CR 86, [1986] JPL 519 and *Wigan Metropolitan Borough Council v Secretary of State for the Environment* (1987) 54 P & CR 369, [1987] JPL 575.
8a [1989] JPL 424.

(s 86(3)). However, as the objectives of the structure plan will inevitably be expressed broadly, it would take an extreme case to show the local planning authority had failed to comply with this duty.[9] It would also seem that this duty is only directed at the local planning authority and not the Secretary of State.

Other non-statutory policy statements

A matter which has given rise to some practical difficulty in recent years has been the weight to be given, when determining a planning application, to policies contained elsewhere than in the development plan itself and the relationship between these policies and the development plan. The courts have held that policies in certain other documents are capable of being 'material' considerations as the term is used by s 29(1). However, we have considered the status of such 'policies' separately from the general question of what are material considerations, as the policy or view as to the importance of a material consideration is really a different issue from material considerations themselves.

Draft development plans present particular problems. The local planning authority puts forward certain proposals for the use of land in its draft plan. Local people object to these proposals and a public inquiry is arranged. In the meantime, a planning application is submitted to the local planning authority for the development of the land. If the application is in accord with the proposals in the draft plan the local planning authority may be minded to grant permission. Such a step would effectively pre-empt the decision on the objections to the local plan, and the objectors would, understandably, feel aggrieved. On the other hand, the local planning authority may decide to postpone a decision on the application until the local plan proposals have been settled. As this may be some time away the applicant may well feel aggrieved. This difficulty serves to highlight the relationship between development plans and development control.

In *Link Homes Ltd v Secretary of State for the Environment*[10] Willis J commented that the fact that a development plan was in course of preparation was not a reason which could be used as a rubber stamp objection to refuse all planning applications until the plan had been approved or adopted. On the other hand, in *R v City of London Corpn, ex p Allan*[11] Woolf J, held that a draft plan must be taken into account if it is material to an application, although, as with approved plans, the contents will not bind the authority. What this seems to amount to is that an application for planning permission may properly be refused on the ground that the development will be likely to prejudice the outcome of a draft development plan[12] but that there is no

9 For an unsuccessful attempt see *R v Royal County of Berkshire, ex p Mangnall* [1985] JPL 258. Also see *Carroll Business Parks Ltd v Secretary of State for the Environment* (5 July 1988, not reported at the time of going to press) where Pill J accepted that the Secretary of State had not erred in law in considering that 'there is no positive obligation to implement a particular proposal as distinct from seeking to achieve the general objectives of the Structure Plan ...'

10 [1976] JPL 430. See also *Myton Ltd v Minister of Housing and Local Government* (1963) 61 LGR 556, 16 P & CR 240; and *Thornville Properties v Secretary of State for the Environment* (1980) 258 Estates Gazette 172, [1981] JPL 116.

11 (1980) 79 LGR 223 (cited with approval by the Court of Appeal in *Davies v London Borough of Hammersmith and Fulham* [1981] JPL 682).

obligation to refuse the application in such circumstances.[13] All that is required is that the effect of the proposed development on the policies and proposals in the draft plan should be properly considered before the application is determined.[14]

So, in effect, a grant of planning permission can pre-empt a draft plan and thus undermine the whole process of plan-making as long as the issue of pre-emption is considered and the decision is not perverse or totally unreasonable.[15] The position is therefore one of complete flexibility. The policies in the draft plan can be applied, which, if this results in a grant of permission, will underwrite those policies before they are formally adopted or approved. In contrast, the policies can be rejected, in which case, if it results in a grant, the draft plan will effectively have been rewritten. Finally the issue can be postponed by refusing the application on grounds of prematurity, as long as clear reasons can be shown why the draft plan would be prejudiced. This principle of prematurity has recently been endorsed by the Court of Appeal in *Arlington v Secretary of State for the Environment and Crawley Borough Council*[16] where it was held that a refusal was justified because of the risk of prejudice or error which could arise. The nearer the draft plan is to being adopted or approved the more weight it will be given by the Secretary of State. This was spelt out in circular 22/84 which stated that

'A structure plan, a local plan and proposals for the alteration, repeal or replacement of such plans may be taken account as a material consideration for development control purposes while going through the statutory procedures leading to approval or adoption. The weight to be accorded to such a plan or to such proposals will increase as successive stages are reached in the statutory procedures.' (para 1.12)

This approach was accepted by McCowen J in *J A Pye (Oxford) Estates v Secretary of State for the Environment and Wychavon District Council.*[17] Similar difficulties arise over the weight which may be given to non-statutory policy statements of local planning authorities, whether adopted or in course of preparation. These are policy statements on specific topics which are prepared and adopted by local planning authorities and used to guide development control decisions. No formal procedures govern their preparation and the extent to which the public can influence such policies is entirely in the hands of the local planning authority. It would seem that such policy statements may properly be taken into account in determining a planning

12 See, for example, *Governors of Rugby School v Secretary of State for the Environment* (1975) 234 Estates Gazette 371. In *Thornville* (above) Sir Douglas Frank held that reasons must be given why the application if granted, would prejudice the plan.
13 *Davies v London Borough of Hammersmith and Fulham* [1981] JPL 682; *R v City of London Corpn, ex p Allan* (1980) 79 LGR 223. See also ministerial decisions noted in [1979] JPL 494, [1981] JPL 65 and 541, and [1982] JPL 322.
14 See, for example, *R v Hammersmith and Fulham London Borough Council, ex p People Before Profit Ltd* (1981) 80 LGR 322, 45 P & CR 364.
15 In *Wyre Forrest District Council v Secretary of State for the Environment* (1989) Independent, 31 March, the Court of Appeal, overturning the decision of the High Court, held that a decision of an inspector not to refuse for prematurity was valid despite the fact that a report of a local plan inquiry was pending.
16 [1989] JPL 166.
17 [1987] JPL 363.

application,[18] and that failure to take account of such a statement may render a decision *ultra vires*.[19] As with development plans, a statement of this kind must not bind the authority but should be weighed against any other material considerations.

As to published government policies, the courts have equally held that planning decisions can be based on such policies, and have consistently quashed decisions where there has been a failure to have regard to a relevant policy or to explain why a policy has not been followed.[20]

In *J A Pye (Oxford) Estates Ltd v Wychavon District Council and Secretary of State for the Environment*[1] Glidewell J held that ministerial policies set out in departmental circulars[2] were material considerations which had to be taken into account in determining an appeal; he also held that interpretation of a circular is a matter of law on which the court may review a decision.[3] In *Hatfield Construction Ltd v Secretary of State for the Environment*[4] Mr David Widdicombe QC, sitting as a deputy High Court judge, held that departmental circulars and development control policy notes were part of the background of every planning appeal and must be presumed to have been taken into account in the determination of an appeal unless there was evidence to the contrary.

So the need to have regard to the statement of government policy will depend on the relevance of the particular policy and whether it has been raised by the parties. Thus in *Penwith District Council v Secretary of State for the Environment*[5] Woolf J quashed a decision of an inspector where he granted permission for an amusement arcade without referring to Development Control Policy Note No 11 which had been set out in the written submissions. However, it would seem that the policies do not always have to have been raised by the parties, as, when a circular comes into existence after

18 *Myton Ltd v Minister of Housing and Local Government* (1963) 61 LGR 556, 16 P & CR 240. In *Philglow Ltd v Secretary of State for the Environment and the London Borough of Hillingdon* [1984] JPL 111 (revsd on other grounds 51 P & CR 1, 270 Estates Gazette 1192) the Secretary of State for the Environment was held entitled to take account of a local planning authority's change of attitude on a policy document prepared by the authority. Also see *J A Pye (Oxford) Estates Ltd v Secretary of State for the Environment and Wychavon District Council* [1987] JPL 363, where a non-statutory plan was accepted as a material consideration.
19 See *J A Pye (Oxford) Estates Ltd v Secretary of State for the Environment and Cherwell District Council* (1981) 261 Estates Gazette 368. As to the difficulties which may arise over non-statutory policies see, however, *Westminster City Council v Great Portland Estates plc* [1985] AC 661, [1984] 3 WLR 1035 (p 76 above).
20 See Brian Thompson 'Development Control's "Circular" Triangle' 1984 SPLP 36; and S M Nott and P H Morgan, 'The Significance of Department of the Environment Circulars in the Planning Process' [1984] JPL 623.
1 [1982] JPL 575.
2 In *Peak Park Joint Planning Board v Secretary of State for the Environment and Cyril Kay* [1979] JPL 618 Sir Douglas Frank considered that advice in a department circular relating to the renewal of planning permission was merely some form of administrative policy and was not a relevant planning consideration but this seems clearly wrong.
3 On this point see *Rockhold Ltd v Secretary of State for the Environment and South Oxfordshire District Council* [1986] JPL 130; *E C Gransden & Co Ltd v Secretary of State for the Environment* (1985) 54 P & CR 86, [1986] JPL 519 and *Surrey Heath Borough Council v Secretary of State for the Environment* (1986) 85 LGR 767, 53 P & CR 428.
4 [1983] JPL 605, CA. See too *New Forest District Council v Secretary of State for the Environment and Clarke* [1984] JPL 178.
5 [1986] 1 EGLR 193, [1986] JPL 432.

an inquiry but before the decision,[6] though it could be that an inspector is not presumed to be aware of all the documents that are issued by the Department of Environment.[7]

In *J A Pye (Oxford) Estates Ltd v West Oxfordshire District Council*[8] Mr David Widdicombe QC, sitting as a deputy High Court judge, expressed the view that a *draft* circular was not a material consideration—it might be amended or might never be issued. In that case the circular in question came into operation between the submission of the inquiry inspector's report and the issue of the decision letter; the decision was therefore quashed because of the minister's failure to take it into account. In both *Richmond-upon-Thames London Borough Council v Secretary of State for the Environment*[9] and *Westminster City Council v Secretary of State for the Environment and City Commercial Real Estates Investments Ltd*[10] the report of the Property Advisory Group on 'Planning Gain' was held to be a material consideration: despite its purely advisory status it represented the views of a government-appointed committee. In the latter case Mr David Widdicombe QC stood by what he had said on the status of draft circulars in *J A Pye (Oxford) Ltd* (above) but in the former case Glidewell J said that he did not agree that a draft circular could never be a material consideration.

Where government policies are not readily available from H M Stationery Office it would seem wrong to hold those policies to be material considerations. In *Dimsdale Developments (South East) Ltd*[11] MacPherson J doubted whether an after dinner speech by the then Secretary of State for the Environment should be used in argument. On the other hand it has been accepted that a decision of a Secretary of State could of itself alter or make policy and so one would have to look to those decisions to ascertain that policy.[12] Parliamentary statements have sometimes been used to alter or explain government policies and as such statements are publicly available they would seem to be capable of being 'material' considerations.[13] Where there is a change in government policy this must be stated in clear and unambiquous terms.[13a]

Government policies can be used as reasons for departing from policies in development plans and even for holding a policy in a development plan to be arbitrary.[14] If development plans do not have to be 'slavishly adhered to', the same must apply to government policies but government inspectors in practice feel themselves bound to apply their minister's policies. However, in

---

6 See *Newham London Borough v Secretary of State for the Environment* (1986) 53 P & CR 98, [1986] JPL 607 but compare *Kasperck and Coppen v Secretary of State for the Environment and Lewes District Council* [1988] JPL 785.
7 *Wokingham District Council v Secretary of State for the Environment* [1989] JPL 424.
8 (1982) 47 P & CR 125.
9 [1984] JPL 24.
10 [1984] JPL 27.
11 (1985) 275 Estates Gazette 58, [1986] JPL 276.
12 See *Sears Blok v Secretary of State for the Environment and London Borough of Southwark* [1982] JPL 248.
13 See *R v Secretary of State for the Environment and Charles Church Developments Ltd, ex p Surrey Heath Borough Council* [1988] JPL 783.
13a See *Bromley London Borough v Secretary of State for the Environment* (4 May 1989, unreported).
14 See *Waverley Borough Council v Secretary of State for the Environment* [1987] JPL 202.

Surrey Heath Borough Council v Secretary of State for the Environment[15] Kennedy J held that a failure to take into account local circumstances in applying a policy could amount to a misinterpretation of that policy and in *Wycombe District Council v Secretary of State for the Environment*[16] Graham Eyre QC, sitting as a deputy judge, laid down that whether the policy was contained in a development plan or elsewhere, such as in government circulars, there was no requirement that it should be slavishly followed.

The courts have also warned against a legalistic approach to government policies and have emphasised that circulars and the like have to be read as a whole.[17] This means that on an appeal an inspector's task is one of balancing or weighing various policies or factors and government policies by no means automatically override the policies in the development plans. Local planning authorities, at least in theory, are free, having considered government policy, to decide not to follow it.[18] The position of inspectors is much more questionable. From a literal reading of their jurisdiction to decide appeals (see Sch 9, para 2) they are placed in the same position as the Secretary of State and as such should not see themselves bound by government policies. Yet it is clear that inspectors cannot make policy[19] and should not question the merits of government policy.[20] Also the decisions of inspectors are treated legally as those of the Secretary of State[1] and so where the government policy is so precise as to dictate the answer, it could be that the inspector is bound to apply the policy.[2] However, the principle against fettering discretion is so strong, that it is submitted that in the final analysis even inspectors must be free to depart from government policy.

'Any other material considerations'[3]

In determining an application, a local planning authority must have regard not only to the development plan and to the other matters listed at p 199 above but also to 'any other material considerations' (1971 Act, s 29(1)). A decision which fails to take account of material considerations or which is based on matters which are not material may be quashed by the courts[4] on

---

15 (1986) 85 LGR 767, [1987] JPL 199.
16 (1987) 57 P & CR 177, [1988] JPL 111.
17 See *E L S Wholesale (Wolverhampton) v Secretary of State for the Environment* (1987) 56 P & CR 69, [1987] JPL 844.
18 See *R v Camden London Borough Council, ex p Comyn Ching & Co (London) Ltd* (1983) 47 P & CR 417, [1984] JPL 661.
19 *Chelmsford Borough Council v Secretary of State for the Environment* [1985] JPL 316.
20 *R v Secretary of State for Transport, ex p Gwent County Council* [1988] QB 429, [1987] 1 All ER 161, CA.
1 See para 2(3) of Sch 9.
2 See on this Kennedy J in *Bolton Borough Council v Secretary of State for the Environment and Barratts (Manchester) Ltd* [1987] JPL 580 where he seemed to suggest that the inspector was *bound* to apply the policy.
3 See Michael Purdue, 'The Scope of Planning Authorities' Discretion: or What's Material?' [1977] JPL 490; Martin Loughlin, 'The Scope and Importance of "Material Considerations"' (1980) 3 *Urban Law and Policy* 171; and Paul Q Watchman, 'Planning Considerations' 1983 SPLP 36 and 72.
4 The onus of proving that an irrelevant consideration was taken into account or a relevant one ignored rests with the person seeking to challenge the decision—see, for example, *Fawcett Properties Ltd v Buckingham County Council* [1959] Ch 543, [1959] 2 All ER 321, per Pearce LJ; and *Bell and Colvill Ltd v Secretary of State for the Environment and Guildford Borough Council* [1980] JPL 823.

the ground that it is *ultra vires* the authority.[5] It is therefore important to define the scope of the matters embraced by this term. As one writer has put it: 'The question of material considerations is a crucial one for development control, and indeed for the whole town and country planning system, since it is through this concept that the limits to public intervention in the planning sphere are defined.'[6]

These 'other material considerations' are not specifically defined in the 1971 Act and it is difficult to discern their scope by implication from the legislation. The courts, for their part, have tended to confine themselves to deciding upon the validity of the particular consideration in issue in any given case and to eschew the giving of general guidance about their range. As a great deal turns on the particular circumstances of each case, it is not possible to reconcile all the decisions in this area and it is difficult to extract from them any yardstick which may readily be used as a measure of the validity of any given consideration.

Although it is well established that these 'other material considerations' must be of a 'planning' nature,[7] this merely serves to rephrase the question in terms of 'what is planning'? Here, too, there is a lack of definition. There is no explicit statement in the 1971 Act of the objectives of planning or of the planning system. This may be because planning is not an end in itself. It is not the function of the system to build houses or roads or hospitals but rather to provide a framework within which such investments can be made. The nearest that the Act comes to a statement of an objective is the very generally expressed requirement that development plans should set out policies and proposals for the development and the use of land in the local planning authority's area.[8] This suggests that the scope of development plans is delimited by physical land use matters. It does not, however, mean that the policies and proposals for the development and use of land can only be related to physical or amenity factors. Section 7(4) expressly requires the local planning authority to have regard to the economic planning and

5 *Associated Provincial Picture Houses Ltd v Wednesbury Corpn* [1948] 1 KB 223, [1947] 2 All ER 680. The presence of an irrelevant factor or a failure to take account of a relevant factor may not be fatal if the court considers that the defect did not affect the decision, or operated in favour of the complainant—see, for example, *Hanks v Minister of Housing and Local Government* [1963] 1 QB 999, [1963] 1 All ER 47; *Bradwell Industrial Aggregates v Secretary of State for the Environment* [1981] JPL 276; and *Chichester District Council v Secretary of State for the Environment and Hall Aggregates (South Coast) Ltd* [1981] JPL 591. It seems that any relevant matter arising up to the date of the decision (e g between the holding of a public inquiry and the decision) must be taken into account—see, for example, *J A Pye (Oxford) Estates Ltd v West Oxfordshire District Council* (1982) 47 P & CR 125; and *Price Bros (Rode Heath) Ltd v Department of the Environment* (1978) 38 P & CR 579. A person exercising a statutory discretion may be under a duty to call his own attention to relevant matters—see, for example, *Prest v Secretary of State for Wales* (1982) 81 LGR 193, 266 Estates Gazette 527; and *F J Tierney v Secretary of State for the Environment and Spelthorne Borough Council* [1983] JPL 799. However, this may not apply so strictly to inspectors; see *Wokingham District Council v Secretary of State for the Environment* [1989] JPL 424.

6 J Underwood, *Development Control: A Review of Research and Current Issues* (Pergamon Press, 1981), p 199.

7 *East Barnet UDC v British Transport Commission* [1962] 2 QB 484, [1961] 3 All ER 878; *Stringer v Minister of Housing and Local Government* [1971] 1 All ER 65, [1970] 1 WLR 1281; *Newbury District Council v Secretary of State for the Environment* [1981] AC 578, [1980] 1 All ER 731, per Lords Scarman and Fraser; and *Westminster City Council v Great Portland Estates plc* [1985] AC 661, [1984] 3 WLR 1035.

8 1971 Act, ss 7(1A) and 11(3).

development of the region as a whole and the Structure and Local Plans Regulations prescribe a range of matters that must be contained in such plans, including a statement of the regard that has been paid to social and economic policies.[9] So the policies and proposals in the plans are concerned with the implications which these matters may have for the physical environment.

As the control of development is intended to operate within the framework of the policies and proposals in the development plan, it would seem to follow that the development control process is similarly circumscribed by physical land use factors. Although 'other material considerations' are matters outside the development plan, it appears that they too must follow this general pattern and be concerned with the use of land. In *Stringer v Minister of Housing and Local Government*[10] Cooke J defined these other considerations as 'any consideration which relates to the use and development of land'.

However, as a yardstick for measuring the validity of a consideration this definition clearly has its problems. The list of matters which could be said to be concerned with the use and development of land is open-ended, as the courts are beginning to recognise.[11] Some further qualification of the yardstick is desirable. This further qualification is a test of remoteness of the relationship between the proposed development and the material considera- tion. The consideration must be shown to be 'material' to the particular application. In *Stringer* Cooke J went on to say: 'Whether a particular consideration falling within that broad class is material in any given case will depend on the circumstances.' Also in *R v Westminster City Council, ex p Monahan*[12] Staughton LJ said that like conditions, considerations, to be material, must 'fairly and reasonably relate to the development permitted'.

Thus although the list of considerations could be said to be open-ended, a local planning authority in determining an application must take into account only those planning considerations which are relevant in the particular circumstances of the case. In some cases the courts have been prepared to determine whether a particular factor, relevant to planning in general, is in fact relevant in the circumstances of a particular case,[13] in other cases it has, however, been said that it is for the local planning authority (or the minister) to decide whether, in the circumstances of an individual case, a particular issue is material.[14] The weight to be attached to a particular consideration is generally for the local planning authority or the Secretary of

9　See reg 9 of the Town and Country Planning (Structure and Local Plans) Regulations 1982 and paras 4.8 and 4.10 of circular 22/84.
10　[1971] 1 All ER 65, [1970] 1 WLR 1281.
11　See, for example, *Clyde & Co v Secretary of State for the Environment* [1977] 1 All ER 333, [1977] 1 WLR 926, per Sir David Cairns. In general, however, the courts treat it as a matter of statutory interpretation, and therefore as a matter for judicial determination, whether a particular consideration is capable in law of being relevant to town and country planning.
12　[1989] JPL 107, CA; but see *Northumberland County Council v Secretary of State for the Environment* [1989] JPL 700.
13　See, for example, *Brown v Secretary of State for the Environment* (1978) 40 P & CR 285.
14　See, for example, *Sovmots Investments Ltd v Secretary of State for the Environment* [1977] QB 411, [1976] 1 All ER 178, per Forbes J; and *Vale of Glamorgan Borough Council v Secretary of State for Wales and Rhys-Williams* (1985) 52 P & CR 418, [1986] JPL 198 where Woolf J said that the Secretary of State's decision as to whether an alternative site was relevant could only be challenged in the courts if it was unreasonable.

State to determine;[15] however, if the authority or the minister attach undue or insufficient weight to a particular consideration the court may be prepared to intervene and quash the decision as perverse or unreasonable.[16] It is also important to remember that the courts will not quash a decision if the factor wrongly taken into account or omitted was insignificant or insubstantial and that it is clear that it did not affect the outcome.[17]

It would seem, therefore, that the 'other material considerations' in s 29(1) must satisfy two tests. First of all, they must be 'planning' considerations, that is they must have consequences for the use and development of land. Secondly, they must be material in the circumstances of the case, that is they must relate to the proposed development. Further it would appear that material considerations are not confined to the consequences of the proposed development looked at in isolation. The decisions of the courts make clear that local planning authorities are not, for example, confined to the question 'whether the character of the building or the proposed building is objectionable in itself'[18] and it has been held to be quite proper for a local planning authority to refuse an application, which might be unobjectionable in itself, on the grounds that it was desirable to preserve an existing permitted use of the land[19] or that if permission were granted it would be difficult to resist further applications for the development of other sites.[20]

Clearly, such tests provide only general guidance for those engaged in the development control process. Difficult questions will inevitably arise at the margins and much will depend on the particular circumstances of each case. In town and country planning the doctrine of relevant and irrelevant considerations has given rise to what H W R Wade describes[1] as 'incessant litigation' and some illustration of the scope of the matters which have been accepted or rejected in particular cases as 'other material considerations' may therefore be helpful.

'Amenity'. In *Stringer* (above) Cooke J found it impossible to accept that planning considerations are limited to matters relating to amenity.[2] 'Amenity' considerations are, however, often important in the determination of planning applications. Though the concept of 'amenity' is impossible to define with precision—one official report described it as 'that element in the appearance and lay-out of town and country which makes for a comfortable and pleasant life [and] the quality which a well-designed building estate or

---

15 See *Sovmots* (above), per Forbes J; and *Clyde & Co v Secretary of State for the Environment* [1977] 1 All ER 333, [1977] 1 WLR 926.
16 See, for example, *South Oxfordshire District Council v Secretary of State for the Environment* [1981] 1 All ER 954, [1981] 1 WLR 1092. See too *Niarchos (London) Ltd v Secretary of State for the Environment* (1977) 76 LGR 480, 35 P & CR 259.
17 See *Hanks v Minister of Housing and Local Government* [1963] 1 QB 999 at 1020, and *Simplex G E (Holdings) Ltd v Secretary of State for the Environment* [1988] JPL 809, CA.
18 *Clyde & Co v Secretary of State for the Environment* [1977] 1 All ER 333, [1977] 1 WLR 926, per Sir David Cairns.
19 *Clyde & Co* (above).
20 *Collis Radio Ltd v Secretary of State for the Environment* (1975) 73 LGR 211, 29 P & CR 390. and p 212 below.
1 *Administrative Law* (Clarendon Press, Oxford, 6th edn. 1988). p 370.
2 See too the comments of Sir David Cairns in *Clyde & Co v Secretary of State for the Environment* [1977] 1 All ER 333, [1981] 1 WLR 926.

neighbourhood will have[3]—it is clear that the scope of amenity considerations is very wide. As the same report put it: 'Anything ugly, dirty, noisy, crowded, destructive, intrusive or uncomfortable may "injure the interests of amenity" and, therefore, be of concern to the planning authority.' In *Copeland Borough Council v Secretary of State for the Environment*,[4] for example, Lord Widgery CJ said that 'the purpose of all town and country planning is to preserve amenities and the sensible and attractive layout of properties.'

Compatibility with other uses. In *Collis Radio Ltd v Secretary of State for the Environment*[5] Lord Widgery CJ declared:

'Planning . . . deals with localities and not individual parcels of land and individual sites. In all planning cases it must be of the greatest importance when considering a single planning application to ask oneself what the consequences in the locality will be . . . In so far as an application for planning permission on site A is judged according to the consequence on sites B, C and D, in my judgment no error of law is disclosed but only what is perhaps the most elementary principle of planning practice is being observed.'

Thus in *Stringer* (above), after quoting Widgery J's dictum that 'an essential feature of planning must be the separation of different uses or activities which are incompatible the one with the other',[6] Cooke J held that the likelihood that a proposed development would interfere with the work of the Jodrell Bank telescope was a material planning consideration. Similarly, in *R M C Management Services Ltd v Secretary of State for the Environment*[7] it was held that in dealing with an application for a ready-mixed concrete plant, the local planning authority could properly take into account the effect which dust created by the concrete plant would have on neighbouring factories manufacturing precision products and requiring clean air.

The desirability of preserving a balance of uses (e g in a shopping area) will be a material consideration, and it will, it seems, be proper to take account of the desirability of safeguarding the future development potential of neighbouring land,[8] and of the danger that development would prejudice public proposals for the land in question. In *R v Doncaster Metropolitan District Council, ex p British Railways Board*[9] Scheiman J concluded that whilst it was not a function of land use planning to protect commercial interests, it was relevant to consider the degree to which the opening of a new store might lead to the decay of existing centres. He therefore concluded that:

'In principle, planning authorities were entitled to refuse planning permission for a large new outlet if its operation was likely to lead to such decay on a significant scale.'

3 Ministry of Town and Country Planning. *Town and Country Planning Progress Report 1943–1951* (Cmd 8204, 1951).
4 (1976) 31 P & CR 403.
5 (1975) 73 LGR 211, 29 P & CR 390.
6 See *Fitzpatrick Developments Ltd v Minister of Housing and Local Government* (1965) 194 Estates Gazette 911.
7 (1972) 222 Estates Gazette 1593. See too, for example, [1973] JPL 120, [1974] JPL 425, and [1983] JPL 398.
8 See appeal decision reported in [1987] JPL 685.
9 [1987] JPL 444.

In this regard, it would seem doubtful whether any distinction can be made between preventing development which might have a deleterious effect in relation to other land users and a case where the proposals are opposed on the grounds of the existence of an incompatible established land use in proximity to the site. Thus it has been held that the proximity of a sewage works or an explosives factory could be a reason for refusing permission for a use which was therefore incompatible.[10]

Private interests. In *Stringer*[11] Cooke J could not accept that the local planning authority 'must have regard only to public interests as opposed to private interests', and declared that in his view 'the protection of the interests of individual occupiers is one aspect, and an important one, of the public interest as a whole'. He considered that in this context no assistance was to be derived from the decisions in *Buxton v Minister of Housing and Local Government;*[12] *Simpson v Edinburgh Corpn*[13] and *Gregory v Camden London Borough Council.*[14] These cases were, he said, 'concerned with the right of an individual to maintain proceedings in the courts. An individual may well have no such rights and yet be a person whose interests may very properly be considered at an anterior stage when the question whether or not to grant planning permission is being dealt with.'

It is, for example, a material consideration that a proposed development would result in loss of privacy, sunlight, daylight or amenity enjoyed by a neighbouring householder.[15] This applies whether or not the neighbour has any legal rights at private law,[16] but see below, page 225.

Retaining the existing use. The desirability of retaining the existing permitted use of premises is a matter which can validly be taken into account in determining a planning application, provided that the local planning authority's reason for seeking the continuation of the existing use is a proper planning one.[17] In *Clyde & Co v Secretary of State for the Environment,*[18] for example, the Court of Appeal held that permission for a change from residential to office use could properly be refused on the ground that the existing residential use of the building in question was one which, given the shortage of housing accommodation in the area, ought to continue.[19]

---

10 See *Ricketts and Fletcher v Secretary of State for the Environment and Salisbury District Council* [1988] JPL 768.
11 [1971] 1 All ER 65, [1970] 1 WLR 1281.
12 [1961] 1 QB 278, [1960] 3 All ER 408.
13 1960 SC 313, 1961 SLT 17.
14 [1966] 2 All ER 196, [1966] 1 WLR 899.
15 See, for example, *Barratt Developments (Eastern) Ltd v Secretary of State for the Environment and Oadby and Wigston Borough Council* [1982] JPL 648; and [1972] JPL 660, [1977] JPL 685 and [1985] JPL 336.
16 *Brewer v Secretary of State for the Environment* [1988] JPL 480.
17 See *Clyde & Co v Secretary of State for the Environment* [1977] 1 All ER 333, [1977] 1 WLR 926; *Granada Theatres Ltd v Secretary of State for the Environment* (1980) 43 P & CR 253; *L O Finn & Co v Secretary of State for the Environment and Barnet London Borough* [1984] JPL 734.
18 [1977] 1 All ER 333, 1 WLR 926.
19 Since the discontinuance of a use is not in itself development, the planning authority have no way of ensuring that premises are actually used for the permitted purpose; the owner might simply prefer to leave the premises empty.

Alternative permitted uses, if any, may also be taken into account,[20] and it will normally be material to consider what could happen if an application is refused. In *Clyde & Co* Sir David Cairns said that it was enough that there was 'at least a fair chance' that the refusal of permission for the proposed use would result in the existing use being continued. However, in *Westminster City Council v British Waterways Board*[1] Lord Bridge expressed the view that a rather higher standard was appropriate; in his view it was necessary to show 'a balance of probability' that a refusal would result in the preferred use being continued.

In *Westminster City Council v British Waterways Board*[2] Dunn LJ held that preservation of the existing use of land is not to be confused with the preservation of use by a particular existing occupier, which is not generally a material planning consideration; planning is concerned, he said, 'with development of land, and not with the protection of existing occupiers'.

However, in *Westminster City Council v Great Portland Estates*[3] Lord Scarman approved a policy of protecting special industrial activities considered important to the diverse character, vitality and functioning of Westminster as 'a powerful piece of positive thinking' even though it also had the effect of protecting existing occupiers.

Precedent and ministerial decisions. As each application for planning permission must be considered on its own merits, it might be thought that fear of creating an undesirable precedent was not a proper planning consideration. In *Collis Radio Ltd v Secretary of State for the Environment*,[4] however, the Divisional Court held that a local planning authority can properly take into account the possibility that to grant planning permission for a particular development, unobjectionable in itself, might set a precedent and make it difficult for the authority to refuse planning permission for similar development on other sites and thus lead to undesirable proliferation of such development. Mere fear or generalised concern is not enough; there must be evidence in one form or another for the reliance on precedent.[5] This does not mean that previous decisions, whether by local planning authorities or by the Secretary of State, form binding precedents. However, it does seem that previous ministerial decisions are capable of being material considerations even though, as stated above, the decisions of inspectors cannot be treated as forming government policy.[6] In *Rockhold Ltd v Secretary of State for the Environment and South Oxfordshire District Council*[7] Forbes J, while accept-

20 *South Oxfordshire District Council v Secretary of State for the Environment* [1981] 1 All ER 954, [1981] 1 WLR 1092 (see p 217 below).
1 [1985] AC 676, [1984] 3 All ER 737. Also see *London Residuary Body v Secretary of State for the Environment* [1989] EGCS 116.
2 (1983) 82 LGR 44 CA; upheld in the House of Lords; [1985] AC 676, [1984] 3 All ER 737.
3 [1985] AC 661, [1984] 3 WLR 1035.
4 (1975) 73 LGR 211, 29 P & CR 390; followed in *Tempo Discount Warehouses Ltd v Enfield London Borough and the Secretary of State for the Government* [1979] JPL 97; and *Anglia Building Society v Secretary of State for the Environment and Medina Borough Council* [1984] JPL 175. Contrast *Walter Hermans & Sons Ltd v Secretary of State for the Environment* (1974) 234 Estates Gazette 47, [1975] JPL 351.
5 *Poundstretcher Ltd v Secretary of State for the Environment* [1989] JPL 90.
6 See *Sears Blok v Secretary of State for the Environment and London Borough of Southwark* [1982] JPL 248. Also see *Chelmsford Borough Council v Secretary of State for the Environment and E R Alexander Ltd* [1985] JPL 316 where Woolf J stated that a failure to take into account a previous decision could show evidence of unfair or improper treatment.
7 [1986] JPL 130.

ing that one inspector could always decide to disagree with the approach of a previous inspector, accepted that reasons for the disagreement should be given. This can be defended on the ground of the need for consistency in decision-making but where there is disagreement on matters of opinion it will be hard to give reasons. In *Ainley v Secretary of State for the Environment and Fylde Borough Council*[8] Taylor J seemed to suggest that inspectors were entitled to form their own views on matters of opinion and need not give their reasons for disagreement with another inspector; and in *Lee v Secretary of State for the Environment*[9] it was pointed out that in *Rockhold* the case was concerned with three successive applications and appeals in respect of the same site and it was held that where an inspector was dealing with a different site, he did not have to give reasons for adopting a different approach. It is also clear that the principle of issue estoppel does not apply to the exercise of administrative discretions.[10]

Safety. The possible consequences of a development on the safety of the public and of users of the premises, whether from its potentially hazardous nature or from its likely effect on traffic flow, has been regarded as a planning matter.[11] Indeed, local planning authorities are required by the GDO to have regard to representations made to them in appropriate cases by the Health and Safety Executive and by the highway authority.[12]

In *Stringer*[13] Cooke J said: 'if permission is sought to erect an explosives factory adjacent to a school, the minister must surely be entitled and bound to consider the question of safety.' Control over hazardous development has been reinforced by amendments to the GDO and the UCO and the Housing and Planning Act 1986 has introduced a separate system of consents for the introduction of hazardous substances; see chapter 18, p 520.

Economic and financial considerations.[14] Difficult questions arise as to how far the economic or financial implications of a proposed development are relevant planning considerations.

In *J Murphy & Sons Ltd v Secretary of State for the Environment*[15] the minister, in considering whether to grant planning permission for local authority development, had refused to take into account the fact that the site would, because of its nature and situation, be a particularly expensive one to develop. Ackner J held 'as a matter of law' that the minister's view was correct; there was nothing in the planning legislation which required a local

8 [1987] JPL 33.
9 [1989] JPL 521.
10 See *Thrasyvoulou v Secretary of State for the Environment* [1988] QB 809, [1988] 2 All ER 781.
11 See, for example, circular 9/1984 on planning controls over hazardous development; *Development Control Policy Note No 1* (MHLG, 1969); and appeal decisions noted in [1970] JPL 112, 162 and [1975] JPL 751.
12 Art 18. GD.O
13 [1971] 1 All ER 65, [1971] 1 WLR 1281.
14 For analyses of the courts' decisions on this matter see M Purdue, 'The Economics of Development—Its Status as a Planning Consideration' [1979] JPL 146; J Alder, 'Planning Permission and the Eccentric Millionaire' (1979) 129 New LJ 704; M Loughlin, 'Planning Control and the Property Market' (1980) 3 *Urban Law and Policy* I; A F Footner, 'The Financial Consequences to an Applicant—Are They Material in Determining a Planning Application?' [1983] JPL 724. F H Stephen and E Young, 'An Economic Insight on the Judicial Control of Planning Authorities' Discretion' (1985) 7 *Urban Law and Policy* 133.
15 [1973] 2 All ER 26, [1973] 1 WLR 560.

planning authority to look beyond the proposed development's effect on land use and to enquire into costs.[16] 'The planning authority', said Ackner J, 'exercises no paternalistic or avuncular jurisdiction over would-be developers to safeguard them from their financial follies.' To somewhat similar effect, Sir Douglas Frank stated in *Walters v Secretary of State for Wales*[17] that if the inquiry inspector's decision letter in that case were to be construed 'as conveying that permission would be refused if it were shown that the development could only be carried out at a loss because of design constraints and the market demand, then I would hold he was wrong'.

However, in *Sovmots Investments Ltd v Secretary of State for the Environment*[18] Forbes J, said (obiter) that if Ackner J was intending to say in *Murphy* that cost could never be a relevant planning consideration, he was unable to agree. In Forbes J's view local planning authorities were entitled to bear in mind the likelihood of a development being carried into effect.

In *Sosmo Trust Ltd v Secretary of State for the Environment and London Borough of Camden*[19] Woolf J said that although the various authorities on the relevance of the cost or economic viability of a proposed development appeared at first sight to be in conflict, it was possible to reconcile these authorities once it was appreciated that 'what could be significant was not the financial or lack of financial viability of a particular project but the consequences of that financial viability or lack of financial viability'. In that case planning permission for office development had been refused. On appeal to the Secretary of State the applicants argued that if their scheme was not approved, the site would remain derelict. However, in the letter giving the decision on the appeal it was said that in general the financial aspects of a proposed development were not relevant to planning. Founding strongly on what was said by Forbes J in *Sovmots* (above), Woolf J held that the present case was one where no reasonable Secretary of State could have concluded that the economic factor was not relevant. It must, said Woolf J, 'be a planning consideration that a consequence of not granting planning permission was that an existing building was going to be left unoccupied and derelict'.

Woolf J's view that the cost or viability of a proposed development will be relevant where it is likely to have some significance in planning terms would seem to be borne out by the decisions in a significant number of cases.[20] In

16 However, in *Hambledon and Chiddingfold Parish Council v Secretary of State for the Environment* [1976] JPL 502 Ackner J said he might have stated the general principle too widely in *Murphy*.
17 (1978) 77 LGR 529.
18 [1977] QB 411, [1976] 1 All ER 178.
19 [1983] JPL 806.
20 See *Kent Messenger Ltd v Secretary of State for the Environment* [1976] JPL 372; *Clyde & Co v Secretary of State for the Environment* [1977] 1 All ER 333, [1977] 1 WLR 926; *Niarchos (London) Ltd v Secretary of State for the Environment* (1977) 76 LGR 480, 35 P & CR 259; *Richmond-upon-Thames London Borough Council v Secretary of State for the Environment* (1978) 37 P & CR 151, [1979] JPL 175; *James Miller & Partners (Guildford) Ltd v Secretary of State for the Environment and Guildford Borough Council* [1980] JPL 264; *Brighton Borough Council v Secretary of State for the Environment* (1978) 39 P & CR 46; *Calflane Ltd v Secretary of State for the Environment* (1981) 260 Estates Gazette 1191, [1981] JPL 879; *R v East Yorkshire Borough of Beverley Council, ex p Wilson* [1989] JPL 183; *Wordie Property Co Ltd v Secretary of State for Scotland* 1984 SLT 345. *Finn & Co Ltd v Secretary of State for the Environment* [1984] JPL 734. See too *Prest v Secretary of State for Wales* (1982) 81 LGR 193 [1983] JPL 112; and *Green v Secretaries of State for the Environment and Transport* (1984) 271 Estates Gazette 551 (decisions on compulsory purchase orders). See too [1977] JPL 537 and [1979] JPL 54.

Brighton Borough Council v Secretary of State for the Environment,[1] for example, planning permission had been refused for residential development on an unused part of playing fields attached to a school. The school building was 'listed' as a building of special architectural or historic interest and occupied a prominent position in a conservation area. The inspector who determined the appeal against the refusal of permission took account of the fact that the building's future would only be assured if capital could be realised from the proposed development. Sir Douglas Frank held that the building's restoration was an important planning matter and that the inspector was therefore entitled to take into account the possibility that a planning benefit would result from the grant of permission. Similarly in *R v Westminster City Council, ex p Monahan*[2] the Court of Appeal held that where commercial development was proposed as part of a package which would result in improvements to the Royal Opera House in Covent Garden, this was capable of being a material consideration. Kerr LJ firmly stated that:

'Financial constraints on the economic viability of a desirable planning development are unavoidable facts of life in an imperfect world. It would be unreal and contrary to common sense to insist that they must be excluded from the range of considerations which may properly be regarded as material in determining planning applications. Where they are shown to exist, they may call for compromises or even sacrifices in what would otherwise be regarded as the optimum from the point of view of the public interest. Virtually all planning decisions involve some kind of balancing exercise. A commonplace illustration is the problem of having to decide whether or not to accept compromises or sacrifices in granting permission for development which could, or would in practice, otherwise not be carried out for financial reasons. Another, no doubt rarer, illustration would be a similar balancing exercise concerning composite or related developments, ie related in the sense that they can and should properly be considered in combination, where the realisation of the main objective may depend on the financial implications or consequences of others. However, provided that the ultimate determination is based on planning grounds and not on some ulterior motive, and that it is not irrational, there would be no basis for holding it to be invalid in law solely on the ground that it has taken account of, and adjusted itself to, the financial realities of the overall situation.'

So while the personal financial consequences of the proposed development should not normally be material (but see p 220 below), the planning consequences of those financial considerations can be material.

In the *Royal Opera House* case the desirable and the undesirable developments were all part of one composite or related development, proposed by the applicant and so this was held to justify the balancing exercise carried out by Westminster City Council. Staughton LJ at least was of the mind that this balancing exercise could not be carried out where there were two separate

1 (1978) 39 P & CR 46.
2 [1989] JPL 107.

developments which were entirely unconnected.[2a] There is still doubt over whether the local planning authority can refuse planning permission because they consider that the proposed development is not economically viable.

In *Sosmo Trust* it was not necessary for Woolf J to decide this point but he said that while some support for that argument was to be found in *Walters* (above), he had reservations about the general applicability of what had been said in that case. In Woolf J's view the accumulation of planning permissions which were incapable of implementation could be undesirable. Further, what was said in *Walters* was to some extent contrary to Forbes J's view in *Sovmots* that it would be right for a local planning authority to treat more favourably a wise commercial development than one which could only be implemented by an eccentric millionaire.

There is little doubt that the general economic impact of a development is a proper planning consideration.[3] It is common practice for a developer to support his application by reference to the economic benefits, whether national, regional or local, which will flow from it (sometimes expressed in terms of economic 'need'), and a local planning authority will clearly have these in mind when reaching a decision. Circular 14/85 on Development and Employment firmly endorses this argument stating that:

'New development contributes to economic activity and the provision of jobs. It is in the national interest to promote and encourage it. The planning system must respond positively and promptly to proposals for development. Delay adds to the cost of development.'(para 2)

Equally, local planning authorities will wish to take account of any undesired economic effects which may result from the proposal and it would seem to be quite proper to do so.[4] However this should always be justified by reference to the planning consequences and circular 2/86 on 'Small Businesses' warns that 'Planning Control is not intended to enable local planning authorities to intervene in the normal operation of market forces' (para 11).

The adequacy of existing public services to serve the needs of a proposed development and the cost of providing necessary new infrastructure are planning considerations.[5]

However, it seems that the conferring of a direct financial benefit on the local planning authority (or the avoidance of direct financial disadvantage to them) cannot be a material consideration in dealing with a planning

---

2a But see *Northumberland County Council v Secretary of State for the Environment* [1989] JPL 700 where it was held that a composite development project was not essential for financial considerations to be material. There the profit from the proposed development was held to be relevant because it would be used to subsidise other unspecified developments.

3 See ministerial decision noted at [1972] JPL 403. See too *J Sainsbury Ltd v Secretary of State for the Environment and Colchester Borough Council* [1978] JPL 379; and *R v Doncaster Metropolitan District Council, ex p British Railways Board* [1987] JPL 444.

4 In *Wain Leisure Centre Ltd v Secretary of State for the Environment* [1989] JPL 190 Malcolm Spence QC (sitting as deputy judge) accepted that economic effects which would mean the loss of some valuable development or loss of employment were material considerations.

5 See, for example, *Esdell Caravan Parks Ltd v Hemel Hempstead RDC* [1966] 1 QB 895, [1965] 2 All ER 1011; *George Wimpey v Secretary of State for the Environment and Maidstone District Council* [1978] JPL 773 and [1974] JPL 307.

application.[6] The fact that an applicant for planning permission has offered to provide some form of 'planning gain'[7] which will overcome some planning objection to the proposal may justify the grant of planning permission where it would otherwise have had to be refused, but failure to provide any 'planning gain' or to offer to carry out something which it is the planning authority's duty to do is not in itself a legitimate reason for refusal of permission.[8] As the *Royal Opera House* case[9] shows it will be material when the planning gain is part of a proposed composite development and that gain cancels out an undesirable feature of the overall development.

Existing rights and planning history. Existing use rights attaching to the land in question and its planning history may be relevant considerations. Thus in *Wells v Minister of Housing and Local Government*[10] the fact that planning permission had already been granted (though not implemented) for a particular development was held to be a matter which ought to have been taken into account in considering whether planning permission should be granted for a similar,[11] though larger, development. In *South Oxfordshire District Council v Secretary of State for the Environment*[12] Woolf J held that a time-expired planning permission was a relevant consideration; the minister was, however, wrong to regard such a permission as a 'vitally material consideration'.

The purpose for which land is presently used and the fact that a particular use is immune from enforcement action may be relevant considerations in considering whether planning permission should be granted for the erection of buildings to be used for that purpose.[13] It may also be relevant to consider the uses to which land could be put without the risk of enforcement action being taken, so long as there is a likelihood of such a use being taken up,[14]

6 See appeal decision noted in [1975] JPL 424. In *Davy v Spelthorne Borough Council* [1984] AC 262, [1983] 3 All ER 278. Lord Fraser doubted if it would be proper for a local planning authority to allow themselves to be influenced by the threat of an action for damages.
7 See p 222 below.
8 See *Westminster Renslade Ltd v Secretary of State for the Environment* (1983) 48 P & CR 255, [1983] JPL 454; and *Richmond-upon-Thames London Borough Council v Secretary of State for the Environment* [1984] JPL 24.
9 *R v Westminster City Council, ex p Monahan* [1989] JPL 107, CA.
10 [1967] 2 All ER 1041, [1967] 1 WLR 1000; see too *Walter Hermans & Sons Ltd v Secretary of State for the Environment* (1974) 234 Estates Gazette 47, [1975] JPL 351; *North Surrey Water Co v Secretary of State for the Environment* (1976) 34 P & CR 140; *Millard v Secretary of State for the Environment* (1979) 254 Estates Gazette 733; *Spackman v Secretary of State for the Environment* [1977] 1 All ER 257, and appeal decision reported in [1984] JPL 132.
11 The existence of a permission for development of a different kind is not likely to be relevant—see *North Surrey Water Co v Secretary of State for the Environment* (1976) 34 P & CR 140, [1977] JPL 100.
12 [1981] 1 All ER 954, [1981] 1 WLR 1092. However, in *Peak Park Joint Planning Board v Secretary of State for the Environment and Cyril Kay* [1979] JPL 618 Sir Douglas Frank expressed the view that an expired planning permission was no longer of any account. In *R (Thallon) v Department of the Environment* [1982] NI 26, an invalid planning permission was held not to be a material consideration—see Brian Thompson, 'Relevance in the Determination of Planning Applications' [1983] JPL 97.
13 *Western Fish Products Ltd v Penwith District Council* [1981] 2 All ER 204; *Newbury District Council v Secretary of State for the Environment and Reading Borough Council* [1983] JPL 281; and *Philglow Ltd v Secretary of State for the Environment and the London Borough of Hillingdon* [1984] JPL 111 (revsd on other grounds 51 P & CR 1, 270 Estates Gazette 1192).
14 *Snowden v Secretary of State for the Environment and Bradford City Council* [1980] JPL 749; and *Lewstar Ltd v Secretary of State for the Environment* [1984] JPL 116.

although whether the planning history of a site is a material consideration will depend greatly on the circumstances of the individual case.[15] Where a building had been destroyed by fire the Secretary of State for the Environment considered that some weight had to be given to the fact that, but for the fire, the premises would still have been in use.[16]

However, it seems that, where an enforcement notice has been served requiring certain uses to cease and it is too late to challenge the validity of this notice, this pre-empts any argument that there might have existed established user rights.[17] It might though be possible to raise a personal hardship argument; see later at p 218.

Social considerations. There is some uncertainty about how far what might be described as social considerations may be taken into account in determining planning applications. In *R v Hillingdon London Borough Council, ex p Royco Homes Ltd*[18] the Queens Bench Division quashed a planning permission for the development of land for residential purposes which was subject to conditions restricting the first occupiers of the proposed houses to persons on the council's housing waiting list and according them security of tenure for ten years. The court took the view that the conditions effectively required the applicants to take on a significant part of the local authority's housing duties and, as such, were unreasonable. Again, in *David Lowe & Sons Ltd v Musselburgh Town Council*[19] the First Division of the Court of Session quashed a planning permission for residential development which was subject to a condition allocating four out of every five of the houses to meet local authority housing needs. Although the court's decision turned upon ambiguity in the phrasing of the condition, both the Lord President (Lord Emslie) and Lord Cameron would have been prepared to hold that a planning permission could not competently be qualified by such a condition; in their view the condition went far beyond matters relating to the development of land.

On the other hand, the Structure and Local Plans Regulations (see p 51 above) specifically require planning authorities to have regard to social policies and considerations in the preparation of development plans and it would seem strange that they should be ignored for the purposes of development control. In *Clyde & Co v Secretary of State for the Environment*[20] Sir David Cairns accepted that 'the need for housing is clearly a planning consideration'; and in *Bradwell Industrial Aggregates v Secretary of*

---

15 See *Tower Hamlets London Borough Council v Secretary of State for the Environment and Lane* [1983] JPL 315; and *Peacock Homes Ltd v Secretary of State for the Environment* [1983] JPL 541 (planning history relevant); and *Chris Fashionware (West End) Ltd v Secretary of State for the Environment* (1980) 256 Estates Gazette 1009, [1980] JPL 678; and *G A Whistlecraft v Secretary of State for the Environment and North Bedfordshire Borough Council* [1983] JPL 809 (planning history not relevant).
16 [1977] JPL 608.
17 See *Nash v Secretary of State for the Environment and Epping Forest District Council* (1985) 52 P & CR 261, [1986] JPL 128 but also see *Weitz and FDS (Market Research) Ltd v Secretary of State for the Environment and Camden London Borough Council* [1985] JPL 171 where Woolf J suggested that lost user rights might just be relevant.
18 [1974] QB 720, [1974] 2 All ER 643.
19 1973 SC 130, 1974 SLT 5.
20 [1977] 1 All ER 333, [1977] 1 WLR 926.

State for the Environment[1] Sir Douglas Frank listed among the questions which the minister should have asked himself the question 'how important, taking into account economic and social factors, was the continuance of this undertaking?' More recently in *Severn Trent Water Authority v Secretary of State for the Environment and South Staffordshire District Council*[2] David Widdicombe QC (sitting as a deputy judge) accepted that the need for a period of social stability and consolidation was a good reason for refusing permission.

Need. Whilst it seems that the need for a particular development or type of development in economic or social terms may be a valid consideration,[3] lack of need for a particular development is not a planning reason which would support its refusal unless it is a development which would not otherwise be allowed. For example, the availability of land for private house building is a crucial issue in determining applications for private houses; see circular 15/84.

Alternative sites. The question whether a better alternative site is available for a proposed development can be a material consideration.[4] For example, a proposal to site a development in a green belt may be supported by the applicant on the ground that the need for the development in that area outweighs its disadvantages. In such a case, the question of whether there is a suitable alternative site outside the green belt is likely to be material. In *R v Royal County of Berkshire, ex p Mangnall*[5] Nolan J held that although it was the duty of the local planning authority to consider and evaluate a suggested alternative site, the planning legislation did not require the comparative evaluation of the two sites to be carried out on an equal basis in order to choose the 'better' site; it was sufficient for the local planning authority to have proper regard to the suggested other site as a possible alternative. In *Ynystawe, Ynyforgan and Glais Gipsy Site Action Group v Secretary of State for Wales and West Glamorgan County Council*[6] Glidewell J stated that an inspector at a public inquiry was not bound to look around for alternatives, but if evidence about suitable alternatives was offered to him in such a case, he was bound to consider and evaluate it.

Even though as a matter of law an alternative site may be a material consideration, it is a question for the local planning authority or the

---

1 [1981] JPL 276. See also *Commercial and Residential Property Development Co Ltd v Secretary of State for the Environment* (1981) 80 LGR 443; and appeal decisions noted in [1979] JPL 418, [1980] JPL 843 and 853.

2 [1989] JPL 21.

3 See *Stringer v Minister of Housing and Local Government* [1971] 1 All ER 65, [1970] 1 WLR 1281, per Cooke J; and *Clyde & Co v Secretary of State for the Environment* [1977] 1 All ER 333, [1977] 1 WLR 926, per Sir David Cairns.

4 See *Rhodes v Minister of Housing and Local Government* [1963] 1 All ER 300, [1963] 1 WLR 208; *Banks Horticultural Products v Secretary of State for the Environment* (1979) 252 Estates Gazette 811; *Brown v Secretary of State for the Environment* (1978) 40 P & CR 285; *Ynystawe, Ynyforgan and Glais Gipsy Site Action Group v Secretary of State for Wales and West Glamorgan County Council* [1981] JPL 874; and *Prest v Secretary of State for Wales* (1982) 81 LGR 193.

5 [1985] JPL 258.

6 [1981] JPL 874.

Secretary of State to determine in the particular circumstances whether or not alternative sites should be considered and this determination can only be overturned by the courts if it is unreasonable.[7]

The courts have ruled that alternative sites will generally be relevant in two main situations. First, where the development itself will have inevitable adverse effects or disadvantages. In *Trusthouse Forte Hotels Ltd v Secretary of State for the Environment*[8] Simon Brown J suggested that this class would include proposals for airports, coalmining, petrochemical plants, nuclear power stations and gypsy encampments. In contrast, developments such as dwellinghouses, offices and superstores would generally not require alternative sites to be considered.[9] Where the proposed development will have inevitable disadvantages, Oliver LJ in *Greater London Council v Secretary of State for the Environment and London Docklands Development Corpn*[10] also suggested the following three characteristics were needed: firstly, the presence of a clear public convenience or advantage; secondly, the existence of an alternative site which would not have the disadvantages or would not have them to the same extent and thirdly, a situation in which there could only be one permission granted for such a development or at least only a very limited number of permissions. Even where these characteristics apply it seems alternative sites will not be relevant if the environmental impact is relatively slight and the planning objections are not especially strong.[11]

The second situation is where the planning objections turn on the site on which the development is proposed rather than on the proposed development itself. In such a case, where it is sought to overcome the planning objections by the need for the proposed development it is not essential for those opposing the development to identify precisely the alternative sites and it may be incumbent on the developer to establish the need for the proposed development on the application or appeal site rather than for an objector to establish that such need could and should be met elsewhere.[12]

Personal circumstances and attributes. Where an adverse decision on a planning application would cause an applicant great hardship then it seems that, other considerations being equal, this factor may tip the balance in favour of a grant of permission.[13]

In *Great Portland Estates plc v Westminster City Council*[14] Lord Scarman stated that 'It would be inhuman pedantry to exclude from the control of our

7 See *Rhys Williams v Secretary of State for Wales* [1985] JPL 29, CA and *Vale of Glamorgan v Secretary of State for Wales and Rhys-Williams* (1985) 52 P & CR 418, [1986] JPL 198.
8 (1986) 53 P & CR 293, 279 Estates Gazette 680.
9 See *Rhodes v Minister of Housing and Local Government* [1963] 1 All ER 300, [1963] 1 WLR 208; *Greater London Council v Secretary of State for the Environment and London Docklands Development Corpn* (1985) 52 P & CR 158, [1986] JPL 193 and *R v Carlisle City Council, ex p Cumbrian Co-operative Society Ltd.* [1985] 2 EGLR 193, [1986] JPL 206 but see *Lakin Ltd v Secretary of State for Scotland* 1988 SLT 780.
10 (1985) 52 P & CR 158, [1986] JPL 193.
11 *Rhys Williams v Secretary of State for Wales* [1985] JPL 29, CA.
12 See *Trust House Forte's Ltd* case supra.
13 See *New Forest District Council v Secretary of State for the Environment and Clarke* [1984] JPL 178; *Tameside Metropolitan Borough Council v Secretary of State for the Environment* [1984] JPL 180; and *Westminster City Council v Great Portland Estates plc* [1985] AC 661, [1984] 3 WLR 1035. And see ministerial decisions noted at [1969] JPL 159 and [1979] JPL 132.
14 [1984] 3 All ER 744, HL.

environment the human factor' but he emphasised that such factors fell to be considered as exceptions to a general rule to be met in special circumstances. For example, the minister has said that where a dwelling has been destroyed by fire or other disaster or is to be demolished because of, say, road proposals, an application for a replacement dwelling has 'a very strong claim to sympathetic consideration'.[15]

Otherwise, it seems that the personal circumstances or attributes of the applicant will not generally be of much relevance in the consideration of a planning application. Nor will the identity[16] or attributes of the person who is to occupy premises normally be a material consideration. In *Birmingham Corpn v Minister of Housing and Local Government*[17] Lord Parker CJ accepted that a local planning authority were not concerned with the characteristics of the particular people living in a house, whether unruly or well behaved. So far as the internal space standards of proposed houses are concerned, it has been held in a number of appeal decisions made by the minister or his inspectors that these are matters for the developer and his customers and not for the local planning authority.[18] Once a building has been erected, internal alterations can be made without the need for planning permission and it can therefore be argued that the internal arrangements of a building for which planning permission is sought cannot generally be a proper planning consideration. That question was, however, left open by Lord Widgery CJ in *R v Hillingdon London Borough Council, ex p Royco Homes Ltd*.[19] In *Newham London Borough v Secretary of State for the Environment*[20] Webster J held that, where it was proposed to convert single dwelling houses into flats, the likelihood of the noise from one flat disturbing the others was a material consideration. This would suggest that normally internal arrangements will only be material, if they will have an impact on the locality. It is not clear how far planning control can properly be used to regulate the quality of work carried out under planning permission.[1]

Miscellaneous. Moral considerations cannot normally be taken into account by the planning authority[2] but in *Finlay v Secretary of State for the Environment and London Borough of Islington*[3] it was held to be a material consideration that the showing of sexually explicit films in premises might be detrimental to the character and amenities of the area. Equally, political considerations such as the political persuasion of the developer or an

15 [1973] JPL 123.
16 See *Westminster City Council v British Waterways Board* [1985] AC 676, [1984] 3 All ER 737.
17 [1964] 1 QB 178, [1963] 3 All ER 668. See too *R v Hillingdon London Borough Council, ex p Royco Homes Ltd* and *David Lowe & Sons Ltd v Musselburgh Town Council* (see p 218 above). Contrast, however, *Fawcett Properties Ltd v Buckingham County Council* [1961] AC 636, [1960] 3 All ER 503 (see p 229 below). Also see *North Tyneside Borough District Council v Secretary of State for the Environment* [1989] JPL 196.
18 See, for example, [1978] JPL 579, [1979] JPL 191, [1980] JPL 704, [1983] JPL 407, 694 and 836 and [1984] JPL 458. See, however, *R v Hillingdon London Borough Council, ex p Royco Homes Ltd* [1974] QB 720, [1974] 2 All ER 643.
19 [1974] QB 720, [1974] 2 All ER 643.
20 (1986) 53 P & CR 98, [1986] JPL 607.
1 See *Sutton London Borough Council v Secretary of State for the Environment* (1975) 29 P & CR 350; see also appeal decisions noted at [1980] JPL 704, and [1981] JPL 108.
2 See, for example, appeal decision reported in [1968] JPL 108, and the decisions noted in 1983 SPLP 54.
3 [1983] JPL 802. See too appeal decision reported in [1980] JPL 58.

ideological dislike of the proposed development (as in the case of private schools or hospitals) will not be material. Thus the Secretary of State in considering an appeal against a refusal of a nuclear shelter agreed with his inspector that much of the opposition stemmed from non-planning considerations and that there were no grounds for treating the proposal differently in planning terms from any other development.[4] On the other hand, the weight to be given to proper planning considerations will inevitably be influenced by political views and the courts have accepted that politics is part of the context of local government.[5]

It seems that undertakings or agreements to achieve a planning gain or advantage[6] can be material. In *Bearsden Town Council v Glasgow Corpn*[6] it was held that undertakings given by the applicants, though not legally enforceable, were material considerations which could properly be taken into account in considering a planning application. In *McLaren v Secretary of State for the Environment and Broxbourne Borough Council*[7] it was held that the minister was entitled to take account of the fact that the local planning authority and the applicants proposed to enter into an agreement relating to certain aspects of a proposed development if permission were granted.

Fairness to the applicant may be a relevant, though probably not important, consideration. In *Ynys Mon Isle of Anglesey Borough Council v Secretary of State for Wales and Parry Bros (Builders) Co Ltd*[8] it was held that provided other planning considerations did not compel a different view, the Secretary of State was entitled to treat it as a factor supporting the grant of planning permission that, having regard to the planning history of the surrounding area, it would be inequitable to refuse permission.

Among the matters which cannot, it seems, properly be taken into account by the local planning authority are the existence of title restrictions which might prevent the carrying out of the proposed development.[9]

Provision of access for the disabled is, it seems, a proper planning consideration,[10] and s 29A now imposes a duty upon local planning authorities to draw to applicants' attention their statutory responsibilities to the disabled.[11]

Planning and other controls. Given the nature of planning, there will be occasions when 'planning' considerations may overlap with 'highway' or

4 [1984] JPL 909.
5 See *R v Rushmoor Borough Council, ex p Crawford* (1981) Times, 28 November; *R v Amber Valley District Council, ex p Jackson* [1984] 3 All ER 501, [1983] JPL 742; and *R v Waltham Forest London Borough Council, ex p Baxter* [1988] QB 419, [1987] 3 All ER 671, CA.
6 1971 SC 274, 1971 SLT 66. See too *Augier v Secretary of State for the Environment* (1978) 38 P & CR 219 (in which it was, however, said that the applicants would be barred from going back on their undertakings).
7 [1981] JPL 423.
8 [1984] JPL 646; see also *R v Beverley Borough Council, ex p Wilson* [1989] JPL 183 where Glidewell J held that the fact that the council were under a moral obligation to the applicant was relevant.
9 See note attached to decision of Lands Tribunal for Scotland in *Gorrie & Banks Ltd v Musselburgh Town Council* 1974 SLT (Lands Tr) 5, in which the planning history of a particular site is recounted. See too appeal decision reported in [1983] JPL 764 (right of way). It may, however, be relevant to take into account the fact that a neighbour's legal rights might have the effect that the applicant could not implement some aspect of the proposed development without which it should not be allowed to proceed.
10 See, for example, appeal decision reported in [1983] JPL 136.
11 This was inserted by s 3 of the Disabled Persons Act 1981.

'housing' or 'educational' considerations and so on. An attempt to further delimit the scope of 'other material considerations' has sometimes been made by those who argue that planning powers should not be used to regulate matters which can be dealt with under other, more specific, statutes. This is a view which has been expressed by the Secretary of State and his inspectors on a number of occasions. In determining an application to increase the number of caravans on a site it has been held that internal site matters should be left to the caravan site licensing authority.[12] Radio and television interference was felt to be a matter for British Telecom under the Wireless Telegraphy Act[13] but a different view was taken in a later decision.[14] The Secretary of State has agreed with his inspectors' view that health planning should be effected wholly through the Health Service Acts rather than partly through the town and country planning legislation.[15] Again the Secretary of State considered that in the majority of cases the control of operations on a waste disposal site should be left to the waste disposal licence stage under the Control of Pollution Act.[16] Finally the durability of materials of construction has been held to be a matter for Building Regulations control and not a planning issue.[17]

Circular 1/85 on 'The Use of Planning Conditions in Planning Permissions' warns against the duplication of controls. This equally applies where matters are the subject of specific control elsewhere in the planning legislation and a planning condition prohibiting advertisements has been held by the Secretary of State to be *ultra vires*.[18]

There is also a principle of statutory interpretation that general powers in an Act should not derogate from powers granted specifically in other legislation—*generalia specialibus non derogant*. Also, powers will often not be truly concurrent, as different statutes have different purposes and contexts, but so far as planning and other statutes are concerned the courts have shown little inclination to construe different statutory codes as if Parliament had allocated mutually exclusive areas of jurisdiction to each code. In any event, the presumption would seem to be specifically rebutted by s 289 of the 1971 Act which provides that powers conferred by the planning legislation may be exercised in relation to any land notwithstanding any provision for regulating development of land made by an enactment in force at the passing of the 1947 Act.[19] In *Esdell Caravan Parks Ltd v Hemel Hempstead RDC*[20] the Court of Appeal held that the various considerations relating to the use of land as a caravan site could not be divided into two watertight groups, one

12 [1972] JPL 407.
13 [1983] JPL 75.
14 [1983] JPL 760.
15 [1983] JPL 142.
16 [1983] JPL 695.
17 [1985] JPL 70.
18 [1982] JPL 733.
19 The reference to an enactment in force at the passing of the 1947 Act appears to include a later re-enactment of the same provision—see *Westminster Bank Ltd v Minister of Housing and Local Government* [1971] AC 508, [1976] 1 All ER 734, per Lord Reid.
20 [1966] 1 QB 895, [1965] 3 All ER 737. See too *Hanks v Minister of Housing and Local Government* [1963] 1 QB 999, [1963] 1 All ER 47 (a rigid distinction could not be drawn between 'planning' and 'housing' considerations). 'Housing need' was upheld as a material consideration in *Clyde & Co v Secretary of State for the Environment* [1977] 1 All ER 333, [1977] 1 WLR 926.

a group of 'planning' considerations which might relevantly be taken into account by the local planning authority considering the grant of permission for the site and the other a group of 'site' considerations which could properly be taken into account only by the authority considering the grant of a caravan site licence; many considerations fell into both categories and could therefore be taken into account by both authorities.[1]

In *Westminster Bank Ltd v Minister of Housing and Local Government*[2] it was held that in refusing an application for planning permission on the ground that the land would be required for future road widening the local planning authority had not acted outside their powers, even though the result of using planning powers rather than highway powers to achieve this objective was to deprive the landowners of a right to immediate payment of compensation. The House of Lords held that as Parliament had imposed no limit on the use of either method of preventing development which would interfere with road proposals, the use of one method rather than the other was not an abuse of power.[3]

In *Ladbroke (Rentals) Ltd v Secretary of State for the Environment and Royal Borough of Kensington and Chelsea*[4] it was argued that, having regard to the specific powers of the licensing authority under the gaming legislation to impose restrictions on permitted opening hours in order to prevent disturbance to occupiers of property in the vicinity, it was not open to the Secretary of State to impose such restrictions in the exercise of his powers under the planning legislation. Sir Douglas Frank said that while it would no doubt be right 'as a matter of sensible administration' that such matters should be left to the licensing authority, the court was not entitled to imply that simply because the licensing authority possessed these express powers, the wide powers given to local planning authorities were thereby diminished. It may therefore be appropriate for a local planning authority to ask (as did Parker J in his capacity as inspector at the Windscale inquiry) whether some other system of control can be relied upon to achieve the desired result; if it can, he said, 'it is the task of that system to afford the necessary protection and not that of the planning authority'.[5]

So, while in some cases it will be *ultra vires* to use a general planning power for what is strictly the concern of another set of controls, in most cases it will be a question of discretion as to what is the most appropriate control. As circular 1/85 recognises, there may be circumstances where it would be unwise to rely on the alternative control being exercised in the manner or to

---

1 Some matters will, of course, be more appropriately dealt with under one or other of the codes—see *Babbage v North Norfolk District Council* [1989] EGCS 117.
2 [1971] AC 508, [1970] 1 All ER 734. See also *Hoveringham Gravels Ltd v Secretary of State for the Environment* [1975] 1 QB 754, [1975] 2 All ER 931 (the fact that a site was known to the local planning authority to be a site of great archaeological importance was 'a perfectly legitimate reason for refusing planning permission'); *Allnatt London Properties Ltd v Middlesex County Council* (1964) 62 LGR 304, 15 P & CR 288; and *Maurice v LCC* [1964] 2 QB 362, [1964] 1 All ER 779.
3 However, in *British Airports Authority v Secretary of State for Scotland* 1979 SC 200, 1979 SLT 197 Lord Cameron appears to have drawn support for his view that a condition was *ultra vires* for unreasonableness from the fact that the matter in question could more appropriately be dealt with under other legislation.
4 [1981] JPL 427.
5 Report of the Windscale Inquiry, p 41, quoted in *Planning for Industry* (JPEL Occasional Paper, 1980), p 62.

the degree needed to secure planning objectives. It also may turn out as in the case of *Harwich Harbour Conservancy Board v Secretary of State for the Environment*[6] that the alternative controls do not in fact give the necessary power. There it was held that the Harwich Harbour Acts 1863 and 1865 and the Coast Protection Act 1949 did not give controls over the effect of an additional user of a harbour on the use of other vessels. The generation of traffic by the development of a marina would have a detrimental affect on the commercial operations of the port and was a planning matter.

That duality of control may give rise to legal difficulties is, however, demonstrated by the decision of the Court of Session in *Glasgow District Council v Secretary of State for Scotland*.[7] The court held that where development is carried out under the compulsion of a building authority in the interests of public safety, the work is not subject to planning control. The problem facing the court was whether the building or planning code took priority in the exceptional situation in which the landowner found himself— on the one hand he was faced with a requirement to demolish his building but on the other hand was refused planning permission for the work. Faced with two such conflicting orders, the landowner was entitled to know where he stood. The court concluded that in such circumstances common sense demanded that public safety should prevail.

The relevance of private law. The fact that an action might lie at common law to restrain noise or smell or some other adverse effect that might result from a proposed development does not prevent the planning authority taking account of that factor but it may be relevant to consider whether some potential damage to amenity could be reduced by private law remedies.[8]

On the other hand, the fact that it would not be possible to restrict the development by private law, will certainly be irrelevant to the question of determining an application for planning permission. In *Brewer v Secretary of State for the Environment*[9] David Widdicombe QC, sitting as a deputy judge, held that both the absence and the existence of private law rights of light were irrelevant. He stated 'Planning was concerned with land use from the point of view of the public interest and as a generality it was not concerned with private rights as between landowners.'

The need to bring development plan policies and other material considerations to the attention of the decision-maker

As a matter of general principle it is up to the parties to raise what they consider to be the material considerations and it has been held that the Secretary of State could not be blamed for failing to take into account a point which had not been brought to his attention.[10] In *Tierney v Secretary of State for the Environment and Spelthorne Borough Council*[11] Sir Douglas Frank

---

6 (1974) 233 Estates Gazette 263, [1974] JPL 724.
7 1980 SC 150, 1982 SLT 28 (see p 92 above).
8 See *Fitzpatrick Developments Ltd v Minister of Housing and Local Government* (1965) 194 Estates Gazette 911, per Widgery J. Also see *R v Exeter City Council, ex p Thomas (J.L.) & Co Ltd* (1989) Times, 11 May.
9 [1988] JPL 480.
10 See Forbes J in *Chris Fashionware (West End) Ltd v Secretary of State for the Environment* (1980) 256 Estates Gazette 1009, [1980] JPL 678.
11 [1983] JPL 799.

specifically denied that in the earlier case of *Bradwell Industrial Aggregates v Secretary of State for the Environment*[12] he had quashed a decision of the Secretary of State for ignoring matters not raised by the parties. Sir Douglas Frank stated that 'The questions which he said the inspector and the Secretary of State should ask themselves [in *Bradwell*] were those which were raised either expressly or by necessary implication at the inquiry.'

On the other hand it may be that where an issue has been raised, the decision-maker may be under a duty to take into account new information which relates to that issue and is within the knowledge or deemed to be within the knowledge of the decision-maker.[13]

It has also been held that the Secretary of State was wrong not to refer to a circular which was published between the submission of the inspector's report and the decision of the Secretary of State.[14] Equally, where there is material available in the department which would show that what had been put before the inspector was wrong, then this must be deemed to be within the knowledge of the Secretary of State and his decision may be quashed if he fails to refer to this material.[15] However, in *Wokingham District Council v Secretary of State for the Environment*[16] Malcolm Spence QC sitting as a deputy judge held that this principle only applies to the case where an inspector has been given wrong information and not to the case where fresh information becomes available after the inquiry. He went on to state that:

It is impossible to conceive that an inspector is obliged as a matter of law to have regard to every consideration, be it in the form of structure plan alterations or modifications to them, other decisions of inspectors or of the Secretary of State on nearby sites and the like, without such matters having been brought to his attention.'

It is hard to square this with David Widdicombe's approach in the *Pye* case[17] but it may be that the issue depends on whether the decision is made by the inspector or by the Secretary of State. This is because Malcolm Spence also considered, without deciding the point, that inspectors, unlike the Secretary of State, cannot be deemed to know all about the documents which are in the possession of the Department of the Environment.

12 [1981] JPL 276.
13 See *Prest v Secretary of State for Wales* (1982) 81 LGR 193 [1983] JPL 112.
14 See *J A Pye (Oxford) Estates Ltd v West Oxfordshire District Council* (1982) 47 P & CR 125, [1982] JPL 577.
15 *Hollis v Secretary of State for the Environment.* [1983] JPL 164.
16 [1989] JPL 424.
17 See fn 14, above.

CHAPTER 9
CONTROL OF DEVELOPMENT
3: CONDITIONS

General

In terms of s 29(1) of the 1971 Act local planning authorities are empowered to grant planning permission 'subject to such conditions as they think fit'. Section 30(1), which is expressed to be without prejudice to the generality of s 29(1), goes on to list certain specific types of condition which may be imposed. These may regulate the development or use of any land under the control of the applicant (whether or not it is land in respect of which the application is made) or require the carrying out of works on any such land, 'so far as appears to the planning authority to be expedient for the purposes of or in connection with the development authorised by the permission' (s 30(1)(a)).

It is not clear whether s 30(1)(a) should be construed as amplifying or restricting the scope of the general power conferred on local planning authorities by s 29(1). The relationship between the two provisions has been aptly described as 'somewhat obscure'.[1] In *British Airports Authority v Secretary of State for Scotland*[2] the First Division of the Court of Session appear to have taken the view that all conditions must satisfy the 'expediency' test contained in the Scottish equivalent of s 30(1). Lord Cameron stated, for example, that: 'The power to impose conditions is governed by s 27(1)(a) of the Town and Country Planning (Scotland) Act of 1972 and the "expediency" there referred to is "for the purposes of or *in connection with*" ... the development authorised by that permission.' However, in *Hall & Co Ltd v Shoreham-by-Sea UDC*[3] the Court of Appeal rejected the argument that the 'expediency' test should be treated as restricting a local planning authority's general powers to impose conditions. Willmer LJ pointed out that the subsection, in which the 'expediency' test appears, declares those special powers to be without prejudice to the more general powers on conditions. He therefore refused to treat the provision relating to the special powers 'as imposing a limitation on the wide words' of the general provision.

The Court of Session's approach in *British Airports Authority* appears to necessitate a somewhat strained construction of the legislation. It seems much more natural to read s 30(1)(a) as amplifying rather than restricting the scope of the power conferred by s 29(1). Section 30(1)(a) would appear to be intended to permit the local planning authority to impose particular types of condition which might not otherwise be competent. In particular, s 30(1)(a) seems to extend the local planning authority's powers (which under s 29(1)

1 See [1979] JPL 315.
2 1979 SC 200, 1979 SLT 197.
3 [1964] 1 All ER 1, [1964] 1 WLR 240.

appear to relate only to land comprised in the application) by enabling them to impose conditions affecting other land under the applicant's control. Thus in *Atkinson v Secretary of State for the Environment and Leeds City Council*[4] Woolf J accepted that generally s 30(1)(a) only applied where the application did not include the land to which the proposed condition related.

Section 30(1)(b) provides for what may be described as a 'limited period permission'. This is a permission granted subject to a condition requiring the removal of any buildings or works authorised by the permission, or the discontinuance of any use of land so authorised, at the end of a specified period, and the carrying out of any works required for the reinstatement of land at the end of that period. A grant of planning permission for development consisting of the winning and working of minerals might be described as a special type of limited period permission. Section 44A of the 1971 Act[5] provides that every such permission shall be subject to a condition as to the duration of the development (see p 515 below).

In addition to the general provisions of ss 29 and 30, there are a number of provisions in the 1971 Act dealing with particular types of condition. Section 30A[6] provides that where planning permission for mineral workings is granted subject to a condition requiring the restoration of the site on completion of the development, then the local planning authority may also impose what is termed an 'aftercare' condition requiring certain steps to be taken to bring the land up to a specified standard (see p 518 below). Sections 41 and 42 and Sch 24 provide that, subject to certain exceptions, every planning permission shall be subject to a condition that the development must commence within a stipulated period, failing which the permission will lapse (see p 261 below). Section 59 imposes a duty on the local planning authority to ensure, whenever it is appropriate, that in granting planning permission for any development adequate provision is made, by the imposition of conditions, for the preservation or planting of trees.

Although the general power to impose conditions in s 29(1) is, in the words of Lord Jenkins, 'expressed in language apt to confer an absolute discretion on a local planning authority to impose any condition of any kind they may think fit',[7] the power has not been interpreted as unlimited by the courts and there are several possible grounds on which a condition may be challenged (either in the courts or on appeal to the Secretary of State) as being invalid in law.[8]

In *Pyx Granite Co Ltd v Minister of Housing and Local Government*,[9] Lord Denning declared, in the course of a judgment approved by the House of Lords in *Fawcett Properties Ltd v Buckingham County Council*:[10]

4 [1983] JPL 599.
5 Added by the Town and Country Planning (Minerals) Act 1981, s 7.
6 Added by the Town and Country Planning (Minerals) Act 1981, s 55.
7 *Fawcett Properties Ltd v Buckingham County Council* [1961] AC 636, [1960] 3 All ER 503, HL.
8 See Mungo Deans, 'Planning Conditions and the Courts' 1984 SPLP 10. Department of the Environment circular 1/85 provides guidance on the use of conditions in planning permissions. For a critique of circular 1/85 see A J Scrase 'Planning Conditions—The Law and the Policy Context' [1987] JPL 323.
9 [1958] 1 QB 554, [1958] 1 All ER 625, CA.
10 [1961] AC 636, [1960] 3 All ER 503; and in *Mixnam's Properties Ltd v Chertsey UDC* [1965] AC 735, [1964] 2 WLR 1210, sub nom *Chertsey UDC v Mixnam's Properties Ltd* [1964] 2 All ER 627; and *Newbury District Council v Secretary of State for the Environment* [1981] AC 578, [1980] 1 All ER 731, HL.

'Although the planning authorities are given very wide powers to impose "such conditions as they think fit", nevertheless the law says that those conditions, to be valid must fairly and reasonably relate to the permitted development. The planning authority are not at liberty to use their powers for an ulterior object, however desirable that object may seem to them to be in the public interest.'

'It follows', said Viscount Dilhorne in *Newbury District Council v Secretary of State for the Environment*,[11] 'that the conditions imposed must be for a planning purpose and not for any ulterior one,[12] and that they must fairly and reasonably relate to the development permitted. Also they must not be so unreasonable that no reasonable planning authority could have imposed them.' In addition to the three tests laid down by Viscount Dilhorne, conditions may also be void for uncertainty[13] and it seems that they could be open to challenge on the ground that they are unnecessary.[14] These tests are considered in turn.

The condition must be imposed for a planning purpose and not for an ulterior one

This is another way of saying that in deciding to impose conditions a local planning authority may be influenced only by planning considerations. The difficulty of defining the proper scope of planning considerations was discussed in the preceding chapter and that discussion is relevant here. To say that these considerations or purposes are to be derived from the development plan so far as material to the application, from the response to publicity and consultations and from any other material considerations does little to narrow the field.

Argument about the proper scope of planning has occurred in the context of conditions imposing a limitation on the class of people who may occupy development. Planning control is concerned primarily with the use of land rather than with the user.[15]

However, provided the purpose of a condition is one which relates to the use of the land, it would seem that this purpose may be secured through a condition which has the consequence of limiting the categories of user.[16] In *Fawcett Properties Ltd v Buckingham County Council*[17] planning permission for a pair of cottages had been granted subject to a condition providing that

---

11 [1981] AC 578, [1980] 1 All ER 731, HL.
12 In the same case Lord Fraser said that a condition 'may have other purposes as well as its planning purpose. But if it is imposed solely for some other purpose or purposes, such as furtherance of the housing policy of the local authority, it will not be valid as a planning condition.'
13 *Fawcett Properties Ltd v Buckingham County Council* [1961] AC 636, [1960] 3 All ER 503; *David Lowe & Sons Ltd v Musselburgh Town Council* 1973 SC 130, 1974 SLT 5.
14 *British Airports Authority v Secretary of State for Scotland* 1979 SC 200, 1979 SLT 197.
15 See *Westminster City Council v Great Portland Estates plc* [1985] AC 661, [1984] 3 WLR 1035, and *Westminster City Council v British Waterways Board* [1985] AC 676, [1984] 3 All ER 737.
16 *Westminster City Council v Great Portland Estates plc* [1985] AC 661, [1984] 3 WLR 1035, and *Fawcett Properties Ltd v Buckingham County Council* [1961] AC 636, [1960] 3 All ER 503.
17 [1961] AC 636, [1960] 3 All ER 503.

occupation of the cottages was to be limited to persons employed in agriculture or forestry. The House of Lords held that although the wording of the condition might be open to criticism and might produce anomalies, the condition was reasonably related to planning purposes—in particular, the furtherance of the local planning authority's green belt policy—and did not place an unreasonable restriction on the use of the cottages.

In such cases it is important to note that there are usually two planning purposes involved. First there will be a policy of restricting development, usually to preserve amenities; the green belt policy in the case of *Fawcett*. There is then the purpose behind the justification of limited exceptions to that policy: in the case of *Fawcett* meeting the agricultural needs of the area. It is the combination of the two which justifies the restriction on certain types of occupant.

However, there could be situations where restrictions on the type of occupant may not be justified in planning terms. In *Fawcett* Lord Keith said 'There might be personal attributes or circumstances required of the occupants which had no conceivable relevance to planning policy and if so, such requirements would be bad.' The only judicial decisions which have come close to this have concerned conditions imposed for housing purposes. In the Scottish case of *David Lowe & Sons Ltd v Musselburgh Town Council*,[18] planning permission had been granted to a local authority for residential development subject to a condition that:

'The sites are approved for the burgh's estimated future local authority and private housing needs over the next 20 years which cannot be accommodated within the existing burgh boundaries, in the proportion of one private house to four local authority houses.'

The First Division of the Court of Session held the condition to be so ambiguous as to be unenforceable but it was also held that the condition was invalid as planning was not concerned with ownership or occupation of buildings. *Fawcett* was apparently cited in argument but was not mentioned by either the Lord President or Lord Cameron. It is therefore hard to reconcile this case with *Fawcett*. It is also arguable that housing needs come under the umbrella of planning considerations. However, as the decision in *R v Hillingdon London Borough Council, ex p Royco Homes Ltd*[19] shows, a condition will be invalid if it is imposed for an ulterior purpose. The conditions in question provided that the first occupiers of the residential development in question should be persons on the council's housing waiting list and that for a period of ten years from the date of first occupation the occupiers of the dwellings should have security of tenure under the Rent Acts. In the Divisional Court Lord Widgery CJ, who delivered the main judgment, considered that the conditions were 'the equivalent of requiring the applicants to take on at their own expense a significant part of the duty of the council as housing authority'; 'however well intentioned and however sensible such a desire on the part of the council may have been', there was, in Lord Widgery's view, no doubt that these conditions were *ultra vires*.

18 1973 SC 130, 1974 SLT 5. See Eric Young, 'Planning Condition Apportioning Land Between Private and Local Authority Housing' [1975] JPL 139.
19 [1974] QB 720, [1974] 2 All ER 643.

In practice, local planning authorities have shown a continuing interest in the use of occupancy conditions, most commonly to restrict new houses in the countryside to agricultural workers.[20] The minister has accepted that occupancy conditions may have a role to play in the control of office and industrial development, although he has emphasised the importance of wording the condition so that a developer can ascertain with a degree of certainty whether a particular prospective occupier is included in the specified class.[1]

Further, circular 1/85 gives detailed advice on when conditions should be imposed restricting the occupancy of buildings and land and the form that such conditions should take; see paras 72 to 80. In particular the circular warns against restricting occupation to a worker on a named farm or small holding; see para 80.[2] The circular also advises that conditions restricting the occupation of commercial or industrial premises to local firms should only be imposed where there is a need for local firms to expand. In *Slough Industrial Estates Ltd v Secretary of State for the Environment*[3] the reasons for imposing such a condition were challenged but no challenge was made to the legality of the condition.

The condition must fairly and reasonably relate to the development permitted

Not only must a condition be imposed for a planning purpose, there must also be a relationship between the development proposed and the condition. This is a rather more stringent test than is applied to grounds of refusal. The latter must be supported by a sound planning reason but the link between the particular development proposed and the ground of refusal can be relatively slight,[4] though the minister requires as a matter of policy that it be shown that the development would cause demonstrable harm to interests of acknowledged importance.[5] It has been argued that this particular limitation on conditions does not apply but it would seem to be firmly entrenched.[6]

Inevitably, difficult questions can arise in determining whether there is a sufficiently direct relationship between a particular development and a

---

20 See *Alderson v Secretary of State for the Environment* (1984) 49 P & CR 307, [1984] JPL 429 (p 243 below).
1 See generally the decisions noted at [1975] JPL 556, [1979] JPL 412 and 414, [1980] JPL 212 and 845, [1981] JPL 918, [1982] JPL 543, [1984] JPL 368 and [1986] JPL 390. Also see Martin Loughlin's comprehensive study, 'Local Needs Policies and Development Control Strategies' which examines the role of occupancy restrictions; Working Paper 42 of School for Advanced Urban Studies, University of Bristol.
2 Martin Loughlin in his study of occupancy conditions, note 11, argues on the grounds of *Wakelin v Secretary of State for the Environment* (1978) 77 LGR 101 46 P & CR 214, CA that such a condition would be valid but this seems doubtful.
3 [1986] 2 EGLR 201, [1987] JPL 353.
4 See, for example, *Collis Radio Ltd v Secretary of State for the Environment* (1975) 73 LGR 211, 29 P & CR 390; *Clyde & Co v Secretary of State for the Environment* [1977] 1 All ER 333, [1977] 1 WLR 926; and *Ynystawe, Ynyforgan and Glais Gipsy Site Action Group v Secretary of State for Wales and West Glamorgan County Council* [1981] JPL 874. See too appeal decision reported in [1983] JPL 833. However, it should be noted that in *R v Westminster City Council, ex p Monahan* [1989] JPL 107 Staughton LJ held that material considerations to which regard may be had in determining a planning application must also fairly and reasonably relate to the development proposal.
5 See circular 14/85, para 3.
6 See John Lannon, 'Planning conditions. The main difficulty with Newbury' [1988] JPL 460.

condition attached to permission for that development. In *British Airports Authority v Secretary of State for Scotland*[7] it was argued that before a condition could be said to be fairly and reasonably related to the permitted development there had to be a causal relationship between the development and the mischief which the condition was designed to suppress. Lord Cameron did not consider this method of approach to be of real assistance, saying:

'It does not in my opinion really matter whether the development can be said to be directly causative of the state of affairs to which the condition is intended to apply, or whether that state of affairs is merely consequential upon the use to which the development is or will be or may be applied. It is enough that there should be a recognised and real relationship between the development and the condition and that it can be affirmed that it is one that is fair and reasonable.'

In this regard the courts only intervene on the ground of gross unreasonableness or if the planning authority or the Secretary of State misdirect themselves in law. In *Newbury District Council v Secretary of State for the Environment*[8] Viscount Dilhorne expressed the position:

'If in the circumstances of this case, the condition imposed was not, in the Secretary of State's opinion fairly and reasonably related to the permission granted, the courts cannot interfere with his conclusion unless it is established that the Secretary of State had misdirected himself or reached a conclusion to which he could not reasonably have come.'

However, this is a distinction which courts themselves do not always keep in mind and in many of the cases they give the impression of deciding for themselves whether the condition fairly and reasonably relates, rather than reviewing the Secretary of State or the local planning authority's judgment on this.

The application of this test in practice may be illustrated by reference to four cases: *Pyx Granite Co Ltd v Minister of Housing and Local Government*,[9] *British Airports Authority v Secretary of State for Scotland*,[10] *Newbury District Council v Secretary of State for the Environment*,[11] and *Elmbridge*

---

7 1979 SC 200, 1979 SLT 197.
8 [1981] AC 578, [1980] 1 All ER 731.
9 [1958] 1 QB 554, [1958] 1 All ER 625; revsd on other grounds by the House of Lords [1960] AC 260, [1959] 3 All ER 1.
10 1979 SC 200, 1979 SLT 197.
11 [1981] AC 578, [1980] 1 All ER 731. See too *Kingston-upon-Thames Royal London Borough Council v Secretary of State for the Environment* [1974] 1 All ER 193, [1973] 1 WLR 1549; *AI & P (Stratford) Ltd v London Borough of Tower Hamlets* (1976) 237 Estates Gazette 416; *Penwith District Council v Secretary of State for the Environment* (1977) 34 P & CR 269; *Peak Park Joint Planning Board v Secretary of State for the Environment and ICI* (1979) 39 P & CR 361, [1980] JPL 114; *Kember v Secretary of State for the Environment* [1982] JPL 383; *Gill v Secretary of State for the Environment and North Warwickshire District Council* [1985] JPL 710; and *R v St Edmundsbury Borough Council, ex p Investors in Industry Commercial Properties Ltd* [1985] 3 All ER 234, [1985] 1 WLR 1168. Also *Selected Enforcement and Allied Appeals*, pp 44 and 45; and ministerial decisions noted in [1977] JPL 742, [1983] JPL 259, 762, 764 and 833, and [1984] JPL 199.

Borough Council v Secretary of State for the Environment and Hill Samuel & Co Ltd and Case Poclain Corpn Ltd.[12]

In *Pyx Granite* the Court of Appeal had to consider whether conditions, affecting plant situated on land which was not the subject of the planning application, were reasonably related to the quarrying operations with which the planning permission was concerned. As mentioned above, the local planning authority are entitled to impose conditions on land under the applicant's control, whether or not it is land in respect of which the application was made, but only 'so far as appears to the local planning authority to be expedient for the purposes of or in connection with the development authorised by the permission'. The Court of Appeal held the conditions valid; they were imposed for a proper planning purpose and they required the carrying out of works on land which was so near to the site of the permitted quarrying operations as to make the works 'expedient for the purposes of or in connection with' that development. Lord Denning considered that it might have been otherwise had there been an attempt 'to impose like conditions about plant and machinery a mile or so away ... But here the plant and machinery is on the spot and the conditions are so closely "in connection with" the permitted development as to be valid.'

In *British Airports Authority v Secretary of State for Scotland* the First Division of the Court of Session had to consider the validity of conditions, varied by the Secretary of State for Scotland on appeal, attached to three permissions for development at Aberdeen Airport. The first application was by the British Airports Authority for permission to construct a new terminal building and improved aircraft handling facilities. The permission was subject to conditions restricting operational hours so as to prevent night flying and limiting the direction of take off and landing so as to avoid over-flying built up areas. The court held that the conditions were designed to serve a proper planning purpose, namely the protection of the area surrounding the airport by limiting the time and place of aircraft noise. They also held that the Secretary of State was entitled to find on the evidence that the development was required to cater for the intensification of the use of the airport as such. There was a close relationship between the permitted development and future noise levels and the conditions designed to control the mischief of aircraft noise were fairly and reasonably related to that development.

The second application was by Bristow Helicopters Ltd for permission to extend their terminal building. The permission was subject to a condition restricting operational hours to prevent night flying. Here, too, the court held that the Secretary of State was entitled to find on the evidence that the development was required to enable the company to handle the expected growth in helicopter traffic and that there was, accordingly, a clear relationship between the appellants' future use of the airport for helicopter traffic and the permitted development of their terminal.

The third application was by British Airways Helicopters Ltd for permission to erect a one storey building as an office for their flight operations headquarters for the United Kingdom and as accommodation for ground training for flying personnel. This permission was also subject to a condition restricting operational hours so as to avoid night flying. In this case the court

12 [1989] JPL 277.

found that there was no connection whatever between the permitted develop-ment and the helicopter operations of the appellants at the airport. The condition could not therefore be said to be fairly and reasonably related to the development in question and was quashed.

In *Newbury District Council v Secretary of State for the Environment* planning permission had been granted in 1962 for the use of two existing hangars on a disused airfield as warehouses. The permission was subject to a condition requiring the removal of the buildings at the end of 1972. The buildings were not removed and in due course an enforcement notice was served. On appeal, the Secretary of State decided that the condition was not sufficiently related to the change of use for which the planning permission had been granted and that the 1962 permission was therefore void. The local planning authority appealed and the matter eventually came before the House of Lords. The court held that the condition had been imposed for a planning purpose, the hangar being an undesirable intrusion into the landscape. However, they found that on the evidence the Secretary of State was entitled to conclude that the condition requiring the removal of the hangars was not fairly and reasonably related to the permission for a temporary change in their use and was therefore *ultra vires*.[13]

Finally in *Elmbridge Borough Council v Secretary of State for the Environment and Hill Samuel & Co Ltd and Case Poclain Corpn Ltd*[14] an application was made to occupy a building without complying with a condition that the building be only occupied by a particular body. This was granted subject to a condition that the windows of the building which overlooked homes should be obscurely glazed. The court upheld a decision by the Secretary of State's inspector that the condition was invalid as it did not fairly and reasonably relate to the permitted development having regard to the nature of the planning application.

Malcolm Spence QC sitting as a deputy judge stated:

'The local planning authority is not entitled to take advantage of the later application relating solely to the identity of the occupier to impose a condition which with the benefit of hindsight it would have liked to impose on the original permission: If, for example there was something special about the occupation by Case Poclain [the applicant], such as a hugely increased number of employees that would have made obscure glass desirable, that would have been another matter.'

Conditions must not be unreasonable

A condition may be imposed for a planning purpose and be fairly and reasonably related to the permitted development, yet be so unreasonable as to be *ultra vires* the local planning authority. As was pointed out by Lord Reid in *Westminster Bank Ltd v Minister of Housing and Local Government*,[15] the word 'unreasonable' as used in this context has a somewhat artificial meaning; a condition attached to a grant of planning permission will be held

13 The House of Lords did not rule out the possibility, though it might only arise in exceptional cases, that a condition requiring the removal of a building might fairly and reasonably relate to a grant of permission for a change in the use of the building.
14 [1989] JPL 277.
15 [1971] AC 508, [1970] 1 All ER 734. See too *Kent County Council v Kingsway Investments (Kent) Ltd* [1971] AC 72, [1970] 1 All ER 70.

by the courts to be void for 'unreasonableness' only if it is one 'which no reasonable authority acting within the four corners of their jurisdiction could have decided to impose'.[16] There may well be room for disagreement as to whether a particular condition is unreasonable or not.[17]

Situations in which conditions have been challenged as unreasonable may be divided for illustrative purposes into three broad categories.[18] (1) Factors beyond the control of the applicant, (2) restrictions on existing use rights, and (3) financial and other obligations. These categories are considered in turn.

(1) *Factors beyond the control of the applicant*

In *British Airports Authority v Secretary of State for Scotland*[19] Lord Cameron said:

'A condition imposed under the planning legislation can be enforced by enforcement orders in terms of s 84 of the 1972 Act [the Scottish equivalent of s 87 of the 1971 Act]. Failure to comply with such an order involves exposure to substantial penal sanctions. In my opinion it follows from this that the necessary assumption on which this structure of conditions and powers of enforcement rests, is that nothing shall be imposed upon a developer with which it is plain he does not possess the capacity to comply.'

In that case a condition imposed on the applicants, the British Airports Authority, an obligation to control the direction of take off and landing of aircraft at Aberdeen Airport. That was a matter which only the Civil Aviation Authority could control and there were no steps which the applicants could take to secure the result required by the condition. The requirement was therefore 'no "condition" at all' and was *ultra vires*.

The decision suggests that the fact that the applicants would not be able to comply with the condition and the fact that it would be unenforceable were both factors demonstrating the condition's unreasonableness. In *Peak Park Joint Planning Board v Secretary of State for the Environment and ICI*[20] Sir

16 *Associated Provincial Picture Houses Ltd v Wednesbury Corpn* [1948] 1 KB 223, [1947] 2 All ER 680, per Lord Greene MR.
17 Contrast, for example, Lord Reid's view of the conditions at issue in *Mixnam's Properties Ltd v Chertsey UDC* [1965] AC 735, [1974] 2 WLR 1210, sub nom *Chertsey UDC v Mixnam's Properties Ltd* [1964] 2 All ER 627 with that of Lord Upjohn in the same case, or the judgment of Salmon LJ with that of Diplock LJ in *Westminster Bank Ltd v Beverley Borough Council* [1969] 1 QB 499, [1968] 2 All ER 104. See too the divergent views expressed in *Kingsway Investments (Kent) Ltd v Kent County Council* [1969] 2 QB 332, [1969] 1 All ER 601, CA; revsd sub nom *Kent County Council v Kingsway Investments (Kent) Ltd* [1971] AC 72, [1970] 1 All ER 70, HL.
18 It may also be that a condition which has the effect of making a planning permission radically different from what was applied for would be treated as unreasonable—see the remarks of Forbes J in *Bernard Wheatcroft Ltd v Secretary of State for the Environment* (1980) 43 P & CR 233 (p 254 below).
19 1979 SC 200, 1979 SLT 197. Contrast *Kent County Council* (above). See too ministerial decision noted in 1982 SPLP 85.
20 (1979) 39 P & CR 361. See too *Bizony v Secretary of State for the Environment* (1975) 239 Estates Gazette 281. In *R Bell & Co (Estates) Ltd v Department of the Environment for Northern Ireland* [1982] NI 322 (and see 1983 SPLP 79) it was held that a condition which, though capable of implementation at the time of its imposition, had subsequently become impossible, had to be disregarded. And see *Commercial and Residential Property Development Co Ltd v Secretary of State for the Environment* (1981) 80 LGR 443.

Douglas Frank said that an unenforceable condition (which may well also be impossible to comply with) had to be distinguished from one which might be difficult to enforce; he did not think it anything to the point that a condition otherwise desirable should not be imposed merely because it might be difficult to enforce. Further, in *Bromsgrove District Council v Secretary of State for the Environment*[1] Mann J rejected the submission that there was an independent head of invalidity based on the practical difficulties of enforcement. So it would seem a distinction must be made between conditions which are unreasonable because they are impossible to comply with and those which are simply impractical for the local planning authority to enforce.

In *Grampian Regional Council v City of Aberdeen District Council*[2] the House of Lords held that a condition which prescribed that development was not to begin until a particular result had been achieved was, in the circumstances of the case, valid, notwithstanding that it did not lie within the applicants' sole power to bring about the result required by the condition. In that case the reporter who had held a public inquiry into a deemed refusal of planning permission said in his decision letter that he would have favoured granting permission had it not been that increased traffic from the proposed development would in his view result in unacceptable traffic danger at a road junction some distance from the appeal site. He considered that a condition requiring closure of part of the road between the appeal site and the junction would be incompetent since the applicants could not themselves ensure closure of the road. (A closure order would be open to objection and would require confirmation by the Secretary of State.)

Before the Court of Session[3] the applicants accepted that on the authority of *British Airports Authority* (above) a condition requiring them to secure the road's closure would have been invalid for unreasonableness. They argued, however, that the reporter had misdirected himself in failing to consider whether to impose a condition to the effect that development was not to commence until the road in question had been closed. That argument found favour with the First Division.

On appeal to the House of Lords, the planning authority attacked the First Division's decision on the ground that the imposition on a planning permission of any negative condition relating to the occurrence of an uncertain event was unreasonable. They argued that there was no practical distinction between a positive condition requiring the road to be closed (which had been conceded to be *ultra vires*) and the negative condition sanctioned by the Court of Session; in either case the practical effect was to require the applicants to bring about something that was not within their power to secure. It was further argued for the planning authority that it was undesirable that there should be prolonged uncertainty as to whether the development would be able to proceed.

The House of Lords held that there was no substance in the planning authority's contentions. In the first place, there was in this context a crucial difference between the positive and negative type of condition; the latter was enforceable while the former was not. Secondly, the reasonableness of any condition had to be considered in the light of the circumstances of the

1 (1987) 56 P & CR 221, [1988] JPL 257.
2 1984 SLT 197.
3 *Grampian Regional Council v Secretary of State for Scotland* 1983 SLT 526.

individual case and in this case the applicants' proposals had been found by the reporter to be generally desirable in the public interest; the only aspect he considered disadvantageous was the traffic problem and that could be solved in a way which had reasonable prospects of coming about. Not only, therefore, would it not have been unreasonable to grant planning permission subject to the suspensive condition, it would have been highly appropriate to do so. Further, in the House of Lords' view, s 198 of the Town and Country Planning (Scotland) Act 1972 (which makes provision for the stopping up of highways in order to enable development to be carried out; see s 210 of the 1971 Act) told strongly in favour of the reasonableness of a negative condition relating to road closure; it could be inferred that such a condition was contemplated by the legislature. As to the argument on uncertainty, it was, the House of Lords considered, sufficient to notice that the Act makes provision as to the duration of planning permission (see p 261 below) and thus recognises that development which has been granted planning permission may not be carried out within any particular time scale or at all; uncertainty might be said to be a natural feature of the planning process. On the other hand it can be argued that a condition worded this way will only be reasonable if there is some prospect of the facts on which it is based coming into effect. If there is no prospect, then it could be that the condition is as bad as if it were requiring the developer to carry out the impossible. However, a *Grampian* condition (as it is now known) was upheld in *Daws v Secretary of State for the Environment*[4] even though compulsory purchase would be needed to effect the works required.

Where a condition relates to land which is not owned or in some way under the control of the applicant, it might be thought that this would be a prime example of factors beyond the control of the developer. However, in *Atkinson v Secretary of State for the Environment and Leeds City Council*[5] Woolf J accepted that such a condition was valid if the land to which the condition related was part of the application. As a consequence, if, as in *Atkinson*, the development goes ahead, it is possible for the person who owns the land the subject of the condition to be required to carry out the works. In most cases, he should be able to recover his expenses from the actual developer under s 91(2) but not if, as in *Atkinson*, the developer has gone bankrupt. The solution suggested by Woolf J is, as in *Grampian*, for the condition to be worded negatively and to state that the development should not commence until the works on the other land have been carried out.[6]

Section 30(1)(a) of the 1971 Act makes clear that a condition may be validly imposed in respect of land other than the land which is the subject of the application for planning permission, but that such other land must be under the 'control' of the applicant.[7] In *Birnie v Banff County Council*,[8] for

---

4 (20 November 1987, unreported.)
5 [1983] JPL 599.
6 For a discussion of these problems see Stephen Tromans 'Planning and Access Problems' [1985] JPL 827.
7 The relevant time is, it seems, the date of the decision rather than the date of the application—see *Atkinson* (above).
8 1954 SLT (Sh Ct) 90. See too *Peak Park Joint Planning Board v Secretary of State for the Environment and ICI* (1979) 39 P & CR 361; *Ladbroke (Rentals) Ltd v Secretary of State for the Environment* (1981) 258 Estates Gazette 973; and ministerial decisions noted in [1967] JPL 615 and 617; [1968] JPL 306; and [1980] JPL 423. Contrast, however, the decision noted in [1983] JPL 415.

example, the owners of a piece of ground were granted planning permission for the erection of a house, the permission being subject to a condition that an access lane be formed on ground that had been retained in other ownership. The condition was not complied with and the planning authority served an enforcement notice requiring the owners to form the lane. The Sheriff held that the condition sought to be enforced was *ultra vires* in that it required the carrying out of works on land which was not under the applicant's control.

To avoid such problems the planning authority may have to refuse planning permission until the necessary land is brought within the applicant's control. However, in *George Wimpey & Co Ltd v New Forest District Council*[9] Sir Douglas Frank stated that 'control' did not necessarily involve 'having an estate or interest in the land but only such right as was required to implement the condition'. It was 'a question of fact and degree for the Secretary of State whether the control was of a degree and kind sufficient to satisfy him that the condition would be complied with'. It was, however, held in this case that the Secretary of State ought to have considered the possibility of overcoming a difficulty over access to a site by imposing a negative condition to the effect that development should not commence until satisfactory arrangements had been made.

Where the land is neither part of the application nor in the control of the applicant, it would seem that a condition requiring works on that land would not be valid but that a negative condition following the *Grampian* formula might be appropriate.[10]

(2) *Restrictions on existing use rights*

The effect of the 1947 planning legislation was to subject all new development to control by local planning authorities but to leave landowners with the right to carry on the existing use of the land. In general, the only way in which the local planning authority can of their own initiative require the discontinuance of an existing lawful use of land, or impose conditions on the continuance of such a use, or require the removal of existing buildings or works, is by making an order under s 51 of the 1971 Act; compensation is payable in respect of any loss suffered as a result of the making of such an order.[11]

It would seem, however, that in granting planning permission for the development of land the local planning authority may be able, without payment of compensation, to impose a condition which has the effect of restricting 'existing use' rights, provided the condition is imposed for a planning purpose and is fairly and reasonably related to the permitted development. Where, for example, an authority grant planning permission for the extension of an existing factory, they may be entitled to impose a condition requiring the formation of a new access to the site and the closing of an existing access.[12] This would seem to be borne out by the wording of s 30(1) which authorises the imposition of a condition for regulating not only

9 (1979) 250 Estates Gazette 249, [1979] JPL 314. See too *Hayns v Secretary of State for the Environment* (1977) 36 P & CR 317; *Augier v Secretary of State for the Environment* (1978) 38 P & CR 219; and appeal decision noted in [1980] JPL 425.
10 Again see *Tromans* above for discussion of the possibilities.
11 See ch 15.
12 See, for example, [1969] JPL 287.

the development but also the *use* of any land under the control of the applicant. It was thus possible for Talbot J to hold in *City of London Corpn v Secretary of State for the Environment*[13] that a condition which had the effect of prohibiting change from one use to another use within the same class in the Use Classes Order—a change which would not amount to development—was valid. It is, of course, the case that if the applicant does not wish to comply with a condition restricting 'existing use' rights he need not implement the permission.

It has been argued that the same would not apply to a condition restricting the operation of the classes of permitted development under the General Development Order[14] but in *Gill v Secretary of State for the Environment*[15] it was conceded before Glidewell J that rights under the GDO could be removed by a condition in appropriate circumstances.

The power of a local planning authority to attach to a grant of planning permission conditions abrogating 'existing use' rights was considered by the Divisional Court in *Kingston-upon-Thames Royal London Borough Council v Secretary of State for the Environment.*[16] In that case the local planning authority granted planning permission for the reconstruction of a railway station subject to a condition that an area of land, shown on the plan which accompanied the application as allocated for car parking purposes, should be available for those purposes at all times and should be used for no other purpose. Compliance with the condition would have necessitated the removal from this area of land of the main electric traction cable. Reconstruction of the station was carried out but the condition was not complied with. Following an appeal against an enforcement notice issued by the local planning authority, the Secretary of State held the condition *ultra vires* in that its effect would be to restrict, without payment of compensation, existing activities which would be legal under planning law if the permitted development had not taken place.

Though the minister's conclusion appeared to be supported by the decision of the House of Lords in *Minister of Housing and Local Government v Hartnell,*[17] by the decision of Glyn-Jones J in *Allnatt London Properties Ltd v Middlesex County Council*[18] and by a dictum of Lord Denning in *Pyx Granite Co Ltd v Minister of Housing and Local Government,*[19] the Divisional Court held in the *Kingston* case that the proposition relied on by the minister was untenable and that the condition, being reasonably related to the permitted development and not unreasonable, was valid. Lord Widgery CJ considered

---

13 (1971) 71 LGR 28, 23 P & CR 169. See *Carpet Decor (Guildford) Ltd v Secretary of State for the Environment* (1981) 261 Estates Gazette 56, [1981] JPL 806 where Sir Douglas Frank appeared to accept that a local planning authority could exclude the operation of the General Development Order by condition on a planning permission.

14 See J E Alder 'Planning Conditions and Existing Rights' (1972) 36 Conv (NS) 421 and 'The Effect of a Planning Condition upon Existing Rights' [1973] JPL 701.

15 [1985] JPL 710; see above.

16 [1974] 1 All ER 193, [1973] 1 WLR 1549. See too *Prossor v Minister of Housing and Local Government* (1968) 67 LGR 109; *Leighton and Newman Car Sales Ltd v Secretary of State for the Environment* (1975) 30 P & CR 23, per Lord Widgery CJ; *Peak Park Joint Planning Board v Secretary of State for the Environment and ICI* (1979) 39 P & CR 361; and *Penwith District Council v Secretary of State for the Environment* (1977) 34 P & CR 269.

17 [1965] AC 1134, [1965] 1 All ER 490.

18 (1964) 62 LGR 304, 15 P & CR 288.

19 [1958] 1 QB 554, [1958] 1 All ER 625.

that *Hartnell's* case 'was a very special one ... decided purely on its own facts' and that it 'had nothing to do with the present case except that the phrase about removing existing use rights without compensation may have found its roots in those very different factual circumstances'. *Hartnell* had concerned the transitional provisions of the Caravan Sites and Control of Development Act 1960 by which the applicant had effectively no choice but to apply for planning permission if he wished to get a site licence even though he had established user rights.

His Lordship did not cast doubt upon the correctness of the decision in *Allnatt's* case but considered that the reason given for the decision in that case was wrongly expressed. Bridge J just felt that *Allnatt* was wrongly decided.

A similar view was expressed by the Lord President (Lord Emslie) in *British Airports Authority v Secretary of State for Scotland.*[20] After examining a number of authorities he stated that he was:

'clearly of the opinion that they do not establish the particular proposition for which they were cited, namely that the powers of s 27(1) may never be used to restrict, without compensation, existing rights of use of land under the control of an applicant for planning permission. There is, in my opinion, no such general principle to be discovered from a construction of the 1972 Act.'

(3) *Financial and other obligations*

Difficult questions can arise over conditions which require a payment in money or in kind by the developer. Department of the Environment circular 1/85 states that:[1]

'No payment of money or other consideration can be required when granting a permission or any other kind of consent required by a statute, except where there is specific statutory authority. Conditions requiring for instance, the cession of land for road improvements or for open space, or requiring the developer to contribute money towards the provision of public car parking facilities, should accordingly not be attached to planning permissions.'

The Secretary of State has on several occasions expressed the opinion that the making of a payment to the local planning authority—for example, as a contribution to infrastructural costs[2] or to the cost of provision of parking spaces by the planning authority—cannot properly be made a condition of a planning permission. In a recent appeal decision an inspector concluded:

'Government advice and Ministerial decision, however, combine to make clear that in lieu of providing parking spaces, either on-site or on other nearby land available to him, the option of offering a commuted sum

---

20 1979 SC 200, 1979 SLT 197.
1 Para 63.
2 See, for example [1974] JPL 106, and [1980] JPL 841. Woolf J appeared to agree in *McLaren v Secretary of State for the Environment and Broxbourne Borough Council* [1981] JPL 423.

towards the cost of providing additional public car parking is one which at first instance is exercisable solely at the discretion of the developer.'[3]

The minister has also said that it is improper to impose a condition requiring a developer to make over land to the local planning authority[4] or to find security for the fulfilment of a condition contained in a planning permission[5] or requiring a developer to enter into an agreement with the local planning authority.[6]

The principle that no payment of money or other consideration can be required when granting planning permission appears to be derived from the well-settled rule of law that any charge upon a subject may only be imposed by clear and unambiguous language in a statute.[7]

The nearest the 1971 Act comes to a clear and unambiguous provision is to be found in s 30(1)(a). This provides that, without prejudice to the general power in s 29(1), conditions may be imposed on a grant of planning permission requiring the carrying out of works on the land which is the subject of the application and on any other land under the control of the applicant.

Such conditions must fulfil the tests discussed earlier in this chapter. Thus they must be imposed for a planning purpose and be fairly and reasonably related to the permitted development. A condition requiring the provision of, or a contribution towards the cost of providing, infrastructure unrelated to the development would therefore be *ultra vires* the local planning authority.[8] On the other hand, it is commonplace to find conditions on planning permissions requiring the provision of car parking, the carrying out of landscaping, the planting of trees and so on—conditions which impose a financial burden on the developer but which serve a planning purpose, are fairly and reasonably related to the development and are reasonable in the circumstances.

However, in *Hall & Co Ltd v Shoreham-by-Sea UDC*[9] the Court of Appeal categorised as unreasonable a condition which required the developers of an industrial site to construct, at their own expense, a service road along the frontage of the site and to give a right of passage over the road to and from adjoining sites. The object sought to be obtained by the local planning authority—a restriction on the number of access points to a congested main road—was a proper planning purpose and the condition was held to be fairly and reasonably related to the permitted development. However, the court took the view that the condition effectively took away the plaintiffs' rights of property without compensation by requiring them to construct at their own expense what would virtually amount to a public highway and was thus unreasonable and *ultra vires*. A similar conclusion was reached by Woolf J in *M J Shanley Ltd v Secretary of State for the Environment and South*

3 [1982] JPL 463. See also the ministerial decisions noted at [1967] JPL 493, [1975] JPL 620, and [1982] JPL 665. See also circular 22/83, Appendix B, para 3.
4 *Bulletin of Selected Appeal Decisions*, II/17 and XI/1.
5 *Bulletin of Selected Appeal Decisions*, III/16.
6 See [1980] JPL 841.
7 See J M Evans, *de Smith's Judicial Review of Administrative Action* (4th edn, Stevens, 1980), p 100.
8 *R v Bowman* [1898] 1 QB 663.
9 [1964] 1 All ER 1, [1964] 1 WLR 240.

Bedfordshire District Council[10] about a proposed condition which would have required the provision for public recreation of 40 acres of land.

More recently the Court of Appeal in *Bradford City Metropolitan Council v Secretary of State for the Environment*[11] held that a condition that required, before houses could be occupied, that road widening works should be carried out to a bordering public road, was invalid. The condition did not expressly require the developer to carry out the works and to dedicate the new strip to the public but this was how it was interpreted by the court. The Court of Appeal said such a condition had to be 'manifestly unreasonable' as no relevant distinction could be made between the condition and that in *Hall v Shoreham*. If the condition was manifestly unreasonable in *Hall v Shoreham*, so it was here. The local planning authority had tried to distinguish *Hall* on the ground that in the *Bradford* case the road widening was in fact part of the application and the developer was agreeing to the condition. This was disputed by the developer but the court held that the willingness of the developer did not make the condition any less unreasonable. *Vires* could not be conferred by consent. However, in a tantalising aside, the court commented that if the condition could have been construed as imposing a purely negative obligation, that the development should not proceed, or the houses not be occupied, until the road had been widened, then the condition could well have been valid. The court then referred to the *Grampian* case which has already been discussed above. For such a condition to be reasonable, it is arguable that there should be a reasonable prospect that the works would be carried out by the Highway Authority. It must be doubtful whether a condition would be reasonable where it is plain that the developer would have to contribute to their cost or carry them out himself.[12] However, in *Daws v Secretary of State for the Environment*,[13] Bernard Marder QC, sitting as a deputy judge, upheld such a negative condition where it was plain that the applicant would have to carry out the highway works and presumably dedicate the land to the public.

So just how far a local planning authority can go in using conditions to redistribute the cost of infrastructure provision from the public to the private sector is still uncertain. For example, a condition requiring the provision of a children's play area in a residential development may be said to serve a planning purpose and if the need for the provision of such infrastructure arises solely from the development in question then the condition is fairly and reasonably related to the proposal. The question is whether such conditions are unreasonable in terms of the decision in *Hall*.

The decisions in *Britannia (Cheltenham) Ltd v Secretary of State for the Environment* and *Robert Hitchins Builders Ltd v Secretary of State for the Environment*[14] suggest that such conditions may be valid in respect of matters which are incidental or ancillary to the permitted development, provided they are to be located on land within the control of the developer. In these cases, which were heard together, Sir Douglas Frank held that permission for large scale residential development could properly be made the subject of

10 [1982] JPL 380. See also the decision by the English minister reported in [1979] JPL 485.
11 (1986) 53 P & CR 55, [1986] JPL 598.
12 See p 237, above.
13 (20 November 1987, unreported.)
14 (1978) 247 Estates Gazette 301, [1978] JPL 554 (subsequently quashed on other grounds by the Court of Appeal (1979) 251 Estates Gazette 467, [1979] JPL 534).

conditions requiring the provision and layout of adequate play areas and open spaces although he accepted that a requirement to dedicate them to the public would be unreasonable. This qualification seems rather artificial since a provision for public space is not much use if the public have no right to use the space. In *Britannia*, the condition was being backed up by a planning agreement by which the public was given access.

It seems unlikely that conditions can be used to require the provision of infrastructure, or a contribution towards the cost of its provision, on land beyond the control of the developer, even if the need for it derives solely from the development. The local planning authority in such circumstances can, of course, refuse the application on the ground that the present systems of sewage disposal, water supply, roads, etc. are inadequate or that the development is premature, although this may, in some cases, seem an unduly negative response. Alternatively, and in order to overcome such a blockage of his application, a developer may voluntarily agree to provide, or to contribute towards the cost of, the necessary infrastructure. In view of the uncertainty in this area it is not uncommon to find such matters dealt with by way of planning agreements (see chapter 11) or by some equivalent proced-ure under the Highways Act.[15]

In conclusion it would therefore seem that most of the problems can be solved by a combination of separate agreements and negative conditions.

Uncertainty

In addition to the three tests laid down by Viscount Dilhorne in *Newbury District Council v Secretary of State for the Environment*,[16] a condition attached to a grant of planning permission may be held void for uncertainty, though strictly this may be an aspect of the principle of unreasonableness. In *Fawcett Properties Ltd v Buckingham County Council*[17] the House of Lords held by a majority of 4 to 1 that although the wording of a particular condition was imperfect and might give rise to problems of construction, the condition was not void for uncertainty. Lord Denning declared:

'a planning condition is only void for uncertainty if it can be given no meaning or no sensible or ascertainable meaning and not merely because it is ambiguous or leads to absurd results. It is the daily task of the courts to resolve ambiguities of language and to choose between them; and to construe words so as to avoid ambiguities or to put up with them.'

Applying Fawcett, in *Alderson v Secretary of State for the Environment*[18] the Court of Appeal held that a condition which required occupation of a dwelling to be restricted to a person employed 'locally in agriculture', had a perfectly intelligible meaning although some doubtful cases might arise. Fox LJ argued that the fact that doubtful cases might, and almost certainly

15 As Grant points out in 'Urban Planning Law' at p 381, s 278 of the Highways Act 1980 is often used, by which highway authorities accept contributions towards the cost of proposed highway works.
16 [1981] AC 578, [1980] 1 All ER 731.
17 [1961] AC 636, [1960] 3 All ER 503. See too *Hall & Co Ltd v Shoreham-by-Sea UDC* [1964] 1 All ER 1, [1964] 1 WLR 240; and *M J Shanley Ltd v Secretary of State for the Environment and South Bedfordshire District Council* [1982] JPL 380.
18 (1984) 49 P & CR 307, [1984] JPL 429.

would, arise could not be a reason for invalidating the decision: 'They were really questions of degree and must be dealt with upon the facts of the individual cases as they arose.' It was probably significant that the words used in *Alderson* were almost the same as those recommended for an agricultural worker's condition by the Department of the Environment.[19]

On the other hand in *M J Shanley Ltd v Secretary of State for the Environment and South Bedfordshire District Council*[20] Woolf J held that a condition requiring the first opportunity to buy houses to be given to local people was invalid and unenforceable. This was because it did not give any indication at all as to the method or terms upon which the first opportunity was to be offered.

Conditions which leave the details to be worked out later by the local planning authority are not invalid.[1] So, conditions are often imposed which require schemes to be agreed with or approved by the authority. However, the local planning authority should be careful to make plain that the development has to be operated according to such schemes and to ensure that they are enforceable. Thus in *Penwith District Council v Secretary of State for the Environment*[2] on an appeal the Secretary of State granted permission subject to a condition that 'Before the development hereby permitted is commenced a scheme shall be agreed with the Local Planning Authority to cover the following points: A Noise insulation, B Shopfront type, C Opening hours'. In challenging the validity of this condition, it was pointed out that the condition did not expressly state that the development (an amusement arcade) had to be operated according to such a scheme. Woolf J indicated that it might be possible to imply this but went on to hold that in the case of opening hours, which were of great importance, it would not be practical or desirable that the condition should depend on having something read into it.

Where the matter comes to the courts by way of a challenge to an appeal against a refusal of planning permission or the service of an enforcement notice, the tendency is to interpret conditions benevolently but it seems that this liberalism may not apply when the condition is the subject of a prosecution in the criminal courts.[3]

It would also seem that the standard of certainty required may vary according to whether the permission is granted on an application for full planning permission or merely for outline permission.[4]

Necessity[5]

Department of the Environment circular 1/85 suggests that in deciding whether to impose a condition consideration should be given by the local planning authority to the need which the condition will fulfil.[6]

19 Circular No. 1/85 uses the words 'in the locality'.
20 [1982] JPL 380. Also see appeal decision noted in [1984] JPL 837.
 1 See *Roberts v Vale Royal District Council* (1977) 78 LGR 368, [1977] JPL 369 s 36(1); provides a right of appeal against a refusal to approve details; see p 266 below.
 2 [1986] 1 EGLR 193, [1986] JPL 432.
 3 See *Warrington Borough Council v Garvey* [1988] JPL 752.
 4 See *Inverclyde District Council v Inverkip Building Co Ltd* 1981 SC 401, 1982 SLT 401, and *Britannia (Cheltenham) Ltd v Secretary of State for the Environment* (1978) 247 Estates Gazette 301, [1978] JPL 554.
 5 See Eric Young, 'Is an Unnecessary Condition *Ultra Vires*?' [1983] JPL 357.
 6 Paras 12–14.

Now there is an important difference between conditions which the Secretary of State considers should not be imposed as a matter of policy and conditions which *cannot* be imposed as a matter of law. Necessity would appear to be primarily a matter of policy. However, in *British Airports Authority v Secretary of State for Scotland*[7] the First Division of the Court of Session broke new ground in holding that certain conditions which they found to be unnecessary were 'inexpedient' and therefore *ultra vires* in terms of the Scottish equivalent of s 30(1)(a). The permission granted to the British Airports Authority for development at the airport was subject to a condition which stated that the developers 'shall take such steps as are necessary to secure that all aircraft using the airport, shall, whenever it is safe and practicable to do so, take off towards the north and land from the north'. One of the grounds on which this condition was challenged by the applicants was that it was unnecessary; by the time the Secretary of State came to make his decision the Civil Aviation Authority had taken the steps necessary to ensure that aircraft landed and took off in the desired direction. This submission was upheld by the court. The Lord President (Lord Emslie) declared that 'it can never be "expedient . . . in connection" with a permitted development within the meaning of s 27(1) of the 1972 Act, to impose a condition which is unnecessary'. Lord Cameron, agreeing with the Lord President, drew attention to the existence of other statutory powers, specifically intended for the regulation of the matters with which the condition was concerned; these showed, he said, 'that in a very real sense the imposition of the condition is unnecessary for the purpose for which it was apparently designed'.

In the same case a condition attached to the planning permission granted to one of the companies engaged in helicopter operations at the airport was challenged on similar grounds. The condition prohibited night flying from the company's helicopter terminal. It was pointed out by the company that there had been no evidence before the Secretary of State that there was any likelihood of helicopters operating from this land. They argued that the Secretary of State's planning objective in imposing the condition—the control of aircraft noise—was covered by a condition attached to the planning permission granted to the British Airports Authority, since it was from their runways that all flying took place. The court accepted that the condition was 'both pointless and unnecessary'. It could not be said to be 'expedient' and was therefore *ultra vires*.

Whilst it is clearly desirable that conditions should serve some worthwhile purpose, the full implications of this particular aspect of the judgments are difficult to foresee. The issue of necessity was not dealt with at any length and it is uncertain what measure of need the courts will apply and what effect it may have, for example, on the use of overlapping and concurrent powers (see p 222 above). We therefore submit that the courts will only interfere with the local planning authority's or Secretary of State's view of the need for the condition, where it is manifestly unnecessary and is so much decoration.

Severance of invalid conditions and the legal consequences

If a condition is held to be void there may have to be considered the question whether the planning permission to which the condition was attached

7 1979 SC 200, 1979 SLT 197.

remains in force, shorn of the invalid condition, or whether the whole permission falls with the invalid condition. In the first place it must be considered whether it is a decision of a local planning authority that is being questioned or whether it is a decision of the Secretary of State on appeal or on a 'called in' application.

In the latter case, the decision can only be challenged by an aggrieved person by way of an application to the High Court in the terms of s 245(1)(b). Section 245(4)(b) provides, *inter alia*, that if the court is satisfied that the action of the Secretary of State is not within the powers of the Act it may quash the action (see chapter 20). In *British Airports Authority v Secretary of State for Scotland*[8] the First Division of the Court of Session held that the word 'action' in the equivalent Scottish section referred to the 'decision' of the minister and the 'decision' in that case was the composite confirmation of the grant of planning permission subject to certain conditions. The section did not empower the court to excise the *ultra vires* conditions from the decision. If the conditions were *ultra vires*, the whole composite decision failed and would be quashed. It would seem therefore, that if the decision in question is that of the Secretary of State then the possibility of the severance of invalid conditions does not arise.

Where the decision in question is that of a local planning authority (and not therefore subject to the statutory provisions on challenge) then the law is not clear. It has been said on the one hand, that it is never possible to mutilate a planning permission by removing a condition and that if any one of the conditions attached to a grant of permission is held to be bad, the whole planning permission falls with it.[9] At the other extreme the view has been expressed that an *ultra vires* condition is always severable, since if it is void it can have no effect on the force of the planning permission itself.[10]

The most widely held view appears to be that severance of an invalid condition is possible in some circumstances.[11] In *Hall & Co Ltd v Shoreham-by-Sea UDC*[12] the Court of Appeal, having held certain conditions void for unreasonableness, held that the conditions were not severable—they were fundamental to the planning permission in the sense that the planning authority would not have granted planning permission without the conditions and thus the whole planning permission fell with the conditions.

In *Kent County Council v Kingsway Investments (Kent) Ltd*[13] the House of Lords held by a 3 to 2 majority that a condition requiring approval of

8 1979 SC 200, 1979 SLT 197.
9 See *Pyx Granite Co Ltd v Minister of Housing and Local Government* [1958] 1 QB 554, [1958] 1 All ER 625, per Hodson LJ; and *Kent County Council v Kingsway Investments (Kent) Ltd* [1971] AC 72, [1970] 1 All ER 70, per Lord Guest.
10 See *Kingsway Investments (Kent) Ltd v Kent County Council* [1969] 2 QB 332, [1969] 1 All ER 601, per Winn LJ.
11 See *Fawcett Properties Ltd v Buckingham County Council* [1958] 3 All ER 521, [1958] 1 WLR 1161, per Roxburgh J; *Hall & Co Ltd v Shoreham-by-Sea UDC* [1964] 1 All ER 1, [1964] 1 WLR 240; *Allnatt London Properties Ltd v Middlesex County Council* (1964) 62 LGR 304, 15 P & CR 288; *Kingsway Investments (Kent) Ltd v Kent County Council* [1969] 2 QB 332, [1969] 1 All ER 601, CA; revsd sub nom *Kent County Council v Kingsway Investments (Kent) Ltd* [1971] AC 72, [1970] 1 All ER 70, HL; and *R v Hillingdon London Borough Council, ex p Royco Homes Ltd* [1974] QB 720, [1974] 2 All ER 643.
12 [1964] 1 All ER 1, [1964] 1 WLR 240; followed in *Royco Homes* (above).
13 [1971] AC 72, [1970] 1 All ER 70.

detailed plans within three years of the grant of outline planning permission was not void for unreasonableness. Though it was not necessary to the decision, the majority (Lords Morris of Borth-y-Gest, Donovan and Guest) expressed the view that if the condition had been invalid it could not have been severed from the outline permission. The minority (Lords Reid and Upjohn) differed from the majority in both respects. All of their Lordships except Lord Guest considered that severance of an invalid condition was possible in certain circumstances but the judgments exhibit considerable differences of view as to what those circumstances are.

Also the tests offered tend to be based on rather subjective judgments as to whether the condition is trivial or important, or goes to the root of the permission or changes its character. More recently in *R v St Edmundsbury Borough Council, ex p Investors in Industry Commercial Properties Ltd*[14] Stocker J said that he would have severed a condition, which required a supermarket development to have independent retail outlets, because 'The condition is not so fundamental as to render the whole permission granted void.'[15] More precisely Lord Reid in the *Kingsway Investments* case said that where a condition was imposed for a non-planning purpose it always could be severed. He also made a distinction between conditions which limited the manner in which the land could be developed (not severable) and a procedural condition (severable).

The uncertainty means that an applicant could risk losing a permission altogether by challenging a condition by way of judicial review. The safer route is to use the statutory machinery which now provides for application to be made for a condition to be revoked before the development has been implemented (see 1971 Act, s 31A).

In the situation where the development is carried out but there is non-compliance with a condition, it is still possible to argue on appeal against an enforcement notice that the condition is invalid. This was the case in *Newbury District Council v Secretary of State for the Environment*[16] where Lord Fraser rejected the idea that estoppel prevented the developer raising the invalidity of the condition. In *Elmbridge Borough Council v Secretary of State for the Environment*[17] the ingenious argument was raised that the condition had to be treated as valid until it had been pronounced invalid by a court. This was firmly rejected by Malcolm Spence QC (sitting as a deputy judge) who stated:

'In my judgement, the inspector was fully entitled to pronounce upon the validity or otherwise of the condition and having done so, was not constrained to uphold the legality of the enforcement notice by virtue of the fact that as at the date of service it had not yet been pronounced invalid.'

14 [1985] 3 All ER 234, [1985] 1 WLR 1168.
15 Also see *British Airports Authority v Secretary of State for Scotland* 1979 SC 200, 1979 SLT 197 and *Inverclyde District Council v Inverkip Building Co Ltd* 1981 SC 401, 1982 SLT 401; affd 1983 SLT 563.
16 [1981] AC 578, [1980] 1 All ER 731. See also *Birnie v Banff County Council* 1954 SLT (Sh Ct) 90 and *Inverclyde District Council v Inverkip Building Co Ltd* 1981 SC 401, 1982 SLT 401.
17 [1989] JPL 277.

Where there is no appeal against the enforcement notice, it would appear that s 243 would prevent the validity of a condition being raised as a defence to a prosecution in the criminal courts. This excludes challenge in any proceedings on any of the grounds on which an appeal can be brought. One of these grounds is that the matters alleged in the notice do not constitute a breach of planning control: an attack on the validity of the condition amounts to such a ground.[18]

Conditions attached to applications under ss 31A and 32

Where development has been granted subject to conditions, there is provision for application to be made for the development to be carried out without complying with the conditions. This can apply when the development has already been implemented (s 32(1)(a)) or where the development has not yet been implemented (s 31A). In the case of s 31A, there is an express power to impose alternative conditions and although there is not an express power with regard to s 32, it was assumed in *Elmbridge Borough Council v Secretary of State for the Environment*[19] that there was a similar power.

In that decision the deputy judge had no doubt that the principle, that conditions should fairly and reasonably apply to the proposal, applied to a s 32 application. It must therefore be that the general principles set out above apply with any necessary modifications to both s 32 and s 31A applications.

18 However, see *Warrington Borough Council v Garvey* [1988] JPL 752, where Judge Woolley went into the validity of a condition on a criminal prosecution in the Crown Court. He also argued that the standards as to the validity of conditions should be tighter in criminal proceedings.
19 [1989] JPL 277.

CHAPTER 10

CONTROL OF DEVELOPMENT
4: LOCAL PLANNING AUTHORITY'S
DECISION AND OTHER MATTERS

Having considered an application for planning permission, the local planning authority may:

(a) grant planning permission unconditionally, or
(b) grant planning permission subject to such conditions as they think fit, or
(c) refuse planning permission (1971 Act, s 29(1)).

So long as they confine themselves to proper planning considerations and observe the appropriate procedural requirements (see chapters 7 and 8), local planning authorities have a wide discretion to grant or refuse planning permission.

Local planning authorities also enjoy a wide discretion to attach conditions to a grant of planning permission; some control over that discretion is, however, exercised by the courts (see chapter 9). The courts also exercise a certain amount of control over the more general powers of local planning authorities to determine planning applications.

The scope of the local planning authority's discretion: limitations

While the local planning authority must take account of the various matters mentioned in chapters 7 and 8[1] they are in no way bound by these matters and must consider each planning application on its own merits. They must not (in the absence of statutory authorisation) act under the dictation of another person or body[2] or so tie their hands in advance as to disable themselves from properly exercising their discretion.[3] In *Steeples v Derbyshire County Council*[4] Webster J considered that a planning authority's prior

---

1 In *R v London Borough of Haringey, ex p Barrs* [1983] JPL 54 (below) one of Comyn J's reasons for holding a grant of planning permission *ultra vires* for unreasonableness was that the authority did not appear to have paid any real attention to objections but this decision was reversed by the Court of Appeal (1983) *Times*, 7 July. Contrast, however, *R v Hammersmith and Fulham London Borough Council, ex p People Before Profit Ltd* (1981) 80 LGR 322, 45 P & CR 364.

2 See, for example, *H Lavender & Son Ltd v Minister of Housing and Local Government* [1970] 3 All ER 871, [1970] 1 WLR 1231, in which the minister's decision was held *ultra vires* in that he had in effect surrendered his discretion to another minister. See too *R v Worthing Borough Council, ex p Burch* (1983) 50 P & CR 53, [1984] JPL 261, in which an expression of opinion by the Secretary of State for the Environment as to the future use of a piece of Crown land was held to be an unlawful constraint on the free exercise of the planning authority's discretion.

3 See chs 8 and 11.

4 [1984] 3 All ER 468, [1985] 1 WLR 256.

obligation to use their best endeavours to obtain planning permission for a particular development would have indicated to a reasonable man that the local planning authority had imposed upon themselves a fetter on their freedom to discharge their statutory duty and would have suggested to the reasonable man that there was a real likelihood that the authority would be biased in their consideration of an application for planning permission for the development in question; the grant of planning permission was held to be in breach of the rules of natural justice and *ultra vires*.

However, in *R v Sevenoaks District Council, ex p Terry*[5] Glidewell J disagreed with the test propounded by Webster J in *Steeples*. He pointed out that:

'it is not uncommon for a local authority to make a decision relating to land or other property in which it has an interest. In such a situation the application of the rule designed to ensure that a judicial officer does not appear to be biased would, in my view, often produce an administrative impasse.'

Glidewell J therefore concluded that the correct test was whether it was clear in the circumstances that the authority could not exercise proper discretion. This approach has since been followed by Stocker J in *R v St Edmundsbury Borough Council, ex p Investors in Industry Commercial Properties Ltd*[6] who said there was no need to speculate on what the reasonable man might have thought and that the test was whether the local planning authority had taken into account all proper considerations and excluded all improper considerations. As it will usually be difficult to prove that improper considerations such as the corporate interest of the council have been taken into account, this approach means that decisions will be invulnerable in law however much there may be an appearance of bias.

Again in *R v Amber Valley District Council, ex p Jackson*[7] a meeting of the local Labour party decided, prior to consideration of a planning application for a particular development, to support the development in question. The Labour group were in control on the council. Objectors to the proposed development sought an order of prohibition to prevent the authority considering the application, arguing that any reasonable person knowing the relevant facts would regard the outcome of the planning application as a foregone conclusion and that in the circumstances the local planning authority could not fairly determine the application. Woolf J held that although there was an obligation on the local planning authority to act fairly and without bias on an application for planning permission, here there was no evidence of bias. Woolf J said that all that the evidence indicated was that the local planning authority were 'politically predisposed' in favour of the development; it was, in his view, 'almost inevitable now that party politics played so large a part in Local Government, that the majority group on a Council would decide on the Party line', but it would be wrong to infer that the planning committee would not take into account all relevant factors.[8] It may be, however, that a decision taken on the basis of a pre-determined group policy which members felt themselves obliged to follow would be of questionable validity; in such circumstances it might be inferred that members had closed their minds to matters they were bound to take into account.[9]

While the determination of a planning application can be classified as an administrative rather than a judicial function, it is now plain that the rules of natural justice or to use the modern expression, the duty to act fairly, applies to such determinations. So, although a corporate interest in the subject matter of the planning application will only invalidate the decision where it has in fact affected the exercise of the discretion, where a member of the planning committee has a personal interest in the outcome, a much stricter approach will be taken. In *R v Hendon RDC, ex p Chorley*[10] the Divisional Court quashed a decision of a planning committee granting permission where a member of the committee who took part and voted, was acting as estate agent for the vendor of the property.[11] In the case of a financial interest, this in itself will be sufficient to constitute a likelihood of bias, but in the case of other types of interest or potential bias the test would probably be whether a reasonable man would have thought there was a real likelihood or a reasonable suspicion of bias.[12] In any case, the Local Government Act 1972 disqualifies members from participating in particular decisions in which they have any pecuniary interest and imposes a duty to disclose 'any pecuniary interest direct or indirect in any contract, proposed contract or other matter'.[13]

The duty to act fairly could also impose procedural requirements over and above those already imposed by the statutory rules. However, the courts fashion the extent or content of the duty according to the context of the decision and have shown a disinclination to imply additional rules at the level of decision-making by local planning authorities. Thus it has been held that the owner of the property has no right to be given an opportunity to be heard by the planning committee[14] and in *Gaiman v National Association for Mental Health*[15] Megarry J pointed out that thousands of planning applications are refused every year without any hearing, yet he knew 'of no suggestion that local planning authorities are thereby universally acting in contravention of the principles of natural justice'. In practice many authorities do provide for

8　See too *Cardiff Corpn v Secretary of State for Wales* (1971) 115 Sol Jo 187, 22 P & CR 718 in which Thesiger J said that 'local planning authorities consist of democratically elected members and the members are, in my view, in practice constantly considering what their voters want and may, in dealing with any question, deal with it in accordance with what they think will be satisfactory to those whose votes they have solicited in the past and intend to solicit in the future.'

9　However, in *R v Waltham Forest London Borough Council, ex p Baxter* [1988] QB 419, [1987] 3 All ER 671, the Court of Appeal held that it did not matter, even if the member might find the whip withdrawn if he did not abide by party policy, as long as he was free to remain a member and made the final decision himself.

10　[1933] 2 KB 696.

11　It was held not to matter that he did not speak and no formal vote was taken.

12　*R v London Rent Assessment Panel Committee, ex p Metropolitan Properties Co (FGC) Ltd* [1969] 1 QB 577, [1968] 3 All ER 304.

13　See ss 94 and 95 of the Local Government Act 1972.

14　*Hanily v Minister of Local Government and Planning* [1952] 2 QB 444, [1952] 1 All ER 1293.

15　[1971] Ch 317, [1970] 2 All ER 362.

an opportunity for applicants and others to speak to planning committees but the decision in *R v Secretary of State for the Environment, ex p Kent*[16] would suggest that such general practices cannot be translated into a legal right by way of the doctrine of legitimate expectations. It would be different if the local planning authority were to specifically undertake to provide a hearing or to give one party an unfair advantage over another.[17]

On the basis of the '*Wednesbury* principles' the courts also exercise a degree of control over discretionary decision-making through the concepts of relevancy, reasonableness and purpose (see chapter 20). All three concepts are considered in chapter 9 in connection with the imposition of conditions on planning permissions, while the concept of relevancy in the determination of applications is considered in chapter 8. However, brief mention may be made here of examples of cases in which the courts have treated decisions on planning applications as *ultra vires* for unreasonableness or as involving a use of discretionary powers for an ulterior purpose or improper motive.[18]

In *Niarchos (London) Ltd v Secretary of State for the Environment*[19] a local planning authority had refused to grant a further temporary permission for the use of premises as offices, the development plan containing a policy to the effect that temporary office permissions should not be renewed in respect of any premises 'reasonably capable' of adaptation for residential use. On appeal, the minister refused planning permission, stating that he did not think that the financial considerations which allegedly made conversion of the offices to houses unprofitable were of such importance as to merit an exception to the development plan policy. Sir Douglas Frank, sitting as a deputy judge of the High Court, held that the minister had misinterpreted the policy. What he should have asked himself was whether the premises could reasonably be adapted for housing. The deputy judge considered that the minister should have taken the financial implications into account and that had he done so the inevitable conclusion would have been that the premises could not reasonably be adapted for residential use. (The inspector who held the inquiry into the appeal had concluded that the only alternative to continuation of the office use was that the premises would be left empty.) The minister's decision was therefore, unreasonable and had to be quashed.

Though much quoted and analysed, the '*Wednesbury*' test for unreasonableness is, however, notoriously difficult to apply in practice. In *R v Haringey London Borough Council, ex p Barrs*,[20] for example, a local

16 [1988] JPL 706.
17 *R v Great Yarmouth Borough Council, ex p Botton Bros Arcades Ltd* (1987) 56 P & CR 99, [1988] JPL 18. See Hinds 'Third Party Objections to Planning Applications: An Expectation of Fairness' [1988] JPL 742 for an analysis of the issue.
18 As Lord Greene pointed out in *Associated Provincial Picture Houses Ltd v Wednesbury Corpn* [1948] 1 KB 223, [1947] 2 All ER 680, the various grounds on which a discretionary decision may be attacked run into one another and some of the decisions dealt with in chapter 8 in the context of 'material considerations' could equally be treated under the heading of 'improper purpose'.
19 (1977) 76 LGR 480, 35 P & CR 259. Contrast *Granada Theatres Ltd v Secretary of State for the Environment* (1980) 43 P & CR 253; and *Wessex Regional Health Authority v Salisbury District Council and Secretary for the Environment* [1984] JPL 344. In *Bell and Colvill Ltd v Secretary of State for the Environment and Guildford Borough Council* [1980] JPL 823 Forbes J said that he 'profoundly disagreed' with the decision in *Niarchos*.
20 (1983) Times, 1 July, reversing [1983] JPL 54. See too *Buckinghamshire County Council v Hall Aggregates (Thames Valley) Ltd and Sand and Gravel Association* [1985] JPL 634.

planning authority, having purchased a site with an existing planning permission for four houses, subsequently granted themselves planning permission for seven houses. Comyn J held, applying the *Wednesbury* principles, that the permission was *ultra vires* for unreasonableness in that the facts suggested that the authority had granted themselves a permission they would not have granted to a private individual. On appeal, however, the members of the Court of Appeal found themselves unable to conclude on the evidence that the planning authority had acted unreasonably.

Certainly the trend would seem to be towards a very strict test. In *Council of Civil Service Unions v Minister for the Civil Service*[1] Lord Diplock used the term 'irrationality' to cover *Wednesbury* unreasonableness and said: 'It applies to a decision which is so outrageous in its defiance of logic or of accepted moral standards that no sensible person who had applied his mind to the question to be decided would have arrived at it.' This means that in practice, if not in theory, a decision will normally only be quashed for being unreasonable if the unreasonableness is linked to other heads of review such as relevancy and improper purpose.[2] However, there are the rare cases where a decision has been overturned on what can be called 'pure' *Wednesbury* unreasonableness.[3]

So far as concerns the use of development control powers for an ulterior object or for improper purposes, it has been held that a local planning authority are not entitled to refuse planning permission to the owners of land simply in order to protect the authority's own possession of the property,[4] and that it is improper to use planning powers to impose on a developer some burden which should properly be shouldered by the planning authority themselves in some other capacity.[5] The minister has held that a local planning authority are not entitled to refuse planning permission for a private hospital in order to protect National Health Service staffing resources.[6] In *Paul v Ayrshire County Council*[7] it was said that it would clearly be a misuse of planning powers for a planning authority to attempt by means of a refusal of planning permission to create a right of way.

Where a local planning authority had made a firm statement that it was going to grant permission, it might be held by the court that it was an abuse of power to refuse permission without first giving the applicant an oppor-

---

1 [1985] AC 374, [1984] 3 All ER 935.
2 Though the courts seem more willing to review procedural powers (such as the power to grant an adjournment on the grounds that the decision is unreasonable or wrong); see *Niarchos (London) Ltd v Secretary of State for the Environment and Westminster City Council (No 2)* [1981] JPL 118 and *R v Secretary of State for the Environment, ex p Mistral Investments* [1984] JPL 516.
3 See *Wyre Forest District Council v Secretary of State for the Environment and the Order of the Holy Trinity Convent* [1989] JPL 270 for a recent example; but this was in the event revsd; see (1989) Times, 29 March.
4 *Westminster City Council v British Waterways Board* [1985] AC 676, [1984] 3 All ER 737. Contrast *Westminster City Council v Great Portland Estates plc* [1985] AC 661, [1984] 3 WLR 1035.
5 See *Westminster Renslade Ltd v Secretary of State for the Environment* (1983) 127 Sol Jo 444, 48 P & CR 255; *Hall & Co Ltd v Shoreham-by-Sea UDC* [1964] 1 All ER 1, [1964] 1 WLR 240 (see p 241 above); and *R v Hillingdon London Borough Council, ex p Royco Homes Ltd* [1974] QB 720, [1974] 2 All ER 643 (see p 234 above).
6 See appeal decision reported in [1983] JPL 142.
7 1964 SC 116, 1964 SLT 207.

tunity to comment.[8] Otherwise it would seem that an agreement by which a local planning authority undertook to grant permission would not be valid.[9]

The decision on an application for planning permission

The question whether a local planning authority may grant a planning permission which departs from the terms of the application made to them — whether, for example, the authority may grant planning permission for the erection of 30 houses on a site for which application was made to build 40 houses—does not admit of a straightforward answer. In *Glacier Metal Co Ltd v London Borough of Hillingdon*[10] Judge Stabb declared that a local planning authority 'may grant planning permission if they approve the whole of the application, but must refuse if they disapprove of part, because they have no power to grant planning permission as to part only'.[11] However, though it seems clear that an authority are not entitled to grant planning permission for a development substantially different from that for which application was made, Judge Stabb's statement appears to be too sweeping.

In *Kent County Council v Secretary of State for the Environment and Burmah Total Refineries Trust*[12] Sir Douglas Frank accepted that where an application was made up of a number of separate and divisible elements, it was lawful for these elements to be separately dealt with; it was held in this case that the decision of the minister to grant permission for part of the development applied for and to refuse permission for the remainder was valid. A rather different approach was adopted in *Bernard Wheatcroft Ltd v Secretary of State for the Environment*.[13] In this case the minister had concluded that where application had been made for planning permission for the erection of 420 houses on 35 acres of land, the proposed development was not severable and that it would therefore be improper for him to grant planning permission for an alternative scheme, put forward by the applicants, for 250 houses on 25 acres. Forbes J held that there was no principle of law that unless the proposed development was severable there could not be imposed on a planning permission a condition which would have the effect of reducing the permitted development below that for which planning permission had been sought. Accordingly, the Secretary of State had misdirected himself in law. The true test was whether the effect of the conditional planning permission would be to allow development which was in substance not that for which planning permission had been sought. Forbes J expressed the view that the main, but not the only, criterion for judging whether the substance of an application would be altered is whether the development 'is so changed that to grant it would be to deprive those who should have been consulted on the changed development of the opportunity of consultation'.

---

8 See *Costain Homes Ltd and Milton Hutchings Ltd v Secretary of State for the Environment and Hillingdon London Borough Council* [1988] JPL 701; but compare *R.v Secretary of State for the Environment ex p, Barratt (Guildford) Ltd* (1989) Times, 3 April.

9 See *Stringer v Minister of Housing and Local Government* [1971] 1 All ER 65, [1970] 1 WLR 1281 and *Windsor and Maidenhead Royal Borough Council v Brandrose Investments* [1983] 1 All ER 818, [1983] 1 WLR 509, CA.

10 (1975) 239 Estates Gazette 573.

11 Judge Stabb suggested, however, that the powers of the minister on appeal might be rather wider.

12 (1976) 75 LGR 452, 33 P & CR 70. See also *Boddington Breweries v Secretary of State for the Environment* (27 January 1988, unreported).

13 (1980) 43 P & CR 233; followed in *Wessex Regional Health Authority v Salisbury District Council and Secretary for the Environment* [1984] JPL 344.

Where, as in the case before him, the proposed development had been the subject of consultation and had produced root-and-branch opposition to any development at all, it was difficult to accept that it should be necessary to repeat the consultation process on a smaller development.[14] Forbes J said that he had come to his general conclusion 'with a certain feeling of satisfaction', as it seemed to him 'to permit a welcome degree of flexibility in the conduct of planning applications and appeals while at the same time maintaining adequate safeguards for the interests of those in whose favour the provisions for consultation were enacted'.

Also, in *Britannia (Cheltenham) Ltd v Secretary of State for the Environment*[15] (which was not referred to in *Wheatcroft*) Sir Douglas Frank said that it must be beyond doubt that the development described in a planning application includes any development ancillary or incidental to the proposed development. He concluded in that case that conditions requiring that provision be made in the plans for public open space and a social and shopping centre were incidental to an application for a large housing development; and that in dealing with an application for outline planning permission it was permissible to attach conditions excluding an area from development in order to preserve it for some type of development other than that for which application had been made.[16]

Local planning authorities sometimes seek to limit the scope of a planning permission, not by way of condition but by way of a restriction contained in the permission itself—for example, by granting planning permission for the use of a building for agricultural purposes. In *Wilson v West Sussex County Council,*[17] for example, planning permission was granted for an 'agricultural cottage'. The Court of Appeal held that since the permission specifically incorporated the terms of the application for permission it was necessary to refer to the application in construing the permission (see p 271 below), and that the word 'agricultural' had a functional significance and was to be construed as limiting the proposed dwelling to one intended to be occupied by an agricultural worker. In *Waverley District Council v Secretary of State for the Environment*[18] permission for the use of buildings as a 'depot for cattle lorries' had been granted following an application for permission to use land and buildings for agricultural purposes. Hodgson J held that it could not be said that the use of the buildings for general haulage purposes unconnected with agriculture came within the terms of the permission.

It seems that such restrictions or limitations are not enforceable as conditions or implied conditions.[19] Failure to comply initially will technically

---

14 See, however, *Wessex Regional Health Authority* (above) where the court reluctantly decided that it could not interfere with a decision of an inspector that a reduction from 48 to 37 houses differed substantially from the development originally proposed and that there might be objectors to the 37 layout.

15 [1978] JPL 554 (revsd on different grounds by the Court of Appeal [1979] JPL 534).

16 See too *Inverclyde District Council v Inverkip Building Co Ltd* 1983 SLT 563.

17 [1963] 2 QB 764, [1963] 1 All ER 751. See too *Trinder v Sevenoaks RDC* (1967) 204 Estates Gazette 803; *East Suffolk County Council v Secretary of State for the Environment* (1972) 70 LGR 595; *Williamson v Cambridgeshire County Council* [1977] RVR 132, 34 P & CR 117; and *Kwik Save Discount Group Ltd v Secretary of State for Wales* (1980) 79 LGR 310, 42 P & CR 166.

18 [1982] JPL 105. See also *Uttlesford District Council v Secretary of State for the Environment* [1989] JPL 685.

19 *Carpet Decor (Guildford) Ltd v Secretary of State for the Environment* (1981) 261 Estates Gazette 56, [1981] JPL 806.

mean that the whole development is unauthorised.[20] However, where the development as authorised is implemented and, thereafter, there is a change of use which contravenes the restrictions or specifications in the permission, there will only be a breach of planning control if the change constitutes development as being material. In *East Suffolk County Council v Secretary of State for the Environment*,[1] for example, the Divisional Court held that the minister had not erred in law in ruling that where planning permission had been granted for the erection of a house 'for the purpose of dwelling accommodation for an agricultural worker', a change from occupation by an agricultural worker to occupation by someone who was not so employed was not a material change of use and that the restriction in the permission could not therefore be enforced. It seems that in such circumstances a local planning authority should impose a specific condition rather than rely on a restriction in the permission itself. Where the limitation is set out in the application itself, there is no power to grant an unrestricted permission but it is possible to impose a condition as well as a limitation.[2]

Although planning permission is normally to enure for the benefit of the land and of all persons for the time being interested therein (see s 33(1)), in appropriate circumstances the local planning authority may grant a 'personal' planning permission, expressed to be for the benefit of a particular individual only. Permission may also be granted for a limited period (s 30(1), (2)—see p 228 above).

The local planning authority may grant planning permission for the retention on land of buildings or works constructed or carried out before the date of the application or for the continuance of a use of land instituted before the date of the application, whether the development in question was carried out without permission or under a permission granted for a limited period; any such permission may be expressed to have retrospective effect (s 32). Permission can also be granted for the retention of such buildings or works or the continuation of such a use without complying with some condition subject to which a previous planning permission was granted (s 32(1)(b)). Alternatively, permission can be granted to develop land without compliance with conditions previously attached to a grant of permission (s 31A).

Planning permission granted for the erection of a building may specify the purposes for which the building may be used; if no purpose is specified, the permission is to be construed as including permission to use the building for the purpose for which it is designed (s 33(2)).[3] Thus, a building designed for use as a factory could, unless a particular class of industry is specified in the permission, be used for any factory purpose consistent with its design.

20 See *Copeland Borough Council v Secretary of State for the Environment* (1976) 31 P & CR 403 and *Kerrier District Council v Secretary of State for the Environment and Brewer* (1980) 41 P & CR 284, [1981] JPL 193.
1 (1972) 70 LGR 595.
2 See *Uttlesford District Council v Secretary of State for the Environment* [1989] JPL 685.
3 The effect of this provision was considered in *Wilson v West Sussex County Council* [1963] 2 QB 764, [1963] 1 All ER 751; see too *Peake v Secretary of State for Wales* (1971) 115 Sol Jo 507, 22 P & CR 889; and *Wood v Secretary of State for the Environment* [1973] 2 All ER 404.

In *Wilson v West Sussex County Council*[4] the Court of Appeal held that 'designed' as used by s 33 meant 'intended to be used' and did not mean an architectural design suitable for a particular use, at least in the case of an outline permission. This intention will usually be gleaned from the terms of the grant of permission.

When granting planning permission relating to a building or premises in respect of which a duty exists to include, where it is reasonable and practicable to do so, provision for the needs of the disabled,[5] the local planning authority are to ensure that the applicant is aware of the duty (1971 Act, s 29A).[6] There is a similar duty on local planning authorities when granting permission for educational buildings to draw attention to the duties with regard to the disabled in such buildings.[7] Circular 10/82 suggests that developers be made aware of their duties by means of a note accompanying the grant of permission.

Outline planning permission and approval of reserved matters

Having granted an application for outline planning permission (see p 173 above), the local planning authority have in effect committed themselves in principle to the type of development specified in the permission. The subsequent approval of the planning authority is, however, required with regard to 'reserved matters', i e, matters of detail which are reserved by way of condition in the outline permission for later consideration (see p 174 above).

In *Inverclyde District Council v Inverkip Building Co Ltd*[8] the Second Division of the Court of Session held that although a particular matter included in a condition attached to a planning permission under the umbrella of 'reserved matters' did not in fact relate to a matter which was capable of being a reserved matter in terms of the GDO, its inclusion as a 'reserved matter' did not make the grant of outline permission invalid. In this case the Lord Justice-Clerk (Lord Wheatley) expressed the opinion that the distinction between conditions relating to reserved matters and 'ordinary' conditions is that in respect of reserved matters the planning authority *must* impose conditions reserving these matters for their subsequent approval whereas any other conditions attached to a grant of planning permission are at the discretion of the planning authority.

Having granted outline planning permission and thus given their approval in principle to the type of development proposed, it is not open to the local planning authority, in dealing with a subsequent application for approval of reserved matters, to refuse approval except on grounds which arise from and relate to matters which were reserved in the outline permission.[9] The

---

4 [1963] 2 QB 764, [1963] 1 All ER 751.
5 See ss 4 to 7 of the Chronically Sick and Disabled Persons Act 1970 which includes buildings or premises to which the public are admitted and offices, shops, railway premises and factories.
6 Added by the Disabled Persons Act 1981.
7 See ss 29B and 8 of the Chronically Sick and Disabled Persons Act 1970.
8 1983 SLT 563.
9 See *Cardiff Corpn v Secretary of State for Wales* (1971) 22 P & CR 718; *Chelmsford Corpn v Secretary of State for the Environment* (1971) 22 P & CR 880; *Lewis Thirkell Ltd v Secretary of State for the Environment* (1978) 248 Estates Gazette 685, [1978] JPL 844; and appeal decisions noted in [1969] JPL 156, and [1976] JPL 555 and 726.

authority cannot at the stage of consideration of reserved matters consider such questions as whether the development is desirable in principle or is premature. An application for approval of reserved matters must also be within the ambit of the outline permission and must accord with the conditions annexed to that permission,[10] and where what purports to be an application for approval of details does not accord with the terms of the outline permission, the local planning authority are entitled to treat the later application as a completely new application and to refuse it on grounds of principle.[11] Where, for example, outline planning permission had been granted for a warehouse for wholesale and retail distribution, the local planning authority were held entitled to refuse an application for approval of details which was not in accordance with the outline permission in that it showed that the applicants' real intention was to erect a supermarket.[12] Where, however, an application for approval of reserved matters includes matters which are not within the ambit of the outline permission, it may sometimes be possible for the local planning authority to grant only that part of the application falling within the scope of the outline permission.[13]

Further, in *R v Hammersmith and Fulham London Borough Council, ex p Greater London Council*[14] the Court of Appeal held that where outline permission had been granted for a major redevelopment, setting out various permitted uses, the local planning authority had the power to grant approval to a submission of reserved matters which omitted some of the uses specified. Glidewell LJ held that, using Lord Denning's test in *Heron Corpn*, the application was still within 'the ambit of the outline permission'. He said that:

'If for instance . . ., the application for approval of detail showed some added uses, it would often be easy to say "That is not within the ambit of the outline" but where the application for approval of detail omitted one or more of the uses, it seems to be more difficult to decide the question.'

Application for approval of reserved matters must be made with a specified time limit (see p 261 below). However, in *Cardiff Corpn v Secretary of State for Wales*[15] Thesiger J said that 'a local planning authority cannot eliminate an outline planning permission merely by failing to consider and approve the detailed plans which have been submitted in time for an appeal to be entered to the Minister against either a refusal or a mere failure to approve.' However it would be up to the applicant to challenge the failure to approve either by appealing to the minister against a deemed refusal or by applying for judicial review.

10 See *Inverclyde District Council v Secretary of State for Scotland* 1980 SC 363, 1981 SLT 26 (Second Division); affd 1982 SC (HL) 64, 1982 SLT 200; *Heron Corpn Ltd v Manchester City Council* [1978] 3 All ER 1240, [1978] 1 WLR 937; and see p 175.
11 See *Shemara Ltd v Luton Corpn* (1967) 18 P & CR 520; *Calcaria Construction Co (York) Ltd v Secretary of State for the Environment* (1974) 27 P & CR 435; *Chalgray Ltd v Secretary of State for the Environment* (1976) 33 P & CR 10, and appeal decisions noted in [1974] JPL 45 and [1980] JPL 354.
12 *Calcaria Construction* (above).
13 See *Inverclyde District Council v Lord Advocate* 1982 SLT 200.
14 (1985) 51 P & CR 120, [1986] JPL 528.
15 (1971) 22 P & CR 718.

On an application for approval of reserved matters it is not clear whether the local planning authority have power to impose further conditions relating to that matter[16] or whether their powers at this stage are restricted to outright approval or rejection of the detailed proposals. This point was raised in *Chelmsford Corpn v Secretary of State for the Environment*[17] and was said by Browne J to raise 'very difficult and fundamental problems', but in the circumstances of that case it was not necessary to deal with the question.

Notice of decision

Notice of the local planning authority's decision on an application for planning permission or for approval of reserved matters is to be in writing (GDO, art 25). Despite doubts by some commentators[18] case law appears to have established that it is the notice of the authority's decision rather than the resolution of the authority which constitutes the grant or refusal of permission.[19] Most recently in *R v West Oxfordshire District Council, ex p C H Pearce Homes Ltd*[20] Woolf J affirmed this view. He held that he was bound by the previous decision of *R v Yeovil Borough Council*[1] and rejected arguments that the Court of Appeal decision in *Slough Estates*[2] could be distinguished because of the different wording in a previous GDO. This means that until the written notification is issued, the council can always change its mind and refuse permission. It may, however, be possible to show that what purports to be a planning permission is in fact no permission at all because it was issued by mistake (see *Norfolk County Council v Secretary of State for the Environment*)[3] or because it was issued without authority (see *A-G (HM), (Co-operative Retail Services Ltd) v Taff-Ely Borough Council*).[4] The date of the decision is presumably the date when the notification is signed and for the purposes of the time limit on appeals it seems clear time runs from the date that the notification is received (GDO, art 25 and Pt II of Sch 3). It is also important in determining whether development has been begun within the statutory time limit to establish the exact date when a decision on a planning application was made.

The period within which the local planning authority are to give notice to an applicant of their decision is eight weeks commencing on the date of receipt of the application or (except where the applicant has already given notice of appeal to the Secretary of State) such extended period as may be

---

16 However, such a decision seems to be envisaged by art 25(a) of the GDO.
17 (1971) 70 LGR 89, 22 P & CR 880.
18 See, for example, J F Garner, 'When is a Planning Permission?' [1972] JPL 194, and M Albery, 'What and When is a Planning Decision?' (1974) 70 LQR 351.
19 See *R v Yeovil Borough Council, ex p Trustees of Elim Pentecostal Church* (1971) 33 P & CR 29, and *Co-operative Retail Services v Taff-Ely Borough Council* (1978) 38 P & CR 156. See too *Slough Estates Ltd v Slough Borough Council (No 2)* [1969] 2 Ch 305, [1969] 2 All ER 988, [1969] 2 WLR 1157, CA; on appeal [1971] AC 958, [1970] 2 All ER 216, HL.
20 [1986] JPL 523.
1 Ibid.
2 Ibid.
3 [1973] 3 All ER 673, [1973] 1 WLR 1400.
4 (1981) 42 P & CR 1, HL.

agreed in writing between the applicant and the local planning authority (GDO, art 23(2)).[5] If the local planning authority do not give notice of their decision within the proper period, the applicant is entitled to appeal to the Secretary of State as if permission had been refused (1971 Act, s 37).

In *Bovis Homes (Scotland) Ltd v Inverclyde District Council*[6] the planning authority failed to give notice of their decision on an application for approval of reserved matters within the time limit. The applicants raised an action seeking (1) declarator that the local planning authority were bound to consider the application and give notice of their decision thereon; and (2) decree ordaining the authority to give such notice within two months of decree. The planning authority argued that the applicants could have appealed to the Secretary of State within the six month period following the 'deemed refusal' of planning permission and that since they had not done so their action was incompetent because a common law remedy was not available to the pursuers where they had failed to avail themselves of the statutory machinery for appeal. The planning authority also argued that even if there was a duty upon them to give a decision within the period following receipt of the application, the duty 'flew off' at the end of that period. Founding strongly upon the decision in *London and Clydeside Estates Ltd v Aberdeen District Council*[7] (in which the House of Lords had to consider similar provisions in the Land Compensation (Scotland) Act 1963), Lord Wylie held that the obligation to deal with an application was a continuing one, notwithstanding the expiry of the period specified in the GDO. An order, requiring notice of the decision to be given, was therefore granted.

Where, on an application for planning permission or for approval of reserved matters, the local planning authority decide to grant permission or approval subject to conditions or to refuse permission or approval, the notice is to state the reasons for the decision (GDO, art 25). The 1988 order now makes it explicit that the local planning authority must state their full reasons clearly and precisely. Failure to give any reason for the imposition of a condition does not, however, automatically invalidate the condition.[8] Where as in *Brayhead (Ascot)*[9] the challenge is made long after the failure, the courts will be reluctant to grant a remedy. In a case where relief is sought quickly, the courts might use their discretion to quash a determination especially if the reasons are illogical or inadequate.[10] Where there was a total failure to give reasons the better remedy might be to grant mandamus requiring reasons to be given. Where no reasons are given the court is, it seems, entitled to look at all the surrounding circumstances in order to

---

5 As to the date on which an application is to be taken as having been received, see art 23(3) of the GDO (p 189 above).
6 1982 SLT 473. See too *James v Minister of Housing and Local Government* [1965] 3 All ER 602, sub nom *James v Secretary of State for Wales* [1966] 1 WLR 135, CA (overruled on other grounds in the House of Lords [1968] AC 409, [1966] 3 All ER 964; and *London Ballast Co Ltd v Buckinghamshire County Council* (1966) 65 LGR 227, 18 P & CR 446.
7 [1979] 3 All ER 876, 1980 SC (HL) 1, 1980 SLT 81.
8 *Brayhead (Ascot) Ltd v Berkshire County Council* [1964] 2 QB 303, [1964] 1 All ER 149, [1964] 2 WLR 507.
9 Ibid.
10 See *Main v Swansea City Council* (1984) 49 P & CR 26 and *R v London Borough of Lambeth Council, ex p Sharp* (1986) 55 P & CR 232, [1987] JPL 440.

ascertain what the authority's reasons are.[11] Even before the change in the wording it had been held that it is the duty of the local planning authority to give all their reasons and not just some of them.[12]

Notice of a refusal or conditional grant of planning permission or of a refusal or conditional grant of approval of reserved matters is to be accompanied by a notification informing the applicant of his right to appeal to the Secretary of State and of his rights in certain circumstances to serve a purchase notice or make a claim for compensation[13] (GDO, art 25 and Sch 3, Pt II).

Register

Under s 34 of the 1971 Act it is the duty of local planning authorities to keep a register containing prescribed information with respect to planning applications. This function is carried out by the local planning register authority which is the district planning authority except in Greater London, a metropolitan county or a National Park[14] (GDO, art 27). The register is to be available for inspection by the public at all reasonable hours (s 34). The register is to be kept in two parts[15] (GDO, art 27(2)). Part I is to contain a copy of every application for planning permission and of every application for approval of reserved matters submitted to the authority and not finally disposed of, together with copies of plans and drawings submitted in relation thereto. In this way full information about any application which has not been finally disposed of is available to the public. Part II of the register provides a record of every application made to the authority and the particulars of subsequent decisions or directions. Every entry in the register is to be made within 14 days of the receipt of an application or of the giving or making of the relevant direction, decision or approval, as the case may be (GDO, art 27(8)). Local planning authorities are empowered to keep copies of the relevant part of the register at local offices (GDO, art 27(9)). The register is to include an index in the form of a map for enabling a person to trace any entry in the register (GDO, art 27(7)).

Time limits upon planning permission

Before the coming into operation of the Town and Country Planning Act 1968 a planning permission which was not acted upon remained effective for an indefinite period; unless there was imposed upon the grant of permission a condition setting a time limit for the commencement or completion of development or for the submission for approval of 'reserved matters'

---

11 See *RKT Investments Ltd v Hackney London Borough Council* (1978) 36 P & CR 442.
12 *Hamilton v West Sussex County Council* [1958] 2 QB 286, [1958] 2 All ER 174.
13 The effects of failure to comply with similar statutory provisions relating to the issue of a certificate of appropriate alternative development were considered by the House of Lords in *London and Clydeside Estates Ltd v Aberdeen District Council* [1979] 3 All ER 876, [1980] 1 WLR 182, 1980 SC (HL) 1, 1980 SLT 81.
14 In Greater London and the metropolitan counties, it is the London Borough or the local planning authority and in national parks, the county council.
15 In *Steeples v Derbyshire County Council* [1984] 3 All ER 468, [1985] 1 WLR 256 it was held that the keeping of a file of all applications could not be said to amount to the keeping of a register.

following an outline planning permission,[16] a developer could be as dilatory as he pleased over beginning or completing a development or over submission of detailed plans. Provision was, however, made by the 1968 Act for the imposition of time limits upon planning permissions; that Act also enabled a local planning authority to take certain action where there is unreasonable delay in completing development.

The 1971 Act, re-enacting the provisions of the 1968 Act, provides that, subject to certain exceptions, every planning permission[17] shall be granted or, as the case may be, shall be deemed to be granted, subject to a condition that the development must be begun not later than the expiration of:

(a) five years beginning with the date on which the permission is granted or deemed to be granted (s 41(1)(a)), or

(b) such other period (whether longer or shorter) as the authority concerned with the terms of the planning permission may direct, having regard to the provisions of the development plan and to any other material considerations (s 41(1)(b)).[18]

If a time limit is not imposed by express condition attached to a grant of planning permission, that permission is deemed to have been granted subject to a condition that development must be begun within five years (s 41(2)).

There is excluded from the operation of s 41:[19]

(a) any planning permission granted by a development order;

(b) any planning permission granted by an enterprise zone scheme;

(c) any planning permission granted by a simplified planning zone scheme;

(d) any planning permission granted for a limited period;

(e) any planning permission for the mining or working of minerals where there is a condition limiting the life of the permission to a period following the completion of other development rather than from the time of the granting of the permission;

(f) any planning permission granted under s 32 of the 1971 Act on an application relating to buildings or works completed, or a use of land instituted, before the date of the application;

(g) any outline planning permission (such permission is dealt with separately under s 42 (below)); or

(h) any planning permission granted or deemed to have been granted before 1st April 1969.

Section 42 provides that every outline planning permission (as defined in s 42(1)) shall be granted subject to conditions to the following effect:

(a) that application for approval of any reserved matter must be made

---

16 A condition requiring approval of reserved matters within a specified period was held valid in *Kent County Council v Kingsway Investments (Kent) Ltd* [1971] AC 72, [1970] 1 All ER 70.

17 As regards planning permission for mining operations see p 514 below.

18 In *L A Ames Ltd v North Bedfordshire Borough Council* (1979) 253 Estates Gazette 55, [1980] JPL 183, CA it was held that a condition requiring development to commence within three years of a contingent future event, the date of which could not be foreseen at the date of the grant of planning permission, would not comply with the provisions of s 41(1)(b).

19 See s 41(3).

within three years[20] of the grant of outline permission;[1] and
(b) that the development must be begun before the expiry of five years from
the date of the outline permission or before the expiry of two years from
the date of final approval of any reserved matter, whichever is the later
(s 42(2)).

If these time limits are not imposed by express condition, they are deemed
to have been imposed on a grant of outline planning permission (s 42(3)). The
authority concerned with the terms of an outline permission may substitute
for the periods of five, three and two years referred to in the statute such
other periods as, having regard to the provisions of the development plan
and to any other material considerations, they consider appropriate (s 42(4),
(6)).

Sections 41 and 42 do not apply to any planning permission or outline
planning permission granted before 1st April 1969, but, unless development
under such a permission had been started before the beginning of 1968, any
such permission was deemed to have been granted subject to the time limits
specified in paras 19 and 20 of Sch 24 to the 1971 Act.[2] There is no statutory
time limit in a case where development under a permission was begun before
the beginning of 1969; this also means that in such a case no completion
notice (see p 265 below) can be issued under s 44 and the developer can take
as long as he pleases over completing the development.

In *R v Secretary of State for the Environment, ex p Percy Bilton Industrial
Properties Ltd*[3] outline planning permission had been granted in respect of a
22 acre site in 1952 and parts of the site had been developed in accordance
with subsequent detailed approvals. Applications made in 1973 for approval
of details in respect of undeveloped portions of the site were held invalid by
the minister as having been made outside the statutory time limits. The
Divisional Court held, however, that for the purposes of the statutory
provisions on the duration of planning permission, the 22 acre site was not to
be treated as consisting of separate parcels of land and that development had
to be taken to have begun on the whole site; the land was not therefore

---

20 In *R v Bromley London Borough Council, ex p Sievers* (1980) 41 P & CR 294 outline planning
 permission had been granted on 24th June 1974. An application for approval of details was
 completed on Saturday 22nd June 1977 but the local planning authority's offices were shut
 on that and the following day, with the result that the application was not handed in until
 24th June. Shaw LJ held that the Saturday and Sunday did not count in computing the time
 and that the lateness of the application, if any, was *de minimis* and had to be disregarded.
1 This would seem to mean that the applicant 'is entitled to submit plan after plan, details after
 details, within the three years in the hope of getting them approved; but, if none of those is
 approved, the condition prevents any more being submitted after the three years' (*Kingsway
 Investments (Kent) Ltd v Kent County Council* [1969] 2 QB 332, [1969] 1 All ER 601, per Lord
 Denning MR). See too *Cardiff Corpn v Secretary of State for Wales* (1971) 115 Sol Jo 187, 22
 P & CR 718; and appeal decision noted in [1975] JPL 364.
2 Paras 19 and 20 impose similar time limits on planning permissions granted before 1st April
 1969 which have not been commenced prior to 1968. However, in *Colley v Canterbury
 County Council* [1989] JPL 532, Millett J held that in the case of an outline permission which
 is subject to a condition that application for approval of reserved matters should be made
 not later than a specified date or period, para 20(2) has the effect of exempting the permission
 from any time limit on commencement. He said this equally applied to a condition that
 required approval to be given within a specified date or period.
3 (1975) 31 P & CR 154. See too *Salisbury District Council v Secretary of State for the
 Environment and Parnwell* [1982] JPL 702, and *Etheridge v Secretary of State for the
 Environment* (1983) 48 P & CR 35.

subject to the statutory time limits. So there can still be cases of planning permissions granted before 1st April 1969, where details regarding an outline permission can still be submitted for approval, because details with regard to part of the site were approved and work commenced before the beginning of 1968.

For the purposes of ss 41 and 42 development is to be taken to be begun on the earliest date on which any 'specified operation' comprised in the development is carried out (s 43(1)). The 'specified operations', detailed in s 43(2), include any work of construction in the course of the erection of a building, the digging of a trench for the foundations of a building, the laying of any underground main or pipe to the foundations, any operation in the course of laying out or constructing a road or part of a road, and any change in the use of land, where that change constitutes 'material development' as defined in s 43(3).

As Eveleigh LJ said in *Malvern Hills District Council v Secretary of State for the Environment*:[4] 'Very little need be done to satisfy the section. That which is done, however, must genuinely be done for the purpose of carrying out the development.' Marking out an estate road with pegs has been held to amount to a 'specified operation',[5] as has the digging of trenches which were immediately back-filled.[6] To qualify as a 'specified operation' the work must, however, involve implementation of the development authorised by the permission.[7]

In *Salisbury District Council v Secretary of State for the Environment and Parnwell*[8] it was accepted that the beginning of part of a development is sufficient to lift the time limit for all of the development granted unless the permission was severable. Thus, where permission for seven bungalows is granted, the commencement of the building of one lifts the time limit for all.

There is a right of appeal against conditions imposed by virtue of ss 41 and 42 (s 43(6)) but the imposition of such conditions is mandatory and an appeal in respect of the imposition of a time limit can in effect be made only against the specified period and not against the principle of such a condition.

If a condition imposed under s 41 or s 42 is not complied with, development, which is carried out after the date by which it is required to be carried out, shall be treated as unauthorised and if an application for approval of reserved matters is made out of time it shall be treated as not made in accordance with the terms of the permission (s 43(7)).

Where development has not been started, application for renewal of a permission which is subject to a time limit under s 41 or s 42 can be made

4 (1983) 81 LGR 13, 46 P & CR 58.
5 *Malvern Hills* (above). See too *Spackman v Secretary of State for the Environment* [1977] 1 All ER 257, and *United Refineries Ltd v Essex County Council* (1976) 241 Estates Gazette 389, [1978] JPL 110.
6 *High Peak Borough Council v Secretary of State for the Environment and Courtdale Developments Ltd* [1981] JPL 366.
7 See *South Oxfordshire District Council v Secretary of State for the Environment* [1981] 1 All ER 954, [1981] 1 WLR 1092, and [1980] JPL 764. For development to be 'begun' it will normally have to be authorised by the permission in question (see *Etheridge v Secretary of State for the Environment* (1983) 48 P & CR 35), but development in breach of a condition may suffice (see *Clwyd County Council v Secretary of State for Wales and Welsh Aggregates* [1982] JPL 696 (upheld on other grounds by the Court of Appeal sub nom *Welsh Aggregates Ltd v Secretary of State for the Environment and Clwyd County Council* [1983] JPL 50)).
8 [1982] JPL 702.

under reg 3(3)(a) of the Town and Country Planning (Applications) Regulations 1988 at any time before the expiry of the time limit simply by making written application to the local planning authority, and giving sufficient information to enable the authority to identify the previous grant of permission; there is no need to supply plans and drawings with such an application. If such an application is refused there is a right of appeal to the Secretary of State. The Secretary of State has advised authorities that as a general rule such applications should only be refused if there has been some material change in planning circumstances or where continued failure to begin development would cause unacceptable uncertainty or where there is still reasonable time left to run on the existing permission (circular 1/85). The validity of this advice has been questioned[9] but it would appear to be quite proper; and in any case a time expired permission is capable of being a material consideration.[10] The conditions referred to in ss 41 and 42 cannot found a compensation claim, nor can such conditions give rise to a purchase notice (see 1971 Act, ss 147, 169, and 180).

Completion notice

Once development has been begun under a planning permission, that permission is given an indefinite life, subject, however, to the right of the local planning authority to serve a completion notice under s 44 of the 1971 Act. A completion notice can be served where:

(a) a planning permission is, by virtue of ss 41 or 42 or paras 19 or 20 of Sch 24, subject to a condition that development must be begun before the expiration of a particular period; and
(b) the development has been begun within that period but the period has elapsed without the development having been completed; and
(c) the local planning authority are of opinion that the development will not be completed within a reasonable period (s 44(1), (2)).

A completion notice is to state that the planning permission will cease to have effect at the expiration of a period specified in the notice, being a period of not less than twelve months after the notice takes effect (s 44(2)). The notice is to be served on the owner and on the occupier of the land and on any other person who, in the opinion of the local planning authority, will be affected by the notice (s 44(3)(a)). It is to take effect only if and when it is confirmed by the Secretary of State (s 44(3)(b)). If, within such period (being a period of not less than 28 days from service of the notice) as may be specified in a completion notice, any person on whom the notice is served so requires, the Secretary of State must afford to that person and to the local planning authority an opportunity of being heard by a person appointed for the purpose by the Secretary of State (s 44(4)). In confirming a notice the Secretary of State may substitute some longer period for that specified in the notice as the period at the expiry of which the planning permission is to cease to have effect (s 44(3)(b)).[11]

9 *Peak Park Joint Planning Board v Secretary of State for the Environment and Cyril Kay* [1979] JPL 618.
10 See *South Oxfordshire District Council v Secretary of State for the Environment and Faherty Bros Ltd* [1981] JPL 359.
11 For examples of decisions of the Secretary of State on completion notices see [1979] JPL 184 and 480, [1981] JPL 605, [1983] JPL 483, [1984] JPL 820 and [1985] JPL 125.

If a completion notice takes effect, the planning permission referred to in the notice, in so far as it relates to development not carried out, becomes invalid at the expiration of the specified period (s 44(5)). The local planning authority may withdraw a completion notice at any time before the expiry of the period specified in the notice (s 44(6)). The section does not expressly state that any works carried out before the period when the permission became invalid are retrospectively unauthorised. Yet the Secretary of State in confirming an enforcement notice has held that an uncompleted building had not been constructed under a 1968 permission (on which a completion notice had been confirmed) 'because what has been built differs materially from the completed dwelling authorised by the permission.'[12]

Duration of mineral permissions

Any planning permission for the winning and working of minerals has a defined life (see p 515 below).

Appeal to Secretary of State

Where application is made to a local planning authority for planning permission or for any approval required under a development order, or for any consent, agreement or approval required by a condition imposed on a grant of planning permission, and that permission, consent, agreement or approval is refused by the authority or is granted by them subject to conditions, the applicant, if he is aggrieved by the decision, is entitled to appeal to the Secretary of State (1971 Act, s 36).

Where the local planning authority fail to give notice of their decision within the prescribed period (see p 259 above), appeal may be made to the Secretary of State as if the application had been refused and notification received by the applicant at the end of the prescribed period (s 37).

The procedure for making an appeal to the Secretary of State is set out in art 26 of the GDO. Notice of appeal, stating the grounds on which the appeal is made, is to be given to the Secretary of State, on a form obtained from him, within six months of the decision or of the expiry of the time allowed for the giving of notice of the local planning authority's decision or within such longer period as the Secretary of State may at any time allow. With the notice of appeal the appellant is to furnish the Secretary of State with a copy of the application made to the local planning authority and all relevant plans and documents submitted with it, any notices or certificates under ss 26 and 27 where relevant, a copy of the notice of the decision, all other relevant correspondence with any planning authority and any other plans, documents[13] or drawings relating to the application which have not already been sent to the authority. At the same time the appellant must serve on the local planning authority a copy of the notice of appeal and, if relevant, copies of any plans, documents or drawings relating to the application which the authority has not seen. This requirement was introduced in 1987.[14] The

---

12 See [1985] JPL 496 and article by Harold Brown 'The Consequences of a Completion Notice' [1985] JPL 466. Also see *Pilkington v Secretary of State for the Environment* [1974] 1 All ER 283, [1973] 1 WLR 1527.
13 The word 'documents' was added by the 1988 GDO.
14 See Town and Country Planning General Development (Amendment) Order 1987.

objective is to speed up appeals and local planning authorities are asked to treat the receipt of the copy of the notice of appeal as the start of the appeal rather than wait to hear from the department.[15] Notice of all appeals must be given by the appellant to owners and agricultural tenants of the land (1971 Act, s 36(5)).

Before determining an appeal the Secretary of State must, if either the appellant or the local planning authority desire it, afford to each of them an opportunity of a hearing before a person appointed by the Secretary of State. Such a hearing will normally take the form of a public local inquiry but recently, if both parties agree, a more informal hearing may be held. In the majority of cases this right to a hearing is waived and the appeal is heard by way of written representations.[16]

Most planning appeals are now determined by persons appointed for the purpose by the Secretary of State. Appeal procedures generally are discussed in chapter 19.

The Secretary of State or appointed person may allow or dismiss an appeal against the decision of a local planning authority, or may reverse or vary[17] any part of the authority's decision, whether the appeal relates to that part of the decision or not, and may deal with the application as if it had been made to him in the first instance.[18] Since the whole matter is before him, the Secretary of State or appointed person may, for example, have to consider whether, instead of refusing planning permission, there is any form of condition which might achieve a satisfactory result.[19]

However, where the issue of conditions has not been canvassed on appeal there is no duty on the Secretary of State or his inspectors to look around to see if there is some possible condition which might save the application.[20]

It might be different if it was proposed to grant an application.[1] Also if the Secretary of State or his inspector does decide to impose a condition (apart from the standard conditions) which had not been canvassed before the parties, they should be given an opportunity to comment before it is imposed.[2]

15 See circular 18/86, para 15.
16 There is now a strict timetable for written representations; see Town and Country Planning (Appeals) (Written Representations Procedure) Regulations 1987 and ch. 19.
17 See p 254 above. As to amendment of the application at this stage see *Inverclyde District Council v Secretary of State for Scotland* 1980 SC 363, 1981 SLT 26 (Second Division); affd 1982 SC (HL) 64, 1982 SLT 200.
18 This means that the Secretary of State has power to deal with the application even though the decision of the local planning authority from which the appeal arose is in fact a nullity—see *Stringer v Minister of Housing and Local Government* [1971] 1 All ER 65, [1970] 1 WLR 1281.
19 See, for example, *Grampian Regional Council v Secretary of State for Scotland* 1983 SLT 526; *George Wimpey & Co Ltd v New Forest District Council* (1979) 250 Estates Gazette 249, [1979] JPL 314; and *M J Shanley Ltd v Secretary of State for the Environment and South Bedfordshire District Council* [1982] JPL 380. See also *Brittania (Cheltenham) Ltd v Secretary of State for the Environment* [1979] JPL 534 where the Court of Appeal held that if Secretary of State regards conditions proposed by the local planning authority as objectionable or *ultra vires*, he was not obliged to dismiss the appeals and could consider if any other condition was suitable.
20 See *Finlay v Secretary of State for the Environment and London Borough of Islington* [1983] JPL 802 and *Mason v Secretary of State for the Environment* [1984] JPL 332.
1 See *Jillings v Secretary of State for the Environment and the Broads Authority* [1984] JPL 32.
2 See *Mason v Secretary of State for the Environment*, above.

The Secretary of State can also take into account facts and arguments not put forward by the parties at the time of the decision being appealed.[3] He is however bound by the rules as to fairness and must give parties an opportunity of dealing with new arguments.[4] An appellant should therefore bear in mind that in determining an appeal against a conditional grant of planning permission the Secretary of State or appointed person is entitled to impose more onerous conditions or even to refuse planning permission altogether.[5]

The Secretary of State does not have the power to enter into a planning agreement on appeal but he can encourage the applicant and the local planning authority to enter into such an agreement and take it into account if it is agreed.[6]

The decision on any appeal under s 36 is declared to be final (s 36(6)). This is a decision disposing of the appeal and not a decision in the course of an appeal.[7] Any person aggrieved by the decision is entitled to make application to the High Court under s 245 of the 1971 Act to have such a decision quashed (see chapter 20 below).

Reference to Planning Inquiry Commission

The 1971 Act empowers the Secretary of State to refer development proposals of a far-reaching or novel character to a Planning Inquiry Commission constituted by the minister under s 47 of the Act (see p 562 below).

Effect of planning permission

The 1971 Act provides that any grant of planning permission to develop land shall (except in so far as the permission otherwise provides and without prejudice to the statutory provisions as to duration, revocation or modification of permission) enure for the benefit of the land and of all persons for the time being interested therein (s 33(1)).

Any number of planning applications may be made in respect of the same land, even though the proposals in the applications are mutually inconsistent, and the local planning authority are obliged to deal with each application on its own merits, regarding each application as a proposal for separate and independent development.[8] There can therefore be a number of unimplemented planning permissions outstanding in respect of the same area of land and the owner of land may be able to choose which of several mutually inconsistent planning permissions he will exercise. Where, however, one of two or more permissions is acted upon, it will not thereafter be

3 *Price Bros (Rode Heath) Ltd v Department of the Environment* (1978) 38 P & CR 579; *New Forest District Council v Secretary of State for the Environment and Clarke* [1984] JPL 178 and the ministerial decision at [1969] JPL 484.
4 *Lewis Thirkell Ltd v Secretary of State for the Environment* (1978) 248 Estates Gazette 685, [1978] JPL 844.
5 See [1974] JPL 482 and 739, and [1975] JPL 556.
6 See *McLaren v Secretary of State for the Environment and Broxbourne Borough Council* [1981] JPL 423.
7 *Co-operative Retail Services v Secretary of State for the Environment* [1980] 1 All ER 449, [1980] 1 WLR 271, (1979) 39 P & CR 428.
8 See *Pilkington v Secretary of State for the Environment* [1974] 1 All ER 283, [1973] 1 WLR 1527.

possible for the landowner to implement any other inconsistent permission. In *Pilkington v Secretary of State for the Environment*[9] permission had been granted in 1953 for the erection of a bungalow at the northern end of a strip of land, the bungalow to be ancillary to a smallholding which was to occupy the remainder of the land. In 1954 permission was given for the erection of a house in the centre of the strip of land, the remainder of the strip again being shown as associated with the permitted development. The 1954 permission was implemented. It was then proposed (and would have been physically possible) to erect the bungalow referred to in the 1953 permission. The Divisional Court held that the 1953 permission could not now be imple-mented—it permitted a house on the site as ancillary to the smallholding which was to occupy the rest of the site and it was not now possible, consistently with the (implemented) 1954 permission, to erect a house on those terms.

It would seem, however, that a planning permission can sometimes be regarded as divisible, and in *F Lucas & Sons Ltd v Dorking and Horley RDC*[10] Winn J held that a developer who had been granted two planning per-missions in respect of the same area of land, the earlier permission allowing the erection of twenty-eight houses on the site, the later permitting six houses in accordance with a quite different layout plan for the same site, was entitled to develop part of the land in accordance with the later permission and the remainder of the site in accordance with the earlier permission. Winn J considered that the planning permission for twenty-eight houses was not to be regarded as permitting only the complete development but was properly to be regarded as allowing the erection of any one or more of the houses comprised in the scheme.[11]

The mere fact that planning permission has been applied for and granted does not in itself detract from existing use rights in any way; it is only if the permission is acted upon that any such question can arise[12] and there is, of course, no compulsion upon a landowner to implement a permission. A grant of planning permission does not preclude the landowner subsequently contending that no such permission was necessary.[13]

Equally, it is only if a planning permission is implemented that any condition attached to the permission can come into effect.[14] However, even though a particular development departs from the terms of a planning permission, carrying out the development may be treated as an implemen-

---

9 [1974] 1 All ER 283, [1973] 1 WLR 1527; approved by the Court of Appeal in *Hoveringham Gravels Ltd v Chiltern District Council* (1977) 76 LGR 533, and by the House of Lords in *Pioneer Aggregates (UK) Ltd v Secretary of State for the Environment* [1985] AC 132, [1984] 2 All ER 358. See too *Ellis v Worcestershire County Council* (1961) 12 P & CR 178; and *Lobb v Secretary of State for the Environment and South Wight Borough Council* [1984] JPL 336. Contrast *Salisbury District Council v Secretary of State for the Environment and Parnwell* [1982] JPL 702.
10 (1964) 62 LGR 491, 17 P & CR 111; compare ministerial decision noted in [1974] JPL 45.
11 See too *Sheppard v Secretary of State for the Environment* (1974) 233 Estates Gazette 1167.
12 See p 111 above on the circumstances in which implementation of a planning permission may lead to a new chapter in the planning history of the site.
13 *Newbury District Council v Secretary of State for the Environment* [1981] AC 578, [1980] 1 All ER 731. See too *Mounsdon v Weymouth and Melcombe Regis Corpn* [1960] 1 QB 645, [1960] 1 All ER 538; *East Barnet UDC v British Transport Commission* [1962] 2 QB 484, [1961] 3 All ER 878; and *Sheppard v Secretary of State for the Environment* (1974) 233 Estates Gazette 1167.
14 See *Sheppard* (above).

tation of the permission with the result that a condition attached to the permission can be enforced.[15]

In *Pioneer Aggregates (UK) Ltd v Secretary of State for the Environment*[16] Lord Scarman said that planning control was a creature of statute and that it was a field of law in which the courts should not introduce principles or rules derived from private law unless expressly authorised to do so by Parliament or unless it was necessary in order to give effect to the purpose of the legislation. His Lordship pointed out that planning permission was not a private right but a right which is declared by statute to enure for the benefit of the land (see 1971 Act, s 33(1)—above); the House of Lords therefore held that there is no principle in planning law that a valid planning permission capable of being implemented can be held to have been abandoned or lost by the act of a person entitled to the benefit of the permission.[17] The Court of Appeal were therefore held to have erred in law in holding in *Slough Estates Ltd v Slough Borough Council (No 2)*[18] that by taking action inconsistent with the retention of any rights under a planning permission a landowner might be held to have waived or abandoned his rights under the permission.

Conditions cannot be implied from the wording of a planning permission.[19] In the somewhat special circumstances of the case it was held in *R v Derbyshire County Council, ex p North East Derbyshire District Council*[20] that a condition attached to a grant of planning permission might be treated in effect as granting permission for that which the condition required.

Even though a planning permission contains an error it will, it seems, be effective 'if it so accurately describes the development to be carried out that anyone taking the permission and its accompanying plans and applications to the land will be able to see, without doubt, precisely what it is which has been authorised'.[1]

The mere grant of planning permission for development may not, of course, be enough to enable a developer to proceed with the projected development; he may, for example, require consents under other legislation.

15　See, for example, *Kerrier District Council v Secretary of State for the Environment and Brewer* (1980) 41 P & CR 284; and *J Toomey Motors Ltd v Basildon District Council* (1982) 264 Estates Gazette 141, [1982] JPL 775 (see p 308 below).

16　[1985] AC 132, [1984] 2 All ER 358.

17　However, once fully implemented a permission may be 'spent' in the sense that it will not authorise further development; see *Cynon Valley Borough Council v Secretary of State for Wales* (1987) 53 P & CR 68, but compare *Durham County Council v Secretary of State for the Environment* [1989] JPL 603.

18　[1969] 2 Ch 305, [1969] 2 All ER 988.

19　See *Trustees of Walton-on-Thames Charities v Walton and Weybridge UDC* (1970) 68 LGR 488. See too *East Suffolk County Council v Secretary of State for the Environment* (1972) 70 LGR 595; *Sutton London Borough v Secretary of State for the Environment* (1975) 29 P & CR 350; and *Carpet Decor (Guildford) Ltd v Secretary of State for the Environment* (1981) 261 Estates Gazette 56, [1981] JPL 806. Contrast, however, *Kwik Save Discount Group Ltd v Secretary of State for Wales* (1980) 79 LGR 310, 42 P & CR 166, in which, on the interpretation of the permission in question, a restriction could be implied on the goods to be sold in a showroom; and see p 255 above.

20　(1979) 77 LGR 389. See too *Irlam Brick Co Ltd v Warrington Borough Council* [1982] JPL 709; *Welsh Aggregates Ltd v Secretary of State for the Environment and Clwyd County Council* [1983] JPL 50; and *R v Surrey County Council, ex p Monk* (1986) 53 P & CR 410, [1986] JPL 828. Contrast *Alexandra Transport Co Ltd v Secretary of State for Scotland* 1974 SLT 81.

1　See *R v Secretary of State for the Environment, ex p Reinisch* (1971) 70 LGR 126, 22 P & CR 1022, per Lord Widgery CJ.

The fact that planning permission has been granted for a particular development is no defence to a nuisance action in respect of the activities authorised
by the permission. A grant of planning permission does not override any land
obligation to which the land in question may be subject but the fact that such
permission has been granted or refused may be taken into account by the
Lands Tribunal in considering an application under s 84 of the Law of
Property Act for variation or discharge of a land obligation.[2] In *Re Martins
Application*[3] Fox LJ held that, even if the obligation was created by a
planning agreement, a subsequent grant of permission does not discharge the
obligation and is merely a circumstance which can and should be taken into
account by the Lands Tribunal.

Construction of planning permission

In *Miller-Mead v Minister of Housing and Local Government*[4] Lord Denning
MR said: 'A grant of [planning] permission runs with the land and may come
into the hands of people who have never seen the application . . .' In general,
such people may take a planning permission at face value in that it is
generally competent, in construing a planning permission, to consider only
material to be found within the four corners of the document granting
planning permission,[5] including any reasons stated therein.[6] It is not normally permissible to look at the application for permission as an aid to
interpretation.[7] Where, however, the planning permission expressly incorporates the application or a plan which accompanied the application or
correspondence relating to the application, it will be proper and necessary to
have regard to the incorporated documents.[8] In *Chalgray Ltd v Secretary of
State for the Environment*[9] Slynn J said that this applied even where the
permission by itself was unambiguous. Now that the application is a public
document which is open to be inspected, it would seem proper to look to the
application for guidance even if it is not expressly incorporated, at least if
there are doubts as to the meaning and validity.[10] On the other hand it will
still be improper to take into account a local planning authority's knowledge

2 See *Re Beechams Application* (1980) 41 P & CR 369, [1981] JPL 55.
3 [1989] JPL 33, CA.
4 [1963] 2 QB 196, [1963] 1 All ER 459.
5 *Slough Estates Ltd v Slough Borough Council (No 2)* [1971] AC 958, [1970] 2 All ER 216;
   Miller-Mead (above); and appeal decisions noted in [1980] JPL 61 and 352.
6 *Crisp from the Fens Ltd v Rutland County Council* [1950] WN 72, 1 P & CR 48; *Fawcett
   Properties Ltd v Buckingham County Council* [1961] AC 636, [1960] 3 All ER 503; *Centre
   Hotels (Cranston) Ltd v Secretary of State for the Environment* [1982] JPL 108; and *Irlam
   Brick Company v Warrington Borough Council* [1982] JPL 709.
7 See *Slough Estates and Miller-Mead* (above).
8 *Wilson v West Sussex County Council* [1963] 2 QB 764, [1963] 1 All ER 751; *Slough Estates*
   (above); *Chalgray v Secretary of State for the Environment* (1976) 33 P & CR 10; *Manning v
   Secretary of State for the Environment and London Borough of Harrow* [1976] JPL 634; *Kwik
   Save Discount Group Ltd v Secretary of State for Wales* (1980) 79 LGR 310, 42 P & CR 166;
   and *Edmunds v Secretary of State for Wales and Powys County Council* [1981] JPL 52
   (competent to have regard to letter 'inextricably attached' to the planning application).
9 (1976) 33 P & CR 10.
10 See *Wivenhoe Port Ltd v Colchester Borough Council* [1985] JPL 396 where Oliver LJ without
   deciding the point seemed inclined to the view that it was right to look to the application.

of an applicant's intentions in construing a permission.[11] However, in *R v Basildon District Council, ex p Martin Grant Homes Ltd*[12] it was held that a planning committee of a district planning authority must be presumed to have knowledge of all the information that is known to the council. Therefore a grant of planning permission was interpreted to include permission to carry out work previously permitted by the building regulation approval granted by the engineering department of that council, as the planning committee must be taken to have intended that all necessary and reasonable work for the implementation of the planning permission was being incorporated within the general grant of consent.

It is not normally competent to consider the resolution of the local planning authority in order to construe or explain the terms of a permission.[13] Where, however, the issue is whether planning permission was in fact granted or whether the decision was within the power of the local planning authority, the court is entitled to go behind the document in question in order to ascertain the true facts.[14]

A planning permission is not to be construed *contra proferentes*.[15] Where a planning permission incorporates words which are defined in the 1971 Act or related legislation it seems that they are to be given their natural meaning and not the meaning as set out in the planning legislation.[16]

Enterprise zones and planning permission

The Local Government, Planning and Land Act 1980[17] makes provision for the designation of enterprise zones, the purpose of such designation being to encourage industrial and commercial activity in such areas through the removal or streamlining of certain statutory or administrative controls and the removal of certain fiscal burdens. The scope and procedure under which an area may be designated an enterprise zone (by order made by the Secretary of State) and the effects of such designation are set out in Sch 32 to the 1980 Act, and are discussed in chapter 16.

One of the important effects of an order designating an enterprise zone is that planning permission is thereby granted for any particular development specified in the enterprise zone scheme[18] or for development of any class so specified; such permission may be subject to conditions or limitations and certain matters may be reserved for approval by the enterprise zone authority. If the Secretary of State approves, the enterprise zone authority may direct that any permission granted by the scheme is not to apply in

11 *Meadows v Secretary of State for the Environment and Gloucester City Council* [1983] JPL 538 but see *Kent v Guildford R D C* (1959) 11 P & CR 255.
12 (1986) 53 P & CR 397.
13 *Slough Estates Ltd v Slough Borough Council (No 2)* [1969] 2 Ch 305, [1969] 2 All ER 988, per Lord Denning MR.
14 *Co-operative Retail Services Ltd v Taff-Ely Borough Council* (1979) 39 P & CR 223, CA; affd sub nom *A-G (HM) (Co-operative Retail Services Ltd) v Taff-Ely Borough Council* (1981) 42 P & CR 1, HL and *Norfolk County Council v Secretary of State for the Environment* [1973] 3 All ER 673, [1973] 1 WLR 1400.
15 *Crisp from the Fens Ltd v Rutland County Council* [1950] WN 72, 1 P & CR 48, per Singleton J.
16 See *Wyre Forest District Council v Secretary of State for the Environment* [1989] JPL 362.
17 See s 179 and Sch 32.
18 An enterprise zone scheme is to be prepared, on the invitation of the Secretary of State, by a district council, London Borough Council, new town corporation or urban development corporation.

relation to a specified development or class of development or to a specified class of development in a specified area within the zone.

A permission ceases to have effect once an area ceases to be an enterprise zone except where the development authorised has already been commenced.[19] Similarly any modifications to a zone do not affect any planning permission under a scheme which has been begun before the modifications take effect.[20] However, a completion notice can be served if the development is unreasonably delayed.[1]

Simplified planning zones and planning permission

Building upon the concept of the enterprise zone, the Housing and Planning Act 1986[2] introduced the simplified planning zone (SPZ). The effect of an SPZ scheme when adopted is to grant planning permission within the zone for the types of development specified in the scheme. There is no requirement to submit a planning application or to pay a fee. The scope and procedures of such schemes are discussed in chapter 16, below.

An SPZ may grant planning permission for any type of development except for certain mineral and waste disposal proposals which have been excluded by order of the Secretary of State under a power provided by s 24E(3).[3] Also circular 25/87 advises that SPZs should not grant planning permission for hazardous development. Planning permissions granted may be unconditional or can be subject to such conditions, limitations or exceptions as may be specified in the scheme (1971 Act, s 24A(3)) and s 24B(1) provides that the conditions and limitations can be in respect of all development permitted by the scheme or in respect of particular classes or descriptions of development. In this regard, it seems SPZs will be rather similar to the classes of permitted development set out in the GDO which are also subject to conditions and limitations. The validity of an SPZ can only be challenged by way of s 244 as if it were a structure plan (1971 Act, ss 242(1)(a) and 244(7)). This means that after six weeks of its adoption or approval, its validity cannot be challenged in any legal proceeding whatsoever (see chapter 20). Therefore, although breaches of conditions and limitations attached to an SPZ are to be enforced under the normal power provided by s 87 (see chapter 12 below), it will not be possible to argue on appeal that such conditions are *ultra vires*. Also, as the *Encyclopaedia of Planning* points out, it remains to be seen if the grounds of challenge will be the same as for normal planning conditions; see para 2-837/4.

Planning permission granted by an SPZ ceases to have effect at the end of 10 years from the date of adoption or approval of the scheme except where the development authorised has begun (1971 Act, s 24C(2)). In the case of the last exception it is still possible to serve a completion notice under s 44.

19 See para 22(1) to Sch 32.
20 See para 21 to the Schedule.
 1 See para 22(2) and p 265 above.
 2 See ss 24A to 24E and Sch 8A to the 1971 Act inserted by s 25 of the Housing and Planning Act 1986. Also see the Town and Country Planning (Simplified Planning Zones) Regulations 1987 and the Town and Country Planning (Simplified Planning Zones) (Excluded Development) Order 1987.
 3 See Excluded Development Order 1987 which excludes development of any of descriptions which is a 'county matter as defined by para 32 of Schedule 16 to the Local Government Act 1972.'

SPZs can be altered under s 24D and the result can be to withdraw a planning permission or to impose new or more stringent conditions. This takes effect from the end of the period of twelve months from the date of the adoption or approval of the alteration but does not apply to planning permissions where the development has been begun before the permission is withdrawn or the conditions changed (1971 Act, ss 24D(5) and (6)).

Development by local authorities

Where a local authority propose to carry out development they must, unless planning permission for that development is granted by development order (see p 150 above) or is deemed to be granted as a result of a direction attached to a sanction granted by a government department (see p 150 above), obtain planning permission in one of the following ways.

Where a local authority require planning permission for development which they propose to carry out[4] in the area for which they are themselves the local planning authority, the procedures contained in the Town and Country Planning General Regulations 1976 apply. There are two main stages; the resolution that permission should be sought and the resolution that the development should be carried out. The procedures laid down in the regulations are similar to those for applications by private individuals. Following s 27, notice in writing must be given to all persons, who at the date of the resolution to seek permission were entitled to a 'material interest'[5] or were agricultural tenants, that permission is being sought and the notice must describe the development and the site (reg 4(2)(a)). Where ss 26 and 28 would apply to an ordinary planning application, notices describing the development sought must be published in a local newspaper and, in the case of s 28 developments, site notices must be displayed for not less than 7 days on or near the land to be developed (reg 4(2)(b) and (c)). All such notices shall state that any objection to the proposal should be made to the authority in writing within a specified period, to be not less than 21 days (reg 4(2)). These provisions were considered in the case of *R v Lambeth London Borough Council, ex p Sharp.*[6] The Court of Appeal held that, for compliance with reg 4(2)(c), the notice published in the newspaper had to state a period within which objections could be made and that a failure to specify such a period was a fundamental breach which was fatal to the whole process. Croom-Johnson LJ at first instance also held that the notice was also defective because it failed to refer to 'representations' rather than objections and it had not been proved that it had been there for seven days. He also held that only *one* site notice need be displayed despite the use of the plural 'notices'.

A copy of the resolution to seek permission must be placed in Pt I of the register of planning applications (reg 4(6)) and in *Steeples v Derbyshire County Council*[7] Webster J held that a failure to lodge meant that there was

---

4 This does not perhaps include the situation where a development is to be a joint venture with private developers on a profit-sharing basis or where the proposal is speculative—see *Sunbell Properties Ltd v Dorset County Council* (1979) 253 Estates Gazette 1123.
5 As defined in s 6(1) and (2) of the Community Land Act 1975.
6 (1985) 50 P & CR 284; affd sub nom *R v London Borough of Lambeth Council, ex p Sharp* (1986) 55 P & CR 232, [1987] JPL 440, CA.
7 [1984] 3 All ER 468, [1985] 1 WLR 256.

no power to pass the second resolution as this is conditional on the copy having been lodged for 21 days.

Once the various periods for objections have elapsed, the local planning authority can resolve to carry out the development. In which case, provided the Secretary of State has not required the application to be made to him, the permission is deemed to have been granted by the Secretary of State. Such a permission enures only for the benefit of the authority passing the resolution and so is a permission personal to that authority (reg 4(7)).

Very similar procedures apply to the case where the development is not to be carried out by the local planning authority but the land, on which the development is to be carried out, is vested in the authority (reg 5). The main difference is that the deemed permission can be subject to conditions and is treated for all purposes of the Act as if it were a permission granted on a planning application (reg 5(4)(b) and (6)).

In *R v London Borough of Lambeth Council, ex p Sharp*[8] Stephen Brown LJ stated that:

'It had to be borne in mind that this [the 1976 regulations] was a special form of procedure to be operated where the authority was in effect seeking to grant permission to itself.'

This means, as the authorities show, that the procedures have to be followed strictly and even relatively minor breaches can result in the permission being quashed by the courts. It would also support the argument that the procedures laid down by the regulations are exclusive and that local planning authorities cannot apply for planning permission unless they either own the land or intend to carry out the development.[9]

Both the county and district planning authority can utilise the procedures but each must consult the other (reg 10(2)).

The rules about environmental assessment[10] apply to these procedures. Under reg 17 of the Town and Country Planning (Assessment of Environmental Effects) Regulations 1988, local planning authorities are prohibited from resolving under reg 4 or 5 of the 1976 regulations to seek planning permission for their own development or development on their own land without preparing an environmental statement, where the relevant development comes within the regulations. The regulation also prohibits them from passing a further resolution whereby planning permission is granted without first considering the available environmental information. The crucial judgment as to whether there is a requirement for environmental assessment is left to the local planning authorities themselves but they may request a direction by the Secretary of State.

Development by statutory undertakers

Except where planning permission is deemed to be granted or is granted by the GDO (see p 150 above), statutory undertakers[11] must make application for planning permission in the normal way before carrying out development.

8 [1987] JPL 440, CA.
9 See Grant *Urban Planning Law* for a discussion of this issue at p 241.
10 See p 177 below.
11 As defined in s 290 of the 1971 Act. See too *British Airports Authority v Secretary of State for Scotland* 1979 SC 200, 1979 SLT 197.

Where, however, an application is made by statutory undertakers in respect of their 'operational land'[12] or certain other land, and that application is 'called in' by the Secretary of State or an appeal is made to the Secretary of State from the planning authority's decision on such an application, the application or appeal is to be dealt with by the Secretary of State acting jointly with the 'appropriate minister', ie the minister responsible for the undertaking in question[13] (s 225). Special provision is made in a number of other respects by the 1971 Act in relation to the operational land of statutory undertakers (see Pt XI of the Act).

Stopping up and diversion of roads, etc

In order that development of land may be carried out in terms of a planning permission, it may be necessary to stop up or divert a road; there are contained in Pt X of the 1971 Act provisions which enable such action to be taken.

Where the Secretary of State is satisfied that it is necessary to do so in order to enable development to be carried out in accordance with planning permission or to be carried out in accordance with an enterprise zone scheme or to be carried out by a government department, he may by order authorise the stopping up or diversion of any road[14] (s 209(1)). Such an order may deal with the provision or improvement of any other road and may contain such other incidental and consequential provisions as appear to the Secretary of State to be necessary or expedient (s 209(2), (3)); in particular, the order may require a specified authority or person to pay, or to make contributions in respect of, the cost of the carrying out of any work provided for by the order or of any increased expenditure attributable to the order. In this way the person carrying out the development which necessitates the stopping up may have to contribute towards the cost of the closure.

Section 215 lays down the procedure to be followed in connection with the making by the Secretary of State of such an order. If any objection to the making of the order is received by the Secretary of State a local inquiry will be held unless the Secretary of State is satisfied that 'in the special circumstances of the case' the holding of such an inquiry is unnecessary (s 215(3)). If objection is made by an authority or person required to make a financial contribution under the order, the order is to be subject to special parliamentary procedure (s 215(6)). It was formerly the case that the procedure for making an order stopping up or diverting a road could not be begun until planning permission for the development to which the order related had been granted. It is now provided, however, that in specified circumstances— where, for example, an application for planning permission has been 'called in' or where an appeal has been made to the Secretary of State—the procedure for making the order may be carried on concurrently with the

12 On the meaning of 'operational land' see ss 222 and 223. See too *R v Minister of Fuel and Power, ex p Warwickshire County Council* [1957] 2 All ER 731, [1957] 1 WLR 861; *East Barnet UDC v British Transport Commission* [1962] 2 QB 484, [1961] 3 All ER 878 and the ministerial decision noted at [1967] JPL 51.
13 As defined in s 224 of the 1971 Act.
14 Although this provision cannot be used where the permitted development has been completed, it can be employed if development has been started but not completed and the order is needed to enable the development to be completed, see *Ashby v Secretary of State for the Environment* [1980] 1 All ER 508, [1980] 1 WLR 673.

proceedings relating to planning permission (s 216). In this way the stopping up order may be made earlier than would otherwise be possible; the order cannot, however, be finally made until planning permission has been granted (s 216(5)).

Local planning authorities may themselves make orders stopping up or diverting footpaths or bridleways if this is necessary in order to enable development to be carried out in accordance with planning permission or to be carried out by a government department (1971 Act, ss 210).[15] Section 214 of the 1971 Act also provides for the extinguishment of public rights of way over land held by a local authority for planning purposes. This can be done by order of the Secretary of State or by the local authority themselves. Modified provisions apply to urban development corporations.[16]

Such orders are advertised and, if no objections are received, are confirmed by planning authorities themselves. If objections are received, the order is to be submitted to the Secretary of State for confirmation (1971 Act, s 217 and Sch 20).

15 For a discussion of the various stopping up powers: see M Williams 'Footpaths and Bridleways Affected by Development' [1989] JPL 651.
16 See s 149(3)(b) and Sch 29, Pt II to the Local Government, Planning and Land Act 1980.

CHAPTER 11

PLANNING AGREEMENTS

Introduction

Section 52 of the 1971 Act provides that a local planning authority may enter into an agreement with any person interested in land in their area for the purpose of restricting or regulating the development or use of the land. Research has shown widespread use of the provision.[1]

The purpose of this sort of agreement, said Walton J in *Western Fish Products Ltd v Penwith District Council*,[2] is to 'enable the local planning authority to control matters which it might otherwise have no power to control by the imposition of conditions on any planning permission.' Such agreements are used, it would seem, to duplicate normal development control powers; they offer an alternative enforcement mechanism and their content is not susceptible to variation or discharge by way of an appeal to the Secretary of State.

Section 52 enables local planning authorities to achieve these purposes by empowering them to enter into a special form of agreement. The agreement is special in two ways. First of all, if registered as local land charge, it will be enforceable at the instance of the planning authority against individual successors in title (s 52(2)). Local authorities have a general power to enter into contracts in pursuance of their functions. That power is given statutory recognition in s 111 of the Local Government Act 1972, which empowers local authorities to do anything which is calculated to facilitate or is conducive or incidental to the discharge of any of their functions. A local planning authority may, therefore, enter into an agreement with a landowner for the purpose of restricting or regulating the development or use of land without recourse to s 52 of the 1971 Act. However, whilst such an agreement may be adequate where an immediate 'one off' obligation is involved, it may be of limited value if the development which underlies the agreement is to be carried out by some third party or if the agreement imposes a postponed or continuing obligation. Such an agreement will be enforceable between the original contracting parties but will not bind successors in title. Section 52 of the 1971 Act overcomes this difficulty by providing that an agreement made under that section may be enforced by the local planning authority against persons deriving title to the land from the person with whom the agreement was entered into (1971 Act, s 52(2)).

Secondly, an agreement under s 52 is special in the sense that it could be used by the planning authority to impose some fetter on the exercise of their

---

1 See, in particular, J Jowell, 'Bargaining in Development Control' [1977] JPL 414, and J N Hawke, 'Planning Agreements in Practice' [1981] JPL 5 and 86.
2 19 November 1977, unreported.

discretionary powers. It is often said that public bodies which have been entrusted with the exercise of statutory powers and duties 'cannot enter into any contract or take action incompatible with the due exercise of their powers or the discharge of their duties'.[3] A public authority cannot, as it were, disable itself by contract from exercising its powers or from performing its statutory duties. However, as Wade says: 'There will often be situations where a public authority must be at liberty to bind itself for the very purpose of exercising its powers effectively.'[4] The problem is that the courts have not provided any very clear guidelines as to how and where the line is to be drawn between, on the one hand, a contract which is an improper restriction on an authority's discretion and, on the other hand, a contract which is a legitimate exercise of that discretion. This is not the place for a detailed discussion of this very difficult area of law,[5] but it is of some importance to consider how far planning authorities can, by means of agreements, validly restrict the future exercise of their powers. Can they, for example, bind themselves to grant planning permission or to refrain from taking enforcement action? These are questions we examine in more detail below; at this stage it is sufficient to say that despite words in s 52(3) which appear to go some way towards allowing for this, the courts are reluctant to allow such fetters.

There is nothing very new about the power to enter into agreements for planning purposes; what is new is the extent to which the power is now being used. Provision for planning agreements was first made, in a somewhat more limited form, in the Town and Country Planning Act 1932.[6] The object of that provision would seem to have been to enable planning authorities to keep land free of development without becoming liable to pay compensation. The power was subsequently extended almost to its present form by the Town and Country Planning Act 1947, although the exercise of the power was subjected to ministerial approval. There seems little doubt that the requirement to obtain this approval had an inhibiting effect on the use of agreements. The requirement was abolished by the Town and Country Planning Act 1968. Since then, and particularly since local government reorganisation in 1974, there has been a very substantial increase in the use of such agreements.[7]

The increasing use of agreements has, not surprisingly, caused some concern, particularly amongst developers. The main focus of concern has been the use of agreements to secure what is commonly referred to as

---

3 *Birkdale District Electric Supply Co Ltd v Southport Corpn* [1926] AC 355, per Lord Birkenhead.
4 H W R Wade, *Administrative Law* (Clarendon Press, Oxford, 6th edn, 1988), p 339.
5 For such discussion see J M Evans, *de Smith's Judicial Review of Administrative Action* (Stevens, 4th edn, 1980), pp 317–320; H W R Wade, *Administrative Law* (above), pp 335–341; P Rogerson, 'On the Fettering of Public Powers' [1971] PL 288; and E Young and J Rowan-Robinson, 'Section 50 Agreements and the Fettering of Powers' [1982] JPL 673.
6 In *Ransom and Luck Ltd v Surbiton Borough Council* [1949] Ch 180, [1949] 1 All ER 185, CA it was held that the sole purpose of this provision was to allow local authorities to accept undertakings from landowners and to enable authorities to enforce such undertakings; it did not permit a local authority to contract not to use its statutory powers or to use those powers in a particular way.
7 For studies of the use of such agreements see Dr Hawke, 'Planning Agreements in Practice' [1981] JPL 5 and 86 and D Henry, 'Planning by Agreement: A Local Survey' [1984] JPL 395.

'planning gain'.[8] The term has no precise definition but generally refers to some sort of benefit to the community which was not part of the original proposal by a developer, and was therefore negotiated, and is not of itself of any commercial advantage to the developer. There is, broadly, some attempt to extract a community benefit from the profits of a particular development.[9]

As a result of this concern, the Property Advisory Group was asked by the Secretary of State for the Environment in 1980 to prepare a report on the subject of 'planning gain'. Their report, published in 1981,[10] was very critical of the practice of bargaining for planning gain. Subject to certain exceptions, the Property Advisory Group categorised the practice as unacceptable, their main objection being that if planning decisions were generally to be linked to the willingness of developers to offer collateral benefits by way of agreements, the whole planning system would fall into disrepute. The report went on to advocate the provision of guidance by the Secretary of State. Such guidance was subsequently issued by the Secretary of State for the Environment in DoE circular 22/83. In general terms, circular 22/83 recommends that obligations imposed by agreement should be reasonable in the circumstances, should be fairly and reasonably related in scale and kind to the development proposed and should represent a reasonable charge on the developer.[11]

Whilst considerable attention has been focused on attempts by some local planning authorities to secure planning gain, rather less attention has been given to the consequences of the use of agreements on the development control process as a whole. Development control is a process of regulation; the local planning authority 'adjudicates' in public on proposals for development. Planning by agreement might fairly be described as the antithesis of this; the process of public adjudication gives way to negotiation carried on in private. Although the development control process can accommodate with advantage the occasional use of agreements to overcome objections to development which might otherwise prove insurmountable, it would seem that the widespread use of agreements could only be accommodated at a cost to the adjudicatory nature of the process. As Grant says of the position: 'The consequence of increased reliance by authorities on planning agreements as an instrument in development control was that the traditional regulatory model of control in many cases was superseded by a consensual, negotiated model.'[12] None the less, it is clear from the overall scheme of the legislation

---

8 See, for example, J Jowell, 'Bargaining in Development Control' [1977] JPL 414; J Jowell, 'The Limits of Law in Urban Planning' [1977] CLP 63; M Grant, 'Developers' Contributions and Planning Gain: Ethics and Legalities' [1978] JPL 8; S Byrne, 'Conditions and Agreements: The Local Authority's Viewpoint', in JPEL Occasional Paper, *Development Control—Thirty Years On* (Sweet and Maxwell, 1979); Sir D Heap and A J Ward, 'Planning Bargaining: The Pros and Cons' [1980] JPL 631; J Ratcliffe, 'Planning Gain—An Overview' (1981) 258 Estates Gazette 407; and I Simpson, *Planning Gain: the Implications for Planning in the UK* (University of Strathclyde, 1984).

9 Also see M Loughlin, 'Planning Gain: Law Policy and Practice', 1 Oxford Journal of Legal Studies 61 for a conceptual analysis of the purposes of such agreements.

10 *Planning Gain* (HMSO, 1981). And see *Richmond-upon-Thames London Borough Council v Secretary of State for the Environment* [1984] JPL 24; and *Westminster City Council v Secretary of State for the Environment and City Commercial Real Estates Investments Ltd* [1984] JPL 27.

11 See J Jowell and M Grant, 'Guidelines for Planning Law' [1983] JPL 427 for a critique of the draft circular.

12 Malcolm Grant, *Urban Planning Law* (Sweet and Maxwell, 1982), p 364.

that the role of the planning authority was never intended to be solely one of regulation; the authority is endowed with wide promotional powers (see chapter 16). The difficulty lies in the reconciliation of these powers when they are used in combination.

However, there are statutory alternatives to the use of s 52. These will be discussed after a detailed examination of the complexities of s 52.

The parties

Section 52(1) provides that a local planning authority (a term which for this purpose refers to a county or district planning authority[13]) 'may enter into an agreement with any person interested in land in their area.' Subsection (2) states that such an agreement may be enforced by the local planning authority against persons deriving 'title under that person in respect of the land . . .',

The phrase 'any person interested in the land' is one that gives rise to some difficulty. In *Pennine Raceway Ltd v Kirklees Metropolitan Council*[14] Eveleigh LJ observed that the provision was not confined to interests in land in the strict conveyancing sense. In that case it had been argued that the reference in sub-s (2) to 'person deriving title under that person' indicated that a person could only be interested in land if it was possible to 'derive title from him'. Eveleigh LJ rejected this and stated 'I read it as saying that if in a particular case the person interested had such an interest which was transferable and had transferred it, then the agreement may be enforced against the transferee.' So the main limitation may be that the interest must be capable in law of being transferred. In the case of any lesser interest, the agreement might still be enforceable as an ordinary contract against the person entering into the agreement but would not be binding on the land. It would also seem that the interest must be an actual and not a prospective interest.[15]

A person with a sufficient interest can, of course, only bind his own interest. A landlord cannot, for example, burden a tenant's interest (unless there is some provision to that effect in the lease). It appears, therefore, that the local planning authority will have to make sure that any person with whom they propose to enter into an agreement under s 52 has the necessary capacity to do so. They will have to investigate the title and they will have to consider whether, in order to ensure that the agreement is effective, other parties with different interests in the land need to be joined.

If an obligation affecting land is to be effective in the short term as well as in the longer term, then it may be that all persons who currently have some interest in the land should be joined as parties to the agreement, including those with interests which are incapable of binding the land. If the latter were omitted, they might be able to ignore the agreement for as long as their interest subsists. It may be necessary for the local planning authority to employ other powers to achieve the desired effect.

---

13 S 1(2A) of the 1971 Act and s 182(2) of the Local Government Act 1972.
14 [1983] QB 382, [1982] 3 All ER 628, CA.
15 See *Jones v Secretary of State for Wales* (1974) 72 LGR 583, 28 P & CR 280; though as Lord Denning pointed out in that decision, local authorities can enter into contracts with prospective owners under other powers.

The scope of the agreement

Subsection (1) of s 52 provides that a local planning authority may enter into an agreement with any person interested in land:

> 'for the purpose of restricting or regulating the development or use of the land ... and any such agreement may contain such incidental and consequential provisions (including provisions of a financial character) as appear to the local planning authority to be necessary or expedient for the purposes of the agreement.'

The phrase 'for the purpose of restricting or regulating' the development or use of land appears to impose some limit upon the scope of agreements but it is a limit which it is difficult to define with any precision. While the words 'restricting or regulating' clearly permit the inclusion in a s 52 agreement of negative obligations—for example, provisions placing restrictions upon the use of premises—the extent to which the agreement can impose obligations of a positive nature—obligations requiring, for example, the provision of infrastructure or the allocation of land for some public purpose—is far from certain.

It seems clear that an agreement can only be said to 'restrict' the development or use of land if it is of a negative character, in the sense that it imposes some prohibition or limitation upon what is to be done on the land or permits the doing of something subject to conditions or within certain limits.

'Regulating' presents rather more difficulty. The ordinary meaning seems to overlap with that of 'restrict'.[16] In so far as they are distinguishable, 'restrict' would seem to be concerned primarily with limiting what can be done, whereas 'regulate' is concerned with ensuring that something is done in a particular way.

However, we think it unlikely that a court would insist that every provision in an agreement must be of a restrictive or regulatory nature. It seems to us that the question that has to be asked in every case is whether the agreement, taken as a whole, could properly be said to have been made for the purpose of restricting or regulating the development or use of land. Such an approach opens the door to the inclusion in a s 52 agreement of obligations which are positive in character. 'Provided', says Grant, 'that the main clear purpose of an agreement is to restrict or regulate use or development, that purpose may be achieved through positive or negative consequential or incidental terms.'[17]

Whether, read as a whole, a particular agreement can be said to be restrictive or regulatory of the development or use of land is a question which will depend very largely on the terms of the agreement and generalisations on the question would appear to be unsafe. Nevertheless, we find it difficult to see how an agreement which, for example, required a developer to make what amounted to a gift of works unconnected with a development could be said to be restrictive or regulatory in nature. On the other hand, a provision in an agreement requiring a financial guarantee for the reinstatement of land

16 The *Shorter Oxford English Dictionary* (1978), for example, defines 'regulate' as 'to control, govern or direct by rule or regulation; to subject to guidance or restrictions; to adjust, in respect of time, quantity, etc.'
17 Paper presented to a conference on 6 June 1979, quoted in (1979) 251 EG 1262.

would seem to come within the scope of s 52, the reinstatement of the land being the main purpose of the agreement.

Difficult questions arise in connection with agreements which impose an obligation on a developer to provide or to contribute towards the cost of providing sewers, roads, open spaces and so on generated by a proposed development. However, we think such a requirement might fairly be said to be regulatory of the development in the sense of ensuring that it meets a certain standard and that such an obligation could be described as 'incidental or consequential' on the attainment of that purpose.

The courts have recently given some guidance on the issue. In *Bradford City Metropolitan Council v Secretary of State for the Environment*,[18] it was argued that a condition, requiring the developer to carry out the widening of a public road at his own expense, would have been lawful, if incorporated in a s 52 agreement. Lloyd LJ rejected this, stating:

'If the condition was manifestly unreasonable, and so beyond the powers of the Planning Authority to impose it, whether or not the developers consented, it had to follow that it was also beyond the powers of the Planning Authority to include the condition as "an incidental or consequential provision" of an agreement restricting or regulating the development or use of the land under section 52.'[19]

However, he went on to suggest that a *contribution* to the cost of widening could be reasonable because of the 'increased use of the road resulting from the development and the benefit to the occupiers of the residential development.' Lloyd LJ then referred to circular 22/83 on 'Planning Gain' which lays down that the obligation should only be imposed on the developer when (1) it enables the development to go ahead; (2) the extent of the obligation is related in scale and kind to the benefits the proposed development will get from the obligation and (3) the facility to be provided or financed is directly related to the development in question or the use of the land after development; see paras 6 to 8.

Such tests are similar to the requirements of the United States' courts that exactions should have a 'rational nexus' or a 'reasonable relationship' to the development being allowed and also resemble the tests which are applied to planning conditions. However, if the tests as to the validity of conditions and the scope of s 52 agreements become too subsumed one in another, it will defeat the whole purpose of the agreements. In many cases developers may be willing to pay more than their share of needed infrastructure if this is the only way to get the desired permission, but local planning authorities may be reluctant to enter into agreements if there are doubts about their validity.

The most recent decision of the courts, *R v Gillingham Borough Council, ex*

---

18 (1986) 53 P & CR 55, [1986] JPL 598.
19 In *R v Westminster City Council, ex p Monahan* [1989] JPL 107 Kerr LJ, while not deciding the point commented that such agreements were 'no doubt far less vulnerable to the risk of successful appeals or applications for judicial review, which was to be welcomed. But if a particular condition would be illegal—on grounds of manifest unreasonableness or otherwise—if it were imposed upon an applicant for planning permission, then it could not acquire validity if it was embodied in a section 52 agreement, whether at the instance of the applicant himself or not.'

p Parham Ltd,[20] takes a much more flexible approach to the scope of planning agreements. In this case a planning agreement had been entered into under which a developer covenanted to modify and to extend an existing public highway and subsequently to dedicate the land as a public highway. The local planning authority had resolved that, at the same time as this agreement was made, they would grant planning permission for residential development which would be served by the highway. The dispute turned on the length that the highway was to be extended. Under the agreement the road stopped short of the land owned by another developer and thus created a 'ransome strip' which would have to be acquired by that builder if he was to develop the land. This second developer argued that the local planning authority, in line with their policy of ensuring progressive and continuous residential development, should not have entered into an agreement which left this strip and should have insisted that the highway was extended as far as the second developer's land. As a result the second developer submitted that both the resolution and subsequent grant of permission were invalid. This was rejected by Roche J who held that the decision of the local planning authority, not to try to insist that the road should be extended all the way to the next site, was not irrational or unreasonable. Importantly, in doing so, while Roche J accepted that, as with planning conditions, planning agreements should only be entered into to achieve planning objectives and their terms should not be manifestly unreasonable, he held that planning agreements, unlike planning conditions, did not have to be limited to matters that fairly or reasonably related to the development that was being permitted. Indeed Roche J found that the planning agreement in question was not for the benefit of the actual development which was being granted at the same time but was intended to facilitate the progressive and continuous development of other land.

While this approach goes against the prescription in circular 22/83, we would submit that it is correct. Section 52 does not contain any explicit reference to the undertaking having to be related to a grant of planning permission and therefore it would be wrong to impose such a restriction just because in fact the undertaking is in return for the grant of permission. On the other hand, where the undertaking in no way makes the proposed development more acceptable in itself, this could be grounds for holding the undertaking to be manifestly unreasonable. In this regard the undertaking in the *Gillingham* case would appear to have been substantially the same as that in *Bradford* as it required the developer to build a public road at his own expense. Yet there seems to have been no suggestion that the agreement was therefore bad. Lloyd LJ in the *Bradford* case seemed to be suggesting that such a requirement could be valid as long as the undertaking benefited the proposed development and yet Roche J held that the extension was not for the benefit of the development which was being granted!

It is suggested that a combination of *Bradford* and *Gillingham* could seem to produce a reasonable solution. An undertaking to contribute towards infrastructure either in cash or in kind would be valid as long as the contribution was not disproportionate to the benefits to be derived by the proposed development while as long as an undertaking was designed to achieve a planning purpose, there would be no separate requirement that it

20 [1988] JPL 336. Also see *R v Wealdon District Council ex p Charles Church South East Ltd* (1989) Times, 12 April.

had fairly and reasonably to relate to any grant of permission on which the agreement was conditional.

Finally it is worth noting that the *Gillingham* case suggests the possibility of attacking a planning agreement by way of the grant of planning permission. For example a developer might undertake in a planning agreement a restriction or regulation which clearly did not fairly or reasonably relate to a proposed development but which nevertheless was reasonable and achieved a planning purpose. Even if the undertaking was therefore valid, third parties might be able to attack the grant of planning permission on which the agreement was conditional, on the ground that the undertaking was not a factor which should have been taken into consideration in granting permission. This involves accepting the argument put forward but not determined in *R v Westminster City Council, ex p Monahan*,[1] that a material consideration must not only serve a planning purpose but must also fairly and reasonably relate to the permitted development. The answer essentially depends on whether it is considered right as a matter of policy that a development should be considered acceptable not because an undertaking solves planning problems related to *that* development but because it creates planning benefits elsewhere.

Enforcement of agreements

A prime advantage of planning agreements under s 52 is that there is no need to serve an enforcement notice and the local planning authority can go directly for an injunction.[2] This was so held by the Court of Appeal in *Avon County Council v Millard*[3] where a company had entered into a s 52 agreement that all mining operations would cease after a certain date unless further permission was granted and a new access road constructed. The Court of Appeal granted an interim injunction when the operations continued in breach of the undertaking. Fox LJ stated that:

'There was nothing in s 52 which indicated that ordinary civil remedies for breach of contract were not available, indeed subsection (2) suggested they were since the local authority would not normally suffer damage and was normally not in search of damages, injunction would normally be the only appropriate remedy under the contract.'

It seems that an enforcement notice had also been served and an appeal lodged but the court held that there was no need to exhaust the statutory procedure before obtaining an injunction.[4]

Fox LJ in *Avon County Council v Millard* referred to the agreement as a contract. This raises the possibility that an undertaking by a developer might not be enforceable against him if there was no reciprocal undertaking or consideration from the local planning authority.[5] It has therefore been argued that s 52 creates a special statutory obligation which does not require consideration.[6] Nevertheless local planning authorities would be prudent to

1 [1988] JPL 557; on appeal [1989] JPL 107, CA, per Staughton LJ at pp 117–18.
2 See ch 12 for the delays and technicalities inherent in the statutory system of enforcement.
3 [1986] JPL 211; see also *Beaconsfield District Council v Gams* (1974) 234 Estates Gazette 749.
4 Compare the use of injunction as supplement to statutory enforcement where normal statutory machinery must have been tried and found wanting; see ch 12 at p 373.
5 An undertaking to grant planning permission would very likely be void; see p 287.
6 See M Grant, 'Planning by Agreement' [1975] JPL 501.

ensure that agreements are made under seal to ensure that the covenants are enforceable at common law by way of injunction and damages.

Section 52(2) expressly provides for the agreement to be enforceable by the local planning authority against persons deriving title from the original covenantor.[7] However the subsection goes on to add the words 'as if the local authority were possessed of adjacent land and as if the agreement had been expressed to be made for the benefit of the land.' This has caused a good deal of discussion, in academic and professional texts and journals, of the question of the enforceability of positive obligations contained in agreements.[8] Positive covenants imposed on a sale of land can bind the person who originally undertakes the obligation but cannot, either at common law or in equity, bind his successors in title. Negative or restrictive covenants will bind successors in title in equity provided the covenants conform to certain strict requirements.[9] The wording therefore has been taken to be designed to put the local planning authority notionally in a position whereby they could conform to these strict requirements and thus enforce negative or restrictive covenants through the medium of an agreement which will bind successors in title. This could mean that positive covenants could not be enforced against successors in title and even throws doubt on the enforcement of restrictive covenants unless they are capable of benefiting adjoining land rather than conferring some broad public benefit. This latter course would be very artificial and in *Gee v National Trust for Places of Historic Interest and Natural Beauty*[10] Lord Denning concluded of a similar provision that it was simply machinery to give standing to enforce the restriction where the body would have no standing at common law. It was not necessary to deem any particular land to be in the ownership of the enforcing body. The arguments that only restrictive covenants can be enforced against successors in title have more weight as the wording of the whole section does suggest that it is primarily concerned with negative covenants. Certainly in *Abbey Homesteads (Developments) Ltd v Northamptonshire County Council*[11] Nourse LJ appeared to assume that it was only restrictive covenants which ran with the land. Whatever the true position, it should not cause trouble in practice as there is now a separate statutory provision for enforcing positive covenants against successors in title.[12] There is no provision in s 52 for the enforcement of any undertaking made by the local planning authority by the successor in title of the person entering into the agreement, but the benefit of such a covenant would run with the land and be enforceable.[13]

---

7 Any restriction or prohibition should be registered as local land charge under the Local Land Charges Act 1975.
8 See in particular J F Garner, 'Agreements Under Section 25' [1949] JPL 628; Malcolm Grant, 'Planning by Agreement' [1975] JPL 501; Michael Aves, 'Enforcing Section 52 Agreements' [1976] JPL 216; John Alder, *Development Control* (Sweet and Maxwell, 1979), pp 129–132; L R Tucker, 'Planning Agreements—The Twilight Zone of Ultra Vires' [1978] JPL 806; and M Loughlin, 'Planning Gain: Law, Policy and Practice' (1981) 1 Oxford Jo of Legal Studies 61.
9 These requirements were spelt out in *Tulk v Moxhay* (1848) 1 H & Tw 105, 2 Ph 774.
10 [1966] 1 All ER 954, [1966] 1 WLR 170; Salmon and Davies LJJ both left the point open.
11 (1986) 130 Sol Jo 482, 278 Estates Gazette 1244.
12 See s 33 of the Local Government (Miscellaneous Provisions) Act 1982 and p 293 below.
13 See s 78 of the Law of Property Act 1925 and *Smith and Snipes Hall Farm Ltd v River Douglas Catchment Board* [1949] 2 KB 500, [1949] 2 All ER 179.

Finally, to be enforceable the covenant must obviously be reasonably clear and certain.[14]

Agreements and the local planning authority's discretion

From the point of view of the local planning authority, one of the attractions of planning agreements is that they enable the authority to broaden the scope of their development control powers. In particular, an agreement under s 52 can enable a planning authority to get round some of the limitations and uncertainties connected with planning conditions (see chapter 9). Local planning authorities clearly have a wide discretion to enter into agreements under s 52 and a further wide discretion as to the content of any such agreement, but there are, inevitably, certain legal constraints.

In the first place, since the power to make agreements under s 52 is conferred by the planning legislation, it seems reasonable to suppose that the courts would require a local planning authority to demonstrate that a s 52 agreement had been entered into for a 'planning' purpose. For example in *R v Gillingham Borough Council, ex p F Parham Ltd*[15] Roche J held that it would be undesirable to permit a practice whereby s 52 agreements were entered into as a condition precedent to the granting of planning permissions to achieve objectives other than planning objectives. It is clear that the scope of the planning legislation is wide. In *Stringer v Minister of Housing and Local Government*[16] Cooke J commented: 'In principle, it seems to me that any consideration which relates to the use and development of land is capable of being a planning consideration.' On this view, the requirement that an agreement must have a 'planning' purpose would not seem to impose much of a constraint.

Secondly, and more significantly, if an agreement relates in some way, as the great majority do, to the exercise by a local planning authority of their development control powers—for example, the granting of planning permission or the taking of enforcement action—then the agreement is likely to have to be confined to dealing with matters which can be said to be 'material planning considerations'. The reason for this is that ss 29 and 87 of the 1971 Act stipulate the matters which may be taken into account by a local planning authority in determining a planning application or in deciding whether or not to take enforcement action. The principal such matters are the development plan and 'any other material considerations'. In deciding whether or not to grant permission or serve an enforcement notice the authority may well be influenced by the outcome of any negotiations over a planning agreement. Such agreements must, therefore, either be the consequence of a policy or proposal in the development plan or a 'material consideration'. If they are not, then, as indicated above at p 285, the validity of the development control decision (although not, it would seem, the agreement) may be open to question on the ground that it has been influenced by an immaterial consideration.

14 See *National Trust for Places of Historic Interest or Natural Beauty v Midlands Electricity Board* [1952] Ch 380, [1952] 1 All ER 298.
15 [1988] JPL 336.
16 [1971] 1 All ER 65, [1970] 1 WLR 1281; see also *Westminster City Council v Great Portland Estates plc* [1985] AC 661, [1984] 3 WLR 1035, per Lord Scarman, and generally the discussion in chapter 8.

Agreements which are the consequence of a policy or proposal in the development plan are now more commonplace. A number of examples have been noted.[17] Further encouragement has been given to local planning authorities in circular 22/83 to give guidance in their development plans about the circumstances in which agreements may be sought. Where a development plan contains a policy statement of this kind, then a failure to have regard to the policy when determining an application or an appeal in an appropriate case will lay the decision open to challenge. This can cause complications.

In *Richmond-upon-Thames London Borough Council v Secretary of State for the Environment*[18] Glidewell J held that the inspector would have been wrong to have ignored a policy in the development plan, that office developments should provide planning advantages, just because the Property Advisory Group in their report on planning gain had condemned the practice of bargaining for planning gain. This raises the difficult issue of the relationship between the policies on planning gain in the development plans and the guidance provided by circular 22/83. It would seem that both have to be regarded but neither automatically overrules the other.[19] Of course neither should urge a policy which is unlawful but in the case of the development plan it might be too late to challenge its legality.[20]

The expression 'material considerations' would appear to be narrower in scope than 'planning considerations'. In *Stringer* (above) Cooke J said: 'Whether a particular consideration falling within that broad class [ie of planning considerations] is material in any given case will depend on the circumstances.' In other words, it would seem that material considerations are those considerations relating to the use and development of land which arise out of or are relevant to the matter in hand. A planning permission which was dependent on an agreement which, for example, sought to impose on a developer the cost of providing public services unrelated to his development would arguably be concerning itself with something that was not a material consideration.

Equally, the local planning authority will have to ensure that the advantages they envisage arising from an agreement do not cause them to ignore other relevant considerations. Failure in this respect will also lay their decision on the planning application open to challenge.[1]

It would seem that if the parties to a planning appeal indicate their willingness to enter into an agreement, that is a matter which the Secretary of State will have to take into account in reaching his decision.[2]

17 See, for example, M Grant, 'Developers' Contributions and Planning Gain: Ethics and Legalities' [1978] JPL 8; M Loughlin, 'Planning Gain: Law, Policy and Practice' (1981) 1 Oxford Jo of Legal Studies 61; and *Planning Gain* (Report of the Property Advisory Group, HMSO, 1981).
18 [1984] JPL 24.
19 See the *Richmond* case; and *Westminster City Council v Secretary of State for the Environment* [1984] JPL 27.
20 See *Westminster City Council* case.
 1 See, for example, *Steeples v Derbyshire County Council* [1984] 3 All ER 468, [1985] 1 WLR 256. Contrast *R v Sevenoaks District Council, ex p Terry* [1985] 3 All ER 226, [1984] JPL 420.
 2 See *McLaren v Secretary of State for the Environment and Broxbourne Borough Council* [1981] JPL 423. Compare, however, *Tarmac Properties v Secretary of State for Wales* (1976) 33 P & CR 103 in which it was held that the Secretary of State had not acted unreasonably in not taking into account an agreement which had been drafted but never executed by the parties.

Agreements and the fettering of powers

We mentioned earlier that a public authority cannot disable itself by contract from exercising its powers and from performing its statutory duties.[3] For example, in *Stringer* (above) an undertaking given by a local planning authority to Manchester University to the effect that they would discourage development which might prejudice the operation of the Jodrell Bank telescope was held by Cooke J to be inconsistent with the proper performance of the authority's statutory duties. The effect of the agreement was to bind the authority to disregard considerations relevant to a planning application, considerations which, under the planning legislation, the authority were obliged to take into account.

The presumption underlying the decision in *Stringer* is that Parliament cannot have intended that authorities should be able, by agreement, to disable themselves from carrying out their statutory responsibilities. If, however, Parliament manifests an intention that authorities should be able to bind themselves in particular ways, there is, of course, no place for the operation of such a presumption. As regards planning agreements, it can be argued that such a manifestation of parliamentary intention appears in sub-s (3)(a) of s 52. That sub-section is somewhat obscurely worded but it would seem that it is intended to preserve the exercise of any planning powers in accordance with the provisions of the development plan or in accordance with any direction given by the Secretary of State as regards matters to be included in such a plan, notwithstanding anything to the contrary contained in an agreement. Put another way, sub-s (3) would seem to mean that an authority may by agreement pre-determine the way in which it will exercise a particular power—for example, the determination of a planning application or a decision on enforcement action—but such an agreement will not bind the authority if it requires an exercise of power contrary to the provisions of the development plan or of a direction by the Secretary of State.

The sub-section came under judicial scrutiny in *Windsor and Maidenhead Royal Borough Council v Brandrose Investments*.[4] In that case, a local planning authority, in accordance with an agreement made under s 52 of the Town and Country Planning Act 1971, granted planning permission for the redevelopment of a site. The development necessarily involved the demolition of buildings on the site. Before demolition of these buildings took place, the planning authority decided to extend an existing conservation area in such a way that it included the development site. One effect of the designation of an area as a conservation area is that the consent of the local planning authority is required for the demolition of any buildings in the area. When the developers began to demolish buildings on the development site, the local planning authority sought an injunction to restrain them from doing so. The main issue before the court was whether the authority could lawfully enter into an agreement which would operate so as to exclude the exercise of the

---

3 For discussion of the application of this doctrine see E Young and J Rowan-Robinson, 'Section 52 Agreements and the Fettering of Powers' [1982] JPL 673 and the texts and articles cited in that article. See too *R v Sevenoaks District Council, ex p Terry* [1984] JPL 420.
4 [1981] 3 All ER 38, [1981] 1 WLR 1083, revsd [1983] 1 All ER 818, [1983] 1 WLR 509, CA; and see Malcolm Grant, 'The Planning After Effects of the Brandrose Litigation', *Local Government Chronicle*, 15 July 1983, p 768.

authority's statutory powers to prevent the demolition of buildings on the site.

Fox J, at first instance, held that an agreement under s 52 could validly fetter such powers. There was, he said, 'nothing in principle to prevent the exercise of a statutory power being limited by the previous exercise of another statutory power'. This was the effect of the s 52 agreement and the local planning authority were, accordingly, not entitled to use their statutory powers to prevent such demolition.

The Court of Appeal, however, after confessing that they shared the bemusement of counsel for the plaintiffs as to what s 52(3) meant, held that local planning authorities were not empowered to inhibit themselves by agreement from including land in a conservation area or from requiring consent for the demolition of buildings in such an area. In the court's judgment sub-s (3) could not be construed 'as restricting the exercise of a local planning authority of any of their statutory powers which they have a public duty to exercise'. This emphasis on public duties could mean that a local planning authority is free to restrict the future exercise of a mere power, but powers and duties in public law cannot be separated into watertight compartments. There will usually be an element of choice written into most duties and invariably a power will involve a duty to consider using that power.[5] Certainly in the case of s 29, although the local planning authority has a discretion as to how it determines an application, the authority is under a public duty to make a determination and is constrained in the way it exercises its discretion. So, if the approach of the Court of Appeal is followed, it would seem that an agreement by a local planning authority to grant planning permission is strictly unenforceable. By declining to attempt to interpret sub-s 3, the court has effectively made it redundant.

In practice, the decision does not make much difference. Local planning authorities are unlikely to renege on their part of the agreement, unless the planning circumstances should radically alter their view as to whether the planning gain warrants the granting of permission. Also as Lawton LJ pointed out in the *Windsor and Maidenhead* case, if 'an agreement made pursuant to section 52 before planning permission had been granted ... it might become irrelevant if planning permission was not granted or ineffective if conditions were imposed inconsistent with the agreement ...'. It could be irrelevant because it was completely dependent on the proposed development or it even might be unenforceable as an undertaking without consideration if the undertaking was not made under seal. In any case most developers' undertakings will be made expressly conditional on the planning permission being granted and the development taking place.

Variation and termination of s 52 agreements

Section 52(1) states that agreements may be entered into 'either permanently or during such period as may be prescribed by the agreement'.

The agreement itself may provide for its termination either after a prescribed period or after the carrying out of specified works. It may sometimes be implicit that the agreement is to end after certain works have been carried out.

5 See *R v Stroud District Council, ex p Goodenough, Usborne and Tomlin* (1980) 43 P & CR 59, [1982] JPL 246 and for further discussion of this point see the article cited in n 33.

An agreement may become less relevant with the passage of time. For example, planning policies may change, there may be a change of circumstances, or the planning permission to which the agreement is related may be revoked. It may be desirable to make provision in the agreement for revocation or modification of the agreement in such circumstances. The parties can of course agree to a revocation or modification at any time. Also an application can be made to the Lands Tribunal under s 84 of the Law of Property Act 1925 for the variation or discharge of a restrictive covenant contained in an agreement made under s 52 of the Town and Country Planning Act 1971.[6]

With regard to s 84, the first point to note is that the Lands Tribunal's jurisdiction only relates to restrictive covenants and not to positive covenants. In distinguishing the two, it would seem that it is the effect rather than the wording that is important. This is shown by the Court of Appeal decision in *Abbey Homesteads (Developments) Ltd v Northamptonshire County Council*.[7] This decision concerned a covenant in a s 52 agreement which required that 'An area of 1.3 hectares adjacent to the playing field and amenity open space areas shall be reserved for school purposes.' Overturning the views of the Lands Tribunal, the Court of Appeal held that this wording did create a restrictive covenant running with the land. It was irrelevant that it did not expressly prohibit other uses, the clear effect was that the land should *not* be used for other than school purposes. The court held that the restriction was sufficiently certain to be enforceable even though it did not specify which 1.3 hectares was to be reserved for school purposes: this was left to the discretion of the developers. It was also concluded that the restriction did not lapse once the land had been acquired for school purposes; it continued to require the land to be used for such purposes indefinitely.

The Lands Tribunal may discharge or modify a restriction if it is satisfied that any of four possible grounds apply. These grounds are that:

(1) by reason of changes in the character of the property or the neighbourhood or any other material circumstances, the restriction ought to be deemed obsolete;

(2) the continued existence of the restriction would impede some reasonable public or private user of the land, without securing any practical benefits of substantial value or advantage for the persons entitled to the benefit of the covenant and that money would be adequate compensation for any loss or disadvantage suffered;

(3) the persons entitled to the benefit of the restriction have agreed either expressly or by implication, by their acts or omissions, to the same being discharged or modified;

(4) the proposed discharge or modification will not injure the persons entitled to the benefit of the restriction.

It is not easy to apply these grounds to covenants contained in planning agreements. This is not surprising. In private law, restrictive covenants are a

---

6 See *Gee v National Trust for Places of Historic Interest and Natural Beauty* [1966] 1 All ER 954, [1966] 1 WLR 170; *Re Beecham Group Ltd's Application* (1980) 41 P & CR 369, 256 Estates Gazette 829; *Re Bovis' Homes Southern Ltd's Application* [1981] JPL 368 and *Abbey Homesteads (Developments) Ltd v Northamptonshire County Council* (1986) 278 Estates Gazette 1244.

7 (1986) 278 Estates Gazette 1244.

means by which individual land owners can protect the amenities and value of their land. Planning agreements are essentially part of the public system of development control. They are imposed in the public interest and for planning considerations which are not just concerned with questions of amenity. It is the accident of the use of the private law mechanism of the restrictive covenant which brings into play s 84.

The main difficulty with the way the grounds are drafted is that they tend to assume the existence of a particular person who owns land which benefits from the covenant. In the case of a covenant in a planning agreement, it is not intended to benefit any particular piece of land owned by the local planning authority and so there is no question of any particular person being or not being injured by the removal of the covenant (see ground (4) above). Also monetary damages will not normally be suitable compensation for the removal of a restriction imposed for the general interest (see ground (2) above). Fortunately the courts have interpreted the grounds flexibly. In *Abbey Homesteads* Nourse LJ accepted that there was obvious difficulty in fitting s 52(2) and ground (4) together but he thought that the persons entitled to benefit from the restriction must be taken to be those members of the general public who will benefit from the permitted use of the land which is subject to the restriction.[8] Then in *Re Martin's Application*[9] the Court of Appeal upheld findings by the Lands Tribunal that a covenant preventing building on land benefited a local authority because 'the interference with visual amenity would be an injury to the Corporation in its capacity as custodian of the public interest.' The Lands Tribunal also had held that the covenant was of substantial advantage to the corporation for which money would not be an adequate compensation.

So in the case of planning agreements it will be the issue of whether the restriction should now be deemed obsolete because of 'changes in the character of the property or the neighbourhood or any other material considerations' which will be crucial as this clearly involves planning considerations. In *Abbey Homesteads* the Court of Appeal held that it was wrong to treat the covenant that the land should not be used otherwise than as a school as obsolete just because the land had been acquired for school purposes. The covenant was still in full effect and Nourse LJ stated that in any case this reason (relied upon by the tribunal for concluding that the restriction was obsolete) did not come within s 84. The reference to other material circumstances, in ground (1), had to be construed *eiusdem generis* with the particular words used by the section. Parker LJ added that:

'The fact that at a particular time the owner or prospective owner of the land does not wish to breach the covenant or may even be under a statutory duty to comply with it does not render the covenant obsolete.'

In *Re Martin's Application*[10] the Court of Appeal held that the test for obsolescence was whether the original object of the restriction can still be

8 Compare *Re Beecham Group Ltd's Application* (1980) 41 P & CR 369 where the Lands Tribunal, in ordering the modification of a restriction, did so principally on the ground that the local planning authority would suffer no injury: though it may be that by injury the tribunal was considering the impact on the public planning policies of the authority.

9 [1989] JPL 33, CA.

10 Ibid.

achieved. In the case of a planning agreement the original object must have been a planning objective and so the Lands Tribunal is inevitably involved in making a planning judgment. The Lands Tribunal is not a planning authority and so there arises the difficult question of the extent to which the tribunal must accept the views of the legitimate planning authorities. This question was directly at issue in *Re Martin's Application.* The Court of Appeal had to consider the effect of a grant of planning permission on an application to have a restrictive covenant discharged. An agreement had been entered into under s 37 of the Town and Country Planning Act 1962 that certain land 'should not be used for any purpose other than as a private open space and that accordingly no building, structure or erection (other than fencing, a summer house or garden shed if the owner shall so require) shall be placed thereon.' Years later the Secretary of State upheld an appeal against a refusal to grant planning permission to build a dwelling on that land but the local authority was not prepared to release the owners of the land from the covenant as they still considered that it was in the interests of the amenities and the environment of the area that the land remained undeveloped. Upholding a decision of the Lands Tribunal not to discharge the covenant on grounds (1), (2) and (4), the Court of Appeal said that the entering into of a planning agreement and the granting of planning permission constituted two independent systems of control. While the two regimes impinged on each other to some extent, the granting of planning permission was merely a circumstance which the Lands Tribunal can and should take into account when exercising jurisdiction under s 84 and was not conclusive. In determining a planning application or an appeal the local planning authority or the Secretary of State is making a policy judgment by weighing conflicting factors and arguments. *Re Martin's Application* would suggest that the Lands Tribunal's role is essentially different. In granting permission a local planning authority may accept that a proposed development will interfere with the visual amenities of the area but yet determine that the need for housing outweighs this disadvantage. It would appear that the Lands Tribunal's role is to make a determination on the evidence as to whether the planning objective is still being achieved and, if it concludes that it is, the application to discharge the restriction must be rejected. However, in this regard s 84 does allow the Lands Tribunal to take into account any material considerations and in *Re Cox's Application*[11] a restriction on separate occupancy of an extension to a dwelling was discharged because it was no longer practical to fulfill the restrictions. The tribunal instead substituted an agricultural occupancy covenant.

We would argue that the present position is unsatisfactory and that it might be more appropriate in the case of planning agreements for an application for discharge to be made to the Secretary of State on planning grounds.

Alternatives to s 52 agreements

Following the recommendations of the Sheaf Committee[12] s 126 of the Housing Act 1974 provided a means of enforcing positive covenants against successors in title. This section has now been superseded by s 33 of the Local

---

11 (1985) 51 P & CR 335, [1985] JPL 564.
12 Report of the Working Party on Local Authority/Private Enterprise Partnership Schemes (1972) para 3.

Government (Miscellaneous Provisions) Act 1982. This applies when a principal authority[13] and any other person are parties to an instrument under seal which has the purpose of securing the carrying out of works or facilitating the development or regulating the use of land in the council's area (s 33(1)(a)).[14] Provided the covenant is expressed to be one to which the section (or its predecessor s 126) applies and defines the land in which the person executing the covenant has an interest, obligations to carry out works or do any other thing are enforceable (without time limit of any kind) against any person deriving title from the original covenantor (s 33(2)).[15]

Such an instrument can be enforced by injunction but s 33 in addition confers powers on the authority to enter on the land concerned and to carry out the works or do anything required to be carried out or remedy anything which has been done and which the covenant required not to be done; costs of such works are recoverable from any person against whom the covenant is enforceable (s 33(3)).[16]

It would seem plain that s 33 only provides a method of enforcing positive covenants.[17] This means that, if an agreement is to contain both positive and restrictive covenants, it should make clear which are made under s 52 and which under s 33.

There used to be numerous Private Acts which gave particular local authorities special powers of entering into and enforcing agreements.[18] However, s 262 of the Local Government Act 1972 provided that most local legislation should cease to have effect by the end of 1984. It is of course open to local authorities to promote replacement local Acts but circular 14/75 made clear that only a small percentage would justify re-enactment. The government's view was that many of the provisions should more appropriately be contained in public general Acts.[19] Nevertheless, local Acts have been successfully promoted which contain special powers for local authorities to enter into agreements.[20] Also, any agreements entered into under the local Acts, which have now ceased to have effect, are still enforceable.

There also exist specific statutory provisions by which developers can assist in the provision of public services which may be needed before it is suitable to allow the development to take place. In the case of highways, agreements can be entered into under s 38 and s 278 of the Highways Act 1980. In the case of s 38, the developer constructs the highway at his own expense and on his own land. The local authority in return agrees to adopt the highway once it has been constructed and to take over the cost of maintenance after an agreed

---

13 This includes county and district councils as well as London boroughs but not the London Docklands Development Corporation or any other development corporations (s 33(9)).
14 It also applies where the purpose is facilitating the development or regulating the use of land outside the council's area.
15 S 33(2) makes clear that it can also be enforced against persons deriving title in lesser interests—tenants and others.
16 S 33(4) requires not less than 21 days' notice to be given to any person with an interest in the land or against whom the covenant is enforceable.
17 But note sub-s (3)(a) refers also to restrictions.
18 See *Beaconsfield District Council v Gams* (1974) 234 Estates Gazette 749 for an example of the enforcement of such a local Act.
19 The Local Government (Miscellaneous Provisions) Act 1982 being an example of such an Act.
20 See for example the Oxfordshire Act 1985, s 4 and the West Glamorgan Act 1987, s 52. Also note the Greater London Council (General Powers) Act 1974, s 16.

period. Section 278 applies where the construction work is to be carried out by the Highway Authority and authorises the authority to agree to additional works or to bring forward the date of construction in return for a contribution to the cost of the works. Such an agreement can only be entered into with a person who would derive a special benefit from the agreement and the authority should not enter into an agreement unless they are satisfied that it will be of benefit to the public. Section 278 agreements can be used for 'off site' highways, ie highways outside the confines of the development site. It seems that s 278 agreements are sometimes used for entirely new highways proposed and built by the developers but this is stretching the scope of the provision.

Similarly, under s 18 of the Public Health Act 1936 and s 16 of the Water Act 1973, arrangements can be made with respect to the construction of sewers. Under s 18 water authorities may agree with a developer proposing to construct sewers that if the construction is undertaken in a manner agreed by the water authority, then the water authority will adopt the sewer. Where the developer does not own the necessary land to construct adequate sewers, there is power under s 16 for the developer to force the authority to provide a public sewer for domestic purposes.[1] The duty to construct the sewer only applies if several conditions are met.[2] These include an undertaking being given to meet, for a period of 12 years, a proportion of the cost of providing the sewers. Planning permission for the proposed development must have already been granted and there must be two existing hereditaments served with private drains. These conditions make s 16 inappropriate for 'green field' sites but agreements can be made conditional on these conditions being fulfilled.

1 Domestic purposes as defined would extend to commercial development as well as residential, see s 16(12) of the Water Act 1973.
2 See s 16(1).

CHAPTER 12

THE ENFORCEMENT OF PLANNING CONTROL

Introduction

There is not much point in having a sophisticated system for controlling development unless there are effective provisions for enforcing control. Part V of the 1971 Act provides the machinery for enforcement.

The present chapter is primarily concerned with those provisions of Pt V which deal with the enforcement of control over development which has been carried out without planning permission or in contravention of a condition or limitation attached to a grant of planning permission. The remaining provisions of Pt V, which relate to the enforcement of control in relation to listed buildings, hazardous substances, trees, waste land, advertisements and orders under s 51 of the 1971 Act, are summarised in the chapters dealing with those matters.

In 1975 Dobry commented that: 'Over the years, enforcement, because of legal technicalities involved, has probably been the weakest link in the planning control system.'[1] The provisions of Pt V of the 1971 Act have twice been amended (by the Town and Country Planning (Amendment) Act 1977 ('the 1977 Act') and the Local Government and Planning (Amendment) Act 1981 ('the 1981 Act')) in an effort to overcome some of the weaknesses highlighted by Dobry and others. These changes, together with the less strict approach to the construction of enforcement notices adopted by the courts,[2] may have gone a little way towards reducing the technical complexity of this area of planning law but it is doubtful if they have done much to reduce the cumbersome and time-consuming nature of the enforcement process.[3]

A TAKING ENFORCEMENT ACTION

Power to issue an enforcement notice

A breach of planning control may take one of three forms:

(i) an unauthorised operation;
(ii) an unauthorised material change of use;

---

1 G Dobry QC, 'Review of the Development Control System: Final Report' (HMSO, 1975).
2 See, for example, *Miller-Mead v Minister of Housing and Local Government* [1963] 2 QB 196, [1963] 1 All ER 459, per Lord Denning MR; *Eldon Garages Ltd v Kingston-upon-Hull County Borough Council* [1974] 1 All ER 358, [1974] 1 WLR 276, per Templeman J; and *Ferris v Secretary of State for the Environment* (1988) 57 P & CR 127, [1988] JPL 777.
3 See J Jowell and D Millichap, 'The Enforcement of Planning Law' [1986] JPL 482 for both a study of the way the system works and a proposal for reform. Also note the Report on 'Enforcing Planning Control' (HMSO) published in April 1989 which makes various recommendations for reform.

(iii) a breach of a condition or limitation subject to which planning permission has been granted.

Although a breach of planning control is unlawful,[4] it is not, of itself, a criminal offence.[5] Instead, s 87 of the 1971 Act provides that, where it appears to a local planning authority that a breach of planning control has occurred since 1963, then they may issue what is termed an 'enforcement notice' requiring the breach to be remedied. Contravention of the terms of an effective enforcement notice may result in sanctions, including prosecution.

Despite the criminal consequences of disobeying an enforcement notice the courts have held that the jurisdiction to serve a notice does not depend on there actually having been a breach of planning control.[6]

The use of the work 'appear' has been taken to mean that the local planning authority does not have to be satisfied that a breach has occurred,[7] and it is enough that a prima facie case exists. Further, the authority are under no obligation to satisfy themselves whether the development in question is permitted under the GDO or whether there are grounds upon which a notice can be successfully challenged.[8]

In *Ferris v Secretary of State for the Environment*[9] Graham Eyre QC justified this on the grounds of the difficulties that any other approach would place on local planning authorities. He said:

'An authority may well have insufficient information. The burden of monitoring each planning unit in its administrative area in order to discern a change of use and answer the question whether it is material in relation to unidentifiable use bases would collapse the administration of the whole scheme of legislation and the proposition has only to be stated to be seen as an absurdity.'

As a result the onus is very much on those affected by the enforcement notice to rebut the allegation of the breach of control.[10]

The bodies primarily responsible for the enforcement of planning control are the district planning authorities.[11] The county planning authority can serve an enforcement notice where it appears to the county that it relates to a matter which should properly be considered a county matter and the district should consult the county first before serving a notice if it appears to the

---

4 S 23(1) of the 1971 Act requires planning permission to be obtained for the development of land.
5 Contrast the situation where there has been an infringement of listed building control (s 55 of the 1971 Act).
6 See *Jeary v Chailey RDC* (1973) 26 P & CR 280.
7 See *Miller-Mead v Minister of Housing and Local Government* [1963] 2 QB 196, [1963] 1 All ER 459.
8 See *Tidswell v Secretary of State for the Environment* (1976) 34 P & CR 152 and *Ferris v Secretary of State for the Environment* (1988) 57 P & CR 127, [1988] JPL 777. However an enforcement notice cannot be served in anticipation of a future breach; see *R v Rochester City Council ex p Hobday* (1989) Times, 22 February.
9 Ibid.
10 An unreasonable issue of an enforcement notice could result in costs being awarded on an appeal; see circular 2/87, para 14.
11 Local Government Act 1972, s 182, Sch 16, para 24(1).

district to relate to a county matter.[12] If, after consultation with the appropriate planning authority,[13] the Secretary of State considers it expedient to do so, he may himself issue an enforcement notice (1971 Act, s 276(5A)). In metropolitan areas, the Greater London area and in areas covered by an urban development corporation the enforcement body will be the single local planning authority; see chapter 2.

Even if it appears to the relevant local planning authority that a breach of control has occurred, there is no obligation to issue an enforcement notice. Section 87 provides that they *may* issue a notice 'if they consider it expedient to do so having regard to the provisions of the development plan and to any other material considerations'.[14] It is therefore clear that the Act gives the authority a discretion as to whether to take enforcement action or not.[15] This does not mean that the exercise of the discretion is unchallengeable in the courts. (See p 586 below.) In the case of a clear breach of planning control, it is arguable that the local planning authority are under a duty at least to consider taking enforcement action,[16] and in coming to their decision, they must not act for ulterior motives, take into account irrelevant factors or otherwise offend the *Wednesbury* principles.[17]

As compared with the exercise of the discretion in determining a planning application under s 29, there is little case law on what are the proper considerations to be regarded in issuing an enforcement notice but the employment of the same formula would suggest that generally the same principles would apply. In *Donovan v Secretary of State for the Environment*[18] it was argued that it was unfair to take action against one street trader, while several cases of unauthorised trading went on unheeded. Otton J held that:

'the fact that the local authority had not taken enforcement action against others (assuming that to be so) was not a material consideration, either in enforcement proceedings or in the deemed planning application. The fact that others had got away with an unauthorised user cannot put Mr Donovan in the right or make his user lawful.'

However, it would be invalid to issue a notice for improper motives and in *Davey v Spelthorne Borough Council*[19] Lord Frazer doubted if it would be proper for a planning authority to allow their decision on whether to take enforcement action to be influenced by the threat of a possible action for damages. As with planning applications and appeals, it must be now accepted that published government policies are material considerations to

---

12 See para 24(2) and (3) of Sch 16. The validity of an enforcement notice cannot be called into question in any proceedings on the grounds that the district failed to consult the county or that the county had no jurisdiction to serve the notice; see para 51(2) of Sch 16. As to the meaning of county matters; see p 17 above.

13 By para 47 of Sch 16, this will either be the district planning authority or the county planning authority depending which the Secretary of State considers appropriate.

14 The same phrase as is used in s 29; see ch 8.

15 See *Perry v Stanborough (Developments) Ltd* (1977) 244 Estates Gazette 551.

16 See *R v Stroud District Council, ex p Goodenough, Usborne and Tomlin* (1980) 43 P & CR 59, where it was held there was a duty to consider using powers relating to listed buildings.

17 Laid down by Lord Greene in *Associated Provincial Picture Houses Ltd v Wednesday Corpn* [1948] 1 KB 223, [1947] 2 All ER 680.

18 [1988] JPL 118.

19 [1984] AC 262, [1983] 3 All ER 278, HL.

be considered in deciding whether to take enforcement action.[20] In this respect government circulars have emphasised that enforcement should not be taken lightly.

Circular 22/80 recommends that enforcement notices should only be issued where planning reasons clearly warrant such action and there is no alternative to enforcement proceedings; see para 15. The circular goes on in Annex B to advise that in the case of small businesses that:

'The first step in considering whether enforcement action is necessary should be to explore, in discussion with the owner or operator of a small business whether it is practicable to reach a compromise which will allow his activities to continue at their present level or if necessary less intensively.'

and in the new Planning Policy Guidance Note Number 1 (PPG1) it is advised that 'where the activity involved is one which would not give rise to insuperable planning objections if it were carried on somewhere else then the planning authority should do all it can to help in finding suitable alternative premises before initiating enforcement action' para 30. An appeal against an enforcement notice requires the payment of a fee appropriate to a planning application for the development: see p 188; but circular 20/85 warns against local planning authorities initiating enforcement action solely with a view to securing payment of a fee; see (para 6 of Appendix 1).

Where a local planning authority consider that they would be likely to grant planning permission in regard to the apparent breach of control, circular 20/85 advises that the developer should be informed of the breach and invited to submit a planning application, warning him at the same time of the difficulties he might face in selling his interest in the land and the risk of enforcement action.

A failure to take enforcement action could result in a complaint of maladministration to the Commission for Local Administration if the authority had been at fault in not issuing the notice.

Although the power to take enforcement notice is discretionary, in special circumstances the planning authority may be barred from taking action because of previous statements made by the authority or on the authority's behalf (see p 334 below).

There is nothing to prevent a planning authority taking enforcement action while an appeal against a refusal of planning permission is pending.[1]

Entry and information

If a local planning authority believe that a breach of planning control has occurred, they will, before embarking upon formal enforcement action, wish to ensure that they are in possession of as much information as possible as to the activities carried on upon the land in question and as to the persons having an interest in the land. Section 280 of the 1971 Act allows a person duly authorised in writing by the planning authority to enter upon land for

---

20 See ch 8, p 204.
1 See *Davis v Miller* [1956] 3 All ER 109, [1956] 1 WLR 1013, but the fact of an impending appeal can be mitigating circumstances in sentencing for failure to comply; see *R v Newland* (1987) 54 P & CR 222, [1987] JPL 851, CA.

the purpose of surveying it in connection with the service of an enforcement notice. Admission to occupied land cannot be demanded as of right unless twenty-four hours' notice has been given (s 281). In addition, s 284 of the 1971 Act[2] empowers an authority to serve a notice on the occupier of land, or on a person in receipt of rent from the land, requiring him to state the nature of his interest in the land, the name and address of any other person known to him as having an interest in the land, and details of the purpose for which the land is currently being used. An authority can now also require to know the date when that use began, the name and address of any person who had used the premises for that purpose and information as to the time that any activities being carried out on the premises began. The distinction between 'use' and 'activities' reflects the distinction between operational development and a material change of use and the power enables an authority to judge whether service of an enforcement notice or stop notice is restricted by the passage of time.

It seems that local planning authorities sometimes use these powers in order to pressurise compliance without having to serve an enforcement notice. Failure to respond to the notice or knowingly making a mis-statement in response to the notice is a criminal offence.

Issuance and service of an enforcement notice

The Local Government and Planning (Amendment) Act 1981 introduced a change by which the notice is first 'issued' by the authority and copies are then served on interested parties. This change was introduced to overcome the difficulties that could arise if a notice was served on several persons and was drafted to take effect within 28 days of service. This could result in a notice purporting to take effect at different dates and so probably being invalid.[3] The new requirement to 'issue' a notice is interpreted as meaning that the authority should prepare a properly authorised document and retain it in their records (circular 26/81, para 3 of Annex). Details must be entered in the register of enforcement notices and stop notices.[4]

Copies of the enforcement notice then have to be served on the owner[5] and the occupier of the land to which it relates, and on any other person having an interest in that land if, in the authority's opinion, that interest is materially affected by the notice[6] (s 87(5)). Service is to be effected by service of a copy of the notice on each such person. This makes it clear that there is only one notice in respect of a breach of control but that copies of it must be served on

---

2 As amended by s 5(4) of the Town and Country Planning (Amendment) Act 1977.
3 See *Bambury v London Borough of Hounslow* [1966] 2 QB 204, [1966] 2 All ER 532; and *Stevens v Bromley London Borough Council* [1972] Ch 400, [1972] 1 All ER 712, CA where Salmon LJ left the point open to further argument.
4 See s 92A and art 28A of the GDO.
5 'Owner' is defined by s 290 to mean a person, other than a mortgagee not in possession, entitled to receive the rack rent or who would be so entitled if it is let at less than the rack rent. According to *London Corpn v Cusack-Smith* [1955] AC 337, [1955] 1 All ER 302, HL this means that a freeholder who lets at less than a rack rent is not the owner. The owner is the tenant who is entitled to let at a rack rent.
6 'Interest' probably means a legal interest of some sort in the land; see *Stevens v Bromley London Borough Council* [1972] Ch 400, [1972] 1 All ER 712, per Salmon LJ and appeal decision reported in [1976] JPL 113. See too [1983] JPL 826. But lesser interests could require service as occupiers.

each person with an interest in the land.[7] Copies must be served not later than 28 days after the date on which the notice is issued, which will be the date on which the notice is formally drawn up. Where there are several interested parties, they can be served with their copies on different days but they must all be served at least 28 days before the issued notice states that it is going to take effect (s 87(5)). In other words, having issued the notice, the local planning authority must ensure that everyone receives copies both 28 days after issue and 28 days before the notice takes effect.

The issuing of a notice cannot be delegated to a single member even if he is the Chairman of the Planning Committee. A notice authorised by a single person will be a nullity and it is doubted whether it could be retrospectively validated by the full committee.[8] However, even where standing orders of the council provide that a particular officer shall be delegated the powers of issuing notices, the issue of a notice by some other officer will be valid if actual practice shows that arrangements have been made for the discharge of the function in this way.[9]

Difficult questions can arise as regards the definition of 'occupier' for the purposes of s 87(5). In *Stevens v Bromley London Borough Council*[10] a majority of the Court of Appeal took the view that it is in each case a question of fact and degree whether a licensee, such as a person permitted to station a caravan on land, is an 'occupier' for the purpose of the statutory requirement as to service of an enforcement notice. In that case the court held (distinguishing *Munnich v Godstone RDC*[11]) that where the owner of a caravan had, under a licence from the owner of the land, stationed the caravan on a site, had used it as a permanent home for some seven months, and appeared 'to have exercised a degree of control on the site indistinguishable from that of a tenant', he was in all the circumstances an occupier of the land in the sense of the statute and was therefore entitled to be served with an enforcement notice relating to the land.

In *Scarborough Borough Council v Adams and Adams*[12] Watkins LJ concluded that in view of the length of time and the exclusive nature of their occupation, mere squatters were, in the circumstances of the case, 'occupiers' for the purposes of the planning legislation. In that case it was held that so far as issue of an enforcement notice was concerned it was irrelevant and had no effect on the validity of the notice that the recipients were described as 'occupiers' even if they were only trespassers. In considering what the word 'occupier' means for the purposes of the planning legislation it is doubtful whether much assistance is to be derived from decisions on the meaning of the word in other branches of the law.[13] As a consequence, persons can be occupiers for the purpose of s 87(5) and yet not be owners of the land nor

7 This would seem to overcome the difficulty that occurred in *Skinner v Secretary of State for the Environment* (1978) 247 Estates Gazette 1173, [1978] JPL 842.
8 See *R v Secretary of State for the Environment, ex p Hillingdon London Borough Council* [1986] 1 All ER 810, [1986] 1 WLR 192 which was affirmed by the Court of Appeal; see [1986] 2 All ER 273, [1986] 1 WLR 807. Also see *R v Rochester City, ex p Hobday* (1989) Times, 22 February.
9 See *Cheshire County Council v Secretary of State for the Environment* [1988] JPL 30.
10 [1972] Ch 400, [1972] 1 All ER 712. See too ministerial decisions noted in [1976] JPL 113 and [1983] JPL 271.
11 [1966] 1 All ER 930, [1966] 1 WLR 427, CA.
12 (1983) 147 JP 449, 47 P & CR 133.
13 See *Caravans and Automobiles Ltd v Southall Borough Council* [1963] 2 All ER 533, [1963] 1 WLR 690, per Lord Parker CJ.

have some other legal interest which will be materially affected by the notice. As only persons with an 'interest in the land' can appeal (s 88(1)), the reasoning would seem to be that occupiers may have a right to be informed of the notice and so avoid breaching the criminal law; but they may not have sufficient interest in the land to justify being able to challenge the notice.

The fact that the legislation requires service on certain classes of people does not preclude the local planning authority serving notice on someone who does not belong to those classes.[14]

Section 88(2)(f) of the 1971 Act provides that an appeal can be made to the Secretary of State on the ground inter alia that the notice was not served as required by s 87(5) (see p 343 below). Further, s 243(1) provides that the validity of an enforcement notice 'shall not, except by way of appeal [to the Secretary of State], be questioned in any proceedings whatsoever' on any of the grounds on which appeal can be made to the Secretary of State.

The effect of similar provisions was considered in the Scottish case of *McDaid v Clydebank District Council*.[15] In that case the planning authority served three enforcement notices on the occupier of land but omitted to serve the owners even though the planning authority knew of the interest in the land of one of the owners. The occupier failed to appeal against the notices and the owners did not become aware of the notices until after the time for appeal to the Secretary of State had expired. The owners petitioned the Court of Session for suspension of the notices and for an interdict prohibiting the authority taking action on the notices. The Lord Ordinary (Lord Allanbridge) refused the petition on the ground that s 85(10) (the equivalent Scottish provision to s 243(1)) excluded the court's jurisdiction.

On appeal, the First Division held that the court's powers were not excluded by s 85(10) and that as the enforcement notices had not been properly served, they were nullities. This was not, said Lord Cameron, 'a mere error in the manner or requirements of service; so far as the petitioners are concerned there was no service on them at all'. Since the notice was lacking 'an essential element',[16] it was 'not such a notice as the statute required and thus a nullity'. The petitioners had lost their right of appeal as a result of a breach of precise obligations laid on the planning authority and the authority ought not to be entitled, the court thought, to take advantage of their failure to comply with the legislation.

However, the Court of Appeal in *R v Greenwich London Borough Council, ex p Patel*[17] declined to follow the Scottish interpretation and upheld the exclusion clause. Again, an enforcement notice had been served on the occupier of property but not on the actual owner. This was not surprising in the circumstances as the occupier, the sister-in-law of the owner, had held herself out to be the owner. There was no appeal against this notice and when notice was given under s 91 that the council would enter the property to remove the unauthorised operations, the real owner challenged by way of judicial review the council's power to carry out the proposed demolition. The Court of Appeal rejected the argument that the enforcement notice was a

---

14 See *Scarborough Borough Council* (above).
15 1984 SLT 162.
16 It may be noted that in *Scarborough Borough Council v Adams and Adams* (above) Watkins LJ said that the legislation makes it 'imperative' that the planning authority serve notice on certain classes of people.
17 [1985] JPL 851.

nullity because of the failure to serve it on the owner. This was justified on the grounds that the consequences of failure to serve a notice on a person with an interest in the land are dealt with in other parts of the Act which attempt to protect the interests of such a person. In particular it was pointed out by Neill LJ that one of the grounds of appeal to the Secretary of State is that the notice has not been served as required by s 87(4) and the Secretary of State is empowered to disregard the fact that a person required by s 87(4) to 'be served with a notice' was not served 'if neither the appellant nor that person has been substantially prejudiced by the failure to serve him' (s 88(4)). Neill LJ also pointed to s 243(2), which gave a person charged with a criminal offence under s 89(5), but who had not been served with an enforcement notice, the right to question its validity on any of the grounds specified in s 88(1)(b) to (e). Again this only applies if the person charged could show that he had been substantially prejudiced by the failure to serve the notice on him (s 243(2)(c)(ii)).[18]

These and other provisions mean that the likelihood of injustice is rare though the value of an owner's property could be reduced by being unable to challenge a notice. In *McDaid*, the planning authority failed to serve the notice on one of the owners even though it was known that the person had an interest in land. Neill LJ distinguished *McDaid's* case because of this and it seemed to be accepted in all three judgments that the validity of the notice could have been challenged if there had been a deliberate failure to serve a copy of the notice on an owner.[19] Sir John Megaw also suggests that relief might be granted if there had been carelessness on the part of the administrative body in failing to give effect to the statutory requirements but he made this point on the presumption that the notice was subject to review on the grounds of lack of notice.[20]

The local planning authority may withdraw an enforcement notice at any time before it takes effect: s 87(14). For example, it may have come to their notice that the breach of control is immune from enforcement action or that the notice has been wrongly served. Notice of the withdrawal must be given to every person who was served with a copy of the enforcement notice (s 87(15)). Any such withdrawal does not prevent the authority serving a fresh enforcement notice in respect of the breach of control. A second enforcement notice can, it seems, be served before the first becomes effective.[1]

Where an enforcement notice is a nullity or is quashed for material error there would seem to be nothing to prevent a local planning authority from serving a fresh enforcement notice in respect of the breach of control unless in the meantime the breach has become immune from enforcement action under one of the 'limitation periods'. However where it has been held on appeal that no breach of planning control has taken place, the principle of

---

18 The defendant must also satisfy the court that he did not know and could not reasonably be expected to know that the enforcement notice had been issued; s 243(2)(c)(i).
19 Neill LJ referred to Lord Fraser's judgment in *Davey v Spelthorne Borough Council* [1984] AC 262, where Lord Fraser pointed out that notice could be challenged if it was vitiated by fraud or bribery or if it had been issued without authority, at 272.
20 Carelessness is not yet in itself a ground for judicial review though it could be evidence of negligence if the local planning authority could be held to be under a duty of care in issuing and serving enforcement notices; see on this *Davey v Spelthorne Borough Council* above.
1 See *Edwick v Sunbury-on-Thames UDC* (1965) 17 P & CR 1.

issue estoppel applies and, if another enforcement notice is issued, this point cannot be reopened on appeal.[2]

The formalities of service

Section 283 sets out the ways in which service may be effected. Where the usual or last known place of abode of the person is known or where the person has given an address for service, service can be effected by leaving the copy at that place or by sending it in a prepaid registered letter or by recorded delivery service (s 283(1)(b)(c)).[3] The methods set out in s 283 are not mandatory and it is clear that service can be effected by the ordinary postal service.[4] The advantage of complying with the methods set out in s 283 is that s 7 of the Interpretation Act 1978 will apply. This provides that where service is authorised to be made by post, unless the contrary intention appears, 'the service is deemed to be effected by properly addressing, prepaying and posting a letter containing the document and, unless the contrary is proved, to have been effected at the time at which the letter would be delivered in the ordinary course of post.'

The reference to proving the contrary in s 7 means that evidence can be admitted to show that service was not effected by the ordinary course of the post, where time is of the essence.[5] Yet in *Moody v Godstone RDC*[6] it was held that, in the case of enforcement notices, proof of receipt was not necessary even where there was evidence that the notice had not been received. However, as it is important that a copy of the notice should be served within a certain period (s 87(5)) and an appeal lodged before the notice takes effect, it can be argued that *Moody v Godstone* should be distinguished on its facts and that an individual should be able to lead evidence to show he never received the copy.[7] Service at a place of business to somebody else who promises to give the document to the person to be served, has been held to be good service[8] and in *Steeples v Derbyshire County Council*[9] Webster J found that where a box was placed at the end of a path, so inviting anyone having anything which did not require a signed receipt to leave it in the box, this constituted service in accordance with s 283(1)(b).

Where there are numerous occupiers of a site, it may be difficult to obtain all the names. Section 283(2) provides for service where names cannot be ascertained after reasonable inquiry. In such a case the notice can be addressed to 'the owner' or 'the occupier' and, among other methods of service, can be affixed conspicuously to some object on the premises. The fact that a fictitious name had been provided does not deprive the local planning

---

2 See *Thrasyvoulou v Secretary of State for the Environment* [1988] QB 809, [1988] 2 All ER 781, [1988] JPL 689.
3 In the case of an incorporated company or body, service is to be made to the secretary or clerk at their registered or principal office s 283(1)(d).
4 See *R v Secretary of State for the Environment and Bromley London Borough Council, ex p Jackson* [1987] JPL 790.
5 See *R v County of London Quarter Sessions Appeal Committee, ex p Rossi* [1956] 1 QB 682, [1956] 1 All ER 670.
6 [1966] 2 All ER 696, [1966] 1 WLR 1085.
7 See *R v County of London Quarter Sessions Appeal Committee, ex p Rossi* [1956] 1 QB 682, [1956] 1 All ER 670; *Hewitt v Leicester City Council* [1969] 2 All ER 802, [1969] 1 WLR 855, 20 P & CR 629; and *Maltglade Ltd v St Albans RDC* [1972] 3 All ER 129, [1972] 1 WLR 1230.
8 *Morecombe and Heysham Corpn v Warwick* (1958) 56 LGR 283, 9 P & CR 307.
9 [1984] 3 All ER 468, [1985] 1 WLR 256.

authority of this method of service.[10] Regulation 15 of the Town and Country Planning General Regulations 1976 lays down that the words 'Important—This Communication affects your Property' must be inscribed clearly and legibly on the notice. If a person appeals against a notice this prevents any later claim that this person was not properly served.[10a]

The content of an enforcement notice

There is no prescribed form of notice but model forms are set out in the Appendix to circular 38/1981. In terms of the 1971 Act and the Town and Country Planning (Enforcement Notices and Appeals) Regulations 1981 (the 1981 regulations) an enforcement notice must specify certain matters. These are:

1. the matters alleged to constitute a breach of planning control (s 87(6));
2. the steps required to be taken to remedy the breach or to make the development comply with the terms of any planning permission or alleviate injury to amenity (s 87(7) and 87(10));[11]
3. the date on which the notice is to take effect (s 87(13));
4. the period or periods within which any steps specified are to be carried out (s 87(8));[12]
5. the boundaries of the land to which the notice relates (reg 3 of the 1981 regulations);
6. the reasons why the authority consider it expedient to serve an enforcement notice (reg 3 of the 1981 regulations); and
7. an explanation of the rights of persons to appeal against the enforcement notice (reg 4 of the 1981 regulations).

Each of these matters is considered in detail below but it is necessary first to discuss the significance of the formalities of drafting a notice.

Since 1947 there has been much litigation about the way in which the prescribed matters should be dealt with in enforcement notices and in several decisions under the Town and Country Planning Act 1947 the courts adopted a very strict approach.[13] However, the substantial amendments to the legislation on enforcement notices which were effected in 1960 were such that Lord Denning was able to say in *Miller-Mead v Minister of Housing and Local Government*[14] that the legislature had 'disposed of the proposition that there must be a strict and rigid adherence to formalities.' This was done principally by making certain grounds of challenge exclusive to the Secretary of State, in that they could only be raised on appeal to him and by giving him a wide power to amend mistakes and other errors in a notice. The result has been that it will generally only be possible to argue that a notice is of no legal effect or a nullity, if it is clear from the face of the notice that the local

---

10 *Hammersmith London Borough Council v Winner Investments Ltd* (1968) 66 LGR 625, 20 P & CR 971.
10a See s 110(2) and *Marshall v Ruttle* [1989] JPL 681.
11 The alternatives were added by the Local Government and Planning (Amendment) Act, 1981 s 1 and Schedule 1, para 1.
12 As substituted by the Local Government and Planning (Amendment) Act, 1981 s 1 and Schedule 1, para 1.
13 See for example *Francis v Yiewsley and West Drayton UDC* [1958] 1 QB 478, [1957] 3 All ER 529; *Cater v Essex County Council* [1960] 1 QB 424, [1959] 2 All ER 213; and *East Riding County Council v Park Estate (Bridlington) Ltd* [1957] AC 223, [1956] 2 All ER 669.
14 [1963] 2 QB 196, [1963] 1 All ER 459.

planning authority have failed to comply with an important statutory requirement. In this the guiding principle is that laid down by Upjohn LJ in the *Miller-Mead* case. This is that the notice must tell the recipient fairly 'what he has done wrong and what he must do to remedy it.' Further in *Eldon Garages Ltd v Kingston-upon-Hull County Borough Council*[15] Templeman J accepted that notices must be construed against the history and background and state of knowledge of the recipient.[16]

Failure to draw up the notice as prescribed may mean that it will be quashed on appeal by the Secretary of State but it may also be possible to apply directly by way of judicial review for a declaration that the notice is invalid or to raise invalidity as a defence to a criminal prosecution. As explained below at p 350, difficult distinctions have been drawn between grounds of invalidity which can only be raised by way of appeal and those that can also be raised before the courts without going to appeal. Distinctions can further be made between faults which can be cured on appeal and faults which require the Secretary of State to quash on appeal.

1 Matters alleged to constitute a breach of control

An enforcement notice must specify the matters alleged to constitute a breach of planning control (s 87(6)).

It is probably still the case that the notice must make clear which of two types of breach of planning control is alleged; the notice must allege either that development has been carried out without a grant of planning permission or that there has been a breach of a condition subject to which planning permission was granted.[17] This used to be specifically required by the legislation but the wording was changed by the Town and Country Planning Act 1968. Nevertheless Templeman J in *Eldon Garages Ltd v Kingston-upon-Hull County Borough Council*[18] rejected the argument that the new wording meant that it was necessary only to set out the facts. Templeman J said:

'. . . the notice is null and void unless it makes plain what the plaintiffs have done wrong, meaning by that making it clear inter alia whether they have developed without planning permission or whether they have committed a breach of condition subject to which planning permission was granted.'

This necessity has been doubted[19] and in *Rochdale Metropolitan Borough*

15 [1974] 1 All ER 358, [1974] 1 WLR 276.
16 This could make it difficult for subsequent owners or occupiers to know exactly what was being required of the notice and so risk committing a criminal offence. In *Coventry Scaffolding Co (London) Ltd v Parker* [1987] JPL 127 Kerr LJ suggested that such fears were unlikely as you would need to prove an element of intention for a criminal offence under s 89 to be committed.
17 See *East Riding County Council v Park Estate (Bridlington) Ltd* [1957] AC 223, [1956] 2 All ER 669; *Francis v Yiewsley and West Drayton UDC* [1958] 1 QB 478, [1957] 3 All ER 529; *Miller-Mead v Minister of Housing and Local Government* [1963] 2 QB 196, [1963] 1 All ER 459; *Eldon Garages Ltd v Kingston-upon-Hull County Borough Council* [1974] 1 All ER 358, [1974] 1 WLR 276, *Garland v Minister of Housing and Local Government* (1968) 20 P & CR 93, per Lord Denning MR; and *Pilkington v Secretary of State for the Environment* [1974] 1 All ER 283, [1973] 1 WLR 1527, per Lord Widgery CJ.
18 [1974] 1 All ER 358, [1974] 1 WLR 276.
19 See *Pilkington v Secretary of State for the Environment* [1974] 1 All ER 283, [1973] 1 WLR 1527, per Lord Widgery CJ.

Council v Simmonds[20] the Divisional Court, without apparently being referred to *Eldon Garages*, concluded that it was not necessary to specify the nature of the breach and that all that was required was that the matters alleged to constitute the breach should be specified. Mr David Widdicombe QC, sitting as a deputy judge, in *Scott v Secretary of State and Bracknell District Council*[1] noted the conflict between the two decisions but did not have to choose between them. However, he did hold that it was not necessary to specify the exact category of unauthorised development in the notice; ie whether it was operational development or a material change of use. But it would seem that the notice should indicate sufficiently precisely what is the nature of the breach and so, in the case of the placing of a structure on land, make clear whether it is the placing that is the breach or the particular use to which the land or caravan is being put.[2] However, such a mistake will normally be capable of amendment on appeal.[3]

The difference between *Eldon Garages* and *Rochdale* is more apparent than real, as Templeman J in the *Eldon Garages* case emphasised that no special magic formula had to be used and the nature of the breach will usually be apparent from the notice as a whole and the general context. Thus in *Epping Forest District Council v Matthews*[4] Stephen Brown LJ held that a notice, which, by a slip, alleged both types of breach of control, was not a nullity as it was plain to the recipients that what was being alleged was the breach of condition. He held that this was an error which could be properly corrected on appeal as there was no fundamental ambiguity.

If the notice is valid on its face, it will not be a nullity because the allegation is shown to be false or incorrect. It used to be thought that a notice which alleges unauthorised development instead of a breach of condition or vice versa will have to be quashed on appeal. In *Kerrier District Council v Secretary of State for the Environment and Brewer*[5] Lord Lane CJ said:

'It is clearly established by many decisions that, if a planning authority wishes to serve an enforcement notice, it must decide whether the breach alleged is development without planning permission or failure to comply with some condition or limitation. If, on the facts of any particular case, the planning authority puts the case in the wrong pigeon-hole, the enforcement notice will be set aside.'

Yet in *Garland v Minister of Housing and Local Government*[6] it was said that it might be necessary to reconsider whether such a mistake made the notice irretrievably bad and in *R v London Borough of Tower Hamlets ex p Ahern*[6a] Roch J held that such a mistake was capable of correction on appeal. It has

---

20 (1980) 40 P & CR 432.
1 [1983] JPL 108.
2 See *Restormel Borough Council v Secretary of State for the Environment and Rabey* [1982] JPL 785.
3 *Woodspring District Council v Secretary of State for the Environment* (1982) 46 P & CR 425, [1982] JPL 784 and *Burner, Burner and Burner v Secretary of State for the Environment and South Hams District Council* [1983] JPL 459.
4 [1987] JPL 132.
5 (1980) 41 P & CR 284.
6 (1968) 20 P & CR 93 per Lord Denning at 101. Also see *West Oxfordshire District Council v Secretary of State for the Environment* [1988] JPL 324.
6a (1989) Times, 29 March.

also been held that a mistake as to the type of unauthorised development ca
be altered under the power of variation (s 88A(2)).[7]

Selecting the correct 'pigeon-hole' will not always be easy. In *Kerrie
District Council* (above), for example, planning permission was granted fo
the erection of a bungalow subject to a condition restricting the occupatio
of the dwelling to persons employed in agriculture. The bungalow when bui
was occupied by people who were not 'agricultural workers' within th
meaning of the condition. The planning authority served an enforcemen
notice on the occupiers alleging a breach of the condition. On appeal, th
Secretary of State found that the bungalow as built differed materially fron
that which had been approved. It included a basement not shown on th
plans attached to the grant of planning permission. The minister therefor
concluded that the bungalow had been built without planning permissio
and that, as the planning permission which had been granted had not bee
implemented, there could be no question of a breach of condition; th
enforcement notice would have to be quashed as it alleged the wrong type o
breach. The Divisional Court took a different view. They considered tha
without the grant of planning permission the bungalow would never hav
been built. 'Having relied on the permission to build a house, it would seem
strange that the occupiers should not be bound by the condition, particularl
if it was by reason of their own default that the plans were not complied with
If the house had complied with the plans, the occupiers would have beer
bound by the condition. They can hardly be in a better position because th
house did not comply with the plans.'

The decision in *Kerrier District Council* suggests that development carried
out on the strength of a grant of planning permission will bring any
conditions into operation and allow for their enforcement notwithstanding
that the development departs in a material way from the grant of permission.
Donaldson LJ reached a similar conclusion in *J Toomey Motors Ltd v
Secretary of State for the Environment*.[8] He did not think 'that it was possible
to repudiate a permission, where one was doing that which one had been
given planning permission to do, and there was no other basis upon which
one could do it'.

There will, of course, be cases where the development being carried on
departs to such an extent from any grant of planning permission that it will,
as a matter of fact and degree, have to be treated as development without
planning permission rather than as a breach of condition.

In *Hilliard v Secretary of State for the Environment*[9] the Divisional Court
accepted that it may be possible on occasions to allocate a breach of control
to either 'pigeon-hole', ie development without planning permission or the
breach of a condition or limitation. In that case planning permission had
been granted for the erection of a building on a farm subject to a condition
that the building should only be used for the storage of agricultural produce

---

7 See *Wealden District Council v Secretary of State for the Environment and Innocent* [1983] JPL
   234 and *Harrogate Borough Council v Secretary of State for the Environment* (1986) 55 P &
   CR 224, [1987] JPL 288; but compare *Copeland Borough Council v Secretary of State for the
   Environment* (1976) 31 P & CR 403.
8 [1981] JPL 418; affd by the Court of Appeal (1982) 264 Estates Gazette 141. See also *Clwyd
   County Council v Secretary of State for Wales and Welsh Aggregates* [1982] JPL 696.
9 (1978) 37 P & CR 129; see too the comments of Shaw LJ giving the judgment of the Court of
   Appeal (*loc cit*).

and farm implements in conjunction with the use of the farm for agricultural purposes. Subsequently, it was used for the storage and wholesale distribution of fruit and vegetables not produced on the farm. The local planning authority served an enforcement notice alleging an unauthorised material change of use. The appellant argued that the authority were wrong in law to assert a material change of use and that they ought to have alleged a breach of condition. This argument was rejected by the Divisional Court. Lord Widgery said:

'I think it was a strange administrative action to take the course which the council took but to say that it was wrong in law is something which I cannot accept. I think that if the council could make out their case either on breach of condition or intensification of activity it was up to them as a matter of law to choose which they wanted.'

Also in *West Oxfordshire District Council v Secretary of State for the Environment*[10] it was held that, where permission was granted to use a building as 'a house and meeting place for christians' subject to a condition that excluded its use for any other purpose and the building was then used as a school, it could either be alleged that the change was an unauthorised material change of use *or* a breach of the condition. It was also held that the permission was not spent or irrelevant because a material change had taken place. However, in *Camden London Borough Council v Backer and Aird*[11] Donaldson LJ expressed some doubt about whether the same activity could amount to both unauthorised development and a breach of a condition. In that case planning permission was granted for the erection of a second storey on a building for use as a loft. The permission was subject to a condition restricting the use of the loft to storage in connection with the residential use of the remainder of the premises. The loft was subsequently occupied as a separate residential unit and the planning authority served an enforcement notice alleging breach of the condition. The notice was quashed for reasons which are not material to the present discussion. However, Donaldson LJ went on to say that it seemed to him to be arguable 'that the condition applied and limited and restricted the loft user, and that it was only if you were using the premises as a loft otherwise than in accordance with the condition that then it can be said to be a breach of the condition'. If you were not using it as a loft at all, he would have thought it arguable that you were simply acting without planning permission.

In any case, in *Britt v Buckinghamshire County Council*[12] it was held that the planning authority could overcome any difficulty about selecting the correct 'pigeon-hole' by serving two enforcement notices making alternative allegations, provided that the authority made clear that the notices were served in the alternative.

The decision in *Copeland Borough Council v Secretary of State for the Environment*[13] illustrates the degree of precision that may be required. In that case planning permission had been granted for the erection of a house, the plans indicating that the roof was to be constructed of tiles of a particular

---

10 [1988] JPL 324.
11 [1982] JPL 516, CA.
12 (1962) 60 LGR 430, 14 P & CR 332. See too *Harding v Secretary of State for the Environment and Bridgnorth District Council* [1984] JPL 503.
13 (1976) 31 P & CR 403. And see the cases mentioned at pp 353–355 below.

colour. The wrong colour of tiles was used and the planning authority served an enforcement notice describing the breach as consisting of construction of the roof with the wrong colour of tiles. The court held that in reality the breach consisted of the erection of a building which did not comply with the approved plans; the enforcement notice contained what Lord Widgery described as a 'gross error' and was 'so groggy' that it could not be saved.

It would have seemed more logical to have treated the requirement as to the colour of the tiles as a 'limitation' with the result that the use of the wrong tiles would have been a breach of a limitation rather than totally unauthorised development. Indeed s 87(3)(b) provides that there is a breach of planning control 'if any conditions or limitations subject to which planning permission was granted have not been complied with' and s 87(9)(b) refers to steps for securing compliance with conditions or limitations. However, the word 'limitations' is not defined in the Act and in *Peacock Homes Ltd v Secretary of State for the Environment and Epsom and Ewell Borough Council*[14] Dillon LJ said that the word does not carry any technical meaning and would seem to be surplus in that any limitation on a planning permission would have to be imposed by way of a condition. He said, however, that insofar as it has any weight, the word 'limitations' would seem apt to cover a limitation in time subject to which planning permission is granted. But, in *Wilson v West Sussex County Council*[15] the Court of Appeal held that in a planning permission for an agricultural cottage, the word 'agricultural' had a functional significance and was to be construed as limiting the proposed building to one intended to be occupied by an agricultural worker or by a person engaged in agriculture.

So the position is that a limitation imposed in the description of the development granted governs what can be legally carried out on the land but is not treated as a 'limitation' as used in s 87 for the purposes of enforcement.

The courts have similarly taken a narrow interpretation of the limitation as used in the classes of permitted development in the General Development Order. They have taken the view that the limit on cubic capacity prescribed in relation to certain types of development permitted by the GDO is not a 'limitation' on the permission. Where the limit prescribed by the GDO has been exceeded, the whole of any such development is unauthorised and an enforcement notice should treat the breach as the carrying out of development without planning permission.[16]

So long as it specifies the alleged breach with sufficient clarity, an enforcement notice need not specify the former or base use of the land.[17] In

---

14 (1984) 83 LGR 686, 48 P & CR 20.
15 [1963] 2 QB 764, [1963] 1 All ER 751. Also see *Uttlesford District Council v Secretary of State for the Environment* [1989] JPL 685.
16 See *Garland v Minister of Housing and Local Government* (1968) 20 P & CR 93; *Copeland Borough Council v Secretary of State for the Environment* (1976) 31 P & CR 403; and *Rochdale Metropolitan Borough Council v Simmonds* (1980) 40 P & CR 432. Yet in *Cynon Valley Borough Council v Secretary of State for Wales* (1986) 85 LGR 36, [1986] JPL 760, the Court of Appeal held that, for the purposes of s 23(8), descriptions of the class of development in column (1) of Sch 1 to the GDO were limitations subject to which the development was granted; see Leach, 'Conditions and Limitations' [1986] JPL 584 for an analysis of the meaning of limitation.
17 See *Ross v Aberdeen County Council* 1955 SLT (Sh Ct) 65; *Clarke v Minister of Housing and Local Government* (1966) 64 LGR 346, 18 P & CR 82; and *City of Westminster v Secretary of State for the Environment* [1983] JPL 602. An error as to the previous use can be corrected on appeal—see appeal decision noted in [1982] JPL 121.

Ferris v Secretary of State for the Environment[18] it was held that, not only does the planning authority not have to specify in the notice the previous or base use, but that, if it does identify that base use, it need not be established by evidence. From *Bristol Stadium Ltd v Brown*[19] it would seem the enforcement notice must describe the general activity complained of but need not go into any great detail. There is no reason why an enforcement notice should not specify two separate breaches of planning control.[20] An enforcement notice is not a nullity merely because it overstates the case and alleges more than can be proved; any such error can be corrected on appeal.[1] It has also been held that a notice is not invalid because it is not stated that the alleged operational development has taken place within the last four years.[2]

2 *Steps required to be taken to remedy the breach of planning control*

Subsection (7) of s 87 requires an enforcement notice to specify:

(a) any steps required by the local planning authority to be taken in order to remedy the breach of planning control;
(b) any steps referred to in sub-s (10) which are required by the local planning authority to be taken for the purpose of 'making the development comply with the terms of any planning permission which has been granted in respect of the land' or 'removing or alleviating any injury to amenity which has been caused by the development.'

This wording was the result of the Local Government and Planning (Amendment) Act 1981 which substantially recast s 87. The old wording was that an enforcement notice shall specify 'the steps required by the authority ... for restoring the land to its condition before the development took place.'[3] This language suggested that the local planning authority had very little discretion as to the steps it could require. If it served an enforcement notice, the authority *had* to require the alleged breach of control to be completely remedied: no more and no less could be required. This 'Shylock' dilemma meant that it was taken that a local planning authority could not 'underenforce';[4] although there were some suggestions by the courts that this might be possible.[5]

Section 87(7) still uses the word *shall* but by substituting the term 'any works' for 'the works' it would seem to give the local planning authority a

18 (1988) 57 P & CR 127, [1988] JPL 777.
19 (1979) 252 Estates Gazette 803, [1980] JPL 107.
20 See appeal decision noted in [1979] JPL 547.
1 *Brooks and Burton v Secretary of State for the Environment* [1978] 1 All ER 733, [1977] 1 WLR 1294.
2 See *Harrogate Borough Council v Secretary of State for the Environment* (1986) 55 P & CR 224, [1987] JPL 288 where Webster J disagreed with Hodgson J in *Hughes v Secretary of State for the Environment and Fareham Borough Council* (1985) 51 P & CR 134, [1985] JPL 486. But note that reg 4 of the Town and Country Planning (Enforcement Notices and Appeals) Regulations 1981 requires that a notice shall be accompanied by a copy of ss 87 to 88B or a summary thereof, which should explain that the operational development is immune if it has taken place more than four years ago.
3 This was set out in s 87(6)(b).
4 *Garland v Minister of Housing and Local Government* (1968) 112 Sol Jo 841, 20 P & CR 93, CA.
5 See *Iddenden v Secretary of State for the Environment* [1972] 3 All ER 722, [1972] 1 WLR 1433; *Copeland Borough Council v Secretary of State for the Environment* (1976) 31 P & CR 403.

choice as to whether it wished to require any steps to be taken. If the planning authority did not want any steps to be taken to remedy the breach then there would be nothing to specify in the notice under that particular head. In such a situation the notice can instead of requiring steps to remedy the breach require either that the development must comply with the terms of any planning permission which has been granted or that steps be taken to remove or alleviate any injury which has been caused by the development.

Circular 26/81 (which sets out to explain the changes) argues that the former possibility deals with the difficulties highlighted by the *Copeland* decision.[6] Thus where a planning permission has been granted but a development is unauthorised, because of a failure to comply exactly with the terms of the grant, an enforcement notice can now allege that the development is totally unauthorised and then require, not complete demolition, but compliance with the terms of the planning permission. While the requirements relating to injury to amenity cover the situation where the local planning authority would be prepared to grant planning permission provided that steps are taken to make the development more environmentally acceptable. Thus the enforcement notice, having recited that unauthorised development has taken place, can then require remedial works. Circular 26/81 gives the examples of landscaping, tree planting, fencing or restriction on opening hours (see para 8). But the injury to the amenity which the works are alleviating must have been caused by the authorised development.[7] Grant has pointed out that because the new powers set out in s 87(1) are expressed as additions rather than alternatives, a local planning authority may still have to require steps to be taken to remedy the alleged breach.[8] However, the use of the term 'any steps' in s 87(7)(b) would suggest that the steps under this head are also at the discretion of the local planning authority. If this is right, a local planning authority has complete flexibility. It can require steps either under (a) or (b) or a combination of both.[9]

The amended wording also defines more precisely what is meant by 'steps to be taken in order to remedy the breach'. These are defined as steps for the purpose:

(a) of restoring the land to its condition before the development took place; or

(b) of securing compliance with the conditions or limitations subject to which planning permission was granted (s 87(9)).

Thus in *Green v Secretaries of State for the Environment and for Transport*[10] Woolf J held that where a dwellinghouse was being constructed rather than a calf-rearing unit, it came within s 87(9)(a) rather than s 87(9)(b) as the development was not authorised by Class VI of the GDO and there was no question of there being a non-compliance with conditions or limitations.

6   Ibid.
7   So you cannot extraneously require improvements unconnected with the development; see *Bath City Council v Secretary of State for the Environment* [1983] JPL 737.
8   See *Urban Planning Law* at pp 412–13.
9   The courts, as yet, have not been asked to make a ruling on the effect of the new provisions but the equivalent provisions regarding listed building enforcement notices were discussed in *Bath City Council v Secretary of State for the Environment* [1983] JPL 737. However, these provisions make clear that where restoration is impracticable or undesirable, remedial works are an alternative.
10 [1985] JPL 119.

The new wording also makes clear that under these heads there can be included steps for the demolition or alteration of any buildings or works, the discontinuance of any use of land or the carrying-out of any buildings or other operations (s 87(9)(b)(i) to (iii)). This would seem to indicate that where a material change of use has involved changes to the physical state of the land, then the notice can require operational-type works to be carried out.[11]

There is also now special provision for breaches of control by the deposit of refuse or waste materials on land (which will normally be a material change of use; see p 140 above). A notice may require that the contours of the resulting waste tip be modified by altering the gradient of its sides in a specified manner (s 87(11)). So where there has been unlawful tipping, the local planning authority will be able to require the sides of the tip to be modified.[12]

Where buildings or works have been carried out without permission and an enforcement notice has required remedial steps under s 87(10)(b), planning permission is deemed to be granted for the retention of the building or works which have resulted from complying with the notice (s 87(16)). The section does not specify any procedure for such a deemed grant of permission and circular 26/81 suggests that all local planning authorities have to do is to notify the recipient on a copy of the enforcement notice that permission is deemed to be granted at the time when, in the local planning authority's view, the required steps have been taken to completion. It also suggests that the deemed grant be entered in the enforcement notice and stop notice register, when it takes effect (para 14).

Where the enforcement notice is requiring steps to be taken to remedy the breach of control, the notice must not require *more* than is necessary to restore land to the condition it was before the unauthorised development or to comply with the condition which has been broken.

In *Cleaver v Secretary of State for the Environment and Warwick District Council*,[13] an enforcement notice described the breach of control as 'the carrying out of unauthorised development, namely the reception, storage and breaking up of any vehicle, metal, wood, plastic, asbestos or product of metal, wood, plastic or asbestos or any other such items'. The notice went on to require the recipient, amongst other things, to 'discontinue the operation of a trade or business comprising the sale or exchange of any such item or material'. The notice was successfully challenged in the Divisional Court on the ground that the steps required to be taken exceeded what was necessary to remedy the breach. In particular, while the notice required the recipient to discontinue business activities, the breach alleged in the notice made no reference to such activities. Whilst the steps proscribed the sale of items of the sort described in the breach, the notice did not relate the retail activity to the storage and breaking business.

The steps required to be taken in a notice may also be treated as excessive if they purport to restrict established rights. This is sometimes referred to as the

11 See *Murfitt v Secretary of State for the Environment and East Cambridgeshire District Council* (1980) 40 P & CR 254; *Perkins v Secretary of State for the Environment and the Rother District Council* [1981] JPL 755; and *Somak Travel Ltd v Secretary of State for the Environment* (1987) 55 P & CR 250, [1987] JPL 630 and see p 324 below.
12 See *Rhymney Valley District Council v Secretary of State for Wales and Isaac* [1985] JPL 27.
13 [1981] JPL 38.

'*Mansi* rule' after the decision in *Mansi v Elstree RDC*.[14] In that case an enforcement notice alleged a material change in the use of a glasshouse from use for agriculture to use for the sale of goods and required the latter use to be discontinued. The appellant argued that the notice purported to restrict his activities further than it legitimately might by forbidding all sales, including subsidiary sales of home-grown produce and other goods which had previously been carried on quite lawfully in association with the use of the glasshouse for agricultural purposes. This argument was accepted by the court, Widgery J saying:

> 'True that use was a subsidiary one, but nevertheless it should be protected and, in my judgment, this appeal should be allowed to the extent that the decision in question should be sent back to the Minister with a direction that he ought to amend the notice so as to safeguard the appellants' established right . . .'

This decision was followed in *Newport v Secretary of State for the Environment and Bromley London Borough*[15] in which Waller LJ commented that 'it is important, where criminal prosecution is a possibility, that the limits of what can and what cannot be done should be set out.'

Just what rights are to be safeguarded in the notice may be difficult to determine, particularly where a material change through intensification has occurred. In *de Mulder v Secretary of State for the Environment*,[16] enforcement notices were served in respect of an intensification of use and required the recipients to reduce the activities on the site to their level in 1970, being the point in time when it was alleged that the intensification had become material. Lord Widgery CJ said:

> 'In those so-called intensification cases the material change of use occurs at a point when the landowner has already exercised every right which the planning Acts give him, in other words it is not until the material change of use occurs that enforcement action can be taken, and when the enforcement action is taken any latitude of the kind to which I referred in *Mansi's* case has already been absorbed and enjoyed. It seems to me, therefore, in the present case if the Secretary of State is allowed to do as he has purported to do, namely, to cut the appellant down to the level of general dealing appropriate in April 1970, he will on the way, as it were, have made the necessary adjustment required in *Mansi's* case.'

Although the '*Mansi* rule' needs to be borne in mind when specifying the steps to be taken to remedy a breach of planning control, an enforcement notice must be read as a whole and there are circumstances in which it will be

14 (1964) 16 P & CR 153. See M Purdue, 'The Complexities of Enforcing the Development Control System and the *Mansi* Rule' [1981] JPL 154.
15 (1980) 40 P & CR 261. See also *Trevors Warehouses Ltd v Secretary of State for the Environment* (1972) 23 P & CR 215; *Day and Mid-Warwickshire Motors Ltd v Secretary of State for the Environment and Solihull Metropolitan District Council* (1979) 78 LGR 27; *Lee v Bromley London Borough Council* (1983) 45 P & CR 342, [1982] JPL 778; *Haigh v Secretary of State for the Environment and Kirklees Borough Council* [1983] JPL 40; *Choudhury v Secretary of State for the Environment* (1983) 265 Estates Gazette 345, [1983] JPL 231; and *Denham Developments Ltd v Secretary of State for the Environment* (1983) 47 P & CR 598.
16 [1974] QB 792, [1974] 1 All ER 776.

unnecessary for the notice to spell out established rights. It is not, it seems, 'necessary for the Secretary of State or the local authority to have to go so far as to put in an enforcement notice that which must be obvious to everybody'.[17] In particular, it is not necessary for the notice to make specific provision for safeguarding a use which is obviously ancillary to the permitted use of the premises. In *Monomart (Warehouses) Ltd v Secretary of State for the Environment*,[18] for example, planning permission had been granted, *inter alia*, for a 'builders' merchants' warehouse'. The appellants used the premises as a 'do-it-yourself supermarket', retailing builders' supplies. The planning authority served an enforcement notice requiring the discontinuance of the retail sales. The Secretary of State on appeal added the words 'except as may be incidental to the use of the premises as a builders' merchants' warehouse'. The Divisional Court considered that the addition was not strictly necessary. Construing the notice as a whole, it was clear that the breach with which the notice was concerned was retail sales in excess of retail sales permissible as ancillary or incidental to the main use. It was quite impossible to make sense of the notice unless it was assumed that the reference to the retail sale of goods was a reference to the retail sale of goods in excess of the rights which might be incidental to the warehouse use.

Similarly, in *Jones v Secretary of State for the Environment*,[19] Lord Widgery stated that he could see 'no reason in law or commonsense' why an enforcement notice should make provision for safeguarding an ancillary use which had ceased by the time enforcement had become necessary. This is presumably because the steps required to be taken can only relate to the alleged breach of control and if an activity is not being carried on at the time when the breach occurs, then there can be no question of the activity being discontinued.

It therefore would seem from the cases that a distinction has to be made between an established subsidiary use, ie a use which is not ancillary to another main use and ancillary uses which have been or could be carried out on the site. In the case of the former the notice always should make clear that the established subsidiary use is excluded from the ambit of the notice. While in the case of the latter, in *Haigh v Secretary of State for the Environment and Kirklees Borough Council*[20] McCullough J said that it was only desirable that it should be made plain that ancillary uses were not being forbidden and it might not always be necessary.[1]

Clearly, there will be occasions when it may be difficult to determine whether the '*Mansi* rule' applies. In *Cord v Secretary of State for the Environment and Torbay Borough Council*[2] Donaldson LJ suggested that:

'It might be a useful test, where this question arose, to write out the terms of the enforcement notice and then to write below it the things which the person concerned was entitled to do without further planning permission.

17 *Cord v Secretary of State for the Environment and Torbay Borough Council* [1981] JPL 40, per Kilner-Brown J.
18 (1977) 34 P & CR 305. See also *Cord* (above), and *North Sea Land Equipment v Secretary of State for the Environment* (1981) 262 Estates Gazette 668, [1982] JPL 384.
19 (1974) 28 P & CR 362.
20 [1983] JPL 40.
1 So it was held in that case that on appeal the Secretary of State should have at least considered whether it was necessary to use his powers to amend the notice; see p 350 below.
2 Ibid.

They should then consider whether the second paragraph derogated from the first paragraph. If one was plainly a derogation from the other there was a strong case for writing it into the enforcement notice for the avoidance of doubt. But if the chronicle of matters which the landowner was entitled to do did not constitute a derogation from the requirements of the enforcement notice it was a waste of time and might even, in some circumstances, be a source of confusion to specify what was obvious.'

Finally in *Swinbank v Secretary of State for the Environment and Darlington Borough Council*[3] David Widdicombe QC (sitting as a deputy judge) suggested that future litigation might be avoided if in enforcement notices concerned with change of use a statement were to be included that the enforcement notice did not affect any existing use rights or uses which were not development.[4] He added that:

'If adopted, it should serve to bring the *Mansi* series of cases, which now runs to some fifteen or sixteen reported decisions to an end, a consummation devoutly to be desired.'

The '*Mansi* rule' does not cause the same problems to cases involving operational development (as opposed to cases involving change of use). A local planning authority may, for example, quite properly require the demolition of the whole of an unauthorised extension to a house; there is no obligation upon the authority to safeguard in the enforcement notice that part of the extension which would have been permitted under the general development order. This is because the building of the extension is treated as one operation and not as a series of separate operations.[5] On the other hand, if there are two buildings on a site, one unauthorised and the other authorised, obviously the local planning authority can only require the unauthorised to be demolished.

In the case of a material change of use, there is no question of requiring the former use of land to be resumed. As Lord Justice-Clerk (Lord Grant) pointed out in the Scottish decision, *Paul v Ayrshire County Council*,[6] while the planning authority may enforce the discontinuance of a new use and the restoration of land to its previous state, there is no power to compel the restoration and continuance of the previous use.

The steps required also must not be hopelessly ambiguous, otherwise it seems that the notice will be a nullity, but the authorities show that the courts are appreciative of the problems of local planning authorities and will not strike down a notice just because its wording may result in some doubtful cases.[7]

---

3   (1987) 55 P & CR 371, [1987] JPL 781.
4   On the facts of the case he held that it was not necessary to protect the right to agricultural use as it was clear from the terms of the notice that it was not aimed at farming activities.
5   *Prengate Properties Ltd v Secretary of State for the Environment* (1973) 71 LGR 373, 25 P & CR 311; *Ewen Developments Ltd v Secretary of State for the Environment and North Norfolk District Council* [1980] JPL 404; *Rochdale Metropolitan Borough Council v Simmonds* (1980) 40 P & CR 432 and *Green v Secretaries of State for the Environment and for Transport* (1984) 271 Estates Gazette 551, [1985] JPL 119.
6   1964 SC 116, 1964 SLT 207.
7   See *Ivory v Secretary of State for the Environment and North Hertfordshire District Council* [1985] JPL 796 where Kennedy J applied the Court of Appeal's approach in *Alderson v Secretary of State for the Environment* (1984) 49 P & CR 307, [1984] JPL 429 to conditions. However, the courts may be stricter in the case of a criminal prosecution; see *Warrington Borough Council v Garvey* [1988] JPL 752.

In particular the courts have not been prepared to hold enforcement notices to be nullities, which fail to spell out precisely the degree of use or the condition of the land *before* the unauthorised development took place. In *Ormston v Horsham RDC*,[8] for example, the Court of Appeal held that a notice which required the restoration of land to its condition before unauthorised development took place but did not specify the land's condition prior to the development was sufficiently certain. The owner knew what the site was like before he began the development and could therefore restore it accordingly. In *Bath City Council v Secretary of State for the Environment*[9] it was held (in the context of a listed building enforcement notice) that there would be nothing uncertain in a requirement to restore the roof of a building to its condition prior to the carrying out of unauthorised works. Woolf J said that it would not be open to the landowner in such a case to say that he could not remember the precise state of the roof at the appropriate time; in such circumstances it may, he said, be an indirect consequence of unauthorised development that the person who carried out the works has to carry out more work to comply with an enforcement notice than is strictly required by the notice, but that would not be a ground for challenging the validity of the notice—the person who carried out the unauthorised works should be in the best position to know what steps are required to rectify the breach and if he does not know, he cannot complain if it means he has to do more work than would otherwise be necessary.

In *Trevors Warehouses Ltd v Secretary of State for the Environment*[10] Lord Widgery CJ upheld the validity of a notice which required the discontinuance of a use except to the extent to which it had been carried on prior to 1 January 1964. Lord Widgery CJ accepted that he saw some practical difficulty in determining precisely what had been the extent of the use but considered that there was no practical alternative and that the notice was not ambiguous. On the other hand in *Lee v Bromley London Borough Council*[11] May LJ appeared to hold that where there had been an appeal on the grounds that there had not been a breach of planning control, the Secretary of State or his inspector should make a finding which was couched in sufficiently precise terms to enable the user of land to know clearly that which he is and is not permitted to do. It was not made clear how this left cases where there was no appeal or where the occupier did not have available the inspector's report containing such findings.[12] Also s 88B(1)(c) specifically provides that the Secretary of State may on an appeal determine the purpose for which land can lawfully be used and in *Ferris v Secretary of State for the*

---

8 (1965) 17 P & CR 105.
9 (1983) 47 P & CR 663. See too *Lipson v Secretary of State for the Environment* (1976) 75 LGR 361, 33 P & CR 95 and *Eldon Garages Ltd v Kingston-upon-Hull County Borough Council* [1974] 1 All ER 358, [1974] 1 WLR 276, per Templeman J.
10 (1972) 23 P & CR 215. Also see *Bristol Stadium Ltd v Brown* (1979) 252 Estates Gazette 803, [1980] JPL 107; and *Rhymney Valley District Council v Secretary of State for Wales and Isaac* [1985] JPL 27.
11 (1983) 45 P & CR 342, [1983] JPL 778.
12 Also see Scottish case of *McNaughton v Peter McIntyre (Clyde) Ltd* High Court of Judiciary (21 March 1978 unreported) but see 1981 SPLP 15) where an enforcement notice which required the removal of material from the foreshore was held bad for lack of specification as it was unclear how much material had to be removed.

Environment[13] it was held that the use of the word 'may' meant that the matter was discretionary. A determination had to be requested and could be refused if there was not sufficient information. Also in *R v Runnymede Borough Council, ex p Seehra*,[14] Schiemann J, after a detailed review of the authorities, held that it was admissible to use wording, in both enforcement notices and stop notices, which was such that matters of fact and degree were incorporated in them. There, an enforcement notice had been issued which alleged a material change from residential to mixed residential and religious purposes and included a requirement to cease using the land except for the purposes incidental to the employment of a dwellinghouse. Schiemann J accepted that such a wording could mean that an occupier of the house in order to avoid possible prosecution might refrain from doing things he was perfectly entitled to carry out, but he nevertheless held that the notices were not void and did, within the spirit of the authorities, give an indication as to what had to be done.

While there are some doubts as to the level of specificity required, there is no doubt that an enforcement notice which is very imprecise or ambiguous as to the steps to be taken will be treated as a nullity. In *Metallic Protectives Ltd v Secretary of State for the Environment*,[15] for example, an enforcement notice alleged a breach of a condition which provided in effect that no nuisance was to be caused to the residential properties in the area by reason of the emission from a factory of noise, vibration, smoke, smell, fumes, soot, ash, dust or grit. The notice required the appellants to install satisfactory sound-proofing for a compressor and to take all possible action to minimise the effects of using acrylic paint. The Divisional Court considered that these requirements were far too imprecise; the notice was so defective as to be a nullity and incapable of amendment. Similarly, in *Hounslow London Borough Council v Secretary of State for the Environment and Indian Gymkhana Club*,[16] the Divisional Court concluded that two enforcement notices which required the recipients 'to comply or seek compliance' with a condition attached to a planning permission did not tell the recipients with sufficient clarity what steps they had to take and were so ambiguous as to be nullities.

Then in *Dudley Bowers Amusements Enterprises Ltd v Secretary of State for the Environment*[17] where an enforcement notice required an amusement arcade to cease during the period of 'summer time', it was felt that 'summer time' could have three different meanings and was 'hopelessly ambiguous'.

In this regard there is an important distinction between the requirements which are totally ambiguous and steps which exceed what can in fact be required. The first is grounds for holding the notice to be a nullity, while in the case of the second, it is only a ground for holding that the notice is invalid on an appeal (s 88(2)(9)) and it may be that the error can be corrected on an appeal[18] (see p 350).

---

13 (1988) 57 P & CR 127, [1988] JPL 777.
14 (1986) 151 JP 80, [1987] JPL 283.
15 [1976] JPL 166.
16 [1981] JPL 510. See also *Sykes v Secretary of State for the Environment* [1981] 1 All ER 954, [1981] 1 WLR 1092, 42 P & CR 19.
17 (1985) 52 P & CR 365, 278 Estates Gazette 313.
18 See *Epping Forest District Council v Scott* (1985) 53 P & CR 79, [1986] JPL 603.

3 *The date on which the notice is to take effect*

An enforcement notice must specify the date on which it is to take effect (s 87(13))[19] and, as explained earlier, the local planning authority must ensure that copies are served 28 days before it takes effect (ss 87(5) and (13)).

If there is an appeal to the Secretary of State against an enforcement notice, the notice is of no effect pending the final determination or withdrawal of the appeal (s 88(10)). It seems, however, that it is unnecessary to state in the notice that the specified date is subject to the provisions of s 88(10) although in the interests of clarity this may be desirable.[20]

4 *The period for compliance with the notice*

In addition to specifying the date on which it is to take effect, an enforcement notice must also specify the period for compliance with the notice (s 87(8)). In other words, it must state the period, commencing with the date when the notice takes effect, within which the steps specified in the notice are required to be taken. Because local planning authorities can now require a range of steps to be taken to remedy a single breach of planning control, s 87(8) also provides for a notice to specify that different steps be taken within different periods of time. It is a ground of appeal that the period specified for compliance falls short of what should reasonably be allowed.

It seems that there will be sufficient compliance with the statutory provisions if a notice requires the steps to be taken by a certain date rather than within a specified period. All that is required is that the period should be capable of deduction within the four corners of the notice, if necessary by subtracting the date on which the notice is to take effect from the date specified for compliance.[1] However, it still appears that the notice must make clear both the date on which it is to take effect and the time within which the steps required by the notice are to be taken; a notice which does not specify both of these is a nullity. Thus in *Burgess v Jarvis and Sevenoaks RDC*[2] an enforcement notice which required the demolition of houses built without planning permission 'within five years after the date of service' of the notice but which did not specify the date when the notice took effect was held to be bad.

5 *Boundaries of the land*

An enforcement notice must specify the precise boundaries of the land to which it relates, whether by reference to a plan or in some other way.[3] The Secretary of State considers that this identification is best done by a plan

19 It would seem that a notice which fails to do so is invalid; see *Burgess v Jarvis and Sevenoaks RDC* [1952] 2 QB 41, [1952] 1 All ER 592; and *Swallow and Pearson v Middlesex County Council* [1953] 1 All ER 580, [1953] 1 WLR 422.
20 *King and King v Secretary of State for the Environment and Nuneaton Borough Council* [1981] JPL 813.
 1 *King and King v Secretary of State for the Environment and Nuneaton Borough Council* (above).
 2 [1952] 2 QB 41, [1952] 1 All ER 592; followed in *Mead v Chelmsford RDC* [1953] 1 QB 32, sub nom *Mead v Plumtree* [1952] 2 All ER 723; *Swallow and Pearson v Middlesex County Council* [1953] 1 All ER 580, [1953] 1 WLR 422; and *Godstone RDC v Brazil* [1953] 2 All ER 763; [1953] 1 WLR 1102.
 3 See reg 3 of the 1981 regulations.

attached to the notice which indicates the boundaries of the land by means of a coloured line.[4] In *Coventry Scaffolding Co (London) Ltd v Parker*[5] the Divisional Court held that an enforcement notice which had failed to specify the property to which the notice related was not a nullity as the persons to whom the notice was addressed knew it was aimed at a particular property. This concerned a notice issued before the regulation was made requiring the boundaries to be identified but it does suggest that such an error does not automatically invalidate the notice and that it could be cured on appeal.[6] However, in *Warrington Borough Council v Garvey*[7] Judge Wooley held that the word precise must mean what it said and he held a notice to be invalid which did not identify the land precisely.

In determining whether a material change of use has occurred, regard must be had to the correct 'planning unit'.[8] And when an enforcement notice is served alleging a material change of use, it is, as was said by Widgery LJ in *Hawkey v Secretary of State for the Environment:*[9] 'always open to the landowner to contend, if he can, that the planning unit is something larger than that specified in the notice and that, if the true planning unit is looked at, no material change of use has occurred at all' (and that there has, therefore, been no breach of planning control).

Although the enforcement notice has to specify the land on which it is alleged that a breach of planning control has taken place, it is not essential that the enforcement notice should identify the planning unit.[10] Nor is it necessary that the enforcement notice be directed towards the whole planning unit; it is open to the authority to bring enforcement proceedings either in respect of the whole planning unit or in respect of some smaller portion on which the alleged breach of planning control has occurred.[11] In *de Mulder v Secretary of State for the Environment*[12] Lord Widgery CJ put the matter thus:

'It is in my judgment quite proper ... for the planning authority to say: although the material change of use is to be observed all over the site, the activities which give rise to that are in one place or in one corner, and we will direct our enforcement action to the place where the offensive activity takes place.'

In *de Mulder* the planning authority had, however, served a number of enforcement notices, each directed to a different part of a farm which was the appropriate planning unit. The separate enforcement notices had the effect of restricting the appellants' use of the land to the intensity of use existing in

---

4 See circular 38/81, para 31.
5 [1987] JPL 127.
6 See also *Patel v Betts* (1977) 243 Estates Gazette 1003, [1978] JPL 109.
7 [1988] JPL 752.
8 The question of the appropriate planning unit is discussed in ch 5.
9 (1971) 22 P & CR 610.
10 See *Hawkey* (above).
11 See *Hawkey* (above) and *Morris v Secretary of State for the Environment* (1975) 31 P & CR 216. See too ministerial decisions noted in [1976] JPL 120, 590 and 710, [1977] JPL 264, and [1978] JPL 338.
12 [1974] QB 792, [1974] 1 All ER 776.

each of the separate areas on a particular date, whereas if a single enforcement notice relating to the whole planning unit had been served, the
appellants would have been able to increase the intensity of use in any one of
those separate areas so long as the overall intensity of use of the planning
unit lid not exceed the level existing on the date in question. The Divisional
Cou t held that a planning authority could not, by arbitrarily dividing up a
site into a number of smaller areas and directing a separate enforcement
notice to each of those smaller areas, impose more severe restrictions on a
landowner than might have been imposed on him by a single enforcement
notice applicable to the whole planning unit and that in this case the separate
enforcement notices were therefore unduly restrictive.[13]

In *Thomas David (Porthcawl) Ltd v Penybont RDC*[14] the Court of Appeal
employed the concept of the appropriate 'planning unit' in order to determine the question whether too wide an area had been specified in an
enforcement notice concerned with unauthorised operations.[15] In that case a
company had for some time carried on, without the grant of planning
permission, mining operations on two small areas of land. The enforcement
notice served by the planning authority was not, however, confined to the
two areas actually being worked but required the company to discontinue[16]
the extraction of sand and gravel from any part of a much larger area which
included the two small areas. A licence granted by the owners of the land
entitled the company to work an area rather larger than that to which the
notice applied. The company argued that the notice was invalid in that it
should have been confined to the two areas actually worked. The Court of
Appeal held that the notice was valid; as the planning unit was not confined
to the two small areas worked but 'extended to the whole area which might
be regarded as suitable for excavation by the developers if they could get
planning permission for it', the notice was not too wide. In the Divisional
Court[17] Lord Widgery CJ declared:

'I do not think that it can possibly have been the intention of Parliament
that, when an enforcement notice is served in regard to mining operations
such as the present, the effect of the enforcement notice should be
meticulously restricted to the very square yardage which is being the
subject of an actual cut by the shovel or bulldozer as the case may be. I
think it is permissible and indeed right in mining operation cases to ask
whether the land on which the actual cut is taken is not in truth and in fact
part of a wider area which is being started in development by the particular
immediate activity referred to. If as a matter of fact and common sense it is
clear that the first cut is a cut relative to a larger area, then it is right for the

13 See also *Burdle v Secretary of State for the Environment* [1972] 3 All ER 240, [1972] 1 WLR
1207, per Bridge J; *TLG Building Materials Ltd v Secretary of State for the Environment*
(1980) 41 P & CR 243, and *Dunton Park Caravan Site Ltd v Secretary of State for the
Environment and Basildon District Council* [1981] JPL 511.
14 [1972] 3 All ER 1092, [1972] 1 WLR 1526.
15 Prior to this case the concept of the planning unit had been employed only in cases involving
change of use.
16 Generally, an enforcement notice cannot require the discontinuance of 'operations' but the
discontinuance of mining operations is treated for this purpose as a use of land (see Town
and Country Planning (Minerals) Regulations 1971, reg 3(b)).
17 [1972] 1 WLR 354.

tribunal of fact to determine if it thinks fit that the larger area is a planning unit for present purposes.'

6 Reasons for notice

In any enforcement notice they serve, the local planning authority must specify the reasons why they consider it expedient to serve the notice.[18] The Secretary of State regards this as an important initial means of enabling the recipient of a notice to understand from the outset the reasons why the planning authority have taken this course of action. It also means that a person who could be affected by the notice might apply for judicial review on the grounds that the reasons were outside the scope of planning or in some way showed an abuse of power.[19]

7 Explanatory note

An enforcement notice has to be accompanied by an explanatory note which shall include:

(1) a copy of ss 87 to 88B of the 1971 Act or a summary of those sections. In particular it must be explained that there is a right of appeal to the Secretary of State and that any appeal must be in writing and set out the possible grounds of appeal;
(2) notification that an appeal to the Secretary of State must be supported by a statement in writing within 28 days of being required by the Secretary of State and that this statement must specify the grounds and the supporting facts of the appeal.

The terms of this notice are prescribed by reg 4 of the 1981 regulations.

Crown land

Provided that the Crown grants consent to the service of an enforcement notice, enforcement action is competent against a person who holds an interest in Crown land (see 1971 Act, s 266(1)(b)). Any person entitled to occupy Crown land by virtue of a contract in writing is deemed to have an interest in the land for this purpose.[20]

Where unauthorised development was carried out on Crown land by a person without an interest in the land (in Parliament the example mentioned was that of mobile snack bars operating on laybys on trunk roads) it was formerly impossible to take enforcement action. The Town and Country Planning Act 1984 seeks to close this loophole by providing in s 3 that a planning authority may, with the consent of the appropriate government department, serve a 'special enforcement notice'. This is somewhat narrower in scope than an ordinary enforcement notice and the grounds of appeal are more restricted. The Secretary of State is empowered to make regulations applying to Crown land such provisions of the 1971 Act as he considers expedient.[1]

---

18 See reg 3 of the 1981 regulations.
19 *Davey v Spelthorne Borough Council* [1984] AC 262, [1983] 3 All ER 278.
20 See Town and Country Planning Act 1984, s 4.
 1 See s 287(2) of the 1971 Act as applied by s 6(2) of the Town and Country Planning Act 1984 and the Town and Country Planning (Special Enforcement Notices) Regulations 1984.

Register of enforcement notices, etc

Section 92A of the 1971 Act[2] imposes a duty on all district planning authorities and on metropolitan districts or London boroughs to maintain a register of enforcement notices and stop notices. The information to be kept in this register is prescribed by art 28 of the General Development Order.

B IMMUNITY FROM ENFORCEMENT ACTION

The question whether the operations or uses being carried on upon land are subject to the risk of enforcement action will clearly be an important factor in any transaction affecting that land. In order to introduce some certainty into this area, it has been considered desirable to impose what might be described as 'limitation periods' on the power to take enforcement action. Somewhat paradoxically, therefore, it can sometimes be advantageous for a developer to seek to prove that a breach of planning control has persisted for some time.

Limitation periods

For this purpose breaches of planning control may be divided into the following five categories:

1. An enforcement notice may only be served within four years of the carrying out of an unauthorised building, engineering, mining or other operation (s 87(4)(a)).

Building and engineering operations may be made up of many component parts. The building of a house, for example, might be said to comprise the laying of foundations, the construction of walls and the placing of the roof. However, it seems that, subject to any special provision in the planning permission itself, building or engineering operations are to be treated as a single operation and not as a multitude of operations.[3] Thus the building of a house will be treated as one operation. The difficulty is that the various parts of the operation may be carried out over a period of time and this has given rise to some uncertainty as to the date from which the four year period is to be calculated. The reference in s 87(4)(a) to 'the carrying out' of the operation suggests that if activities are to be treated as one operation then time runs from the date of substantial completion and it now seems clear that this is the correct approach.[4] In *Ewen Developments Ltd v Secretary of State for the Environment and North Norfolk District Council*,[5] for example, the local

---

2 Inserted by the Local Government and Planning (Amendment) Act 1981, s 1 and Schedule, para 6.
3 See *Ewen Developments Ltd v Secretary of State for the Environment and North Norfolk District Council* [1980] JPL 404; *Copeland Borough Council v Secretary of State for the Environment* (1976) 31 P & CR 403. See too *Garland v Minister of Housing and Local Government* (1968) 20 P & CR 93, and ministerial decisions noted in *Selected Enforcement and Allied Appeals*, pp 48–52. Compare, however, *F Lucas & Sons Ltd v Dorking and Horley RDC* (1964) 62 LGR 491, 17 P & CR 111, and the judgment of Stephenson LJ in *Thomas David (Porthcawl) Ltd v Penybont RDC* [1972] 3 All ER 1092, [1972] 1 WLR 1526.
4 See *Howes v Secretary of State for the Environment and Devon County Council* [1984] JPL 439; and *Ewen Developments Ltd v Secretary of State for the Environment and North Norfolk District Council* [1980] JPL 404.
5 Above.

planning authority served an enforcement notice requiring the removal of a number of embankments which had been constructed over a period of years. The developer argued that he could only be required to reduce the height of the embankments to the height at which they were four years before the enforcement proceedings began. The Divisional Court rejected this argument, holding that the construction of the embankments should be viewed as one operation and that individual elements of the construction could not be singled out as time-barred.

It seems that the question whether particular building works should be viewed as a single operation or as two or more separate operations will normally depend on the appearance of the building in question.[6] So a building operation will not normally be considered complete until the roof has been put on.[7]

Although time appears to run from the date of substantial completion of building and engineering operations, there is nothing to prevent a local planning authority serving an enforcement notice as soon as unauthorised operations are started.

Different considerations would seem to apply as regards the 'limitation period' for mining operations. In *Thomas David (Porthcawl) Ltd v Penybont RDC*,[8] the Court of Appeal had to consider the effect of an enforcement notice which required a company to discontinue mining operations carried out without the grant of planning permission on two areas of land. The company claimed that as the extraction of sand and gravel from the two areas had begun more than four years before service of the enforcement notice, the operations were immune from enforcement action and the company was entitled to continue mining operations in the future within the two areas. The Court of Appeal held that in mining operations each shovelful extracted or each cut by the bulldozer is a separate act of development in itself and is not merely part of one continuing development; in this case, therefore, the court held that although those mining operations which had taken place more than four years before service of the enforcement notice were not subject to enforcement action, the enforcement notice had been validly served in respect of extractions made within the four years preceding the notice. Tipping operations are in a sense the reverse of mining operations. However, in a ministerial decision the substantial completion test was applied to tipping operations which amounted to 'other operations' rather than a material change of use and it was found that the operations were immune from enforcement as they had been substantially completed more than four years before the service of the enforcement notice.[9]

It would seem that there will be occasions when building, engineering, mining or other operations which are themselves immune from enforcement action under the four year limitation period may nonetheless be caught by an enforcement notice alleging an unauthorised material change of use. In *Murfitt v Secretary of State for the Environment and East Cambridgeshire*

---

6 See *Worthy Fuel Injection Ltd v Secretary of State and Southampton City Council* [1983] JPL 173.
7 See, for example, ministerial decisions [1982] JPL 55 and [1984] JPL 601.
8 [1972] 3 All ER 1092, [1972] 1 WLR 1526.
9 [1987] JPL 520.

District Council[10] an enforcement notice required the discontinuance of the use of a site for the parking of heavy goods vehicles and the restoration of the site in accordance with a scheme to be agreed with the local planning authority or in default of agreement to be determined by the Secretary of State. The developer argued that the requirement to restore the site could not include a requirement to remove hardcore which had been laid on the site more than four years before the date of service of the notice; that was an 'operation' which was protected by the limitation period. The Divisional Court disagreed. After pointing out that the Act specifically requires that an enforcement notice should set out the steps to be taken to restore the land to its condition before the unauthorised development took place, Stephen Brown J said:

'That is, of course, a mandatory duty that is placed on a local authority, and it would make a nonsense of planning control, in my judgment, if it were to be considered in the instant case that an enforcement notice requiring discontinuance of the use of the site in question for the parking of heavy goods vehicles should not also require the restoration of the land, as a physical matter, to its previous condition, that requirement, of necessity, being the removal of the hardcore.'

The decision in *Murfitt* was followed in *Perkins v Secretary of State for the Environment and Rother District Council.*[11]

There was some suggestion by counsel for the Secretary of State in *Murfitt* that a 'change of use' enforcement notice could catch only those operations which were integral to the change of use but the judgments of Stephen Brown J and Waller LJ are couched in terms which appear to be wide enough to catch any sort of operations, integral or otherwise. Further in *Perkins* Glidewell J was inclined to agree that the words were sufficiently wide to cover the situation where operational development was caught by the requirements of the change of use enforcement notice, even though the operational development was not an integral part of the change of use. *Murfitt* and *Perkins* were both dealing with the old wording of s 87. The new wording introduced by the 1981 Amendment Act is more explicit in that it specifically states that the steps, requiring the land to be restored to its condition before the development took place, include the demolition or alteration of buildings or the carrying out of any building or other operations. In *Somak Travel Ltd v Secretary of State for the Environment*[12] Stuart-Smith J held that this wording meant that where, in carrying out a material change of use to a building, a spiral staircase had been constructed, the enforcement notice could require the removal of the staircase even though, as works which did not materially affect the external appearance of the building, the construction of the staircase was deemed not to be development by s 22(2)(a). Stuart-Smith J followed Stephen Brown LJ in *Murfitt* in holding that the construction of the staircase was part and parcel of or integral to the material change of use. He therefore did not have to decide

---

10 (1980) 40 P & CR 254.
11 [1981] JPL 755.
12 (1987) 55 P & CR 250, [1987] JPL 630.

whether it would be different if it was not so integral, but he expressed the view that s 87(9) was so widely phrased that it would not matter.

So the weight of authority indicates that even where operational development has become immune (or as in *Somak* is deemed not to be development) enforcement action may be taken regarding it where it took place in association with a material change of use which is not immune. On the other hand, as the *Mansi* line of cases emphasises, the requirements of a notice must turn on the alleged breach of control and so there must be a nexus between the two. This must mean that you cannot require steps to be taken which are not in the least connected to that breach of planning control.[13]

Quite apart from the situation which arose in *Murfitt* and *Perkins*, there will be occasions where the carrying out of operations may be accompanied by a material change in the use of the land on which the operations have taken place. In a case where four years have elapsed since operations were carried out and no enforcement notice can, therefore, be served in respect of those operations, it would seem that it may still be possible in some circumstances to serve an enforcement notice in respect of a change of use which accompanied the carrying out of the operations and to which the four year limitation does not apply.[14]

2. An enforcement notice may only be served within four years of a failure to comply with a condition or limitation which relates to the carrying out of building, engineering, mining or other operations and subject to which planning permission was granted (s 87(4)(b)).

In *Peacock Homes Ltd v Secretary of State for the Environment and Epsom and Ewell Borough Council*[15] the Court of Appeal held that a condition, attached to a planning permission for the erection of a building, which provided that the use was to be discontinued and the building demolished at the end of a specified period could fairly be said to relate to the erection of the building. Dillon LJ said that the words 'which relates to' were not words of art and might often mean little more than 'which has to do with'. This is a very flexible interpretation and any condition attached to a permission granting operational development could be said to 'have to do with' operations. However, the Court of Appeal stopped short of holding that *all* conditions attached to permission for operational development come within the four year rule. It could be that it is only conditions, which *relate* to the carrying out of operations in the sense that they involve operations or are closely akin or connected to such operations, that come within s 87(4)(b).

In the case of mining operations, it is specifically provided that the four-year period runs from the date when non-compliance with the condition has come to the planning authority's knowledge.[16]

3. An enforcement notice may only be served within four years of the making without planning permission of a change of use of any building to use as a single dwellinghouse (s 87(4)(c)).

---

13 See Woolf J in *Bath City Council v Secretary of State for the Environment* (1983) 47 P & CR 663.

14 See *Burn v Secretary of State for the Environment* (1971) 219 Estates Gazette 586, and appeal decision reported in [1974] JPL 733. One could thus have a building which the local planning authority cannot require to be demolished but which cannot lawfully be used.

15 (1984) 83 LGR 686, 48 P & CR 20.

16 See Town and Country Planning (Minerals) Regulations 1971, reg 4.

Such a change of use can, it seems, take place before the building is actually used as a dwellinghouse.[17] The phrase 'use as a single dwellinghouse' is narrower in its meaning than 'residential use'.[18]

4. An enforcement notice may only be served within four years of a failure to comply with a condition which prohibits, or has the effect of preventing, a change of use of a building to use as a single dwellinghouse (s 87(4)(d)).[19]

5. All other breaches of control, ie all unauthorised material changes of use other than to a single dwellinghouse, and all breaches of conditions or limitations other than those falling within categories 2 and 4 above, are immune from enforcement action if the breach occurred before 1964 (s 88(2)(e)).

The courts have not given any very clear guidance on the application of the time limits to a breach of a condition attached to a planning permission (categories 2, 4 and 5 above). If, for example, a condition prohibiting a certain use was first broken prior to the end of 1964 and the breach has continued since that date, is it now too late to serve an enforcement notice or can the planning authority still serve a notice on the basis that there has been a breach of planning control after the end of 1964? In *Bilboe v Secretary of State for the Environment*[20] an application to use an old stone quarry as a tip was granted in 1950 subject to a condition requiring the approval of the planning authority to be obtained for the materials to be deposited. Between 1950 and 1963 rubble was tipped on the site without the approval of the planning authority having been obtained. No further tipping took place until after 1975 when, although the planning authority's approval was obtained for the deposit of certain materials, other materials which had not been approved were tipped on the site. An enforcement notice was served alleging a breach of the condition attached to the permission of 1950. The Court of Appeal held that non-compliance with the condition had taken place once and for all in or about 1950, so that the breach of control was now immune from enforcement action. No consideration appears to have been given to whether this might have been a 'continuing' as opposed to a 'once and for all' breach and counsel for the developers had expressly argued that the breach of the condition was immune from enforcement if the first breach had taken place before 1964.

On the other hand in a case where sales of certain categories of articles took place intermittently in breach of a condition prohibiting the sales of such articles, the Minister of Housing and Local Government took the view that as there was no connection or continuity between one sale in breach of the condition and another such sale on another date, each sale constituted a complete and separate breach in itself and the time for serving an enforcement notice therefore began afresh from the date of each breach.[1] Where the

---

17 See *Impey v Secretary of State for the Environment* (1980) 47 P & CR 157, and *Backer v Secretary of State for the Environment* (1982) 47 P & CR 149.
18 See *Backer* (above).
19 Added by the Local Government and Planning (Amendment) Act 1981, Schedule, para 1. This provision fills the gap noted by the Divisional Court in *Backer v Secretary of State for the Environment* (1980) 42 P & CR 98 (upheld by the Court of Appeal sub nom *Camden London Borough Council v Backer and Aird* [1982] JPL 516).
20 (1980) 78 LGR 357, 39 P & CR 495.
1 See [1961] JPL 691 and (1961) 12 P & CR 406.

failure to comply with a condition has been continuous, the minister has, in a number of cases where the 'four year rule' applied, quashed enforcement notices served more than four years after the initial breach, holding that the time for service began to run from the first date of non-compliance with the condition.[2] This approach is supported by s 94(1)(b) which provides that a use of land is established if 'it was begun before the beginning of 1964 under a planning permission in that behalf granted subject to conditions or limitations which either have never been complied with or have not been complied with since the end of 1963.' So what is needed to stop time running anew is a continuous breach.

Even though a particular breach of a condition has in this way become immune from enforcement action, that does not necessarily mean, however, that the condition is entirely unenforceable—such a condition could still be enforced, according to the minister, 'if any further breaches of a demonstrably different nature occurred'.[3]

The operation of the time limits on service of an enforcement notice can clearly give rise to difficult problems. In the case of an unauthorised change of use there may well be practical difficulties in determining when the material change of use occurred, especially if the change took place gradually over a period.[4] From *Cheshire County Council v Secretary of State for the Environment*[5] it seems that if the change of use is gradual, you compare the pre-1964 position with the present position to see if there has been a material change since 1964.

In order to alleviate such difficulties, a person having an interest in the land in question may, except in cases to which the four year time limit applies (categories 1 to 4 above), ask the planning authority to issue an 'established use certificate'.[6]

If granted, this establishes conclusively for the purposes of an appeal against an enforcement notice the facts as stated in the certificate. This will usually mean that the use in question has secured immunity from enforcement action.

Certification of established use

In the case of all unauthorised material changes of use (except those relating to a change to use as a single dwellinghouse) the only restriction on service of an enforcement notice is that the breach of planning control must have occurred after the end of 1964 (see p 327 above). This might make it difficult for a person with an interest in land to establish (notably for the benefit of intending purchasers) that the use to which the land is being put is safe from enforcement. In order to overcome this difficulty, which is likely to increase with the passage of time, the 1971 Act provides that where a person having an interest in land claims that a particular use of that land has become

---

2 See, for example, [1963] JPL 813, [1966] JPL 348, [1968] JPL 294 and 351, and [1971] JPL 57.
3 [1968] JPL 294.
4 See *Britt v Buckinghamshire County Council* (1962) 60 LGR 430, 14 P & CR 332, per Widgery J.
5 (1971) 222 Estates Gazette 35.
6 See 1971 Act, s 94 and below.

'established', he may apply to the planning authority for a certificate to that effect (s 94(2)). Such a certificate is termed an established use certificate.[7]

An established use certificate is, as regards the matters stated therein, conclusive[8] for the purposes of an appeal against an enforcement notice served in respect of any land to which the certificate relates, provided that application for the certificate was made before the notice was served (s 94(7)). An established use certificate is not equivalent to a grant of planning permission (see p 333 below); it merely provides a protection against enforcement action. It has also been held that in determining a s 53 application the existence of a s 94 certificate is irrelevant in deciding whether a proposed change of use amounts to development.[9]

For the purposes of Pt V of the 1971 Act, a use of land is established if:

(a) it was begun before the beginning of 1964 without planning permission in that behalf and has continued since the end of 1963; or

(b) it was begun before the beginning of 1964 under a planning permission in that behalf granted subject to conditions or limitations,[10] which either have never been complied with or have not been complied with since the end of 1963; or

(c) it was begun after the end of 1963 as a result of a change of use not requiring planning permission and there has been, since the end of 1963, no change of use requiring planning permission (s 94(1)).

Paragraph (c) would seem to be intended to cover the case where the use which is claimed to have become established was begun after the end of 1963, but the previous use was in the same use class, with the result that the change of use was not such as to require planning permission. It could also cover the case of a material change of use which took place before 1964 but was then followed by a change in the method of use but which change did not constitute a material change.

Before it can be claimed that a use has become established in terms of para (a) or para (b) above, it must be shown that there has been a continuous breach of planning control from a date before 1 January 1964; a use cannot therefore become established under s 94 of the 1971 Act if there has been a grant of planning permission which, for any part of the time since 31

---

7 A consultation paper issued by the Department of the Environment in 1984 stated that with the passage of time applications and appeals relating to established use certificates are becoming increasingly difficult to decide; in particular, it is increasingly difficult to obtain firm factual evidence on which to base a decision. The consultation paper therefore proposed that the statutory provisions relating to the making of applications for established use certificates should be repealed. A lengthy period of grace would be allowed before these changes became operative in order to allow persons who wished to secure immunity from enforcement action to apply for a certificate. An established use certificate would still, as at present, provide conclusive evidence that the use specified therein was immune from enforcement action. However, on 11 November 1985 in reply to a Parliamentary question it was stated that the government did not intend to pursue the proposal to withdraw the system (HC Debates, Vol 86, Col 18).

8 The certificate cannot subsequently be 'explained' by evidence as to the actual use at the time the certificate was granted—see *Broxbourne Borough Council v Secretary of State for the Environment* [1980] QB 1, [1979] 2 All ER 13 (below).

9 In *Moran v Secretary of State for the Environment and Mid-Sussex County Council* [1988] JPL 24, McCullough J held that the comparison had to be made between the present actual use and the proposed use, not the use as set out in the certificate.

10 Presumably this means that the permission may be one granted by the GDO.

December 1963, rendered the use lawful or made the condition inoperative, as the case may be.[11]

Subsection (2) of s 94 provides that application may be made for an established use certificate where it is claimed that a 'particular use' of land has become established. The Secretary of State for the Environment takes the view that by virtue of that sub-section a certificate can be sought only in respect of the particular purpose for which the land was used at the appropriate time and that it is not, for example, open to the planning authority or the minister 'to issue a certificate generally for "industrial use" or for "use for industrial purposes"':[12] these are not descriptions of particular uses of land but general references to a type of use.[13] A class of use specified in the Schedule to the Use Classes Order cannot be regarded as a 'particular use'; the certificate must specify the precise use to which the land was put, eg timber storage ancillary to the use of the adjoining land as a sawmill and wood products factory.[14] An application for an established use certificate must relate to the primary use of the planning unit.[15]

Application for an established use certificate may only be made in respect of a use subsisting at the time of the application (s 94(2)). Article 29(1)(b) of the Town and Country Planning General Development Order 1988, which lays down the procedures for applying for a certificate, requires that the use applied for must be 'a use subsisting on the date when the application is made'. The Secretary of State therefore used to take the view that the use had actually to be taking place 'on the ground' even though it had not been abandoned.[16] But this view has been repudiated. Now in order to establish that a use is not subsisting at the date of the application, there has to be, in the opinion of the Secretary of State for the Environment, 'positive evidence either of a change of use or of abandonment of the former use'.[17] In *Vaughan v Secretary of State for the Environment and Mid-Sussex District Council*[18] McNeill J held that an application could not be made for an established use certificate where the use was illegal, as it contravened the requirements of a valid enforcement notice which had taken effect. McNeill J relied on the earlier decision in *Glamorgan County Council v Carter*[19] where it was held that 'use' as generally used in the planning legislation means lawful use and cannot include 'use which' constitutes the commission of a criminal or quasi-criminal offence.[20] An application for an established use certificate may not be made in respect of the use of land as a single dwellinghouse (s 94(2)). The Secretary of State has held that this provision did not bar an application in which it was alleged that a condition relating to the class of persons who

11 See *Bolivian and General Tin Trust v Secretary of State for the Environment* [1972] 3 All ER 918, [1972] 1 WLR 1481; see too appeal decisions reported in [1972] JPL 226 and 230, and [1974] JPL 239.
12 Unless the use in question is so general it cannot be described with greater precision—see appeal decision noted in [1981] JPL 449 ('general storage').
13 [1971] JPL 463. See also [1972] JPL 171, [1974] JPL 293 and [1981] JPL 449.
14 See [1971] JPL 463.
15 See appeal decision reported in [1977] JPL 188.
16 [1979] JPL 780.
17 [1971] JPL 463. See also [1981] JPL 449 and [1982] JPL 800. For discussion of the arguments see Bourne, 'The Status of Established Use' [1983] JPL 348.
18 [1986] JPL 840.
19 [1962] 3 All ER 866, [1963] 1 WLR 1.
20 Also see [1972] JPL 230, [1974] JPL 490, [1975] JPL 106 and 686, [1976] JPL 247, [1981] JPL 691 and [1986] JPL 770.

might occupy a dwellinghouse had not been complied with; such a condition, the minister thought, 'did not itself concern the use of the building as a single dwellinghouse'.[1]

Detailed provision as to the method of applying for an established use certificate and as to the procedure on appeal against refusal of such a certificate is made by Sch 14 to the 1971 Act and art 29 of, and Sch 6 to, the GDO. An application for an established use certificate must describe the use in respect of which a certificate is sought and, if there is more than one use of the land on the date when the application is made, there must be provided a full description of all uses of the land at the date of the application, giving, where appropriate, an indication of the part of the land to which each of the uses relates (GDO, art 29(1)(c)). Unless the applicant is himself the owner of the whole of the land to which the application relates he must give notice of the application to all owners of the land (GDO, art 29(4)).[2] It is an offence to give false information or to withhold material information in order to procure a particular decision on an application for an established use certificate (s 94(8)). An application for an established use certificate may be accompanied by an application for planning permission to continue the use (s 32).[3] Circular 109/77 contains a Department of the Environment memorandum which states: 'The making of such an application is not to be regarded as an admission of doubt about the immunity of a use from enforcement action nor be allowed to prejudice in any way the full consideration on its merits of the claim for an established use certificate.' (See para 20 of the memorandum.)

If and in so far as they are satisfied that the applicant's claim is made out, the local planning authority must grant an established use certificate (s 94(4)). The onus is therefore on the applicant to establish his claim[4] but the planning authority may, of course, take account of any information in their possession. The planning authority's jurisdiction (or the Secretary of State's on appeal) is not limited by the exact description of the use set out in the application. In *Bristol City Council v Secretary of State for the Environment*[5] Stuart-Smith held that a certificate can be granted for a lesser degree of use than that set out in the application. The application had sought a certificate of established multiple paying occupation comprising seven units and nine occupiers in total but on appeal the Secretary of State had granted a certificate for six units and a total of six occupiers. In holding this, Stuart-Smith J disagreed with a statement by David Widdicombe QC (sitting as deputy judge) in *Hipsey v Secretary of State for the Environment and Thurrock Borough Council*.[6] However, it will be different, if, as in *Hipsey*, an application is made for an established use and it is decided that the material change by way of intensification took place after 1964 and not before.

The determining authority is not seized with the question of whether prior to 1964 there were established subsidiary rights but with whether the

---

1 [1971] JPL 417.
2 'Owner' is defined in art 29(5) of the GDO and includes an occupier of any part of the land.
3 Note Secretary of State's powers to grant planning permission on an appeal against a refusal of an established use certificate: s 95(3).
4 See appeal decisions noted in [1979] JPL 247 and 780. The standard of proof is 'the balance of probabilities' rather than 'beyond all reasonable doubt' — see [1981] JPL 527.
5 [1987] JPL 718.
6 [1984] JPL 806.

intensified use had been established before 1964. The important difference would seem to be between a misdescription in the detail of the use in the application and the use turning out to be entirely different from that described. So, if it turns out that the use had only been established on part of the land which is the subject of the application, a certificate can be granted with regard to that part only. The Secretary of State, going back on previous decisions,[7] has held that the use of land must not invariably attach to the 'planning unit' as a whole[8] and so a certificate can be granted which only confirms that a use has been established on a particular part of a planning unit. On the other hand, the fact that a use has been established on part of a planning unit will often mean that the use can be extended to the rest of the planning unit and in *Enticott and Fullite Ltd v Secretary of State for the Environment*[9] Woolf J pointed out that '. . . activity on part of the planning unit can affect the established use of the whole planning unit'.

The importance of describing the established use with some precision in the certificate is borne out by the decision of the Divisional Court in *Broxbourne Borough Council v Secretary of State for the Environment*.[10] The local planning authority granted an established use certificate certifying that 'the use of the above land and building for the storage, sawing, re-sawing and disposal of timber in the round and the storage, maintenance, repair and overhaul of vehicles and plant incidental thereto' was established. The site subsequently changed hands and in due course came to be used, amongst other things, as a bulk storage depot for timber planks. The planning authority took enforcement action requiring the discontinuance of the use of the land for the purpose of the stacking and storage of planks of timber. On appeal the Secretary of State considered that the present use of the site was not so different from that described in the established use certificate as to constitute a material change of use. The court upheld the Secretary of State's decision. The certificate was wholly silent as to the scope and intensity of the use at the time it was issued and the established use was therefore to be treated as without limit as regards these matters; the whole purpose of an established use certificate was to preclude the necessity of reopening investigation of past events. As Robert Goff J commented, the case demonstrated 'that planning authorities should exercise great care concerning the terms of established use certificates which they issue'.

An application for an established use certificate may specify two or more uses, in which case the certificate may be granted either for all those uses or for some one or more of them (s 94(3)). It would seem that a certificate may not be granted in respect of a use not described in the application[11] though a misdescription of the type of use in the application would not rule out a certificate being granted in a different form of words.[12]

If an application for an established use certificate is refused in whole or in part by the planning authority or if the authority fail to give notice of their decision within eight weeks (or such extended period as may be agreed) the

---

7 See [1977] JPL 188 and [1981] JPL 527.
8 [1985] JPL 801.
9 [1981] JPL 759.
10 [1980] QB 1, [1979] 2 All ER 13.
11 See [1971] JPL 467.
12 See *Bristol City Council v Secretary of State for the Environment* [1987] JPL 718.

applicant may appeal to the Secretary of State (s 95(2)).[13] Before determining an appeal, the Secretary of State must, if either the applicant or the local planning authority so desire, afford to each of them an opportunity of appearing before and being heard by a person appointed by the Secretary of State for the purpose (s 95(4)).[14] Where the planning authority have granted an established use certificate in respect of part of the land covered by an application and an appeal is made in respect of the remaining part of the land, the Secretary of State has no power to revoke the certificate already granted.[15] In determining an appeal the Secretary of State is, however, entitled to uphold the planning authority's decision on grounds different from those of the authority.[16]

On an appeal under s 95(2) the Secretary of State may grant planning permission in respect of any use of land for which an established use certificate is not granted (s 95(3)); in the case of any use of land for which the Secretary of State has power to grant planning permission under s 95, the appellant is deemed to have made application for such permission (s 95(6)) and a fee must be paid.[17] The fee is due at the time when written notice of the appeal is given to the Secretary of State but will be refunded in the event of an established use certificate being granted.

An established use certificate is not equivalent to a grant of planning permission—an established use certificate would not, for example, be a substitute for the express grant of planning permission which is necessary before a caravan site licence can be granted—so that in some cases it might be wise for an applicant for an established use certificate to apply also for planning permission in order that the two applications can be dealt with together. It would seem, by virtue of s 94(2), which provides that application for a certificate can only be made in respect of a use subsisting at the time of the application, that the Secretary of State has no jurisdiction to grant planning permission under s 95 for a use not subsisting at that date.[18]

Except as provided in s 245 of the 1971 Act, the validity of any decision of the Secretary of State on an appeal relating to an established use certificate shall not be questioned in any legal proceedings whatsoever (s 242) (see chapter 20).

A form of established use certificate is set out in Pt 3 of Sch 6 to the General Development Order. The date on which application for the certificate was made is to be the date at which the use will be certified as established if the certificate is granted (1971 Act, Sch 14, para 4(c)). The form of established use certificate contains a note emphasising that the certificate is not a grant of planning permission and that it 'does not necessarily entitle the owner or occupier of the land to any consequential statutory rights which may be conferred where planning permission has been granted under Pt III

13 For the procedure, see 1971 Act, Sch 14, and GDO, art 29(12). Strangely there is no express provision that a failure to determine an application within eight weeks is a deemed refusal but see art 29(12) of the GDO.
14 If a public local inquiry is held the procedure is governed by the Town and Country Planning (Enforcement) (Inquiries Procedure) Rules 1981.
15 See the comments of Woolf J in *Cottrell v Secretary of State for the Environment and Tonbridge and Melling District Council* [1982] JPL 443.
16 *Cottrell* (above).
17 See Town and Country Planning (Fees for Applications and Deemed Applications) Regulations 1989, reg 10(1)(b), (6) and (9) and Sch 1, para 11.
18 See appeal decisions noted in [1971] JPL 117.

of the Town and Country Planning Act 1971'. Thus the fact that a use is referred to in a certificate will not imply that it is a use of land which can lawfully be resumed without planning permission under the provisions of s 23(5), (6) and (8) of the 1971 Act[19] (see p 145 above). Also it could be that, even though an established use certificate has been granted, planning permission will still be required for a change from the 'established' use to another use within the same class, on grounds that the established use is not lawful.[20] Also, the fact that a use has been established, does not mean that it cannot be abandoned or superseded (see chapter 5 above). The certificate is simply conclusive as to the facts stated in the certificate for the purposes of an appeal against an enforcement notice.

A register of established use certificates must be maintained by the planning authority.[1]

Estoppel

In *Pioneer Aggregates (UK) Ltd v Secretary of State for the Environment*[2] Lord Scarman stated that

> 'Planning control is a creature of statute. It is an imposition in the public interest of restrictions upon private rights of ownership of land. The public character of the law had been recognised by the House of Lords in *Newbury District Council v Secretary of State for the Environment.*[3] It is a field of law in which the courts should not introduce principles or rules derived from private law unless it be expressly authorised by Parliament or necessary in order to give effect to the purpose of the legislation. Planning law, though a comprehensive code imposed in the public interest, is of course based on land law. Where the code is silent or ambiguous, resort to the principles of the private law (especially property and contract law) may be necessary so that the courts may resolve difficulties by application of common law or equitable principles. But such cases will be exceptional.'

One of the areas where the courts have been tempted to resort to private law principles is enforcement. In special circumstances, it appears that a local planning authority may be estopped from issuing an enforcement notice because of previous conduct, even though technically a breach of planning control may have taken place.

A s 53 determination that planning permission is not required, or an actual grant of planning permission, should prevent an enforcement notice being issued with regard to activities covered by such documents. In such circumstances, it can hardly appear to the local planning authority that there has been a breach of planning control as required by s 87(1). If an enforcement notice were to be issued, an appeal, on the grounds that the matters alleged do not constitute a breach of planning control (s 88(2)(b)), would be bound

19 See appeal decision noted in [1976] JPL 117.
20 See *Young v Secretary of State for the Environment* (1983) 81 LGR 389 but note this case concerned the GDO rather than Use Classes Order. For a discussion of this issue, see ch 5, p 128.
1 1971 Act, Sch 14, para 6 and GDO, art 29(14).
2 [1985] AC 132, [1984] 2 All ER 358.
3 [1981] AC 578, [1980] 1 All ER 731.

to succeed. On the other hand, it would probably be too late to challenge the validity of the enforcement notice if an appeal was not lodged in time (s 243(2)(b)), unless it could be shown that the local planning authority had acted in bad faith.[4]

The courts have held that a valid s 53 determination may exist even though the formal procedures have not been followed (see p 141 above). This is on the basis that the authority is entitled to waive any legal formalities or technicalities governing the s 53 procedures.[5] The practical result is that a s 53 determination operates in the same way as if all the formalities had been observed. However since the Court of Appeal's decision in *Western Fish Products Ltd v Penwith District Council*[6] it is clear that the courts will be reluctant to deem the waiver of statutory procedures where the outcome could affect members of the public.[7]

The position is more difficult where the person making the representation has not got the formal authority to make that kind of decision.

In *Southend-on-Sea Corpn v Hodgson (Wickford) Ltd*[8] it was held that a planning authority were entitled to serve an enforcement notice notwithstanding that one of their officials had earlier written to the developer stating that planning permission was not required for the development in question. At the time of that decision there was, however, no statutory provision for the delegation to officials of the power to make planning decisions. By the time *Lever Finance Ltd v Westminster (City) London Borough Council*[9] was decided, statute permitted the delegation of certain planning functions to officials and in *Lever*, which seems almost indistinguishable on its facts from the *Southend* case, the Court of Appeal held that where, in the course of a telephone conversation, a planning officer, acting within his ostensible authority, had informed a developer that proposed variations from approved plans were not material and did not require consent, the planning authority was bound by the officer's statement and could not take enforcement action in respect of development carried out on the strength of the official's assurance. Sachs LJ considered that the continuance, after the coming into operation of the statutory provisions permitting delegation of certain functions to officials, of the practice of allowing a planning officer to decide whether an alteration to a detailed planning permission was material or not, resulted in an implied delegation to the officer of power to deal with an application as to whether any further permission was required; and that the formalities for such an application were sufficiently observed if the decision on the application was recorded by the respective parties. Lord Denning MR, with whom Megaw LJ concurred, also reached the conclusion that the planning authority were bound by the officer's statement but seems to have applied a wider principle. He said:[10]

4 See *Davy v Spelthorne District Council* [1984] AC 262, [1983] 3 All ER 278.
5 See *Wells v Minister of Housing and Local Government* [1967] 2 All ER 1041, [1967] 1 WLR 1000 and Sachs LJ in *Lever Finance Ltd v Westminster (City) London Borough Council* [1971] 1 QB 222, [1970] 3 All ER 496.
6 [1981] 2 All ER 204.
7 See on this *Kerrier District Council v Secretary of State for the Environment and Brewer* (1980) 41 P & CR 284, [1981] JPL 193.
8 [1962] 1 QB 416, [1961] 2 All ER 46.
9 [1971] 1 QB 222, [1970] 3 All ER 496.
10 [1971] 1 QB 222 at 230.

'If the planning officer tells the developer that a proposed variation is not material, and the developer acts on it, then the planning authority cannot go back on it. I know that there are authorities which say that a public authority cannot be estopped by any representations made by its officers. It cannot be estopped from doing its public duty: see, for instance, the recent decision of the Divisional Court in *Southend-on-Sea Corpn v Hodgson (Wickford) Ltd.*[11] But those statements must now be taken with considerable reserve. There are many matters which public authorities can now delegate to their officers. If an officer, acting within the scope of his ostensible authority makes a representation on which another acts, then a public authority may be bound by it, just as much as a private concern would be. A good instance is the recent decision of this court in *Wells v Minister of Housing and Local Government.*[12] It was proved in that case that it was the practice of planning authorities, acting through their officers, to tell applicants whether or not planning permission was necessary. A letter was written by the council engineer telling the applicants that no permission was necessary. The applicants acted on it. It was held that the planning authority could not go back on it. I would like to quote what I then said:

"It has been their practice to tell applicants that no planning permission is necessary. Are they now to be allowed to say that this practice was all wrong and their letters were of no effect? I do not think so. I take the law to be that a defect in procedure can be cured, and an irregularity can be waived, even by a public authority, so as to render valid that which would otherwise be invalid."'

The fact that a representation has been acted upon may not, however, be sufficient to make that representation binding on the planning authority; as was pointed out by Lord Widgery CJ in *Norfolk County Council v Secretary of State for the Environment,*[13] 'the mere fact that my agent has made a representation within his ostensible authority on which you act is not enough to estop me from denying his actual authority unless you have acted to your detriment'. In this case it was held that since applicants for planning permission had not suffered any loss by acting upon a permission issued in error by an official, the planning authority were entitled to deny the validity of the permission.

In *Brooks and Burton Ltd v Secretary of State for the Environment,*[14] Lord Widgery warned against further extension of the doctrine expressed in *Lever.* In *Brooks and Burton* it was argued that the planning authority were barred from serving an enforcement notice because of earlier statements by officials to the effect that the activities in question would not require planning permission. The Divisional Court held that it had not been shown that the appellants gave the officials sufficient information for them to give a precise answer so as to bind the authority. Lord Widgery declared that 'any attempt to expand the doctrine of estoppel in *Lever* was to be deprecated' because it was extremely important that a planning authority's officers should feel free to help applicants 'without all the time having the shadow of estoppel

11 [1962] 1 QB 416, [1961] 2 All ER 46.
12 [1967] 2 All ER 1041, [1967] 1 WLR 1000.
13 [1973] 3 All ER 673, [1973] 1 WLR 1400.
14 [1978] 1 All ER 733, [1977] 1 WLR 1294.

hanging over them and the possibility of their immobilising the authority by some careless remark'.

Lord Widgery's concern was received with sympathy by the Court of Appeal in *Western Fish Products Ltd v Penwith District Council*.[15] The decision in that case has virtually reinstated the *Southend* position and, whilst not overturning *Lever* in so many words, has cast much doubt upon the generous elaboration of the doctrine of estoppel in that case. *Western Fish Products* again concerned a situation in which a planning official had indicated by letter to a developer (in this case of a fish processing plant) that the proposed development could proceed without further planning permission on the basis of established use rights. The council subsequently requested applications for planning permission, refused them when submitted, and started enforcement proceedings.

The Court of Appeal upheld the council's action on several grounds. In particular, they held that, on the facts of this case, the letter sent by the officer was not to be regarded as a representation as to existing use rights nor could the developer be seen as having relied on it to his detriment. More significantly, however, the court propounded the general principle that 'an estoppel cannot be raised to prevent the exercise of a statutory discretion or to prevent or excuse the performance of a statutory duty'. To this principle they recognised only two kinds of exception.

One exception was that referred to earlier where a procedural requirement was taken to be waived and so the authority was estopped from relying on the lack of formality. The other exception was where an officer is wrongly assumed to have been given delegated powers to determine specific questions, such as applications under ss 53 or 94 of the Act. Any decisions made by such officers could not be revoked. In this regard Megaw LJ, giving the judgment of the court, disagreed with Lord Denning's view in *Lever* that local planning authorities would automatically be bound by representations made by officers which were within their ostensible authority. Megaw LJ stated:

'In the court's opinion that principle laid down by Lord Denning was not an authority for the proposition that every representation made by a planning officer within ostensible authority bound the planning authority which employed him. For an estoppel to arise there had to be some evidence justifying the person dealing with the planning officer for thinking that what the officer said would bind the planning authority.'

Megaw LJ said that this would depend on the circumstances (in *Lever* there had been a past history of planning officers being allowed to determine such questions), but that Lord Denning had gone too far in stating that a person dealing with the authority could automatically assume that the local planning authority have passed all the necessary resolutions to give the officer authority. In conclusion, estoppel only operates to validate informal decision-making in these two specific cases: waiver of statutory procedures and lack of formal delegation. Otherwise representations or conduct cannot cure what is done without authority. Thus in *Bedfordia Plant Ltd v Secretary of State for the Environment and North Bedfordshire District Council*[16] it was

15 [1981] 2 All ER 204.
16 [1981] JPL 122.

held that a Rural District Council could not make a binding statement as to established use rights as it had no power to grant established use certificates.

All the above authorities basically dealt with cases where the doctrine of estoppel was being used in an attempt to cure a failure to follow a statutory procedure leading up to a statutory decision. It is unlikely that the courts would allow representations or conduct unrelated to a statutory process, to affect the decision to take enforcement action. For example, a promise not to issue an enforcement notice or to prosecute would founder on the doctrine that public authorities cannot bind themselves as to how they will exercise their statutory functions.[17] However, it has been suggested that the House of Lords' decision in *Re Preston*[18] means that the issue of an enforcement notice in such circumstances might be challenged as an abuse of power.[19] In that decision it was held that where a public body has made a representation and subsequently acted contrary to that representation, the body may thereby be held to have abused its powers. However it was stressed by Lord Scarman that the court would only consider it to be an abuse of power, if, had not the commissioners been a public authority, their conduct would be the equivalent of a breach of contract or a breach of a representation giving rise to estoppel. So the principle in *Preston* will have limited application, but it has since been applied to a representation by the Secretary of State on a planning appeal.[20] Where estoppel applies, it would seem that a developer can apply for judicial review to stop the issue of an enforcement notice or alternatively get a declaration that the local planning authority is estopped from taking enforcement action.[1] Finally there is always the remote possibility of suing for damages on the basis that the local planning authority have committed the tort of negligence by giving faulty advice or making a negligent misstatement.[2]

C CHALLENGING ENFORCEMENT NOTICES

Introduction

The legislation on enforcement appears to be designed to ensure that in the majority of cases a person who wishes to challenge an enforcement notice should, in the first place at least, follow the statutory avenue of appeal to the Secretary of State for which provision is made by s 88(1) of the 1971 Act. The eight grounds of appeal set out in s 88(2), which include certain matters of fact, planning merits and law, cover the matters on which one is most likely to wish to challenge an enforcement notice. In providing that an enforcement notice is not to be questioned on specified grounds other than by way of appeal to the Secretary of State, the legislation seeks to ensure that in the majority of cases it is only after the appeal process has been exhausted that

---

17 See *Stringer v Minister of Housing and Local Government* [1971] 1 All ER 65, [1970] 1 WLR 1281 and the *Western Fish* case above.
18 [1985] AC 835, [1985] 2 WLR 836.
19 See Rutherford, Peart and Pickard, 'Estoppel and Development Control Counter Service' [1986] JPL 891.
20 See *Costain Homes Ltd v Secretary of State for the Environment* [1988] JPL 701.
 1 See *Lever Finance Ltd v Westminster London Borough Council* and *Western Fish Products Ltd v Penwith District Council*.
 2 *Davy v Spelthorne Borough Council* [1984] AC 262, [1983] 3 All ER 278; but see *Ryeford Homes Ltd v Sevenoaks District Council* [1989] NLJR 255.

enforcement action may be challenged in the courts. Certain of the grounds on which it might otherwise have been possible to attack the *vires* of an enforcement notice in court are thus made the exclusive preserve of the Secretary of State and if in such a case the notice is not challenged by way of appeal the opportunity to challenge the notice may be lost for good. Further, in determining an appeal the Secretary of State or appointed person may correct certain types of defects in enforcement notices; the scope for challenging notices in the courts on technical grounds is thus reduced.

Although the grounds on which appeal to the Secretary of State may be made embrace a number of matters on which the *vires* of a notice might, in the absence of the specific statutory provisions, be open to attack in the courts, they do not cover all the grounds on which it may be possible to challenge the validity of an enforcement notice; in some circumstances it is possible to challenge the *vires* of an enforcement notice in court, either directly or as a defence to proceedings for non-compliance with an enforce-ment notice. In theory, it has been said, 'the statutory appeals system and the challenge of notices by other means ought to be mutually exclusive',[3] and that the matters which may be the subject of an appeal to the minister do not go to the *vires* of a notice. The distinction has, however, been blurred both by the way in which the legislation is drafted and by the courts. The interplay between the statutory provisions and the courts' general powers have resulted in very considerable complexity in this area.[4]

This section deals firstly with appeal to the Secretary of State and then with challenge in the courts.

Appeal to the Secretary of State

A person having an interest in the land to which an enforcement notice has been served may appeal to the Secretary of State whether or not a copy of the notice has been served on him. Prior to 1971, a person on whom an enforcement notice had been served had a right to appeal, but the Local Government and Planning (Amendment) Act 1981 changed the law so that someone who had been sent the notice as a matter of information should not automatically have a right of appeal. In *Scarborough Borough Council v Adams and Adams*[5] it was therefore accepted that squatters and trespassers had not got an interest in land and could not appeal. In a ministerial decision, the Secretary of State held that persons, who were not owners, mortgagees or tenants but had a licence to occupy land, also had no right of appeal.[6] However, s 4(2) of the Town and Country Planning Act 1984 amended the position so that a person who is in occupation of land or buildings by virtue of a licence in writing now has a right of appeal. While it is not a ground of

---

3 J Davis, 'Enforcement', in *Development Control—Thirty Years On* (JPEL Occasional Paper, 1979); see also J Alder, *Development Control* (Sweet and Maxwell, 1979), pp 148–150.

4 See M Purdue, 'The Methods of Challenging Enforcement Notices' [1973] JPL 84; J E Alder, 'Challenging Enforcement Notices' [1978] JPL 160; and M Purdue, 'The Secretary of State's Power to Repair Defective Enforcement Notices' [1981] JPL 483.

5 (1983) 147 JP 449, [1983] JPL 673. Also see *R v Secretary of State and South Shropshire District Council, ex p Davis* (1989) Times, 15 May where the court refused to upset the Secretary of State's decision that the would-be appellant was a trespasser and did not have adverse possesion.

6 [1983] JPL 826.

appeal to the Secretary of State that a notice is *ultra vires*, as was said in one appeal,[7] 'where in the course of an appeal such issues are raised the Secretary of State has no alternative but to consider them, since they go to the question of his jurisdiction.' The minister, and indeed the court in the event of a challenge of the minister's decision on the appeal,[8] may conclude that the notice is a nullity.[9] In any case, since it may not be clear, until a court pronounces on it, that an enforcement notice is *ultra vires*, even if it is decided to challenge a notice in the court, it may be wise to consider also the lodging of an appeal to the Secretary of State, thus safeguarding this avenue of challenge in the event of the court action proving unsuccessful. Where the minister or appointed person concludes that the notice is *ultra vires*, the notice is incapable of correction or variation by the minister because the appeal cannot validate a nullity.[10] Indeed, the appeal itself might arguably be regarded as a nullity. Unlike appeals under s 36 of the 1971 Act (see p 267 above) the minister, in determining an appeal under s 88 of the Act, may not deal with the matter anew. The notice could merely be disregarded but, so that there should be no doubt in the matter, the minister may decide that it should be formally quashed.[11] When an appeal is lodged, the enforcement notice is of no effect pending the final determination or withdrawal of the appeal (s 88(10)); in the meantime, unless a stop notice has also been served (see p 368 below), the breach of control may continue. An appeal can therefore serve as a holding device and a high proportion of enforcement appeals are withdrawn prior to determination.

Even though s 246 provides a right to appeal to the High Court on a point of law against the decision of the Secretary of State upholding an enforcement notice, the courts at first held that the notice takes effect on the date of the appeal decision.[12] This meant that the time for compliance ran from the date of appeal decision and not from the date when it is too late to apply to the court under s 246. In *London Parachuting Ltd and Rectory Farm (Pampisford) Ltd v Secretary of State for the Environment*[13] the Court of Appeal held that if an appeal to the court is made, the appellant can also seek an order from the High Court staying any proceedings being brought under the enforcement notice until the appeal is determined by the court. However, it is unsatisfactory that an individual could potentially face criminal prosecution or have his rights affected by an enforcement notice when he is still in the process of challenging the notice. Also there was the strange potential consequence that, if the court on an appeal remitted the notice back to the

---

7 [1982] JPL 48.
8 See 1971 Act, s 246.
9 See, for example, *Metallic Protectives Ltd v Secretary of State for the Environment* [1976] JPL 166; and *Hounslow London Borough Council v Secretary of State for the Environment* [1981] JPL 510. Where there has been an appeal to the Secretary of State it would seem that an allegation that the notice is a nullity would be made under s 246 and not by judicial review; see *Dudley Bowers Amusements Enterprises Ltd v Secretary of State for the Environment* (1985) 52 P & CR 365, 278 Estates Gazette 313; cf *Rhymney Valley District Council v Secretary of State for Wales and Isaac* [1985] JPL 27.
10 *Ridge v Baldwin* [1964] AC 40, [1963] 2 All ER 66.
11 See, for example, *Hounslow London Borough Council v Secretary of State for the Environment* [1981] JPL 510.
12 *Dover District Council v McKeen* [1985] JPL 627 and *London Parachuting Ltd and Rectory Farm (Pampisford) Ltd v Secretary of State for the Environment and South Cambridgeshire District Council* (1985) 52 P & CR 376, [1986] JPL 279.
13 Above.

Secretary of State and the notice was then quashed, an enforcement notice having come into legal effect, then ceased to have effect.[14]

Subsequently, in *R v Kuxhaus*[15] the Court of Appeal reluctantly went back on the obiter dicta in the *London Parachuting* case and held that, as long as the s 246 appeal process is still alive, the appeal under s 88 has not been finally determined and so the enforcement notice has not taken effect. In other words the s 88 appeal and the s 246 appeal are not two self-contained and completely separate procedures. The practical result is that as long as an appeal has been lodged and not finally dismissed by the courts, the notice cannot take effect. An appeal under s 246 should be brought within 28 days but even after 28 days it cannot be assumed that the notice will take effect as leave to extend the appeal can be granted. Again, even if the appeal to the High Court is dismissed, there is always the possibility of getting leave to appeal to the Court of Appeal and then to the House of Lords. However, in *R v Kuxhaus* the Court of Appeal made clear that in this regard miracles in litigation are not to be assumed and when application has not been made within a year to apply out of time, it can be taken that the s 88 appeal has been finally settled; see *Garland v Westminster City London Borough Council*.[16]

On the other hand, the Court of Appeal in *Kuxhaus* held that the actual decision in *Dover District Council v McKeen*[17] is right and that, where there is no appeal under s 246, the time for complying with the enforcement notice runs concurrently with the time for appealing. Thus the date that the enforcement notice takes effect, in such circumstances, is the date of the Secretary of State's decision.

The Court of Appeal accepted that the right to appeal to the court under s 246 could be abused. As the judgment put it:

'The legal history of the enforcement of enforcement notices is not a happy one. Infringing uses of land are often profitable uses of land. Determined infringers were initially able to exploit technicalities, and even after certain statutory improvements to the machinery of enforcement were then able to use the delays inevitable in busy courts to continue infringing planning requirements while their often hopeless appeals were working their way to the top of the list.'

R v Kuxhaus is itself a good example of how long the statutory machinery can be strung out. By the time the Court of Appeal finally dismissed the second challenge to the notice and their petition for leave to appeal to the House of Lords was dismissed, the enforcement notices were more than six years old. The notices then took effect but as the prosecutions for breach of the notices were brought prematurely the convictions had to be quashed. The solution suggested by the court was that, as with an application for judicial review, there should be a need to get leave from the High Court to bring a s 246 appeal. This would enable the court quickly to screen out hopeless and unworthy appeals.

14 See G Kirkwood, 'The Suspension of Enforcement Notices' [1986] JPL 482 for a discussion of the issues.
15 [1988] QB 631, [1988] 2 All ER 705.
16 (1970) 68 LGR 587, 21 P & CR 555.
17 Above.

Grounds of appeal

Appeal to the Secretary of State may be made on any one or more of the eight grounds set out in s 88(2) of the 1971 Act. If made out, certain of the grounds of appeal lead inevitably to the quashing of the enforcement notice. The grounds of appeal are as follows:

(a) That planning permission ought to be granted for the development to which the enforcement notice relates or, as the case may be, that a condition or limitation alleged in the enforcement notice not to have been complied with ought to be discharged.

Section 88B(3) provides that where an appeal is brought against an enforcement notice, the appellant shall be deemed to have made an application for planning permission for the development to which the notice relates. It would seem, therefore, that the planning merits of the alleged breach of control will be in issue in the appeal whether or not ground (a) is specifically pleaded. Also it has been held that the Secretary of State can allow the appeal on grounds not specifically pleaded by the appellant.[18]

(b) That the matters alleged in the enforcement notice do not constitute a breach of planning control.

The appellant may be able to show, for example, that the activity complained of does not constitute 'development' within the meaning of s 22 of the 1971 Act (see chapter 5) or that the development is permitted by the general development order (see chapter 6). In an appeal on ground (b) the question of whether a breach of planning control has occurred is to be judged as at the date the enforcement notice was served.[19] The fact that planning permission has been sought and granted subject to a condition does not preclude a later appeal on ground (b).[20]

(c) That the breach of planning control alleged in the notice has not taken place.

This ground of appeal was introduced by the Local Government and Planning (Amendment) Act 1981[1] and meets the point made by Lord Widgery CJ in *Hammersmith London Borough Council v Secretary of State for the Environment*[2] in which his Lordship said: 'It is a little odd that the Act of 1971 at no point authorises the Secretary of State to accept an appeal against an enforcement notice merely because the allegation in the notice does not fit the factual position on the ground.' The new provision allows an appeal to be lodged on the ground that there has 'in fact', as opposed to 'in law' (ground (b)), been no breach of planning control.[3]

(d) In the case of a notice which, by virtue of s 87(4) of the 1971 Act, may be served only within the period of four years from the date of the breach of planning control to which the notice relates, that the period has elapsed at the date of service.

---

18 *Chelmsford RDC v Powell* [1963] 1 All ER 150, [1963] 1 WLR 123.
19 *Prengate Properties Ltd v Secretary of State for the Environment* (1973) 71 LGR 373, 25 P & CR 311.
20 See *East Barnet UDC v British Transport Commission* [1962] 2 QB 484, [1961] 3 All ER 878.
 1 See Schedule.
 2 (1975) 30 P & CR 19. See, however, *Jeary v Chailey RDC* (1973) 26 P & CR 280, CA.
 3 See [1985] JPL 63 for an example of the way grounds (b) and (c) relate to each other.

(e) In the case of a notice not falling within para (d) (above), that the breach of planning control alleged by the notice occurred before the beginning of 1964. Grounds (d) and (e) allow for an appeal on the basis that the breach of control is immune from enforcement action under one or other of the 'limitation periods' (see p 323 above). These grounds are mutually exclusive.

(f) That the enforcement notice was not served as required by s 87(5) of the Act (see p 300 above).

(g) That the steps required by the notice to be taken exceed what is necessary to remedy any breach of planning control or to achieve a purpose specified in s 87(10). This would include the plea successfully advanced in *Mansi v Elstree RDC*[4] that the notice seeks to restrict a use of the land which may legitimately be carried on (see p 314 above). To succeed on this ground the appellant must show that the enforcement notice requires more than is necessary to undo the contravention, or that it goes beyond what can be required under s 87(10). If it is desired to argue that it would be reasonable to require something less than full restoration, that argument would seem more logically to come within ground (a).

(h) That the specified period for compliance with the notice falls short of what should reasonably be allowed. It would seem that the reasonableness of the period allowed is to be tested as at the date of service of the notice.[5] In considering whether in terms of ground (h) the specified period falls short of what should reasonably be allowed, the minister is apparently entitled to take into account the previous planning history of the site. In *Mercer v Uckfield RDC*[6] an appeal against a refusal of planning permission was dismissed in November 1959. In December 1960 an enforcement notice was served requiring the owner to remove vehicles and other articles from the site within 28 days of the notice taking effect. At the date of service there were some 300 vehicles on the site and the owner appealed to the minister on the ground that the period allowed for compliance with the notice was unreasonably short. Taking the previous planning history of the site into account, the minister found the period reasonable. The Divisional Court held that the owner, knowing that an enforcement notice could have been served at any time after November 1959, kept the vehicles on the site after that date at his peril and that the previous planning history was relevant and was properly taken into account by the minister.

Appeal procedure

An appeal must be made in writing to the Secretary of State (s 88(3)) and must be made before the date specified in the enforcement notice as the date on which it is to take effect (s 88(1)). The Secretary of State has no power to extend the time for appeal. The requirements that an appeal be made in writing and within the specified time are imperative and cannot be waived by the Secretary of State.[7] It is not enough that an appeal is posted before the specified date; the notice of appeal must be received by the Secretary of State

4 (1964) 16 P & CR 153.
5 *Smith v King* (1969) 68 LGR 40, 21 P & CR 560.
6 (1962) 14 P & CR 32.
7 *Howard v Secretary of State for the Environment* [1975] QB 235, [1974] 1 All ER 644, CA.

before the relevant date.[8] Where the notice takes effect on a day following a weekend or a bank holiday, it has been held that the appeal can be effected by posting the appeal on the weekend or bank holiday through a letter box provided.[9]

There is no prescribed form for a notice of appeal (though a form of appeal is obtainable from the Department of the Environment; DoE No 14069) and in the Scottish case of *Pirie v Bauld*[10] it was held that a letter which referred to the equivalent section to s 88 but did not specifically state that it was intended to give notice of appeal was to be treated as a valid appeal. A person giving notice of an appeal must submit to the Secretary of State a statement specifying the grounds on which he is appealing against the enforcement notice and stating briefly the facts[11] on which he proposes to rely in support of each of these grounds; if this statement is not submitted at the time of making the appeal, or any statement received is inadequate and the Secretary of State has to request further information, the minister may require the information to be supplied within 28 days.[12] If that requirement is not complied with, the Secretary of State may dismiss the appeal (s 88(6)(a)). Circular 38/81 stated that if an appeal is dismissed under s 88(6) then any planning fee already paid will be returned as the Secretary of State will not have considered the deemed planning application (see below).

Local planning authorities have been asked to send all recipients an extra copy of the enforcement notice, which can be sent to the Secretary of State with any appeal which may be made.[13] In any case there exists a power for the Secretary of State to require the local planning authority to send him, within 14 days of the authority having been told that an appeal has been made, a copy of the enforcement notice and the names and addresses of those served with copies.[14] If this is not done the enforcement notice can be quashed (s 88(6)(b)).

A fee is generally payable in respect of the 'deemed' planning application associated with the enforcement appeal (above) and should be paid to the Secretary of State when the appeal is lodged.[15] The fee will be refunded if the Secretary of State declines jurisdiction, or if the enforcement notice is

---

8 See *Lenlyn Ltd v Secretary of State for the Environment* (1984) 50 P & CR 129, [1985] JPL 482; and *Cookham RDC v Bull* [1972] 225 Estates Gazette 2104, CA. In *R v Melton and Belvoir Justices, ex p Tynan* (1977) 75 LGR 544, 33 P & CR 214 notice of appeal was sent one day late but was initially accepted by the Secretary of State; the Divisional Court took the view that the purported acceptance did not render the appeal valid. Also see *R v Secretary of State and Bromley London Borough Council, ex p Jackson* [1987] JPL 790.

9 *Rv Secretary of State for the Environment ex p JBI Financial Consultants* [1989] JPL 365.

10 1975 SLT (Sh Ct) 6.

11 It is necessary to state facts even if it is proposed only to raise matters of law on appeal—see *PAD Entertainments Ltd v Secretary of State for the Environment* (1982) 264 Estates Gazette 1005, [1982] JPL 706.

12 1971 Act, s 88(4) and reg 5 of the Town and Country Planning (Enforcement Notices and Appeals) Regulations 1981. These provisions give statutory recognition to the decision in *Howard v Secretary of State for the Environment* [1975] QB 235, [1974] 1 All ER 644, CA.

13 See circular 32/1983, para 41.

14 See s 88(6)(e) and reg 8 of the Town and Country Planning (Enforcement Notices and Appeals) Regulations 1981.

15 See the Town and Country Planning (Fees for Applications and Deemed Applications) Regulations 1989, reg 10.

withdrawn, or if the appeal is withdrawn before the date of the public inquiry or site inspection, or if the appeal succeeds on any of the grounds (b) to (f) in s 88(1) or is held to be invalid.[16] A fee is payable in respect of each appeal made by different persons against an enforcement notice.

In cases where the appeal is to be decided by written representations, the local planning authority must submit to the Secretary of State and to the appellant a statement of the submissions which they propose to put forward.[17] This statement is to include a summary of the authority's response to each ground of appeal advanced by the appellant and a statement as to whether the authority would be prepared to grant planning permission for the development alleged in the enforcement notice to have been carried out, and, if so, the details of any conditions they would wish to attach to such a permission.

If the authority's statement is not submitted within 28 days of the date that the statement was required by the Secretary of State,[18] the Secretary of State may allow the appeal without further procedure and quash the enforcement notice (s 88(6)(b)). The Secretary of State will, it seems, not invoke this power when he considers there are extenuating circumstances.[19] Where a local inquiry is to be held to consider the appeal, the statement must be served not later than 28 days before the date of the inquiry, unless a later date is mutually agreed by the Secretary of State and the parties to the appeal.[20]

The appeal procedure is similar to that for appeals against refusal or conditional grant of planning permission (see p 266 above and chapter 19). The Secretary of State must, if either the appellant or the local planning authority so desire, afford to each of them an opportunity of appearing before, and being heard by, a person appointed by the minister for the purpose (s 88(7)).[1] However, this right is expressly overridden by s 88(8) which provides that the Secretary of State is not required to afford such an opportunity if he proposes to dismiss an appeal because the appellant has not provided the statement of his grounds of appeal and supporting facts when required to do this by the Secretary of State. If a statement is provided which specifies more than one ground of appeal but the appellant has not provided facts to support each of the grounds within 28 days of being required under reg 5 to provide a statement, then the Secretary of State may determine the appeal without considering any of the grounds which have not been backed up with information (s 88(9)). So the position would seem to be that, where there has been partial compliance with reg 5, the Secretary of State may instead of dismissing the appeal summarily, determine it exclusively on the grounds that have been supported by facts. Similarly, if the local planning authority has failed to supply its statement within the required time and in the prescribed form or has failed to send copies of the enforcement notice with details of the persons served (s 88(5)(c)(e) and regs 6 and 8), the

---

16 See reg 10(8) to (12) above. But note the exemption regarding a notice alleging use of land as caravan site.
17 1971 Act, s 88(5)(b) and reg 6 of the Town and Country Planning (Enforcement Notice and Appeals) Regulations 1981.
18 See reg 6(2)(b), ibid.
19 See circular 38/81, para 39.
20 See reg 6(2)(a) of the 1981 regulations.
1 The procedures for such a hearing, generally dealt with by way of local inquiry, are governed by the Town and Country Planning (Enforcement) (Inquiries Procedure) Rules 1981.

Secretary of State may allow the appeal and quash the notice without giving the authority an opportunity for a hearing (s 88(6)(b) and (8)).

Appeals against enforcement notices are among the classes of appeals which have been delegated to appointed persons (see chapter 19); however, the Secretary of State retains power to direct that any particular appeal is to be determined by him.[2]

Where it is not proposed to hold a public inquiry, the local planning authority must give notice of the appeal to the occupiers of property in the neighbourhood of the appeal site who in the authority's opinion are affected by the breach of planning control. This notification must include a description of the alleged breach, reasons for serving the notice, grounds of appeal and a time limit within which interested parties can submit written comments to the authority (s 88(5)(d) and reg 7). Failure to comply with this requirement does not empower the Secretary of State to quash the notice summarily.[3]

Widgery J in *Nelsovil v Minister of Housing and Local Government*[4] held that it was for the appellant to make good his grounds of appeal. However, in *LWT Contractors Ltd v Secretary of State for the Environment and Broxbourne Borough Council*[5] Woolf J stressed that the burden of proof in enforcement appeals was not the criminal burden of 'beyond reasonable doubt' but the ordinary civil burden of 'the balance of probabilities'. Nevertheless, as the onus is on the appellant this means that on an appeal the planning authority does not have to provide evidence as to the previous use to show that the change was material. If the appellant does not produce evidence that satisfies the Secretary of State or his inspector on the balance of probabilities that the change was not material, then it must be accepted that a breach of control has taken place.[6]

Determination of appeal

On the determination of an appeal against an enforcement notice the Secretary of State (or, in a delegated case, the inspector)[7] is to give directions for giving effect to his determination including, where appropriate, directions for quashing the enforcement notice or for varying its terms (s 88A(1)). There would appear to be two distinct powers of variation: one contained in s 88A(1) and the other set out in s 88A(2). The wording of s 88A(1) indicates that this power of variation only applies where variation is necessary to give effect to the final outcome of the appeal. It therefore applies when the appellant has convinced the Secretary of State or his inspector that the steps

---

2 See the Town and Country Planning (Determination of Appeals by Appointed Persons) (Prescribed Classes) Regulations 1981 and Sch 9, para 3 to the 1971 Act.

3 But it could be grounds on which a third party (not so informed) might challenge the legality of any subsequent grant of planning permission; see *Wilson v Secretary of State for the Environment* [1988] JPL 540.

4 [1962] 1 All ER 423, [1962] 1 WLR 404. See also *Britt v Buckinghamshire County Council* [1964] 1 QB 77, [1963] 2 All ER 175, CA; *Wild and AGM Car Hire Ltd v Secretary of State for the Environment* (1976) 241 Estates Gazette 235, [1976] JPL 432; and *Ross v Aberdeen County Council* 1955 SLT (Sh Ct) 65.

5 [1981] JPL 815; see too *Thrasyvoulou v Secretary of State for the Environment* [1984] JPL 732.

6 See *Ferris v Secretary of State for the Environment* (1988) 57 P & CR 127, [1988] JPL 777.

7 In the determination of an enforcement notice appeal the appointed person has the same powers and duties as are conferred upon the Secretary of State by s 88(4) to (6) of the 1971 Act (1971 Act, Sch 9, para 2(1)).

required by the notice are excessive (ground (g)) or too pre-emptory (ground (h)). The other power of variation is more general and is provided to deal with initial faults in the notice as drafted (see below).

The Secretary of State may grant planning permission for the development to which the enforcement notice relates or for part of that development or for the development of part of the land to which the notice relates (s 88B(1)(a)). This wording does not get round the difficulties highlighted in *Richmond upon Thames Borough Council v Secretary of State for the Environment*.[8] There it was held that it was not open to the Secretary of State to grant permission for development different from the unauthorised development, the subject of the enforcement notice. However, the power to grant permission for part of the unauthorised development gives the Secretary of State a certain amount of flexibility and may mean that he can grant permission for a more restricted activity than the actual material change of use.[9] It would seem that it is not open to the minister to grant planning permission in respect of land which was not covered by the notice.[10] A grant of planning permission may include permission for the retention or completion of any buildings or works without compliance with a condition attached to a previous planning permission (s 88B(2)(a)). The permission may also be subject to such conditions as the Secretary of State thinks fit (s 88B(2)(b)). In considering whether to grant planning permission, the minister must, as in a planning appeal, have regard to the provisions of the development plan, so far as material to the subject matter of the enforcement notice, and to any other material considerations (s 88B(2)).[11]

The Secretary of State may discharge any condition or limitation on a grant of planning permission for the development to which the enforcement notice relates (s 88B(1)(b)); it appears that this power is not confined to a condition or limitation in respect of which a breach of planning control is alleged. Furthermore, he may substitute for it any other condition or limitation whether more or less onerous (s 88B(2)).

The Secretary of State may also determine any purpose for which the land may, in the circumstances obtaining at the time of the determination, be lawfully used, having regard to any past use thereof or to any planning permission relating to the land (s 88B(1)(c)). A determination under this provision will make clear the use to which the land may lawfully be put and will avoid the need for exploratory applications for planning permission. A determination under s 88B(1)(c) does not, of course, oblige a person with an interest in the land to use the land in accordance with the determination, but he may do so at any time after the determination without further authorisation under the planning legislation. The Secretary of State will apparently not make such a determination unless specifically asked to do so by one of the parties and even when asked has sometimes had to decline to do so because

---

8 (1972) 224 Estates Gazette 1555.
9 See *Hansford v Minister of Housing and Local Government* (1969) 213 Estates Gazette 637 in which it was held that planning permission could not be granted for part of the offending development.
10 See appeal decision noted in [1973] JPL 261.
11 See *ELS Wholesale (Wolverhampton) Ltd v Secretary of State for the Environment* (1987) 56 P & CR 69, [1987] JPL 844 where May LJ sets out the principles which apply to the exercise of this discretion.

insufficient evidence was presented to the inquiry to enable him to form a view on the question.[12]

Even if appeal to the Secretary of State against an enforcement notice has not been made on ground (a) of s 88(2) (ie, on the ground that planning permission ought to be granted for the development to which the enforcement notice relates or, as the case may be, that a condition or limitation alleged in the enforcement notice not to have been complied with ought to be discharged), the appellant is deemed to have made an application for planning permission for the development to which the notice relates (s 88B(3)).

A decision that a use is immune from enforcement action because it began before the beginning of 1964 is not equivalent to a grant of planning permission (see p 333 above) and even where an appeal succeeds on ground (d) of s 88(2) (ie that the alleged breach occurred before the beginning of 1964) and the enforcement notice is quashed, the Secretary of State will still have to consider the application for planning permission which the appellant is, by virtue of s 88B(3), deemed to have made.

The application of issue estoppel to appeals. In the course of an appeal the Secretary of State or his inspector will make several important findings: whether a breach of control as alleged took place; whether the use was established prior to 1964 etc. These findings will be crucial to the outcome of the actual appeal but it appears that it will also be impossible to challenge the correctness of these findings in other subsequent appeals. This is because the Court of Appeal in *Thrasyvoulou v Secretary of State for the Environment*[13] held that the principle of issue estoppel applied to a decision in an appeal against an enforcement notice under s 36 and s 88 of the 1971 Act. In 1982 enforcement notices had been served alleging that properties were being used as hostels and that this amounted to a material change of use. On appeal, the enforcement notices were quashed mainly on the grounds that the properties in the circumstances were being used as hotels rather than hostels and a material change had not taken place. Then in 1985 new enforcement notices were issued by the council with respect to the same properties alleging a material change of use 'to use as a hostel for homeless families'. This time round on appeal, the inspector upheld the notices 'on the basis of a very considerable body of evidence and submissions as to the law put before me much of which may not have been available to my predecessor'. These decisions were challenged in the court by way of s 246 and it was held that the inspector was bound in law not to reopen the findings made by his predecessors and that this meant that, in respect of certain of the notices, he had erred in law in not quashing the notices.

The principle as laid down in the judgment of Ralph Gibson LJ is that the onus is on the party which raises the estoppel, to prove that in previous proceedings a final determination had been made of a point which properly belonged to those proceedings:

'It is not open to the planning authority to relitigate the same issue: that

---

12 See *Selected Enforcement and Allied Appeals*, p 62. This interpretation has been endorsed by Graham Eyre QC in *Ferris v Secretary of State for the Environment* (1988) 57 P & CR 127, [1988] JPL 777.
13 [1988] QB 809, [1988] 2 All ER 781.

means that the estoppel can not for example, be displaced by a more copious citation of authority, or demonstration of the fact that the current exercise of discretion or of judgment on matters of fact and degree has been operating differently from the exercise of those powers at an earlier time, or by more detailed evidence of the nature of the activities, if there has been no material change in fact, in their nature between the time of the first decision and the later proceedings.'[14]

However, Ralph Gibson LJ made clear that there will be circumstances where the issue can be reopened as when false or misleading evidence has been given at the time of the previous decision. The principle will also not apply where the facts have materially changed since the last decision.

On the other hand the principle of issue estoppel has no application to the exercise of an administrative discretion as to whether to grant planning permission[15] but it may apply to a s 36 appeal where the decision relates to the existing use rights of a party.

Parker LJ also pointed out that it could be argued that, because para 2(3) of Sch 9 to the 1971 Act provided that the validity of an inspector's decision on an enforcement appeal 'shall not be questioned in any proceedings whatsoever' except by way of appeal under s 246, the reopening of an issue decided by the inspector on such an appeal would be violating that prohibition. However, this requires the words 'validity of his decision' in Sch 9 to be read to include not only the decision on the outcome of the appeal but the decisions on issues on which that final decision was based. In the event Parker LJ had no concluded view on the matter as it had not been argued, but he used it as a strong supporting reason for the applicability of issue estoppel to a s 88 appeal.

Ralph Gibson LJ justified the application of issue estoppel to enforcement notice appeals on the ground that it was 'necessary for the protection as a matter of right of the occupier of land against the unfair, although well intentioned, repetition of proceedings which in my judgment Parliament cannot be taken to have intended to authorise.' But this seems to neglect Lord Scarman's warning in *Pioneer Aggregates (UK) Ltd v Secretary of State for the Environment*[16] against the application of private law principles to comprehensive statutory codes unless it was expressly authorised by Parliament or was necessary to give effect to the purpose of the legislators. Ralph Gibson LJ in effect is reversing the burden of proving that the private law principle is necessary. An alternative and, we would submit, preferred solution, would be to leave it to the applicant to argue that the re-issue of the notice in the circumstances was so unfair as to be an abuse of power.[17]

There is a specific power on an appeal for the Secretary of State to disregard the fact that a person required to be served with a copy of the enforcement notice has not been served if neither the appellant nor that person has been substantially prejudiced. In *Mayes v Secretary of State for*

---

14 Ibid at p 695.
15 See *Rockhold Ltd v Secretary of State for the Environment and South Oxfordshire District Council* [1986] JPL 130 which was distinguished in *Thrasyvoulou*.
16 [1984] AC 132, [1984] 2 All ER 358, HL; and see p 334 above.
17 See *Re Preston* [1985] AC 835 and see p 388 above. This argument could be raised either by an application for judicial review or on appeal.

Wales[18] Sir Graham Eyre QC, sitting as a deputy judge, held that the test was whether there was any reasonable prospect that the position of the person would have been different if he had been properly served.

Defects in enforcement notices

On an appeal against an enforcement notice, the Secretary of State or appointed person may correct any informality, defect or error in the notice or give directions for varying its terms if he is satisfied that the correction or variation can be made without injustice to the appellant or the local planning authority (s 88A(2)). However, some defects will be regarded as so serious as to render the notice *ultra vires*, with the result that no question of correction or variation can arise.

In *Miller-Mead v Minister of Housing and Local Government*[19] Upjohn LJ stated that if on its face the notice does not comply with the requirements of [s 87] then it is a nullity and 'so much waste paper'. He said: 'A notice has to specify certain matters. If it does not so specify, the notice is plainly inoperative as a notice under the Act.' It would seem, therefore, that a failure to specify the breach of control, the steps required to be taken to remedy the breach, the date on which the notice is to take effect and the period for compliance will nullify the notice. Thus in *Burgess v Jarvis and Sevenoaks RDC*[20] the Court of Appeal held that a notice which did not specify the period at the expiration of which it was to take effect was a nullity.

Upjohn LJ went on to define a further category of defects which will nullify a notice. He said:

'Supposing, then, on its true construction the notice was hopelessly ambiguous and uncertain, so that the owner or occupier could not tell in what respect it was alleged that he had developed the land without permission or in what respect it was alleged that he had failed to comply with a condition or, again, that he could not tell with reasonable certainty what steps he had to take to remedy the alleged breaches. The notice would be bad on its face and a nullity.'

This category may be illustrated by the decision of the Divisional Court in *Metallic Protectives Ltd v Secretary of State for the Environment*.[1] The court considered that a notice which required the installation of satisfactory sound-proofing of a compressor and for all possible action to be taken to minimise the effects created by the use of acrylic paint was so uncertain in its terms as to be a nullity. As such, it was incapable of amendment.

At the same time it is important to emphasise that the courts will not lightly hold an enforcement notice to be a nullity. In particular it is now clear that you can look beyond 'the four corners' of the notice and have regard to the surrounding context. Thus in *Coventry Scaffolding Co (London) Ltd v Parker*[2] an enforcement notice failed to specify the property to which the

---

18 (1989) Times, 1 February.
19 [1963] 2 QB 196, [1963] 1 All ER 459.
20 [1952] 2 QB 41, [1952] 1 All ER 592.
 1 [1976] JPL 166.
 2 [1987] JPL 127. Also see *Epping Forest District Council v Matthews* [1987] JPL 132.

notice related. On subsequent prosecution for failure to comply with the notice, the occupiers of the property (a company) were fined a small amount. The company appealed to the High Court by way of case stated alleging that the enforcement notice was a nullity and that no prosecution could be based on it. The copy of the notice had been served on the company at its office which adjoined the premises the subject of the notice and previous correspondence with the company had referred to the address of those premises. The Divisional Court upheld the conviction on the grounds that the enforcement notice was not a nullity and Kerr LJ who gave the main judgment said that:

'What had to be decided in each instance was whether, in the light of the surrounding circumstances, the recipient of the notice was sufficiently and clearly apprised of the effect of the notice, and of what he had to do pursuant to it to render it just or unjust to hold him to it.'

Also, certain matters on which it might have been possible to challenge the *vires* of an enforcement notice at common law are included in the statutory grounds of appeal to the Secretary of State under s 88 (above) and the provision of a statutory right of appeal suggests that these matters do not go to the *vires* of an enforcement notice. As a result of his powers of correction and variation the Secretary of State will in some circumstances be able to uphold an enforcement notice which might otherwise have had to be quashed as invalid. The answer to the question whether the Secretary of State is able to correct or vary an error in an enforcement notice will, of course, be important for the recipient of the notice because if the power is not available then the notice will have to be quashed by the minister. For the recipient the end result may, therefore, be much the same as if the notice was a nullity.

Speaking of the similarly-worded provision in the Town and Country Planning Act 1962, Lord Denning said in *Miller-Mead* that the minister:

'can correct errors so long as, having regard to the merits of the case, the correction can be made without injustice. No informality, defect or error is a material one unless it is such as to produce injustice. Applied to misrecitals, it means this—if the misrecital goes to the substance of the matter then the notice may be quashed, but, if the misrecital does not go to the substance of the matter and can be amended without injustice, it should be amended rather than that the notice should be quashed or declared a nullity.'

This statement of Lord Denning brings together two tests. First there is the question of whether the mistake goes to the substance of the notice and second there is the likelihood of injustice being caused by amendment. Lord Denning seemed to be stating that, even if there is no risk of injustice, a notice cannot be amended if the mistake goes to the substance of the notice, even though he also seemed to suggest that a mistake cannot be material if it will not produce injustice!

The Local Government and Planning (Amendment) Act 1981 changed the wording of the Secretary of State's powers to which Lord Denning had been referring in *Miller-Mead*. Previously, informalities, errors and defects could be corrected as long as the Secretary of State was satisfied that they were not material. Now the only limitation on the powers of correction is that the Secretary of State must be satisfied that the corrections can be made without injustice. It is difficult to decide whether this is different from the formula laid down by Lord Denning in *Miller-Mead*. Although the requirement of materiality has been dropped (it may have been assumed, following Lord Denning, that it was otiose since something which will not cause injustice cannot be material), it may still be that mistakes which go to the substance of the notice cannot be regarded as informalities, defects or errors and so cannot be corrected. In *H T Hughes & Sons Ltd v Secretary of State for the Environment*[3] Hodgson J, after quoting Lord Denning in *Miller-Mead*, decided that a misrecital which went to the substance of the notice could not be corrected even if it would not cause injustice. But in *Harrogate Borough Council v Secretary of State for the Environment*[4] Webster J assumed that the attention of Hodgson J could not have been drawn to the legislative changes since *Miller-Mead* and concluded that it followed that notions of materiality or substance were no longer relevant to the construction of the meaning of 'correct' in s 88A(2). Nevertheless Webster J did accept there could be changes that were so fundamental that they were beyond the powers of the Secretary of State on appeal.[4a]

The other change introduced by the 1981 Act was in respect of the power of variation. Prior to 1981 a notice could only be varied if the variation was in favour of the appellant. There is now no such restriction on either of the two powers of variation to be found in s 88A. There is no express limitation on the power of variation in s 88A(1) and the second power (s 88A(2)) is only limited in that, as with corrections, variations can only be made where the Secretary of State is satisfied that injustice will not be caused to either the appellant or the local authority. As stated above, it would appear that the first power of variation applies where the appellant has succeeded on grounds (f) and (h), while the second applies where the notice is generally found to be faulty; though there may well be some overlap between the two. The importance of the new wording on variation is that, if an error is so grave that it cannot be corrected, it may still be capable of variation. Thus in *Wealden District Council v Secretary of State for the Environment and Innocent*[5] David Widdicombe QC (sitting as deputy judge) held that, although an amendment of a recital which had alleged a material change of use in such a way that it alleged operational development was beyond what in ordinary language could be called a correction, it could be amended under the power of variation. In the *Harrogate* case Webster J agreed with David Widdicombe that 'variation' was a wider term than 'correction' but did not agree with his observation that 'To satisfy the description "variation" I think there must be sufficient continuity of identity before and after the change.' Indeed Webster J thought it undesirable to attempt to define either word or to draw any fine line of distinction between them. Further it has already been

---

3 (1984) 51 P & CR 134, [1985] JPL 486.
4 (1986) 55 P & CR 224, [1987] JPL 288.
4a Since then in *R v London Borough of Tower Hamlets ex p P.F Ahern (London) Ltd* (1989) Times 29 March Roch J held that the Secretary of State may correct *any* defect or error if he is satisfied that the correction can be made without injustice to either party.
5 [1983] JPL 234.

held that it does not matter if the Secretary of State or his inspector confuses the two as long as he has the power to make the change under one of them.[6] So it would seem that the major issue will be whether the change is so fundamental that it cannot be made without causing injustice.

The statutory changes mean that cases decided on the old law must be looked at carefully but they can still provide some guidance.[7] It used to be that if the planning authority allege the wrong breach of control—for example, if they allege development without planning permission when the notice should refer to a breach of a condition—then the error would be regarded as material and incapable of correction.[8] But in *R v London Borough of Tower Hamlets ex p P.F Ahern (London) Ltd*[9] Roch J held that even this kind of error could be corrected if this would not cause injustice. Serious misdescriptions of the alleged breach have been held to be incapable of correction.[10]

In *Kensington and Chelsea Royal Borough v Secretary of State for the Environment and Mia Carla Ltd*[11] Donaldson LJ said that the power to correct a notice was 'distinctly limited'. It would not extend to correction of a misdescription in the alleged unauthorised material change of use. The notice in that case referred to 'a material change in the use of the garden of the said land to a use for the purposes of a restaurant'. The local planning authority argued that it could be amended so as to refer instead to a material change of use by way of intensification of the restaurant use. 'Plainly', said Donaldson LJ, 'such an amendment would not be the correction of any informality or defect; it would be producing a totally different enforcement notice.'

The decision in *Mia Carla* appears to go further than that in *Birmingham Corpn v Minister of Housing and Local Government and Habib Ullah*.[12] There Lord Widgery CJ said that the minister was perfectly right to refuse to amend a notice which alleged as the breach of control 'house-let-in-lodgings' rather than 'use as separate dwellings'. Lord Widgery did not specifically rule out such an amendment but stated that 'it would be wrong in these circumstances for the minister to amend an enforcement notice to cover a development which had never been put forward or argued' at the inquiry into the appeal. In other words, such an amendment or correction would cause injustice.

Misdescriptions of the breach of control which are not of a serious nature would seem to be capable of correction. Thus, in *Hammersmith London*

6 *Morris v Secretary of State for the Environment* (1975) 31 P & CR 216.
7 For a critique of the old powers of correction see M Purdue, 'The Secretary of State's Power to Repair Defective Enforcement Notices' [1981] JPL 483. Examples of appeal decisions raising the question whether correction could be made are to be found in [1977] JPL 116, 397 and 675, [1978] JPL 568 and 785, [1979] JPL 47, 188 and 786, [1980] JPL 469, [1983] JPL 449 and 826, and [1984] JPL 451. See too *Selected Enforcement and Allied Appeals*, pp 11, 12, 21 and 29.
8 *Garland v Minister of Housing and Local Government* (1968) 20 P & CR 93; and *Kerrier District Council v Secretary of State for the Environment and Brewer* (1980) 41 P & CR 284; but see *West Oxfordshire District Council v Secretary of State for the Environment* [1988] JPL 324.
9 (1989) Times, 29 March.
10 *Copeland Borough Council v Secretary of State for the Environment* (1976) 31 P & CR 403; *Kensington and Chelsea Royal Borough v Secretary of State for the Environment and Mia Carla Ltd* [1981] JPL 50; and *Choudhury v Secretary of State for the Environment* (1983) 265 Estates Gazette 345, [1983] JPL 231.
11 [1981] JPL 50.
12 [1964] 1 QB 178, [1963] 3 All ER 668.

Borough Council v Secretary of State for the Environment[13] it was held that where the Secretary of State considered that an enforcement notice contained an unsuitable description of the use of premises he was entitled, and indeed bound,[14] to attempt to obtain accuracy in the notice by substituting a more suitable description in the notice, provided that no injustice would thereby be done to either party; in this case the Secretary of State had erred in concluding that an inappropriate allegation of change of use to guest-house (rather than 'hostel' or some such similar description) was a material error which he could not correct.

Although the description of the breach as a material change of use rather than as operational development can be varied if it will not cause injustice David Widdicombe QC in *Wealden*[15] stated that:

'In most cases which come to mind, a variation from material change of use to operational development would be very likely to cause injustice. The issues which can arise in respect of these two types of development can be quite different. Further there was no time limit for enforcement in cases of material change of use, but there was a four-year time limit in cases of operational development and this limitation period could be an issue.'

Widdicombe did not make clear whether such problems could be overcome by re-opening the hearing or having further exchange of written representations but the implication seems to have been that where the time limit was relevant the notice could not be varied. The local planning authority could then issue another notice but by then it might be absolutely clear that the operations were substantially completed more than four years from the issue of the notice.

It appears that any correction which has the effect of enlarging the scope of the enforcement notice will generally be regarded as material and beyond the powers of the minister. For example, in *TLG Building Materials v Secretary of State for the Environment*,[16] Donaldson LJ commented that it seemed to him that it was:

'beyond a mere formality to call upon somebody to stop using some land for the storage of building materials and to amend it to the much wider concept of prohibiting use as a builders merchants yard ... [A]ny wider condemnation—if that was the right word—in an enforcement notice must be material, except in somewhat exceptional circumstances.'

In the same case Hodgson J said that it was 'only in the most unusual circumstances that one could say that the correction of a notice that altered the planning unit to which the enforcement notice was directed was not material'. Similarly, the minister has held that it would be beyond his powers

13 (1975) 30 P & CR 19. See also *Brooks and Burton Ltd v Secretary of State for the Environment* [1978] 1 All ER 733, [1977] 1 WLR 1294; *Patel v Betts* [1978] JPL 109; and *Bevan v Secretary of State for Wales* (1969) 211 Estates Gazette 1245.
14 See also on this point Ackner J in *Hounslow London Borough Council v Secretary of State for the Environment and Indian Gymkhana Club* [1981] JPL 510. See too *Wealden District Council v Secretary of State for the Environment and Innocent* [1983] JPL 234; and *Bath City Council v Secretary of State for the Environment* (1983) 47 P & CR 663.
15 [1983] JPL 234.
16 (1980) 41 P & CR 243.

to correct a plan attached to an enforcement notice so as to extend the area covered by the notice.[17]

The decision in *Morris v Secretary of State for the Environment*[18] would seem to provide an illustration of the 'somewhat exceptional circumstances' referred to by Donaldson LJ in *TLG Building Materials* when a 'wider condemnation' will not be regarded as material. The enforcement notice alleged as the breach of control the use of premises for the sale, repair and respraying of motor vehicles. The notice required the discontinuance of the use of the site for repairing and respraying vehicles and the removal of the vehicles. Through an oversight it omitted to proscribe the sale of vehicles. The court held that the notice could be corrected to include the sale of vehicles. No injustice would be caused as the omission was a pure error and it was obvious that it should have been there from the start. Similarly, in *Sanders v Secretary of State for the Environment and Epping Forest District Council*[19] the Divisional Court held that a notice could be corrected so as to proscribe the use of land for the repair of boilers in addition to the storing and cutting up of scrap metal. The additional use had been in issue in the appeal against the enforcement notice and could not be carried on independently of the other proscribed activities; together they formed a composite mixed use of the land. The correction would not, therefore, cause injustice.

Subject to the question of injustice, any correction which has the effect of enlarging the scope of the notice is likely to be regarded as material, but a reduction in the scope of the notice will usually be within the minister's powers.[20] Thus, for example, the minister has been prepared to correct a notice which referred to a larger area than was actually used for the purpose enforced against.[1] The court will return a notice to the minister for correction if there is a risk that it may prohibit a lawful use.[2]

Challenging the validity of the Secretary of State's decision

Section 246(1) provides that a 'decision in proceedings on an appeal' against an enforcement notice can be appealed against on a point of law.[3] The term 'decision in proceedings on an appeal' would clearly cover a final determination of the appeal; such as the quashing or upholding of the enforcement notice. It would also seem to cover decisions to dismiss an appeal or to quash the notice because of failures to comply with the appeal procedures (see p 347). But in *Lenlyn Ltd v Secretary of State for the Environment*[4] Hodgson J

---

17 [1971] JPL 348; see too [1974] JPL 734, [1975] JPL 166, and [1976] JPL 710.
18 (1975) 31 P & CR 216.
19 [1981] JPL 593.
20 See *Camden London Borough v Secretary of State for the Environment* (1978) 252 Estates Gazette 275, [1979] JPL 311, and *Burner, Burner and Burner v Secretary of State for the Environment and South Hams District Council* [1983] JPL 459.
1 [1974] JPL 159; see too [1974] JPL 248 and 426.
2 *Mansi v Elstree RDC* (1964) 16 P & CR 153; *Newport v Secretary of State for the Environment and Bromley London Borough* (1980) 40 P & CR 261; *Trevors Warehouses Ltd v Secretary of State for the Environment* (1972) 23 P & CR 215; and *Day and Mid-Warwickshire Motors Ltd v Secretary of State for the Environment* (1979) 78 LGR 27 and p 314 above.
3 See ch 20 for detailed discussion of s 246.
4 (1984) 50 P & CR 129, [1985] JPL 482.

held that where the Secretary of State made a decision to decline jurisdiction to hear an appeal, the correct way to challenge the legality of such a decision was by way of an application of judicial review and not under s 246. However, Hodgson J would seem not to have been referred to a previous line of the authorities where it had been held that such a decision could be challenged under s 246.[5] The difference could be important as an application under s 246 has to be made within 28 days, while with judicial review it can be made within three months as long as there is not undue delay.[6] It remains to be seen whether a failure to apply for judicial review in time means that it is too late to challenge the validity of the decision in any later proceedings. The courts had previously held that a failure to take up the matter under s 246 meant that the decision to refuse the appeal was effective and the enforcement notice took effect, even though there might have been a valid appeal.[7]

As an appeal against an enforcement notice is deemed to be an application for planning permission (s 88B(3)), a decision on an appeal is also a determination of that deemed planning application. Although s 245 is the more appropriate remedy to challenge the determination of the planning application, there is a right to go under s 246 as an alternative.[8]

Challenge of enforcement notice directly in the courts

The recipient of an enforcement notice which is *ultra vires* may be able to challenge it directly in the High Court on ordinary administrative law principles, or might take the risk of simply ignoring the notice, raising the question of *vires* as a defence to proceedings for non-compliance with the notice. However, even if the recipient of an enforcement notice is satisfied that the notice is a nullity, as an enforcement notice 'runs with the land' (see p 361 below), he may consider it desirable to get a formal pronouncement from the court so as to remove any doubts which might arise in the future. As Lord Denning remarked in *Lovelock v Minister of Transport*:[9] 'The plain fact is that, even if such a decision as this is "void" or a "nullity", it remains in being unless and until some steps are taken before the courts to have it declared void.'

The right to challenge an enforcement notice in the courts on ordinary administrative law principles is restricted by s 243(1)(a) of the 1971 Act which provides[10] that: 'The validity of an enforcement notice shall not, except by way of appeal under Pt V of this Act be questioned in any proceedings

---

5 *Button v Jenkins* [1975] 3 All ER 585; *Horsham District Council v Fisher* [1977] JPL 178; *Chalgray Ltd v Secretary of State for the Environment* (1976) 33 P & CR 10, [1977] JPL 176; and *Wain v Secretary of State for the Environment* (1978) 39 P & CR 82, [1979] JPL 231.

6 See *R v Stratford-on-Avon District Council, ex p Jackson* [1985] 3 All ER 769, [1985] 1 WLR 1319.

7 See *Button v Jenkins* and *Wain v Secretary of State for the Environment* above. For criticism of these cases see John Alder, 'Challenging Enforcement Notices' [1978] JPL 160.

8 See *Gill v Secretary of State for the Environment* [1985] JPL 710, explaining *Broxbourne Borough Council v Secretary of State for the Environment* [1980] QB 1, [1979] 2 All ER 13. See also *J Toomey Motors Ltd v Secretary of State for the Environment and Basildon District Council* [1981] JPL 418.

9 (1980) 78 LGR 576, 40 P & CR 336. See too *London and Clydeside Estates Ltd v Aberdeen District Council*, [1979] 3 All ER 876, [1980] 1 WLR 182 1980 SC (HL) 1.

10 Subject to the exception mentioned in s 243(2) (below).

whatsoever on any of the grounds on which such an appeal may be brought.'[11]

The purpose of this preclusive clause would therefore seem to be that if it is considered that the local planning authority are in error in alleging that the activities in question constitute a breach of control or that a breach of control has taken place, or are in error in describing the breach of control, on questions of immunity from enforcement action or in the service of the notice, or in their requirements as to the steps to be taken or the time in which those steps have to be taken, the only way in which the mistake may be challenged is by way of an appeal to the Secretary of State under s 88 and thence to the courts by way of s 246. If no appeal is lodged then the opportunity to challenge such errors is in general lost for good. In *Miller-Mead v Minister of Housing and Local Government*[12] Lord Denning explained the legislation's effect in the following terms:

'You used previously to be able to raise any of these matters before the courts. But by reason of s 33(8) of the Act of 1960 [the terms of which were very similar to those of s 243(1)(b) of the 1971 Act] you can no longer do so. You cannot raise it by an action for a declaration. You cannot raise it by appeal to the justices. Nor by waiting until there is an attempt to enforce it by criminal proceedings. You can only raise it by an appeal to the Minister. And even if you succeed in your appeal, the Minister can at the most quash it. He cannot declare it to be a nullity or hold it to be void from the beginning. In this way the legislature has disposed of the suggestion that an enforcement notice is a "nullity" on any such ground.'

The courts have refused to give a narrow interpretation to s 243(1)(b). In *R v Thomas George Smith*[13] the Court of Appeal rejected the argument that 'proceedings' should be confined to proceedings by way of judicial review and did not cover criminal proceedings. In the judgment of the court the word 'proceedings' in s 243(1)(a) included criminal proceedings under s 89(1) and (5).[14]

The Court of Appeal in *R v Keeys*[15] further held that, even if it turns out on a prosecution that the facts as alleged in the enforcement notice do not fit what has actually taken place, this cannot be raised as a defence as it is a ground which could have been raised on appeal to the Secretary of State (ground (c)). In this case, the enforcement notice required the stationing of a 'mobile home' and a 'caravan' to be discontinued. It was therefore held that s 243 prevented it being argued that the enforcement notice was not being disobeyed as the structures, which were admittedly still on the site, could not

---

11 Formerly s 243 had not excluded challenge on grounds (a), (f) and (g) and the courts had held that challenges could be made on the grounds that the steps required were excessive or the time allowed unreasonably short in the magistrates court; see *Smith v King* (1969) 68 LGR 40, 21 P & CR 560; *Hutchinson v Firetto* [1973] JPL 314; and *Redbridge London Borough v Perry* (1976) 75 LGR 90. However, even then you could not challenge the merits of an enforcement notice; see *Rochdale Metropolitan Borough Council v Simmonds* (1980) 40 P & CR 432, [1981] JPL 191.
12 [1963] 2 QB 196, [1963] 1 All ER 459, CA.
13 (1984) 48 P & CR 392.
14 See also *Prosser v Sharp* [1985] 1 EGLR 175, [1985] JPL 717; and *Epping Forest District Council v Scott* (1985) 53 P & CR 79, [1986] JPL 603.
15 (1987) 152 JP 107, [1989] JPL 28.

be described as a 'mobile home' or 'a caravan'. However, s 243 can only prevent it being argued that the facts as alleged in the notice did not exist at the time the notice was served. It must be still open to a defendant to raise the defence that he has *since* complied with the notice by carrying out works or altering his activities.

In *Jeary v Chailey RDC*[16] the Court of Appeal held that the similarly-worded privative clause in the Town and Country Planning Act 1962 could not be construed as directed only to groundless challenges of enforcement notices but had to be read as directed also to preventing the assertion of vested rights; even if the appellant in this case had, as he alleged, a vested right to use the premises in question for the purpose which the enforcement notice alleged was in breach of planning control, he was still precluded by the statutory provision from questioning the validity of the notice in the courts.

In *Davy v Spelthorne Borough Council*[17] Lord Fraser said that the word 'validity' as used in s 243(1)(a) was not to be understood in its strict legal sense but was to be taken as meaning 'enforceability', so that an action questioning an enforcement notice, even indirectly, on any of the specified grounds would be caught by the privative clause.[18] In that case Lord Wilberforce said that there may be some warrant for not giving the preclusive clause a restricted meaning and it has been held that in certain circumstances the preclusive clause may act as a bar to proceedings begun before the service of an enforcement notice.

In *Square Meals Frozen Foods Ltd v Dunstable Borough Council*,[19] in anticipation of an enforcement notice being served, the occupiers applied to the High Court for a declaration that they were not in breach of planning control. An enforcement notice was then served after the commencement of the proceedings for the declaration. The Court of Appeal considered that the proceedings were debarred by s 243(1)(b). Lord Denning and Scarman LJ also thought that even if proceedings were not debarred, the courts would stay the action for declaration as the matters were better dealt with by way of appeal to the Secretary of State.[20]

On the other hand in *Flashman v London Borough of Camden*[1] the Court of Appeal, distinguishing the *Square Meals* judgment, held that s 243 did not require that an action should be immediately struck out if the grounds of challenge went beyond the grounds protected by the privative clause or where there was at least an arguable question as to whether s 243 afforded a

16 (1973) 26 P & CR 280.
17 [1984] AC 262, [1983] 3 All ER 278, HL.
18 The House of Lords doubted whether a claim for damages for negligence involved a challenge of the validity of an enforcement notice but held that even if it did, the plaintiff's assertion that he had acquiesced in an enforcement notice because of the planning authority's negligent advice was not a ground covered by s 243(1)(a).
19 [1974] 1 All ER 441, [1974] 1 WLR 59 (which was referred to without disapproval by Lord Wilberforce in *Davy* (above).
20 Also see *James Barrie (Sand and Gravel) Ltd v Lanark District Council* 1979 SLT 14 where the Court of Session similarly held that where the planning authority had resolved to take enforcement action, including the service of a stop notice, the occupiers could not apply for a declarator that they were immune from enforcement action and an interdict to prevent the service of a stop notice. Lord Cowie held that the validity of an enforcement notice could not be challenged on one of the grounds reserved to the Secretary of State which was effectively what the applicants were attempting to do.
1 (1979) 130 NLJ 885. Also see *R v Secretary of State for the Environment, ex p Davidson* (1988) Times, 23 June.

defence. Similarly, in the Scottish case of *McDaid v Clydebank District Council*[2] Lord Cameron held that where a notice was not served on an owner, this did not come within the grounds made exclusive to the Secretary of State as it went beyond arguing that the notice had not been served as required by the Act, which was the ground made exclusive to the Secretary of State. This argument is very dubious and was not even raised in the similar English decision of *R v Greenwich London Borough Council, ex p Patel*.[3]

More important is the argument, accepted in the *McDaid* case, that such a privative clause is not effective to exclude the courts declaring that an enforcement notice is a nullity.[4] This argument is of course based on the landmark decision in the House of Lords of *Anisminic Ltd v Foreign Compensation Commission*.[5] However, in *R v Greenwich London Borough Council, ex p Patel*, Neill LJ, while accepting that 'a court was entitled to investigate whether a decision was a nullity' notwithstanding a statutory provision that the decision 'shall not be called in question in any court of law', held that the provisions in the 1971 Act and the authorities showed that a failure to serve a copy on the owner did not make the enforcement notice a nullity. Neill LJ was presumably referring in particular to Lord Denning's statement in *Miller-Mead* that by making certain grounds exclusive to the Secretary of State the 'legislature had disposed of the suggestion that an enforcement notice is a nullity on any such ground'.[6] It therefore seems fairly certain that it cannot be argued that an enforcement notice is a nullity on any of the grounds set out in s 88(2).

Section 243(1)(a) is not to apply where criminal proceedings are brought under s 89(5) of the 1971 Act in respect of non-compliance with an enforcement notice against a person who:

(a) has held an interest in the land since before the enforcement notice was issued;
(b) did not have the enforcement notice served on him; and
(c) satisfies the court that:
  (i) he did not know and could not reasonably have been expected to know that the enforcement notice had been issued; and
  (ii) his interests have been substantially prejudiced by the failure to serve him with a copy (s 243(2)).

An enforcement notice can of course be challenged on some ground other than those contained in the relevant paragraphs of s 88(1). Lord Fraser of Tullybelton pointed out in *Davy v Spelthorne Borough Council*[7] that:

'If, for example the respondent has alleged that the enforcement notice had been vitiated by fraud, because one of the appellant's officers had been bribed to issue it, or had been served without the appellant's authority, he

---

2 1984 SLT 162.
3 [1985] JPL 851.
4 Also accepted by the Court of Appeal in *Jeary v Chailey RDC* (1973) 26 P & CR 280.
5 [1969] 2 AC 147, [1969] 1 All ER 208 but see *R v Secretary of State for the Environment, ex p Ostler* [1977] QB 122, [1976] 3 All ER 90.
6 See *Miller-Mead v Minister of Housing and Local Government* [1963] 2 QB 196 at 221.
7 [1984] AC 262, [1983] 3 All ER 278. See also *Jeary v Chailey RDC* (1973) 26 P & CR 280, per Orr LJ.

would indeed have been questioning its validity, but not on an of the grounds on which appeal may be brought under Part V.'

A complicating factor here is that largely as a result of the influential decision of the Court of Appeal in *Miller-Mead v Minister of Housing and Local Government*[8] there has been a tendency to draw a sharp distinction between notices which are nullities as being bad on their face and notices which are invalid for other reasons;[9] in the latter case the notice stands, says Grant, 'until it is quashed by the Secretary of State or the court'.[10] However, rigid classifications of this sort are not now followed in administrative law generally[11] and in *R v Greenwich London Borough Council, ex p Patel*[12] Sir John Megaw argued that even where a mandatory statutory provision was breached, the court still retained a residual discretion whether or not to nullify the decision under review. So the court may take into account factors such as whether anyone has been prejudiced or the delay in bringing the action, depending on the importance of the provision.[13]

With that important proviso it is suggested that an enforcement notice will be *ultra vires* in the following circumstances:

(a) A notice which fails to specify some essential statutory requirement will be *ultra vires*. If, for example, the notice fails to specify the breach of control, the steps required to remedy the breach, the date on which the notice is to take effect or the period for compliance,[14] the notice will be *ultra vires*. Although a mere technical error will not have the effect of nullifying a notice,[15] failure to comply with the statutory requirements as to identification of the land and as to provision of reasons and a statement of the rights of appeal might do so.[16] It will not render a notice *ultra vires* that it proceeds on a false basis of fact and that there has in reality been no breach of planning control;[17] a planning authority may serve an enforcement notice where it *appears* to them that there has been a breach of planning control and, in the words of Upjohn LJ,[18] 'a *prima facie* case only need be shown to satisfy the prerequisites of a valid notice'.

(b) An enforcement notice which is uncertain in the sense that it does not fairly tell the recipient what he has to do will be *ultra vires* (see p 318 above).

8 [1963] 2 QB 196, [1963] 1 All ER 459.
9 See M Grant, *Urban Planning Law*, pp 402–409.
10 Ibid, p 408.
11 See, in particular, *London and Clydeside Estates Ltd v Aberdeen District Council* [1979] 3 All ER 876, [1980] 1 WLR 182, 1980 SLT 81, in which Lord Hailsham stated that 'in the field of the rapidly developing jurisprudence of administrative law' the courts will not consider themselves bound 'to fit the facts of a particular case and a developing chain of events into rigid legal categories or to stretch or cramp them on a bed of Procrustes invented by lawyers for the purposes of convenient exposition'.
12 See above.
13 See *Main v Swansea City Council* (1984) 49 P & CR 26; and *R v London Borough of Lambeth Council, ex p Sharp* (1986) 55 P & CR 232, [1987] JPL 440, CA.
14 See *Miller-Mead v Minister of Housing and Local Government* [1963] 2 QB 196, [1963] 1 All ER 459, CA.
15 See *Patel v Betts* (1977) 243 Estates Gazette 1003, [1978] JPL 109, and *Coventry Scaffolding Co (London) Ltd v Parker* [1987] JPL 127.
16 See *London and Clydeside Estates Ltd v Aberdeen District Council* 1980 SC (HL) 1, 1980 SLT 81; and *Warrington Borough Council v Garvey* [1988] JPL 752.
17 See *Jeary v Chailey RDC* (1973) 26 P & CR 280; and *Miller-Mead* (above).
18 In *Miller-Mead* (above).

(c) An enforcement notice may also be *ultra vires* on the ground that the planning authority have in some way misused their discretionary powers. The validity of a notice might, for example, be challenged on the grounds that in deciding to serve the notice the authority had failed to take account of some relevant factor[19] or that the notice was vitiated by fraud or had been served without the authority's sanction.[20]

D CONSEQUENCES OF ENFORCEMENT NOTICE

Enforcement notice to have effect against subsequent development

Section 93(1) of the 1971 Act provides that compliance with an enforcement notice, whether in respect of the demolition or alteration of any building or works or the discontinuance of any use of land or in respect of any other requirement contained in the notice, does not discharge the notice. Any provision of an enforcement notice requiring a use of land to be discontinued is to operate as a requirement that it shall be discontinued permanently to the extent that it is in contravention of Pt III of the 1971 Act and accordingly any resumption of the use at any time after its discontinuance is to that extent in contravention of the enforcement notice (s 93(2)).[1] If development is carried out on land by reinstating or restoring buildings or works which have been demolished or altered in compliance with an enforcement notice, the notice, even though its terms may not be apt for the purpose, is deemed to apply in relation to the reinstated or restored building or works as it applied in relation to the building or works before they were demolished or altered (s 93(3)).[2] Any person who, without the grant of planning permission, carries out development by way of reinstating or restoring buildings or works which have been demolished or altered in accordance with an enforcement notice is guilty of an offence and is liable on summary conviction to a fine not exceeding level 5 on the standard scale (at present £2,000). Presumably the local planning authority may also enter upon the land and carry out works under s 91 of the 1971 Act (below).

Effect of subsequent planning permission

An enforcement notice cannot be withdrawn once it has taken effect (s 87(14)). It will however cease to have effect in so far as it requires works to be carried out or a use to be discontinued, once planning permission has been

---

19 See, for example, *Flashman v London Borough of Camden* (1979) 130 NLJ 885 (in which the Court of Appeal distinguished *Square Meals Frozen Foods Ltd v Dunstable Borough Council* [1974] 1 All ER 441, [1974] 1 WLR 59).
20 See *Davy v Spelthorne Borough Council* [1984] AC 262, [1983] 3 All ER 278, per Lord Fraser; *Scarborough Borough Council v Adams and Adams* (1983) 147 JP 449, 47 P & CR 133, per Watkins LJ; and *R v Secretary of State for the Environment, ex p Hillingdon London Borough Council* [1986] 1 All ER 810, [1986] 1 WLR 192.
1 See in this regard *Prosser v Sharp* [1985] 1 EGLR 175, [1985] JPL 717 where the occupier removed one caravan and then replaced it by another; Stephen Brown LJ held the effect of s 93 was to preclude the further use of the land for a similar purpose.
2 In *Broxbourne Borough Council v Small* [1980] CLY 2638 it was held that where a barn which was the subject of enforcement action was replaced by a smaller Nissen hut used for the same purpose, that was a replacement or restoration of the barn.

granted for the retention on land of buildings or works or for the continuance of a use of land (s 92(1)).[3] Similarly, a grant of planning permission to
retain buildings or works or continue a use without complying with a
condition means that an enforcement notice ceases to have effect in so far as
it requires steps to be taken to comply with the condition. Where the new
planning permission granted, after the service of a copy of the notice, only
relates to part of the requirements of the notice, it is in effect a variation of
the terms of the notice.[4] It may cause difficulties for the local planning
authority; if, for example, after service of an enforcement notice, they grant
planning permission subject to conditions but the developer does not comply
with the conditions, the authority will have to issue a fresh enforcement
notice.[5]

Reversion to 'lawful' use after service of enforcement notice

Where an enforcement notice has been issued in respect of any development
of land, planning permission is not required for the use of that land for the
purpose for which (in accordance with the provisions of Pt III of the 1971
Act) 'it could lawfully have been used if that development had not been
carried out' (s 23(9)).[6]

Non-compliance with an enforcement notice

The possible consequences of failure to comply with the requirements of an
effective enforcement notice depend upon the nature of the requirements
which have not been complied with. The legislation makes a distinction in
this respect between the carrying out of a use of land in contravention of an
enforcement notice, a 'desist notice' (s 89(5)) and a failure to carry out steps
(other than the discontinuance of a use of land) required to be taken by the
notice, a 'do notice' (s 89(1)).[7] The distinction is not between unauthorised
development by material change of use and unauthorised development by
operational development, as with a material change of use steps can be
required to restore the land to its condition before the change. Also under
s 89(5) the offence can be committed by failing to desist from operations
where there has been non-compliance with a condition or limitation. So the
distinction is between failing to *do* something required and failing to *desist*.

3 The notice is not, however, rendered a nullity—see *R v Secretary of State for the
Environment, ex p Three Rivers District Council* [1983] JPL 730. As a result the Secretary of
State has power to award costs on an appeal against an enforcement notice because of the
local planning authority's failure to withdraw the enforcement notice in good time, even
where the notice has ceased to have effect. Also, until the enforcement notice is withdrawn,
the appeal would allow the Secretary of State to grant planning permission, which could be
on more favourable terms than the grant which had meant that the enforcement notice
ceased to have effect.
4 *Dudley Borough Council v Secretary of State for the Environment and Electronic and
Mechanical and Engineering Co Ltd* [1980] JPL 181.
5 See *Havering London Borough Council v Secretary of State for the Environment* (1983) 45 P &
CR 258, [1983] JPL 240.
6 See p 145 above.
7 See *Hodgetts v Chiltern District Council* [1983] 2 AC 120, [1984] 2 WLR 577, where the terms
were used by Lord Roskill.

'Do notice' offences

Section 89(1) makes it an offence if there is a failure to comply with any steps required by an enforcement notice to be taken, other than a requirement that a use of land be discontinued. The offence is committed by the person who, at the time a copy of the enforcement notice was served on him, was the owner of the land to which the notice relates. The penalty on summary conviction is a fine not exceeding £2,000. For conviction on indictment no maximum fine is prescribed. It has been held that the prosecution must prove that the owner of land was served with a copy of the notice and the fact of an appeal by the person who was alleged to be the owner did not absolve the local authority from proving that fact.[8]

The offence committed is a single once-and-for-all offence and so there is no problem of the charge being bad for duplicity.[9] It would appear that the offence incorporates an element of *mens rea* even if full *mens rea* is not required. In *South Cambridgeshire District Council v Stokes*[10] an owner, who was served with an enforcement notice, did not appeal. His tenant did appeal but later withdrew the appeal. The owner tried to argue on a subsequent prosecution under s 89(1) that he had not committed the offence as he did not know how long he had to comply since he did not know when the notice took effect. Forbes J said that he thought it doubtful whether knowledge of the actual time for compliance with the notice was an essential ingredient of the *mens rea* required for the commission of the offence. In any case, he went on to hold that there was a duty in such circumstances for the person to take all proper care to inform himself of when the notice was going to take effect.[11] The owner could have easily found out from the local planning authority about the progress of the appeal and so discovered when the notice was to take effect. So the effect of this decision is that the prosecution has to establish that the defendant either had the necessary knowledge or reasonably should have had it because he had the means of knowledge.[12]

After copies of the enforcement notice have been served, it is of course possible for the ownership of the land to change. Section 89 deals with this potentiality by allowing the original owner to have the new owner brought before the court. For this to happen, he must have ceased to be owner at some time before the end of the period allowed for compliance with the notice and the prosecution must be given three days clear notice (s 89(2)). Then, if it can be proved that the failure to take the steps, which have not been complied with, was attributable in whole or in part to the default of the subsequent owner, the subsequent owner can be convicted and, provided that the original defendant can prove that he had taken all reasonable steps to secure compliance, the original owner shall be acquitted (s 89(3)). In this regard, where there is evidence that a person is the owner of the land at one

---

8 See *R v Ruttle, ex p Marshall* (1988) 153 JP 134, [1989] JPL 68.
9 *St Albans District Council v Norman Harper Autosales Ltd* (1977) 35 P & CR 70; and *Chiltern District Council v Hodgetts* [1983] 1 All ER 1057. The problem in the *St Albans* case concerning time limits on bringing a prosecution no longer applies because of s 127 of the Magistrates' Courts Act 1980. See p 365 below.
10 [1981] JPL 594.
11 This duty was derived from Lord Diplock's judgment in *Sweet v Parsley* [1970] AC 132, [1969] 1 All ER 347, HL.
12 As explained by Kerr LJ in *Coventry Scaffolding Co (London) Ltd v Parker* [1987] JPL 127.

date, it may be presumed that he is the owner at a later date unless there is some ground for thinking otherwise.[13]

Once a person has been convicted of an offence under s 89(1), that person commits a further offence, if he does not as soon as practicable do everything in his power to secure compliance (s 89(4)). He can then be fined on summary conviction £200 for each day following the first conviction that there has not been compliance. On conviction on indictment the fine is unlimited. In *Tandridge District Council v Powers*[14] after the owner had been acquitted of an offence under s 89(4) (presumably because he had done everything in his power to secure compliance), another prosecution was subsequently brought. Woolf J quashed the justices' decision that there was no case to answer and held that s 89(4) created a continuing offence. This means that a fresh offence could be committed, if it could be proved that circumstances had now changed and the owner was not doing everything practical to secure compliance. In this regard Woolf J pointed out that, if the owner was convicted, he could only have a fine imposed on him which was calculated from a date subsequent to the period in regard to which he had been acquitted. In other words the fine could not be inflated by reference to a period in which the defendant had been found not guilty of a s 89(4) offence.

However, in *Chiltern District Council v Hodgetts*,[15] the House of Lords held that s 89(4) was not a continuing offence but a single one. Lord Roskill in a speech, with which the rest of their lordships agreed, stated:

'... it is plainly contemplated that the further offence of non-compliance with a "do notice" created by subsection (4), though it too is a single offence, might take place over a period of time, since the penalty for it was made dependent upon the number of days on which it took place.'

It has therefore been suggested that s 89(4) should *only* be taken as a single offence for the purpose of charging.[16] Otherwise it would seem to mean that after being convicted under s 89(1) and s 89(4), the owner is not in breach of the criminal law by still refusing to secure compliance with the enforcement notice. In such a case the local planning authority could either seek to execute the works themselves under s 91 or attempt to get an injunction (see p 373).

'Desist notice' offences

Section 89(5) creates two types of offence. The first limb of the subsection provides that where an enforcement notice requires a use of land to be discontinued or any conditions or limitations are required to be complied with in respect of a use of land, then if any person[17] uses the land or causes or permits it to be used in contravention of the notice he commits an offence. This wording would seem to suggest that where there has not been compliance with a condition attached to a grant of permission for a change of use, it is the continued use without compliance with the condition that is the

---

13 *Whitfield v Gowling* (1974) 28 P & CR 386; but see *R v Ruttle, ex p Marshall* [1989] JPL 681.
14 [1982] JPL 645.
15 [1983] 1 All ER 1057.
16 See *Encyclopaedia of Planning*, Vol 2, 2–1092.
17 Occupiers, squatters and even trespassers may be guilty of an offence, regardless of their status, if they act in breach of the terms of a notice—see *Scarborough Borough Council v Adams and Adams* (1983) 147 JP 449, 47 P & CR 133.

offence and not the breach of the condition. The sub-section also makes it an offence, where any conditions or limitations are required to be complied with in respect of the carrying out of operations, to carry out those operations or cause or permit them to be carried out in contravention of the notice. This again would suggest that, where a grant of permission for operational development has been subject to conditions, and the conditions have not been complied with, an offence is committed if the operations are continued in contravention of an enforcement notice. The penalty on summary conviction is a fine not exceeding £2,000. For a conviction on indictment no maximum fine is prescribed. In *Hodgetts v Chiltern District Council*[18] the House of Lords held that this initial offence, though it may take place over a period, is a single offence and not a series of offences committed each day that non-compliance prior to conviction continues.

It was however suggested that, although there was no objection to charging the single offence as having occurred 'on or since' a specific date, it would be preferable to charge that the offence had been committed between two specific dates; that is between the date that compliance with the enforcement notice first became due and a date not later than the date when the information was laid (or some earlier date if the enforcement notice had been complied with by the time information was being laid).

The second limb of s 89(5) creates a 'further offence' of continuing the use after conviction; this offence can only be committed by someone who has already been convicted of the initial offence. A person convicted of this offence is liable on summary conviction to a fine not exceeding £200 for each day on which the offence continues. On conviction on indictment of this further offence no maximum fine is prescribed.

In *Hodgetts* Lord Roskill also held that this further offence was also a single offence and not a series of separate offences.[19] While it makes sense that the first part of s 89(5) should be a single offence (otherwise theoretically a person would have to be charged with hundreds of offences), it would seem strange if a second conviction has the effect of preventing any further prosecutions. This goes against previous authorities[20] and it may be that a further single offence arises if there is still non-compliance following the second conviction. Otherwise the local planning authority would have to seek an injunction (see p 373 below) or serve a fresh enforcement notice. It used to be important whether only one offence rather than a series of offences had been committed, when the prosecution had to be brought within six months of the date that the offence was committed, but now there is no time limitation on an offence which can be prosecuted by indictment.[1]

There is some doubt as to whether *mens rea* is required for an offence

---

18 [1963] 2 AC 120, [1984] 2 WLR 577.
19 Overriding *Parry v Forest of Dean District Council* (1976) 34 P & CR 209.
20 Apart from above, see *St Albans District Council v Norman Harper Autosales Ltd* (1977) 35 P & CR 70. See also *R v Chertsey Justices, ex p Franks* [1961] 2 QB 152, [1961] 1 All ER 825; and *Tandridge District Council v Powers* (1982), 80 LGR 453 (which turned on the interpretation of s 89(1) and (4)).
1 S 127 of the Magistrates' Courts Act 1980.

under s 89(5) of the 1971 Act. In *Stevens v Bromle   London Borough Council*[2] two members of the Court of Appeal apparently considered that *mens rea* was not required for the commission of an offenc   Edmund Davies LJ said that the effect of the provision is that 'provided an enforcement notice is validly served on someone, *any* person who thereafter uses the land in a manner contravening it is *ipso facto* rendered guilty of a criminal offence, regardless of whether or not he has himself been served and even regardless of whether he has knowledge that a notice has been served at all.' However, in *Coventry Scaffolding Co (London) Ltd v Parker*[3] Kerr LJ took the view that the approach of Forbes J in *South Cambridge District Council v Stokes*[4] applied to all offences under s 89 and so to get a conviction under s 89(5) it had to be established that the defendant had the necessary knowledge or reasonably should have had it because he had the means of knowledge. Also in the Scottish case of *Pirie v Bauld*[5] the sheriff held that the accused lacked the *mens rea* necessary for the commission of the offence of non-compliance with an enforcement notice in that they believed that they had appealed to the minister against the enforcement notice in question.

Where the owner of land is not himself in occupation of that land it would seem that he runs the risk of prosecution under this provision only if he does something 'which can be said to amount to a using of the land for the unauthorised purpose, or causing or permitting it to be so used'—see *Johnston v Secretary of State for the Environment*.[6] The Divisional Court held in that case that an offence was committed only if a person was in a position to discontinue the unlawful use and, notwithstanding the notice, either continued to use the land in defiance of it or caused or permitted some other person to do so. In *Ragsdale v Creswick*[7] the Divisional Court held that the failure of a landowner to take legal proceedings to evict a trespasser on his land who had been acting in breach of an enforcement notice might amount to a failure to take reasonable steps to secure compliance with the notice. Much would depend, it was said, on the nature, cost and prospect of success of the proceedings and also upon the prospect of the planning authority securing the cessation of the offending use by the use of criminal sanctions. It also appears that the prosecution must correctly allege *either* permitting or using and a mistake in this regard will invalidate the prosecution.[8]

Otherwise, whether an offence has been committed under s 89(5) will depend on the construction put on the terms of the enforcement notice. In *Cord v Secretary of State for the Environment and Torbay Borough Council*[9] the Divisional Court accepted that in this regard it could usually be implied that enforcement notices did not extend to activities which could otherwise be carried on without permission. However, in *Epping Forest District Council v Scott*[10] Stephen Brown LJ rejected the argument that an enforcement notice enforcing conditions had to be construed in the light of the actual terms of

2 [1972] Ch 400, [1972] 1 All ER 712. See too *Maidstone Borough Council v Mortimer* [1980] 3 All ER 552 (knowledge of existence of tree preservation order) and *R v Wells Street Metropolitan Stipendiary Magistrates, ex p Westminster City Council* [1986] 3 All ER 4, [1986] 1 WLR 1046 (knowledge of building being listed).
3 [1987] JPL 127.   4 [1981] JPL 594.
5 1975 SLT (Sh Ct) 6.
6 (1974) 28 P & CR 424. See too *Test Valley Investments Ltd v Tanner* (1963) 15 P & CR 279; *Bromsgrove District Council v Carthy* (1975) 30 P & CR 34; and *Redbridge London Borough v Perry* (1976) 75 LGR 90.
7 (1984) 276 Estates Gazette 1268.   8 *Waddell v Winter* (1967) 65 LGR 370.
9 [1981] JPL 40.   10 (1985) 53 P & CR 79, [1986] JPL 603.

the condition. This can have the harsh consequence that if requirements beyond the terms of the condition are imposed, it would seem to be too late to raise this on a prosecution even as a question of construction of the enforcement notice. However, it could be different if the words used were ambiguous and it is a general principle that instruments having penal consequences should be interpreted narrowly. In *Warrington Borough Council v Garvey*[11] Judge Woolley in the Crown Court said that the usual benevolent approach to the interpretation of enforcement notices did not apply in a criminal prosecution.

In criminal proceedings the validity of an enforcement notice may not be questioned on any of the grounds specified in s 88(2) of the 1971 Act[12] except in the very limited circumstances mentioned in s 243(2).[13] This means that, as in the *Epping Forest* case, it will be too late to argue that the allegation of the breach of planning control in the notice is factually incorrect.[14]

Execution of works by planning authority and costs of compliance

Section 91 provides an additional method of obtaining compliance in the case of a 'do notice'. Where steps have not been taken within the required period[15] the local planning authority may enter the land and take those steps. This only applies to steps which may be required under s 87(7)(a) and so does not include the new powers to require works to comply with a grant of planning permission or to carry out alleviating work to any injury to amenity.

The planning authority need not carry out all the steps required by the enforcement notice; they are entitled to take such of those steps as they consider appropriate.[16] There seems no reason why direct action should not be taken to secure the removal of items associated with an unauthorised use of land, provided the enforcement notice specifically requires such removal. For example, although s 91 cannot be used to secure the discontinuance of an unauthorised use of land as a caravan site, it seems arguable that s 91 would support the taking of direct action to remove unauthorised caravans. In *Midlothian District Council v Stevenson*[17] the Court of Session held that where an enforcement notice was served which required, *inter alia*, the removal of caravans, the council were entitled to enter and remove the caravans.[18] In *Waverley Borough Council v Hilden*[19] Scott J in the case of an unauthorised use of a site for residential occupation of caravans said that he was not sure whether or not s 91(1) could be used to forcibly remove the caravans from the site but he accepted that it could be used to carry out other steps such as removing fencing and hardcore. The planning authority are

11 [1988] JPL 752.
12 1971 Act, s 243(2)(b); see p 360 above. And see *R v Smith* (1984) 48 P & CR 392, [1985] JPL 183, CA and *Prosser v Sharp* [1985] 1 EGLR 175, [1985] JPL 717.
13 See p 359 above.
14 But see *Warrington Borough Council v Garvey* [1988] JPL 752.
15 The period set out in the enforcement notice can be extended (s 89(6)). From *St Albans District Council v Norman Harper Autosales Ltd* (1977), 35 P & CR 70 this must be done before the original period expires.
16 See *Arcam Demolition and Construction Co Ltd v Worcestershire County Council* [1964] 2 All ER 286, [1964] 1 WLR 661.
17 1985 SLT 424, [1986] JPL 913.
18 Also see *Tandridge District Council v Powers* [1982] JPL 645; and *Prosser v Sharp* [1985] 1 EGLR 175, [1985] JPL 717 which hold that it is an offence under s 89(1) to refuse to remove caravans; but see *R v Jefford* [1986] JPL 912.
19 [1988] 1 All ER 807, [1988] 1 WLR 246, [1988] JPL 173.

entitled to recover from the person who is at that time the owner of the land any expenses reasonably incurred in carrying out the steps (s 91(11)).

The power to execute works is conditional on there being a valid enforcement notice but it will not be possible to challenge the validity of a notice on any of the grounds set out in s 88(2) except by way of appeal to the Secretary of State (s 243(2)(b)). However, in *R v Greenwich London Borough Council, ex p Patel*[20] it was held that it would be possible to challenge a decision to resort to s 91 by way of judicial review. Neill LJ said that there was a duty on the planning authority to investigate facts which tended to show, for example, that the matters alleged did not constitute a breach of planning control (ground in s 88(2)(b)), where these facts were put forward by owners or other interested person who had not been served with copies of the notice and had not appealed. An unreasonable refusal to investigate such facts would be a ground for reviewing not the validity of the enforcement notice but the decision to enter the land and execute the works. Lord Donaldson MR similarly thought that an individual, who had not been served with a copy of the notice, could seek judicial review if the local planning authority had not given appropriate consideration and effect to any representations which he had raised concerning matters which he had had no opportunity of raising by way of appeal.

The person who committed the original breach of planning control may not be either the owner or the occupier at the time the notice is issued. His breach may therefore cause the owner or occupier to incur expenses in having to comply with the notice. These expenses and any sums paid by the owner under s 91(1) are deemed to be incurred or paid for the use and at the request of the person who committed the breach of planning control and so will be recoverable in civil law (s 91(2)).[1]

E STOP NOTICES AND INJUNCTIONS

Stop notices

As mentioned above, an enforcement notice does not take effect until any appeal against the notice has been finally determined or withdrawn (s 87(10)) (see p 340).

A lengthy period can therefore elapse between service of an enforcement notice and the time when the recipient of the notice needs to comply with it. If allegedly unauthorised operations continue during that period, proper consideration of the merits of an enforcement notice can be prejudiced; it is one thing to tell a developer to remove the foundations of an unauthorised building, but quite a different matter to tell him to pull down a completed building.

Furthermore, the alleged breach of control may cause serious planning problems, for example of a polluting or hazardous nature. Planning authorities have, therefore, been given power to serve what is known as a 'stop notice'. As the name suggests, the effect of the notice is to prohibit the

---

20 [1985] JPL 851.
1 This was referred to as a 'doubtful remedy' by the Sherriff Principal in the Scottish case of *MacDonald v Glasgow Corpn* 1960 SLT (Sh Ct) 21 and also see *Atkinson v Secretary of State for the Environment and Leeds City Council* [1983] JPL 599 where this remedy was not available as the developer had gone into liquidation.

carrying out of the alleged breach of control until such time as any appeal against the enforcement notice has been finally determined or withdrawn.[2]

The power to serve a stop notice arises where an enforcement notice has been issued and a copy served and the local planning authority consider it expedient to prevent, before the expiry of the period allowed for compliance, the carrying out of any activity which is, or is included in, a matter alleged by the notice to constitute the breach (s 90(1)).

It is clear from the wording of the sub-section that a stop notice need not prohibit the whole of an activity alleged to be in breach of planning control; the planning authority could, for example, restrict the operation of a stop notice to particular aspects of the unauthorised activity or to a particular part of the planning unit on which the unauthorised activity is being carried on.

There are certain activities which cannot be prohibited by a stop notice. Firstly a stop notice may not prohibit the use of any building as a dwellinghouse (s 90(2)(a)). Secondly it is provided that a stop notice may not prohibit the use of any land as a site for a caravan occupied by any person as his only or main residence (s 90(2)(b)). In *Runnymede Borough Council v Smith*[3] Millett J held that this protected both the users at the time of the service of the copy of the notice and future users. So a stop notice cannot have the effect of preventing the future use of a site for a caravan occupied by any person as his only or main residence, even though future use would be in breach of the terms of the enforcement notice which would cover both present and future use as a caravan site. In that decision, it was also accepted by the parties and the judge that s 90(2)(b) protected more than a single caravan; though it was left open whether, if a family occupied more than one caravan as their main or only residence, more than one caravan would be protected per family. With respect to the last point, the spirit of the protection would suggest that all should be protected. However, Millett J made clear that a stop notice could stop the use of land for the parking and storage of lorries, trailers and other equipment which were not occupied as residences. Thirdly, a stop notice cannot prohibit the taking of any steps specified in the enforcement notice as required to be taken in order to remedy the breach of planning control (s 90(2)(c)). Finally, where an activity has been begun more than twelve months earlier, whether or not this use has been continuous, a stop notice may not prohibit the carrying out of that activity on the land unless it is or is incidental to, building, engineering, mining or other operations or the deposit of refuse or waste materials (s 90(2)). This means that, once twelve months have elapsed since a use of land commenced, a stop notice is generally ineffective to prevent its continuance. This protection applies even if the use was lawfully commenced but has since become unlawful because of the expiration of a limitation period.[4] However, circular 4/87 suggests that even where the material change of use occurred more than twelve months ago, new ancillary activities which began during the past twelve months can be prohibited by a stop notice.[5]

If a stop notice purports to prohibit any of the above activities, it does not

2 The law and practice relating to stop notices is usefully explained in circular 4/87.
3 (1986) 53 P & CR 132, [1986] JPL 592.
4 *Scott Markets Ltd v Waltham Forest London Borough Council* (1979) 77 LGR 565, 38 P & CR 597, CA.
5 See para 7 of Annex 2 to the circular 4/87. Also see *R v Epping Forest District Council, ex p Strandmill Ltd* [1989] EGCS 101.

mean that the stop notice is invalid, it means that the notice will be legally ineffective in that respect and non-compliance will not have any legal consequences.[6]

A stop notice, as its name suggests, is an instrument of negative control. As was pointed out in *Pirie v Bauld*,[7] the notice 'does not oblige the person on whom it is served to remedy the breach of planning control alleged in the enforcement notice'. Whilst it can prohibit the carrying on of an activity alleged in the enforcement notice to constitute a breach of planning control it cannot require the carrying out of positive conditions, notwithstanding that the failure to implement the condition constitutes a breach of planning control. Furthermore, if it purports to prohibit the carrying on of an activity which is not a matter alleged in the enforcement notice to constitute a breach of planning control then the stop notice will be invalid.[8]

A stop notice must refer to and have annexed to it a copy of the relevant enforcement notice (s 90(1)). It seems that where a stop notice incorporates the terms of the enforcement notice then any deficiency of particularity in the stop notice may be cured by reference to the enforcement notice.[9]

A stop notice must specify the date that it takes effect. This date must be not earlier than three days nor later than twenty-eight days from the day on which it is first served on any person (s 90(3)). As a stop notice cannot be contravened until it takes effect, a failure to specify a valid date would make the notice invalid. A stop notice may be served on any person who appears to the local planning authority to have an interest in the land or to be engaged in any activity prohibited by the notice (s 90(5)). As well as service, the local planning authority may display on the land to which the stop notice relates a site notice publicising the terms, timing and consequences of the notice (s 90(5)). Unlike the case with enforcement notices, there is no statutory requirement that a stop notice shall be served on the owners and occupiers of the land or other persons with an interest in the land.

Where a site notice has been displayed, any person commits an offence[10] if he contravenes or causes or permits the contravention of the stop notice, provided, of course, it has come into effect (s 90(7)).[11] Where a site notice has not been displayed the offence can only be committed by a person who has been served with the stop notice and then only two days after service.[12]

There is no right of appeal against a stop notice. Unless previously withdrawn by the planning authority,[13] a stop notice stands or falls with the enforcement notice to which it relates; a stop notice ceases to have effect when the enforcement notice to which it refers takes effect or is quashed or withdrawn (s 90(4)). Where the enforcement notice is varied so that it no

---

6   See *Runnymede Borough Council v Smith*, above.
7   1975 SLT (Sh Ct) 6.
8   *Clwyd County Council v Secretary of State for Wales and Welsh Aggregates* [1982] JPL 696.
9   *Bristol Stadium Ltd v Brown* (1979) 252 Estates Gazette 803, [1980] JPL 107.
10 The maximum penalty for non-compliance with a stop notice was increased to £2,000 by the Criminal Penalties etc (Increase) Order 1984; while the maximum fine for a continuing contravention was raised to £200 by the Housing and Planning Act 1986 (s 49 and Sch 11 para 13).
11 It is, however, a defence to prove that the accused had not been served with the notice and that he did not know or could not reasonably be expected to know of its existence (s 90(8)).
12 In any case the stop notice cannot take effect until three days after the first service. So the two days only affects persons who are served later.
13 The procedure to be followed on withdrawal of a stop notice is set out in s 90(6).

longer relates to an activity prohibited by the stop notice, the stop notice ceases to have effect in relation to that activity (s 90(4)). A stop notice, in any case, ceases to have effect once the period for compliance with the notice expires, as from then on non-compliance with the enforcement notice will be a criminal offence (s 90(4)(b)) and the stop notice is in effect superseded by the enforcement notice.

Although there is no right of appeal against a stop notice, there is nothing to prevent a person seeking judicial review of the planning authority's action in deciding to serve a stop notice on the ground that the authority would be acting outside their powers.[14] However, Scottish case law suggests that to get an interim injunction there must be some evidence that the local planning authority have no power to serve a stop notice or are abusing their power to serve a notice.[15] The normal remedy would be to ask for a declaration that a stop notice, which has already been served, is invalid.[16] This could be on the grounds that the terms of the notice were hopelessly ambiguous or that there had been a fundamental breach of the statutory requirements or there was no authority to serve the stop notice or some other head of review.

On a prosecution for a failure to comply with a stop notice, it is possible to raise as a defence the argument that the activities complained of had been commenced more than twelve months earlier. In *R v Jenner*[17] Watkins LJ rejected the argument that such a challenge could only be raised by way of judicial review and stated:

'The process of judicial review, which rarely allowed the reception of oral evidence, was not suited to resolving the issues of fact involved in deciding whether an activity, said to be prohibited by it was caught by section 90.'

So the magistrates will first have to decide whether the notice is legally capable of requiring the activities to cease and then whether there has been a failure to comply. It would also seem that a prosecution can be defended on the ground that the notice is a nullity.[18] There is also the specific defence provided by s 90(8) that the defendant had not been served with the notice and did not know and could not reasonably have been expected to know of its existence. It is specifically provided that a stop notice shall not be invalid because the enforcement notice to which it relates was not served as required by s 87(4) of the 1971 Act, if it is shown that the planning authority took all reasonably practicable steps to effect proper service (s 90(9)).

Details of stop notices are to be entered in the register which local planning authorities are required to keep (see p 323 above).

Compensation for loss due to stop notice

Section 177 of the 1971 Act provides that where a stop notice ceases to have

14 *Scott Markets Ltd v Waltham Forest London Borough Council* (1979) 77 LGR 565, CA.
15 See *Central Regional Council v Clackmannan District Council* 1983 SLT 666; *James Barrie (Sand and Gravel) Ltd v Lanark District Council* 1979 SLT 14; *Earl Car Sales (Edinburgh) Ltd v City of Edinburgh District Council* 1984 SLT 8; but see *Marine Associates Ltd v City of Aberdeen Corpn* 1978 SLT 41.
16 *R v Runnymede District Council, ex p Seehra* (1986) 151 JP 80, [1987] JPL 283.
17 [1983] 2 All ER 46, [1983] 1 WLR 873.
18 *Bristol Stadium Ltd v Brown* (1979) 252 Estates Gazette 803, [1980] JPL 107.

effect the local planning authority will in some circumstances have to pay compensation in respect of any loss or damage 'directly attributable to the prohibition contained in the notice' (see s 177(1)). Subsection (2) details the precise circumstances in which compensation will be payable for loss due to a stop notice. Broadly speaking, a compensation claim will arise where the stop notice is itself withdrawn independently of the enforcement notice to which it refers, or where the enforcement notice is withdrawn by the planning authority otherwise than in consequence of a grant by them of planning permission, or where the enforcement notice is varied so that the breach ceases to include the activity prohibited by the stop notice, or where the enforcement notice is quashed on any of the grounds mentioned in s 88(2)(b), (c), (d) or (e), (f) and (h) (see p 342 above). As difficult questions of law may arise on an appeal under s 88(2)(b)[19] and as the facts to support an appeal on s 88(2)(d) or (e) may be outside the knowledge of the planning authority, this compensation provision may have a deterrent effect on the use of stop notices. In this regard circular 4/87 argues that there is widespread misunderstanding as to when compensation is payable and states that compensation has in fact been paid infrequently; see Annex 3 to the circular.

If, however, the local planning authority decide to grant planning permission and for that reason withdraw the enforcement notice, or if, on appeal, the Secretary of State decides on the planning merits to grant planning permission for the development to which the enforcement notice relates and for that reason quashes the enforcement notice, compensation will not be payable for loss resulting from service of a stop notice.

If a stop notice turns out to be invalid, there is no right to compensation. This is because in theory a stop notice, which is invalid, should not be followed; ie compensation only arises from non-use resulting from a lawful command in a stop notice.[20] In *Clwyd County Council v Secretary of State for Wales and Welsh Aggregates*[1] Forbes J got round this by making an order that the stop notice, which was hopelessly invalid, should be withdrawn. The withdrawal then gave rise to rights to compensation. However, unless a person affected by a stop notice is prepared to go to the lengths of challenging it by judicial review, he may be faced with a dilemma of either defying the possibly invalid notice but so risking conviction of a criminal offence or obeying the notice but therefore having no rights to compensation unless the enforcement notice is subsequently quashed or withdrawn.[2]

A claim for compensation[3] under s 177 may only be made by a person who had an interest in or occupies the land in question at the time when the notice was first served; it is not necessary to the making of a claim that the stop notice should have been served on the claimant. The loss or damage in respect of which compensation is payable may include a sum payable in respect of a breach of contract caused by the taking of action necessary to comply with the stop notice (s 177(5)). In the assessment of any compensa-

19 See, for example, *Malvern Hills District Council v Secretary of State for the Environment* (1983) 81 LGR 13, 46 P & CR 58, CA.
20 See Millett J in *Runnymede Borough Council v Smith* [1986] JPL 592 at 595–6.
1 [1982] JPL 696.
2 See *R v Runnymede Borough Council, ex p Seehra* (1986) 151 JP 80, [1987] JPL 283 where Scheimann J recognised this problem.
3 As to the time limit for making a claim see the Town and Country Planning General Regulations 1976, reg 14(2).

tion under s 177 there is to be taken into account any failure on the part of
the claimant to comply with the provisions of s 284 of the 1971 Act (relating
to the powers of authorities to require information as to interests in land and
as to the purpose for which land is being used) to the extent that such failure
has contributed to the circumstances in which the enforcement notice was
withdrawn or varied or quashed, or the stop notice withdrawn (s 177(6)).[4]

Compensation for loss 'directly attributable' to the prohibition in a stop
notice which delayed completion of a house was found to be payable in
Sample (Warkworth) Ltd v Alnwick District Council.[5] The Lands Tribunal
held that compensation was payable in respect of the idle time of the builders'
labour force and the cost of work needed to rectify deterioration resulting
from the delay. The tribunal also awarded compensation in respect of loss of
interest on the purchase price of the house from October 1981, the estimated
date of completion, to March 1982, the date of actual completion, even
though the planning authority had permitted building work to restart in
December 1981 and argued that interest should only be payable up to that
time; in the tribunal's view the fact that there was likely to be a delay in
completing the house, which could be aggravated by the holiday period and
the onset of severe weather, was sufficiently contemporaneous in following
the prohibition in the stop notice that causation was not broken. The
builders were also held entitled to be reimbursed for a payment they had
made in respect of the cost of temporary accommodation for the purchasers
of the house since it avoided the possible loss of the sale or an action which
might have involved greater loss. Compensation was claimed in respect of the
costs of the builders' appeal against the enforcement notice, the builders
arguing that although planning permission had been granted in December
1981, the enforcement notice and stop notice had not been withdrawn and
they were therefore forced to proceed with the appeal in order to qualify for
compensation for loss due to the stop notice. The Lands Tribunal held,
however, that the costs of the appeal were not 'directly attributable' to the
stop notice, the remedy for recovering these costs being exerciseable at the
time of the appeal decision itself. The tribunal expressed the view that the
words 'directly attributable' as used in the legislation were not to be qualified
by the concept of reasonable foreseeability.[6]

The enforcement of planning control by injunction

A minority of developers are prepared to continue to defy enforcement and
stop notices, despite being convicted in the magistrates' courts, because of
the financial advantages. As a remedy of last resort, it is now established that
local planning authorities can resort to seeking an injunction in the High
Court. This is a formidable weapon of enforcement. If granted, the indivi-

---

4 Inserted by the 1977 Act.
5 (1984) 48 P & CR 474.
6 For other Lands Tribunal decisions on the right to compensation see *Robert Barnes and Co
Ltd v Malvern Hills District Council* [1985] 1 EGLR 189, (1985) 274 Estates Gazette 733 (no
right to interest on amount of compensation except from date of award) and *Texas
Homecare Ltd v Lewes District Council* (1985) 51 P & CR 205, [1986] JPL 50 (no requirement
that claim has to be in any particular form: all that is needed is an unequivocal claim). Also
see *Graysmark v South Hams District Council* [1989] O3 EG 75 where the Court of Appeal
held that damage which was too remote under the doctrine of the *Liesbosh* [1933] AC 449
could not be recovered.

dual who defied an injunction would risk committal to prison or an unlimited fine for contempt of court. It also cuts through the complicated and cumbersome statutory procedures of enforcement.

There are, however, constitutional objections to the use of an injunction as a means of enforcing the criminal law. If Parliament in its wisdom has set up a particular machinery with its own procedures and penalties, too ready use of the injunction could be seen as flouting the will of Parliament. So the injunction cannot be sought as a convenient alternative to the statutory machinery; its use must always be specially justified.

Prior to the coming into force of the Local Government Act 1972, local planning authorities had to invoke the assistance of the Attorney-General by way of a relator action. As Buckley J said in *A-G v Ashborne Recreation Ground Co*:[7] 'The Attorney-General suing in respect of the invasion of public rights has at least as large a right to invoke the protection of the Court as a private owner suing in respect of his rights.' Thus in *A-G (on the relation of Hornchurch UDC) v Bastow*[8] an injunction was issued to restrain the defendant from using land as a caravan site, the defendant having been repeatedly prosecuted for so using his land in contravention of the terms of an enforcement notice. Devlin J stated:

'When Parliament makes provision which enables local authorities to exercise powers over the use of land, that provision is plainly made with the object of conferring a right upon the public because Parliament considers that the public is entitled not to have the land used in ways which may be considered to be unhealthy or offensive ... [T]here is the creation of a public right and the Attorney-General is therefore entitled to come to this court to have it enforced.'

Section 222 of the Local Government Act 1972 now allows local authorities in England and Wales to institute civil proceedings where they consider it expedient to do so for the promotion or protection of the interests of the inhabitants of their area. The addition of the words 'in their own name' to the equivalent section in the previous Local Government Act 1933 was held by the House of Lords to give local authorities this important independence.[9] As the Attorney-General put it in *Stoke-on-Trent City Council v B and Q (Retail) Ltd*,[10] this conferred 'a substantial measure of autonomy on local authorities in respect of law enforcement within their areas'. On the other hand it may well be that the courts will scrutinise an application by a local authority more carefully than when it had the backing of the Attorney-General.[11] It would seem that to get an injunction it will be normally necessary to show that the criminal law has been broken or is about to be

7 [1903] 1 Ch 101.
8 [1957] 1 QB 514, [1957] 1 All ER 497. See also *A-G v Ashborne Recreation Ground Co* [1903] 1 Ch 10; *A-G v Sharp* [1931] 1 Ch 121; *A-G (on the relation of Hornchurch UDC) v Bastow* [1957] 1 QB 514, [1957] 1 All ER 497; *A-G (at the relation of Egham UDC) v Smith* [1958] 2 QB 173, [1958] 2 All ER 557.
9 See, in particular, *Stoke-on-Trent City Council v B and Q (Retail) Ltd* [1984] AC 754, [1984] 2 All ER 332, HL.
10 See above.
11 See Devlin J in *A-G (on the relation of Hornchurch UDC) v Bastow* (above) where he stated that the courts should only refuse an application by the Attorney General in exceptional circumstances.

broken. This has never been expressly laid down as an absolute precondition and it might in extreme circumstances be possible to obtain an injunction to prevent a breach of planning control which although 'unlawful' is not in itself a criminal offence.[12] However, in most of the cases where an injunction has been granted, it was alleged that the criminal law had been broken, but it is not always necessary to show there have been frequent and repeated offences committed. Thus in *Westminster City Council v Jones*[13] the local planning authority successfully sought an interlocutory injunction in its own name under s 222 restraining the defendant from using premises as an amusement arcade. The use of the premises for that purpose was in breach of planning control, an enforcement notice had been served together with a stop notice, and a summons had been issued for failure to comply with the stop notice and was to be heard shortly.

On the other hand, it is not enough just to show that the criminal law is being broken. In *Stoke-on-Trent City Council v B and Q (Retail) Ltd*[14] Lord Templeman stated that 'there must certainly be something more than mere infringement before the maintenance of civil proceedings can be invoked and accorded for the protection of the interests of the inhabitants of the area'. The phrase 'a deliberate and flagrant flouting of the law' has evolved as a description of the situation when an injunction would be granted.[15] However, in *Runnymede Borough Council v Ball*[16] the Court of Appeal made clear that this phrase was not a test of jurisdiction and an injunction could be granted in other circumstances. The underlying question will always be whether the statutory remedies available would be adequate to protect the interests of the local inhabitants: which in the context of the planning legislation means doing all in the authority's power to protect through properly observed planning control the natural amenities of the area. So injunctions will be granted where it is clear from past conduct that prosecutions will not result in compliance either because the penalties are inadequate or because of the financial rewards or for some other reason.[17] But injunctions will also be granted where the activities must be immediately stopped either because of the serious injury they will cause or because the development is in practice irreversible.[18]

It would also usually be necessary to show that there has been a clear and

---

12 See *A-G (at the relation of Egham UDC) v Smith* [1958] 2 QB 173, [1958] 2 All ER 557 where an injunction was granted which restrained future breaches of planning control on other land where as yet no enforcement notices had been served, though there had been breaches of the criminal law with regard to a particular site. Also see *Bedfordshire County Council v Central Electricity Generating Board* [1985] JPL 43 where Piers Ashworth QC (sitting as a deputy judge) appeared to accept that an injunction could be granted to stop anticipatory breach of planning control, although he referred in his judgment to anticipatory breaches of the *criminal* law when it would seem that the criminal law was not in issue. Finally, see *City of London Corpn v Bovis Construction Ltd* [1989] JPL 263 and *Southwark London Borough v Frow* [1989] JPL 645.

13 (1981) 80 LGR 241, [1981] JPL 750.   14 See above.

15 It seems it originated from Oliver J (as he then was) in *Stafford Borough Council v Elken Ltd* [1977] 2 All ER 519, [1977] 1 WLR 324, CA; see Purchas LJ in *Runnymede Borough Council v Ball* [1986] JPL 288.

16 [1986] 1 All ER 629, [1986] 1 WLR 353. See also *City of London Corpn v Bovis Construction Ltd* [1989] JPL 263.

17 See *Kent County Council v Batchelor* [1978] 3 All ER 980, [1979] 1 WLR 213; and *Westminster City Council v Jones* (1981) 80 LGR 241, [1981] JPL 750.

18 See *Kent County Council v Batchelor* [1978] 3 All ER 980, [1979] 1 WLR 213; and *Runnymede Borough Council v Ball* [1986] 1 All ER 629, [1986] 1 WLR 353, [1986] JPL 288.

manifest breach of the law[19] and in *Runnymede Borough Council v Smith*[20] an injunction was refused because it was concluded that the defendants were not in fact committing a criminal offence because the stop notice could not prohibit the use of the caravans as main or only residences.[1]

Where an injunction is granted, its terms can be very broad and may prohibit not only activities which are breaches of the criminal law but future breaches of planning control. In *A-G (at the relation of Egham UDC) v Smith*[2] an injunction was granted restraining the defendant from using any land within the local authorities boundaries as a caravan site. Only local authorities apart from the Attorney-General can bring proceedings for an injunction in their own name. The power does not extend by implication to urban development corporations even though they are often given planning control functions.[3] Private individuals with sufficient interest could seek to prevent a local authority acting in breach of planning control by seeking an application for judicial review[4] but would have to seek the assistance of the Attorney-General by way of a relator action against another private individual who was committing offences under the planning legislation.[5]

The normal way to contest a planning authority's decision to seek an injunction is by defending the action but it would seem that the decision to seek an injunction is itself capable of being subject to judicial review. It is the exercise of a statutory discretion and as such is challengeable on the normal grounds on which discretionary powers are challengeable.[6]

In *Waverley Borough Council v Hilden*[7] Scott J held that, where the person against whom the injunction was being sought was arguing that the council's decision to seek the injunction was invalid, this was not a defence in the true sense but an assertion that the council had no jurisdiction. He went on to hold that such an assertion should be dealt with by way of judicial review and not as a defence to the injunction. In that case an injunction was granted against gypsies who were violating the planning laws, even though the county (but not the district who were seeking the injunction) were alleged to be in breach of the duty to provide sites for gypsies under the Caravan Sites Act 1968. Scott J, however, also stated that injunctions 'ought not to be granted if other less draconian means of securing obediance to the law are available' and cut down the scope of the injunction where s 91 (the power to execute works: see p 367) could be used to achieve the same ends. This decision has since been approved by the Court of Appeal.[8]

---

19 See *Westminster City Council v Jones* (above).
20 (1986) 53 P & CR 132, [1986] JPL 592.
 1 Millett J in that case also held that in any case he would have refused to grant the injunction as it was not a case of deliberate and flagrant breach of the criminal law nor a case of irreparable damage.
 2 [1958] 2 QB 173, [1958] 2 All ER 557 and *A-G, ex rel East Sussex County Council v Morris* [1973] JPL 429.
 3 *London Docklands Development Corpn v Rank Hovis Ltd* (1985) 84 LGR 101, CA.
 4 See *Steeples v Derbyshire County Council* [1984] 3 All ER 468, [1985] 1 WLR 256, [1981] JPL 582.
 5 *A-G, ex rel Hing v Codner* [1973] 1 NZLR 545.
 6 See *Stoke-on-Trent City Council v B and Q (Retail) Ltd* [1984] 2 All ER 332, per Lord Templeman at 341.
 7 [1988] 1 All ER 807, [1988] 1 WLR 246, [1988] JPL 175. See also *West Glamorgan County Council v Rafferty* [1987] 1 All ER 1005, [1987] 1 WLR 457, CA.
 8 See *Avon County Council v Buscott* [1988] QB 656, [1988] 1 All ER 841, CA.

CHAPTER 13

ADVERSE PLANNING DECISIONS: COMPENSATION

A INTRODUCTION

'[I]t is quite clear', said Lord Reid in *Westminster Bank Ltd v Minister of Housing and Local Government*,[1] 'that when planning permission is refused the general rule is that the unsuccessful applicant does not receive any compensation.' There are, as we shall see, three limited exceptions to this rule; these are discussed below.

The general rule, which applies as much to the imposition of conditions as to a refusal of permission, would seem to be in line with the way in which public controls over the use and management of land have developed over the years. During the last one hundred and fifty years owners of property have been increasingly compelled, without compensation, to comply with certain requirements regarding their property, all imposed ostensibly in the public interest. 'Ownership of land', observed the Uthwatt Committee in 1942, 'involves duties to the community as well as rights in the individual owner. It may involve complete surrender of the land to the State or it may involve submission to a limitation of rights of user of the land without surrender of ownership or possession being required.'[2] The question is: at what stage are the rights of the individual owner so circumscribed by the requirements of the public interest that compensation should follow?

The conventional approach has been to draw a line between the complete surrender of land and a mere limitation of the landowner's freedom to use his land as he pleases. There is a line of cases which supports the judicial presumption that an intention to take away the property of a subject without giving him a legal right to compensation for its loss is not to be imputed to the legislature unless that intention is expressed in unequivocal terms.[3] On the other hand, a mere limitation on use would seem to give rise to no such presumption.[4] 'A mere negative prohibition', said Wright J in *France, Fenwick & Co v R*,[5] 'though it involves interference with an owner's enjoyment of property, does not, I think, merely because it is obeyed, carry with it at common law any right to compensation.' In the absence, therefore,

---

1 [1971] AC 508, [1970] 1 All ER 734, HL.
2 *Report of the Expert Committee on Compensation and Betterment* (Cmnd 6386, 1942), para 32.
3 *Burmah Oil Co (Burma Trading) Ltd v Lord Advocate* 1963 SC 410; on appeal 1964 SC (HL) 117; *Tiverton and North Devon Rly Co v Loosemore* (1884) 9 App Cas 480, HL; *Cannon Brewery Co v Gas Light and Coke Co* [1904] AC 331, HL; *Colonial Sugar Refining Co Ltd v Melbourne Harbour Trust Comrs* [1927] AC 343, PC; and *Bond v Nottingham Corpn* [1940] Ch 429, [1940] 2 All ER 12, CA.
4 *Belfast Corpn v OD Cars Ltd* [1960] AC 490, [1960] 1 All ER 65, HL; and *Westminster Bank Ltd v Minister of Housing and Local Government* [1971] AC 508, [1970] 1 All ER 734, HL.
5 [1927] 1 KB 458.

of any specific provision in the legislation, the position is that, subject to the three exceptions discussed below, there is no entitlement to compensation for any loss resulting from an adverse decision on a planning application.

However, simple though the distinction between expropriation and limitation may seem in theory, in practice the effect on a landowner of a limitation may be every bit as severe as an expropriation. The Uthwatt Committee conceded: 'It will always be a matter of difficulty to draw the line with any satisfactory logic, ie, to determine the point at which the accepted obligations of neighbourliness or citizenship are exceeded and an expropriation is suffered—particularly as the standard of obligation will vary with the political theory of the day.'[6]

The 1971 Act recognises that planning proposals and decisions made in the public interest can have an effect on a landowner similar to expropriation. Part IX of the Act contains provisions which enable a landowner to require a public body to purchase his interest in certain circumstances—a sort of inverse expropriation. These provisions are discussed in detail in chapters 14 and 17.

However, the provisions in Pt IX of the 1971 Act only come into operation in narrowly defined circumstances. There may be occasions when obligations imposed by local planning authorities on developers through the development control process do not bring these provisions into operation, yet might fairly be described as expropriation without compensation. In *Hall & Co Ltd v Shoreham-by-Sea UDC*,[7] for example, the local planning authority granted planning permission for industrial development subject to a condition that the developers 'shall construct an ancillary road over the entire frontage of the site at their own expense and as and when required by the local planning authority, and shall give right of passage over it to and from such ancillary roads as may be constructed on adjoining land'. The Court of Appeal held the condition to be so unreasonable as to be *ultra vires*. Willmer LJ observed: 'I can certainly find no clear and unambiguous words in the Town and Country Planning Act 1947 authorising the defendants in effect to take away the plaintiffs' rights of property without compensation by the imposition of conditions such as those sought to be imposed.' And in *R v Hillingdon London Borough Council, ex p Royco Homes Ltd*,[8] where planning permission for residential development was granted subject to conditions that the houses built should be occupied by people on the local authority's waiting list, with security of tenure for ten years, Lord Widgery CJ described the conditions as 'a fundamental departure from the rights of ownership and so unreasonable that no planning authority, appreciating its duty and properly applying itself to the facts, could have imposed them'. In cases such as these, where the proper scope of planning powers is in issue, the applicant's remedy lies, not in a claim for compensation, but in having the obligation struck out on appeal to the Secretary of State or by way of recourse to the courts. The scope of planning control is discussed in detail in chapters 8, 9 and 10.

Where there are available to an authority alternative statutory powers of control over development, one providing for payment of compensation and the other not, the authority are not obliged to adopt the procedure which

6 Cmnd 6386 (1942), para 35.
7 [1964] 1 All ER 1, [1964] 1 WLR 240.
8 [1974] QB 720, [1974] 2 All ER 643.

provides for payment of compensation if the use of the planning power is otherwise being exercised properly.[9] Thus in *Westminster Bank Ltd v Minister of Housing and Local Government*[10] the House of Lords held that a planning authority were entitled to refuse an application for planning permission on the ground that the land would be required for road-widening, notwithstanding that the authority could have achieved their objective by the alternative method of prescribing an improvement line under the highways legislation, a course of action which would have meant the immediate payment of compensation. Lord Reid expressed the view that an authority would be entitled to employ their planning powers in preference to some alternative power even if their sole reason for so doing was a desire to avoid payment of compensation.

B THE EXCEPTIONS TO THE GENERAL RULE

We mentioned above that there are three limited exceptions to the general rule that no compensation is payable for an adverse decision on an application for planning permission for the development of land. These exceptions concern:

(a) an adverse decision in respect of certain categories of development not constituting 'new development';
(b) an adverse decision on an application consequent on the modification or withdrawal of a planning permission granted by development order;
(c) an adverse decision on an application for 'new development' on land in respect of which there exists an unexpended balance of established development value.

The first two exceptions are discussed in detail in chapter 15 which deals with control of the existing use of land; in this chapter, we confine ourselves to a brief outline of the relevant statutory provisions. It is, however, appropriate to deal with the third exception in full in this chapter.

Development not constituting 'new development'

The categories of development which do not constitute 'new development'[11] are defined in Pts I and II of Sch 8 to the 1971 Act. They are commonly referred to as 'existing use development' because they comprise relatively minor activities closely related to the existing use of the land.

Section 169 of the 1971 Act deals with the position where an adverse decision is made by the Secretary of State on an application for planning permission for any of the classes of existing use development specified in Pt II of Sch 8. If, as a result of the decision, it can be shown that the value of a

---

9 *Westminster Bank Ltd v Minister of Housing and Local Government* [1971] AC 508, [1970] 1 All ER 734. See, too, *Stringer v Minister of Housing and Local Government* [1971] 1 All ER 65, [1970] 1 WLR 1281; and *Hoveringham Gravels Ltd v Secretary of State for the Environment* [1975] 1 QB 754, [1975] 2 All ER 931, CA.
10 Above.
11 'New development' is simply a reference to any development other than those categories specified in Pts I and II of Sch 8 to the 1971 Act (1971 Act, s 22(5)).

person's interest in the land is less than it would have been if permission had been granted, or been granted unconditionally, the planning authority must compensate that person for the difference in value.

The modification or withdrawal of planning permission granted by development order

Section 24 of the 1971 Act empowers the Secretary of State to grant planning permission for development by way of development order. Article 3 of the Town and Country Planning General Development Order 1988, for example, grants planning permission for the numerous categories of development listed in Sch 2 to the order. A planning permission granted by development order may, however, be withdrawn or modified as a result of the revocation or amendment of the order or by the issuing of a direction under powers contained in the order (for example, a direction under Art 4 of the general development order). The effect is to require any proposed development caught by the revocation, amendment or direction to be the subject of a formal application to the planning authority for planning permission in the normal way.

Section 164 provides for compensation where a specific planning permission has been revoked or modified by an order under s 45, and s 165 provides for the same right to compensation in the case of the alteration of the rights under a development order, in the event of the refusal of such an application or the imposition of conditions other than those which would originally have been imposed by the development order.

Compensation will be paid by the planning authority to any person with an interest in the land who can show that he has incurred abortive expenditure or has otherwise sustained loss or damage as a direct result of the revocation, amendment or direction.

The unexpended balance of established development value

The third exception to the general rule that no compensation is payable in respect of an adverse decision on an application for planning permission can be explained, as a JUSTICE report *Compensation for Compulsory Acquisition and Remedies for Planning Restrictions* (1969) commented, 'historically but not logically'. Although little now remains of the complex scheme for the control of land values contained in the Town and Country Planning Act 1947, in order to explain this third exception it is necessary to make brief mention of certain aspects of that scheme.

Proceeding on the basis that 'development value'—broadly, the value which land may have over and above its 'existing use' value because of the possibility that it may be put to some more profitable use—is created by the efforts of the community as a whole, the 1947 Act provided, in effect, for the expropriation by the state of the prospective development value of all land. To achieve this objective, it was laid down that when development was carried out under planning permission the developer was to pay a 'development charge' equal to the amount by which the value of the land was estimated to have increased as a result of the grant of permission. As development value was thus secured to the state it was logical to provide, as the 1947 Act did, that where planning permission was refused or was granted subject to conditions, with the result that the prospective development value of land could not be fully realised, there would generally be no entitlement to compensation in respect of the adverse decision.

In recognition of the hardship which might have resulted in some cases if no payment were made in respect of the loss to individual owners of the development value of their land, there was established, for Britain as a whole, a global fund of £300 million against which claims for loss of development value might be made under Pt V of the 1947 Act. It was intended that payment of established claims would be made on a once and for all basis in 1953, but before any such disbursement took place the scheme of the 1947 Act for the control of land values was largely dismantled by the Town and Country Planning Act 1953 and the Town and Country Planning Act 1954.

The abolition of development charge by the 1953 Act meant that development value was in effect restored to landowners; the landowner who obtains planning permission presently enjoys, subject to possible fiscal liabilities, any gain which accrues as a result of that permission. Landowners who are unable, because of planning restrictions, to realise the full development value of their land are, however, seldom entitled to compensation. Parliament was, as Davies says,[12] unwilling to see such owners 'totally deprived of compensation ... and yet at the same time could not face the logical consequence of awarding full compensation in lieu of lost development value'; as the same writer states, a 'kind of "Alice-in-Wonderland" compromise was worked out' in that it was decided that claims on the £300 million fund made and accepted under the 1947 Act, 'although truly redundant now that development charges were abolished, should be applied to this new situation. To have asked for one thing was now to be made the qualification for getting something different.' The 1954 Act provided that from 1 January 1955 compensation might be payable by central government on a refusal or conditional grant of planning permission for 'new development', that is, development falling outside the categories of 'existing use' development specified in the Third Schedule to the 1947 Act,[13] the right to the once and for all payment out of the global fund was replaced, in effect, by a right to compensation if and when loss of development value actually occurred. Payment of compensation for restrictions upon 'new development' was, however, made conditional upon a claim on the £300 million fund for loss of prospective development value having been made under the 1947 Act. On 1 January 1955 any such claim established under the 1947 Act was (with the addition, in lieu of interest, of one seventh of the amount of the established claim, but under deduction of any payment already made) converted into what is termed the 'original unexpended balance of established development value', attached to and running with the land in respect of which the claim was made.

Compensation is now payable under Pt VII of the 1971 Act (re-enacting provisions originally contained in the 1954 Act) in respect of a planning decision restricting 'new development' only if there is attached to the land in question an unexpended balance of established development value. If, therefore, no claim was established on the £300 million fund at the appropriate time, compensation will not now be payable in respect of such a decision.

---

12 *Law of Compulsory Purchase and Compensation* (Butterworths, 4th edn, 1984), p 294.
13 See now 1971 Act, Sch 8.

The amount of any compensation payable for restrictions on 'new development' may not exceed the unexpended balance of established development value; since that balance derives from claims made on the basis of market values prevailing in 1947 and is unaffected by factors such as development plan zoning, any compensation now payable is likely to be much less than the actual loss of development value.[14] It may also be observed that payment of compensation in respect of a decision restricting 'new development' is by no means automatic—even where an unexpended balance attaches to the land in question the right to claim compensation is restricted in a number of important ways. The provisions of Pt VII of the 1971 Act, dealing with compensation for restrictions on 'new development', are considered in section C of this chapter.

C COMPENSATION FOR PLANNING DECISIONS RESTRICTING NEW DEVELOPMENT

Where planning permission for the carrying out of 'new development' is refused or is granted subject to conditions, compensation may be payable under Pt VII of the 1971 Act. 'New development' means 'any development other than development of a class specified in Pt I or Pt II of Sch 8 to the 1971 Act (1971 Act, s 22(5)). It is not essential to the making of a claim that the adverse planning decision should have been the subject of an appeal to the Secretary of State.

Unexpended balance of established development value

Payment of compensation under Pt VII of the 1971 Act is entirely dependent on there being an unexpended balance of established development value attaching to the land. Brief mention has been made above of the way in which the original unexpended balance derives from claims made under Pt VI of the 1947 Act (see ss 135 to 139 of the 1971 Act); if no such claim was made no balance can now be established.

The original balance may be reduced or become wholly expended in a number of ways. If compensation becomes payable under Pt VII of the 1971 Act in respect of depreciation in the value of an interest in land by virtue of a planning decision, the balance is reduced by the amount of that compensation (s 140). If new development on land is permitted and the owner is thus able to realise some of the development value of the land, the unexpended balance is reduced by the value of that new development as at the time when the unexpended balance has to be calculated (s 141). The unexpended balance of established value attaching to any land may also be reduced or extinguished by acquisition of the land under compulsory powers (s 142), by the payment in certain circumstances of compensation for severance or injurious affection (s 143) and by payment in some circumstances of compensation in respect of the revocation or modification of planning permission (s 166). Where necessary, the unexpended balance will be apportioned (s 144).

On application made by any person, the Secretary of State must issue a certificate stating whether particular land had an original unexpended balance; if it did, the certificate must (a) give a general statement of what was

14 See, for example, *Avis v Minister of Housing and Local Government* (1959) 11 P & CR 26.

taken by the Central Land Board to be the state of the land on 1 July 1948 and (b) specify the amount of that original balance (s 145(1)). Such a certificate *may*, if the Secretary of State thinks fit, include additional information with respect to acts or events in consequence of which a deduction is required to be made from the original unexpended balance (s 145(2)). A prospective purchaser of land may have to make his own calculations as to what deductions fall to be made from the original balance. If the issue of a certificate under s 145 involves a new apportionment, only a person who is for the time being entitled to an interest in the land in question may apply for a certificate (s 145(4)). Notice of the proposed apportionment must be given to persons who will be affected and an opportunity provided for the making of objections (s 145(4)). Any dispute may be referred to the Lands Tribunal (s 145(5)). After service of a notice to treat, an authority possessing compulsory purchase powers may obtain a certificate showing the *unexpended* balance attaching to the land in question; notice of any proposed deduction from the original balance must be given to affected parties (see s 145(3)–(5)).

Right to compensation

To succeed with a claim for compensation under Pt VII, a claimant has to show that he is entitled to an interest in land, the value of which has been depreciated by an adverse planning decision (s 146). A favourable decision may, however, be treated as subject to a notional condition (and may, therefore, be treated as an 'adverse' decision) if the Secretary of State certifies that he is satisfied that particular buildings or works were included in the application only because the applicant had reason to believe that without their inclusion permission for the development to which the application relates would not have been granted (s 150). It is not incumbent upon a person whose application for permission to develop is refused to prove affirmatively that if permission had been granted, development would in fact have followed.[15]

Excluded cases

The 1971 Act contains a number of provisions which have the effect of excluding payment of compensation under Pt VII even though there is an unexpended balance of established development value attached to the land in question.

An important exclusion is made by s 147(1) which states that compensation is not payable in respect of the refusal of planning permission for any development 'which consists of or includes the making of any material change in the use of any buildings or other land'. Despite the wide terms of this subsection, assurances were given in Parliament that in a case where development consisted of, say, building operations but also involved a material change in the use of land only the change of use would be excluded from compensation.

In *Overland v Minister of Housing and Local Government*[16] where an outline application for industrial development had been refused by the planning authority, the minister came to the conclusion that compensation in

---

15 See *Overland v Minister of Housing and Local Government* (1957) 8 P & CR 389.
16 Above.

respect of that refusal was excluded on the ground that the development consisted of or included a material change in the use of land. The Lands Tribunal held, however, that since an outline application can only be made in respect of operations, the refusal in this case amounted to a refusal of permission to erect industrial buildings and that the payment of compensation was not therefore excluded by the statute.

Compensation is not payable in respect of the imposition of any condition relating to (a) the number or disposition of buildings on any land; (b) the dimensions, design, structure or external appearance of any building or the materials to be used in its construction; (c) the manner in which any land is to be laid out, including the provision of facilities for the parking, loading or fuelling of vehicles; (d) the use of any buildings or other land; (e) the location or design of any means of access to a road or the materials to be used in the construction of any such means of access ('means of access to a road' does not, for this purpose, include a service road); or (f) in respect of any conditions subject to which planning permission is granted for the winning and working of minerals (s 147(2)).

No compensation is payable in respect of a refusal of permission where one of the reasons for refusal is that development of the kind proposed is premature having regard to either or both of the following matters: (a) the stages by which development is to be carried out, as indicated in the development plan; and (b) any existing deficiency in water supplies or sewerage services, and the period within which any such deficiency may reasonably be expected to be made good (s 147(4)). As regards a refusal based on (a) above this sub-section ceases to apply seven years after the date of the first refusal on this ground.[17]

Section 147(1) excludes payment of compensation in respect of any decision on an application for consent to the display of advertisements. Compensation is not payable in respect of the imposition of conditions relating to the duration of planning permission (s 147(3)) nor is it payable in respect of a refusal of permission where one of the reasons for refusal is that the land is unsuitable for the proposed development on account of its liability to flooding or subsidence (s 147(5)).

Planning permission granted subject to a condition prohibiting development on a specified part of land to which an application relates is, for the purposes of s 147, to be treated as a decision refusing permission with respect to that part (s 147(6)).

Under s 148 no compensation is payable under Pt VII of the 1971 Act in respect of a refusal of planning permission if, notwithstanding that refusal, there is in force immediately prior to the Secretary of State giving notice of his decision on the claim, a grant of planning permission or an undertaking by the Secretary of State to grant permission for 'any development of a residential, commercial or industrial character, being development which consists wholly or mainly of the construction of houses, flats, shop or office premises, or industrial buildings (including warehouses), or any combination thereof'.

Section 149(1) provides that where an interest in land has been compulsorily acquired by or sold to an authority possessing compulsory purchase powers (other than statutory undertakers and the National Coal Board) no

17 1971 Act, s 147(4), amended by the Water Act 1973, s 40(2), Sch 8.

compensation is payable to the authority, or to any person deriving title from them after 1 July 1948, in respect of a planning decision made after service of the notice to treat or after the making of the contract of sale. There are also exclusions in respect of land appropriated by a local authority for a purpose for which the authority could have been authorised to acquire the land compulsorily and in respect of operational land of statutory undertakers and certain land of the National Coal Board (s 149(2), (3)).

Where a claim for compensation under Pt VII has been made, the Secretary of State is entitled under s 38 of the 1971 Act to review the planning decision which has given rise to the claim. Where there has been no appeal against the planning authority's decision, the Secretary of State may give a direction substituting for that authority's decision a decision more favourable to the applicant[18] (s 38(2)). Even if there has been an appeal the Secretary of State is entitled in any case to give a direction granting permission for development other than that to which the application related (irrespective of whether or not the claimant wishes to carry out such development) (s 38(3)). Before making a direction under s 38 the Secretary of State must give notice of the proposal to the planning authority and to the claimant and must afford to each of them an opportunity of appearing before and being heard by a person appointed by the Secretary of State for the purpose (s 39). Where the Secretary of State gives a direction under s 38, the claim for compensation then has effect as if it had been made in respect of the modified or substituted decision (s 155). The giving of such a direction may, of course, mean that compensation will not in fact be payable.

Measure of compensation

Where compensation is payable under Pt VII of the 1971 Act the amount of the compensation is to be either the amount by which the value of the claimant's interest is depreciated by the planning decision or the amount of the unexpended balance of established development value, whichever of these two amounts is the lesser (s 152). 'Depreciation' must be calculated in accordance with the provisions of s 153 and 'value' is to be calculated in accordance with rules (2) and (4) of the rules set out in s 5 of the Land Compensation Act 1961 (s 163). Where compensation is payable in respect of two or more interests in land and the aggregate amount of compensation payable would exceed the unexpended balance, then that balance will be allocated between those interests in proportion to the depreciation of the value of each interest (s 152(3)). The balance will be allocated between those interests in respect of which a claim has been made and a late claimant might therefore find that no balance remained. Section 152 also makes provision for determination of the amount of compensation where an unexpended balance attaches to only a part of the land to which the decision relates or where a depreciated interest subsists in only a part of that land.

Claims for and payment of compensation

A claim for compensation under Pt VII of the 1971 Act must be made within six months of the adverse planning decision or such longer period as the Secretary of State may allow (s 154(1)–(3)) and is to be made on a form issued

18 As to the meaning of the phrase 'decision more favourable to the applicant', see s 38(4).

by the Secretary of State (Town and Country Planning (Compensation and Certificates) Regulations 1974, reg 3). A claimant may be required to furnish certain supporting material (1974 regulations, reg 5). Where the Secretary of State considers that the claim is not justified, he will so notify the claimant, giving him an opportunity to withdraw the claim (s 154(5)(a)). In any case where the claim is not withdrawn, the Secretary of State may, under s 38 of the 1971 Act, review the decision which gave rise to the claim (see p 385 above). The Secretary of State must, unless the claim is withdrawn, give notice of the claim to every other person appearing to him to have an interest in the land (s 154(5)(b)) and must then 'cause such investigations to be made and such steps to be taken as he may deem requisite to enable him to determine the claim' (1974 regulations, reg 6(1)). Notice of the Secretary of State's determination, stating the compensation payable and the amount of the unexpended balance, must be given to the claimant and, if the determination includes an apportionment, to any other person whose interest in the land is substantially affected by the apportionment (1974 regulations, reg 6(4)). Any dispute as to the determination or an apportionment included therein may be referred to the Lands Tribunal (1974 regulations, reg 7).

Compensation under Pt VII of the 1971 Act is paid by the Secretary of State (s 157). Where the compensation payable exceeds £20 the Secretary of State shall, if it appears practicable, apportion the compensation between different parts of the land to which the claim relates according to the way in which those different parts of the land appear to be differently affected by the planning decision (s 158(1), (2)). A notice that compensation exceeding £20 has become payable (a 'compensation notice') should be registered as a local land charge under the Local Land Charges Act 1975, and notice must be given to the London Borough or the County District in which the land is situated (s 158(4)).

Repayment of compensation

In certain circumstances compensation paid in respect of a planning decision restricting new development may have to be repaid. No person is to carry out new development of certain specified types on land in respect of which a compensation notice has been registered until such amount of the compensation as is recoverable under s 159 of the 1971 Act has been repaid or secured to the satisfaction of the Secretary of State (s 159(1)). Such repayment may therefore have to be made by someone other than the person who received the compensation.

Repayment of compensation may be required where it is proposed to carry out any new development:

(a) of a residential, commercial or industrial character, consisting wholly or mainly of the construction of houses, flats, shop or office premises or industrial buildings (including warehouses) or any combination thereof;
(b) which consists in the winning or working of minerals;
(c) 'to which, having regard to the probable value of the development, it is in the opinion of the Secretary of State reasonable' that the provisions as to repayment should apply (s 159(2)).

The repayment provisions will not apply where, on application made to him, the Secretary of State certifies that, having regard to the probable value of the development, it would not be reasonable to require repayment (s 159(3)) and the Secretary of State may remit the whole or part of any compensation recoverable if he is satisfied that the development in question is not likely to be carried out unless he does so (s 159(2)).

Minerals

Certain of the provisions of Pt VII of the 1971 Act are modified in their application to minerals by the Town and Country Planning (Minerals) Regulations 1971.

Conclusion

The unexpended balance of established development value has little practical significance today. Most of the land which had development potential in 1948 will either have been developed long since and the development value realised; alternatively, it will, for whatever planning reasons, have remained undeveloped and compensation will have been paid. Either way, the balance of established development value will have been extinguished. For those relatively few cases where an unexpended balance remains, the compensation, based as it is on 1948 development values, will be unlikely to reflect the development value foregone as a result of an adverse planning decision today.

The real anomaly in this area of law, as the JUSTICE report (above) observed in 1969, 'is not that many people receive no compensation, but that a few people receive some in the shape of the "unexpended balance of established development value" attached to their land'. The report continued: 'We believe that the community has now accepted that there should in general be no payment of compensation for such restrictions.' Its conclusion was that the right to claim compensation should be redeemed over a fixed and limited period of time.

Similarly the consultation paper 'Planning Compensation' published by the Department of the Environment in 1986 concluded that:

'These provisions are increasingly anachronistic and there is little justification for their continuance. The amounts paid to individual claimants are generally small, there are few claims and the numbers are diminishing. It is therefore proposed that Pt VII should be repealed, subject to a transitional period of not less than 2 years to allow potential claimants to submit planning applications and to enter a claim if necessary.'

As yet there is no indication that any amending legislation will be brought forward.

CHAPTER 14

ADVERSE PLANNING DECISIONS: PURCHASE NOTICES

In certain restricted circumstances the owner of land in respect of which an adverse planning decision[1] or order has been made may be able to compel the local planning authority (or some other authority) to acquire his interest in the land. This 'inverse compulsory purchase' procedure is set in motion by service on the local planning authority of a purchase notice. The object of the purchase notice procedure is simply to enable a landowner who, in the public interest, is denied the opportunity to put land to any potentially useful purpose to rid himself of the land.

Conditions for service of purchase notice following an adverse planning decision

Section 180 of the 1971 Act provides that where, on an application for planning permission to develop land, permission is refused or is granted subject to conditions, then if any owner[2] claims:

(a) that the land has become incapable of reasonably beneficial use in its existing state; and

(b) in a case where planning permission was granted subject to conditions, that the land cannot be rendered capable of reasonably beneficial use by the carrying out of the permitted development in accordance with those conditions;[3] and

(c) in any case, that the land cannot be rendered capable of reasonably beneficial use by the carrying out of any other development for which planning permission has been granted or for which the local planning authority or Secretary of State has undertaken to grant planning permission,

---

1 Ie, a refusal or conditional grant of planning permission. Where land is affected by adverse planning *proposals*, it may be possible, by service of a blight notice, to compel the appropriate authority to acquire the land—see chapter 17.

2 Owner is defined by s 290 of the 1971 Act and must be a person who is entitled, at the time of the service of the purchase notice, to receive the rack rent of the land, or if the land is not let at a rack rent, would be so entitled if it were so let. From *London Corpn v Cusack–Smith* [1955] AC 337, [1955] 1 All ER 302, HL, this means that where a rack rent is charged to a lessee, that occupant cannot serve a purchase notice. However, in the ministerial decision notice at [1980] JPL 53 it was held that where land is let under a building lease at a ground rent, this is not to be regarded as a rack rent even if the land is not developed. So the tenant was held to be able to serve the purchase notice. Also see *Rakusson Properties Ltd v Leeds City Council* (1978) 37 P & CR 315 where the Lands Tribunal held that ownership by a subsidiary or associated company was not sufficient for the service of a purchase notice.

3 For the purpose of s 180, conditions under ss 41 and 42 of the 1971 Act, limiting the duration of planning permission, are to be ignored (s 180(4)).

he may serve on the planning authority[4] in whose area the land is situated a purchase notice, ie a notice requiring the authority to purchase his interest in the land.

Where, through the failure of the local planning authority to issue a decision within the period specified in the General Development Order, there is a 'deemed' refusal of planning permission, it seems that refusal cannot form the basis for service of a purchase notice,[5] appeal against the deemed refusal will first have to be made to the Secretary of State and that appeal refused.

Difficult questions can arise over the interpretation of s 180 and, in particular, in relation to the need to show that the land has become incapable of reasonably beneficial use in its existing state. The provision has been the subject of considerable judicial scrutiny.

In *Smart and Courtenay Dale Ltd v Dover RDC*[6] the Lands Tribunal took the view that wherever the words 'the land' are used in the purchase notice provisions, they denote the whole of the land which was the subject of the planning decision; the tribunal held that a purchase notice served by claimants who did not own the whole of the land which had been the subject of an adverse planning decision was on that account invalid. The memorandum to circular 13/83, however, states that '... if permission has been granted for part of the land to which an application related and refused for the remainder, a purchase notice relating to that remainder can be served' (para 7). The memorandum goes on to declare 'that a purchase notice will also be acceptable where land covered by the planning decision comprises parcels of land in different ownerships, and the owners of those parcels combine to serve a single purchase notice relating to their separate interests, if the notice as served relates to the whole of the land covered by the planning decision' (para 9).

In *Purbeck District Council v Secretary of State for the Environment*[7] the planning authority argued that the use by Parliament of the words 'has become' indicated that there should be an identifiable change of circumstances which led to the existing situation. Accordingly, it was argued, an area of marshland, which had always been marshland, could not be described as land which 'had become' incapable of reasonably beneficial use. Woolf J rejected this argument. The section had to be looked at from the point of view of the situation which arose on an adverse decision. Unless the application for planning permission resulted in an adverse decision the section could not apply. If the decision was favourable, it could not be said that the land had become incapable of reasonably beneficial use. It was in this sense that the adverse decision on a planning application could lead to a situation where land could be said to have become incapable of reasonably beneficial use.[8] It is not therefore incumbent upon the server of a purchase notice to show that there is a causal connection between the adverse planning

---

4 The purchase notice will be served on the district council or in London the London Borough or City of London.
5 See ministerial decision noted in [1950] JPL 794.
6 (1972) 23 P & CR 408; see too ministerial decisions noted in [1978] JPL 195; and [1980] JPL 193. See, however, ministerial decision noted in [1976] JPL 647.
7 (1982) 80 LGR 545.
8 See, too, ministerial decision noted in [1970] JPL 276.

decision occasioning the notice and the fact that the land is incapable of reasonably beneficial use.[9]

Incapable of reasonably beneficial use

The phrase which has caused the greatest difficulty is 'incapable of reasonably beneficial use'.[10] The question to be considered in every case is not merely whether the land is of less use or value to the owner in its present state than it would have been if he had been able to develop the land and realise its development potential, but whether, as a matter of fact and degree, the land in its existing state (taking account of any existing permissions and any undertakings to grant permission) is incapable of reasonably beneficial use. As Lord Parker CJ said in *R v Minister of Housing and Local Government, ex p Chichester RDC*:[11] 'I suppose that in every case where land is worth developing and permission to develop is refused, the existing use of the land will be of less beneficial use, it will be less useful to the owner, than if it were developed. The test is whether it has become incapable of reasonably beneficial use in its existing state.'

The memorandum to circular 13/83[12] provides some illustrations of the application of this test. The circular states: 'In considering what capacity for use the land has, relevant factors are the physical state of the land, its size, shape and surroundings, and the general pattern of land-uses in this area; a use of relatively low value may be reasonably beneficial by being used in conjunction with neighbouring or adjoining land, provided that a sufficient interest in that land is held by the server of the notice or by a prospective owner of the purchase notice land' (para 13). The memorandum goes on to state that: 'Profits *may* be a useful test in certain circumstances but the absence of profit (however calculated) is not necessarily material: the concept of reasonable beneficial use is not synonymous with profit.' For example, in appropriate circumstances use as a garden may be a reasonably beneficial use (whether independently or in conjunction with adjoining land).[13]

On the other hand, in *Adams and Wade Ltd v Minister of Housing and Local Government*[14] Widgery J held that 'beneficial use' must mean a use which could benefit the owner or prospective owner of the land and the fact that land in its existing state conferred some benefit on the public at large was no bar to service of a purchase notice. However, if for some reason an owner is unwilling to put land to what could be a beneficial use and there is a demand for the land for that use then it seems that a purchase notice will not succeed.[15]

Not only must the purchase notice relate to the whole of the land which was the subject of the planning decision,[16] but it seems that the whole of the land must be shown to be incapable of reasonably beneficial use. In *Wain v*

9 See *Hoddesdon UDC v Secretary of State for the Environment* (1971) 115 Sol Jo 187. See, too, ministerial decision noted in [1959] JPL 897.
10 See W A Leach, 'Reasonably Beneficial Use' [1977] JPL 283.
11 [1960] 2 All ER 407, [1960] 1 WLR 587. See, too, *General Estates Co Ltd v Minister of Housing and Local Government* (1965) 194 Estates Gazette 201.
12 See, too, ministerial decision noted in [1976] JPL 649.
13 See ministerial decisions noted in [1980] JPL 194 and [1982] JPL 257.
14 (1965) 18 P & CR 60.
15 See ministerial decision noted in [1982] JPL 257.
16 *Smart and Courtenay Dale Ltd v Dover RDC* (1972) 23 P & CR 408.

Secretary of State for the Environment[17] a purchase notice was served in respect of some 37 acres of land, half of which was covered by grass and thorn bushes and some dilapidated buildings and was described as gently undulating, and half of which was covered with a mixture of grass, weed and reed, with concrete protrusions and containing a reed-covered pond. After an inquiry, the inspector concluded that the gently undulating land could be used for grazing and hay in the spring and summer months and that, if the buildings were made good—which could be done without planning permission—the land could be put to a reasonably beneficial use. He concluded, however, that the outlay required to reclaim the other land would not be justified by the likely return and that that part of the 37 acres was incapable of beneficial use. The Secretary of State refused to confirm the notice, holding that the owner of the land had to show that the whole of the land which was the subject of the planning decision was incapable of reasonably beneficial use. The Court of Appeal upheld his decision. Lord Denning commented that it seemed to him that: '. . . the true interpretation was that the owner could not claim the right to have the council purchase his land compulsorily except when all the land had become incapable of reasonably beneficial use. If part of the land was capable of reasonably beneficial use, then he could not insist on a compulsory purchase.'[18] There would, however, seem to be nothing to prevent a landowner in this situation from applying for planning permission to develop that part of the land which is incapable of beneficial use and then serving a purchase notice in the event of an adverse decision.

An owner of land cannot render it incapable of reasonable beneficial use simply by fencing it off or otherwise artificially separating it from other land that he owns. This was so held in *Whiston v Secretary of State for the Environment and Stoke on Trent City Council*[19] where the Secretary of State had determined that land was capable of beneficial use as a garden of a house owned by the applicant. No significant works would be needed to reincorporate the land into the curtilage of the house and it would not involve a material change of use requiring planning permission. David Widdicombe QC, upholding the Secretary of State's decision, held that he was entitled to take into account the fact that the site could be incorporated into other land owned by the applicant.

Where land is rendered incapable of reasonably beneficial use as a result of a breach of planning control by the landowner, it appears that the landowner will be able to take advantage of the breach by serving a purchase notice provided that it is too late for enforcement action to be taken. In *Purbeck District Council v Secretary of State for the Environment*[20] permission had been granted for the use of land, previously used for clay extraction operations, as a rubbish tip subject to controls designed to secure the reinstatement of the site in a satisfactory form. As a result of what appeared to be total disregard of these controls by the owner's tenant, the land had become incapable of reasonably beneficial use. Woolf J interpreted the purchase notice provisions as 'excluding a situation where the land had

17 (1981) 44 P & CR 289.
18 See too ministerial decision noted in [1976] JPL 649.
19 [1989] JPL 178.
20 (1982) 80 LGR 545.

become incapable of beneficial use because of unlawful activities on the land', ie, activities being carried on in breach of planning control. However, in *Balco Transport Services Ltd v Secretary of State for the Environment (No 2)*[1] the Court of Appeal further explained the position. Here land which could only be legally used for agriculture had become incapable of such use because hardcore had been laid down without planning permission. Because of the four-year rule (see p 323) it was too late to take enforcement action against the unauthorised operation. Glidewell LJ (with whose judgment the rest of the Court of Appeal agreed) stated that, 'the maxim that a man could not take advantage of his own wrong had no application to the question whether land had become incapable of reasonable beneficial use in its existing state'. In any case, Glidewell LJ pointed out that it could well be that enforcement action had not been taken because the planning authority did not object to the operations which had added to the value of the land. He then made clear that the position would be different if, as in *Purbeck*, it were not too late to take enforcement action. If by the service of an enforcement notice the landowner could have been required at his expense to put the land in a state in which it would have been capable of reasonable beneficial use, the landowners could not be heard to say that the land in its existing state was incapable of such a use. Glidewell LJ therefore laid down that if at the time when the purchase notice was served:

(i)   the land to which it related was in a state which had been caused by development carried out without planning permission; and,

(ii) a valid enforcement notice in respect of that development either had already been served or could be served; and,

(iii) such an enforcement notice could require the owner or occupier to take steps to restore his land to its condition before the development took place; and

(iv) in such a condition the land would be capable of reasonably beneficial use

then the conditions for confirming the purchase notice had not been fulfilled.

The practical consequence is that with regard to operations, if the local planning authority are to fend off a notice, they must serve an enforcement notice within four years. If permission were to be granted to retain the works on appeal against the enforcement notice, this would presumably enable the purchase notice to go ahead. In the case of a material change of use the four-year rule does not apply to any cases where a purchase notice would be relevant. So, unless the material change or breach of condition had occurred before 1964, it would still be possible to take enforcement action many years after the actual breach. The owner could, of course, seek to have the position regularised by putting in an application for permission under s 32(1)(a) or (b) but this would in all likelihood be refused. The obvious example is, as in *Purbeck*, the unauthorised use of land as a refuse tip, but other uses of land can render it incapable of beneficial use; the sorting of scrap comes to mind. Difficult practical problems could arise where the unauthorised use had ceased several years before, but in such a case it would still seem possible to serve an enforcement notice requiring the land to be restored. This in itself would be sufficient to defeat a purchase notice.

1 [1986] JPL 123.

It is implicit that any use of land which requires and has not got the benefit of a grant of planning permission is to be ignored in determining whether the land is capable of beneficial use; such a use would be necessarily unlawful (1971 Act, s 23(1)). Thus in deciding whether land could be beneficially used as a garden, it would have to be asked whether this would be a material change of use.[2]

On the other hand, the Secretary of State takes the view that in considering whether land has become incapable of reasonably beneficial use in its 'existing state', there can be taken into account alterations and improvements which could be carried out without the need for planning permission:[3] he therefore refused to confirm a purchase notice relating to land which had become semi-derelict and incapable, without improvement, of reasonably beneficial use for agriculture but which could, with normal husbandry and improvement of security, have been made suitable for grazing purposes.[4]

At the time the purchase notice is served, perforce it will only be grants of planning permission and undertakings then in existence, which will be relevant for condition (c), i e whether the land cannot be rendered capable of reasonably beneficial use by carrying out development authorised by such permissions or undertakings.[5] However, where a purchase notice is not accepted, the Secretary of State in deciding whether to confirm the notice under s 183 (see above) has to consider whether the conditions in s 180(1)(a) to (c) apply. The Secretary of State now takes the view that this means whether the conditions are fulfilled at the time of his decision and that this necessitates taking into account, *inter alia*, any relevant planning permission, whether granted before or after service of the purchase notice.[6] The relevant time for considering whether land has become incapable of reasonably beneficial use is therefore not the date of service of the purchase notice but the time the minister considers it.

Even where permission has been or will be granted for a prospective development which would render the land capable of a reasonable beneficial use, it is still necessary to judge whether that permission will be taken up. In *Gavaghan v Secretary of State for the Environment*[7] it was held that the Secretary of State had acted irrationally in holding that there was a prospective purchaser for the land which could lawfully be used as curtilage land.

In determining any question as to what is or would be a reasonably beneficial use of land, no account is to be taken of any prospective use of the land which would involve the carrying out of 'new development'[8] (s 180(2)). It may be relevant to consider whether land is denied any prospective

2 See *Whiston v Secretary of State for the Environment* [1989] JPL 178.
3 The Secretary of State for the Environment takes the view that account cannot be taken of works for which planning permission would be required—see [1978] JPL 195 and 197.
4 See [1976] JPL 189. Cf appeal decisions noted in [1982] JPL 792; and [1984] JPL 817.
5 A promise 'to give favourable consideration' would not be a binding undertaking; see circular 13/83, para 14.
6 See appeal decisions noted in [1981] JPL 762; and [1984] JPL 817 and circular 13/83, para 14.
7 [1989] JPL 596.
8 Ie, development outside the classes of 'existing use' development specified in the Eighth Schedule to the 1971 Act—see chapter 15. For the purposes of any determination under s 180(2), the Eighth Schedule is modified (see s 180(3)). In addition, for the purposes of any such determination no account is taken of any prospective use of the land which would contravene the condition set out in Sch 18 to the 1971 Act (s 180(2)) (see p 416 below).

usefulness by lack of permission for development specified in the Eighth Schedule[9] to the 1971 Act but the fact that the land could be rendered capable of more beneficial use by Eighth Schedule development is not conclusive evidence that it is incapable of reasonably beneficial use in its existing state.[10] Indeed, the Secretary of State now takes the view that Sch 8 rights cannot affect the issue of whether land has or has not got reasonably beneficial use.[11]

Section 180(2) is concerned with the standards by which the present and potential lawful uses of the land are to be judged. It cannot therefore be interpreted as preventing account being taken of a prospective use of land (for which permission has been granted or an undertaking given) when considering whether the condition in sub-s 180(1)(c) applies. Thus, in *Gavaghan v Secretary of State for the Environment*[12] Lionel Read QC, sitting as a deputy judge, held that, where land was otherwise incapable of reasonably beneficial use, account could be properly taken of an undertaking by the local planning authority to grant permission for the use of the land as part of the curtilage of a neighbouring house, in considering whether the land *could* be rendered capable of reasonably beneficial use by carrying out that change of use. Lionel Read QC stated:

'So it cannot be argued, for example, that agricultural land is not reasonably beneficial because if permission *were* to be granted for offices (ie new development) it would be worth millions. But it can be argued that a useless piece of scrub for which permission for offices *has* been granted can be rendered capable of reasonably beneficial use and so falls outside s 180(1)(c).'

Procedure

There is no prescribed form of purchase notice but a model form is given in Appendix 1 to the Memorandum in circular 13/83. It seems that a letter addressed to the relevant council in whose area the land is situated will suffice: see para 5 of the circular. A purchase notice must be served within twelve months of the adverse decision; it is to be served on the council in whose district the land is situated[13] (s 180(1) and Town and Country Planning General Regulations 1976, reg 14). The Secretary of State has power to extend the period for service (reg 14(2)), but the council do not.

The council should, within three months of service of a purchase notice, themselves serve notice on the owner or lessee by whom the purchase notice was served. If the council are willing to comply with the notice, or if another body has agreed to comply with it in their place, the counter-notice will so state; on the service of such a counter-notice, stating that the council or another local authority or statutory undertaker or new town or urban development corporation[14] are prepared to purchase the land, the appropriate authority are deemed to be authorised to acquire compulsorily the

---

9 See chapter 15.
10 See *Brookdene Investments Ltd v Minister of Housing and Local Government* (1970) 21 P & CR 545 (but see doubts expressed by Fisher J at p 550); see too ministerial decisions noted in [1978] JPL 483; and [1982] JPL 259; also circular 13/83, para 14 of memorandum.
11 See ministerial decision noted at [1986] JPL 374.
12 [1989] JPL 596.
13 See note 3 above.
14 See Local Government, Planning and Land Act 1980, s 149(3)(b) and Sch 29 Pt II.

relevant interest in accordance with the provisions of Pt VI of the 1971 Act, and to have served a notice to treat[15] in respect thereof[16] (s 181(1), (2)). In such cases no reference to the Secretary of State is required. If the council are not willing to comply with the purchase notice and have not found any other body willing to comply with it, the counter-notice must so state and should specify the council's reasons for not complying with the notice[17] and state that copies of the counter-notice and the purchase notice have been transmitted to the Secretary of State (s 181(1)(c)); since a purchase notice cannot, in such a case, become effective unless it is confirmed by the Secretary of State, the council must transmit to the minister a copy of the purchase notice, together with a copy of the counter-notice they propose to serve before they take steps to serve the counter-notice (s 181(3)).

If the authority were to fail to serve a counter-notice within the three-month period, then after nine months of service of the purchase notice, it will be deemed to have been confirmed by the Secretary of State (s 186(2) and (3)(a)).[18]

Action by Secretary of State

Where a purchase notice is transmitted to the Secretary of State, he may take one of the several courses of action specified in s 183 of the 1971 Act. If he is satisfied that the conditions specified in s 180(1)(a) to (c) (above) are fulfilled, he may confirm the notice; in so doing he may substitute for the council on whom the notice is served some other authority.[19] In this regard, the Department of the Environment have advised that the Secretary of State is required to have regard to the 'probable ultimate use' of the land or building or site of the building. He will accordingly exercise his power of substitution only if it is shown that the land or building is to be used in the reasonably near future for the purposes of the functions of that other body (s 183(1), (4)). Where the notice is confirmed, the relevant authority are deemed to be authorised to acquire compulsorily the relevant interest and to have served in respect thereof a notice to treat (which cannot be withdrawn under the power conferred by s 31 of the Land Compensation Act 1961) (see 1971 Act, ss 186(1) and 208).

In lieu of confirming the notice the minister may grant planning permission for the development in respect of which permission was refused, or, where permission was granted subject to conditions, may revoke or amend those conditions so far as seems necessary to render the land capable of reasonably beneficial use (s 183(2)). Alternatively, if satisfied that the land, or

---

15 Which cannot be withdrawn under the power conferred by s 31 of the Land Compensation Act 1961 (1971 Act, s 208).
16 Ss 49 and 50 of the Land Compensation Act 1973, relating to severance of agricultural land, have effect in relation to a case where notice to treat is deemed to have been served by virtue of the purchase notice provisions.
17 In the Memorandum annexed to circular 13/84 it is stated that it is not sufficient to merely state that the site has a reasonably beneficial use and full and clear reasons should be given, para 26.
18 If the purchase notice was nevertheless transmitted to the Secretary of State, it would be deemed to be confirmed six months after the date of transmission, (1971 Act, s 186 (3)(b)).
19 A different authority may only be substituted if the Secretary of State first offers a hearing to that authority—see *Ealing Borough Council v Minister of Housing and Local Government* [1952] Ch 856, [1952] 2 All ER 639.

part of it, could be rendered capable of reasonably beneficial use within a reasonable time by the carrying out of any other development for which planning permission ought to be granted, the Secretary of State may, in lieu of confirming the purchase notice, or in lieu of confirming it so far as relates to that part of the land, direct that planning permission for that development shall be granted (s 183(3)).[20] If the Secretary of State considers that the conditions specified in s 180(1)(a) to (c) (above) are not fulfilled, he will refuse to confirm the notice; by virtue of s 184 he may also refuse to confirm a notice served in respect of land which has a restricted use by virtue of a previous planning permission (below).

Before taking any action with respect to a purchase notice, the Secretary of State must give notice of his proposed action to the parties concerned, any one of whom then has the right to require that the parties be afforded the opportunity of a hearing before a representative of the minister (s 182(1)–(3)); after such a hearing the Secretary of State is entitled to deviate from the course of action originally proposed without giving the parties the opportunity of a further hearing (s 182(4)).[1]

If the Secretary of State has not, within six months of transmission to him of the purchase notice, confirmed the notice or taken such action as is mentioned in s 183(2) or (3) (ie has neither made a more beneficial planning decision nor directed that permission for some other development be granted) and has not notified the server of the notice that he does not propose to confirm the notice, then the notice is deemed to be confirmed (s 186(2), (3)). Somewhat oddly, provided the minister gives notice within the time limit that he does not propose to confirm, he then has unlimited time to come to his decision.[2] Also the Secretary of State has unlimited time where an appeal has been lodged against the refusal or conditional grant of planning permission (1971 Act, s 186(3A)).[3]

The validity of the Secretary of State's decision on a purchase notice may be challenged under s 245 of the 1971 Act but not otherwise (s 243) (see chapter 20). Where a decision of the Secretary of State is cancelled, the purchase notice is treated as cancelled and the owner is entitled to serve another notice in its place (s 186(4)). There is no power to suspend a purchase notice except as an interim measure.[4]

Land with restricted use by virtue of previous planning permission

Section 184 of the 1971 Act is designed to deal with the type of situation which arose in *Adams and Wade Ltd v Minister of Housing and Local Government*.[5] In that case planning permission for housing development had been granted subject to a condition that a strip of land be reserved as amenity

---

20 For illustrations of the exercise of this power see ministerial decisions noted in [1976] JPL 649; and [1982] JPL 792.
1 Thus in *Whiston v Secretary of State for the Environment* [1988] JPL 178 the Secretary of State proposed to confirm the notice but following a hearing at the insistence of the applicant, he then decided the conditions did not apply and refused to confirm.
2 See *Sheppard v Secretary of State for the Environment* (1974) 233 Estates Gazette 1167.
3 See Housing and Planning Act 1986, Sch 11, para 7.
4 *Whiteacre Estates (UK) Ltd v Secretary of State for the Environment and Tunbridge Wells Borough Council* [1984] JPL 177.
5 (1965) 18 P & CR 60.

land. After the houses were built application was made for permission to develop the amenity land and on the refusal of permission the owners served a purchase notice. It was argued for the Secretary of State that the owner of a piece of land which was, as a whole, capable of reasonably beneficial use could not sever the land and serve a purchase notice in respect of a part which was, in isolation, incapable of reasonably beneficial use. Widgery J rejected that argument and quashed the Secretary of State's decision not to confirm the purchase notice.

Section 184 of the 1971 Act relates to land which has, by virtue of a previous planning permission, a restricted use. Land is to be treated as having a restricted use by virtue of a previous planning permission if it is part of a larger area in respect of which permission was previously granted and either it is an express condition of that planning permission or the planning application contemplated (expressly or by necessary implication) that that part of the land should 'remain undeveloped or be preserved or laid out in a particular way as amenity land in relation to the remainder' (s 184(2)). In the view of the Secretary of State the word 'undeveloped', as used in this provision, stands by itself and is not connected with the words 'as amenity land in relation to the remainder'.[6] This view seems to be borne out by the concluding words of sub-s (3) of s 184 (below). It has been held[7] that land only has a 'restricted use by virtue of a previous planning permission' if the restriction in question is one which is capable of enforcement.

On a refusal or conditional grant of permission, and the consequent service of a purchase notice, in respect of land which has a restricted use by virtue of a previous planning permission, the Secretary of State, even though satisfied that the land has become incapable of reasonably beneficial use in its existing state, is not obliged to confirm the notice if it appears to him that the land having a restricted use by virtue of the previous planning permission ought, in accordance with that previous permission, to remain undeveloped or, as the case may be, remain or be preserved or laid out as amenity land in relation to the remainder of the larger area for which that permission was granted (s 184(3)). This subsection is permissive only and, even though the circumstances of a particular case may satisfy the conditions of s 184, the minister is not obliged to refuse to confirm the purchase notice.[8]

In *Plymouth Corpn v Secretary of State for the Environment*[9] it was held that these provisions only apply where the whole of the land which was the subject of the purchase notice, and not merely part of it, has a restricted use by virtue of a previous planning permission. However, the Housing and Planning Act 1986 has closed this further loophole by amending s 184 so that it applies to 'land which consists in whole or in part of land which has a restricted use' (see s 49 and sch 11, para 6).

Where a grant of outline permission is followed by approval of detailed plans, it is the outline consent which constitutes the planning permission;[10] it would therefore seem that the provisions of s 184 can only apply in relation

---

6 See [1974] JPL 158. So land can be 'restricted' even if not laid out for amenity purposes; see also *Strathclyde Regional Council v Secretary of State for Scotland* 1987 SLT 724.
7 *Sheppard v Secretary of State for the Environment* (1974) 233 Estates Gazette 1167.
8 See, for example, ministerial decisions noted in [1974] JPL 158; and [1983] JPL 753.
9 [1972] 3 All ER 225, [1972] 1 WLR 1347; see too ministerial decision noted in [1978] JPL 394.
10 See p 174 above.

to a planning permission and can have no application in relation to a decision consisting of a mere approval of details.[11]

Compensation

If a purchase notice is accepted or confirmed, compensation is assessed on the normal compulsory purchase basis.[12] The fact that the land in question has been shown to be incapable of reasonably beneficial use in its existing state does not mean that the measure of compensation for the land will necessarily be limited to the value attributable to its existing use. Much will depend on the reason for the adverse decision. For example, planning permission may have been refused because the land is required for a scheme of public works. It may be possible to show that were it not for the scheme the land would have development potential and that that potential should be taken into account in assessing compensation under the provisions of the Land Compensation Act 1961. Also in assessing the compensation, the benefit of permission for Eighth Schedule development may be assumed which could substantially increase the presumed market value of the land.[13]

Where the Secretary of State, in lieu of confirming a purchase notice, directs that planning permission ought to be granted for some alternative development, it is possible that the 'permitted development value' of the land (in effect, the value of the land calculated with regard to that alternative permission but assuming that no other planning permission would be granted—see s 187(5)) may be less than the land's 'existing use value' (in effect, its value on the assumption that permission would be granted for development of any class specified in the Eighth Schedule[14]—see s 187(5)); if that is shown to be the case the planning authority are bound to pay compensation of any amount equal to the difference between the two values (see s 187(2)–(5)).

Other cases in which a purchase notice may be served

It is not only a refusal or conditional grant of planning permission that may form the basis for service of a purchase notice; certain other types of adverse planning decision or order may entitle an owner or lessee of land to serve a purchase notice.[15] In particular, where planning permission is revoked or modified (see p 405) or where an order is made requiring discontinuance of an authorised use or imposing conditions on the continuance of such a use or requiring the alteration or removal of authorised buildings or works (see p 401), an owner may be able to serve a purchase notice; the procedure outlined above is applied, with certain modifications, to such a case (see

---

11 See ministerial decisions noted in [1974] JPL 38; and [1983] JPL 753.
12 As to the appropriate date by reference to which compensation is to be assessed see *W & S (Long Eaton) Ltd v Derbyshire County Council* (1975) 31 P & CR 99, CA. See also *Toogood v Bristol Corpn* (1973) 26 P & CR 132. There is a duty on the planning authority to negotiate in all good faith for the purchase of the property; in *Bremer v Haringey London Borough Council* (1983) Times, 12 May, damages were awarded against a planning authority for breach of that duty.
13 Land Compensation Act 1961, s 15(3).
14 See p 415.
15 See 1971 Act, ss 188–191.

ss 188 and 189). Section 190 of, and Sch 19 to the 1971 Act make similar provision for the service in certain circumstances of a listed building purchase notice in a case where listed building consent is refused, granted subject to conditions, revoked or modified (see chapter 18).

CHAPTER 15

CONTROL OF THE EXISTING USE OF LAND

A INTRODUCTION

The general effect of the comprehensive scheme of planning control introduced in 1947 was to regulate the carrying out of new development on land but to leave the landowner with the right to carry on the existing use. 'The system of planning control, then *and now*', says Davies,[1] 'rests on the assumption that the existing use of land—and the value of that use—is the owner's; but the prospect of developing the land—and the value of that prospect—is the community's'.

However, there will be occasions when a planning authority wish to exert control over the existing use of land, perhaps because of a change in planning policy or because of a change in the character of an area. The 1971 Act makes provision for such control but, as it derogates from the right to carry on the existing use of land, the general rule is that such control may only be exercised on payment of compensation. The purpose of this chapter is to examine these controls and the circumstances in which compensation is payable.

There will also be occasions where the value of the existing use of land is adversely affected, not so much by the exercise of direct control, but from the prospect of the carrying through of planning proposals in the locality—for example, the construction of a new road. In certain circumstances, a person with an interest in land which is adversely affected in this way will be able to obtain compensation or, in some cases, to require a public authority to purchase his interest. These circumstances are beyond the scope of this chapter and are discussed in detail in ch 17.

For the purposes of this chapter we treat the 'existing use' of land as comprising:

(1) activities currently being carried on in conformity with a grant of planning permission, or which are unauthorised but have become immune from enforcement action, or which were instituted prior to the planning legislation coming into force;
(2) other development for which planning permission has been granted either in response to an application or by way of development order but which has not yet been carried out; and
(3) certain classes of development specified in Schedule 8 to the 1971 Act which are so closely related to the existing use of the land that they are effectively treated as forming part of the existing use (generally referred to as 'existing use development').

1 Keith Davies, *Law of Compulsory Purchase and Compensation* (Butterworths, 4th edn, 1984), p 271.

The controls over these categories of existing use are considered in turn below.

The general rule, as we have already indicated, is that the exercise of control over the existing use of land is subject to the payment of compensation. However, as Grant observes:[2] 'Local authorities have rarely been in a position to buy environmental improvements by using the powers of direct intervention'. The result is that the formal controls which we describe below have been little used in practice[3] and the regulation of the existing use of land has been largely opportunistic. Planning authorities may well take the opportunity presented by the submission of an application for planning permission for new development either to negotiate some restriction on the existing use through agreement (see ch 11) or to impose a restriction on the existing use by way of condition on the grant of planning permission for the new development (see ch 9).

B CONTROL OF EXISTING USES, BUILDINGS AND WORKS

For various reasons a local planning authority may wish to modify or prohibit some authorised use of land or may wish to secure the removal or alteration of some authorised building—the authority may, for example, have changed their policy and may now desire the removal of some building for which planning permission was previously granted,[4] or they may wish to remove development which was originally unauthorised but in respect of which enforcement action is now time-barred, or they may wish to put an end to a use which was instituted in an unsuitable location prior to the planning legislation coming into force.

Extent of powers

Section 51 of the 1971 Act empowers a local planning authority to make an order:

(a) requiring that any use[5] of land should be discontinued[6] or imposing conditions on the continuance of a use of land; or

(b) requiring that specified steps be taken for the alteration or removal of any building or works.

The provisions of s 51 were substantially extended in their application to mineral workings by the Town and Country Planning (Minerals) Act 1981 and new sections 51A–F are discussed in full in chapter 18.

An order under s 51 may be made in any case where such action appears to the local planning authority to be expedient in the interests of the proper

---

2 Malcolm Grant, *Urban Planning Law*, p 646.
3 With a view to encouraging planning authorities to make wider use of these controls, certain modifications have been made by the Town and Country Planning (Minerals) Act 1981 to the application of the general rule to mineral operations (see ch 18).
4 If a planning permission has not been implemented it may be revoked or modified under s 45 of the 1971 Act (see below).
5 In *Parkes v Secretary of State for the Environment* [1979] 1 All ER 211, [1978] 1 WLR 1308, CA, it was held that land used for the sorting, processing and disposal of scrap materials was a 'use' of land which could be the subject of a discontinuance order.
6 An order can be made effecting a partial discontinuance of use—see [1973] JPL 181.

planning of their area (including the interests of amenity), regard being had to the development plan and to any other material considerations (s 51(1)).

In a case in which the validity of an order was challenged, Roskill J held that the powers conferred by the section, ie,

(a) to require discontinuance of a use or to impose conditions on the continuance of a use, or
(b) to require alteration or removal of any buildings or works—were alternative and it was not the case that the planning authority could only use power (b) in a case where power (a) would not suffice.[7]

In the same case Roskill J also had to consider the meaning of the word 'amenity' as used in this provision. In confirming an order requiring the removal of a building the minister had accepted his inspector's conclusion that although the building did not in its present condition detract from amenity, it would be advisable, since the building was unsuitable for residential use, to remove it now rather than let it fall slowly into a ruinous condition. It was argued that 'amenity' as used in the section must mean amenity as at the time of making the order and that the minister had exceeded his powers in having regard to future amenity. It was held that there was no reason to limit 'amenity' as used in the section to present amenity, Roskill J declaring: 'I see no reason why the whole concept does not include all amenities, past, present and, in particular, future'. However, in a case where he considered that the existing uses of a site were not sufficiently objectionable to warrant the confirmation of a discontinuance order, the Secretary of State declared that in considering such an order the minister 'is concerned with the way in which the land is being used at present and that in deciding whether or not to confirm the order it is not open to him to anticipate possible intensification of existing uses at some time in the future'.[8]

Procedure

An order under s 51 cannot take effect unless it is confirmed by the Secretary of State (s 51(4)). On confirming an order the minister may make such modifications as he considers expedient.[9] The Secretary of State has, however, expressed the view that on submission of an order requiring discontinuance of a use, it is not open to him to modify the order in such a way as to make it an order imposing conditions on the continuance of that use; such orders are, in his opinion, 'different in kind and effect'.[10]

The functions are normally carried out by the district planning authority but are also exercisable by the county planning authority in a case where it appears to that authority that they relate to a matter which should be properly considered a county matter. Also where it appears to the district planning authority that the case relates to a county matter they shall not exercise the power without first consulting the county planning authority.[11]

---

7 *Re Lamplugh* (1967) 19 P & CR 125, sub nom *Re Watch House, Boswinger* 66 LGR 6.
8 See [1973] JPL 57.
9 The Secretary of State has no specific power to correct defects in an order but in *Miller v Weymouth and Melcombe Regis Corpn* (1974) 27 P & CR 468 the court exercised its discretion not to quash a discontinuance order which contained an obvious clerical error.
10 See [1974] JPL 607.
11 Local Government Act 1972, Sch 16, para 24.

On submission of an order[12] to the Secretary of State the authority must serve notice on the owner and occupier of the land and on any other person who in their opinion will be affected by the order; any person on whom the notice is served has the right to demand a hearing before a person appointed by the Secretary of State for the purpose (s 51(6)). On confirmation of an order the local planning authority must serve a copy on the owner and occupier of the land (s 51(7)). In *K & B Metals Ltd v Birmingham City Council*[13] Sir Douglas Frank QC expressed the view that since it is specifically provided that a discontinuance order shall not take effect until it is confirmed by the minister (see s 51(4)), 'there is no order as such until it is confirmed'.[14]

An order under s 51 may grant planning permission for any development of the affected land (s 51(2)). Where the requirements of an order made under s 51 will involve the displacement of persons residing in any premises, it is the duty of the planning authority, in so far as there is no other suitable residential accommodation available on reasonable terms, to secure the provision of such accommodation in advance of displacement (s 51(8)). The validity of an order made under s 51 may be questioned under s 245 of the 1971 Act but such an order is otherwise unchallengeable (s 242).[15]

Compensation

An order under s 51 will frequently result in the making of a claim for compensation. If, on a claim made in writing to the local planning authority, it is shown that any person has suffered damage in consequence of such an order by depreciation in the value of an interest in the land in question to which he is entitled, or by being disturbed in his enjoyment of the land, the authority are to pay compensation to that person in respect of such damage (s 170(1), (2)).[16] In *K & B Metals Ltd v Birmingham City Council*[17] the Lands Tribunal held (distinguishing *Blow v Norfolk County Council*[18]) that the appropriate date for assessment of compensation on a discontinuance order is the date of confirmation of the order by the minister.

In *Blow v Norfolk County Council*[19] the Court of Appeal held that in assessing the compensation payable in respect of a discontinuance order the Lands Tribunal was entitled to take into account the risks that would influence a prospective purchaser's mind in relation to the price he might pay for the land—in this instance the doubts he would have had as to the extent of 'existing use' rights over the land in question. In *Harrison v Gloucester County Council*[20] account was taken, in assessing compensation, of the fact that planning permission for the development in question had only a short

---

12 There is no prescribed form for such an order.
13 (1976) 33 P & CR 135.
14 Contrast, however, the decision of the Court of Session in *Caledonian Terminal Investments Ltd v Edinburgh Corpn* 1970 SC 271, 1970 SLT 362 (which concerned a modification order— see p 405 below).
15 On recourse to the courts, see ch 20.
16 New ss 170A and 170B have been added to the 1971 Act by s 15 of the Town and Country Planning (Minerals) Act 1981. For a discussion of their effect see ch 18.
17 (1976) 33 P & CR 135.
18 [1966] 3 All ER 579, [1967] 1 WLR 1280, CA.
19 Above. For an example of a case where a discontinuance order resulted in no depreciation, see *Evans v Dorset County Council* (1980) 256 Estates Gazette 503.
20 (1953) 4 P & CR 99.

time to run and that it could be assumed that the permission would not have been renewed after its expiry.

Compensation payable under s 170 may include any expenses reasonably incurred in carrying out any works in compliance with the order (s 170(3)) but compensation will be reduced by the value of any materials removed for the purpose of complying with the order (s 170(4)). A claim for compensation under s 170 is to be made within six months of the making of the order or such longer period as the Secretary of State may allow (see Town and Country Planning General Regulations 1976, reg 14).

Where a purchase notice takes effect in consequence of an order made under s 51 (below), compensation under s 170 is not payable (s 189(4)).

There is no provision for the repayment of compensation paid by the planning authority under s 170.

Purchase notice

If the effect of an order under s 51 is such as to render the land incapable of reasonably beneficial use, a purchase notice may be served under s 180 of the 1971 Act (see ch 15).

Enforcement

Any person who uses land or causes or permits land to be used in contravention of an order requiring the discontinuance of a use of land or imposing conditions on the continuance of a use is liable on summary conviction or on conviction on indictment to a fine (1971 Act, s 108(1)). The present section was substituted by s 11 of the Town and Country Planning (Minerals) Act 1981.[1] The new section provides that it shall be a defence for a person charged with an offence to prove that he took all reasonable measures and exercised all due diligence to avoid commission of the offence by himself or by any person under his control (s 108(6)). The new section also makes provision regarding the procedure to be followed in the event of a person charged with an offence under this section alleging that the commission of the offence was due to the act or default of another person or due to reliance on information supplied by another person (s 108(7)).

Where any step for the alteration or removal of any buildings or works are required to be taken by an order under s 51 but have not been taken within the period specified in the order or within any extended period allowed by the local planning authority, the authority may enter on the land and may themselves take that step (1971 Act, s 108(4)). The authority can recover any expenses reasonably incurred from the person who is then the owner of the land (s 108(4)).

An authority can also sell any materials removed by them from the land, unless the materials are claimed by the owner within three days of their removal. Where an authority sell such materials, they will pay over the proceeds to the owner after first deducting any expenses recoverable by them from the owner.[2]

---

1 Brought into force on 19 May 1986.
2 See s 108(4), applying s 276 of the Public Health Act 1936.

C RESTRICTIONS ON DEVELOPMENT WHICH HAS BEEN GRANTED PLANNING PERMISSION BUT WHICH HAS YET TO BE IMPLEMENTED

Circumstances may arise in which a local planning authority have a change of heart as regards development for which they have granted planning permission. Sections 45 and 46 of the 1971 Act confer on planning authorities powers to revoke or modify a planning permission granted in response to an application under Pt III of the Act. A local planning authority may also wish on occasion to prevent advantage being taken of planning permission granted by way of a development order (see ch 6). Where planning permission has been granted by development order, the order may itself enable a local planning authority to direct that the permission will not apply either in relation to development in a particular area or in relation to any particular development (1971 Act, s 24(5)(b)). In particular, art 4 of the Town and Country Planning General Development Order 1988 ('the GDO') empowers a planning authority to issue such a direction in respect of any of the categories of development granted permission by art 3 of and Sch 2 to the Order. The procedures governing revocation or modification orders and withdrawal of permission granted by a development order are now considered in turn.

1 *Revocation or modification orders*

Extent of powers. Section 45 of the 1971 Act empowers a local planning authority to make an order revoking or modifying, to such extent as they consider expedient, any permission to develop land granted on an application made under Pt III of the 1971 Act.[3] The authority may make such an order in any case where it appears to them, having regard to the development plan and to any other material considerations, that it is expedient to do so. The power conferred by s 45 does not extend to a permission granted by a development order.[4]

An order revoking or modifying planning permission can only be made so long as the planning permission has not been fully implemented.[5] Section 45(4) provides that the power to revoke or modify may be exercised:

(a) where the permission relates to the carrying out of building or other operations, at any time before those operations have been completed; or
(b) where the permission relates to a change of the use of any land, at any time before the change has taken place.

It is also provided that revocation or modification of permission for the carrying out of building or other operations shall not affect so much of those operations as has been carried out before the date on which the order was confirmed.

---

3 Section 8 of the Town and Country Planning (Minerals) Act 1981 has added subss (5) and (7) to s 45 of the 1971 Act. For a discussion of their effect see ch 18.
4 As to withdrawal of such permission see below.
5 The local planning authority have, however, power under s 51 to make an order requiring discontinuance of an authorised use or requiring alteration or removal of authorised buildings or works—see above.

It would seem from the decision of the Court of Session on the equivalent Scottish section in *Caledonian Terminal Investments Ltd v Edinburgh Corpn*[6] that for the purposes of this section a change of use does not 'take place' until the land in question is actually put to the new use. In that case planning permission was granted for change of use from dwelling-house to professional office. On 3 April 1967 work began on internal alterations necessary to make the premises suitable for the new use; on 22 June 1967 the planning authority approved an order modifying the planning permission; the alterations were completed on 5 July 1967; and the premises were opened for business as an insurance office on 10 July 1967. Rejecting the argument that the change of use took place on the date when the alterations began, the Second Division held that the change of use took place after 22 June 1967 (ie, after the date on which the modification order was approved by the authority). The Lord Justice-Clerk (Lord Grant) and Lord Wheatley considered that the change of use did not take place until the date on which the premises actually opened for business.[7]

Procedure. An order revoking or modifying permission[8] will normally be made by a district planning authority but can also be exercised by the county planning authority in a case where it appears to that authority that it relates to a matter which should properly be considered a county matter. Also where it appears to the district planning authority that the case relates to a county matter they shall not exercise the power without first consulting the county planning authority.[9]

Except in the circumstances mentioned below, a revocation or modification order made by a local planning authority does not take effect unless it is confirmed by the Secretary of State (s 45(2)). On submitting an order to the Secretary of State for confirmation, the authority must serve notice on the owner and occupier of the land affected and also on 'any other person who in their opinion will be affected by the order' (s 45(3)). Any person served with such a notice has the right to demand a hearing before a person appointed by the Secretary of State for the purpose (s 45(3)). In confirming such an order the Secretary of State is entitled to modify it (s 45(2)).

In *Caledonian Terminal Investments Ltd v Edinburgh Corpn*[10] the modification order was not confirmed by the Secretary of State until some considerable time after the change of use had taken place. As is mentioned above, the power to revoke or modify planning permission can only be exercised prior to a change of use taking place (s 45(4)) and the appellants' main argument was that the power to revoke or modify is not 'exercised' until the order is confirmed by the minister; the modification order in this case was, they argued, *ultra vires* in that the power had not been exercised until after the change of use took place. The court held that the power was exercised on the date the planning authority made the order; the power had therefore been exercised prior to the change of use taking place and the order was valid.

6 1970 SC 271, 1970 SLT 362.
7 However, note *Backer v Secretary of State for the Environment* (1982) 264 Estates Gazette 535; and *Impey v Secretary of State for the Environment* (1980) 47 P & CR 157 which suggest that acts of conversion can in themselves amount to a material change of use.
8 There is no prescribed form for such an order.
9 Local Government Act 1972, Sch 16, para 24.
10 Above.

Both the Lord Justice-Clerk and Lord Wheatley stressed the practical difficulties that would result from any other conclusion. It may be mentioned, however, that Lord Walker, though he contented himself with expressing 'a doubt rather than a dissent', found 'great difficulty in understanding how the making of the order by the planning authority could ever amount to an exercise of the power to revoke or modify'. The planning authority's order has, he said, 'no effect unless it is confirmed by the Secretary of State'.[11]

The Secretary of State may himself make a revocation or modification order[12] (1971 Act, s 276).

The validity of an order revoking or modifying planning permission may be questioned under s 245 of the 1971 Act but not otherwise (s 242) (see ch 20). The local planning authority cannot unilaterally withdraw a grant of planning permission as an alternative to s 45[13] and a planning permission cannot be abandoned.[14]

Compensation. Where planning permission is revoked or modified by an order made under s 45 of the 1971 Act, then if it is shown that 'a person interested in the land':

(a) has incurred expenditure in carrying out work which is rendered abortive by the revocation or modification;[15] or

(b) has otherwise sustained loss or damage which is directly attributable to the revocation or modification,[16]

the local planning authority must pay to that person compensation in respect of that expenditure, loss or damage (s 164(1)).[17]

The meaning of the phrase 'a person interested in the land' was considered by the Court of Appeal in *Pennine Raceway Ltd v Kirklees Metropolitan Council*.[18] The claimant company had entered into an agreement with a

---

11 Also contrast, *K & B Metals Ltd* (above); and *Iveagh v Minister of Housing and Local Government* [1964] 1 QB 395, [1963] 3 All ER 817, (in which the Court of Appeal held that the word 'made' in relation to a building preservation order meant 'effectively made' and since such an order had no effective operation until it was confirmed by the minister, the order was made on the date it was confirmed).

12 Only in a very exceptional case is the Secretary of State likely to intervene in this way.

13 See *R v Secretary of State for the Environment, ex p Reinisch* (1971) 22 P & CR 1022 at 1025.

14 See *Pioneer Aggregates (UK) Ltd v Secretary of State for the Environment* [1985] AC 132, [1984] 2 All ER 358, HL, disapproving of the Court of Appeal's decision in *Slough Estates Ltd v Slough Borough Council (No 2)* [1969] 2 Ch 305, [1969] 2 All ER 988.

15 See *Holmes v Bradfield RDC* [1949] 2 KB 1, [1949] 1 All ER 381; and *Southern Olympia (Syndicate) Ltd v West Sussex County Council* (1952) 3 P & CR 60.

16 As to the circumstances in which loss or damage may be treated as 'directly attributable' to revocation action see *Hobbs Quarries Ltd v Somerset County Council* (1975) 30 P & CR 286; and *Cawoods Aggregates (South Eastern) Ltd v Southwark London Borough* [1983] RVR 79, 264 Estates Gazette 1087 (both concerned with loss of anticipated profits); but compare *Halford v Oxfordshire County Council* (1952) 2 P & CR 358 and *Evans v Cheshire County Council* (1952) 3 P & CR 50. See too *Burlin v Manchester City Council* (1976) 32 P & CR 115 (LT); and *Pennine Raceway Ltd v Kirklees Metropolitan Council* [1984] RVR 85, 134 NLJ 969.

17 A new s 164A was added to the 1971 Act by s 13 of the Town and Country Planning (Minerals) Act 1981. For a discussion of its effect see ch 18.

18 [1983] QB 382, [1982] 3 All ER 628.

landowner under the terms of which the company, in return for a pecuniary consideration, had been given the sole rights to promote motor car and motor cycle events on an airfield. On the basis of this agreement, the company subsequently erected safety barriers, cleared and surfaced an area of land for pits and for competitors' car parking and created a banking for spectators. Following the withdrawal of their planning permission, the company claimed compensation for abortive expenditure. The local planning authority resisted the claim on the ground that the company was not 'a person interested in the land'. The interest, argued the authority, had to be in the nature of a proprietary interest; the claimants merely had a licence. The Court of Appeal rejected this argument. Eveleigh LJ said that this was a statute which controlled use of and operations on land; it was not a conveyancing statute and the phrase should be interpreted without regard to technical terms. In the court's view, a person who, like the claimants, had an enforceable right as against the owner to use the land in the way which had now been prohibited was 'a person interested in the land' within the meaning of the section.

Any expenditure incurred in the preparation of plans for the purposes of any work, or upon other similar preparatory matters may be included under head (a) above (s 164(2)); but no compensation is payable in respect of any work carried out before the grant of the permission which has been revoked or modified or in respect of any loss or damage (except loss or damage consisting of depreciation in the value of an interest in the land) arising out of anything done or omitted to be done prior to the grant of that permission (s 164(3)). Under head (b) will be included depreciation in the value of any interest in the land resulting from the revocation or modification of permission; the claimant will therefore be entitled to the difference between the value of the interest prior to the making of the order and its value thereafter.[19] Compensation for revocation or modification of planning permission is not dependent on there being attached to the land an unexpended balance of established development value (see ch 13).

In calculating the amount of any depreciation in the value of an interest in land, it is to be assumed that planning permission would be granted for development of any class specified in Sch 8[20] to the 1971 Act (s 164(4)). This provision apparently excludes the making of any other assumptions as to the grant of planning permission; in assessing the post-revocation value of land it can be assumed that Sch 8 development would be permitted but no other assumptions as to the grant of planning permission can be made.[1]

The fact that permission for Eighth Schedule development is to be assumed might cause a problem when it is permission to carry out such development that is revoked or modified. As A E Telling points out,[2] if, in

19 But see *Pennine Raceway Ltd v Kirklees Metropolitan Council* [1984] RVR 85, 134 NLJ 969. In *Loromah Estates Ltd v London Borough of Haringey* (1978) 38 P & CR 234 the Lands Tribunal held that a principle analogous to the principle established in *Pointe Gourde Quarrying and Transport Co v Sub-Intendent of Crown Lands* [1947] AC 565, PC applied to such cases, so that any depreciation in the value of the land having the benefit of the revoked permission, attributable to the revocation order or its confirmation, ought to be left out of account in the assessment of compensation.
20 The classes of development specified in Sch 8 are summarised at p 415 below.
 1 See *Burlin v Manchester City Council* (1976) 32 P & CR 115 (LT).
 2 *Planning Law and Procedure* (Butterworths, 7th edn, 1986), p 324.

such a case, a claim for compensation is disputed, the only remedy would seem to be to re-apply for the permission which has been revoked or modified and on refusal of that application to make a claim for compensation under s 169 (see p 417 below).

A claim for compensation under s 164 should be served on the local planning authority within six months of the date of the decision in respect of which the claim is made, but the Secretary of State has power to extend the period in any particular case (see Town and Country Planning General Regulations 1976, reg 4). For this purpose 'the date of the decision' is presumably the date on which the order is made.

Where compensation becomes payable under s 164 and includes a sum exceeding £20 in respect of depreciation, the local planning authority must, if practicable, apportion the amount between different parts of the land according to the way in which those parts are differently affected by the order in consequence of which the compensation is payable (s 166(1)–(4)).

In a case where the compensation for depreciation exceeds £20 the local planning authority must give notice to the Secretary of State, specifying the amount and any apportionment (s 166(5)) and the notice should be registered as a local land charge. Compensation may have to be repaid (not necessarily by the person by whom it was received) if 'new development' of one of the types specified in s 159 (see p 386, above) is subsequently carried out (s 168). For this purpose the meaning of the expression 'new development' is widened to some extent (see s 168(4)).

Provision is made for the making in certain circumstances of a contribution by the Secretary of State towards the compensation payable by a local planning authority under s 164. Such a contribution may be made where the circumstances of the case are such that the Secretary of State would have been liable to pay compensation under Pt VII[3] of the Act if the permission revoked or modified had been originally refused, or, as the case may be, granted as so modified (s 167(1)). The Secretary of State can only make such a contribution if there is attached to the land an unexpended balance of established development value and the amount of any such contribution may not exceed that balance (s 167(2)). Any contribution so made by the Secretary of State will, of course, reduce the unexpended balance and, in any case, where the Secretary of State proposes to make a contribution, notice must therefore be given to any person with an interest in the land to which the proposal relates or with an interest which is substantially affected by an apportionment included in the proposal and also to any person who appears to be substantially affected by the reduction or extinguishment of the unexpended balance (see Town and Country Planning (Compensation and Certificates) Regulations 1974, reg 14). Any such person may object to the proposal and, if dissatisfied with the Secretary of State's determination, may refer the dispute to the Lands Tribunal (1974 Regulations, reg 15).

Purchase notice. If the effect of a revocation or modification order is to render the land incapable of reasonably beneficial use, an owner or lessee may be able to serve a purchase notice under s 180 (see ch 14).

---

3 Pt VII of the 1971 Act is outlined in ch 13.

Unopposed revocation or modification. Where the local planning authority have made an order under s 45, and the owner and occupier of the land and all persons who, in the authority's opinion, will be affected by the order have notified the authority in writing that they do not object to the order, then the authority may follow the procedure set out in s 46[4] of the 1971 Act and reg 19 of the Town and Country Planning General Regulations 1976; this may result in the order taking effect without confirmation by the Secretary of State.

The authority must advertise the making of such an order; the notice is to specify the period within which any person affected by the order may give notice to the Secretary of State that he wishes to be heard and the date on which, if no such notice is given to the minister, the order may take effect (s 46(2)). A notice containing similar information must be served on the affected parties (s 46(3)). A copy of the advertisement must be sent to the Secretary of State not more than three days after publication (s 46(4)). If no person gives notice to the Secretary of State that he wishes to be heard and the minister does not direct that the order be submitted to him, the order takes effect on the date specified by the authority (s 46(5)).

There is excluded from the operation of s 46 any order revoking or modifying a planning permission granted or deemed to have been granted by the Secretary of State under Pts III, IV or V of the 1971 Act (e g, a permission granted on appeal to the minister) and any order modifying a condition to which a planning permission is subject by virtue of s 41 or s 42 of the 1971 Act (ie, a condition limiting the duration of planning permission) (s 46(6)); any such order will always require confirmation.

2 Withdrawal of permission granted by development order

Article 4: Directions restricting permitted development. If the Secretary of State or the appropriate local planning authority[5] is satisfied that it is expedient that any development permitted by art 3 of and Sch 2 to the GDO, other than Class B of Pt 22 or Class C of Pt 23[6] (see p 151 above), should not be carried out unless permission is granted for it on an application the minister or the authority may under art 4 direct that permission granted by art 3 shall not apply to:

(a) all or any development in any particular area specified in the direction; or

(b) any particular development, specified in the direction.

In this way the minister or the authority can exercise planning control over development which would otherwise be automatically permitted. Such a direction cannot affect the carrying out of:

(a) development permitted under Pt 11 of Sch 2 (Development under Local or Private Acts or Orders);

---

4 As amended by the Local Government Act 1974, s 42(2), Sch 8.
5 The 'appropriate local authority' is the local planning authority whose function it would be to determine an application for planning permission for the development to which the direction relates except in relation to a conservation area in a non-metropolitan county where it is either the county planning authority or the district planning authority.
6 These classes cover mineral workings and mineral deposits and the power of direction is given to mineral planning authorities (see p 18, above).

(b) any development in an emergency; or
(c) any development mentioned in Pt 24 of Sch 2 unless the direction specifically so provides (art 4(2)).

Article 4(3) also exempts certain developments by statutory undertakers unless the art 4 direction so provides.

The need for local planning authorities to get the approval of the Secretary of State. Art 5 of the GDO provides that: a direction by a local planning authority under Art 4 requires the approval of the Secretary of State unless it relates (a) to a listed building or a building notified to the authority by the Secretary of State as a building of special architectural or historic interest or is development within the curtilage of a listed building (Art 5(2)(a) and (b))[7] or (b) relates only to development of land or development in any particular area permitted by Pts 1 to 4 of Sch 2 to the GDO if in the opinion of the planning authority the development would be prejudicial to the proper planning of their area or constitute a threat to the amenities of their area (Art 5(4)).
In giving approval the Secretary of State can modify the direction (art 5(1)).
However, it is only in the case of directions covered by art 5(3) (listed buildings and related developments) that there is no need for the eventual approval of the Secretary of State. In the case of directions relating to Pt 1 to 4, while the direction can come into effect without the Secretary of State's approval, the direction expires if it is disallowed by the Secretary of State or is not approved by him within six months of being made (art 5(5)). Also in the case of Pt 1 to 4, once a direction has been made, a second or subsequent direction of the same kind cannot be made without getting the prior approval of the Secretary of State. So there are, in effect, three categories of art 4 directions. First, directions where the prior approval of the Secretary of State is always needed. Secondly, directions where the subsequent approval of the Secretary of State is needed. Thirdly, directions which never have to be approved by the Secretary of State.
In the first category, once the direction has been approved by the Secretary of State, notice of the direction must be served as soon as practicable on the owner and occupier of every part of the land and the direction comes into force on the date on which it is served on the occupier or, if there is no occupier, on the owner (art 5(10)).
In any other case, the notice of direction has to be served on the owner and occupier as soon as practicable after the direction has been made, and comes into force on the date of service on the occupier or, if there is no occupier, on the owner (art 5(10)). However, in this category, where the eventual approval of the Secretary of State is required, a copy must be sent to him at the same time as service of the direction and the local planning authority must inform the owner and occupier if the Secretary of State disallows the direction or approves it within the six-month period (art 5(9) and (11)).

---

7 Approval is needed even in such situations if the direction would affect the developments of statutory undertakers listed in art 4(3).

Where the direction is made under art 4(1)(a) rather than art 4(1)(b)[8] (ie it is of general rather than individual effect), if the authority consider that individual service is impractical because of the number of owners and occupiers or the difficulty of identification or location, they shall publish notice of the direction, or of the approval, in at least one newspaper circulating in the locality in which the land is situated (arts 5(12) and (14)). Such a notice shall set out the effect of the direction and of any modification made by the Secretary of State and shall name a place where it can be inspected at reasonable hours (art 5(13)). Where notice is given in the above way, the direction shall come into force on the date the notice is first published (art 5(15)).

The Secretary of State can cancel any art 4 directions and the local planning authority can always cancel their own directions without getting the approval of the Secretary of State (art 5(16)).

Directions by mineral planning authorities. Mineral planning authorities have the power to issue directions restricting the drilling of boreholes, seismic surveys and other excavations for the purposes of mineral exploration (Pt 22, Class B) and the removal of material from mineral working deposits. This power is more limited than the general power under Art 4 as Art 6 (which provides the power) spells out the cases when a direction can be made.

Developments already carried out. In *Cole v Somerset County Council*[9] the Divisional Court held that art 4 could not be used retrospectively to withdraw a class of permitted development which had already been acted upon. Donovan J said that the words in Art 4 of the Order of 1950 [the order applicable in the case] 'development' which the minister or local authority 'is satisfied . . . should not be carried out' refer to development which has not yet begun, or if begun, has not yet been carried out in the sense of being completed.

In *Cole*, land which had been used as a golf course was turned into a caravan site for members of the Caravan Club of Great Britain. As the club held a certificate under s 269 of the Public Health Act 1936, this use was permitted under Class V of the 1950 Order; now see Pt 27 of the GDO 1988. Once this use had been instituted and as long as it continued, it could not be made unlawful by an art 4 direction. However, in *South Bucks District Council v Secretary of State for the Environment*[10] the Court of Appeal, overturning a decision of the High Court, held that the position was different in the case of Class IV(2) of the 1977 Order which permits temporary uses for a limited number of days in a calendar year. Making use of Class IV(2), markets were held on Sundays in January and early February 1986. On 19 February 1986 the council gave a direction under art 4(3)(b) of the GDO 1977 that the permission granted by art 3 should not apply to the use of the field for holding markets. In defiance of the notice, the developer, Strandmill Ltd, held markets on the three following Sundays and the council then served

---

8 See *Spedeworth Ltd v Secretary of State for the Environment* (1972) 71 LGR 123, CA where a direction that development of specified land should not be carried out otherwise than as a caravan site was held to a general direction rather than a particular development.

9 [1957] 1 QB 23, [1956] 3 All ER 531.

10 [1989] JPL 351.

an enforcement notice requiring it to cease the use of land for holding markets. The Court of Appeal held that the inspector (who allowed an appeal against the enforcement notice) had erred in law in holding that once the use as Sunday markets had commenced no direction could be given preventing the full quota of 14 days being taken up. The court held that on each Sunday that a market was instituted this amounted to a change of use which needed permission. Therefore art 4 was available to make unlawful any resumption, because such resumption would be once more a change of use, and, until it has taken place, the development it would represent had not been carried out within the meaning of art 4. All their Lordships, however, accepted that once a temporary use had been commenced, it could not be prevented from *continuing* for its full quota of 14 (or 28 days) by being interrupted by the service of an art 4 direction. Nicholls LJ rejected the argument that the intermittent use of land amounted to a 'mixed' or dual use and that therefore the first use as a market was a change to this dual use. This would mean that only one act of development was involved and once it was carried out, it could not be made unlawful by an art 4 direction. In rejecting this argument, Nicholls LJ relied on Diplock LJ's statement in *Webber v Minister of Housing and Local Government*[11] that land could be regarded as used for two activities 'provided that such activity is recurrent and accounts for a substantial part of the total amount of activity taking place upon the land during the appropriate period to be taken for determining what use is to be made of the land'. Nicholls LJ was not satisfied that this test was satisfied in the case of a temporary user under Class IV(2).[12]

In the case of operational development, for the purposes of the four-year rule, time does not run until the development has been substantially completed.[13] This would suggest that an art 4 direction can be effectively made to withdraw permission at any time until such a stage of substantial completion is reached.[14] In the case of s 45, the Act makes clear that revocation does not affect those operations that have already been carried out but there is no such wording in the case of art 4.

Liability for compensation. Where, following the coming into force of a direction under art 4, application is made for planning permission in respect of development of the type specified in the direction and such permission is refused, or is granted subject to conditions other than those imposed in relation to such development by the GDO, compensation may be payable.[15] Section 165 of the 1971 Act states that in any such case the compensation provisions of s 164 shall apply as if the planning permission granted by the development order had been granted by the planning authority under Pt III

---

11 [1967] 3 All ER 981, [1968] 1 WLR 29, CA.
12 But see *Hawes v Thornton Cleveleys UDC* (1965) 17 P & CR 22 where Lord Widgery CJ suggested that where land was held as a racecourse three or four times a year 'no one would suggest that it ceases to be used as a racecourse in the closed season or that a new development occurs on the first day of the next meeting'.
13 See p 323, above.
14 The Court of Appeal decision in *Thomas David (Porthcawl) Ltd v Penybont RDC* [1972] 3 All ER 1092, [1972] 1 WLR 1526, CA, would suggest that in the case of mining operations they cannot be retrospectively withdrawn if they have already been carried out.
15 See, for example, *Fry v Essex County Council* (1959) 11 P & CR 21; and *Pennine Raceway Ltd v Kirklees Metropolitan Council* [1984] RVR 85, 134 NLJ 969.

of the Act and had subsequently been revoked or modified by an order under s 45 of the Act.

From time to time the Secretary of State may decide to vary the terms of the GDO (1971 Act, s 287(3)). The effect of a variation may be similar to that of an art 4 direction. It may bring under the direct control of the planning authority development which hitherto has been permitted under art 3 of and Sch 2 to the Order. For example, the effect of the Town and Country Planning General Development Order 1988 was to remove 'permitted development' status from livestock units which are erected within 400 metres of existing permanent buildings. If an application for planning permission for such development is subsequently refused or is granted subject to more onerous conditions than would have been the case under the GDO, the provisions of s 164 come into operation in the same way as for an art 4 direction (1971 Act, s 165(1)). However, as a result of changes introduced by the Town and Country Planning (Compensation) Act 1985 compensation is only payable if the application for planning permission is made within 12 months from the date when the revocation or amendment came into operation (s 165(1A)). So persons who consider that they have been adversely affected by changes to the GDO will now have to apply in good time for planning permission. This amendment does not apply to the right to compensation following on art 4 directions.

D EXISTING USE DEVELOPMENT

Schedule 8 to the 1971 Act sets out eight categories of development which are described as 'development not constituting new development'. These categories of development are closely related to the existing use of the land and are commonly referred to as 'existing use development'. They are none the less 'development' within the meaning of s 22(1) of the 1971 Act and planning permission is therefore required, either by way of specific grant or by way of a development order, before any such activity can be carried out (1971 Act, s 23(1)). The significance of Sch 8 is that the value of 'existing use development' is treated in effect as if it belonged to the landowner[16] so that, with the exception of the two categories of development set out in Pt I of the Eighth Schedule (see p 415 below), any restrictions on the realisation of this value may only be imposed on payment of compensation.

The explanation for the existence of these categories of development derives from the financial provisions of the 1947 Act (see p 380 above). As a concession to landowners, Sch 3 to the 1947 Act listed certain categories of

---

16 For this reason s 15(3) of the Land Compensation Act 1961 provides that it is to be assumed, for the purpose of assessing compensation in respect of any compulsory acquisition, that planning permission would be granted for development of any class specified in Sch 8 to the 1971 Act. The provisions of the Eighth Schedule must also be taken into account in connection with claims for compensation on revocation or modification of planning permission (see p 408 above). Compensation may be payable under Pt VII of the 1971 Act in respect of restrictions on 'new development'; as mentioned above, 'new development' consists of any development other than development of a class specified in Pt I or Pt II of Sch 8 (1971 Act, s 22(5)). For certain purposes the provisions of Sch 8 must, as mentioned below, be read with the modifications contained in s 278 of, and Sch 18 to, the 1971 Act.

development linked to the existing use of land which were treated as falling within the existing use of land. The result was that a grant of planning permission for such development did not give rise to any liability to development charge; furthermore, if planning permission was refused or was granted subject to conditions, compensation generally had to be paid by the planning authority. Although the financial provisions of the 1947 Act have long since been repealed, subsequent legislation has continued to treat the value of existing use development as belonging to the landowner. The categories of existing use development have remained in substantially similar form and are now set out in Sch 8 to the 1971 Act.

Schedule 8

The classes of development specified in Schedule 8 are broadly as follows:

Part I

1. The rebuilding, as often as may be desired, of any building in existence on 1 July 1948, or destroyed or demolished between 7 January 1937 and 1 July 1948, or in existence at a material date, provided that the cubic content[17] of the original building is not exceeded by more than one tenth or, in the case of a dwellinghouse, by more than one tenth or 1750 cubic feet, whichever is the greater.
2. The use as two or more separate dwellinghouses of any building used at a material date as a single dwellinghouse.

Part II

3. The enlargement, improvement or other alteration,[18] as often as may be desired, of any such building[19] as is mentioned in para 1 or of any building substituted for such a building by the carrying out of any such operations as are mentioned in that paragraph, provided that the cubic content[20] of the original building is not exceeded by more than one tenth or, in the case of a dwellinghouse, by more than one tenth or 1750 cubic feet, whichever is the greater. 'Enlargement' includes the erection of an additional

---

17 As ascertained by external measurement (Sch 8, para 9).
18 In *National Provincial Bank Ltd v Portsmouth Corpn* (1959) 11 P & CR 6 the Court of Appeal held that an application for planning permission, though expressed to be for 'the enlargement, improvement and alteration' of premises, was in substance an application to rebuild the premises and therefore fell within para 1 of the Schedule. In *Camden London Borough Council v Peaktop Properties (Hampstead) Ltd* (1983) 82 LGR 101, the Court of Appeal held that a proposal to build further residential flats by way of the construction of an additional storey on each of two existing blocks of flats should be treated as existing use development (as an enlargement) and not new development. In *Growngrand Ltd v Kensington and Chelsea Royal Borough* (1984) 272 Estates Gazette 676 the Lands Tribunal held that a proposal to construct a two-storey dwelling-house in a garden area held together with existing residential property and to be joined to the existing property by an unroofed pergola was not to be treated as an enlargement, improvement or alteration to the existing property. The link was merely cosmetic and the proposed dwelling would be an additional building.
19 In *Church Cottage Investments Ltd v Hillingdon London Borough Council* (1986) 52 P & CR 439, 280 Estates Gazette 101, a block of 38 flats built in five sections, which were connected together but each section of which had its own entrance, was held by the Lands Tribunal to constitute one building, not five, as the construction was conceived, planned, designed and built as one building and the brickwork was continuous from end to end without a single expansion joint.
20 See note 17 above.

building within the curtilage of, and to be used in connection with, the original building (Sch 8, para 11).[1]

4. The carrying out, on land which was used for agriculture or forestry at a material date, of any building or other operations required for that use, but excluding the erection, enlargement, improvement or alteration of dwelling-houses or of buildings used for the purposes of market gardens, nursery grounds or timber yards or for other purposes not connected with general farming operations[2] or with the cultivation or felling of trees.

5. The winning and working, on land held or occupied with land used for the purposes of agriculture, of minerals reasonably required for the purposes of that use.

6. A change of use of a building or other land from one purpose to another purpose falling within the same general class specified in the Town and Country Planning (Use Classes for Third Schedule Purposes) Order 1948.[3]

7. Where part of a building or land was, at a material date, used for a particular purpose, the use for the same purpose of an additional part of the building or land not exceeding one tenth of the cubic content of the part of the building used for that purpose on 1 July 1948 or on the day thereafter when the building began to be so used, or, as the case may be, one tenth of the area of the land so used on that day.

8. The deposit of waste materials or refuse in connection with the working of minerals, on any land used for that purpose at a material date so far as may be reasonably required in connection with the working of those minerals.

It may be noted that certain paragraphs of Sch 8 employ the expression 'at a material date'; this means either 1 July 1948 or the date by reference to which the Schedule has to be applied (Sch 8, para 12). For the purposes of s 169 of the 1971 Act, which provides for payment of compensation in respect of a planning decision restricting development of a class specified in Pt II of Sch 8 (below), the 'material date' would appear to be the date of the planning decision giving rise to the claim for compensation.

For some purposes Sch 8 is subject to certain modifications originally introduced by the Town and Country Planning Act 1963. These modifications, which have the effect of reducing the scope of the Schedule, were introduced for two reasons. First, it was considered that the reference in paras 1 and 3 to an increase in cubic content of one tenth on the rebuilding or alteration of a building was over-generous, in that an increase of one tenth in cubic content might result, through use of modern building methods, in an increase in floor space of anything up to 40 per cent and it was on the value of

1 In *Growngrand Ltd v Kensington and Chelsea Royal Borough* (1984) 272 Estates Gazette 676 the Lands Tribunal concluded that the phrase 'in connection with' is likely to mean 'ancillary or complementary to'. A new two-storey dwelling to be erected on garden ground held together with existing residential property would not, on the facts of the case, be erected within the curtilage of the existing property and would in no sense be used in connection with the existing property.

2 In *Moxey v Hertford RDC* (1973) 27 P & CR 274 the Lands Tribunal held that a broiler house was not a building connected with general farming operations. And see generally the discussion in *Jones v Stockport Metropolitan Borough Council* (1983) 50 P & CR 299, 269 Estates Gazette 408 of Class VI (now Pt 6) of Sch 1 to the 1977 GDO.

3 The provisions now contained in the Eighth Schedule to the 1971 Act were originally contained in the Third Schedule to the 1947 Act.

that lost floor space that compensation might have to be assessed. Secondly, a planning authority might grant planning permission for development which, in their view, utilised the site to the full, and yet find that refusal of a subsequent application to enlarge the building made them liable to pay compensation. It is therefore provided[4] that in any case where compensation is to be assessed on the assumption that planning permission would be granted for Sch 8 development, it is to be assumed as regards development of any class specified in para 1 or para 3 that such permission would be granted subject to certain limitations on increase in gross floor space; in the case of buildings erected after 1 July 1948 (the date when the 1947 Act came into operation) the tolerances in paras 3 and 8 are not to apply.

The Town and Country Planning Compensation Act 1985 has since further restricted the right to compensation with regard to blocks of flats, following abuse of Class 3 in the case of the so-called 'penthouse flats' applications (see p 418). Much of the development in Pt II of Sch 8 (apart from Class 3) is already permitted by the GDO and the question of compensation does not therefore arise. An account of the rights to compensation follows.

Compensation for restrictions on Eighth Schedule Development

Where, on an application for planning permission to carry out development of any class specified in Pt II of Sch 8 to the 1971 Act, the Secretary of State refuses permission or grants it subject to conditions, any person whose interest in land is depreciated in value as a result of the decision is entitled to claim compensation from the local planning authority (s 169(1), (2)). The decision must be that of the Secretary of State, either on appeal or on reference of the application to him for determination.

A claim for compensation under s 169 must be served on the local planning authority within six months of the date of the adverse decision, unless the Secretary of State agrees to an extension of time in any particular case (Town and Country Planning General Regulations 1976, reg 14).

Where payable, compensation under s 169 is to be an amount equal to the difference between the value of the interest in land following upon the adverse decision and the value that interest would have had if permission had been granted, or had been granted unconditionally, as the case may be (s 169(2)).[4a] It cannot always be assumed that the value of an interest in land would necessarily have been higher if planning permission for Eighth Schedule development had been granted, or had been granted unconditionally, as the case may be.[5]

In determining whether, and to what extent, the value of an interest in land has been depreciated as a result of such a decision, it is to be assumed that any subsequent application for 'the like planning permission would be determined in the same way', but if, in the case of a refusal of planning

---

4 See 1971 Act, s 278 and Sch 18, see too s 169 (below) and the decision of the Court of Appeal in *Camden London Borough Council v Peaktop Properties (Hampstead) Ltd* (1983) 82 LGR 101.

4a *In Richmond upon Thames London Borough Council v Richmond Gateways Ltd* (1989) Times, 12 May, the Court of Appeal held that in calculating the loss caused by the refusal to allow the erection of a penthouse flat there was no requirement that the profits of a notional property developer should be deducted.

5 See *A L Salisbury Ltd v York Corpn* (1960) 11 P & CR 421.

permission, the Secretary of State undertook to grant planning permission for some other development of the land, regard must be had to that undertaking (s 169(3)). In granting planning permission subject to conditions for regulating the design or external appearance of buildings or the size or height of buildings, the Secretary of State may, 'if it appears to him to be reasonable to do so having regard to the local circumstances', direct that those conditions are to be wholly or partially disregarded in assessing compensation (s 169(4)).

It is only a decision restricting development of a class specified in Pt II of the Eighth Schedule that can give rise to a claim for compensation under s 169. For the purposes of s 169 the scope of Pt II of the Eighth Schedule has, for the reasons mentioned above, been materially reduced. In determining for the purposes of s 169 whether and to what extent the value of an interest in land has been depreciated, no account is to be taken of any prospective use which would contravene the condition set out in Sch 18 to the 1971 Act (s 169(3)(c)); that condition is applicable to development specified in para 3 of the Eighth Schedule (enlargement, improvement or other alteration of a building, subject to certain limits as regards increase in the cubic content of the building). The effect of this provision is that in relation to development within para 3 there must be assumed a further condition to the effect that where the building to be altered is the original building,[6] the gross floor space used for any purpose in the altered building may not exceed by more than 10 per cent the gross floor space used for that purpose in the original building, and that where the building to be altered is not the original building no such increase may take place.

In *Camden London Borough Council v Peaktop Properties (Hampstead) Ltd*[7] an application for permission to add an extra storey (of eleven new flats) to each of two blocks of flats was refused. The new flats would have increased the original gross volume of the blocks by less than 10 per cent. The owners claimed compensation in respect of the refusal. The Court of Appeal held that the fact that the proposed development involved the construction of new flats rather than the enlargement of existing flats did not defeat the claim for compensation. However, the proposal would have added 11.49 per cent gross floor space to each of the original blocks of flats and would therefore have breached the '10 per cent additional floor space' rule. The Court held that no account could be taken of any of the prospective use in determining the extent of depreciation resulting from the refusal of planning permission for the enlargement and that no compensation was payable. It seems clear, however, that in such circumstances if the claimant simply redesigned the enlargement so that the additional floor space did not exceed the 10 per cent limitation, the refusal of an application for such development would have given rise to a compensation entitlement.

Such cases could make the planning authorities liable to pay out substantial sums in compensation; the claim in the *Peaktop Properties* case was for £142,500. This potential liability could make planning authorities unwilling to refuse permission and also it seems that some unscrupulous developers put

6 'Original building' means, broadly, a building existing on 1 July 1948, or existing before that date but destroyed or demolished after 7 January 1937, or erected for the first time after 1 July 1948 but not including a building rebuilt after 1 July 1948.
7 (1983) 82 LGR 101.

in applications for developments which were clearly unacceptable under normal planning criteria, with the hope that a refusal would lead to a substantial compensation entitlement.[8] The Town and Country Planning (Compensation) Act 1985 was therefore passed with the aim of closing the loophole. Para 3 of the Eighth Schedule is no longer to be taken to apply where:

(a) the building contains two or more separate dwellings divided horizontally from each other or from some other part of the building; and
(b) the enlargement would result in either an increase in the number of such dwellings contained in the building or an increase of more than 10 per cent in the cubic content of any such dwellings contained in the building.

As a consequence, in the case of blocks of flats, compensation is only payable where permission is refused to enlarge one of the flats by less than 10 per cent of the cubic content of that flat.[9] This new provision only applies to buildings in existence on the appointed day but for the purposes of s 169, para 3 of the Eighth Schedule is to be construed as not extending to works involving any increase in the cubic content of a building erected after the appointed day (1 July 1948). This includes buildings which are original to the site and those resulting from rebuilding operations (s 169(6)(a)).[10] The new provision does not apply to individual dwelling-houses or to industrial properties but they will generally have permitted development rights of enlargement under the GDO (see p 154). More significantly it does not apply to commercial properties.

It would seem that compensation paid under s 169 in respect of a decision restricting Eighth Schedule development cannot be reclaimed by the planning authority even if the decision which originally gave rise to the compensation payment is subsequently reversed. It has also been suggested that s 169 is worded in such a way that it is possible for compensation to be claimed more than once under the section in respect of refusals of planning permission relating to the same property. This would seem doubtful and past payments of compensation would surely have to be taken into account in assessing any new claim.

In the light of all the obscurity and difficulties surrounding s 169, the Department of the Environment has invited comments on the proposal that s 169 should be repealed and the GDO amended so as to give permitted development rights for all the classes of development set out in Pt II of the Eighth Schedule.[11]

Part I of the Eighth Schedule

Compensation is not payable in respect of a planning decision restricting development of a class specified in Pt I of the Eighth Schedule to the 1971 Act. It is not clear why this should be so although Davies[12] suggests that if a

---

8 See Department of the Environment consultation paper 'Planning Compensation', paras 15 and 16.
9 See now s 169(6A).
10 Section 169(6)(b) equally makes clear that para 7 of the Schedule does not apply to buildings erected after the appointed day.
11 See consultation paper 'Compensation Provisions in the Town and Country Planning Acts' published 1986.
12 Keith Davies, *Law of Compulsory Purchase and Compensation* (4th edn), p 319.

refusal to allow the rebuilding of a building (para 1, Pt I of the Eighth Schedule) had qualified for compensation in the period after the Second World War, it would have imposed a very heavy burden on planning authorities. If, however, an adverse decision on an application for permission to carry out development within Pt I renders the land in question incapable of reasonably beneficial use, a purchase notice might be served on the planning authority (see ch 14). If such a purchase notice succeeds it will be assumed, in assessing compensation, that planning permission for development of any class specified in Sch 8 would have been permitted.[13] Otherwise, there is no remedy for a decision restricting development falling within Pt I of the Eighth Schedule.

---

13 See note 8 above. And see *Sorrell v Maidstone RDC* (1961) 13 P & CR 57; and *Walton-on-Thames Charities Trustees v Walton and Weybridge UDC* (1970) 21 P & CR 411, CA.

CHAPTER 16

POSITIVE PLANNING

Introduction

Local planning authorities are sometimes viewed as little more than regulatory agencies whose task it is to resist development which does not conform to the development plan. This is hardly surprising, as for most people, whether as applicants or objectors, the development control process is their point of contact with the planning system. Yet local planning authorities are enabling as well as controlling agencies. They are endowed with wide powers to encourage, assist and undertake development. These are generally referred to as 'positive planning' powers in contrast with development control powers which are seen as essentially 'negative'.[1] 'The essence of positive planning, as we understand it', said the Pilcher Report, 'is that every planning authority should have the power to see that desirable development should happen rather than to have to wait and react to initiatives from others.'[2]

Development plans are intended to have a promotional as well as a controlling influence on development. These plans are to give guidance to prospective developers and should identify the needs and opportunities for development. An important function of the plans is to co-ordinate the planning and provision of infrastructure essential for the development of land. The plans may operate as a trigger for further action by the planning authority. The designation, for example, of an action area is intended to signal the start of a programme of development, redevelopment or improvement in an area requiring comprehensive treatment. Furthermore, development plan allocations may be linked to other initiatives such as industrial promotion, undertaken by the same local authority in a different capacity.

More specific promotional powers include the making of revocation and discontinuance orders to clear the way for more desirable forms of development (see ch 15); the stopping up or diversion of roads affected by development (see ch 10); entering into planning agreements to overcome obstacles to development (see ch 11); and the acquisition of land in connection with development and for other planning purposes (ss 112 and 119 of the 1971 Act).

The Property Advisory Group singled out two functions in particular as likely to be important aids to the promotion of development during this

---

1 See, for example, the White Paper *Land* (Cmnd 5730, 1974). The development control process is generally described as 'negative' because it responds rather than initiatives, although the term is sometimes used pejoratively. The Pilcher Report said of the process that 'the value of the control, the positive contribution which it has made to the urban environment in the last thirty years, and the extent to which the pattern and character of commercial development have thereby been constrained should not be underestimated.' (*First Report of the Advisory Group on Commercial Property Development*, HMSO, 1976).

2 The Pilcher Report (above), para 3.10.

decade: 'The main role of local authorities in development during the 1980s will be in co-ordinating the provision of infrastructure and assembling land where the private sector cannot or will not do so.'[3]

In fact much of this work is done not by local authorities but by specially created corporations. Thirty-two new towns have been built by New Town Development Corporations (see New Towns Act 1981) and today the key to the renewal of the inner city areas is seen in the Urban Development Corporations set up by the Local Government, Planning and Land Act 1980.

Positive planning also encompasses the promotion of new economic activity. This can take the form of fiscal incentives and direct grants. In particular, the Local Government, Planning and Land Act 1980 introduced the mechanism of 'enterprise zones' and the Housing and Planning Act 1986 has increased the scope for financial assistance for urban regeneration. Building on the concept of 'enterprise zones', the Housing and Planning Act 1986 has created 'Simplified Planning Zones' as an additional means of facilitating development. The most important aspects of this form of planning will be covered in this chapter.

Co-ordinating the provision of infrastructure

The term 'infrastructure' is not a statutory one but is generally taken to refer to the services required to support the development of land; it will, for example, include main roads, means of drainage, water supply, public open space, schools and buildings for community use.

Restrictions on public expenditure constrain public authorities in the extent to which they can meet demands for the provision of those supporting services for which they are responsible. Careful co-ordination of the planning and provision of these services is necessary and this is an area in which the development plan can play an important role. The ability of various public bodies to commit resources to infrastructure provision will be a material factor in the allocation of land for development in the plans. Development plans are influenced by and will exert an influence upon the capital programmes of the public bodies responsible for the provision of infrastructure. If development plans are to provide clear guidance to potential developers, planning authorities must, as the Secretary of State has stressed, pay close regard to the resources available for plan implementation. It seems likely that the co-ordinating role of development plans will assume increasing importance in the years ahead. 'The co-ordinated planning and provision of all these services to new development and redevelopment areas becomes even more necessary', commented the Property Advisory Group, 'as restraints on all public expenditure become more severe.'[4]

In very broad terms it may be said that while developers seeking planning permission can in appropriate cases be required to provide services such as private car parking, private drains, estate roads and private open space needed to serve the development in question, the cost of providing services which will be enjoyed as of right by the public at large cannot be *imposed* on a private developer. Conditions seeking, for example, to impose upon a

3 *Structure and Activity of the Development Industry* (HMSO, 1980). The Property Advisory Group was set up in 1978 by the Secretary of State for the Environment as a standing successor to the Pilcher Committee.
4 *Structure and Activity of the Development Industry* (above).

developer the burden of providing a distributor road, public open space or public car parking have been struck down by the courts and by the Secretary of State on appeal.[5]

However, in the absence of any indication that supporting services will be provided by the public sector, a developer may in practice have to take part or all of the burden upon himself if the development is to proceed. While this sort of burden cannot be imposed on a developer, there is considerable scope for varying the conventional distribution of costs between the public and private sectors by way of agreement (see ch 11).

A LAND ASSEMBLY BY LOCAL PLANNING AUTHORITIES

The need for power to acquire land in the public interest has long been accepted; the scope of the power has, however, been the subject of ideological differences between the main political parties. There has been, as Grant observes, a clear difference of opinion about 'the *function*, and consequently the extent, of the intervention'.[6] The Conservative Party see the public acquisition of land as a means to an end; the Labour Party have tended to view the public ownership of land as a desirable end in itself. This divergence of view is reflected in the attempt by the last Labour government to bring development land into public ownership through the Community Land Act 1975 and the subsequent repeal of that Act in 1980 by the succeeding Conservative government.

The present position is that planning authorities have enabling powers to acquire land in connection with development and for other planning purposes. These are set out in Pt VI of the 1971 Act, as amended.[7] These powers are, to employ our earlier phraseology, 'a means to an end', the end being broadly the proper planning of the area, including the implementation of the policies and proposals in the development plan. The Local Government Act 1972 gives local authorities other, more general, powers to acquire land for the discharge of any of their functions;[8] more specific powers to acquire land for particular functions such as housing, education, roads and so on, are to be found in the legislation governing these functions.

The need for planning authorities to have wide powers to acquire land for planning purposes was recognised by the Uthwatt Committee. The Committee declared:

'For the urgent task of reconstructing war-damaged areas and the almost equally urgent task of securing the redevelopment of obsolete and unsatisfactory areas ... it is essential to invest the planning authority with the

---

5 See, for example, *Hall & Co Ltd v Shoreham-by-Sea UDC* [1964] 1 All ER 1, [1964] 1 WLR 240, CA; *R v Hillingdon London Borough Council, ex p Royco Homes Ltd* [1974] QB 720, [1974] 2 All ER 643; *M J Shanley Ltd v Secretary of State for the Environment* [1982] JPL 380; *Westminster Renslade Ltd v Secretary of State for the Environment* (1983) 48 P & CR 255; *Bradford City Metropolitan Council v Secretary of State for the Environment* (1986) 53 P & CR 55, 278 Estates Gazette 1473, CA; and see appeal decisions noted at [1967] JPL 493; [1974] JPL 106; [1975] JPL 620; [1980] JPL 841; and [1982] JPL 463; and see, generally, Circular 1/1985.
6 *Urban Planning Law*, p 500.
7 By the Local Government, Planning and Land Act 1980.
8 See ss 120 and 121.

power to cut through the tangle of separate ownerships and boundary lines and make the whole of the land in the area immediately available for comprehensive re-planning as a single unit. We therefore recommend that for the purpose of securing necessary redevelopment the planning authority should be given the power to purchase the whole of such areas.'[9]

This recommendation was given effect in the Town and Country Planning Act 1944[10] and subsequently in the Town and Country Planning Act 1947.[11] The power was widely employed in dealing with areas of war damage and later in the promotion of town centre redevelopment schemes. The subsequent principal Acts in 1968[12] and 1971 re-enacted the power to acquire land although in different forms.[13] Though the recession had an effect on the level of public acquisition, the Property Advisory Group concluded, as we mentioned earlier, that planning authorities could provide useful support for the development industry by operating as 'land assemblers where the private sector will not or cannot undertake the task for a desirable scheme'.[14]

The first part of this chapter is given over to consideration of the nature of the powers of land assembly in Pt VI of the 1971 Act, the procedures governing their use and the ways in which local authorities may deal with land they have acquired.

1 *Compulsory acquisition of land*

Section 112(1) of the 1971 Act, as amended by s 91(4) of the Local Government, Planning and Land Act 1980, enables county councils, district councils and London borough councils[15] to acquire land compulsorily for planning purposes. Although local authorities may prefer in many cases to proceed by way of negotiation and agreement (see below), recourse to compulsory acquisition may be necessary where a landowner refuses to negotiate, where a large number of interests in land are to be acquired, or where a local authority wish to take advantage of the procedure for expediting the vesting of land in themselves so as to meet a particular timetable.[16]

Local authorities[17] may acquire by compulsory purchase land in their area:

9 *Final Report of the Expert Committee on Compensation and Betterment* (Cmnd 6386, 1942), para 145.
10 Town and Country Planning Act 1944, Pt I.
11 Town and Country Planning Act 1947, Pt IV.
12 Town and Country Planning Act 1968, Pt IV.
13 Before 1968, the power to acquire land compulsorily was conferred for the purpose of comprehensive development and was tied to a designation in the development plan. The 1968 Act dispensed with the need for a development plan designation and slightly extended the purposes for which land could be compulsorily acquired. These powers were repeated in the 1971 Act. An amendment introduced by s 91 of the Local Government, Planning and Land Act 1980 has now broadened still further the purposes for which land may be compulsorily acquired under the 1971 Act.
14 *Structure and Activity of the Development Industry* (above).
15 S 112(5); s 119 of the Local Government, Planning and Land Act 1980 also gives powers under s 112 to Planning Boards.
16 See Compulsory Purchase (Vesting Declarations) Act 1981.
17 The authorities so authorised are county council, district councils, London borough councils, Planning Boards and other local authorities within the meaning of s 29(11) of the 1971 Act.

(i) which is suitable for and is required in order to secure the carrying out of one or more of the following activities, namely, development, redevelopment, and improvements; or

(ii) which is required for a purpose which it is necessary to achieve in the interests of the proper planning of an area in which the land is situated (1971 Act, s 112(1)).[18]

In *R v Secretary of State for the Environment ex p Leicester City Council*[19] it was held that it was not enough to show that the land was 'required' for development, redevelopment or improvement, it also had to be shown that acquisition by the local authority was 'required' to enable that to happen. In this case the local authority did not want to acquire the land provided all the owners agreed to contribute towards the cost of providing new sewers and a road, which were needed for the redevelopment. McCullough J held that the Secretary of State had therefore properly refused to confirm the proposed order on the ground that the local authority was improperly using its powers under s 112 in order to persuade the owners of the land to make financial contributions.

Any such proposal for the compulsory acquisition of land is subject to confirmation by the Secretary of State.

In considering whether land is 'suitable' for development, redevelopment or improvement, the local authority (and the Secretary of State when confirming a proposal) must have regard to a number of factors. These are:

(i) the provisions of the development plan, so far as material:

(ii) whether planning permission for any development on the land is in force; and

(iii) any other consideration which would be material for the purpose of determining an application for planning permission for development on the land (1971 Act, s 112(1A)).

In other words, a proposal to acquire land compulsorily for planning purposes must rest upon sound planning considerations[20] and the onus will be upon the local authority to make the case for acquisition.[1] However, the reference to land being 'required' in connection with development or for other planning purposes does not mean that the acquisition of the land must be shown to be essential; it would appear to be sufficient that the local authority consider the acquisition to be desirable to achieve the proper planning of the area.[2]

Supplementary powers of compulsory acquisition are conferred in respect of (i) adjoining land which is required in order to carry out works designed to facilitate the development or use of the land required for planning purposes—for example, the construction of an access; and (ii) land required to be given in exchange for the land required for planning purposes where the

18 The 'proper planning of an area' might, for example, require the acquisition of land so as to maintain its existing use or to facilitate the development of other land.

19 [1987] JPL 787.

20 For the meaning of this phrase see the discussion in ch 8.

1 *Coleen Properties Ltd v Minister of Housing and Local Government* [1971] 1 All ER 1049, [1971] 1 WLR 433, CA, but see *R v Secretary of State for Tranport, ex p de Rothschild* [1989] 1 All ER 933, [1989] JPL 173.

2 *Errington v Metropolitan District Rly Co* [1882] 19 Ch D 559, CA; and *Company Developments (Property) Ltd v Secretary of State for the Environment* [1978] JPL 107.

latter forms part of a common or open space or fuel or field garden allotment[3] (1971 Act, s 112(1B)).

Section 112 of the 1971 Act refers to the compulsory acquisition of 'land'. 'Land' is defined in s 290 of the Act as including any interest in land or right over land. It would seem, however, that such interests or rights must be in existence at the time of the compulsory acquisition; the power conferred by s 112 does not extend to the compulsory creation and acquisition of new rights over land. Such a power must be conferred in specific terms; expropriation cannot take place by implication.[4] However, under s 13 of the Local Government (Miscellaneous Provisions) Act 1976, where a local authority is authorised to acquire land compulsorily, the Minister can authorise 'new rights' to be acquired. This would include easements.

The procedural provisions of the Acquisition of Land 1981 are applied to the compulsory acquisition of land under the 1971 Act (1971 Act, s 112(4)). These provide for the making of a compulsory purchase order, the giving of notice, the submission of the order to the Secretary of State for confirmation, and the consideration of objections and, where appropriate, the holding of a public inquiry before reaching a decision on the order. The Secretary of State may, however, disregard any objection to the compulsory purchase order which, in his opinion, amounts in substance to an objection to the provisions of the development plan defining the proposed use of the subject land or any other land (1971 Act, s 132(1)).

Although the compulsory acquisition of land for planning purposes will be undertaken by the local authority, the activity or purpose for which it has been acquired may be undertaken or achieved by someone else (1971 Act, s 112(1C)). Thus, a planning authority may undertake land assembly with a view to the subsequent disposal of the land to a developer for development.

Section 113 of the 1971 Act enables the Secretary of State to acquire compulsorily any land necessary for the public service. By contrast with s 112, the section expressly empowers the minister to acquire an easement or other right over land by the grant of a new right. The appropriate procedural provisions of the Acquisition of Land Act 1981 are applied to an exercise of power under s 113.

2 *Acquisition of land by agreement*

Section 119 of the 1971 Act confers wide powers on county councils, district councils and London Boroughs to acquire land for planning purposes by agreement. An authority may acquire land by agreement for any purposes for which they may be authorised to acquire land compulsorily under s 112 (1971 Act, s 119(1) (a)). The power would seem to be available in respect of any land and not just land within their area.

The authorities may also acquire any building appearing to them to be of special architectural or historic interest (it need not be listed) (1971 Act, s 119(1)(b)). Furthermore, they may acquire any land comprising, or contiguous or adjacent to, such a building which is required for preserving the

---

3   S 290 defines all these terms; see also *R v Plymouth City Council and Cornwall County Council, ex p Freeman* [1988] RVR 89, CA; and *R v Doncaster Metropolitan Borough Council ex p Braim* [1988] JPL 35.

4   *Sovmots Investments Ltd v Secretary of State for the Environment* [1977] QB 411, [1976] 3 All ER 720 CA; revsd [1979] AC 144, [1977] 2 All ER 385, HL.

building or its amenities, for affording access to it or for its proper control or management (1971 Act, s 119(1) (c)). While the power contained in s 119 of the 1971 Act may only be exercised in respect of land required for planning purposes, it is not necessary that the land should be required immediately for these purposes. Such land may be purchased by agreement (but not compulsorily) in advance of the authority's requirements and used for the purpose of any of the authority's functions in the interim.[5]

3 *Appropriation of land*

The Local Government Act 1972 gives local authorities a general power to appropriate land which is no longer required for the purpose for which it was originally acquired.[6] The appropriation can be for any purpose for which the council is authorised to acquire land by agreement. So land can be appropriated for planning purposes under the provision. There are, however, special restrictions regarding commons, open space or fuel or field garden allotments.[7] In the case of land acquired or appropriated for planning purposes this provision does not apply (1971 Act, s 122(5)). However, s 122(1) of the 1971 Act confers a similar general power of appropriation for any purpose for which the council is authorised to acquire land. The consent of the Secretary of State is required where the land is or was common land and is held or managed under a local Act (1971 Act, s 122(2)). Also, before appropriating land which consists of or forms part of an open space[8] the authority is required to publish notice of their proposal and to consider any objections made to them (1971 Act, s 122(2B)).

4 *Development*

Often, land will be acquired for planning purposes by local planning authorities with a view to its subsequent disposal to the private sector for development (see below). However, the authorities themselves have wide powers to undertake the development of land held for planning purposes. Section 124(1) of the 1971 Act provides that planning authorities may erect, construct or carry out any building or work on such land providing the building or work is not or could not be authorised under any alternative enactment.[9] They may also repair, maintain and insure any such buildings or works or generally deal with them in the proper course of management (1971 Act, s 124(5)).

Immunity is conferred upon local planning authorities and upon persons deriving title from them against any action for interference with easements or other rights in erecting, constructing, carrying out or maintaining any such building or work, provided it is done in accordance with any planning permission (1971 Act, s 127(1)). Any such interference may, however, give rise to a claim for compensation under ss 63 or 68 of the Lands Clauses Consolidation Act 1845 or under ss 7 or 10 of the Compulsory Purchase Act 1965 (1971 Act, s 127(3)). The immunity does not extend to certain rights vested in or belonging to statutory undertakers for the purpose of carrying

5 Local Government Act 1972, s 120(2).
6 Local Government Act 1972, s 122(1).
7 Local Government Act 1972, s 122(2).
8 As to meaning of open space, see footnote 4 above.
9 See for example, alternative powers under Local Authorities (Land) Act 1963, s 2.

on their undertakings (1971 Act, s 127(1)). Sections 128 and 129 of the 1971 Act deal with the use of land comprising churches or burial grounds and the use of land comprising open space where such categories of land have been acquired for planning purposes.

5 *Disposal*

Planning authorities have considerable flexibility as to the manner of disposal of land held for planning purposes. Section 123(1) of the 1971 Act provides that the authority may dispose of such land to such person, in such manner and subject to such conditions, as may appear to them to be expedient to secure the use and development of the land in accordance with the planning objectives of the area.[10]

The wide terms in which the power is conferred leave the planning authority free to choose whether the planning objectives of the area are best served by disposal of the land before or after development or whether some form of partnership between the public and private sectors is appropriate.[11] Arrangements for disposal may be tied in with a loan from the local authority under the Local Authorities (Land) Act 1963 or in designated districts, under the Inner Urban Areas Act 1978 (see below page 443).

The Secretary of State's consent is not now required prior to disposal except where the land is or was a common and is held or managed under a local act (1971 Act s 123(2) (a)). Consent is also required where the disposal is to be for 'consideration less than the best that can reasonably be obtained', unless the disposal is of a short term[12] leasehold (s 123(2) (b)). The wording of the subsection is such that the price may reflect any difficulties inherent in the development of the site and any restrictions which the planning authority wish to impose on its use and development. But the Court of Appeal has made clear that the qualifying word 'reasonably' does not exempt the authority from their duty to obtain full current open market value of the land. In *Tomkins v Commission for the New Towns*,[13] a case concerning an almost identical provision in the New Towns legislation,[14] it was held that the obligation to obtain the best price may override the principle of fair administration; that where surplus land is being disposed of, the original owner from whom the land was compulsorily acquired should be given the first option of re-purchase.[15] In the particular circumstances the Commission felt that the market in land was so volatile that the only way of ensuring that the land was disposed of at the best consideration was to sell the land on the open market to the highest bidder. The court found that this decision was perfectly proper in the circumstances.

However, where land has been acquired or appropriated for planning

---

10 However the courts may imply restrictions on disposal of land; see *R v Barnet London Borough Council, ex p Pardes House School Ltd* [1989] EGCS 64 and *R v Westminster City Council, ex p Leicester Square Coventry Street Association* (1989) Times, 21 April.
11 For a discussion of the different types of partnership arrangements between the public and private sectors see *Report of the Working Party on Local Authority/Private Enterprise Partnership Schemes* (HMSO 1972); *Structure and Activity of the Development Industry* (above); and generally, M Grant, *Urban Planning Law*, pp 522–528.
12 Seven years or less to run.
13 (1989) 12 EG 59, CA.
14 S 37(3) of the New Towns Act 1981 as amended by the New Towns and Urban Development Corporations Act 1985.
15 The 'Crichel Down' principle; named after the scandal which occurred in 1954.

purposes under s 112(1), any person who was living or working on the land before the work took place, and who wishes to obtain accommodation on the land, must, so far as practicable, be given an opportunity to obtain accommodation suitable to his reasonable requirements (1971 Act, s 123(7)).[16] The terms on which such accommodation is to be provided must be settled with due regard to the price at which any land was initially acquired from such a person. Although this subsection appears at first sight to impose a constraint on a planning authority's freedom of disposal, the qualifications which have been built into it are such that any constraint is likely to be minimal. As Grant comments '. . . the section imposes no duty to offer new accommodation at a low rent, and the small shopkeepers typically displaced by redevelopment schemes can seldom afford the high rents demanded for the new facilities.'[17] And the phrase 'with due regard to the price at which any land was initially acquired' was considered by Paull J in *A Crabtree & Co v Minister of Housing and Local Government*[18] to be 'really a relic from the time when land was often acquired by a planning authority on terms other than its market value and [to] have no real application, except in very exceptional circumstances, to a case where the person dispossessed is entitled, as he is now, to obtain the full market value of such land.'

Part X of the Local Government, Planning and Land Act 1980 provides for the compilation of a register of the land holdings of public authorities and for the issuing of directions by central government for the disposal of such land. For land to be placed on the register it must be:

(a) a freehold or leasehold interest owned by one of the public bodies set out in Sch 16 to the 1980 Act. This includes all the major local authorities, development corporations and public corporations and the list can be varied by statutory instrument (s 93);
(b) situated in an area where Pt X of the Act applies (it now applies to all of England and Wales);
(c) in the opinion of the Secretary of State land which is not being used or not being sufficiently used for the purposes of the relevant body (s 95(2) (c)).

The main legal consequence of entry on the register is that the Secretary of State can issue a direction requiring the body to take steps for the disposal of the interest. Such a direction can include details as to the kind of steps and the conditions on which an offer to dispose is to be made (s 98). The Local Government Act 1988 authorises a direction to prohibit the disposal to certain types of persons or bodies who are associated with the body to whom the direction is given (s 98(2A)). This is clearly aimed at preventing evasion of the spirit of a direction by disposal to associated bodies. A direction has been held to have the effect of an implied consent by the Secretary of State under s 123 of the Local Government Act 1972. This means that the method of disposal in the direction must be followed even if it results in a sale at a price less than that which could otherwise have been reasonably obtained.[19]

It seems that so far, the new provisions have only resulted in a relatively

16 There is no obligation on the authority to offer such accommodation prior to displacement — see *Glasgow Corpn v Arbuckle Smith & Co* 1968 SLT (Sh Ct) 69.
17 *Urban Planning Law*, p 516.
18 (1965) 17 P & CR 232.
19 See *Manchester City Council v Secretary of State for the Environment* (1987) 54 P & CR 212, CA.

small amount of land which has been placed on the register being subject to a direction.[20] The Local Government Act 1988 introduced new provisions aimed at ensuring that land registers are kept up to date and simplifying the direction procedures.[1]

6 Buildings of special architectural and historic interest

Sections 114 to 117 of the 1971 Act contain specific powers relating to the compulsory acquisition of listed buildings in need of repair. These powers ̣e described in ch 18.

Section 125 of the Act requires planning authorities, when exercising their powers of appropriation, development and disposal of land under Pt VI, to have regard to the desirability of preserving[2] listed buildings and other features of special architectural or historic interest.

Where a planning authority have acquired a listed building in need of repair (1971 Act, s 114) or any other building appearing to them to be of special architectural or historic interest (listed or otherwise) (1971 Act, s 119(1)(b)), they may make such arrangements as to its management, use or disposal as they consider appropriate for its preservation (1971 Act, s 126(1)). In *Rolf v North Shropshire District Council*[3] the Court of Appeal held that this section authorised the acquisition of a listed building under s 114 even though the acquiring authority could not afford to repair the building and intended to sell the building to the British Historic Building Trust which did have the funds to restore the building. In any case Russell J had held that disposal could also have been authorised under s 123(1) of the 1971 Act.

B SPECIAL INSTITUTIONS AND MECHANISMS FOR POSITIVE PLANNING

1 Urban Development Corporations

The Urban Development Corporations, provided for by the Local Government, Planning and Land Act 1980 (the 1980 Act) are based on the model of the New Town Development Corporations which were responsible for the development of Britain's new towns.[4] This reflects the shift in the focus of concern from the need to deal with the growth in population to the problems of decay and neglect in the inner city areas of the United Kingdom. However, the remedy is essentially the same. The creation of a single purpose, unelected body which is given wide powers and is financed by central government. Richard Crossman in his Diaries remarked of the new towns that they were

---

20 See [1987] JPL 309 and 706.
1 See s 96A, 97, 99 (5A) to (5E) and 99A in particular, inserted by s 31 and Sch 5 to the Local Government Act 1988.
2 'Preserving' in relation to a building means preserving it either in the existing state or subject only to such alteration or extension as can be carried out without serious detriment to the character (1971 Act, s 125(3)).
3 [1988] JPL 103.
4 The new town legislation is not described in the book. No more new towns are to be designated and the programme is gradually being wound down. The present legislation is to be found in the New Towns Act 1981, and the New Towns and Urban Development Corporation Act 1985.

the greatest creation of his permanent secretary Dame Evelyn Sharp. He went on: 'She is enormously proud of them and convinced that they wouldn't have been built without the completely autocratic constitution of the corporations, which we finance and whose members we appoint. The fact that they can get on with their job without consulting public opinion is the great thing in their favour, according to the Dame.'[5]

Similar observations have been made about the urban development corporations and there has been particular concern about their relationship with the local planning authorities.

Like new towns, urban development corporations have come in waves. The London Docklands and the Merseyside Development Corporations were established in 1981. In 1987 five more development corporations were set up at Trafford, the Black Country, Teeside, Tyne and Wear and Cardiff Bay. Then in 1988, smaller or 'mini' corporations were proposed in Leeds, Bristol and Sheffield, and an additional urban development area was designated in Wolverhampton to be regenerated by the existing Black Country Development. Urban development corporations have been hailed by the Government as a success and the corporations, particularly the London Docklands Development Corporation, have attracted substantial private investment and generated development. On the other hand, a common criticism has been that the local communities have not benefited from the regeneration. In particular, the House of Commons Employment Committee has recommended that the object of urban development corporations should be more precisely defined to include employment and unemployment objectives both in general and for the local community.[6]

The committee also voiced concern about the lack of formal consultation procedures. Section 140 of the Act requires development corporations to prepare a Code of Practice, but the content of the code is entirely at the discretion of the development corporation.

The decision to create an urban development corporation for an area. If the Secretary of State is of the opinion that it is expedient in the national interest to do so, he may designate any area of land as an urban development area (1980 Act; s 134). Such a designation has the legal effect of requiring the Secretary of State to establish an urban development corporation for the purposes of regenerating that area (1980 Act s 135). In practice, both actions will be taken at the same time by one order. The legislation does not set out any criteria by which areas are to be selected to become urban development areas. However, the means of achieving the object of regeneration, which means are set out in s 136 of the 1980 Act, indicate that areas will be selected because of the amount of derelict and vacant land and the need and opportunities for providing employment, housing and a better environment.

The designation of the area and the establishment of the corporation is done by statutory instrument which has to be approved by a resolution of each House of Parliament. Unlike the position with New Towns, there is no statutory right to object or to have a public inquiry held to consider

5 See Richard Crossman's *The Diaries of a Cabinet Minister*, Vol 1, Minister of Housing and Local Government 1964–66 at p 127.
6 See 'The Employment Effects of Urban Development Corporations', HMSO 1988.

objections. On the other hand, the order will normally be classified to be a 'hybrid measure'[7] because it affects private interests in a particular locality. If it is so classified by the Chairmen of Committees this results in the order, after it has been checked for certain technical defects by the Joint Committee of Statutory Instruments, being referred to the Hybrid Instruments Committee of the House of Lords. Petitions can then be deposited against the order and if the committee find that they have *locus standi* they must enquire into the matters complained of in the petitions.[8] In the case of the London Docklands Development Corporation (Area and Constitution) Order 1980, several petitions were lodged by local authorities in the area and other local bodies and interests and these petitioners were found to have *locus standi*. After 50 days of hearing, the committee resolved that, with the exclusion of the Royal Mint, the principle of an urban development area and an urban development corporation should be accepted for the London Dockland. The committee, however, doubted whether it was appropriate for a Parliamentary committee to conduct what was in the nature of a public inquiry and recommended that the Select Committee on the Procedure of the House should examine the implications of the procedure for the future.[9]

No changes in the procedures have since been introduced and subsequent orders creating urban development corporations have gone through more smoothly. This is because the local authorities affected have not been so opposed to the corporations. However, in the case of the Bristol Urban Development Corporation, the Bristol City Council formally petitioned against the Parliamentary Order. In November 1988 the Hybrid Measures Committee of the House of Lords backed the proposal but recommended several changes.

The constitution of urban development corporations. Schedule 26 of the 1980 Act sets out the rules which govern the appointment of members and staff and the decision-making procedures of the corporations. The chairman, deputy chairman and members (there must be not less than 5 and not more than 11) are all appointed by the Secretary of State. In making his appointments the Secretary of State must have regard to 'the desirability of securing the services of people having special knowledge of the locality', and in this regard he must consult such local authorities as appear to him to be concerned with the regeneration of the urban development area (Sch 26; para 2). Apart from this power of appointment, s 138 gives the Secretary of State a general power to issue directions as to how a corporation should exercise any of the powers given to it. In addition, the Secretary of State's consent is required for many of the actions of the corporations.[10]

Central government has therefore ample statutory powers to supervise the work of the corporations closely.

Object and powers. The object of an urban development corporation is to secure the regeneration of its area by in particular:

7 A hybrid measure is one that if introduced as a public bill would be considered hybrid.
8 See Erskine-May's Parliamentary Practice, p 583–585 for an account of the process.
9 See Report of the Select Committee of the House of Lords on the London Docklands Development Corporation (Area and Constitution) Order 1980. (HL) 98. HMSO 1981.
10 Consent is required for payments to local authorities and statutory undertakers and for contribution to the provision of amenities, s 136(5) and for the compulsory purchase of land, s 142.

(a) bringing land and buildings into effective use;
(b) encouraging the development of existing and new industry and commerce;
(c) creating an attractive environment;
(d) and ensuring that housing and social facilities are available to encourage people to live and work in the area. (1980 Act; s 136(2)).

To these ends the corporations are given general powers to deal in property, carry out development, provide services, carry on businesses and generally do anything necessary or expedient. (1980 Act; s 136(3)).

Land acquisition and planning. The two keys to any development project are land ownership and planning permission. In both respects the development corporations are in a very strong position. Under s 141 of the 1980 Act, the Secretary of State may vest land owned by a local authority, statutory undertaker or other public body, in the corporation. Compensation is payable and an order cannot include land used or held by statutory undertakers for the purpose of carrying on their undertaking (1980 Act; s 141(2)). Orders are made by statutory instrument and require the approval of each House of Parliament. As with the orders establishing a corporation, the orders are classified as hybrid and may be petitioned against to the Hybrid Instruments Committee. Petitions were deposited against some of the orders vesting land in the London Docklands Development Corporation but were all rejected. Then under s 142 a corporation may acquire either by agreement or by compulsion land in the urban development area or adjacent to that area where it is required to discharge the corporation's function.'[11] Unlike the normal practice, these acquisition powers are open-ended and the Act does not expressly require the acquisition to be for any particular purpose. However, the Acquisition of Land Act 1981 applies to the compulsory acquisition of land by a corporation and so o:.ners who object will have a right to a public inquiry, where the corporation would presumably have to justify the acquisition.[12]

As to the need for planning permission, under s 148 of the 1980 Act, a corporation can submit proposals for the development of land to the Secretary of State who, if he approves of the proposals, can grant permission by special development order. There must be consultation with the local planning authority[13] and, as well as modifying the proposals, the Secretary of State can impose conditions which can include requiring details to be submitted to the local planning authority. Where such proposals are made, they are the nearest the legislation gets to providing for the preparation of a development plan.

In addition, the order establishing the corporation may make the corporation the local planning authority for development control purposes[14] in place of the existing local planning authorities. This can apply to the whole or any

11 There is even a power to acquire land which is not so adjacent if required for the provision of services in connection with the discharge of the corporations functions in its area.
12 See *R v Secretary of State for Transport, ex p Rothschild* [1989] 1 All ER 933, [1989] JPL 173, CA.
13 As defined in s 148(4) of the 1980 Act.
14 This is for all the purposes contained in Pt III of the Town and Country Planning Act 1971. Of the early urban development corporations, only Cardiff Bay Development Corporation has not been given planning functions.

portion of the urban development area (1980 Act, s 149(1)). This means that the corporations, who are given this function, can not only determine what development is carried out by other persons and bodies but can effectively grant themselves planning permission.[15] As well as development control functions, development corporations may be given various other planning functions found in the 1971 Act. These are set out in Pt I of Sch 29 to the 1980 Act and cover enforcement, tree preservation, advertisement, waste land, conservation area and listed building controls. On the other hand it has been held in *London Docklands Development Corpn v Rank Hovis Ltd*[16] that the London Docklands Development Corporation could not seek in its own name an injunction to prevent the demolition of a building on which the corporation had served a listed building preservation notice. The Court of Appeal held that such a power could not be implied either from the general power contained in s 136(3)(e) or from the development corporation's statutory object of creating an attractive environment. Section 222 of the Local Government Act 1972 has been interpreted as authorising local authorities to seek injunctions but, intentionally or otherwise, Parliament has not given such a power to a development corporation which like any other ordinary person would have to seek the aid of the Attorney General.

Finance. Development corporations are initially to be funded by a mixture of Government grants and loans (1980 Act; s 164 and Sch 31). However, the intention is that most of the work of regeneration will be privately financed. So, the initial outlay of Government monies is a pump-priming exercise and it seems that £1 of Government money is expected to attract about another £7 of private investment. As land prices rise through the regeneration of the area, it may be that a corporation will go into surplus and Sch 31 includes a power that where such a surplus arises, whether on a capital or revenue account, the Secretary of State can direct it to be paid to him.

2 The Land Authority for Wales

The Land Authority for Wales, which was set up by the Community Land Act 1975, has survived the abolition of the Act by the Local Government, Planning and Land Act 1980. The statutory provisions are now in ss 102 to 111 of the 1980 Act. The Land Authority's main duty is to acquire land which in its opinion needs to be made available for development and to then dispose of it for development (1980 Act s 103(1)). To this end, the authority has broad powers to acquire both by agreement and by compulsion land which in the authority's opinion is suitable for development. The authority has no planning powers and its present function is one of land assembly and disposal.

3 Enterprise zones

The concept of the enterprise zone was first floated by Professor Peter Hall in a speech to the annual conference of Royal Town Planning Institute in 1977 when he suggested that the inner city could be regenerated by treating them

---

15 See Pt II of the Town and Country Planning General Regulations 1976.
16 (1985) 84 LGR 101, [1986] JPL 826.

as 'free ports' with minimal controls.[17] The idea was taken up by the Conservative party, but the scheme which was promulgated by s 179 of the Local Government, Planning and Land Act 1980, was far less radical and combined a relaxation of planning controls with fiscal incentives.

Since 1981, enterprise zones have been designated for over 20 localities in England and Wales, though in many of these localities there is more than one zone. On 17 December 1987 the Secretary of State announced in Parliament that he did not intend to designate further enterprise zones in England.[18] Nevertheless, it was made clear that exceptional circumstances could still arise when a particular and localised problem might justify a new enterprise zone. Following the closure of the sole remaining shipyard at Sunderland, the government announced in December 1988 that an enterprise zone would be established in the town.

The policy that in general there will be no more enterprise zones may reflect a government disenchantment with the way the schemes have worked. Monitoring shows that the zones have been successful in attracting firms to the zones. However, this has cost considerable sums of money (by the end of 1986 just under £300 million had been spent on the British zones). There is evidence that the main effect of the zones has been to cause existing firms to transfer into the designated areas. According to a report of the House of Commons Committee of Public Accounts[19] more than £70 million in windfall benefits accrued to businesses already established in enterprise zones. The committee was also concerned about the adverse impact of schemes on neighbouring areas.

In the future, fiscal incentives are likely to take the form of individual development and regeneration grants (see p 443, below). The deregulation side of enterprise zones will continue separately in the form of simplified planning zones (see p 437, below).

Designation procedures. The process begins by the Secretary of State issuing an invitation to a public body to prepare a scheme. The bodies who can be invited to prepare enterprise zones are district councils, London borough councils, new town corporations and urban development corporations (1980 Act, Sch 32, para 1(1)). In making the invitation, the Secretary of State will specify the area for which the scheme can be prepared and may direct its form and content. (Sch 32, para 1(5)). The body chosen then may (there is no legal requirement) prepare and adopt a scheme in accordance with the invitation, which then needs formal designation as an enterprise zone by statutory instrument. Such an order designates the body who prepared the scheme as the enterprise zone authority, defines the boundaries and fixes the period for which the area is to remain an enterprise zone (Sch 32, para 5).

A striking characteristic of the process is that there is no opportunity for a public inquiry into the proposal. 'Adequate publicity' must be given to the scheme prepared by the invited body and any representations considered before it is adopted (Sch 32, para 2), but otherwise the only safeguards are a right to challenge the adoption on legal grounds (para 4) and the fact that the

---

17 See Lloyd and Botham, 'Implementation of Enterprise Zones in Britain', 7 Urban Law and Policy (1985) 33–55 for an account of their origins.
18 See [1988] JPL 73 where the statement is reproduced.
19 House of Lords Paper 293, Session 1985/86.

order is subject to annulment by a resolution of either House of Parliament (para 5(3)). An order, unlike the order setting up an urban development corporation, is not a hybrid measure and so there is no right for private individuals to petition Parliament. This absence of a right to a hearing can be criticised on the grounds that the line of the enterprise zone can seriously affect the interests of individuals.

Once designated, the Secretary of State may invite the enterprise zone authority to submit modifications, which may result in a modification order being made by the Secretary of State by way of a statutory instrument (Sch 32, paras 9 to 15). Such an order can extend the period of the enterprise zone or vary the planning arrangements but cannot reduce the period or alter the boundaries of the zone (para 15).

The planning implications. Professor McAuslan has described an enterprise zone as a 'hybrid of a local plan and a planning permission' as it may cover an area large enough to be the subject of an action area plan ... yet it also operates as a planning permission.'[20] In this respect, it is similar to legal systems which have zoning ordinances which in themselves give rights to development. This consequence is provided by paragraph 17(1) of Sch 32 which states: 'An order designating an enterprise zone under this Schedule shall (without more) have effect on the effective date to grant planning permission for development specified in the scheme or for development of any class so specified'. Such permissions can be made subject to conditions and in addition the enterprise zone authority has a continuing power to issue directions varying the planning regime. A direction can be made that any permission granted shall not apply to a specified development or class of development either in the whole area or a specified area in the zone (para 17(4)). Directions require the approval of the Secretary of State before they can be made.

The wording of the Schedule means that the extent of planning control in enterprise zones can vary considerably both from zone to zone and within a particular zone. Thus it seems that in England enterprise zone schemes grant planning permission for all development except that specified in the individual scheme, while in Wales, the approach is to specify only the specific types of development that can take place without an express grant of planning permission.[1] Zones often differentiate between areas or sub-zones where there exist particular hazards or amenities which require special safeguards. In any case most zones still require permission for developments which are particularly polluting or hazardous.

A modification of the scheme may have the effect of revoking or altering planning rights and, as s 165 is not applicable, there are no rights to compensation. However, a modification order does not affect planning permission where the development was begun before the modification took effect (para 21). Similarly, although a permission granted under a scheme ceases to have effect once an area ceases to be an enterprise zone, this does not apply where the development has commenced[2] (para 22).

20 P McAuslan 'Local Government and Resource Allocation in England': changing ideology, unchanging law (1981) 4 Urban Law and Policy 215 at p 250.
1 See [1984] JPL 218.
2 The Enterprise Zone Authority has, however, power to serve completion notices; see Sch 32, para 22(2).

Most enterprise zone authorities will also be one of the local planning authorities or, indeed, the only local planning authority for the area. However, there is provision for the order designating an enterprise zone to make the enterprise zone authority the local planning authority for all or some of the functions in the 1971 Act (paras 5(7) and 20).

More surprisingly, in determining what planning permissions shall be granted, there is no duty on either the proposing authority or the Secretary of State to have regard to the development plan. Instead, the obligation is the other way round and once an enterprise zone has been designated, as soon as practicable both structure plans and local plans have to be reviewed in the light of the scheme and any alterations which are considered necessary put in process (para 23(1)).

Fiscal implications. The main fiscal benefits available to industrial and commercial businesses located in an enterprise zone are:

(a) Occupiers of commercial and industrial buildings are exempt from paying rates for any period when the building is situated in an enterprise zone[3] (Sch 32 para 27).
(b) Businesses making a profit can set off as capital allowances the total cost of the construction of business premises against corporation tax or income tax liability (s 74 of the Finance Act 1980, applying the Capital Allowances Act 1968).
(c) Employers located in enterprise zones are exempt from paying industrial training levies.

Enterprise zones and environmental assessment. A project for which planning permission is granted by an enterprise zone could well come within Annex II to the European Economic Community directive on environmental assessment and be likely to have significant effect on the environment. In circular 24/88 it is stated that where appropriate the Secretary of State would consider using his powers under Sch 32 to the 1980 Act to require any new or revised enterprise zone to include in its planning regime provisions which either exclude developments which might require an environmental assessment or which require the developer to establish that environmental assessment is not necessary. The same approach has been taken to simplified planning zones and the approach of the Department of the Environment is discussed in more detail under that heading.

4 Simplified Planning Zones

The concept of a simplified planning zone (SPZ) clearly evolved from the experience of granting permission by way of an enterprise zone. The assumption behind SPZs is that developers will be attracted to an area by the certainty of knowing in advance what development they can carry out without having to go through the costly and uncertain business of applying for permission. Circular 25/87 states that: 'Most SPZs are likely to be in older urban areas where an additional stimulus is needed to promote regeneration and encourage economic activity' (para 5). The circular goes on to say that

---

3 The cost to the local authority is refunded from central government by way of grants (Local Government, Planning and Land Act 1980, Sch 32, para 29).

there may be other situations where carefully designed SPZ schemes can be of benefit and Planning Policy Guidance Note 5 (PPG 5) spelt out in detail the possible uses of SPZs.

The examples given are:

(a) land allocated in a development plan for new development such as an 'industrial park'. Here it is advised that the local plan and the SPZ might be prepared in parallel;
(b) large old industrial areas or estates which need regeneration;
(c) areas suitable for mixed industrial warehousing, commercial and retailing development, called 'employment areas';
(d) large sites in single ownership which are unused or underdeveloped;
(e) areas suitable for sizeable new residential developments; and
(f) individual sites for which development briefs have been prepared or could be prepared by the local planning authorities to stimulate interest.

Unlike enterprise zones, SPZs carry with them no automatic fiscal advantages. However, PPG 5 advises that development could be attracted to an SPZ by the provision of needed infrastructure and the availability of government grants and incentives (the range of grants available is discussed at p 443, below).

In contrast to enterprise zones, the process of establishing an SPZ is cumbersome and complicated, and involves a public local inquiry if objections are made to a proposed scheme. The preparation has to be carried out by the local planning authority (the district planning authority or an urban development corporation with planning functions) but any person can, by bringing in the Secretary of State, force the preparation of an SPZ.

It is too soon to judge how frequently the mechanism of the SPZ will be employed. So far it seems that only a handful of schemes have been prepared or are under preparation.[4]

The scope of SPZs. The main legislative framework is set out in ss 24A to 24E of the 1971 Act.

As with enterprise zones an SPZ can grant planning permission for any specified development or class of development either in relation to the whole zone or any part of the zone (1971 Act, s 24A(1)).

There are, however, areas which cannot be included in a SPZ. The areas excluded are:

(a) National Parks;
(b) conservation areas;
(c) land within the Broads;
(d) areas of outstanding natural beauty;[5]
(e) land identified in the development plan as green belt;
(f) areas of special scientific interest[6] (1971 Act, s 24E(1).

Such areas are not excluded if the land became land of such a description *after* the SPZ had been adopted by the local planning authority or approved by the Secretary of State (s 24E(2)). This means that the designation of land

4 See [1988] JPL 665, but see Planning 1989, Issue 809, p 17.
5 As designated under s 87 of the National Parks and Access to the Countryside Act 1949.
6 By notification or order under ss 28 or 29 of the Wildlife and Countryside Act 1981.

within an SPZ as a conservation area does not revoke any planning permission granted by the SPZ, though it will mean that conservation area consents may be required to carry out the development; (see Chapter 18 p 490, below). On the other hand, the Secretary of State now has a power effectively to withdraw the grant of planning permission by making an order that no SPZ schemes shall grant permission in relation to specific areas of land or development of a specified description (1971 Act, s 24E(3)). So far, this power has only been used to exclude minerals and waste disposal development,[7] but it could be used to require environmental assessment (see p 492, above).

Otherwise, s 24A gives the local planning authority a wide discretion as to what can be granted. As PPG 5 puts it 'SPZs could grant permission for a wide range of major developments or one predominant use. Or they might permit a wide range of minor developments including changes of use, extensions and infill developments' (Annex, para 2). The Guidance also points out that as with enterprise zones, SPZs can either be *specific* (by itemising what is allowed) or *general* (by granting almost all types of development except for those specifically listed). Examples of both approaches are set out in Appendices to the guidance. Sub-zones can also be employed to exclude certain classes of development in sensitive areas.

Conditions and limitations. Section 24A(3) provides for planning permission granted by a scheme being subject to 'such conditions, limitations or exceptions as may be specified in the scheme'. This is similar to development orders which may be 'subject to such conditions or limitations as may be specified in the order'. (1971 Act; s 24(4)). In contrast, in the case of express planning permissions s 29(1) empowers local planning authorities to grant planning permission 'subject to such conditions as they think fit'. This would suggest that SPZs are nearer in form to development orders than express grants of permission. This might mean that the courts would treat an SPZ with more deference as a quasi legislative instrument, if the legality of a condition, limitation or exception were to be challenged on legal grounds.[8] More significantly, s 244(7) provides for the validity of an SPZ to be challenged by any person aggrieved within six weeks of adoption or approval, and s 242 states that otherwise its validity shall not be challenged in any other legal proceedings whatsoever. So if a challenge is not mounted within six weeks, it would seem clear that the validity of conditions could not be raised in any subsequent enforcement action. The Act does not expressly exclude the possibility of applying under s 31A or 32(1)(b) for permission to avoid the need for compliance with conditions imposed by an SPZ, but as the SPZs are designed as autonomous schemes it may be that the courts would hold that these provisions are not applicable.

If a legal challenge were to be made against the validity of a condition imposed by an SPZ, presumably the normal tests for validity of conditions laid down in *Newbury District Council v Secretary of State for the*

---

7 See Town and Country Planning (Simplified Planning Zones) (Excluded Development) Order 1987.
8 See *Essex County Council v Minister of Housing and Local Government* (1986) 18 P & CR 531; but see *Council of Civil Service Unions v Minister for the Civil Service* [1985] AC 374, [1984] 3 All ER 935, HL.

Environment[9] would apply except that in considering whether the condition fairly and reasonably related to the development granted, it might be proper to consider the wider context of the whole scheme.

The term 'limitations' would be expected to be given the same meaning as limitations in a development order so that any divergence from those limits would make the whole development unlawful.[10] As to 'exceptions', this is a novel term in planning law and may cover a limitation which is expressed negatively; ie the permission shall not have effect if certain circumstances apply; see in this regard 1988 GDO, Art 3(2).

Section 24B provides that conditions or limitations specified in an SPZ can be imposed generally on all development permitted, or just on particular descriptions of development. Also, conditions or limitations imposed on particular descriptions of development can require the subsequent consent, agreement or approval of the local planning authority (1971 Act, s 24B(2)).

The duration and alteration of SPZs. An SPZ ceases to have effect at the end of ten years beginning from the date of adoption or approval. Any planning permission granted equally ceases to have effect unless development has been begun before the SPZ ceases to have effect. There is provision for the service of completion notices under s 43[11] where development has started but not been completed (1971 Act, s 24C).

Once adopted or approved, SPZs can be altered. Alterations may be favourable in that the area of the zone may be extended, granting further permissions, and conditions, limitations or restrictions[12], to which existing permissions are subject, may be withdrawn or relaxed. Once such alterations are adopted or approved, they take effect forthwith (1971 Act, s 24D(2) to (4)). Alterations can be unfavourable in that they exclude land from the zone, withdraw planning permission or impose new or more stringent conditions, limitations or restrictions; in which case, the alterations do not take effect until twelve months after the date of adoption or approval of the alteration. As alterations do not affect any permission where the development authorised has already begun, this means owners or occupiers of land have twelve months in which to safeguard their planning rights by commencing development. Once again s 43 of the 1971 Act applies (1971 Act, s 24D(5) to (7)).

There would seem to be no right to compensation for any restriction of planning rights, since although an SPZ is similar to a development order, it is not a development order and so s 165 does not apply (see chapter 15 p 414).

The procedures for making or altering an SPZ scheme. The detailed procedures are to be found in Sch 8A to the 1971 Act and in the Town and Country Planning (Simplified Planning Zones) Regulations 1987 (the 1987 Regulations).

Section 24A(4) places a duty on every local planning authority (this is the district planning authority except in urban development areas where development corporations have development control functions) to consider the

9 [1981] AC 578, [1980] 1 All ER 731, HL.
10 See *Garland v Minister of Housing and Local Government* (1968) 20 P & CR 93, 67 LGR 77.
11 See ch 10, p 265, above.
12 The term 'restrictions' appears for the first time in s 24D and may be a form of exception.

desirability of making SPZs for any part of their area, and to keep the question under review. Where the local planning authority consider it desirable, they are required to prepare a scheme. Thus, it is generally left to the discretion of the local planning authority whether an SPZ is prepared. However, any person can force the hand of the local planning authority by requesting the authority to make or alter an SPZ scheme. If the authority refuse to do so or do not decide to do so within three months from the request, the person making the request can require the local planning authority to refer the matter to the Secretary of State unless an SPZ scheme relating to the whole or part of the land specified in the request has been adopted or approved within the 12 months preceding the request. Thereafter, the Secretary of State may, after considering the matter and any written representations by the applicant and the authority, give a direction that an SPZ scheme be prepared or altered (Schedule 8A, para 3). It seems unlikely that this complicated procedure will be frequently put to use because of the effort involved. A would-be developer can always apply directly for planning permission and it would seem dangerous to rely on an unwilling local planning authority to prepare a scheme. Like a local plan, a scheme consists of a map, a written statement and such diagrams, illustrations and descriptive matter as the local planning authority think appropriate for explaining or illustrating the scheme (Sch 8A, para 1).

The procedures for preparing and finalising an SPZ also tend to copy the precedent of local plan procedures (see chapter 4, p 66) and so only a brief summary of the main stages follows.

The authority, which proposes to make or alter an SPZ, must publicise their proposals and, where objections to the scheme have been made in accordance with the 1987 Regulations, the authority must hold a local inquiry or other hearing unless all such objectors indicate that they do not wish to appear (Sch 8A, paras 5 to 8 and the 1987 Regulations). Here the legislation would appear to make a distinction between the need to publicise *the proposals* (which could be in a provisional form) and the right to object to *the proposed scheme or alterations* (which must be in a document form) (Sch 8A, para 5(2) and (3)). This could be taken to mean (as the annotations to the Encyclopaedia of Planning suggest (at 2.837/3) that the publicity stage may take place before the detailed scheme has been finalised.

As with a local plan, the local planning authority do not have to accept the recommendations of the person appointed by the Secretary of State to hold the inquiry. However, Regulation 9 of the 1987 Regulations requires the authority to consider the report of the Inspector and to prepare a statement of their decisions in the light of the report and any recommendation therein. Further, they must give reasons for their decisions.[13]

The authority may adopt the scheme in its original form or may modify it so as to take account of any objections or any other material considerations (Sch 8A, para 9(2)). The Secretary of State, however, may, if it appears to him that the proposals are unsatisfactory, direct the local planning authority to consider modifying the proposals so indicated in his direction and, in such a case, the authority cannot adopt the proposals unless they can satisfy the

---

13 See *Simplex GE (Holdings) Ltd v Secretary of State for the Environment* [1988] JPL 809, CA as to the legal consequences of a failure to give reasons in the context of a local plan.

Secretary of State that they have made the necessary modifications (Sch 8A, para 9(3) and (4)).

The Secretary of State can also 'call-in' proposals for his approval.[14] He may approve the proposals with or without modifications or reject them (Sch 8A, paras 10 and 11).

The SPZ scheme takes effect and planning permission is granted from the date of adoption or approval.

The relationship of SPZs to other planning matters. As SPZs closely resemble local plans, it might have been simpler to have provided that local plans themselves could include grants of planning permission. But the legislation is completely silent as to the relationship between local plans and SPZs. There is no express provision for local planning authorities to have regard to the policies in the development plan in preparing SPZs. Such policies must, however, be capable of being relevant considerations in the *Wednesbury*[15] sense.

There is also a duty imposed on district planning authorities in non-metropolitan areas to consult the county council before preparing a scheme, so that the county can make representations if the SPZ conflicts with Structure Plan policies (Sch 8A, para 5(6)). Nevertheless, it is clearly possible that SPZs could be adopted or approved which conflict with the development plan. There is no requirement in such a case, as with enterprise zones that the development plan should be modified to take account of the SPZ.

These problems are not discussed in circular 25/87, but it is advised that where a local plan or unitary development plan have proposals in common there may be benefits in processing the scheme and the development plan concurrently through one public inquiry (Annex to the Circular, para 31).

An SPZ scheme can only grant planning permission. Consents will still be required in SPZs for cutting down trees subject to a tree preservation order, to alter listed buildings or to do anything which is subject to a separate system of regulation from development control.

The provisions providing for SPZs say nothing about the enforcement of development control in the zones and so enforcement must be the same as elsewhere under the power given to local planning authorities by s 87(1) of the 1971 Act. The only possible complication here is that the use of the term exceptions in s 24B makes it unclear whether a failure to comply with an exception would be unauthorised development or a breach of a condition or limitation (see 1971 Act, s 87(3) and Chapter 12, p 308, above).

SPZs and Environmental Assessment. In order to comply with European Community Directive 85/337, SPZs ought not to grant permission for a project without there being provision for environmental assessment where this is required.[16] Circular 24/88 attempts to deal with this problem. First it is advised that local planning authorities should include in all schemes a provision that 'Development which falls within any of the descriptions

14 The Secretary of State also possesses certain default powers to prepare a scheme himself. To do this he must hold a local inquiry or hearing (1971 Act, Sch 8A, para 12).
15 As laid down by Lord Greene in *Associated Provincial Picture Houses Ltd v Wednesbury Corpn* [1948] 1 KB 223, [1947] 2 All ER 680, CA.
16 See ch 6 for a discussion of the need for environmental assessment.

included in Sch 1 to the Town and Country Planning (Assessment of Environmental Effects) Regulations 1988 is not permitted.' Schedule 2 projects in the Regulations are more difficult to deal with as judgment has to be used as to whether a particular project is likely to have significant environmental effects. Where the SPZ specifies the particular types of development permitted, the Circular advises local planning authorities that such grants can be defined to exclude either development of any description mentioned in Sch 2 or development of any such description which would in their opinion be likely in practice to give rise to significant environmental effects. In the last case Sch 2 development could be authorised which *did* (contrary to the local planning authority's preliminary views) give rise to significant environmental effects. Where the SPZ takes the alternative form of granting permission for *all* development except in particular cases, it is suggested that a provision should be included in the scheme that permission is not given for Sch 2 development unless the authority notify the developer in writing that in their opinion it would not be likely to have significant environmental effects.

5 *Financial aid to promote development*

The decay of the inner city areas has led to the policy of trying to promote regeneration and development by financial incentives. For a long time local authorities have possessed limited powers to make loans for the erection of buildings[17] and central Government has been able to pay grants to local authorities with special social needs.[18] Following the reports on inner city deprivation in Liverpool, Birmingham and Lambeth which were published in 1977, the Inner Urban Areas Act 1978 was enacted which substantially increased the powers of local authorities to give grants and loans with regard to specific areas. The prevailing theme was the need for 'partnership' between local authorities and central Government. There has been criticism of the ineffectiveness of these partnership schemes and since gaining power in 1979, successive Conservative administrations have placed more emphasis on the role of the private sector. Thus, in improving the availability of grants for the reclamation and reuse of derelict land, the law has been changed so that grants can be made direct to private persons. These provisions are now to be found in the Derelict Land Act 1982. Similarly, grants have been issued directly to the private sector to carry out developments rather than through local authorities. This policy can be seen in the way the new provisions in the Housing and Planning Act 1986, for financial assistance for urban regeneration, are worded.

In this area, the law merely sets out the broad powers and the rest turns on administrative practice. The main statutes are now outlined.

The Inner Urban Areas Act 1978. The Act distinguishes between various types of areas. First, if the Secretary of State is satisfied that special social need exists in any urban area and the conditions which give rise to that need could be alleviated by the use of the powers conferred by the Act, he may specify any district which includes the whole or any part of that area as a

17 See s 3 of the Local Authorities (Land) Act 1963. See also s 43 of the Local Government (Miscellaneous Provisions) Act 1982.
18 See Local Government Grants (Social Need) Act 1969.

designated district (1978 Act, s 1). The legal consequences are that the local authorities whose jurisdiction includes the district, can make various loans and grants. Under s 2, loans can be made for the acquisition of land or the carrying out of works on land which the authority is satisfied would benefit the designated district. The loan must be secured by a mortgage on the land and the amount should not exceed 90 per cent of the value of the land, or its value when the works have been carried out. Then, under s 3, loans and grants can be made to common ownership enterprises and co-operative enterprises.[19] Secondly, where the authority is satisfied that conditions in an area, within the designated district, which is predominantly industrial or commercial or would be if developed according to the development plan, could be improved, the authority may declare the area to be an *improvement area*. This triggers off further powers under ss 5 and 6 for the authority to provide loans and grants for improving amenities and grants for converting or improving buildings. Finally, there is provision under s 8 for *special areas* within the district to be specified. These are the so called 'partnership areas' where special social need requires a concerted effort. This 'concerted effort' takes the form of 'arrangements' being entered into by the Secretary of State with the local authorities for the area and other parties (1978 Act, s 7). In special areas the authorities have further powers to lend money for site preparation (1978 Act, s 9), to make grants towards rental payments on buildings intended for industrial or commercial persons (1978 Act, s 10) and to make grants to small firms to help pay the interest on loans made to carry out works (1978 Act, s 11).

It is made clear that these powers are in addition to the power in s 137 of the Local Government Act 1972 to spend the sum of a two-penny rate on purposes which would otherwise be *ultra vires* (1978 Act, s 13).

Most of the funding for financial aid under the Inner Urban Areas Act 1978 has come from central Government in the form of urban development grants. This is not a statutory term and urban development grants can be made to areas which are not designated under the Inner Urban Areas Act 1978. Nevertheless, urban development grants have tended to follow the scheme of the 1978 Act in that the money has been channelled through public authorities rather than being distributed direct to private persons, and aid has been concentrated on the inner urban areas. There is also a non-statutory system of authorities in inner urban areas being selected as 'programme' authorities who are invited by central Government to draw up inner area programmes.

The Derelict Land Act 1982. Under s 1 grants are available towards the costs of acquiring and reclaiming derelict land. There is no statutory definition of 'derelict land' but s 1 only applies to land which is 'derelict, neglected or unsightly, or is likely to become so by reason of actual or apprehended subsidence' (1982 Act, s 1(2)). Also, the Treasury have agreed the definition as 'Land so damaged by industrial or other development that it is incapable of beneficial use without treatment'.[20]

19 Provided for under the Industrial Common Ownership Act 1976.
20 See Department of the Environment Notes for Guidance on Derelict Land Reclamation Grant.

The amount of grant depends on the status of the land. In Assisted Areas[1] and Derelict Land Clearance Areas[2] grants are paid at rates of 100 per cent to local authorities and the English Industrial Estates Corporation and at 80 per cent to other persons.

Grants can be made to private persons and circular 28/85 states that it wishes to see more reclamation carried out on privately owned land. This circular also advises that priority will be given to what it describes as schemes which produce 'hard after-use', that is, schemes leading to private sector commercial, industrial or residential end uses (see para 6).

Compulsory acquisition powers may be needed to carry out the reclamation and s 3 of the 1982 Act extends the power of compulsory purchase under s 89 of the National Parks and Access to the Countryside Act 1949 and s 6(3) of the Local Authorities (Land) Act 1963.

The Housing and Planning Act 1986. Section 27 empowers the Secretary of State to give financial assistance to any person in regard to the cost of certain specified activities. These activities include land acquisition, reclamation, redevelopment, provision of infrastructure and environmental improvements (1986 Act, s 27(2)). The activities must contribute to the regeneration of an urban area by bringing land and buildings into effective use, creating an attractive environment, providing employment for people who live in the area or ensuring that housing and social facilities are available to encourage people to live and work in the area (1986 Act, s 27(1)). The financial assistance can take the form of grants, loans, guarantees or direct expenditure and may be on such terms as the Secretary of State considers appropriate including the repayment or the sharing in the proceeds of disposal (1986 Act, ss 28 and 29).

It will be noted that local authorities are completely left out of the process and applications for urban regeneration grants (as they are non-statutorily termed) are to be made directly to private sector property owners, developers and others in the private sector.[3] It seems that these grants are aimed at tackling medium-sized areas of derelict or neglected land. They thus fall between the major schemes of the urban development corporations and the small activities sponsored by urban development grants. For example, the first urban regeneration grant of £3.25 million was paid to a private firm to help pay for major reclamations work and the provision of infrastructure at a derelict 36-acre site within the Dudley Enterprise Zone.[4]

On 22 June 1988 it was announced in Parliament that in total, 289 urban development grants and eight urban regeneration grants had been approved at a total cost of £175 million.[5] The non-statutory nature of much of the grant system makes changes easy and in May 1988 it was announced that a new city grant will replace urban development and urban regeneration grants. In 57 urban programme areas it will also replace private sector derelict land grant. This means that the private sector now can apply directly

---

1 As designated under the Industrial Development Act 1982; see Assisted Areas Order 1984, SI 1984 No 1844.
2 As designated under the Local Employment Act 1972; see Derelict Land Clearance Areas Orders.
3 See Urban Regeneration Grants, Notes for Guidance.
4 See [1987] JPL 817.
5 Hansard, Vol 135, Issue No 1454.

in all cases, instead of having to go through a local authority to central Government.

Local authorities will still play an important role in providing financial aid for land development. In the past much use has been made of s 137 of the Local Government Act 1972. The Widdicombe report on 'The Conduct of Local Authority Business'[6] found that in addition to expenditure under the Local Authorities (Land) Act 1963 and the Inner Urban Areas Act 1978, £90 million was spent in 1984/5. Apart from various grants, loans, rent subsidies and guarantees to individual firms, it included the acquisition of companies and support for co-operative ventures. A number of companies have also been set up for economic development under the Companies Acts by local authorities. The Widdicombe Report recommended that the proper role of local authorities in economic development should be reviewed and that the law on local authority controlled companies should be amended.[7] These recommendations are being followed up in the Local Government and Housing Bill 1989. Clauses 32 to 34 of the Bill deal with the economic development of their areas by local authorities and create new powers for the providing of financial and other assistance for that function. However the Secretary of State is to be given powers to issue regulations and guidance as to how these powers are to be used. S 137 is to be amended to take into account the new powers, and new restrictions on its use are to be imposed.

The European Community also is an important source for finance for economic development. The European Regional Development Fund[8] makes contributions to publicly provided infrastructure directly linked to industrial handicraft and service activities. Priority should be given to 'national priority areas'.[9]

Finally, it should be remembered that most regeneration projects will require planning permission as well as cash. An offer of a grant gives no exemption from controls. Of course, where the project is backed by central government or the local planning authority, this will not normally be a problem and many projects will be in urban development areas, enterprise and simplified planning zones.

6 1986 Cmnd 9797.
7 See paras 8.143 and 8.117 of the report.
8 Established by Council Regulation 724/75.
9 Art 3 of the Regulation.

CHAPTER 17

PLANNING BLIGHT AND INJURIOUS AFFECTION

A INTRODUCTION

'Planning blight' has been described as 'the depressing effect on existing property of proposals which imply public acquisition and disturbance of the existing use' of the property.[1] The announcement, for example, of the line of a proposed road may well mean that land in the path of that road becomes either completely unsaleable in the open market or saleable only at a price lower than it would otherwise have fetched. Although the proposals in question may not be due to be implemented for some considerable time and although the proposals may not in the meantime have any effect on the use to which the affected land is put, the marketability of land which is likely to be acquired for some public purpose may well be affected immediately.

One solution to the landowner's difficulty is to wait and see what happens. Either the scheme will be dropped or the land will ultimately be acquired for the purpose in question. In the latter event, the price to be paid by the public authority will be the sum the land would have realised on a sale in the open market by a willing seller.[2] This means that any depreciation in value resulting from the compulsory acquisition, or the shadow of compulsory acquisition, will be ignored in determining the price; such depreciation is not a market factor.

However, several years commonly elapse between the first indication that land is required for a scheme of public works and either the eventual demise of the scheme or the acquisition of the land by the public authority. The landowner may not be able to wait that long.

For example, a businessman may find it difficult to make any sensible decisions about future levels of investment in the climate of uncertainty created by the proposed scheme; the best interests of the business may dictate an early move to an area free from uncertainty. A householder may be required to move elsewhere in the ordinary course of his employment and have to place his house on the market immediately. In such cases, since the marketability of the property will be adversely affected, perhaps seriously, by the proposed scheme, hardship might well result.[3]

---

1 *The Future of Development Plans* (HMSO 1965).
2 Land Compensation Act 1961, s 5.
3 There is thus, as the Skeffington Committee said: 'a conflict between, on the one hand, the desirability of giving full publicity at an early stage to proposals the planning authority are considering, so as to stimulate informed public discussion and, on the other hand, the need to avoid causing hardship to individuals by the casting of blight over land or property that may not be required for many years or, indeed, at all'. (*People and Planning: The Report of the Committee on Public Participation in Planning*) (HMSO, 1969).

Statute alleviates the hardship caused in some, but by no means all, cases of planning blight. Certain owner-occupiers of 'blighted' land are entitled, in fairly closely-defined circumstances, to serve on the appropriate authority (in effect, the public body by which the land is liable to be acquired in terms of the blighting proposals) a blight notice requiring that authority to acquire the land. Where a blight notice takes effect, the authority concerned must acquire the property immediately, instead of perhaps waiting until they are ready to proceed with the scheme in question, and must do so at a price which ignores the effect of the blighting proposals.

So far we have used the term 'blight' in the narrow sense of the depressing effect on the value of land resulting from a proposal which implies the eventual public acquisition of the land. It is only where 'blight' in this sense exists that a blight notice may be served under the planning legislation; blight notices and their consequences are considered more fully below. However, the term 'blight' is commonly used in the much wider sense of the depressing effect which the construction and use of a scheme of works may have on the value of surrounding land. In this sense, 'blight' is synonymous with 'injurious affection' or 'worsenment'. The most obvious example of this sort of blight is depreciation resulting from schemes of public works such as the building of a major new road. The noise, vibration and dust from traffic using the road will not only be a source of disturbance to people living nearby but is also likely to have an adverse effect on the value of their property.

Such disturbance is not, of course, limited to public works. Private sector development such as the construction and use of industrial premises or the opening up of a fish and chip shop may seriously disturb neighbours and reduce the value of their property. Indeed, underlying many objections to planning applications is concern about the effect which the proposal will have on the value of neighbouring land.

At common law, activities which seriously disturb a person in the enjoyment of land may be restrained as a nuisance. The law therefore provides a remedy for blight caused by private sector development; it may be restrained as a nuisance by an action for an injunction at the suit of the disturbed neighbour. It should be noted, however, that the key to the remedy is not depreciation in the value of the property (although this will often result) but infringement of the right to comfortable enjoyment of the property. The distinction is important in as much as the courts do not recognise as part of that right a right to a view or a right to privacy although the loss of either may have an adverse effect on value.

What of public sector development? To what extent are major public works such as roads, railways, airports, town centre redevelopment schemes, sewage works and so on open to restraint at the suit of a neighbour who may suffer disturbance and depreciation in the value of his property in consequence of such development? It would seem that the plea of 'public interest' is not, of itself, a sufficient answer to an action for nuisance.[4] It has, however, long been established that where an activity is authorised by statute, whether expressly or by implication, then the person or body carrying on the activity will be immune from an action for nuisance.[5] The Act authorising the activity

---

4 *Duke of Buccleuch v Cowan* (1866) 5 M 214.
5 *Hammersmith and City Rly Co v Brand* (1869) LR 4 HL 171.

does not usually confer an express immunity; rather it is the inevitable consequence of the authorisation.[6]

Where a person or body carrying out a scheme of public works has statutory immunity from an action for nuisance, it seems reasonable to expect that Parliament will make some provision to alleviate the hardship caused by this form of blight. This expectation has been partly fulfilled by the legislature. It is not possible, as with an action for nuisance, to stop the scheme of works; instead, legislation provides for the payment of compensation in respect of some, but by no means all, cases of this sort of blight—what we refer to in this chapter as 'injurious affection'. Only an outline of the law on injurious affection is provided here; more detailed treatments are to be found in works dealing specifically with compulsory purchase and compensation.

B PLANNING BLIGHT

An owner of land the value of which is adversely affected by a proposal which implies its public acquisition may, in certain circumstances, serve a blight notice on the public authority responsible for the proposal giving rise to the blight; a blight notice requires that authority to acquire the land. If the notice takes effect, the authority must acquire the land at a price which ignores the effects of the blighting proposal.

A blight notice is to be distinguished from a purchase notice. The purchase notice procedure may be employed to compel the local planning authority to acquire land which, following the making of an adverse planning decision, has become incapable of reasonably beneficial use in its existing state (see Chapter 14). The statutory provisions on planning blight, on the other hand, are concerned with the situation where adverse *proposals* have affected the *marketability* of land even though the land remains perfectly capable in the meantime of beneficial use.

Proposals giving rise to obligation to purchase

It is only if land falls clearly within one of the 'specified descriptions' of land set out in s 192(1) of the 1971 Act, as amended and extended by the Land Compensation Act 1973[7] that a blight notice can succeed. The specified descriptions are complex and diverse; their common feature is that they all involve proposals which imply that land is likely to be acquired in the future by a body possessing powers of compulsory purchase. Statute lays down in relation to each of the specified descriptions of land the stage which the proposals must have reached before land comes within that description; only when that stage has been reached can a blight notice be served. It may be noted that in some cases a blight notice can be served before the proposals in question have been finally approved.

The specified descriptions of land are broadly as follows:[8]

6 *Hammersmith and City Rly Co v Brand* (1869) LR 4 HL 171; and *Allen v Gulf Oil Refining Co* [1981] AC 1001, [1981] 1 All ER 353, HL. Immunity is only conferred in respect of damage which is the inevitable consequence of operating the works authorised by statute.
7 References in this chapter to the LCA 1973 are references to that Act.
8 The two specified descriptions added by ss 22(6) and 23(8) of the Community Land Act 1975 were repealed by s 101(1) of, and para 2 of Sch 17 to, the Local Government, Planning and Land Act 1980.

1. *Land affected by a development plan or a proposed development plan.* This includes:

(a) Structure Plans

Land indicated in a structure plan as land which may be required for the purposes of any functions of a government department, a local authority, statutory undertakers, the British Coal Corporation, a public telecommunications operator or system, or as land which may be included in an action area;[9] this provision applies if land is earmarked in this way in a structure plan which has come into force, or in a structure plan which has been submitted to the Secretary of State, or in proposals for alterations to a structure plan which have been submitted to the Secretary of State, or in modifications proposed to be made by the minister to any such plan or proposals (1971 Act, s 192(1)(a); LCA. 1973 s 68(1)). However, this does not apply to land in an area for which there is in force a local plan allocating or defining land for the purposes of any such functions (1971 Act, s 192(2)). In such a case, the allocations in the structure plan are superseded by the allocations in the local plan, which is considered next.

(b) Local Plans

Land allocated or defined in a local plan for the purposes of the functions of the same bodies as set out in (a) above. This applies where a local plan is in force, or where copies of a local plan have been made available for inspection prior to adoption or approval, or where proposals for alterations to a local plan have been made available for inspection, or where modifications to such a plan or proposal have been proposed by the local planning authority or the Secretary of State (1971 Act, s 192(1)(b); LCA 1973, s 68(2)).

(c) 'Old Style' Development Plans

Until a relevant local plan comes into operation in any area, land allocated for broadly the same functions as above in an 'old style' development plan, or in proposals for alterations or modifications to such a plan proposed by the Secretary of State, is included within the specified descriptions. (s 138(1)(b) of the Town and Country Planning Act 1962 as incorporated by s 292 of the 1971 Act; para 58 of Sch 24; LCA 1973, s 68(3)).

(d) Unitary Development Plans

The Local Government Act 1985 inserted two new subsections (192(1)(bb) and (bc)) to cater for the unitary plans which now apply to London Boroughs and Metropolitan districts. The specified descriptions now include land indicated or allocated in a unitary plan for the purpose of the functions of the same bodies as set out in (a) above. By virtue of para 20 of Sch 1 to the 1985 Act this extends to unitary plans of which copies have been made available for public inspection, proposals for alteration or replacement of which copies have been made available for inspection, and proposed modifications which have been formally notified.

(e) Non-statutory plans

Land indicated in a plan (other than a development plan approved by a resolution of the planning authority) as land which may be required for the

---

9 On the meaning of the phrase 'may be included in an action area', see *Nowell v Kirkburton UDC* (1970) 21 P & CR 832.

purposes of a government department, a local authority or statutory undertakers or land in respect of which the local planning authority have resolved, or have been directed by the Secretary of State, to take action in order to safeguard the land for development of such purposes[10] (LCA 1973, s 71(1) and (2)).

(f) Road Construction Works in Development Plans
Land indicated in a development plan (otherwise than above) as required for road construction or alteration (1971 Act, s 192(1)(c)).

2. *Highway needs*

(a) Schemes under the Highways Acts
Land on or adjacent to the line of a highway in a proposed or operative order or scheme for the construction, improvement or alteration of a trunk, special or classified road under Pt II of the Highways Act 1980 or the corresponding provisions of Pt II of the Highways Act 1959 or s 1 of the Highways Act 1971. This also applies to land required for the purpose of mitigating the adverse effect which the existence or use of a new or improved road may have on its surroundings (LCA 1973, s 74(1)).

(b) More informal proposals for highways
Land shown on plans approved by a resolution of a local highway authority[11] as comprised in the site of a highway as proposed to be constructed, improved or altered by that authority (1971 Act, s 192(1)(c)) and land identified by the Secretary of State in a written notice to the planning authority as the site of a proposed trunk or special road (1971 Act, s 192(1)(f)).

(c) Land affected by new street orders
Land which comprises all or part of a dwelling or the curtilage of such a dwelling already built (or being built) within the lines of orders prescribing the minimum width of new streets or which fronts onto a highway declared to be a new street and which comes within the prescribed minimum width of the new street (LCA 1973, s 76(1)).

3. *Compulsory Purchase Orders and Housing Needs*

(a) Compulsory Purchase Orders
Land in respect of which a compulsory purchase order is in force but in respect of which notice to treat has not yet been served and land in respect of which a compulsory purchase order has been submitted for confirmation to, or prepared in draft by, a minister (1971, s 192(1)(a); LCA 1973, s 70) or

---

10 In *Hill v Department of the Environment* [1976] NI 43, CA McGonigal LJ expressed the view that since the statutory provisions on blight are clearly designed to assist the owner of blighted property, a benevolent construction should be given to the similar (and potentially somewhat ambiguous) provisions appearing in the legislation applying in Northern Ireland.

11 A plan prepared by a department of the authority but not formally approved by resolution of the authority will not suffice, even though prospective purchasers of property included in the plan have been told that it will be required in the future—see *Fogg v Birkenhead County Borough Council* (1971) 22 P & CR 208; *Page v Borough of Gillingham* (1970) 21 P & CR 973; and *Flanagan v Long Eaton UDC* (1974) 299 Estates Gazette 620.

452 *Planning blight and injurious affection*

where land is authorised to be acquired by special enactment (1971 Act, s 192(1)(i)).

(b) New Towns and Urban Development Areas
Land included in a draft or operative order designating a new town site or within a designated or proposed urban development area (LCA 1973, s 72 and Local Government, Planning and Land Act 1980, s 147).

(c) Housing
Land indicated as proposed to be acquired under s 257 of the Housing Act 1985 as relating to a general improvement area (1971 Act, s 192(1)(h)). Land which is included in a clearance area under s 289 of the Housing Act 1985 or is land surrounded by or adjoining an area declared to be a clearance area where the local authority have determined to purchase that land (LCA 1973, s 73(1)).

Where the statutory provisions refer to land which is 'indicated' in a plan as being required for certain purposes, it would seem that a diagrammatic indication will suffice, provided, of course, that the proposals and the plan in which they appear are such as to satisfy the statutory requirements. In *Bowling v Leeds County Borough Council*[12] the Lands Tribunal held that land was 'indicated' as required for highway purposes even though the indication in the plan was diagrammatic only; in the view of the tribunal the word 'indicated' is 'a word of simple meaning which does not import any requirements of a resolution by the council or programming by it or allocation of money by it'.

Only if land falls squarely within one of the specified descriptions can the statutory requirements as to service of a blight notice be fulfilled. In *Bolton Corpn v Owen*,[13] for example, a development plan provided that a particular area was to be cleared and redeveloped for residential purposes. The owner-occupier of a dwelling-house situated in the area, having failed to find a purchaser for the house, served a blight notice on the local authority, claiming that the land came within one of the specified descriptions of land, being, he claimed, 'land allocated by a development plan for the purposes of any functions of a . . . local authority'. The Court of Appeal held, reversing the decision of the Lands Tribunal, that the claimant had not discharged the onus of showing that the land fell within that category; the statutory provisions require that land should be directly allocated for the functions of a local authority and in this case it was not directly so allocated since the development plan did not specifically state that the clearance and redevelopment was to be carried out by the local authority. The Court considered that the tribunal had erred in speculating upon the probability or otherwise of the redevelopment being carried out by the local authority rather than by private enterprise and in drawing the inference that the area could, 'as a matter of

---

12 (1974) 27 P & CR 531. See too *Mercer v Manchester Corpn* (1964) 15 P & CR 321; *Williams v Cheadle and Gatley UDC* (1966) 17 P & CR 153; and *Smith v Somerset County Council* (1966) 17 P & CR 162.
13 [1962] 1 QB 470, [1962] 1 All ER 101, CA; followed in *Ellick v Sedgemoor District Council* (1976) 32 P & CR 134 (LT). See too *Bone v Staines UDC* (1964) 15 P & CR 450; *Allen and Allen v Marple UDC* (1972) 23 P & CR 368; *Broderick v Erewash Borough Council* (1976) 34 P & CR 214; *Comley and Comley v Kent County Council* (1977) 34 P & CR 218; and *Wyse v Newcastle-under-Lyme Borough Council*, Lands Tribunal, (1979) 129 NLJ 1263.

practical politics', only be redeveloped by a local authority acting under statutory powers.

Discretionary acquisition

Despite the provisions of the Land Compensation Act 1973, which extended the specified descriptions and which enabled an owner-occupier to serve a blight notice at an earlier stage than was previously the case, there may still occur cases of planning blight which cause hardship but which do not fall within any of the statutory categories. Local authorities have been asked to deal sympathetically with cases not covered by the statutory blight provisions (eg cases where blight is caused by non-statutory proposals) and to endeavour, by means of their powers to acquire land in advance of requirements, to alleviate hardship resulting from local authority proposals which are reasonably certain to go ahead.[14]

Interests qualifying for protection

The right to serve a blight notice is restricted, broadly speaking, to those owners or lessees who might be expected to suffer greatest hardship as a result of planning blight.

Where the whole or part of a hereditament[15] or of an agricultural unit[16] is comprised in land of any of the specified descriptions, a blight notice may be served by a person who claims that he is entitled to such an interest in that hereditament or unit as qualifies for protection under the statute (1971 Act, s 193(1)). The interests which qualify for protection are broadly as follows:

(1) in the case of a hereditament:
    (a) the interest of a resident owner-occupier (1971 Act, s 192(4)(b));
    (b) the interest of a (non-resident) owner-occupier of a hereditament the rateable value of which does not exceed a prescribed amount— presently £2,250[17] (1971 Act, ss 192(3),(4)(a); 207(1);
(2) in the case of an agricultural unit, the interest of an owner-occupier (1971 Act, s 192(5)).

For the purposes of the provisions on planning blight the phrases 'owner-occupier' and 'resident owner-occupier' bear the somewhat specialised meanings given them by s 203 of the 1971 Act; it may be observed in particular that in order to qualify as an owner-occupier or resident owner-occupier certain conditions as to period of occupation must be satisfied, and that 'owner-occupier' does not bear the same meaning when used in relation to a hereditament as it does when used in relation to an agricultural unit— occupation of an agricultural unit must be of the whole unit, whereas occupation of a hereditament need only be of a 'substantial part' (1971 Act, s 203). Where the owner of a house had left it empty but had stored certain

14 See MHLG circulars 48/59 paras 63 and 64 and 15/69 para 26. The advice contained in those circulars still applies despite the passing of the 1973 Act; see circular 73/73 para 74.
15 Ie, the aggregate of the land which forms the subject of a single entry in the valuation list— see 1971 Act, s 207(1)—(4). See too *Ley and Ley v Kent County Council* (1976) 31 P & CR 439.
16 As to the meaning of 'agricultural unit' see 1971 Act, s 207(1).
17 See the Town and Country Planning (Limit of Annual Value) Order 1973 (which came into operation on 1 April 1985).

articles in outbuildings, it was held by the Court of Appeal that he could not be said to be an 'owner-occupier' for the purposes of the blight provisions.[18]

An 'owner's interest' means a freehold interest or the interest of a lessee under a lease with at least three years to run at the date of service of a blight notice (see 1971 Act, s 203(4)).[19]

In certain circumstances a mortgagee has power to serve a blight notice (1971 Act, s 201). Where a claimant dies after serving a blight notice, the person who has succeeded to his interest in the hereditament or agricultural unit may carry on the proceedings (1971 Act, s 200), and in certain circumstances the personal representative of a person who at the time of his death was entitled to an interest which would have qualified for protection may serve a blight notice (LCA 1973, s 79). Section 204 of the 1971 Act makes special provision for partnerships.

Injury to interest in land

It is for the person serving a blight notice, the claimant, to establish that the blighting proposals have resulted in injury to his interest in the land in question.

The claimant must show that he has made reasonable endeavours to sell his interest but that in consequence of the fact that the land or a part of it was, or was likely to be, comprised in land of any of the specified descriptions, he has been unable to sell that interest except at a price substantially lower than that for which it might reasonably have been expected to sell if no part of the land were, or were likely to be, included in such proposals (1971 Act, s 193(1)(c), (d); LCA 1973, s 77). It is thus now possible, in contrast to the position prior to the Land Compensation Act 1973, to satisfy the statutory requirements even though the attempts to sell the land were made before the land actually came within one of the specified descriptions.[20]

The onus[1] is upon the claimant to show that his inability to sell the land at a reasonable price is due to the blighting proposals and that the reduction in value resulting from the blighting proposals is substantial. In *Malcolm Campbell v Glasgow Corpn*[2] a blight notice was served in respect of a shop affected by road-widening proposals, the owner-occupiers of the shop claiming that they had been unable to dispose of it at a reasonable price. The authority on whom the notice was served attributed the claimants' failure to sell the shop to a number of factors, including the proximity of a new shopping arcade, an excess of older shops left vacant in the area and traffic restrictions in the vicinity of the shop. The Lands Tribunal for Scotland declined to adopt 'the simple view' that as the claimants had been unable to obtain any offer at all for the shop and since at the very least there was bound

18 *Ministry of Transport v Holland* (1962) 14 P & CR 259; followed in *Segal v Manchester Corpn* (1966) 18 P & CR 112. See, too, *Sparkes v Secretary of State for Wales* (1973) 27 P & CR 545; and *Holmes v Knowsley Borough Council* (1977) 35 P & CR 119.
19 In *Empire Motors (Swansea) Ltd v Swansea City Council* (1972) 24 P & CR 377 it was held that where lessees had two years and nine months of their lease to run, the fact that they had an option to renew the lease did not turn that interest into a qualifying one.
20 See Land Compensation Act 1973, s 77(2).
 1 On onus of proof in relation to blight notices see p 457, below.
 2 1972 SLT (Lands Tr) 8; compare *Bowling v Leeds Borough Council* (1974) 27 P & CR 531; and *Stubbs v West Hartlepool Corpn* (1961) 12 P & CR 365.

to be some element of prejudice attributable to the road-widening proposals, that was enough to entitle the tribunal to declare the notice valid.

The tribunal held that although some element of loss might well be attributable to the road-widening proposals, the claimants had not discharged the onus of proving that it was the road proposals rather than the other adverse factors which had caused a substantial erosion in the value of the shop, nor had they established to the tribunal's satisfaction (a) the price for which the shop might reasonably have been expected to sell if no part had been included in the road proposals and (b) that the only price obtainable was substantially lower; to establish that, it would have been necessary in the circumstances of this case for the claimants to disentangle the effect of the road-widening proposals from the effect of the other adverse factors and that they had failed to do. In this case the tribunal also stated that they did not think that 'simply to invite offers for a property previously advertised for sale at £8,250' sufficiently indicated such willingness on the part of the sellers to reduce their price as to justify the contention by the claimants that they could obtain no price at all for the shop.

What constitutes 'reasonable endeavours to sell' property is a question which will depend on the circumstances of the particular case. Normally it will be necessary to put the property in the hands of estate agents, but in special circumstances it may be sufficient to put a notice in a shop window or to approach particular would-be buyers. For example, in *Lade and Lade v Brighton Corpn*[3] the Lands Tribunal, though they accepted that in most cases the normal procedure would be to advertise the property in the press and to circulate particulars, held in the somewhat special circumstances of the case that, as it was likely that only visiting dealers would have been interested in the antique shop in question, the statutory requirement had been satisfied by the placing of a notice in the shop window and the notification of visiting traders. Nothing short of putting the land on the market will satisfy the statutory provisions; professional advice to the effect that it would be pointless and a waste of time and money to endeavour to sell the land will not suffice.[4]

It will normally not be necessary to set up a forceful selling programme and in *Mancini v Coventry City Council*[5] the Lands Tribunal held that it was sufficient to put the sale in the hands of estate agents. On the other hand in *Glodwick Mutual Institute and Social Club v Oldham Metropolitan Borough Council*[6] the Lands Tribunal found that claimants' endeavours were not reasonable where they informed those who responded to advertisements that the property was subject to a compulsory purchase order but failed to inform them that the authority had indicated that acquisition would not proceed.

Service of blight notice

A blight notice should be in one of the three forms prescribed in Sch 1 to the Town and Country Planning General Regulations 1976 (see reg 18), and should be served on the 'appropriate authority', broadly speaking the government department, local authority or other body by whom, in terms of

3 (1971) 22 P & CR 737.
4 See *Perkins v West Wiltshire District Council* (1975) 31 P & CR 427.
5 (1982) 44 P & CR 114.
6 [1979] RVR 197.

the blighting proposals, the land is liable to be acquired (see 1971 Act, ss 193(1), 205(1). Any question as to which of two or more authorities is the 'appropriate authority' is determined by the Secretary of State (1971 Act, s 205(2)). It seems that it is possible for the same piece of land to come within two specified descriptions at the same time and so there can be two, but not more, appropriate authorities. This was so held in *R v Secretary of State for the Environment, Dorset County Council and Saunders ex p Bournemouth Borough Council*[7] where Mann J upheld a determination of the Secretary of State under s 205(2) that both the county and the borough council were the appropriate authority for part of a piece of land. A blight notice must relate to the whole of the claimant's interest in the hereditament or agricultural unit in question (1971 Act, s 193(1)). The blight notice has to state the specified description of land into which it is claimed that the blighted land falls. Care should be taken to ensure that the correct head is detailed as the Lands Tribunal has no power to allow amendment.[8]

A blight notice may be withdrawn by the claimant within the period set out in s 198 of the 1971 Act.

Counter-notice

Within two months of service of a blight notice the appropriate authority may serve on the claimant a counter-notice,[9] objecting to the blight notice (1971 Act. s 194(1)). Under s 194(2) of the 1971 Act objection may be made by the appropriate authority on one or more of the following grounds: (a) that no part of the land comes within any of the specified descriptions (see p 449 above); or (b) that unless compelled to do so by virtue of the blight provisions, they do not intend to acquire any part of the hereditament or, in the case of an agricultural unit, any part of 'the affected area' (ie, so much of the unit as falls within any of the specified descriptions—1971 Act, s 207(1));[10] or (c) that they intend to acquire only a part[11] of the hereditament or affected area; or (d) that in the case of land falling within paragraph (a) or (bb) or (c), but not paragraph (d), (e) or (f) of s 192(1), the appropriate authority do not propose to acquire any part of the hereditament or, as the case may be, any part of the affected area, during the period of fifteen years (or such longer period as they may specify) from the date of the counter-notice;[12] or (e) that the claimant was not on the date of service of the blight notice entitled to an interest in the land; or (f) that the claimant's interest is not one qualifying for protection (see p 453 above); or (g) that the statutory

---

7 [1987] JPL 357.
8 See *Bryant and Bryant v City of Bristol* (1969) 20 P & CR 742. It may, however, be possible to start afresh with a notice specifying the correct head.
9 A counter-notice should be in the form prescribed in Sch 1 to the Town and Country Planning General Regulations 1976.
10 See, for example, *McDermott and McDermott v Department of Transport* (1984) 48 P & CR 351.
11 In such a case it may be possible for the claimant to employ the compulsory purchase rules on severance in order to compel the authority to acquire the whole of the hereditament or the whole of the affected area—see p 459, below.
12 The Local Government, Planning and Land Act 1980 (Sch 15, para 18) restores the original wording of para (d) as regards counter-notices served on or after 13 November 1980. Between 1 September 1976 and 13 November 1980 the Community Land Act 1975 had reduced the period to ten years and broadened the application of para (d).

provisions relating to endeavours to sell the interest and relating to injury to the claimant's interest (see p 454 above) are not fulfilled.[13]

An authority may not make objection on ground (d) if objection could be made on the grounds specified in paragraph (b) above (1971) Act, s 194(3)); if, therefore, the authority do not intend to acquire the land at all, the 'fifteen year' ground of objection is not to be employed.

Special provision is made as to the grounds on which objection may be made to a blight notice served by mortgagee or by the personal representative of a deceased person (1971 Act, s 201(6) and LCA 1973, s 78(3)).

Where a successful objection is made on grounds (b), (c) or (d) above—ie, where the authority disclaim an intention to acquire—any relevant compulsory purchase orders in force shall cease to have effect (1971 Act, s 199). However, this does not prevent the acquiring authority serving fresh compulsory purchase orders even within the fifteen year period, but an assurance has been given that where a fifteen year disclaimer has been given, very great weight will be given to this fact in deciding whether to confirm the order.[14] A successful counter-notice on the ground that the authority only propose to acquire part (s 194(2)(c)) does not affect any rights to require the whole of the land to be taken (1971 Act, s 202).

Counties, London boroughs and district councils are empowered to make advances to enable any person to acquire a hereditament or agricultural unit in respect of which a counter-notice employing the 'fifteen year' ground of objection has been served, provided that in the case of a hereditament the rateable value does not exceed the amount prescribed for the purposes of s 192(4)(a) (above)—presently £2,250 (1971 Act, s 256).

Reference of objection to Lands Tribunal

Within two months of service of a counter-notice the claimant may require that the objection be referred to the Lands Tribunal (1971 Act, s 195(1)). On such a reference the tribunal is to consider the matters set out in the blight notice and the grounds of objection specified in the counter-notice. The onus of showing to the satisfaction of the tribunal that the objection is not well-founded lies upon the claimant[15] except that where the authority have disclaimed an intention to acquire—ie, where objection has been made on grounds (b), (c) or (d) above—the burden of proof lies upon the authority (1971 Act, s 195(2), (3)).

In *Mancini v Coventry City Council*[16] the Court of Appeal held that the material date, as at which the tribunal has to determine whether an objection is or is not well-founded, is the date when the objection was made, ie, the date of the counter-notice; an event which occurs after the date of service of

13 This ground of objection allows a counter to both s 193(1)(c)—that the claimant has made reasonable endeavours to sell his interest—and s 193(1)(d)—that it has not been possible to sell except at an unduly low price. It would seem that an authority which objects on the ground that one of these conditions is not satisfied cannot put to the Lands Tribunal arguments supporting an objection to the other condition—see *Trustees of St John's Church, Galashiels v Borders Regional Council* 1976 SLT (Lands Tr) 39.
14 See HC Debates Standing Committee G, 28 March 1968, Col 729.
15 See *Bolton Corpn v Owen* [1962] 1 QB 470, [1962] 1 All ER 101, CA.
16 (1983) 270 Estates Gazette 419. See, too, *Louisville Investments Ltd v Basingstoke District Council* (1976) 32 P & CR 419; and *Cedar Holdings Ltd v Walsall Metropolitan Borough Council* (1979) 38 P & CR 715.

the counter-notice—for example, the withdrawal of the compulsory purchase order which gave rise to the blight—will not, it seems, affect the situation. On the other hand, it also means that a change of mind after the service of the blight notice but before the service of the counter-notice can provide the basis for the counter-notice.

It would seem that an objection on the ground that the authority do not intend to acquire the land may not be effective unless the authority take some formal step to remove the blight. In *Sabey and Sabey v Hartlepool County Borough Council*[17] the Lands Tribunal stated that 'in placing the onus on a local authority to show that an objection of this kind is well-founded, Parliament must have intended the Lands Tribunal to look at all the facts of the case and to dismiss the objection unless satisfied that an effective protection against "blight" is provided'. In this case the tribunal found that, in the absence of amendment of the development plan, the simple statement in the counter-notice that the authority did not intend to acquire any part of the land did little to dispel the blight; for that reason the tribunal refused to uphold the objection. The tribunal has, however, no residual discretion to consider hardship.

This was made clear by the Court of Appeal in *Mancini v Coventry City Council*[18] where it was held that hardship and the alleviation of hardship are irrelevant to the question of the validity of an objection in the counter-notice; the earlier decision of the Lands Tribunal[19] suggesting that hardship could be taken into account in assessing the 'reasonableness' of the objection was disapproved.

The Lands Tribunal has no jurisdiction to hear the objections of an authority who have not served a counter-notice within the statutory period, or to deal with any objection not stated in the counter-notice.[20] Thus in cases concerning the Lands Tribunal for Scotland, a failure to serve a counter-notice has been held to mean that the Tribunal could not entertain any challenge to the blight notice.[1] So if a ground of challenge to a blight notice is not specified in s 194, there would seem no way by which this matter can be raised in the Lands Tribunal.[2] It might be possible for an authority to seek a declaration that a blight notice was invalid. However, the reasoning of the House of Lords in *Essex County Council v Essex Inc Congregational Church*

---

17 (1970) 21 P & CR 448. See too *Duke of Wellington Social Club and Institute Ltd v Blyth Borough Council* (1964) 15 P & CR 212; *Rawson v Ministry of Health* (1966) 17 P & CR 239; *Louisville Investments Ltd v Basingstoke District Council* (1976) 32 P & CR 419; and *McKinnon Campbell v Greater Manchester Council* (1976) 33 P & CR 110. Cf *Mancini v Coventry City Council* (above).

18 See, above, and see also *McDermott and McDermott v Department of Transport* (1984) 48 P & CR 351.

19 See *Duke of Wellington Social Club and Institute Ltd v Blyth Borough Council* (1964) 15 P & CR 212.

20 See *Lockers Estates (Holdings) Ltd v Oadby UDC* (1970) 21 P & CR 836 and *Parker and Parker v West Midlands County Council* (1978) 38 P & CR 720. In certain circumstances, however, the authority are empowered to serve a fresh counter-notice specifying different grounds of objection (see LCA 1973, ss 68(6) and 69(3)).

1 *Church of Scotland General Trustees v Helensburgh Council* (1983) 25 P & CR 105 and *Ibbotson v Tayside Regional Council* 1978 SLT (Lands Tr) 25.

2 See *Binns v Secretary of State for Transport* (1985) 50 P & CR 468 where it was held by the Lands Tribunal that a contravention of s 193(2)(a) could not be raised in a counter-notice and so the Lands Tribunal was not concerned with such a defect in the blight notice.

Union[3] would suggest that you must use the statutory machinery and that s 196 has the effect of preventing a challenge to the validity of a blight notice except by way of a counter-notice.

Effect of a valid blight notice

If no counter-notice is served or if a counter-notice is withdrawn or is not upheld by the Lands Tribunal, the appropriate authority are deemed to be authorised[4] to acquire compulsorily the claimant's interest in the hereditament or, in the case of an agricultural unit, the interest of the claimant in so far as it subsists in the affected area, and to have served a notice to treat in respect thereof (1971 Act, s 196(1)). This constructive notice to treat cannot be withdrawn by the authority under the power conferred by s 31 of the Land Compensation Act 1961 (1971 Act, s 208); where, however, the blight notice itself is withdrawn, any deemed notice to treat is thereupon deemed to be withdrawn (1971 Act, s 198(1)).

It may be observed that in the case of an agricultural unit, only the 'affected area' will normally be acquired[5] though it is the unsaleability of the unit as a whole that must be established.

Where the authority have objected on the ground that they intend to acquire part of the land only, and their objection is accepted by the claimant or is upheld by the Lands Tribunal, the authority are deemed to have served notice to treat in respect of that part only (1971 Act, s 198(3)).

Severance of land

In a case where the authority object to a blight notice on the ground that they only require to take part of the land, the right of the claimant under ordinary compulsory purchase principles to require the acquiring authority in certain circumstances to take the whole of the land[6] is preserved by s 202 of the 1971 Act[7] The claimant will thus sometimes be able to compel the authority to acquire the whole of the hereditament or, in the case of an agricultural unit, the whole of the affected area, even though the authority only require part of the hereditament or affected area.[8]

Section 79 of the Land Compensation Act 1973 provides that the owner-occupier of an agricultural unit may include in a blight notice a claim that the 'unaffected area' (ie that part of the unit not falling within any of the specified descriptions of land) is not reasonably capable of being farmed,

---

3 [1963] AC 808, [1963] 1 All ER 326.
4 Under the 'appropriate enactment—see 1971 Act, s 206.
5 See, however, LCA 1973, s 79.
6 See p 462, below.
7 In *Hurley v Cheshire County Council* (1976) 31 P & CR 433 the Lands Tribunal inclined to the view that where an authority objected to a blight notice relating to a house and garden on the ground that they proposed to take only part of the garden for road purposes, the onus lay upon the authority to satisfy the tribunal that the piece of garden ground could be taken without seriously affecting the amenity or convenience of the house. As to the difficulties which may face a claimant who wishes to compel an authority to take the whole rather than part of property see *Lake v Cheshire County Council* (1976) 32 P & CR 143.
8 In *Hill v Department of the Environment* [1976] NI 43 the Court of Appeal in Northern Ireland accepted that a temporary loss in market value could amount to material detriment and thus enable a landowner to require the appropriate authority to acquire the whole of his land.

either by itself or in conjunction with 'other relevant land',[9] as a separate agricultural unit. Where such a claim succeeds, the authority are required to purchase the claimant's interest in the whole unit (see LCA 1973, ss 80 and 81).

Compensation

Where a blight notice takes effect, compensation for the land acquired will be assessed on the normal compulsory purchase basis;[10] any depreciation attributable to the prospect of compulsory purchase is therefore to be disregarded, so that the depressing effect of the blighting proposals must be ignored (see Land Compensation Act 1961, s 9). Where acquisition takes place in consequence of a blight notice there is, however, no entitlement to a home loss or farm loss payment (LCA 1973, ss 29(5) and 34(6)).

C INJURIOUS AFFECTION

In this part of this chapter we are concerned not with the land to be acquired for a scheme of public works, but with neighbouring land the enjoyment of which is adversely affected by the carrying out of the scheme. Subject to one exception (mentioned below) Parliament has not provided a full remedy in such cases but has sought to alleviate hardship by providing for the payment of compensation in some, but by no means all, cases of injurious affection.

The statutory provisions are complex and may conveniently be considered under four separate headings: land held together with land acquired for the scheme; notices of objection to severance; other neighbouring land adversely affected by the *construction* of the works; and other neighbouring land adversely affected by the *use* of the works.

1 *Land held together with land acquired for the scheme*

Section 7 of the Compulsory Purchase Act 1965 (re-enacting s 63 of the Lands Clauses Consolidation Act 1845) provides that in assessing compensation for the compulsory purchase of land regard is to be had not only to the value of the land to be taken 'but also to the damage, if any, to be sustained by the owner of the land by reason of the severing of the land purchased from the other land of the owner, or otherwise injuriously affecting that other land'.[11] Both severance and other injurious affection may arise where part only of a parcel of land is compulsorily acquired. Our concern in this chapter is with 'other injurious affection'. Severance refers to the physical damage caused to land remaining with the owner by severing the part required for the scheme; other injurious affection refers to the depreciation in the value of the retained land caused by the scheme for which the part was acquired. For example, if part of a person's land is acquired for the construction of a major road, he is entitled to claim compensation for the adverse effects (the 'other

---

9 As to the meaning of this phrase, see LCA 1973, s 79(2).
10 Certain special rules on compensation are, however, preserved for the two types of case specified in s 197 of the 1971 Act.
11 Section 20 of the 1965 Act makes provision for the payment of compensation for other injurious affection to persons having no greater interest in land than as tenants for a year or from year to year.

injurious affection') which the construction and use of the road will have on his remaining land.[12]

The remaining land must, however, have been held together with the land acquired. In other words, the pieces of land must have been 'so near to each other and so situated that the possession and control of each gives an enhanced value to all of them'.[13] This requirement may be illustrated by the decision in *Nisbet Hamilton v Northern Lighthouses Comrs*.[14] The Commissioners compulsorily acquired a small island in the Firth of Forth on which to construct a lighthouse. The island formed part of an estate but was located one mile from the mainland and one and a half miles from the main house on the estate. The landowner's claim included an item for damage to the amenity of the main house which would occur if a foghorn was erected on the island. The court held there was no direct link between the land taken and the land alleged to be injuriously affected. They were not 'held together' for the purpose of s 63.

Curiously, it would seem that the scope of a claim for compensation under s 7 for injurious affection may be wider than the scope of an action for nuisance. Although the list of activities which may be recognised by the law as a nuisance is open-ended, there are, as we have indicated already, some activities which in the ordinary sense of the word could be said to disturb a person in the enjoyment of his property and which may depress the value of the property but which will not be regarded as a nuisance. Loss of profits, loss of a pleasant view and loss of privacy are examples.[15] In these cases there is said to be *damnum sine injuria*. The test would appear to be whether the damage is material rather than sentimental or trivial. The dividing line is very much a matter of fact and degree to be determined on the circumstances of each case.

In contrast, the test for compensation for injurious affection would appear to be *damnum* alone. This is illustrated by the decision of the House of Lords in the case of *Duke of Buccleuch v Metropolitan Board of Works*.[16] The claimant leased a house and gardens fronting onto the River Thames together with a causeway jutting out into the river. The Board of Works, who were in process of constructing the Victoria Embankment on the foreshore of the river, acquired the causeway and land along the shore. The embankment was to be used as a public highway, thus cutting off the claimant's direct access to the river. Compensation was clearly due to the claimant for the taking of the land and the causeway and for the injury to the house as a result of its being denied access to the river. The question at issue was whether the claimant was entitled to compensation for depreciation caused to his property by the conversion of the land between it and the river into a highway and its use by the public. The majority of the House of Lords had no

---

12 Section 44 of the Land Compensation Act 1973 provides that compensation for injurious affection shall be assessed by reference to the whole of the works and not only the part situated on the land compulsorily acquired from the claimant. This overcomes the difficulty encountered by the claimants in *City of Glasgow Union Rly Co v Hunter* (1870) 8 M 156; and *Edwards v Minister of Transport* [1964] 2 QB 134, [1964] 2 WLR 515, CA.

13 *Cowper Essex v Acton Local Board* (1889) 14 App Cas 153, per Lord Watson at 167, HL.

14 (1886) 13 R 710. See also *City of Glasgow Union Rly Co v Hunter* (1870) 8 M 156.

15 *White v Works and Public Buildings Comrs* (1870) 22 LT 591; *R v Pearce, ex p London School Board* (1898) 67 LJQB 842; and *Re Penny and South Eastern Rly Co* (1857) 7 E & B 660.

16 (1872) LR 5 HL 418. See too *Cowper Essex v Acton Local Board* (1889) 14 App. Cas. 153.

difficulty in concluding that compensation was due under s 63 of the 1845 Act for any depreciation in the value of the land retained resulting from the exercise of the powers of the acquiring authority, including the depreciating effects of loss of privacy and amenity.

It would seem, therefore, that a landowner, part of whose land has been taken for the scheme, is well placed as a result of this interpretation to recover compensation for all damage resulting from other injurious affection.

2 *Notices of objection to severance*

Where, in the exercise of compulsory powers, an acquiring authority propose to take part only of a parcel of land, the adverse effects of the authority's scheme on the land to be left with the landowner may in some cases be very severe. In such circumstances the landowner may feel that it would be preferable from his point of view for the acquiring authority to take the whole of his land (at its full market value) rather than that he should be left with part, even though he will be compensated for the land and for injurious affection. In such a case statute allows the landowner to serve on the acquiring authority what is generally referred to as a 'notice of objection to severance'.[17]

The broad effect of serving such a notice is to give the acquiring authority a choice. They may decide to proceed no further with the acquisition of any part of the land in question; or they may agree to acquire the lot; or they may persist with their intention to take part only, in which case the notice will be referred to the Lands Tribunal for a decision.

The notice of objection to severance, as its name implies, is concerned principally with severance, ie the physical damage caused to the remaining land by severing the part. The detailed provisions governing such notices are, therefore, outside the scope of this book.

However, an amendment introduced by the Land Compensation Act 1973 indicates that in some cases the injurious effects of the public works for which the land is to be taken may have a material bearing on the outcome of a notice. The test which the Lands Tribunal will apply to a notice of objection to severance directed at a house, building or factory is whether the part can be taken without material detriment or damage to the remainder; and for a park or garden belonging to a house the test is whether the part can be taken without seriously affecting the amenity or convenience of the house.[18] Section 58 of the Land Compensation Act 1973 provides that in applying these tests the tribunal is to take into account not only the effects of severance, but also the use to be made of the part to be acquired, and if the part is being acquired for a scheme of public works extending to other land, then the tribunal is to have regard to the effect of the whole of the use to be made of the other land.

17 See Compulsory Purchase Act 1965, s 8(1); Compulsory Purchase (Vesting Declarations) Act 1981, s 12 and Sch 1; and LCA 1973, ss 53–59.
18 Compulsory Purchase (Vesting Declarations) Act 1981, s 12 Sch 1: Compulsory Purchase Act, s 8(1). The correct way to judge the matter in such a case is to consider whether that part of the property remaining after part has been taken is less useful or less valuable in some significant degree compared with the position obtaining prior to acquisition—see *McMillan v Strathclyde Regional Council* 1984 SLT (Lands Tr) 25.

Where this provision operates, the notice of objection to severance goes further than the compensation provisions of s 7 of the 1965 Act. It provides a full remedy for the landowner in that he can compel the acquiring authority to purchase, at a price which ignores the effects of blight, land which is seriously blighted by their scheme.

3 *Other neighbouring land adversely affected by the construction of the works*

Earlier in this chapter it was suggested that where bodies carrying out schemes of public works have statutory immunity from an action for nuisance, it is reasonable to expect that Parliament will make provision for compensation in lieu. The decision of the House of Lords in *Hammersmith and City Rly Co v Brand*[19] meant that the statutory authorisation of the use of public works could result in the depreciation of the value of land without there being any right of redress. However, s 68 of the Lands Clauses Consolidation Act 1845 (endorsed by s 10 of the Compulsory Purchase Act 1965) provides a right to compensation 'in respect of any lands—which shall have been taken for or injuriously affected by the execution of the works . . .' This section was probably intended to deal with the situation where land was taken *before* compensation was assessed[20] but has been interpreted by the courts to give a right to compensation where no land is taken.

The right to compensation under s 68 is defined by reference to 'four rules' which are said to have been laid down in the House of Lords decision in *Metropolitan Board of Works v McCarthy*.[1]

Rule 1 is that the action giving rise to the depreciation must be authorised by statute. So if the damage is avoidable, then any rights are in tort and not under s 68.[2]

Rule 2 is that the cause of depreciation would be otherwise actionable at common law. So no rights arise, if, as in the case of the loss of a view, there would be no right to obtain damages in nuisance.

Rule 3 is that the claimant must show that the damage is to land or to an interest in land.

Rule 4 is that the loss must be caused by the 'execution of the works' and not by the use of the land after the acquiring authority have carried out those works. This last rule is perhaps the most controversial as it means that the most long-lasting and substantial damage is not compensatable.

4 *Other neighbouring land adversely affected by the use of the works*

In view of the distinction which the courts made between 'construction' and 'use', compensation for blight or injurious affection to land unconnected with land taken for the scheme could fall substantially short of the compensation obtainable under s 7 of the Compulsory Purchase Act 1965. This distinction was brought very forcefully to the notice of the public during the era of the construction of urban motorways. The bringing into use of roads such as Westway in London resulted in many householders being injuriously

19 (1869) LR 4 HL 171.
20 See Davies, *Law of Compulsory Purchase and Compensation*, 4th edn p 174.
 1 (1874) LR 7 HL 243.
 2 See *Clowes v Staffordshire Potteries Waterworks Co* (1872) 8 Ch App 125.

affected by a substantial volume of traffic passing close to their houses at all time of the day and night. As this damage was being caused by the use of the road and not by its construction, it was damage for which no compensation could be claimed. Similar problems resulted from the enlargement of airports. The problem was neatly summarised by JUSTICE in 1969:

> 'We believe it to be a sad commentary on the present law that an owner of land in an area through which a motorway is to be constructed should prefer that the motorway takes the whole of his property rather than go near it.'[3]

The extent of public dissatisfaction coupled with the publication in 1972 of the report of the Urban Motorways Committee[4] led to the issuing in October 1972 of the White Paper *Development and Compensation—Putting People First.*[5] In the White Paper the government recognised this area of hardship and committed itself to a new statutory right to compensation. This right is set out in Part I of the Land Compensation Act 1973. In addition, Part II of the 1973 Act confers upon public bodies certain powers to mitigate the injurious effect of public works. The Act does not alter the position as regards compensation for injurious affection resulting from the construction of public works. Instead, it provides an additional right to compensation for damage resulting from the use of new public works for certain people from whom no land is taken and who are barred from bringing an action at common law for nuisance.[6] The following is a summary of the provisions.

A claim may be made under Pt I of the Land Compensation Act 1973 in respect of depreciation resulting from one or more of the following physical factors caused by the use of the public works: noise, vibration, smell, fumes, smoke, artificial lighting, and a discharge on to the land of any solid or liquid substance[7] (s 1(1) and (2)). The source of the physical factors must be situated on or in the public works in question except that physical factors caused by aircraft arriving at or departing from an aerodrome are to be treated as caused by the use of the aerodrome whether or not the aircraft is within the boundaries of the aerodrome (s 1(5)). Loss of privacy, loss of a view and general loss of amenity are not included in the prescribed factors[8] so that the right to compensation for this form of injurious affection is less generous that that in s 7 of the Compulsory Purchase Act 1965.

---

3 *Compensation for Compulsory Acquisition and Remedies for Planning Restrictions* (Stevens, 1969) and *Supplemental Report* (1972).
4 *New Roads in Towns. Report by the Urban Motorways Committee* (HMSO, 1971).
5 Cmnd 5124 (1972).
6 A claim under the Land Compensation Act 1973 is in effect a substitute for an action for nuisance at common law and can therefore only be made where there is statutory immunity from an action for nuisance. If a claim under the 1973 Act is resisted by an authority on the ground that no statutory immunity exists as regards use of the works, the authority are not entitled to rely on any such immunity in an action for nuisance caused by the physical factors covered by the 1973 Act.
7 The Act does not require that the injury should be of a permanent nature—see *Shepherd v Lancashire County Council* (1976) 33 P & CR 296.
8 Depreciation resulting from the mere proximity of a refuse tip will therefore not give rise to a claim (see *Shepherd v Lancashire County Council* (1976) P & CR 296), nor will depreciation resulting from increased danger or apprehension of danger from traffic (see *Hickmott v Dorset County Council* (1975) 30 P & CR 237).

The public works, the use of which may give rise to a claim, comprise any road, any aerodrome, and any other works or land provided or used in the exercise of statutory powers (s 1(3)). The definition of public works as including land suggests that there could be a right to compensation when, as in opencast coal mining, it is the land rather than any works which is used in the exercise of statutory powers. Depreciation resulting from alterations to the carriageway of an existing road;[9] from runway or apron alterations at an aerodrome, from reconstruction, extension or alterations of other public works, or from a change of use in respect of any public works other than a road or aerodrome may also give rise to a claim (s 9(1), (2) and (3)). Excluded from the list is depreciation resulting from a traffic regulation order or from an intensification in the use of existing public works. For example, the opening of a new major road may substantially increase the volume of traffic on an existing road which now feeds into the new road; the properties adjoining the existing road may suffer depreciation in value as a result but such depreciation will not give rise to a claim under Pt I of the 1973 Act.

The claimant must have a qualifying interest and must have acquired it before the 'relevant date';[10] this is the date on which the public works in question first come into use[11] (ss 1(1) and (9), 2(1) and 9(2)). The qualifying interests are similar, although not identical, to the interests which qualify for protection under the blight notice provisions. They are:

(i) the owner of a dwelling;
(ii) the owner-occupier of an agricultural unit;
(iii) the owner-occupier of a hereditament the annual value of which does not exceed a prescribed amount—presently £2,500[12] (s 2(1), (2) and (3)).

The definition of the terms 'owner's interest'[13] and 'owner-occupier' bear somewhat specialised meanings (see s 2(4) and (5)). An owner's interest includes that of a lessee with at least three years of his lease still to run (s 2(4)). Where the owner's interest in a dwelling carries the right of occupation then the owner must be in occupation to qualify (s 2(2)(b)). Investment owners (other than of dwellings) and owner-occupiers of substantial business premises will not qualify.

A period of twelve months must normally elapse after the relevant date before a claim can be made (the 'first claim day')[14] (LCA 1973, s 3(2) as

---

9 For the purposes of this provision an alteration to a carriageway comprises an alteration (otherwise than by resurfacing) to its location, width or level or the construction of an additional carriageway (see s 9(5)).
10 There is an exception for an interest acquired by inheritance from a person who acquired that interest before the relevant date (s 11). For the position of certain categories of mortgagees and trustees see s 10.
11 As to the date on which works are first used see *Davies v Mid-Glamorgan County Council* (1978) 38 P & CR 727; and *Shepherd v Lancashire County Council* (1976) 33 P & CR 296.
12 Town and Country Planning (Limit of Annual Value) Order 1973.
13 The meaning of this phrase was considered in *Inglis v British Airports Authority* 1978 SLT (Lands Tr) 30.
14 A claim can, however, be made during the twelve month period by an owner who has made a contract for disposing of the land, provided that the claim is made before the land is disposed of; compensation is not payable before the first claim day (s 3(3)). As to the effect of this provision see *Inglis v British Airports* 1978 SLT (Lands Tr) 30.

amended by the Local Government, Planning and Land Act 1980, s 112(2)). This allows time for the use of the public works to build up to something like its normal level so that a realistic assessment can be made of any depreciation in the value of neighbouring property. Claims may be submitted to the responsible authority at any time during the five years following the first claim day.[15]

Compensation is assessed on the basis of the depreciating effect of the level of use of the works as at the first claim day but account may be taken of any intensification of use which may then be reasonably expected (s 4(2)). The assessment is based on rules (2) to (4) of s 5 of the Land Compensation Act 1961 (LCA 1973, s 4(4)(b)) by reference to prices ruling on the first claim day (s 4(1)). The only planning assumption that may be made in valuing the land which is the subject of the claim is that planning permission would be granted for the categories of development set out in Sch 8 to the 1971 Act[16] (LCA 1973, s 5(1), (2) and (4)). Otherwise it is to be assumed that planning permission would not be granted for development (see s 5(3)). Where there is a right to insulation works (below), that benefit will be taken into account for compensation purposes, as will the benefit of remedial works carried out by the authority (s 4(3)). Any appreciation in the value of the land, or of other adjoining land to which the claimant is entitled in the same capacity, which is attributable to the existence or use of the public works is to be set off against any compensation (s 6(1)). No payment will be made on a claim unless the amount of compensation exceeds £50. Interest is due on the compensation from the date of claim until the date of payment (s 18). Any question of disputed compensation is to be referred to and determined by the Lands Tribunal (s 16).[17]

Part II of the Land Compensation Act 1973 contains provisions enabling public authorities to mitigate the injurious effects of their schemes. Section 20 empowers the Secretary of State to make regulations imposing a duty or conferring a power on the responsible authorities to insulate buildings against noise or to make grants available for this purpose. Regulations have been made under this power requiring roads authorities in specified circumstances to install or to make grants in aid of the installation of noise insulation in residential property adversely affected by a road scheme.[18]

Roads authorities are given wide powers to carry out works—for example, the planting of trees and shrubs and the laying out of grassed areas—designed to mitigate the adverse effects of a road scheme, and to acquire land by agreement or compulsorily for this purpose (ss 22(1) and 23). Furthermore, they may arrange for the provision of mitigating works by means of agreements entered into with owners of land in the vicinity of the road (s 24).

Where works for the construction or improvement of a road render the continued occupation of a dwelling impracticable, the roads authority may meet the reasonable expenses of obtaining suitable alternative accommodation until the works are completed (s 28). If the enjoyment of land is seriously affected by the construction, improvement, or use of a road the authority

---

15 Section 113 of the Local Government, Planning and Land Act 1980 safeguards certain claims for compensation for depreciation which were out of time when the 1980 Act was passed.
16 The categories of development specified in Sch 8 are outlined in ch 15.
17 As to the method of assessing such claims see *Marchant v Secretary of State for Transport* [1979] RVR 113.
18 The Noise Insulation Regulations 1975.

may acquire the land by agreement if the interest of the vendor is one which would qualify for protection under the blight notice provisions (s 22(2)).

Similar powers are given to other authorities carrying out public works (with the exception of the power to acquire land compulsorily) for the provision of mitigating works and power to enter into agreements (ss 26(1) and (2), 27 and 28).

D CONCLUSION

Two general points may be drawn from this discussion of the statutory provisions dealing with blight and injurious affection. First of all it would appear that successive governments have been careful to avoid imposing too great a burden on those promoting schemes of public works. Any broadening of the application of the statutory provisions dealing with planning blight or injurious affection might prejudice the carrying out of much-needed schemes. The legislation therefore attempts to achieve a balance between the need for public sector schemes and the alleviation of the most obvious cases of hardship resulting from such schemes. A consequence of this balancing act is, however, that some cases of undoubted hardship will not be alleviated.[19]

The second point is that the legislation concerned with the alleviation of hardship due to blight, and this comment applies particularly to that concerned with injurious affection, has developed in a piecemeal way. The result is legislation which is unnecessarily complicated and, at times, discriminatory. For example, it is difficult to justify the distinction which the statutory provisions make for compensation purposes between a claimant who has had part of his land acquired for a scheme and one who has not. The taking of land is not a prerequisite for injury, yet a person who has had land taken may well receive more in compensation than a person who has not. Nor does there seem to be much justification for continuing the laboured and complicated distinction between injurious affection caused by the construction of the works and that resulting from their use. There would seem to be a strong argument for rationalising these provisions and drawing them together in a separate code.

19 However, in one case where an individual had sustained interference with the enjoyment of her land and had suffered 'intolerable stress' as a result of aircraft and motorway noise, an application to the European Commission of Human Rights was held admissible and the case was settled on the basis of an *ex gratia* payment by the Government—see *Arrondelle v United Kingdom* (Application No 7889/77, 13 May 1982) and [1982] JPL 770.

CHAPTER 18
SPECIAL CONTROLS

A INTRODUCTION

The discussion so far has largely centred on the general control exercised by planning authorities over the use and development of land under Pt III of the 1971 Act. There are, however, numerous other controls exercised by public authorities over use of the land. In some cases it is necessary to comply with these other controls before a planning application can be submitted. For example, the Health Services Act 1976, as amended, provides that an application for planning permission for the construction or alteration of premises to be used for certain hospital purposes outside the National Health Service, or for the conversion of premises for such purposes, is to be of no effect unless it is accompanied by an authorisation issued by the Secretary of State for Social Services. In other cases planning permission must be obtained before approval or consent can be sought under other legislation. A caravan site licence may only be issued under Pt I of the Caravan Sites and Control of Development Act 1960 if the applicant is entitled to the benefit of a planning permission for the use of the land as a caravan site granted otherwise than by a development order. With many controls, no sequence is prescribed and practical considerations will dictate the order in which the necessary approvals are sought. Obtaining approval of building plans under the Building Act 1984 is an example. It is impossible in a book such as this to deal with these other controls.

However, the planning legislation itself has made provision for a number of special controls, the object of which for the most part is, as with general planning control, the protection and improvement of the physical environment. These special controls are directed at advertisements, trees, buildings of special architectural or historic interest, conservation areas, waste land, minerals and now hazardous substances. Any discussion of the planning legislation would be incomplete without coverage of these matters and they are, accordingly, dealt with in this chapter.

The need to provide for special regimes of control rests on a number of considerations. In some cases, general planning control may be ineffective because the activity—for example, the felling of a tree, internal works to a listed building or the demolition of a building in a conservation area—does not constitute development. Some of the activities present problems which are not shared by other forms of development; the display of advertisements and mineral operations are examples. In other cases the additional control allows special emphasis to be given to certain matters such as the protection of the nation's supply of interesting buildings or the preservation of the character of attractive groups of buildings.

Although the object of most of the special controls is the protection and improvement of the environment, the way in which they achieve that object differs. Although there are some similarities, the general nature of the controls and the means by which they are tied into the development control process reflect their different characteristics. The control of waste land, for example, is primarily a remedial process; the controls over important trees and buildings, on the other hand, are essentially preventive in nature. Listed building control is designed to give additional emphasis to certain features and therefore operates as an addition to normal planning control; advertisement control, on the other hand, is designed to cope with the special problems of displaying advertisements and operates as a substitute for normal planning control; whilst control over trees is concerned with an activity which is not development at all and is, therefore, an entirely separate process.

These special controls are now considered in turn.

B BUILDINGS OF SPECIAL ARCHITECTURAL OR HISTORIC INTEREST

General

Under the 1947 Act local planning authorities were empowered to make building preservation orders in respect of buildings of special architectural or historic interest. A building in respect of which a building preservation order had been made (and confirmed by the Secretary of State) could not be demolished or altered without the consent of the planning authority. In order to provide guidance to local planning authorities in the performance of their duties in relation to buildings of special architectural or historic interest the Secretary of State was empowered to compile lists of such buildings. Notice of any proposal to execute works for the demolition of a listed building or for the alteration or extension of such a building in a manner which would seriously affect its character had to be given to the planning authority in order that they might consider making a building preservation order.

As a result of changes made by the 1968 Act the present law[1] on buildings of special architectural or historic interest is fundamentally different from the earlier law. Provision is still made for the compilation or approval by the Secretary of State of lists of buildings of special interest but such 'listing' is now of much greater significance than formerly; under the present law the mere listing of a building means that it thereupon becomes an offence, unless consent has first been obtained, to demolish the building or to alter or extend it in any manner which would affect its character.

The restrictions which follow from the listing of a building may in some circumstances reduce the value of the building. For example, in *Amalgamated Investment and Property Co Ltd v John Walker & Sons*[2] a warehouse was added to the statutory list some two days after a contract had been signed for its purchase for the purposes of redevelopment. The Court of Appeal rejected

---

1 Now mostly contained in the 1971 Act (as amended by the Town and Country Amenities Act 1974, the Local Government, Planning and Land Act 1980, and the Housing and Planning Act 1986) and the Town and Country Planning (Listed Buildings and Buildings in Conservation Areas) Regulations 1987. Throughout the present section of this chapter these regulations are referred to as 'the Listed Buildings Regulations'.
2 [1976] 3 All ER 509, [1977] 1 WLR 164.

an action by the purchaser for recission of the contract. Every purchaser, said the court, should be regarded as being aware of the inherent risk that a building may be listed.

To alleviate the sort of problem that arose in *John Walker* from what is generally referred to as 'spot listing', the Local Government, Planning and Land Act 1980 introduced an immunity certificate procedure.[3] Where an application for planning permission has been made or planning permission has been granted for development involving the alteration, extension or demolition of a building, an individual may ask the Secretary of State to issue a certificate that he does not propose to list the building. The effect of such a certificate is to preclude the minister from listing the building for a period of five years, thus allowing the development to proceed. However, even if a certificate of immunity is granted, consent for demolition will still be required if the building is in a conservation area; see p 490 below.

Unfortunate as the effects of the listing procedure may be for a purchaser in the sort of situation that occurred in *John Walker*, there is another side to this particular coin. The demolition of the Firestone factory in Brentford in 1980 before a decision could be made as to whether or not to add the building to the statutory list (it apparently had a fine Art Deco central façade) focused attention on what the *Journal of Planning and Environment Law* referred to as 'the Achilles heel of the listing process'. 'Faced with the likely prospect of listing reducing the value of the property affected, any professional adviser', commented the *Journal*, 'must surely advise his client as to what the law is[4]— and leave considerations of morality to his client'.[5]

To avoid this sort of difficulty, local planning authorities are empowered to serve a building preservation notice, to give immediate, if temporary, protection to an unlisted building of special architectural or historic interest which is threatened with demolition or alteration in such a way as to affect its character[6] (see p 478 below). During the period that the notice is in force, the building is subject to normal listed building controls including the need to obtain consent for the demolition or alteration of the building. However, the procedure is not a complete answer to the difficulty. It will only be effective if the planning authority are alert to the prospect of demolition. Furthermore, the authority may have to compensate any person having an interest in the building for any loss resulting from the serving of the notice if the building is not subsequently added to the statutory list by the Secretary of State;[7] the prospect of a claim for compensation may deter an authority from using the procedure.

Detailed guidance on law and policy on buildings and areas of special architectural or historic interest is to be found in Circular 8/87 'Historic Buildings and Conservation Areas—Policy and Procedures'.

3 Section 90 and Sch 15, para 5. See also circular 8/87, paras 41 to 45 as to how the process works.
4 In practice, the demolition of a building is not usually treated as development and need not, therefore, be the subject of a planning application (see p 91).
5 [1980] JPL 712, current topic.
6 1971 Act, s 58.
7 1971 Act, s 173.

Listing of buildings

Section 54 of the 1971 Act provides that the Secretary of State is to compile lists of buildings of special architectural or historic interest or to approve, with or without modifications, lists compiled by the Historic Buildings and Monuments Commission for England (the Commission) or by other persons and may amend any list so compiled or approved.[8]

In considering whether a building ought to be listed, the Secretary of State may take into account not only the building itself but also 'any respect in which its exterior contributes to the architectural or historic interest of any group of buildings of which it forms part' (s 54(2)). He may also take into the account 'the desirability of preserving, on the grounds of its architectural or historic interest, any feature of the building consisting of a man-made object or structure fixed to the building or forming part of the land and comprised within the curtilage of the building' (s 54(2)).

Listing of a building can confer protection on both

(a) any object or structure fixed to the building and
(b) any object or structure within the curtilage of the building as long as the object or structure forms part of the land and has done so since before 1 July 1948 (s 54(9)). The limitation with regard to the date that an object or structure became part of the land within the curtilage of the listed building was added by the Housing and Planning Act 1986 to avoid modern erections becoming automatically protected just because they are set up in the curtilage of a listed building. The House of Lords has also given a narrow interpretation to this subsection, so that the protection is not stretched to extreme lengths.

Earlier the Court of Appeal in *A-G ex rel Sutcliffe v Calderdale Borough Council*[9] had given a broad interpretation to s 54(9). The case concerned a terrace of 15 four-storey mill-workers' dwellings linked by a bridge to a mill. The mill was listed. Until 1973 the mill and the the terrace were in the same ownership. In 1973 the terrace but not the mill passed into the ownership of the Calderdale Borough Council. The council proposed to demolish the terrace. The Attorney-General, acting at the relation of local residents who wished to preserve the terrace, argued, *inter alia*, that the terrace was either a structure fixed to the mill or a structure forming part of the land and comprised within the curtilage of the mill[10] and thus fell to be treated as a part of the listed building so that the Secretary of State's consent would be required before demolition of the terrace could take place. Stephenson L J, giving the court's judgment, said that a building had to be considered in its setting as well as with any features of special architectural or historic interest which it possessed. 'The setting of a building', he observed, 'might consist of much more than man-made objects or structures, but there might be objects or structures which would not naturally or certainly be regarded as part of a

---

8 See, too Roger W Suddards, *Listed Buildings: The Law and Practice* (Sweet and Maxwell, 1988, 2nd edition).
9 [1983] JPL 310.
10 It would seem that the two limbs of the subsection are not mutually exclusive (Stephenson LJ in *Calderdale*).

building or features of it, but which nevertheless were so closely related to it that they enhanced it aesthetically and their removal would adversely affect it . . . [I]f the building itself was to be preserved so also should these objects and structures be.' On that approach, he concluded that the terrace was a structure fixed to the mill within the meaning of the subsection.

He also concluded that, notwithstanding the division of ownership, the terrace had not been taken out of the curtilage by the changes which had taken place. The parties were agreed that three factors had to be taken into account in determining whether a structure was within the curtilage of a listed building. These were (1) the physical layout of the listed building and the structure; (2) their ownership past and present; and (3) their use or function, past and present. The terrace, in Stephenson L J's view, 'remained so closely related physically or geographically to the mill as to constitute with it a single unit and to be comprised within its curtilage' in the sense in which those words are used in this subsection.

However, in *Debenhams plc v Westminster City Council*[11] the House of Lords by four to one disapproved of the width of Stephenson LJ's reasoning though they did not overrule the actual decision. The case concerned premises (Hamleys toy shop in the West End of London) which consisted of buildings which had once been connected by a footbridge and a tunnel. One of the buildings had been listed (the Regent Street buildings) but not those in Kingley Street. The question which had to be decided by the courts was whether the whole of the hereditament could claim exemption from rates under the rating legislation because the properties had been unoccupied for more than three months (see General Rate Act 1967, s 17 and paras 1, 2 and 15 of Sch 1, as amended by s 291 of the 1971 Act). It was held, overturning a unanimous Court of Appeal, that the Kingley Street building was an independent building and not listed. It was further held that therefore neither of the buildings could claim exemption from rates. Lord Keith of Kinkel (who gave the main judgment of the majority) said that s 54(9) only contemplates that 'structures' which were ancillary to the listed building itself should be protected and not complete buildings in their own right. He gave the example of the stable block of a mansion house or the steading of a farmhouse as being structures which could come within s 54(9). He added that the subordination of one building to another in terms of use by the occupier could not make it ancillary; thus impliedly discrediting the third factor listed by Stephenson L J. It should be noted that the test as to whether the structure is ancillary to the main building applies to both limbs of subs (9).

After preparation or amendment of any list the Secretary of State is to deposit with the proper officer of the district planning authority or (within Greater London) the London Borough, a copy of so much of the list as relates to that authority (s 54(4)). Any such copy is a local land charge and the council with whom the copy is deposited are to be treated as the originating authority (s 54(6)). The Secretary of State is to keep available for inspection copies of all lists compiled, approved or made by him (s 54(8)). Formal notification of the inclusion of any building in a list, or the exclusion

---

11 [1987] AC 396, [1987] 1 All ER 51.

therefrom of any building, is the duty of the relevant authority[12] in whose area the building is situated (see 1971 Act. s 54(7); and Listed Buildings Regulations, reg 14). Such notification is to be given to every owner and occupier of the building.[13]

There is no direct statutory right of objection to the listing of a building (though if representations against such action are made, the listing will presumably be reconsidered by the Secretary of State) but on a refusal or conditional grant of listed building consent, appeal can be made on the ground that the building is not of special interest and ought to be removed from the list (see p 479 below).

Any building which immediately prior to 1 June 1969 was subject to a building preservation order but was not then listed, is deemed to be a listed building; after consultation with the parties involved the Secretary of State may direct that this provision is not to apply to a particular building (s 54(10) and (11)). Appendix 1 of Circular 8/87 sets out the present principles of selection. An extract from this Appendix follows:

LISTING OF BUILDINGS OF SPECIAL ARCHITECTURAL OR HISTORIC INTEREST—PRINCIPLES OF SELECTION

How the buildings are chosen

The principles of selection for the lists were drawn up by the Historic Buildings Council (the functions of the former Historic Buildings Council for England are now carried out by the Historic Buildings and Monuments Commission (HBMC) and approved by the Secretary of State. They cover four groups:—

> All buildings built before 1700 which survive in anything like their original condition are listed.
> Most buildings of 1700 to 1840 are listed, though selection is necessary.
> Between 1840 and 1914 only buildings of definite quality and character are listed, and the selection is designed to include the principal works of the principal architects.
> Between 1914 and 1939 selected buildings of high quality are listed (see below).

After 1939 a few outstanding buildings are listed.
In choosing buildings, particular attention is paid to:—

> Special value within certain types, either for architectural or planning reasons or as illustrating social and economic history (for instance, industrial buildings, railway stations, schools, hospitals, theatres, town halls, markets, exchanges, alms-houses, prisons, lock-ups, mills).
> Technological innovation or virtuosity (for instance cast iron, prefabrication, or the early use of concrete).
> Association with well-known characters or events.
> Group value, especially as examples of town planning (for instance, squares, terraces or model villages).

---

12 I.e the district planning authority, or the London Borough Council.
13 It has been suggested that failure to notify an owner will not relieve him of liability for an offence under the listed building provisions (see [1980] JPL 778, Practical Point).

A note on interwar buildings

The criteria for selecting buildings of the 1914–1936 period for listing cover two issues: the range of buildings which may be considered, and the quality of the individual buildings actually selected.

The criteria are designed to enable full recognition to be given to the varied architectural output of the period. Three main building styles (broadly interpreted) are represented: modern, classical and others. The building types which may be considered cover nine categories, as follows:—

(a) Churches, chapels and other places of public worship.
(b) Cinemas, theatres, hotels and other places of public entertainment.
(c) Commercial and industrial premises including shops and offices.
(d) Schools, colleges and educational buildings.
(e) Flats.
(f) Houses and housing estates.
(g) Municipal and other public buildings.
(h) Railway stations, airport terminals and other places associated with public transport.
(i) Miscellaneous.

The selection includes the work of the principal architects of the period.

Grading

The buildings are classified in grades to show their relative importance as follows:—

Grade I   These are buildings of exceptional interest (only about 2 per cent of listed buildings so far are in this grade).
Grade II*   These are particularly important buildings of more than special interest (some 4 per cent of listed buildings).
Grade II   These are building of special interest, which warrant every effort being made to preserve them.
Grade III   A non-statutory and now obsolete grade. Grade III buildings are those which, whilst not qualifying for the statutory list, were considered nevertheless to be of some importance. Many of these buildings are now considered to be of special interest by current standards—particularly where they possess "group value"—and are being added to the statutory lists as these are revised.

Certificates of immunity from listing

Under s 54A, where planning permission is being sought or has been obtained, any person may apply to the Secretary of State for a certificate that that it is not intended to list the building (or buildings) shown in the application plans. Once such a certificate is issued, the building cannot be listed for a period of five years nor can it be made the subject of a building preservation notice by a local planning authority within that period. It seems that where a certificate is refused the practice is to list the buildings (see para 3 of circular 8/87). Having got such a certificate, developers can go ahead with a scheme without the fear that it may be suddenly thwarted by a building being listed but, as indicated, an application for a certificate draws attention to the possible qualities of the building. Notice of an application must be given to the local planning authority within whose area the building is situated (s 54A(3) and in London Boroughs the Historic Buildings and Monuments Commission for England must also be notified (s 54A(4)).

Effect of listing

The main effect of the listing of a building is that under s 55(1) of the 1971 Act any person who executes or causes to be executed any works for the demolition of the building or for its alteration or extension in any manner which would affect its character as a building of special architectural or historic interest is guilty of an offence unless written consent for the execution of such works (known as 'listed building consent') has been granted by the planning authority or by the Secretary of State.[14]

In *R v Wells Street Metropolitan Stipendiary Magistrate, ex p Westminster City Council*[15] it was held by the Divisional Court that the offence created was one of strict liability and there was no need to prove that the person executing the works knew that the building was listed. This can still leave problems as to who *caused* works to be executed.

A person guilty of an offence under s 55 is liable to a fine or imprisonment or both. In imposing a fine on a person convicted on indictment the court is to have regard to any financial benefit accruing to the offender in consequence of the offence (s 55(5)).

In proceedings for an offence under s 55 it is a defence to prove that the works were urgently necessary in the interests of safety or health,[16] or for the preservation of the building (s 55(6) and (9)). Following amendments inserted by the Housing and Planning Act 1986 it is now necessary to also prove that it was not practicable to resort to works of repair or works for affording temporary support or shelter (s 55(6)(b)) and that the works were limited to the minimum measures immediately necessary (s 55(6)(c). It was always necessary to give notice of the works in writing as soon as reasonably practicable, but now the notice must justify the detail of the works. The existence of a dangerous structure order made under the Building Act 1984 or the London Building Acts (Amendment) Act 1939 would usually provide a defence under s 55(6), but in *R v Stroud District Council ex p Goodenough*[17] the Divisional Court held that where an owner proposed to demolish (following a dangerous structure order) the authority should have considered urgently whether to use their powers to carry out urgent works or to acquire the building (see p 485). Now a new section 56C, inserted by the Housing and Planning Act 1986, requires the planning authority to consider taking such steps to preserve the listed building *before* taking any steps with the view of making a dangerous structure order. Thus the listed building control now has priority over the power to serve a dangerous structure order.[18]

---

14 For ministerial decisions on what amounts to such works see [1972] JPL 650, [1974] JPL 376, [1975] JPL 690, [1981] JPL 443 and [1984] JPL 55. Also see *Windsor and Maidenhead Royal Borough Council v Secretary of State for the Environment* [1988] JPL 410.
15 [1987] AC 396, [1986] 3 All ER 4.
16 See appeal decision reported in [1981] JPL 835.
17 [1982] JPL 246.
18 This priority is also carried over to the Building Acts themselves, see para 6(2) of Sch 9 to the Housing and Planning Act 1986.

Under s 57 of the 1971 Act it is an offence for any person who, but for the section, would be acting within his legal rights, to commit or permit any act causing or likely to result in damage to a listed building unless that action is taken in the course of works authorised by a specific consent under the Act.

As is indicated in the following section of this chapter, certain buildings are excluded from the operation ss 55 and 57.

Ecclesiastical buildings and ancient monuments

There would seem to be no restriction on the type of building which can listed. There are, however, two types of building which, though they may be listed, are not subject to the control over demolition, alteration or extension which normally follows upon the listing of a building. These are: (i) ecclesiastical buildings for the time being used for ecclesiastical purposes (or which would be so used but for works for their demolition, alteration or extension) but excluding any building used or available for use by a minister of religion as a residence from which to perform the duties of his office: and (ii) buildings included in the schedule of monuments compiled and maintained under s 1 of the Ancient Monuments and Archaeological Areas Act 1979 (ss 56(1) (a) and (b)).

It would seem, however, that listed building consent will be required in respect of the total demolition of a listed ecclesiastical building. In *Trustees of the Howard United Reformed Church, Bedford*[19] the House of Lords held that the words 'for the time being used for ecclesiastical purposes' referred to the time when the works were being carried out; at the time of its demolition a church cannot be said to be so used. Nor could it be said in this case that the ecclesiastical building in question would be used for ecclesiastical purposes 'but for the works' since the real reason why the building would have ceased to be so was the decision of the owners to demolish it and not the carrying out of the demolition works. Only if an ecclesiastical building was being partially demolished and the works would not prevent the rest of the building being used once more for ecclesiastical purposes after the works had been completed could it be said that the building was not being used for ecclesiastical purposes because of demolition works.

The Housing and Planning Act 1986 has inserted a new s 58AA which gives the Secretary of State a power to restrict or exclude the application of the exemption. In doing so the Secretary of State is expressly allowed to discriminate between different faiths and denominations and even different parts of one building or the type of works. Thus consent could be made necessary for the partial demolition of a building if a particular part, such as a spire, or tower was important because of its architectural or historic interest.

In any case, s 2 of the Redundant Churches and Other Religious Buildings Act 1969 provides that listed building control is not to apply to works of demolition where the church is a redundant church of the Church of England and the demolition is to be carried out in pursuance of a pastoral or redundancy scheme made under the Pastoral Measure 1983. In such a case the Church Commissioners have agreed always to ask the Secretary of State

---

19 As to the meaning of the term 'ecclesiastical building' see *A-G v Trustee of the Howard United Reformed Church, Bedford* [1976] AC 363, [1976] 2 All ER 337, and *Phillips v Minister of Housing and Local Government* [1965] 1 QB 156.

whether he wishes to hold a non-statutory local public inquiry where certain named bodies have given reasoned objections. Further, the Church Commissioners have undertaken to accept a recommendation by the Secretary of State that the church be vested in the Redundant Churches Fund and otherwise to engage in further consultation before using their powers to demolish (see para 103 of circular 8/87).

Crown property

Although buildings which are Crown property may be listed, the statutory controls over listed buildings do not apply, subject to what is said below, to the Crown's interest in any such building (see s 266 (1)(c): a tenant of a listed building in Crown ownership would, however, require listed building consent for the demolition, alteration or extension of the building. Furthermore, in order to obtain the benefit of development value on a disposal of Crown land, listed building consent may now be obtained by the Crown in respect of such land but the consent will apply only to work carried out after the land has ceased to be Crown land.[20]

Although Government departments do not require listed building consent they will consult the appropriate local planning authority whenever they propose to demolish a listed building or to alter or extend it in a way which would affect its character: the planning authority will publicise the proposals and notify various bodies and relevant local community societies. Where the local planning authority object to the works and agreement cannot be reached with the developing department, then the matter will be settled by the Secretary of State for the Environment. If the local planning authority themselves do not wish to make representations but objections are received, it will be up to the developing department to decide whether the substance of the objections is such that it would be appropriate for the Secretary of State to decide whether the proposal should proceed.[1]

Historic Buildings and Monuments Commission

The Commission was established under s 32 of the National Heritage Act 1983 and replaced the Ancient Monuments Board for England and the Historic Buildings Council for England. The duties of the Commission are so far as practicable:

(a) to secure the preservation of ancient monuments and historic buildings situated in England;

(b) to promote the preservation and enhancement of the character and appearance of conservation areas situated in England;

(c) to promote the public's enjoyment of, and advance their knowledge of, ancient monuments and historic buildings situated in England and their preservation (National Heritage Act 1983, s 33(1)).

It also gives advice, including advice to the Secretary of State on the inclusion of buildings in the statutory list, and can make grants or loans in relation to historic buildings (s 33(2) and (3)) and can acquire historic buildings. Finally, if so directed, the Commission can exercise certain

20 See Town and Country Planning Act 1984 s 1: and the Town and Country Planning (Crown Land Applications) Regulations 1984.
1 See Circular 18/84, paras 31 to 33 and Annex B.

ministerial functions and has been directed to carry out the functions formerly carried out by the Greater London Council (s 34).

Building preservation notices

If it appears to the local planning authority other than a county authority that a particular building in their area is of special architectural or historic interest but is not listed and is in danger of being demolished or of being altered in such a manner as would affect its character, the authority may employ the powers conferred upon them by s 58 of the 1971 Act to issue a building preservation notice[2] and thus place a temporary standstill on operations affecting the building. While a building preservation notice is in force with respect to a building the provisions of the 1971 Act[3] apply to the building as if it were listed (s 58(4)).

A building preservation notice must normally be served on the owner, and occupier of the building and comes into force as soon as it is served (s 58(1), (3)). Where, however, it appears to the planning authority to be urgent that a building preservation notice should come into force, they may, instead of serving the notice in the normal way, simply affix the notice conspicuously to some object on the building; such action is to be treated as service of the notice (s 58(6)). After service of the notice the planning authority will ask the Secretary of State to consider listing the building. The notice remains in force for six months or until such earlier date as the Secretary of State lists the building or informs the authority of his intention not to list it (s 58(3)). There is no direct right of appeal against a building preservation notice but during the period that such a notice is in force application may be made for listed building consent and an appeal can be lodged against a refusal or conditional grant of such consent (below).

If the Secretary of State notifies the planning authority that he does not intend to list a building which was the subject of a building preservation notice, the authority may not serve another such notice in respect of that building during the next twelve months (s 58(5)). A decision by the Secretary of State not to list the building may result in the planning authority having to pay compensation in respect of any loss or damage directly attributable to the effect of the building preservation notice (including any sum payable in respect of a breach of contract due to the notice) to any person who had an interest in the building at the time the building preservation notice was served (see 1971 Act, s 173 and Listed Buildings Regulations, reg 9).

When is listed building consent required?

Listed building consent is necessary where it is proposed to demolish a listed building[4] or to alter or extend[5] such a building in a manner which would

---

2 A building preservation notice cannot be served in respect of an 'excepted building', ie an ecclesiastical building which is for the time being used for ecclesiastical purposes or a building which is protected under the Ancient Monuments legislation (s 58(2)).
3 Other than s 57 dealing with acts causing or likely to cause damage to listed buildings.
4 'Building' is defined in s 290(1) of the 1972 Act to include any part of a building, so that demolition of part of a building requires listed building consent.
5 The Secretary of State for the Environment has expressed the view that the erection of a free-standing building within the curtilage of a listed building is not an extension—see [1984] JPL 55. Once erected, such a building would previously have become protected but now see s 54(9) as amended by the Housing and Planning Act 1986 and para 1(1) of Sch 9.

affect its character as a building of special architectural or historic interest (s 55(1), (2)). Listed building consent may therefore be necessary in respect of relatively minor works such as painting the front door of a listed building. This was confirmed by the Divisional Court in the decision of *Windsor and Maidenhead Royal Borough Council v Secretary of State for the Environment*.[6]

A listed building enforcement notice had been served alleging the repainting of the exterior of a building without listed building consent. On appeal, the Secretary of State had taken the view that although the painting of the exterior could constitute works of alteration to a listed building, where, as was the case, the façade of the building had already been painted, works of repainting could not be regarded as an alteration to the building: it was accepted that the repainting did affect the character of the building. In a challenge to this determination Mann J held that repainting was capable of being an alteration and that the critical question was whether the repainting affected the character of the building.

Consent will be required for internal alterations which do not in any way affect the external appearance of the building but which affect the building's character in some way.

There may well be cases in which there is doubt as to whether proposed alterations will have an effect on the building's character and whether therefore listed building consent is required. There is no machinery for obtaining a formal determination of that question prior to the execution of works.

Making and determination of application for listed building consent

The need for listed building consent is quite distinct from the requirement in an appropriate case to obtain planning permission.[7]

The procedure for making an application for listed building consent, set out in Sch 11 to the 1971 Act and regs 3 to 7 of the Listed Buildings Regulations, is very similar to that governing an application for planning permission. Application for listed building consent is to be made to the district planning authority or London Borough in Greater London in whose area the building is situated; it is to be made on a form issued by the planning authority and is to be accompanied by a plan and drawings.

The application shall not be entertained by the local planning authority unless it is accompanied by a certificate stating that the applicant is the owner or alternatively certifying that notice has been given or attempted to be given to the owner (reg 6).

Regulation 5 requires the local planning authority to which an application is made; (a) to publish in a local newspaper a notice indicating the nature of the works and where the plans can be inspected; (b) to display for not less than seven days a notice with the same particulars on or near to the listed building.

The Secretary of State has power under para 7(2) and (3) of Sch 11 to

---

6 [1988] JPL 410.
7 It is no longer possible for a grant of planning permission to operate also as listed building consent (s 90 of and para 7 Sch 1 to the Local Government, Planning and Land Act 1980 repealing s 56(2) of the 1971 Act).

direct local planning authorities to notify specified persons of any applications for listed building consent. Directions have been made requiring notice of all applications for consent to demolish a listed building and of the decisions taken thereon to be given to certain specified bodies (circular 8/87, para 81 and Appendix III). Paragraph 5 of Sch 11 also requires the local planning authority to notify the Secretary of State of any application for listed building consent which they propose to grant but pursuant to powers in para 7(1) (1A) and (3) the Secretary of State has made a direction restricting the need for the Department to be notified (see para 86 of circular 8/87). The Direction is very detailed but the main effect is that applications for alterations to Grade II (unstarred) buildings which fall short of demolition of the whole or a significant part of the building, do not have to be notified.[8] Special arrangements apply in Greater London.[9] The main difference in Greater London is the role of the Historic Buildings and Monuments Commission which now supervises the granting of listing building applications by the London Boroughs. The Commission must be notified of all applications and the London Boroughs have no power to grant unless authorised or directed to by the Commission which in turn must notify the Secretary of State if consent to demolition is to be authorised (Sch 11, para 6).

The planning authority are not to decide an application for listed building consent before the expiry of the period during which the application is available for public inspection; in determining the application the authority must take into account any representations received by them during that period (see reg 5). The authority are also to take account of any representations made by an owner of any part of the land to which the application relates (reg 6(4)).

In considering whether to grant listed building consent for any works the local planning authority or the Secretary of State, as the case may be, must have special regard to the desirability of preserving the building or its setting or any features of special architectural or historic interest which it possesses (s 56(3)[10]). Guidance as to the factors which planning authorities should take into account in operating listed building control is contained in circular 8/87 at para 90. As regards applications for consent for demolition of a listed building the circular goes on to state that 'the presumption should be in favour of preservation except where a strong case can be made out for a granting consent. . .'; para 91.[11]

The Secretary of State may call in applications for his own decision (Sch 11, para 4(1)). Where the local planning authority has to notify him that it

---

8 Note that works for the extension of a listed building may also involve the partial demolition of the building, thus requiring notification if the cubic content comes within the specifications set out in the direction (see *R v North Hertfordshire District Council, ex p Sullivan* [1981] JPL 752).

9 See para 6 of Sch 11 to the 1971 Act as amended by para 17 of Sch 2 to the Local Government Act 1985.

10 As amended by the Local Government, Planning and Land Act, 1980 s 90 and Sch 15 para 9.

11 See on this the appeal decisions noted at [1976] JPL 706; [1978] JPL 273 and 638; [1979] JPL 255 and 496; [1981] JPL 72, 304 and 306; and [1984] JPL 363 and 679; and generally, P H Morgan and S M Nott, 'Listed Buildings—Planning Law and Planning Reality' [1980] JPL 715. See too *Kent Messenger Ltd v Secretary of State for the Environment* (1976) 241 Estates Gazette 25; and *Godden v Secretary of State for the Environment* [1988] JPL 99.

proposes to grant consent, if after 28 days, or such longer period as the Secretary of State may in any particular case direct, the minister has not directed that the application be referred to him, or if the Secretary of State informs the authority that he does not intend to call in the application, the authority may then proceed to grant consent (para 5(1)). Before determining an application which he has called in, the Secretary of State must, if either the applicant or the planning authority so desire, afford to each of them an opportunity of being heard by a person appointed for the purpose by the minister (para 4(4)).

Listed building consent may be granted subject to conditions, including conditions as to:

(a) the preservation of particular features either as part of the building or after severance from it;
(b) the making good of any damage caused by the permitted works; and
(c) the reconstruction of the building (or part of it) after the execution of any works, with the use of original materials so far as practicable (s 56(4A))

Listed building consent can now be granted subject to a condition reserving specified details of works to be subsequently approved by the local planning authority (s 56(4B)).[12] The Local Government, Planning and Land Act 1980 also created a new power for consent to demolition of a listed building being granted subject to a condition that the building shall not be demolished before a contract for the carrying out of works of redevelopment of the site is made and planning permission has been granted for the redevelopment for which the contract provides (s 56(5)).[13] This condition is designed to ensure that premature demolition does not take place and leave a gap long before planning permission is sought and rebuilding starts. However, it will not ensure that redevelopment will actually take place or that it will be of a particular quality.[14]

If, in the execution of works, there is a failure to comply with any condition attached to a grant of listed building consent, an offence is committed (s 55(4)). A failure to comply with a condition may also lead to listed building enforcement action where appropriate.

Listed building consents granted after 13 November 1980 are to be subject to a condition that the works will commence within a specified period.[15] If no

---

12 Inserted by Housing and Planning Act 1986, s 40, Sch 9, para 3(1).
13 Inserted by para 10 of Sch 15 to the 1980 Act.
14 As to whether the quality of the proposed replacement building is a relevant factor in determining whether to grant consent, see *Richmond-upon-Thames London Borough Council v Secretary of State for the Environment* (1978) 37 P & CR 151 (where Sir Douglas Frank considered that it could be at least in a conservation area), *Kent Messenger Ltd v Secretary of State for the Environment* [1976] JPL 372 and *Westminster City Council v Secretary of State for the Environment* (1984) Times, 24 March.
15 1971 Act, 56A (inserted by the Local Government, Planning and Land Act 1980, s 90 and Schs 15, para 11). The significance of 13 November 1980 is that it is the date on which this provision was brought into effect. In the absence of any condition to the contrary, listed building consents granted prior to 1 January 1978 are deemed to be subject to a condition that the works shall commence within a period of three years from 13 November 1980. For consents issued between 1 January 1978 and 13 November 1980 the period is five years from 13 November 1980 (1971 Act, s 56A(3) and (4)).

period is specified by the planning authority in the consent, the period will be five years from the date of the grant.

Strangely the commencement of works outside the required period would not make the works unauthorised, (s 55(2) only makes it a term of authorisation that conditions attached under s 56 are followed and time conditions are imposed under s 56A), but it woud be an offence under s 55(4).

Consent for demolition

Where listed building consent has been granted for the demolition of a listed building, the work is authorised only after the successful applicant has given notice of the proposed demolition to the Royal Commissions on the Ancient and Historical Monuments of England or Wales (whichever is relevant)[16] and thereafter the Commission have either been afforded access to the building for recording purposes for a period of at least three months or have stated in writing that they have completed their record or that they do not wish to record the building (s 55(2) and (3)). Failure to observe this provision takes away the authorisation and so renders any works to the building an offence.

Application of listed building control to planning authorities

Section 271 and reg 13 of the Listed Building Regulations require local authorities to make all of their applications for listed building consent, whether or not the application relates to a listed building which they themselves own or not, to the Secretary of State. Most applications have to be to published (reg 13(4) and (5)) and an application by a county council is made to the district who have to forward it to the Secretary of State (reg 13(7)).

Application for variation or discharge of conditions

Section 56 B (inserted by the Housing and Planning Act 1986) creates a new procedure whereby instead of appealing against a condition, 'any person interested in a listed building' can apply for the variation or discharge of the condition. On such an application, as well as varying or discharging the condition the Secretary of State may add new conditions (note parallel procedure provided for planning conditions, s 31A, p 172).

Appeal against refusal or conditional grant of listed building consent

If listed building consent is refused by the local planning authority or is granted subject to conditions, or if the authority fail to give notice of their decision within eight weeks the applicant may appeal to the Secretary of State within six months (see para 8 of Sch 11 to 1971 Act; and reg 8 of the Listed Buildings Regulations). It is specifically provided that an appellant may include as one of the grounds of his appeal a claim that the building is not of special architectural or historic interest and ought to be removed from the list (para 8(2) of Sch 11). If the parties to an appeal agree to dispense with

---

16 The Royal Commissions on Historical Monuments should not be confused with the Historic Buildings and Monuments Commission.

an inquiry[17] the appeal may, if the Secretary of State concurs, be decided on the basis of written submissions (see p 529 below). There is a right of appeal if details reserved for later approval are not approved within eight weeks of the details being received.

Enforcement of listed building control

Where unauthorised works have been carried out on a listed building, the local planning authority may serve a 'listed building enforcement notice.[18] The statutory provisions on enforcement of control over listed buildings, contained in ss 96 to 100 of the 1971 Act, are similar to the provisions for the enforcement of ordinary planning control (see ch 12). The notice must specify either the steps required to restore the building to its former state or the steps required to bring the building to the state it would have been in if the terms and conditions of the listed building consent had been complied with. As a third alternative, the notice may, if the authority consider that restoration would not be reasonably practicable or is undesirable, specify such further works as they consider necessary to alleviate the effect of the unauthorised works.[19] The notice must also specify the period within which the steps are to be taken (1971) Act, s 96(1)(b)).

A stop notice cannot be issued in connection with listed building enforcement action, presumably because the criminal offences created by the Act in relation to unauthorised works on listed buildings render such notices unnecessary.

Among the grounds (set out in s 97(1)) on which appeal may be made against a listed building enforcement notice are the following: (1) that the building is not of special architectural or historic interest; (2) that s 55 has not been contravened (ie, that the works in question have not affected the character of the building); (3) that the works were urgently necessary in the interests of safety or health, or for the preservation of the building, and that it was not practicable to secure safety or health or, as the case may be, the preservation of the building by works of repair or works for affording temporary support or shelter—the works must be also limited to the minimum measures which were immediately necessary; and (4) that the steps required by the notice would not serve the purpose of restoring the character of the building to its former state.

In *R v Leominster District Council, ex p Antique Country Buildings Ltd*[20] Mann J had the problem of applying these provisions to an ancient barn which had been totally dismantled. The majority of the parts were sold by the

---

17 The arrangements for any such inquiry will be governed by the Town and Country Planning (Inquiries Procedure) Rules 1988; see chapter 19.
18 The enforcement procedures and the criminal sanctions are not mutually exclusive but in some circumstances—for example, where a listed building is demolished without consent—the remedial character of the enforcement process may be of no avail.
19 As to the operation of this provision see *Bath City Council v Secretary of State for the Environment* (1983) 47 P & CR 663 where it was held that it did not cover works which were not related to the alleged breach of control and so could not be used to secure an improvement to the listed building by requiring the replacement of tiles by slates because the slates had been removed before the unauthorised works were carried out. Where steps to alleviate the effects of the works are required, listed building consent is deemed to have been granted for the works in question (1971 Act, s 96(7)).
20 [1988] JPL 554.

owner and were going to be shipped to the United States where they would be reassembled. An injunction was obtained preventing the removal of the timbers[1] and they were put in the custody of the district council. A listed building enforcement notice was served on the original owner and on those who now had an interest in the timbers. The notice alleged unauthorised demolition and removal of a listed building and required it to be substantially restored to its former state on its original site. This notice, which was upheld on appeal, was challenged by way of judicial review. It was held that where sufficient parts of the building were still in existence, (it would be different if all that remained was ash or rubble) it was possible to serve an enforcement notice, in the case of total demolition, requiring restoration. The same would apply to a case of partial demolition. Mann J also held that the owner of the re-erectable parts was capable of being the owner of the building and so could be served with an enforcement notice. The translation from realty to personalty with the prospect of reincarnation as a corporeal hereditament was irrelevant. He who owns the parts owns the building, as long as the parts could be fairly described as a building. Mann J laid down that ownership of 70 per cent to 80 per cent of the component parts could render the person capable of describing himself as the owner of the building. It was also held that the notice was not unreasonable in requiring the barn to be re-erected on the same site, as, although the owners did not have rights of access to that site, there was no reason to believe that the owner of the site would not co-operate in re-erection. If she would not co-operate, resort could be made to s 99 which authorised the local planning authority to enter on the land and carry out the steps required in the notice, recovering the expenses from the owner of the land.

Revocation or modification of listed building consent

The statutory provisions on revocation or modification of listed building consent, set out in Pt II of Sch 11 to the 1971 Act, are similar to those governing revocation or modification of planning permission (see ch 15). Compensation may be claimed in respect of abortive expenditure and other loss or damage directly attributable to the making of a revocation or modification order (see 1971 Act, s 172; and Listed Buildings Regulations, reg 9).

Compensation for refusal or conditional grant of listed building consent

Compensation is not payable in respect of the mere listing of a building. Nor is it payable in respect of a refusal of listed building consent to demolish a listed building.[2] Where an application for the alteration or extension of a listed building has been refused, or has been granted subject to conditions, compensation may be payable by the planning authority under s 171 of the 1971 Act. A claim for compensation under s 171 will only succeed if it can be shown:

---

1 [1987] JPL 350.
2 It may be possible to serve a purchase notice in such a case.

(a) that the decision in question was made by the Secretary of State (either on appeal or on the reference of an application to him); and

(b) that the works in question either do not constitute development or, if they do constitute development, that permission for such works is granted by a development order (so that if the building had not been listed no express grant of permission would have been necessary); and

(c) that the value of the claimant's interest in the land is less than it would have been if listed building consent had been granted, or had been granted unconditionally, as the case may be.

Compensation is not payable on a refusal or conditional grant of listed building consent in respect of a building subject to a building preservation notice unless and until the building is listed; a claim may, however, be lodged prior to listing (s 173(2)).

Listed building purchase notice

On a refusal or conditional grant of listed building consent, or on the revocation or modification of such consent, an owner of the land may, if he considers that the land has become incapable of reasonably beneficial use, serve on the planning authority a listed building purchase notices[3] (see 1971 Act s 190 and Sch 19). The statutory provisions on listed building purchase notices are broadly similar to those governing ordinary purchase notices (as to which see ch 14).

Urgent works for preservation of unoccupied listed buildings

There is no obligation upon the owner of a listed building to maintain it in good condition.[4] However, s 101 of the 1971 Act enables the Secretary of State or the local planning authority, on giving not less than seven days' notice to the owner of a listed building (other than excepted buildings)[5] to take any steps urgently required for the preservation of the building.

The crucial feature of s 101 is that if the owner does not carry out the works himself, the expenses of carrying out the works can be recovered from the owner. In the case of *R v Secretary of State for the Environment, ex p Hampshire County Council*[6] the previous wording was found to be inadequate. The council, having given notice, expended £1,356 in erecting and keeping in place scaffolding to support a listed building. The Divisional Court upheld a decision by the Secretary of State that these monies were not recoverable from the owner. This was because, although notice had been given to the owner, the court implied a need for the notice to set out in some

3 See *Leominster Borough Council v Minister of Housing and Local Government* (1971) 218 Estates Gazette 1419 for a case concerning an unsuccessful challenge to the confirmation of such a purchase notice.

4 However, there seems to be no reason why a local planning authority should not take action under s 65(1) of the 1971 Act as amended and re-enacted by the Housing and Planning Act 1986, s 40 and para 7 of Sch 9 (see p 512 below) in respect of a listed building which constitutes a serious injury to amenity.

5 'Excepted buildings' as defined in s 58(2) of the 1971 Act (ie, certain ecclesiastical buildings and ancient monuments) are excluded from this provision. As to the duty to consider the exercise of this power, see *R v Stroud District Council, ex p Goodenough* (1980) 43 P & CR 59.

6 (1980) 44 P & CR 343; see also *R v Camden London Borough Council, ex p Comyn Ching & Co (London) Ltd* (1983) 47 P & CR 417; and appeal decision noted in [1978] JPL 637.

detail the proposed works and the notice had not specified the works. It was also held that the costs of hiring out the scaffolding were not in any case recoverable as the section did not cover works which could involve the owner in a continuing liability. Donaldson LJ (as he then was) observed, 'The section did not fit. It ought to fit and if anybody ever had the time and inclination to put in an amended section in some other Act if would be no bad idea.' The new section now makes clear that the notice of the intention to carry out the works must describe the works: thus giving the owner the opportunity to carry out the works (s 101(4)). Previously the works could only be carried out with respect to 'unoccupied buildings', but now works can be carried out on the parts of an occupied building which are not in use. The problem of works of temporary support and shelter is dealt with by providing that the expenses involved in making available apparatus or materials can be recovered (s 101A(3)).

An owner who is given notice that he will be required to pay the expenses of the works, may within 28 days of receiving such a notice make representations that:

(a) some or all of the works were unnecessary for the preservation of the building;
(b) in the case of works for affording temporary support or shelter, that the temporary arrangements have continued for an unreasonable length of time; or
(c) that the amount specified in the notice is unreasonable or that the recovery would cause him hardship (s 101A).[7]

As to what is meant by 'hardship', in the *Hampshire* case Donaldson LJ said that it clearly covered the personal circumstances of the applicant. He also accepted that it could possibly cover a situation where there was a gross disparity between the cost of the works and the benefit the owner would derive in the terms of the value of the building. This would also seem to go to the reasonableness of the works.[8]

The powers under ss 101 and 101A may be also exercised by the Commission within Greater London (as well as the local authorities) and elsewhere if authorised by the Secretary of State. The powers may be exercised with respect to buildings in conservation areas where the Secretary of State has made a direction on the grounds that the building is important for maintaining the character or appearance of the conservation area (s 101(1) and (2)).

Compulsory acquisition of listed building in need of repair

Although there is no obligation upon the owner of a listed building to maintain it in good condition, either the county or the district council[9] or the Secretary of State may be authorised to acquire compulsorily any listed

7 See *Bolton Metropolitan Borough Council v Jolley* (1988) Independent, 19 December for a case under the old wording.
8 Circular 8/87 sets out the considerations that the Secretary of State will have regard to in the event of an owner making representations: see para 129.
9 In the Greater London area the Commission or the London Borough may be authorised to compulsorily acquire, and although s 114 refers to the Secretary of State authorising the compulsory acquisition, it would seem that the Secretary of State does not have expressly to authorise the initial making of the order and only has to confirm it; see *Robbins v Secretary of State for the Environment* [1988] 2 EGLR 205, [1988] JPL 824.

building[10] which is not being properly preserved (s 114 of the 1971 Act). The Secretary of State is only to make or confirm a compulsory purchase order for the acquisition of such a listed building if he is satisfied that it is expedient to preserve the building (s 114(4)). As a preliminary to compulsory purchase proceedings under s 114 there must be served on the owner of the building a repairs notice specifying the works considered reasonably necessary for the proper preservation of the building (s 115).

In *Robbins v Secretary of State for the Environment*[11] the Court of Appeal held what was necessary for the proper preservation of a building was a question of fact and degree, first for the council when they drew up and served the notice and then again for the Secretary of State when he had to decide whether to confirm the compulsory purchase order. In this regard, works which might normally be considered more appropriate to restoration can be included and the question did not have to be looked at as at the date of the service of the repairs notice. In this case the Secretary of State had concluded that works needed to make an old windmill operational were not reasonably necessary for the proper preservation of the building. The Court of Appeal considered this conclusion to be proper and accepted that if a council sought to include in a repairs notice works which required the restoration of some feature which had already disappeared at the time of the listing, then the Secretary of State would probably conclude that it was not a reasonable step. The Court of Appeal then went on to hold that the inclusion of some items of repair in the notice, which the Secretary of State considered unnecessary, did not make the notice invalid. This means that in practice the local planning authority have a wide discretion as to what works they decide to include in the notice. The exercise of this discretion can only be reviewed indirectly by the Secretary of State in deciding whether to authorise compulsory purchase. It is important to note that a repairs notice under s 115 does not *require* any works. It merely states that they are considered reasonably necessary for the proper preservation of the building.

Notice of the making of the compulsory purchase order may not be served earlier than two months after service of the repairs notice (s 115(1). If the repairs are carried out the authority will presumably not proceed with the acquisition. In any case, any person with an interest in the building may within 28 days of the making of a compulsory purchase order under s 114 make application to the magistrates court which will, if satisfied that reasonable steps have been taken for properly preserving the building, make an order prohibiting further proceedings on the compulsory purchase order (s 114(6)).

Where the planning authority or the Secretary of State is satisfied that a listed building has been deliberately allowed to fall into disrepair for the purpose of justifying its demolition and the development or redevelopment of the site (or any adjoining site), there may be included in a compulsory purchase order under s 114 a direction for minimum compensation payable for the building (below). There is a right of appeal to the magistrates court against such a direction (s 117(5)).

10 Other than an ecclesiastical building in use as such or an ancient monument.
11 [1988] 2 EGLR 205, [1988] JPL 824. The decision of the Court of Appeal has since been upheld on the slightly different grounds that the relevant date for determining what works were required for the preservation of a building was not the date of the notice but the date the building was listed; see [1989] 1 All ER 878, [1989] 1 WLR 201, HL.

These powers were examined by the Court of Appeal in the case of *Rolf v North Shropshire District Council.*[12] There it was held that there was no requirement for the council to take into account the means of the owner in drawing up the repairs notice and that s 126 specifically authorised the compulsory acquisition of a listed building under s 114 where the local authority intended to transfer the building to another body as the local authority itself did not have the means to preserve the building. In this case the building was to be transferred to the British Historic Building Trust.

Further in *Robbins v Secretary of State for the Environment*[13] the Court of Appeal refused to quash a compulsory purchase order where the repairs notice contained works which the Secretary of State considered were not necessary for the proper preservation of the property. This was on the ground that the notice was still valid and so the question of whether a valid notice was a precondition of the compulsory purchase notice did not directly arise.

The whole procedure seems unnecessarily complicated. As Glidewell LJ pointed out, the person on whom the compulsory purchase order is served has two ways of challenging it; by way of application to the magistrates court under s 114(6) or by objecting to the confirmation to the Secretary of State under the Acquisition of Land Act 1981 (when a public inquiry will be held into the objection). It seems those remedies are not alternatives and that both can be tried. It seems strange that both should be available and that potentially both the magistrates court and the Secretary of State should be able to determine whether reasonable steps have been taken for properly preserving the building.

Compensation on compulsory acquisition of listed building

Provision as to the compensation payable on compulsory acquisition of a listed building is made by s 116 of the 1971 Act, as amended by s 6 of the Town and Country Amenities Act 1974. In assessing such compensation it can be assumed that listed building consent would be granted for any works for the alteration or extension of the building. It can also be assumed that consent would be granted for the building's demolition for the purpose of 'existing use' development of the classes specified in Sch 8 to the 1971 Act (see p 415. It is not otherwise to be automatically assumed that listed building consent for demolition would be granted; this means that the compensation payable may well not reflect the value of the site for redevelopment. It will still be possible, however, to take account of the prospects of consent for demolition being granted.

In assessing compensation for a listed building acquired under a compulsory purchase order which contains a direction of minimum compensation (above), it is to be assumed that planning permission or listed building consent would be granted for development or works necessary for restoring the building to, and maintaining it in, a proper state of repair, but that permission or consent would not otherwise be granted at all (s 117(4)).

12 [1988] JPL 103.
13 [1988] 2 EGLR 205, [1988] JPL 824. Upheld by House of Lords; see [1989] 1 All ER 878, [1989] 1 WLR 201.

Grants and loans

All the Secretary of State's powers to make grants towards the costs of repair to historic buildings were transferred to the Commission. These powers are mainly contained in the Historic Buildings and Ancient Monuments Act 1953. The Commission has also powers with regard to the Greater London Area under the Local Government Act 1985 (para 3(1)b of Sch 2). Local authorities may contribute towards the cost of repair and maintenance of a building of architectural or historic interest[14] (see Local Authorities (Historic Buildings) Act 1962).

The National Heritage Memorial Fund 1980 enables the trustees of the National Heritage Memorial Fund to make grants or loans towards the acquisition, maintenance or preservation of land, buildings and other objects which in the opinion of the trustees is of outstanding scenic, historic, aesthetic, architectural or scientific interest (National Heritage Act 1980, s 3). Other sources of funding are set out in circular 8/87: see paras 143 to 149. Alterations to listed buildings are not subject to value added tax provided the works have received listed building consent.

The relation between listed building control and other controls

As seen earlier the need for listed building consent is distinct from the requirement in an appropriate case to obtain planning permission.[15] Nonetheless, the effect of a proposed development on a listed building and its setting will be of concern in the exercise of normal development control powers. This is reflected in the statutory requirement for the local planning authority to publicise a planning application which in their opinion will affect the setting of a listed building[16] (see s 28(1) and p 186, above). Furthermore, in considering whether to grant planning permission for development which affects a listed building or its setting, the planning authority must have special regard to the desirability of preserving the building or its setting or any features of special architectural or historic interest which it possesses (s 56(3) and see p 480, above).

Difficult questions may arise over the relation between listed building control and other controls under, for example, the building, housing or environmental health legislation. The general position appears to be that as these separate codes each have their own distinct purpose, compliance with one does not remove an obligation to comply with another unless this is expressly stated.[17] Section 55(6) of the 1971 Act comes close to such an express statement. Although it does not remove the obligation to comply with listed building control, it does, as we indicated earlier, provide a defence to a prosecution for a breach of listed building control where the works are proved to have been urgently necessary in the interests of safety or health or for the preservation of the building.

14 The building need not be listed.
15 Although the display of outdoor advertisements is controlled under the Town and Country Planning (Control of Advertisements) Regulations 1984, consent under the regulations does not relieve the intending advertiser of the need to comply with listed building control if the advertisement is to be displayed on a listed building in such a manner as to affect its character.
16 See *R v South Hereford District Council, ex p Felton* [1989] EGCS 80 for the scope of this requirement.
17 See s 289 of the 1971 Act.

However *R v Stroud District Council ex p Goodenough*[18] showed the problems that could arise where a dangerous structures notice or order has been served under s 77(1)(a) or s 79(1) of the Building Act 1984 (or s 62(2), 65 or 69(1) of the London Building Acts (Amendment) Act 1939) in respect of a listed building (or an unlisted building in a conservation area).

A new s 56C (introduced by the Housing and Planning Act 1986) now requires that before such orders are made the local planning authority must consider whether they should exercise their powers under s 101 and ss 114 to 115. In addition, amendments have been made to the building legislation by which it is made plain that the works specified in a dangerous structures order require listed building consent. The result is that a prosecution could be brought for failing to obtain consent but s 55(6) could be raised as a defence. However, s 55(6) has also been amended so that it is necessary to show in addition that:

(a) it was not practicable to secure the safety or health or the preservation of the building by works of repair to provide temporary support or shelter;
(b) the works were limited to the minimum measures immediately necessary; and
(c) notice in writing was given as soon as practicable justifying the works.

Although this is not stated expressly, the new wording suggests that listed building consent should be obtained except in cases of emergency. Circular 8/87 suggests that authorities serving dangerous structures orders should remind owners of the need to obtain listed building consent or give notice under s 55(6)(d) (see para 107).

C CONSERVATION AREAS

Designation of conservation areas

Under s 277 of the 1971 Act every local planning authority must from time to time determine which parts of their district are areas of special architectural or historic interest, the character or appearance of which it is desirable to preserve or enhance; they are to designate such areas as conservation areas. Designation of a conservation area does not require the approval of the Secretary of State but notice of any such designation (and of the variation or cancellation of any designation) must be given to the Secretary of State and the Commission ((s 277(6) and (6A)). Notice of any such designation, variation or cancellation, with particulars of its effect, is to be published in the London Gazette and in at least one local newspaper (s 277(7)). Owners and occupiers of property in the area do not have to be individually notified of action under s 277 nor do they have any right of appeal against such action.

The Secretary of State can himself designate any area as a conservation area (s 277(4)).

The main effects of the designation of an area as a conservation area are outlined below.

18 (1980) 43 P & CR 59. Also see *Glasgow District Council v Secretary of State for Scotland* 1980 SC 150.

Preservation and enhancement of conservation area

Designation of a conservation area should, in the words of circular 8/87, 'only be a preliminary to action to preserve or enhance its character and appearance'.

There is imposed on the local planning authority and any other appropriate body a general duty to pay special attention to the desirability of preserving or enhancing the character or appearance of a conservation area whenever they are exercising functions under the 1971 Act or under Pt 1 of the Historic Buildings and Ancient Monuments Act 1953 or under the Local Authorities (Historic Buildings) Act 1962 (1971 Act s 277(8)).

The meaning of this provision has been considered by the High Court in *Steinberg and Sykes v Secretary of State for the Environment and Camden London Borough Council.*[19] In granting planning permission for the erection of a two storey house on derelict land in a conservation area, the inspector made no specific mention of s 277(8) and only asked himself if the proposed development would harm the character of the conservation area. Lionel Read QC, sitting as a deputy judge, held that although it was not necessary for the inspector to specifically refer to s 277(8), the decision letter must show that the inspector had discharged his duty under s 277(8), otherwise either the inference would be that he had not discharged the duty or the inspector would have failed to give adequate reasons as to how he had discharged that duty. He then went on to hold that it was not sufficient for the inspector to show his concern that no *harm* should be caused to the character of the conservation area. That was not the same as paying special attention to the desirability of preserving or enhancing that character as well as its appearance. The deputy judge stated: 'The concept of avoiding harm is essentially negative. The underlying purpose of s 277(8) seems to me to be essentially positive'.

A difficult aspect of the wording of s 277(8) is that it appears to give the decision-maker a choice as to whether to pay special attention to preserving *or* enhancing, the character *or* appearance of the character area. In *Steinberg*, Lionel Read, without deciding the point, doubted whether this meant that the statutory duty could be discharged by considering only whether development would preserve the character of the conservation area and not considering the desirability of enhancement. It may be that the answer is that the authority has to consider *both* preservation *and* enhancement where this is appropriate or, at least, that it cannot choose one duty where the other duty is clearly more appropriate.

More particularly, under s 277B of the 1971 Act it is the duty of the planning authority to formulate and to publish, from time to time, proposals for the preservation and enhancement of any conservation area in their district. These proposals are to be submitted to a public meeting in the area to which they relate and the local planning authority are to have regard to any views expressed by persons attending the meeting. Such proposals are a

---

19 [1989] JPL 258, see also *South Hams District Council v Secretary of State for the Environment* [1988] EGCS 82 where the grant of consent by the Secretary of State for permission to display an advertisement was quashed because of a failure to show that special attention had been paid to the desirability of preserving or enhancing the character or appearance of the area, which was a conservation area. Also see *Bromley London Borough Council v Secretary of State for the Environment and Cope* [1989] EGCS 71.

kind of development plan for the area and, although this is not expressly stated, it must be that such proposals are material, when the authority is exercising its duties under s 277(8). Indeed, these proposals should indicate in a particular case the relative desirability of preservation or enhancement.

Development affecting conservation area

One of the objects of the statutory provisions on conservation areas is to stimulate public interest in the preservation or enhancement of the amenity of such areas. In furtherance of this objective it is provided that publicity must be given by the planning authority to any application for planning permission for development which would, in the opinion of the authority, affect the character or appearance of a conservation area (1971 Act, s 28—see p 186, above). In considering any such application the planning authority must take into account any representations relating to the application (see p 199, above).

Circular 8/87 suggests that planning authorities should consider asking for detailed plans of proposed development within a conservation area rather than grant permission in outline form (see para 61).

Control of demolition in conservation area

Demolition of unlisted buildings in conservation areas is brought under control by s 277A of the 1971 Act. The effect of that section is to apply (with exceptions and modifications) certain of the statutory provisions on listed buildings to buildings in a conservation area.[20] A building[1] to which the provisions of s 277A apply (see below) must not be demolished unless the equivalent of listed building consent has first been obtained. The listed building regulations describe such a consent as a 'conservation area consent' (reg 3) and the provisions in the 1971 Act applied by s 277A(8) are modified accordingly (reg 12 and Sch 3 of the regulations).

An application for such consent is to be made separately from any application for planning permission. If the local planning authority are disposed to grant consent for demolition of a building in a conservation area they do not, as with ordinary applications for listed building consent (see p 480 above), have to notify the Secretary of State (para 5 to Sch 11 does not apply). In the Greater London area the City of London Common Council and the other London Boroughs are required to notify the Commission and to take into account any representations when deciding the application (see para 6 of Sch 11, as modified). Any consent will be of limited duration (s 56A, as applied by s 277A(8)). Circular 8/87 declares that where it is clear that demolition of a building in a conservation area will be followed by redevelopment of the site, 'consent to demolish should normally be given only where there are acceptable and detailed plans for that redevelopment' (para 95). In *Richmond-upon-Thames London Borough Council v Secretary of State for the Environment*[2] it was held that in considering an application for consent to

---

20 See, s 277A(8) and Sch 3 to the Town and Country Planning (Listed Building and Buildings in Conservation Areas) Regulations 1987.
1 Since the word 'building' is defined in s 290(1) of the 1971 Act as including 'any part of a building', it would seem that partial demolition of a building in a conservation area will be subject to the statutory controls.
2 (1978) 37 P & CR 151.

demolish a building in a conservation area, the planning authority or the Secretary of State may legitimately take account of the merits of any proposed redevelopment of the site. Further, in *Westminster City Council v Secretary of State for the Environment*[3] McNeill J said that, in considering an application, the correct approach was to look not at the building alone but at the area and not at preservation alone but at enhancement also. In that case McNeill J upheld a decision granting consent to demolition but subject to a condition that no demolition works should take place until contracts and permission for redevelopment had been finalised.[4]

Such development may in the event not take place and the circular goes on to advise that: 'It may be appropriate to accompany the consent with an agreement enforceable under s 33 of the Local Government (Miscellaneous Provisions) Act 1982' (para 95).

These statutory controls on demolition apply to all buildings in conservation areas other than:

(a) listed buildings (which are already subject to the statutory controls outlined above);

(b) 'excepted buildings' within the meaning of s 56(1) of the 1971 Act (ie certain ecclesiastical buildings and ancient monuments)[5] and

(c) buildings excluded from the operation of s 277A by direction of the Secretary of State under s 277A (4) and (5).

In pursuance of his powers under s 277(4) and (5) the Secretary of State has directed in circular 8/87 that s 277A is not to apply to specified descriptions of buildings.

This replaces the previous direction in circular 23/77. The main change is to remove any references to the classes of permitted development in the General Development Order. It is also made plain that the exemptions do not cover cases where the local authority are making the relevant decision and not the Secretary of State.

The present direction exempts the following descriptions of buildings from control:

(a) any building with a total cubic content not exceeding 115 cubic metres or any part of such building, and in this sub-paragraph 'building' does not include part of a building:

(b) any gate, wall, fence or railing which is less than one metre high where abutting on a highway (including a public footpath or bridleway) or public open space, or two metres high in any other case;

(c) any building erected since 1 January 1914 and used, or last used, for the purposes of agriculture or forestry;

(d) any part of a building used, or last used, for an industrial process, provided that such part (taken with any other part which may have been demolished) does not exceed ten per cent of the cubic content of the original building (as ascertained by external measurement) or 500 square metres of floor space, whichever is the greater;

3 (1984) *Times*, 24 March.
4 Section 56(5), which provides for such a condition, applies to conservation area consents; see Listed Building Regulations, reg 12 and Sch 3.
5 See p 476, above.

(e)   any building required to be demolished by virtue of an order made under s 51 of the Act;

(f)   any building required to be demolished by virtue of any provision of an agreement made under s 52 of the Act;

(g)   any building in respect of which the provisions of an enforcement notice served under s 87, s 96 or s 100 of the Act required its demolition, in whole or in part, however expressed;

(h)   any building required to be demolished by virtue of a condition of planning permission granted under s 29 of the Act, other than a permission deemed to be granted to a local planning authority by virtue of reg 4(5) or reg 5(4) of the Town and Country Planning General Regulations 1976;

(i)   any building to which a demolition order made under Pt IX of the Housing Act 1985 applies;

(j)   any building included in a compulsory purchase order made under the provisions of Pt IX of the Housing Act 1985 and confirmed by the Secretary of State;

(k)   a redundant building (within the meaning of the Pastoral Measure 1983) or part of such a building where demolition is in pursuance of a pastoral or redundancy scheme (within the meaning of that measure).

The Crown and conservation area consent

In order to permit the Crown to obtain the benefit of development value on a disposal of Crown land, 'conservation area consent' may be obtained by the appropriate Crown body in respect of the demolition of Crown buildings in a conservation area.[6] Such a consent applies only to work carried out after the land has ceased to be Crown land.

Urgent works for preservation of unoccupied buildings

If it appears to the Secretary of State that the preservation of a building in a conservation area is important for maintaining the character or appearance of the conservation area, he may direct that s 101 of the 1971 Act is to apply to the building (s 101(2)). Any works urgently necessary for the preservation of the building may then be carried out by the local planning authority or the Secretary of State (see p 485 above).

Protection of trees in conservation areas

Special provision is made by the 1971 Act for the preservation of trees in a conservation area (see p 511 below).

Control of advertisements in conservation areas

Under s 63(3) of the 1971 Act the Secretary of State is empowered, in making regulations for the control of advertisements, to make special provision concerning the control of advertisements in conservation areas.

---

6 See Town and Country Planning Act 1984, s 1; and the Town and Country Planning (Crown Land Applications) Regulations 1984.

Regulations have been made instituting stricter control over advertising in 'areas of special control'.[7]

However, conservation areas are not automatically designated as areas of special control and in circular 8/87 it is stated that there must be 'compelling and relevant planning considerations' to justify the view that the proposed area should be given special protection (para 67).

Financial assistance for conservation areas

Under s 10 of the Town and Country Planning (Amendment) Act 1972 the Commission may give financial assistance by way of grant or loan towards expenditure incurred in the preservation or enhancement of the character of a conservation area of outstanding architectural or historic interest.

D CONTROL OF ADVERTISEMENTS

Because of widespread concern in the late 1940s about the effects of uncontrolled advertising, outdoor advertisements[8] have been subjected to a complex and largely self-contained code of control. This code is currently contained in the Town and Country Planning (Control of Advertisements) Regulations 1989 (the 1989 regulations).[9] The central provision of the 1989 regulations is reg 5 which declares that no advertisement may be displayed without consent granted in that behalf by the local planning authority or the Secretary of State or deemed to be granted by virtue of the regulations themselves.

The display of an advertisement may, of course, involve development—an operation such as the erection of an advertisement hoarding would, for example, constitute development and s 22(4) of the 1971 Act specifically provides that the use for the display of advertisements of any external part of a building not normally used for that purpose is to be treated as involving a material change of use—but planning permission is deemed to be granted in repect of any advertisement which is displayed in accordance with the regulations and in such a case no application for planning permission is necessary (see 1971 Act, s 64).

This means that where an advertisement is displayed without consent under the regulations, the local planning authority may have a choice between taking enforcement action for a breach of planning control or taking out a prosecution under s 109 of the 1971 Act for a contravention of the 1989 regulations. Further, the definition of 'advertisement' in the 1971 Act (s 290(1)) makes a distinction between words, letters etc which actually advertise, announce or direct and 'hoardings or similar structures' which are used for the display of advertisements. Such hoardings are deemed to be advertisements and so it seems their erection does not require planning

---

7 See regs 18 and 19, the Town and Country Planning (Control of Advertisements) Regulations 1989.
8 Certain advertisements displayed within a building are also subject to control—see Town and Country Planning (Control of Advertisements) Regulations 1989, reg 3 and Sch 2, Class J, although some of these advertisements will have the benefit of the deemed consent provisions. See reg 6 Sch 3, Class 12.
9 Made under ss 63, 109, 176 and 257 of the 1971 Act. See also circular 15/1989. The new regulations, as well as changing the substantive law, have completely changed their order and layout.

permission if the display is authorised under the regulations; though it could be argued that s 64 only covers the material change of use involved and not the initial act of development in erecting the hoarding or structure. It could well be that the 'display' only covers the use and not the setting up of the hoarding. In the Scottish decision *City of Glasgow District Council v Secretary of State for Scotland*[10] the Court of Session held that where two canopies were erected above a shop window displaying the shop name they were not covered by s 62 (the Scottish equivalent of s 64) and so required permission. This was on the grounds that the canopies were erected to protect goods and were not the 'display of advertisements'.[11]

Extent of control

The 1971 Act defines 'advertisement' as meaning 'any word, letter, model, sign, placard, board, notice, device[12] or representation, whether illuminated or not, in the nature of, and employed wholly or partly for the purposes of, advertisement, announcement or direction, and (without prejudice to the preceding provisions of this definition) includes any hoarding or similar structure used, or adapted for use for the display of advertisements, and references to the display of advertisements shall be construed accordingly' (s 290 (1)).

The 1984 regulations used to contain a slightly different definition of an advertisement. This has been dropped but reg 2 excludes anything 'employed wholly as a memorial or as a railway signal'.

The word 'site' in relation to an advertisement means any land or building, other than an advertisement, on which an advertisement is displayed (see reg 2(1)). An express grant of consent under the regulations permits the use of the site in question for the display of any advertisement in the manner authorised by the consent.

The regulations apply to the display on any site in England and Wales of an advertisement except in the case of ten classes of advertisements set out in Schedule 2 (reg 3). These include:

(a) an advertisement displayed on enclosed land, and not readily visible from land outside that enclosure or from any part of that land over which the public have a right of way or right of access (class B).

(b) an advertisement displayed inside a building unless the advertisement is either:
   (i) illuminated, or
   (ii) displayed within a building used principally for the display of advertisements, or
   (iii) an advertisement any part of which is within 1 metre of any external door, window (or other opening through which it is visible from outside the building) (Class J)

(c) an advertisement displayed on a vehicle or vessel normally employed as a moving vehicle or vessel. The exception will not, however, apply during

---

10 [1988] CLY 814.
11 But see *Westminster City Council v Secretary of State for the Environment* (1989) EGCS 110 where it was held that canopies and blinds were a display of advertisements.
12 As to the meaning of device; see 1988 JPL 568 and for an exhaustive analysis of the definition; see Millichamp 'Enforcing Advertisement Control' [1988] JPL 382.

any period when such a vehicle or vessel is being used primarily for the display of advertisements (Class C)

(d) an advertisement displayed on or consisting of a tethered balloon flown at a height of not more than 60 metres above ground level[13] on a site which is not within an area of special control, a conservation area, a National Park, the Broads or an Area of Outstanding Natural Beauty, provided:

    (i) no more than one such advertisement is displayed on the site at any one time and,

    (ii) the site is not used for the display of such advertisements on more than 10 days in any calendar year (Class A);

In *Wadham Stringer (Fareham) Ltd v Borough of Fareham*[14] Gibson LJ held that a balloon is displayed on a site if it is attached to that site, even though it might fly over other sites. It was attached to a site if it was tethered to the site whether by being attached to a tree or to a vehicle or to a weight.

(e) an advertisement incorporated in, and forming part of the fabric of, a building (and not merely affixed to or painted on a building), other than a building used principally for advertisements or a hoarding or similar structure (Class D).

(f) an advertisement displayed on an article for sale or on the package or container in which an article is sold, or displayed on the pump, dispenser or other container from which an article, gas or liquid is sold, provided such advertisement:

    (i) refers wholly to the article, gas or liquid, and

    (ii) is not illuminated, and

    (iii) does not exceed 0.1 square metre in area (Class E).

Exceptions are also made in the case of election notices (Class F), Parlimentary requirements (Class G), traffic signs (Class H) and the display of national flags (Class I).

Subject to these exceptions, no advertisement is to be displayed unless it has express consent granted under the regulations or unless consent is deemed to be granted by the regulations themselves.

Deemed consent: the specified classes

The fourteen classes of advertisement specified in Schedule 3 to the regulations fall within the scope of the regulations but may be displayed without express consent[15] from the planning authority because consent is deemed to be granted. The classes are as follows:

13 Including the height of any building to which it is moored; see reg 2(4). Advertising by way of tethered balloon had previously been unlawful so that no provision was made in earlier Advertisement Control Regulations. Following the relaxation contained in the Civil Aviation (Aerial Advertising) (Captive Balloons) Regulations 1984 provision has now been made tying this type of advertising into the general framework of advertisement control. Advertisement by tethered balloon at a height exceeding 60 metres above ground level and 'free flight' advertising remain outside the scope of the Advertisement Control Regulations, but is covered by the Aerial Advertising Regulations; see above.

14 [1987] JPL 715.

15 If, however, application is made for express consent in respect of any advertisement falling within one of the classes specified, then in determining that application the local planning authority is precluded from imposing any condition more limiting than would have applied to the deemed consent (Reg 13(4)).

Class 1. Functional advertisements of local authorities, community councils, statutory undertakers and public transport undertakers.

Class 2. Miscellaneous advertisements relating to the land on which they are displayed, eg direction signs, business nameplates and hotel signs.

Class 3. Certain advertisements of a temporary nature, eg notices relating to the sale of land or the sale of goods or livestock, signs relating to the carrying out of building work by contractors, announcements of local events relating to any demonstration of agricultural methods or processes on the land on which they are displayed.

The provision relating to the sale or letting of land has caused particular problems. The original wording left it unclear whether more than one board per unit of land or premises was authorised. In *Porter v Honey*[16] the House of Lords, while accepting that even under the previous wording only one board for each sale or letting was authorised, however many agents were instructed, held that by implication that the first board displayed remained authorised even though a second unlawful board was later put up. This is now made explicit in the wording of the 1989 Regulations; see Class 3A(1)(b).

Class 4. Illuminated advertisements displayed on business premises within a retail park, which advertisements must be confined wholly to the business carried on and the name of proprietor.

Class 5. Advertisements displayed on business premises[17] with reference to all or any of the following matters: the business carried on, the goods sold[18] or services provided, and the name and qualification of the person carrying on the business or manufacturing or supplying the goods or services on the premises.

Class 6. Advertisements displayed on the forecourt of business premises wholly with reference to the matters specified above in Class 5.[19]

Class 7. An advertisement in the form of a flag which is attached to a single flagstaff fixed in an upright position on the roof of a building.

Class 8. Advertisements on hoardings enclosing land designated in the development plan primarily for commercial, industrial or business purposes and on which building operations are taking place.

---

16 [1988] 3 All ER 1045, [1988] 1 WLR 1420.
17 The term 'business premises' is defined in Part II of Sch 3. On the interpretation of the term see *Dominant Sites Ltd v Berkshire County Council* (1955) 6 P & CR 10; *Cooper v Bailey* (1956) 6 P & CR 261; and *Jones v Merioneth County Council* (1968) 20 P & CR 106.
18 On the scope of this phrase see *Arthur Maiden Ltd v Lanark County Council* [1958] JPL 417.
19 See *Heron Service Stations Ltd v Coupe* [1973] 2 All ER 110, [1973] 1 WLR 502, HL.

Class 9. Advertisements displayed on four-sheet poster panels not exceeding 1.6 square metres in areas where that use is authorised under s 115E (1) of the Highways Act 1980. This Act allows local councils, after consulting the local planning authorities to permit advertising on bus shelters or information kiosks and this class was inserted to avoid the need for a separate advertisement regulation. Circular 2/88 explains the scope of this new class.

Class 10. Advertisements giving notice that a Neighbourhood Watch scheme or similar scheme is in operation in the area.

Class 11. Directional advertisements for the purpose of directing potential buyers and other interested people to a site where residential development is taking place. There are also included in 11B directional advertisements for tourist attractions and facilities in certain designated experimental areas. There are special limitations on this class.

Class 12. Advertisements inside buildings which do not fall within Class J in Schedule 2 (see above).

Class 13. Where a site was being used for the display of advertisements on 1 April 1974 the site may continue to be so used without express consent. Certain specified conditions[20] must, however, be observed.

Class 14. Consent is in certain circumstances deemed to be granted for the continued display of advertisements for which express consent has expired unless a condition to the contrary was imposed or a renewal of consent was applied for and refused.

Each deemed class is subject to its own specific limitations and conditions and Part II of Schedule 3 provides the interpretation of definitions which relate specifically to the deemed consent classes. They are also subject to the standard conditions (see below p 502). Regulation 7 enables the Secretary of State to make a direction, following a proposal to him by the local planning authority to exclude the application of any particular class in any particular case or area. This power does not apply to Classes 11B, 12 and 13 and he must provide an opportunity for objections and publish his reasons for making the direction.

---

20 There must not, for example, be any substantial alteration in the manner of use of the site. That limitation was considered in *Arthur Maiden Ltd v Lanark County Council (No 2)* [1958] JPL 422. See also *Arthur Maiden Ltd v Royal Burgh of Kirkcaldy*, Sheriff Court, Kirkcaldy (18 November 1965, unreported), but see comment at 1980 SPLP 22); and *Mills and Allen v City of Glasgow District Council* 1980 SLT (Sh Ct) 85. Also see Greenwood 'The Advertisement Regulations—a Brief Airing' [1987] JPL 23 for discussion of a magistrates' court case on this point.

Discontinuance action for advertisements displayed with deemed consent

Regulation 8 provides that the local planning authority may serve a notice requiring the discontinuance of the display of an advertisement displayed with deemed consent or the discontinuance of the use of a site for the display of such an advertisement. This means that action can be taken either against a specific advertisement or against a particular site which is used for temporary advertisements. The authority may only invoke the procedure if they are satisfied that this is necessary to remedy 'a substantial injury to the amenity of the locality or a danger to members of the public'. The 1984 Regulations used to provide two tests depending on the class of deemed consent but this duality has been removed. The change means that the higher standard of 'substantial injury to the amenity of the locality' applies throughout rather than the lesser standard of it being 'in the interests of amenity'. The notice must be served on the person displaying the advertisement and on the owner and occupier of the land on which it is displayed.[1]

The discontinuance notice must specify the advertisement or site to which it relates, the period within which the display or use is to be discontinued and must contain a full statement of the authority's reasons for serving the notice. The notice must also specify the period (not being less than 8 weeks after service) at the end of which it will take effect; however, if within that period an appeal is lodged with the Secretary of State, the notice will be of no effect pending the determination or withdrawal of the appeal (see below for a description of the appeal process).

Principles of control

Where express consent is required for the display of advertisements the powers conferred by the 1989 regulations with respect to the grant or refusal of consent (and with respect to the revocation or modification of such consent—see regs 16 and 17 below) are exercisable *only* in the interests of amenity or public safety (1971 Act, s 63(1); 1989 regulations, reg 4(1)).

Regulation 4(1) then sets out some of the relevant factors which must be considered in deciding whether it is in the interests of 'amenity' or 'public safety'. The regulation makes clear that these considerations are not exhaustive and other material factors may be considered. But it would appear to follow that the local planning authority should not concern themselves with the content or subject matter of an advertisement, nor should they consider whether there is a need for any particular advertisement. Express consent cannot be refused because the planning authority consider the advertisement to be unnecessary or offensive to public morals.

Circular 15/89 emphasises that clearly stated and explicit reasons must always accompany a local planning authority's decisions: it is never enough

---

1 In *Swishbrook Ltd v Secretary of State for the Environment* (18 November, 1988, *unreported*) it was held that failure to serve on the advertiser could not be used by the owner as a reason for having an order quashed and there was no need to set out the right of appeal in the order.

merely to state that the display is 'against the interests' of amenity or public safety (see para 30).

Procedure for obtaining express consent

The procedure for obtaining express consent for the display of an advertisement is very similar to that for obtaining planning permission—see regs 9 to 17. The appropriate fee must accompany the application.[2] The planning authority may grant consent subject to the standard conditions specified in Sch 1 to the regulations (below) and to such additional conditions as they think fit, or may refuse consent (see reg 13).

Every grant of express consent must be for a fixed period (see reg 13(5)). This will be five years unless the planning authority specify a longer or shorter period in the consent. Where a shorter period is specified, the authority must, unless the application was for such shorter period, state in writing their reasons for doing so and circular 15/89 advises imposing a specific condition requiring the removal of the display at the end of that period (see para 31).

Within the six months preceding the expiry of an express consent, application may be made for renewal of the consent (reg 13(7)). After expiry of an express consent, however, the advertisement may continue to be displayed unless the consent was granted subject to a condition requiring removal of the advertisement at the expiry of the period specified in the consent or unless renewal of consent has been refused (see Class 14). Such an advertisement which continues to be displayed may be the subject of discontinuance action by the authority.

An express consent for the display of an advertisement may be revoked or modified if it is considered expedient (presumably this can only be done in the interests of amenity or public safety) subject to a possible claim for compensation (see regs 16 and 17).

Appeal to the Secretary of State

An appeal may be made to the Secretary of State against the refusal by a local planning authority to grant express consent; against the grant of express consent subject to conditions; against a deemed refusal arising from the non-determination of an application for express consent; and against a discontinuance notice. Regulation 15 prescribes the procedure for making such an appeal[3] by applying s 36 and 37 of the 1971 Act with necessary modifications (these sections as modified are set out in Part 1 of Sch 4 to the 1989 regs).

Written notice of appeal, stating the grounds on which the appeal is based, is to be given to the Secretary of State within two months from the receipt of notification of the planning authority's decision or within two months of the end of the period within which the decision should have been given. An appeal against a discontinuance notice must be submitted before the notice takes effect (see Pt III of Sch 4, para 1(2)). The appellant must furnish to the Secretary of State within twenty-eight days of giving notice of appeal copies of the documents specified in s 36(2) as modified. The local planning

2 See the Town and Country Planning (Fees for Applications and Deemed Applications) Regulations 1989, reg 11.
3 Also see circular 15/89, paras 36 to 44.

authority, for their part, may be required to submit a statement in writing within a certain period, containing matters relating to the appeal.

Before determining an appeal, The Secretary of State will, if either the appellant or the local planning authority so desire, afford each of them an opportunity of appearing before and being heard by a person appointed by the minister. However, this right does not apply where the Secretary of State is satisfied that he has sufficient information (see s 36(2A) and (4) as modified).

Standard conditions

The five standard conditions to which reference has been made above are contained in Sch 1 to the 1989 regulations. The 1989 regs now make clear that all these conditions apply to all consents granted by or under the regulations (see regs 6 and 13). These conditions provide (1) that all advertisements must be kept clean and tidy; (2) that hoardings etc must be maintained in a safe condition; (3) that when an advertisement is required to be removed under the regulations, the removal shall be carried out to the reasonable satisfaction of the planning authority; (4) that no advertisement is to be displayed without the permission of the owner of the site or any other person entitled to give permission; (5) that an advertisement must not obscure any road, rail or air traffic signal or aid to navigation and must not render hazardous the use of any road, railway, waterway or airfield.

Condition 4 is intended to enable the local planning authorities to deal with the problem of fly posting (see below). Condition 5 used to only apply to deemed consents but in the 1989 regulations applies to express consents as well.

Advertisements relating to travelling circuses and fairs

The 1984 Regulations use to provide that consent may be granted, subject to the standard conditions and other conditions, for the temporary display on unspecified sites of posters, etc relating to the visit of a travelling circus or fair. These are now contained in deemed consent, Class 3G.

Offences and enforcement

Although s 109(1) provides for regulations to be made setting up a system of enforcement notices, no such regulations have as yet been made, but s 109(2) makes it a criminal offence to display an advertisement in contravention of the provisions of the regulations and a person guilty of such an offence is liable on summary conviction to a fine not exceeding level three on the standard scale[4] and to a daily penalty of £40[5] in the case of a continuing offence (see 1971 Act, s 109(2); and 1989 regulations, reg 26). For the purposes of these provisions, and without prejudice to their generality, a person is deemed to display an advertisement if the advertisement is

---

4 See Local Government and Planning (Amendment) Act 1981, s 1 and Schedule, para 16 (which increased the amount to £200) and ss 37 and 46 of the Criminal Justice Act 1982.
5 See Housing and Planning Act 1986, s 49 and Sch 11, para 13.

displayed on land of which he is the owner or occupier or if the advertisement gives publicity to his goods, trade, business or other concerns; such a person is not, however, to be guilty of an offence if he proves that the advertisement was displayed without his knowledge or consent (see 1971 Act, s 109(3)).[6] In *Porter v Honey*[7] Lord Griffiths in the House of Lords pointed out that the burden of proving this defence is placed upon the defendant but it was nevertheless held that this provision showed that Parliament had not intended to create an offence of strict liability. The House of Lords therefore went on to read into the deemed consent for estate agents' boards a provision that the first board which was displayed remains lawful even though a second unlawful board is erected. However, it would seem that it is no defence to prove that you did not know that you had not got the benefit of a deemed consent.

Circular 15/89 gives advice as to how successful prosecutions can be brought against the organisers of events being advertised by 'fly posting' (see para 46). In addition to the power to prosecute, s 109A enables a district council or London Borough Council summarily to remove or obliterate any illegally displayed placard or poster in their area provided they give two days' prior notice of their intention to do so.

Compensation

Only in two sets of circumstances is compensation payable by the planning authority in connection with advertisement control. First, compensation may be payable on revocation or modification of any express consent for the display of an advertisement (see regs 16 and 17). Secondly, where any person, for the purpose of complying with any of the regulations, carries out works for the removal of an advertisement which was being displayed on 1 August 1948 or for the discontinuance of the use of a site used for the display of advertisements on that date, he will be entitled to his reasonable expenses from the planning authority (1971 Act, s 176; and 1989 regulations, reg 20).

Areas of special control

Rural areas or areas other than rural areas which appear to the Secretary of State to require special protection on grounds of amenity may be defined as areas of special control (s 63(3)(b) and (3A)). An order defining an area of special control is made by the local planning authority. It requires the approval of the Secretary of State (see reg 18(2)). The procedure for defining an area of special control is set out in Sch 5 to the 1989 regulations.

The effect of such an order is to restrict very considerably the types of advertisement which may be displayed in the area (see reg 19).

Under s 63(3) of the 1971 Act regulations may make special provision with respect to the display of advertisements in conservation areas, and experimental areas; but no regulations have yet been made for experimental areas. However, there are certain restrictions in conservation areas, National Parks,

---

6 See *John v Reveille Newspapers Ltd* (1955) 5 P & CR 95. On the matter of continuing offences see *Royal Borough of Kensington and Chelsea v Elmton Ltd* (1978) 245 Estates Gazette 10:1.
7 [1988] 3 All ER 1045, [1988] 1 WLR 1420.

areas of outstanding natural beauty and the Broads, on the application of Class 8 of the specified classes of deemed consent (see p 498 above).

Advertisements on listed buildings

Where an advertisement is to be displayed on a listed building and is such as to affect the character of the building, listed building consent will be necessary not only for an advertisement which requires express consent under the 1989 regulations but also for an advertisement that may be displayed with deemed consent (p 478 above).

Controlling advertisements through conditions on planning permissions

The impact of advertisements in an area may be a matter which a local planning authority will wish to take into account in the exercise of their normal development control powers. The question arises whether the general power to impose conditions contained in s 29(1) of the 1971 Act may be used to control matters which are the subject of more specific legislation. As a matter of law this would seem in principle to be an appropriate use of a condition.[8] However, the Secretary of State, presumably as a matter of policy, appears to take the view that the more specific control in the Advertisement Control Regulations should be used in preference to conditions and he has, on a number of occasions, exercised his power on appeal to discharge conditions imposed on planning permissions restricting or regulating the display of advertisements.[9]

E TREE PRESERVATION

Trees make an important contribution to the quality of the landscape. 'Trees', observed a circular issued by the Secretary of State for the Environment, 'enhance the quality of the countryside, provide a habitat for wildlife and soften and add character to built up areas.'[10] In recent years, a number of factors, such as dutch elm disease and changes in agricultural and forestry practices, have resulted in some loss of quality and variety in the landscape. 'If the tree stock is to be maintained for the future', continued the circular, 'the protection and regeneration of our tree cover, and especially the planting of new trees, is essential.'

The 1971 Act recognises the importance of trees by requiring local planning authorities on granting planning permission to make appropriate provision for the planting and preservation of trees (s 59). Although the felling, lopping or destruction of a tree does not constitute development for the purposes of the planning legislation, there are two ways in which an authority may discharge this requirement. First of all, the authority may, in granting planning permission for any development, impose conditions relating to the preservation or planting of trees (s 59(a)). Secondly, the planning authority may make a tree preservation order in connection with the grant of a permission (ss 59(b) and 60).

8 See *Westminster Bank Ltd v Minister of Housing and Local Government* [1971] AC 508, [1970] 1 All ER 734, HL. Contrast appeal decision by the Secretary of State for the Environment noted at [1982] JPL 733.
9 See the appeal decision noted at [1982] JPL 733, circular 1/85, para 17 and Circular 15/89, para 4.
10 Circular 36/78. 'Trees and Forestry', para 2.

The term 'tree' is nowhere defined in the Act. However, circular 36/78 makes a distinction, for the purposes of tree preservation orders, between trees on the one hand and bushes, shrubs and hedges on the other.[11] In *Kent County Council v Batchelor*[12] Lord Denning MR said that a tree in a woodland 'ought to be something over seven or eight inches in diameter', but this measurement was not followed by Phillips J in *Bullock v Secretary of State for the Environment*.[13] Speaking of the relevant statutory provisions he said it seemed to him 'that anything that ordinarily one would call a tree is a "tree" within this group of sections in the Act of 1971. It seems to me that, if it were not so, it would be difficult to apply section 59 which relates to the imposition of conditions for the planting of trees, which in the nature of things are quite likely to be saplings, or s 62 which makes provision for the replacement of trees, which again in the nature of things are likely to be replaced by saplings.'[14]

Conditions

Section 59(a) of the 1971 Act imposes a duty on local planning authorities to ensure, whenever appropriate, that in granting planning permission for any development, adequate provision is made, by the imposition of conditions, for the preservation or planting of trees. Such conditions are widely employed by planning authorities. Model conditions have been published by the Department of the Environment.[15] Establishing a tree screen for a development will take time, perhaps several years. Conditions may require not just the planting of trees but their maintenance during the first few years and the replacement of any trees that die. However, the DoE circular states that it is not reasonable to use conditions to secure the permanent preservation of trees.[16] If this is needed then recourse should be made to tree preservation orders.

Tree preservation order

If a local planning authority consider that 'in the interests of amenity' provision should be made for the preservation of any trees or woodlands in their area, they may make a tree preservation order (s 60(1)). In *Belcross Co Ltd v Mid-Bedfordshire District Council*[17] it was held that the council had not acted improperly by taking into account, in making a tree preservation order, the fact that the tree was not going to be directly damaged by a proposed development. But it would seem that a local planning authority are limited to considerations of amenity in making such orders. This is a notoriously difficult term to define but circular 36/78 suggests that: 'Trees may be worthy of preservation for their instrinsic beauty or for their contribution to the

---

11 Memorandum annexed to circular 36/78, para 44.
12 (1976) 33 P & CR 185, CA.
13 (1980) 40 P & CR 246.
14 See also appeal decision noted at [1979] JPL 483. The Town and Country Planning (Tree Preservation Order) (Amendment) and (Trees in Conservation Areas) (Exempted Cases), Regulations 1975, reg 3(7) exempt trees of less than a prescribed diameter from certain of the controls over trees in conservation areas.
15 Memorandum annexed to circular 36/78, Appendix 4.
16 ibid, para 75. See also circular 1/85, para 40.
17 [1989] JPL 164.

landscape; or because they serve to screen an eyesore or future development; the value of trees may be enhanced by their scarcity; and the value of a group of trees or woodland may be collective only'.[18]

Provision may be made by a tree preservation order:

(a) for prohibiting the cutting down, topping, lopping, uprooting, wilful damage or wilful destruction of trees except with the consent of the planning authority and for enabling that authority to give their consent subject to conditions (s 60(1)(a)), as amended by s 11(1) of the Town and Country Amenities Act 1974);

(b) for securing the replanting of any part of a woodland area which is felled in the course of forestry operations permitted by or under order (s 60(1)(b)); and

(c) for applying in relation to any consent under the order certain of the provisions of the 1971 Act relating to planning permission, applications for such permission, appeals to the Secretary of State, purchase notices, etc. (s 60(1)(c); and s 191(1)).

The order may also provide for payment of compensation in respect of loss or damage resulting from a refusal or conditional grant of any consent required under the order (s 175).

Nothing in a tree preservation order is to prohibit the cutting down, uprooting, topping or lopping of trees that are dead, dying or dangerous; or the carrying out of work in compliance with an obligation under an Act of Parliament or to prevent or abate a nuisance (s 60(6)). There are other exemptions (such as works by certain public authorities) which are included in the form of the order prescribed in the Town and Country Planning (Tree Preservation Order) Regulations 1969[19] (1969 tree regulations).

In certain circumstances a tree preservation order may only be made if the Forestry Commissioners consent to its making (see s 60(7)). Under s 266(2)(a) of the 1971 Act a tree preservation order cannot be made in respect of Crown land unless the 'appropriate authority' consents. Under s 2 of the Town and Country Planning Act 1984 local planning authorities are empowered to make tree preservation orders in respect of Crown land in which there exists no interest other than that of the Crown if the planning authority consider it expedient to do so in order to preserve trees or woodlands on the land in the event of the land ceasing to be Crown land or becoming subject to a private interest. The consent of the 'appropriate authority' is required and such an order does not take effect until the land ceases to be Crown land or becomes subject to a private interest. The Crown is obliged to notify the planning authority of any disposal or granting of an interest. Confirmation procedures can then be commenced.

Procedure for making a tree preservation order

The detailed procedure for the making of a tree preservation order is to be found in the 1969 Tree Regulations.

The order is to be substantially in the form set out in the Schedule to the Regulations and is to include a map defining the position of the trees, groups

18 Memorandum annexed to circular 36/78, para 40.
19 As amended by the Town and Country Planning (Tree Preservation Order) (Amendment) Regulations 1981.

of trees or woodlands to which it relates (reg 4). The planning authority must place on deposit a certified copy of the order and map for inspection in at least one place convenient to the locality (reg 5(a)). In *Vale of Glamorgan Borough Council v Palmer and Bowles*[20] the Divisional Court held that regulation 5(a) was to be interpreted as meaning that a copy of the order and map was to remain deposited for inspection for so long as the order was in force, that the provision was mandatory and not merely directory and that a failure to comply with the provision consequently invalidated an order; 'unless [orders] are so deposited', said Webster J, 'members of the public will be unable to find out what trees in any area are affected by a tree preservation order.'

The planning authority must also serve a copy of the order and the accompanying map on the owners and occupiers of the land affected and on any person known to them to be entitled to work by surface working any minerals in the land or to fell any of the trees affected by the order (reg 5). A period of 28 days is allowed for the making of objections and representations to the local planning authority (reg 7).[1]

Subject to the provisions of s 61 of the 1971 Act (see below), a tree preservation order will not take effect until it is confirmed by the local planning authority (s 60(4)). Before deciding whether to confirm the order, the authority must take into consideration any objections and representations duly made. There is no obligation to afford objectors the opportunity of a hearing but, if a hearing is arranged, the authority must have regard to the report of the hearing (reg. 8). If the authority decide to confirm the order they may make such modifications as they consider expedient (s 60(4)).

After confirmation, a tree preservation order must be recorded in the Local Land Charges Register (s 60(4)).

Provisional tree preservation orders

Normally a tree preservation order does not take effect until it is confirmed by the planning authority (s 60(4)). Since the trees in question might well be destroyed before confirmation, the 1971 Act provides that the planning authority may include in a tree preservation order a direction that the order should take effect provisionally on such date as is specified in the order; in such a case the order continues in force by virtue of s 61 until the expiry of a period of six months from the date the order was made or until the date on which the order is confirmed, whichever occurs first (s 61(1)–(2)).

Consents under tree preservation order

The felling or lopping etc of trees which are subject to a tree preservation order will normally require the consent of the planning authority; if such consent is refused or is granted subject to conditions there is a right of appeal to the Secretary of State (see art 8 of and Third Schedule to the prescribed form of tree preservation order which applies with modifications the procedure for appeals against planning conditions). Before determining an appeal the Secretary of State is obliged to afford to the appellant and the local

---

20 (1982) 81 LGR 678.
1 As amended by the Town and Country Planning (Tree Preservation Order) (Amendment) and (Trees in Conservation Areas) (Exempted Cases) Regulations 1975.

planning authority an opportunity of appearing before and being heard by a person appointed by him for the purpose; however, it seems appeals are usually settled by written representations; see circular 36/78, para 59 of the memorandum.

In a letter published in the *Journal of Planning and Environment Law*, a spokesman for the Department of Environment and Transport indicated that, as the Secretary of State no longer had jurisdiction over the confirmation of tree preservation orders, he would now be exceeding his jurisdiction if, in relation to an appeal against refusal of consent, he took account of the merit of an order at the time it was made.[2] However, on hearing an appeal, the contribution that the tree makes to the amenities of the area (and so too the merits of the original decision to make the Order) will often be relevant.

In certain circumstances the control exercised by the planning authority will interact with the general control over the felling of trees exercised by the Forestry Commission. Under the Forestry Act 1967 a licence issued by the Forestry Commissioners is generally required before trees may be felled.[3] A licence is not, however, necessary in respect of the felling of trees growing in an orchard, garden, churchyard or public open space; nor is a licence needed where felling is immediately necessary for the purpose of carrying out development authorised under the planning legislation (1967 Act, s 9(2)(b),(4)(d)).[4] Where a licence is required in respect of trees which are subject to a tree preservation order, application should be made to the commissioners for a licence (see 1967 Act, s 15(6)) and application for consent need not be made to the planning authority since the licence, if granted, operates as consent under the tree preservation order. If in such a case it is proposed to grant a licence, the local planning authority must be so informed; if the authority object to the grant of a licence the application is referred to the Secretary of State (see 1967 Act s 15(1) to (4)).

Replacement of trees

Where a tree which is the subject of a tree preservation order is removed, uprooted or destroyed in contravention of the order or is removed, uprooted, destroyed or dies at a time when its uprooting or felling is authorised only because it is urgently necessary in the interests of safety, it is the duty of the owner of the land to replace the tree in question with another tree of appropriate size and species as soon as he reasonably can (s 62(1)).[5] On application by the owner of the land the planning authority may dispense with this requirement. The tree preservation order applies to the replacement tree (s 62(2)).

This duty formerly did not apply to woodlands but the Town and Country Planning (Amendment) Act 1985 amended s 62 so that it does apply to the unauthorised removal, uprooting or destruction of trees in a woodland.

2 [1981] JPL 899.
3 See the Forestry (Felling of Trees) Regulations 1979, and *Rutland District Council v Secretary of State for the Environment* (22 June 1989, unreported).
4 See also the Forestry (Exceptions from Restriction of Felling) Regulations 1979 and the Forestry (Exceptions from Restriction of Felling) (Amendment) Regulations 1981.
5 As amended by the Town and Country Planning (Amendment) Act 1985.

However, it does not apply if the action is authorised because of reasons of safety. In the case of woodlands, the duty is to plant the same number of trees either on or near the land on which the trees previously stood, or on some other land if this is agreed between the local planning authority and the owner of that land. The local planning authority in both cases can designate the places for the replanting.

The model order provides for the situation where an unspecified number of trees can be protected within a particular area: referred to as 'Trees Specified by Reference to an Area'. In *Bush v Secretary of State for the Environment and Redditch Borough Council*[6] Graham Eyre QC (sitting as deputy judge) rejected the argument that the replanting duty did not arise in such a case. In such circumstances there is a duty to replant the same number of whatever trees have been removed in the area covered by the order. Enforcement difficulties could however arise if it is not clear how many trees (and of what size and species) have been destroyed.

In granting consent under a tree preservation order the local planning authority may, of course, impose a condition as to replanting or replacement of trees; (see Schedule, art 4 of the Model Order). Such a condition cannot be imposed on a consent relating to a woodland but a direction must be given requiring replanting unless consent is given to allow development to take place or the authority (with the approval of the minister) dispense with replanting (see Schedule, art 4 of the Model Order). It seems that trees planted under a replanting condition are not automatically protected (see circular 36/78, para 60 of the memorandum).

There are now also replanting requirements which arise under the Forestry legislation; see Forestry Act 1986.[7]

Offences and enforcement

A breach of a tree preservation order cannot normally be remedied; the damage to a tree cannot be undone. The sanctions supporting the tree preservation order provisions are, therefore, penal rather than remedial[8] although, as we mentioned above, an owner of land may, in certain circumstances be required to replace a tree.

The penal provisions differentiate between actions which result in the destruction of a tree and actions which cause damage falling short of destruction. The former are dealt with by s 102(1) of the 1971 Act[9] which prescribes penalties on conviction for contravening a tree preservation order by cutting down, uprooting or wilfully destroying a tree or wilfully damaging, topping or looping a tree in such a manner as to be likely to destroy it. A person wilfully destroys a tree if he intentionally inflicts on it injury so radical that in all the circumstances any reasonably competent forester would decide

---

6 [1988] JPL 108.
7 See on this *Rutland v Secretary of State for the Environment*, (22 June 1989 unreported).
8 Local planning authorities have been able to obtain an injunction to support a tree preservation order (see *Kent County Council v Batchelor* [1978] 3 All ER 980, [1979] 1 WLR 213; *A-G v Melville Construction Co Ltd* (1968) 20 P & CR 131).
9 A new s 102(1) was substituted by s 11(3) of the Town and Country Amenities Act 1974.

that it ought to be felled.[10] It would seem that the offence is absolute; knowledge of the existence of an order is not a necessary ingredient.[11]

Section 102(2) of the 1971 Act[12] prescribes lesser penalties for conviction for other offences relating to trees subject to tree preservation orders including causing damage to a tree short of destruction. Section 102(3) makes provision for continuing offences.

Where it appears to the planning authority that the provisions of s 62 of the 1971 Act relating to the replacement of trees (above), or any conditions attached to a consent under a tree preservation order which require the replacement of trees, have not been complied with, they may, within two years from the date when the failure came to their knowledge, serve on the owner of the land a notice requiring him within a specified period to plant a tree or trees of specified size and species (s 103(1)). There is a right of appeal to the Secretary of State against such a notice on the grounds specified in s 103(3) of the 1971 Act. If the notice is not complied with, the planning authority may carry out the required planting themselves and recover their reasonable expenses from the person who is for the time being the owner of the land (see s 103(5)).

Compensation

The mere making of a tree preservation order will not give rise to any claim for compensation. It is only when consent for the felling etc of trees is refused or is granted subject to conditions that such a claim may be made (see 1971 Act s 174 and arts 9 to 12 of the prescribed form of tree preservation order).[13] Compensation will not normally be payable if, on refusing consent or granting consent subject to conditions, the local planning authority certify that they are satisfied either that the refusal or condition is in the interests of good forestry or that the trees have an outstanding or special amenity value. Such a certificate may, however, be the subject of an appeal to the Secretary of State (see Third Schedule of the Model Order).

It used to be the position that a compensation claim could not be headed off in this way, where consent to chop down a woodland was refused. In the case of woodlands, consent can be refused on the grounds that it is necessary in the interests of amenity (see Schedule, art 4 of the Model Order) and where consent is granted a direction requiring replanting must be made (see art 6). In *Bell v Canterbury City Council*[14] the council attempted to forestall a claim

---

10 See *Barnet London Borough Council v Eastern Electricity Board* [1973] 2 All ER 319, [1973] 1 WLR 430.

11 *Maidstone Borough Council v Mortimer* [1980] 3 All ER 552. The order must, however, have been placed on a deposit for inspection so that the public are able to find out what trees in the area are protected— *Vale of Glamorgan Borough Council v Palmer and Bowles* (1982) 81 LGR 678.

12 As amended by the Criminal Justice Act 1982, s 37). It is not altogether clear whether the offence of causing or permitting the destruction of a tree in contravention of a tree preservation order is caught by s 102(1) or (2) of the 1971 Act. If the latter is the case then it attracts a lesser penalty than actual destruction of the tree. For a discussion of this area see C Crawford and P Schofield., 'A Weak Branch of the Law on Trees?' [1981] JPL 316.

13 On the general principles applicable to assessment of compensation following such a decision see *Bollans v Surrey County Council* (1968) 20 P & CR 745; see too *Cardigan Timber Co v Cardiganshire County Council* (1957) 9 P & CR 158.

14 (1988) 56 P & CR 211.

for compensation (where they had refused consent to grub out 39 acres of woodland so that the land could be used for agriculture) resolving that, if consent were to have been granted, the council could have directed replanting under art 6. The Court of Appeal held that art 6 was only applicable in the case of proposed 'forestry operations' and in any case the resolution in the circumstances was totally unreasonable and so invalid. The Court of Appeal also held that the compensation payable included not only the loss of the value of the timber but the diminution in the value of the land caused by not being able to reclaim it for agricultural use. A sum of £38,851 was awarded as compensation. However, this loophole has been closed off and a certificate can now be issued in the case of a group of trees or a woodland, that it has an outstanding or special amenity value.[15]

Where a replanting requirement is imposed in respect of a woodland area, compensation may be payable by the planning authority for loss or damage resulting from the requirement if the Forestry Commissioners decide not to make any advance under s 4 of the Forestry Act 1967 in respect of the replanting on the ground that the requirement frustrates the use of the woodland area for commercial purposes in accordance with good forestry practice (s 175).

Trees in conservation areas

Section 61A[16] of the 1971 Act provides that any person who cuts down, tops, lops, uproots, wilfully damages or wilfully destroys any tree in a conservation area is guilty of an offence unless he has first given notice of his intention to the district council or London Borough in whose area the tree is or was situated. The purpose of this provision is to give the local planning authority an opportunity to consider the making of a tree preservation order. If the local planning authority consent to the proposed works or if the six week period expires without the authority taking action, the proposed works may be carried out.[17] If no specific consent has been given, a further notice will have to be given if the work is not carried out within two years from the service of the original notice.

The provisions of s 61A are not to apply to a tree which is subject to a tree preservation order. Nor do they apply to certain exempted cases specified in regulation 3 of the Town and Country Planning (Tree Preservation Order) (Amendment) and (Trees in Conservation Areas) (Exempted Cases) Regulations 1975.

A person guilty of an offence under s 61A is liable to the penalties applicable in relation to a contravention of a tree preservation order (s 102(4)) (above). Where a tree to which s 61A applies is removed, uprooted or destroyed in contravention of s 61A the owner of the land becomes liable to plant another tree of appropriate size and species, (s 61A(8)).

15 See Town and Country Planning (Tree Preservation Order) (Amendment) Regulations 1988.
16 Section 61A was added by the Town and Country Amenities Act 1974.
17 However it has been held in *R v North Hertfordshire District Council ex p Hyde* (1989) Independent, 14 June, that expiration of the 6 week period does prevent the authority making the trees subject to a tree preservation order.

F LAND ADVERSELY AFFECTING AMENITY OF NEIGHBOURHOOD

If it appears to the local planning authority that the amenity of any part of their area, or any adjoining area, is adversely affected by the condition of land in their area, they may serve a notice on the owner and occupier of the land requiring steps for the condition of the land to be remedied. The notice must specify a period within which these steps must be taken and the notice will take effect, subject to the lodging of an appeal, on a specified date not less than twenty-eight days after service (1971 Act, s 65).

Section 65 is very open-ended in that it does not make clear the nature of the condition of the land which can be taken to have caused the adverse effects nor the nature of the adverse effects. The former wording was much stricter in that it only applied to 'any garden, vacant site or other open land'[18] and it had to be shown that the condition was causing 'serious injury' to amenity. The new wording (introduced by the Housing and Planning Act 1986, s 46) would suggest that it covers both 'built-upon' and 'unbuilt' land; land is defined by s 290 to include buildings. Circular 19/86, however, advises that it should be used with discretion as a means of dealing with relatively isolated severe cases of neglected or unsightly land. It is a ground of appeal that 'the condition of the land to which the notice relates is attributable to, and such as results in the ordinary course of events from, the carrying on of operations or a use of land which is not in contravention of planning control' (1971 Act, s 105(1)(b)). This would suggest that the section is aimed at the physical state of the land rather than at harm caused by active use of the land itself. It is therefore mainly concerned with what are colloquially described as 'eyesores' though it could cover other types of harm: as when the condition of land causes flooding or landslips. However, in *Britt v Buckinghamshire County Council*[19] the Court of Appeal interpreted the old wording as not precluding action where the land is still being put to an active business use, if this is in breach of planning control. There is no ground of appeal that the condition is attributable to operations or uses which are unlawful but immune from enforcement. So the main importance of s 65 would seem to be that it can be used where an enforcement notice could not be served either because the condition of the land is caused by neglect rather than by positive development or where the condition has been caused by development but that development is immune from enforcement.

A person on whom a s 65 notice is served, or any other person having an interest in the land in question, may appeal in writing to a magistrates court on one of the stipulated grounds (1971 Act s 105). The appeal must be lodged before the date on which the notice is to take effect. The lodging of an appeal suspends the operation of the notice until such time as the appeal is determined or withdrawn. The process is similar to that for appealing against an enforcement notice served under s 88 of the 1971 Act except that appeal has to be made to the magistrates court and not the Secretary of State. The magistrates' powers are largely confined to looking at whether the condition of the land has caused adverse effects and at the terms of the notice and they

---

18   In *Stephens v Cuckfield RDC* [1960] 2 QB 373, [1960] 2 All ER 716, CA, this was interpreted as excluding a fenced yard used as a carbreakers' yard which was surrounded by a building.
19   [1964] 1 QB 77, [1963] 2 All ER 175.

have no power to quash the notice on policy grounds. There is a further right of appeal from the magistrates to the Crown Court (1971 Act s 106). It is an offence for any owner or occupier on whom a notice is served to fail to take steps required by the notice within the required period. It is now not necessary to prove in addition that the person has continued or aggravated the injury and so an offence can be committed by simply doing nothing to comply with the notice.[20] There are provisions in s 104 (similar to those in s 89 relating to enforcement notices; see p 363) dealing with the problems of owners or occupiers selling or leaving the land once a notice has been served and making it a further offence to fail to secure compliance after a conviction.

If the steps required by the notice are not taken within the period specified in the notice, the planning authority may themselves take the necessary steps and are entitled to recover their expenses from the person who is then the owner or occupier of the land (s 107).

G MINERALS

Mineral operations,[1] as we indicated earlier,[2] constitute development as defined in s 22(1) of the 1971 Act and are subject, therefore, to planning control. However, it has long been recognised that mineral operations possess certain characteristics which are not shared by other types of development. Building and engineering operations, observed the Stevens Committee in their report *Planning Control over Mineral Working*,[3] are essentially interludes between two successive uses of land; they fit the land for a desired new use which can begin as soon as the operation ends. Mining operations, on the other hand, are an end in themselves; they may continue for many years, often intermittently; they do not fit the land for a desired use; indeed, they are essentially destructive and may render the land unfit for any other use. Furthermore, minerals can only be worked where they exist.

The 1971 Act takes some account of these characteristics by empowering the Secretary of State to make regulations adapting and modifying certain of its provisions in relation to development consisting of mineral operations.[4] Certain adaptations and modifications are currently made by the Town and Country Planning (Minerals) Regulations 1971.[5]

Fuller recognition of these characteristics and their effect followed the publication of the report of the Stevens Committee in 1976[6] and resulted in the Town and Country Planning (Minerals) Act 1981 which made a number of important amendments to the 1971 Act. The regulations and the amendments made by the 1981 Act are now considered in turn.

20 See *Red House Farms (Thorndon) Ltd v Mid Suffolk District Council* (1980) 40 P & CR 119 where it was held that under the old wording an offence could not be committed by simply doing nothing.
1 For the definition of 'mining operations', see s 22(3A) of the 1971 Act; 'development consisting of the winning and working of minerals' and 'mineral-working deposit' are defined in s 264(1A); and 'minerals' is defined in s 290(1).
2 See p 90.
3 HMSO, 1976, ch 3.
4 1971 Act, s 264(1).
5 Made under powers contained in earlier legislation, now superseded by s 264(1) of the 1971 Act, and see amendments made by the Town and Country Planning (Minerals) Regulations 1982.
6 See circular 1/1978 'Report of the Committee on Planning Control over Mineral Workings'.

I *Town and Country Planning (Minerals) Regulations 1971*

The 1971 regulations provide that for certain purposes mining operations are to be treated as if they constituted a 'use' of land rather than 'operations' (reg 3). For example, the carrying out of mining operations may be treated as a use of land for the purposes of s 87 of the 1971 Act, with the result that an enforcement notice can require the discontinuance of mining operations: mining operations are also to be treated as a use for the purposes of s 89 of the 1971 Act, so that where, by virtue of an enforcement notice, mineral development is required to be discontinued and that notice is not complied with, an offence is committed (see reg 3).

As with 'operations' of other sorts, where mining operations are carried out without planning permission an enforcement notice may be served only within four years of the carrying out of the unauthorised development: it was, however, held by the Court of Appeal in *Thomas David (Porthcawl) Ltd v Penybont RDC*[7] that 'each cut by the bulldozer' in the course of mining operations constitutes a separate act of development, so that an enforcement notice can restrain any future unauthorised working and can require reinstatement of land on which unauthorised mining operations took place in the preceding four years. Where there is non-compliance with any condition or limitation attached to a grant of planning permission for mining operations, an enforcement notice may be served at any time within four years after the non-compliance has come to the knowledge of the planning authority (reg 4). This means that, even if such a condition was a condition which relates to 'the carrying out of operations'; (see s 87(4)), the four years do not run from the date of the breach but from the date of knowledge.

Under regulation 6 every planning permission for mining operations granted before 1 April 1969 was, if the development was not begun before the beginning of 1968, deemed to have been granted subject to a condition that the development had to be begun before 1 April 1979. As regards planning permission for mining operations granted on or after 1 April 1969, however, the regulations do not modify the statute and s 41(1) of the 1971 Act provides that any such permission is, unless the local planning authority specify otherwise, deemed to have been granted subject to a condition that the development must be begun within five years.

Circular 60/71 states that in considering what time limit to specify for the commencement of mining operations planning authorities 'should have regard to the mineral operator's reasonable requirement of certainty in planning his production and investing in plant. A period of substantially more than 10 years may well be found to be justified,' (para 6). The circular stresses the mineral industry's need for long-term planning. Section 41(1) must now be read subject to the terms of 41(3)(bb).[8] This excludes from the operation of subs (1) planning permission for the winning and working of minerals which is granted subject to a condition that the development to which it relates must be begun within a specified time after completion of other mineral development which is already being carried out by the applicant. 'In this way', states circular 1/1982, 'the certainty of development is sustained, but a flexibility needed by operators acquiring mineral-bearing

---

7 [1972] 3 All ER 1092, [1972] 1 WLR 1526.
8 Introduced by the Town and Country Planning (Minerals) Act 1981, s 6.

land as it comes onto the market and by mineral planning authorities anxious to safeguard such land is introduced.[9]

II *Town and Country Planning (Minerals) Act 1981*

The Act implements in modified form some of the recommendations of the Stevens Committee. Stevens recognised that, in view of the length of time during which mineral operations continue, conditions imposed at the outset of the process to protect the environment may be rendered less relevant and effective in time by changing circumstances. The Act introduced a series of amendments to the 1971 Act which are designed to tackle this problem.

Duration of mineral permissions. First, s 44A of the 1971 Act[10] provides that mineral permissions, both existing and new, are to have a defined life so that future generations will have an opportunity to review the position. Unless otherwise stated, the term will be sixty years from 22 February 1982[11] or the date of the permission, whichever is the later. In this regard, it has been held that a grant of planning permission is only implemented and so spent when all the minerals have been extracted, which the grant authorises to be extracted.[12]

Duty to review operations. Secondly, s 264A of the 1971 Act[13] imposes a new duty on mineral planning authorities to review mineral operations at such intervals as they see fit with a view to making any changes in the terms of the planning permission which circumstances may require. Such changes will be made by using the existing powers contained in ss 45 and 51 of 1971 Act to modify planning permission or to require that a use be discontinued or that buildings or works be removed or altered. For the purposes of s 51, the winning and working of minerals is to be treated as a use of land (s 51(1A) of the 1971 Act) and an order made under that section may provide for alteration or removal of any plant or machinery used for the winning and working of minerals (s 51A(3)(a)).

The powers contained in ss 45 and 51 are infrequently used at the present time because of the obligation on local planning authorities to compensate for all loss (see p 403 and p 407) including, for example, the depreciation in the value of land resulting from their action. However, the 1971 Act, as amended, provides planning authorities with an incentive to use these powers following a review of mineral operations by enabling the Secretary of State to make regulations modifying the compensation provisions in certain circumstances (s 178A of the 1971 Act).[14]

The modifications operate where certain requirements, referred to as 'mineral compensation requirements' are satisfied. These requirements are complex. Section 164A of the 1971 Act[15] states, for example, that the

---

9 See Annexe to circular; para 25.
10 Added by the Town and Country Planning (Minerals) Act 1981, s 7.
11 The date upon which this provision was brought into effect (Town and Country Planning (Minerals) Act 1981 (Commencement No 1) Order 1982).
12 See *Durham County Council v Secretary of State for the Environment and Tarmac Roadstone Holdings* [1989] JPL 603.
13 Added by the Town and Country Planning (Minerals) Act 1981, s 1(2).
14 Added by the Town and Country Planning (Minerals) Act 1981, s 16.
15 Added by the Town and Country Planning (Minerals) Act 1981, s 13.

compensation provisions for modification orders contained in s 164 (see p 407), will take effect subject to any such modifications where the following requirements are satisfied.

1 the order modifies planning permission for development consisting of the winning and working of minerals (s 164A(2)(a)).

2 the order does not restrict:

(a) the period within which mineral operations are to be commenced;
(b) the size of the area to be used for the winning and working of minerals;
(c) the depth of the operations;
(d) the rate of extraction;
(e) the total quantity of minerals to be extracted; or
(f) the duration of the mineral operations;

(this is as a result of a combination of s 164A(2)(b)(i) and s 178(1) and (2).[16])

3 the order does *not* modify or replace a restriction of the sort referred to in 2 above imposed either by way of condition on the grant of planning permission or by way of an earlier relevant order[17] (s 164A(2)(b)(ii)).

4 the mineral planning authority carried out consultations prior to the making of the order with:

(a) all persons having an interest in the land or the minerals (ss 164A(2)(c) and 178B(1)(a));
(b) in shire counties the district council in whose area the land is situated (ss 164A(2)(c) and 178B(1)(b) and (3)).[18]

5 the permission which is being modified was granted at least five years before the date of the order; or the order imposes what is known as an 'aftercare condition' (see p 518 below) on a planning permission granted prior to 22 February 1982[19] (s 164A(2)(d) and (3));

6 the order is made more than five years after any previous relevant order (s 164A(4)).[20]

Sections 170A[1] and 170B of the 1971 Act[2] specify the mineral compensation requirements which must be satisfied before modified compensation provisions apply to a discontinuance order made under s 51 or to a prohibition order (s 51A), a suspension order or a supplementary suspension order (s 51B) (see below).

Where the mineral compensation requirements are satisfied and a claim for compensation is made, compensation is first calculated in accordance with ss 164 or 170 (whichever is appropriate) as modified by regulations made under s 178A. This section provides for a threshold to be set below which no

16 Added by the Town and Country Planning (Minerals) Act 1981, ss 13 and 16.
17 A 'relevant order' is a reference to a revocation or modification order under s 45 of the 1971 Act, a discontinuance order under s 51 or a prohibition order under s 51A (s 178C(3)).
18 In the case of the Greater London and Metropolitan areas, the district councils are the mineral planning authority and so do not have to consult any other planning authority.
19 The date upon which s 30 A of the 1971 Act which provides for the imposition of aftercare conditions was brought into effect (Town and Country Planning (Minerals) Act 1981 (Commencement No 1) Order 1982).
20 Orders may be made more frequently but will not have the advantage of the modified compensation provisions. For the definition of 'relevant order' see s 178C(3) of the 1971 Act.
1 This section is not yet in force.
2 Added by the Town and Country Planning (Minerals) Act 1981, s 15.

compensation will be paid. The mineral operator will receive in compensation the excess over the threshold. Section 178A(4)–(6) of the 1971 Act[3] sets out the formula for determining the threshold. It is to be 10 per cent of 'the appropriate sum' although a minimum sum is prescribed. 'The appropriate sum' represents the product of the annual value of the right to work the minerals and a multiplier based on the life expectancy of the workings. The details are set out in the Town and Country Planning (Compensation for Restrictions on Mineral Working) Regulations 1985. Regulations 3 and 4 provide for the inclusion of the cost of voluntary amenity works and bring s 170 into line with s 164 as to the expenditure and loss which is compensatable. After the amount of compensation has been calculated under s 164 or 170, regs 5 to 7 provide for the sum to be reduced by the application of various formulae. The calculations are too complicated to be satisfactorily summarized but are explained in circular 11/86 in Appendices 2 and 3.

Prohibition and suspension orders. Thirdly, the 1981 Act recognises the environmental problems that can arise from the intermittent nature of mineral operations and which may become apparent during a review. To cope with such problems, mineral planning authorities are given power to make two new sorts of order.[4]

Section 51A of the 1971 Act provides for a prohibition order. Where no development has been carried out to any substantial extent at a site for a period of at least two years and it appears that the resumption of development is unlikely, the mineral planning authority may by order prohibit the resumption of development and require specific steps to be taken to tidy up the site.[5] Such an order will not take effect unless it is confirmed by the Secretary of State. On submission of the order for confirmation, the authority must also serve notice of the making of the order on the owner or occupier of the land and on any person likely to be affected by the making of the order. Any such person may, within a specified period, require to be heard by a person appointed by the Secretary of State before a decision is made on the order. In the event of the order being confirmed, the planning permission to which it relates will cease to have effect.

Section 51B of the 1971 Act provides for a suspension order to deal with temporary suspensions. Where no development has been carried out to any substantial extent at a site for a period of at least twelve months but it appears that a resumption of development is likely, the mineral planning authority may by order require specified steps to be taken for preserving the environment. The order will specify a period for compliance commencing with the date on which it takes effect; different periods may be specified for different steps. A suspension order requires confirmation by the Secretary of State, and notification and the right to a hearing apply as for a prohibition order.

The object of the suspension order is not to inhibit a resumption of work but to safeguard the environment in the interim. Work may be resumed after

---

3 Added by the Town and Country Planning (Minerals) Act 1981, s 16.
4 Both added by the Town and Country Planning (Minerals) Act 1981, s 10.
5 Where appropriate, the order may include an aftercare condition (s 51A(4)); see p 518 for an explanation of this type of condition.

giving notice to the mineral planning authority and once development has recommenced to a substantial extent[6] the authority must revoke the order (s 51F of the 1971 Act). Application may be made to the Secretary of State to revoke the order should the authority fail to do so.

At any time when a suspension order is in operation, the mineral planning authority may by way of supplementary suspension order direct that steps should be carried out in addition to or in substitution for those required to be taken by the suspension order or by any supplementary suspension order or that the suspension order should cease to have effect. The procedure for the making and confirmation of a supplementary suspension order is the same as for a suspension order (except that no confirmation is required where the order merely revokes a previous order and specifies no further steps to be taken) (ss 51B(5) and 51C).

Suspension and supplementary suspension orders are local land charges (s 51D of the 1971 Act[7]) and orders under ss 45, 51 and 51A are registrable as local land charges under the Local Land Charges Rules 1977.

Suspension orders and supplementary suspension orders must be reviewed as provided in s 51E of the 1971 Act to see whether their provisions need supplementing or whether an order prohibiting resumption of work should be made. Penalties are prescribed for contravention of a prohibition, suspension or supplementary suspension order and planning authorities are given power to enter the land, take the steps specified in the order and recover the costs (s 108 of the 1971 Act[8]).

The compensation provisions of s 170 of the 1971 Act are applied to prohibition, suspension and supplementary suspension orders (s 170A of the 1971 Act) but where the appropriate mineral compensation requirements are satisfied, the modified compensation provisions will operate (ss 170B and 178A of the 1971 Act[9].

Aftercare conditions. Fourthly, s 30A of the 1971 Act[10] enables mineral planning authorities in certain circumstances to impose what are referred to as 'aftercare' conditions on grants of planning permission for mineral operations. Where permission for mineral operations is granted subject to a restoration condition requiring, for example, the replacement of sub-soil and top-soil on the completion of works, then an aftercare condition may also be imposed.[11] This will require the land to be planted, cultivated, fertilised, watered, drained or otherwise treated on completion of the restoration condition for a period of up to five years (or such other maximum period as may be prescribed) so as to make it suitable for use for agriculture, forestry or amenity. The condition may itself detail the steps to be taken or may simply provide for the submission and implementation of an aftercare scheme to be approved by the mineral planning authority.[12] Examples of

6 This provision would seem to be designed to ensure that mineral operators do not get round a suspension order by making a token start.
7 Added by the Town and Country Planning (Minerals) Act 1981, s 10.
8 Substituted by the Town and Country Planning (Minerals) Act 1981, s 11.
9 Added by the Town and Country Planning (Minerals) Act 1981, ss 15 and 16.
10 Added by the Town and Country Planning (Minerals) Act 1981, s 5.
11 Existing permissions may have a restoration condition and an aftercare condition imposed by way of order under ss 45, 51, or 51A of the 1971 Act subject to the payment of compensation, although the compensation may be reduced if the appropriate mineral compensation requirements are satisfied.
12 See s 30A(3)(b) and the right of appeal provided by s 36(1).

aftercare conditions are set out in Appendices II and III of the Explanatory Memorandum attached to circular 1/1982. Consultations with the Ministry of Agriculture, Fisheries and Food are required over the imposition of an aftercare condition specifying agriculture as the after-use and with the Forestry Commission where the after-use is to be forestry.[13]

Where the previous use of the land was for agriculture and the use specified in an aftercare condition is for agriculture, then the land will be considered to have been made suitable for that use when its physical characteristics are restored, so far as practicable, to what they were when the land was previously so used (1971 Act, s 30A(9)). Otherwise, the standard of suitability for use for agriculture or forestry is that the land should be 'reasonably fit for that use' (1971 Act, s 30A(10) and (11)). For amenity use the land is brought to the required standard when it is suitable for sustaining tree shrubs and plants (1971 Act, s 30(12)). A person with an interest in land which is the subject of an aftercare condition may apply for a certificate from the planning authority that the condition has been complied with (1971 Act, s 30A(17)).

Miscellaneous amendments. (1) Because of the widespread concern about the harmful effects of working mineral waste tips and doubts about whether and when such works constitute 'development' and thus fall within the scope of planning control, a new subsection has been added to s 22 of the 1971 Act to clarify the position. Section 22(3A)[14] provides that 'mining operations' are to include:

(a) the removal of material of any description
   (i) from a mineral-working deposit;[15]
   (ii) from a deposit of pulverised fuel ash or other furnace ash or clinker; or
   (iii) from a deposit of iron, steel or other metallic slags; and

(b) the extraction of minerals from a disused railway embankment.

(2) Owners of mineral rights in land are now to be notified of an application for the winning and working of minerals in the same way as the owners of the land (s 27(1A) of the 1971 Act).[16] This implements a recommendation of the Stevens Committee that a person who has an interest in minerals in land should be aware of proposals to work other minerals in the land since this could affect his current or potential operations. However, the owners of rights in oil, gas, coal, gold or silver are excluded from this requirement (1971 Act, s 27(1B)).

(3) In the case of an application for planning permission for underground mining where the appliant is not also the owner of all the land, the applicant's obligation to give notice of the application now extends only to persons whose names and addresses are known to him as being owners of the land to which the application relates (1971 Act, s 27(1)(cc)).[17] This amendment overcomes difficulties encountered in complying with the somewhat stricter

13 See s 30A(3)–(6) of the 1971 Act (added by the Town and Country Planning (Minerals) Act 1981, s 5); also circular 1/1982.
14 Added by the Town and Country Planning (Minerals) Act 1981, s 1(1).
15 For the definition of 'mineral working deposit' see s 264(1A) of the 1971 Act (added by the Town and Country Planning (Minerals) Act 1981, s 1(2).
16 Added by the Town and Country Planning (Minerals) Act 1981, s 4.
17 Added by the Town and Country Planning (Minerals) Act 1981, s 4.

obligation imposed by s 27(1)(b) of the 1971 Act where mining operations are likely to extend under a very large area of land. An applicant taking advantage of s 27(1)(cc) must, however, post a site notice in every parish or community within which any part of the land is situated (1971 Act, s 27(2A) and (2B)[18]).

H HAZARDOUS SUBSTANCES

While safety is a planning consideration[19] it seems that a material change of use does not take place simply because a process becomes more dangerous because of the involvement of hazardous substances. Amendments introduced in 1983 to the Uses Classes Order and the General Development Order (see chs 5 and 6), make clear that the immunity from the need for planning permission and the grant of planning permission respectively bestowed by those Orders did not apply where the activity involved a notifiable quantity of hazardous substances. However, following a consultation paper 'Planning Control over Hazardous Development' issued by the Department of the Environment, a separate system of regulation was inserted in the 1971 Act by the Housing and Planning Act 1986.[20] This new regulatory system has not yet been brought into force[1] and, as it is modelled on the existing system of development control, the following account only brings out its distinctive features.

A 'hazardous substances consent' is required where there is present on, over or under land a hazardous substance in a particular quantity (1971 Act, s 58B(1)). It is left to the Secretary of State to specify by regulations the substances that are considered hazardous and the quantity (s 58B(3)). The control is determined by the aggregate quantity of the substance on under or over land or in or on a structure which is within a radius of 500 metres and is in or on land or structures controlled by the same person (s 58B(1)).[2]

Consent is obtained from the hazardous substances authority. This is, in Greater London, the London boroughs and in the metropolitan counties the district planning authorities. In the non-metropolitan counties control vests in the districts except that the county council exercises control where land is situated in a National Park (outside the Peak Park and Lake District where control is exercised by the Planning Boards) or is used for mineral working or waste disposal (1971 Act, s 1A). An urban development corporation is the authority where it is the local planning authority in relation to all kinds of development (1971 Act, s 1A(4)) and there are special provisions for statutory undertakers where the authority is the appropriate minister (1971 Act, s 1B).

The procedures for the making of applications will be set out in regulations but these regulations may require publicity and consultation (1971 Act, s 58C). In particular, it is envisaged that the Health and Safety Executive

18 Added by the Town and Country Planning (Minerals) Act 1981, s 4.
19 See *Stringer v Minister of Housing and Local Government* [1971] 1 All ER 65, [1970] 1 WLR, 1281 *per* Cooke J.
20 s 31.
 1 A consultation paper on proposed regulations was issued on 17 May 1989.
 2 Thus control is determined essential by drawing a circle of a radius of 500 metres and calculating whether there is sufficient quantity of hazardous material in that circle.

must be consulted (s 58 C(5)(a)). In determining an application, as with a planning application, the authority must have regard to material considerations and may attach conditions (1971 Act s 58D). However, unlike s 29, s 58D goes on to specify particular factors which must be regarded, and particular conditions which may be imposed. While there is an obvious overlap with planning considerations and conditions, a hazardous substances application is a more specialist system of control and demarcation problems may arise (see ch 8, p 222). There are special provisions for the revocation or modification of consents. There is a general power to revoke (which gives rise to a right to compensation) but powers to revoke without paying compensation arise in circumstances where the use of the land has changed or it appears that no hazardous substance has been present on the land for at least five years (1971 Act, s 58H). Consent is automatically revoked without compensation if there is a change of person in control of any *part* of the land to which the consent relates. This does not apply if there is a change of the person in control of the *whole* of the land. Where there is a change in the person in control of part, an application should be made for the continuation of the consent which may lead to it being modified or revoked (1971 Act, s 58J).

Persons causing or allowing hazardous substances to be present on land equal to or exceeding the controlled quantity, commit an offence if they have not got consent. It is also an offence for the person in control of the land to fail to comply with a condition attached to a consent. There are, however, special defences (1971 Act, s 58K). A power to issue a hazardous substance contravention notice requiring steps to be taken to remedy a contravention is contained in s 101B.

The controls have obvious implications for the work of the Health and Safety at Work Executive and s 58N makes explicit that a hazardous substance consent or a contravention notice does not affect their work and that the provisions in the Health and Safety at Work Act 1974 are overriding.

Finally, once the provisions are brought into effect, they apply to any hazardous substances already on land and not just to the introduction of new substances. However, s 34 of the Housing and Planning Act 1986 provides for a six months' transitional period in which applications can be made for existing sites. In such cases there may be a right to a deemed consent if a claim is made.

I INDUSTRIAL DEVELOPMENT CERTIFICATES

Sections 66–72 of the 1971 Act made provision for the exercise of a special form of control over industrial development, but these provisions were repealed by the Housing and Planning Act 1986, s 48, from 7 January, 1987 and in any case had been suspended since 9 January, 1982.

J OFFICE DEVELOPMENT PERMITS

Sections 73–85 of the 1971 Act which refer to office development permits were brought into effect for a temporary period only (s 86(1) of the 1971 Act). The provisions have ceased to have effect and are to be treated as if they had been repealed by another Act (s 86(5) of the 1971 Act).

CHAPTER 19
APPEAL AND OBJECTION PROCEDURES

A GENERAL

As is indicated at many points throughout this book, the planning legislation confers wide discretionary powers upon local planning authorities. These powers include, for example, the making of decisions on applications for planning permission, listed building consent and consent under the advertisement regulations, the initiation of enforcement action and the making of revocation, discontinuance and compulsory purchase orders. Inevitably, the exercise of these powers is a fertile source of conflict between local planning authorities and the individuals or bodies most directly affected by a decision or order. It has long been recognised that if the discretionary nature of planning processes are to retain general acceptance, some means of resolving conflict, a sort of pressure valve, is required. The 1971 Act provides such mechanisms by enabling persons aggrieved[1] by the exercise of many of the powers possessed by planning authorities to appeal or object to the Secretary of State.[2] A right of appeal generally arises as a consequence of an adverse decision by a local planning authority on a proposal (such as an application for planning permission) submitted by an individual or body, while a right to object generally arises in response to a proposal (such as the making of a compulsory purchase order) initiated by a local planning authority. The object of this chapter is to describe the main features of the procedures followed in connection with appeals and objections.[3]

Characteristically, appeal and objection procedures have two complementary purposes—on the one hand, say Wraith and Lamb,[4] 'to give relief to anyone who may consider himself aggrieved and on the other hand to assist a Minister[5] to come to the best possible administrative decision'.[6] They can

---

1 Members of the public at large are not aggrieved persons for these purposes. Whilst they may have an opportunity to make representations in the course of appeal and objection procedures, they cannot initiate the process. Planning control is intended to regulate development in the public interest—not, generally, to confer new rights on members of the public.
2 Objections to a local plan are, however, normally made to and determined by the plan-making authority (see ch 4); and objections to a tree preservation order are made to and determined by the order-making authority (see ch 18).
3 For general discussion of appeal and objection procedures see R E Wraith and G B Lamb, *Public Inquiries as an Instrument of Government* (George Allen & Unwin, 1971); G Ganz, *Administrative Procedures* (Sweet and Maxwell, 1974); and C Harlow and R Rawlings, *Law and Administration* (Weidenfeld and Nicolson, 1984).
4 *Public Inquiries as an Instrument of Government.*
5 The decision on many appeals under the planning legislation is now made by inspectors (see below) and on some objections is made by the local planning authority (see note 2 above).
6 For judicial pronouncements on the purposes and essential characteristics of public inquiries see *Bushell v Secretary of State for the Environment* [1981] AC 75 [1980] 2 All ER 608, HL and *Binney and Anscomb v Secretary of State for the Environment* [1984] JPL 871.

also allow more public participation in decision-making and all three purposes can help justify the eventual decision, thus providing legitimation. More recently the House of Commons Environment Committee endorsed the view of the Town and Country Planning Association that the right of appeal was 'the ultimate safeguard against unfair or unreasonable decisions by local authorities, a mechanism whereby the public can obtain an independent and impartial hearing beyond the realms of local politics and influences'.[7]

Appeals and objections are dealt with in a variety of ways. In some cases a public inquiry will be held before the making of the decisions on an appeal or objection, while in other cases the appeal or objection will be determined on the basis of the parties' written submissions. In some cases the decision is made by the Secretary of State, while in others decision-making powers have been delegated to persons appointed by the Secretary of State for the purpose.

The decision which follows proceedings in connection with an appeal or objection is typically of an administrative or executive nature. Although there can arise under the planning legislation cases in which policy considerations will strictly play no part,[8] and although there are, superficially at least, certain similarities between judicial proceedings and those appeal and objection procedures which involve the holding of a public inquiry, in general it may be said that proceedings in connection with an appeal or objection under the planning legislation are but part of a process leading to the making of an administrative decision, a decision which may be based on the decision-making body's conception of the requirements of planning policy and the public interest.[9]

Procedure

The Secretary of State and the parties involved have a certain amount of discretion as to the procedure to be adopted in the consideration of appeals and objections. Typically, the 1971 Act provides that before determining an appeal or objection the Secretary of State shall afford the appellant or objector and the planning authority, if either so desires, an opportunity of appearing before and being heard by a person appointed by him for the purpose. Where advantage is taken of this opportunity, the Secretary of State will either convene a public inquiry or hold a hearing.[10] Even though the parties may be content to have the case dealt with without their being heard the minister may on his own initiative decide that the issues arising in a particular case are such that a public inquiry should be held.

7 See Fifth Report from the Environment Committee Planning: Appeals, Call-In and Major Public Inquiries, 1986 at p XII.
8 As, for example, where the Secretary of State has to determine an appeal on the question whether particular proposals require planning permission.
9 While a minister or other person or body responsible for making a planning decision is, of course, entitled to have a general policy on planning matters, the effect of that policy must not be such as to prevent the decision-maker fairly judging all the issues relevant to each individual case—see, for example, *Stringer v Minister of Housing and Local Government* [1971] 1 All ER 65, [1970] 1 WLR 1281; *H Lavender & Son Ltd v Minister of Housing and Local Government* [1970] 3 All ER 871, [1970] 1 WLR 1231; and *R v Secretary of State for the Environment, ex p Reinisch* (1971) 22 P & CR 1022.
10 Section 282 of the 1971 Act provides that the Secretary of State 'may cause a local inquiry to be held for the purposes of the exercise of any of his functions under any of the provisions of this Act'.

We suggested that the decision which follows upon an appeal or objection should generally be regarded as being of an administrative nature, in which the decision-maker is free to consider the evidence led against the background of national or local policy. The person responsible for conducting the relevant proceedings and (if different) the person making the decision which follows is not, however, free to act entirely as he pleases. Certain legal requirements (below) have to be obeyed and administrative guidance on procedures, designed to ensure fairness and efficiency, has also been issued. The most important such guidance is contained in circulars issued by the Department of the Environment; in order to complete the procedural picture these are referred to at appropriate points in this chapter.[11]

As for the legal rules governing procedures, these are not to be found in primary legislation. The 1971 Act is virtually silent on the matter. What we do have, however, are rules which derive from two other sources. One source is delegated legislation made either under the 1971 Act or under the Tribunals and Inquiries Act 1971.[12] The other source lies in the judge-made rules of the common law and, in particular, the principles of natural justice or fairness.[13] Within the limits imposed by these legal rules there remains some room for procedural manoeuvre at the discretion of the person conducting the proceedings relating to an appeal or objection.

It was, in part, the widely felt concern that appeal and objection procedures which involved the holding of public inquiries were insufficiently regulated in the interests of fairness and openness that led to the appointment of the Committee on Administrative Tribunals and Enquiries over thirty years ago. That Committee's report[14] (the Franks Report) had a considerable effect on procedures involving public inquiries. Some of the Report's recommendations were implemented by administrative measures. Others were given effect by the Tribunals and Inquiries Act 1958 (now replaced by the Tribunals and Inquiries Act 1971). The 1958 Act made provision for the establishment of the Council on Tribunals; one of the main functions of the council is to consider and report on administrative procedures involving the holding of a statutory inquiry[15] (see now 1971 Act, s 1(1)(c)). There is a right to demand reasons for any decision taken after the holding of a statutory inquiry or hearing, or for any decision taken in a case in which a person concerned could have insisted on a hearing (see 1971 Act, s 12). The Lord Chancellor, after consulting the Council on Tribunals is empowered to make

11 On this see *Johnson and Co (Builders) Ltd v Minister of Health* [1947] 2 All ER 395, CA; *Darlassis v Minister of Education* (1954) 4 P & CR 281; *Essex County Council v Minister of Housing and Local Government* (1967) 18 P & CR 531; and *Bushell v Secretary of State for the Environment* [1981] AC 75, [1980] 2 All ER 608, HL.
12 See Town and Country Planning (Appeals) (Written Representations Procedure) Regulations 1987, (made under s 282B of the 1971 Act), the Town and Country Planning (Inquiries Procedure) Rules 1988 and the Town and Country Planning Appeals (Determination by Inspectors) (Inquiries Procedure) Rules 1988.
13 Statute may, however, exclude the operation of the rules of natural justice—see, for example, s 12(4)(e) of the 1971 Act (exclusion of right to a hearing).
14 Cmnd 218, 1957.
15 References to a 'statutory inquiry' include not only references to an inquiry held in pursuance of a statutory *duty* but also to any inquiry which is held in exercise of a statutory *power* and which is designated by order made under the Tribunals and Inquiries Act; the Tribunals and Inquiries (Discretionary Inquiries) Order 1967 designates, *inter alia*, any inquiry held under s 282 of the Town and Country Planning Act 1971.

rules regulating the procedure to be followed in connection with statutory inquiries or hearings (see 1971 Act, s 11). Procedures in connection with many types of inquiry held under the planning legislation are regulated by the Town and Country Planning (Inquiries Procedure) Rules 1988 and the Town and Country Planning Appeals (Determination by Inspectors) (Inquiries Procedure) Rules 1988.[16] The present rules took effect on 7 July 1988 and, subject to saving and transitional provisions, replace the 1974 rules.

The requirements of these rules are considered in section C of this chapter. A failure to comply with the rules can lead to the decision in question being challenged under s 245 of the 1971 Act. The High Court is empowered to quash a decision if satisfied that the interests of the applicant have been substantially prejudiced by a failure to comply with the rules (see ch 20). There have been very many such challenges, and rulings by the courts have contributed to a fuller understanding of the statutory rules themselves.

When called upon to review the validity of decisions made following upon appeals and objections, the courts have not, however, confined themselves to the content of the express statutory rules. They have also been prepared to infer from the general statutory context the need to observe the common law standards of fair play—the rules of natural justice—although, with the emergence of detailed statutory codes these standards are of less significance for most sorts of planning inquiry. The courts are not, of course, free to infer the existence of rules inconsistent with those laid down under the authority of Parliament; where statutory rules are applicable the rules of natural justice can only apply in so far as they are not inconsistent with the statutory provisions. Indeed, it has been said by some judges that there is a heavy burden on someone seeking to establish a breach of natural justice in respect of procedures at a public inquiry governed by statutory rules.[17] However, in *Reading Borough Council v Secretary of State for the Environment*,[18] David Widdicombe QC, sitting as a deputy judge held that cases outside the scope of the rules had to be dealt with by the normal standards of proof and that there was no question of onus or 'heavy burden'. This judicial difference of opinion has yet to be settled but it is submitted that Widdicombe's approach is to be preferred. The existence of particular procedural rules may infer that that is all which is required but the existence of a set of statutory procedures in itself should not place any heavier burden on an applicant who claims he has not been treated fairly.

The phrase 'natural justice' carries overtones of the procedures followed in the law courts but in recent times the courts have tended simply to declare that appeal and objection procedures must be 'fair'[19] or that the parties must

16 See also the Compulsory Purchase by Public Authorities (Inquiries Procedure) Rules 1976. In many respects the statutory procedure rules go further than the requirements of natural justice but compliance with the statutory rules does not mean there must *ipso facto* have been compliance with the rules of natural justice.

17 See, for example, *Ackerman v Secretary of State for the Environment* (1980) 257 Estates Gazette 1037 CA; *Lake District Special Planning Board v Secretary of State for the Environment* [1975] JPL 220; and *R v Secretary of State for the Environment, ex p London Borough of Southwark* [1987] JPL 587.

18 [1986] JPL 115.

19 See, for example. *Bushell v Secretary of State for the Environment* [1981] AC 75, [1980] 2 All ER 608, HL.

be given 'a fair crack of the whip'.[20] Indeed, in *Council of Civil Service Unions v Minister for the Civil Service*[1] Lord Roskill suggested that the term 'natural justice' should be consigned to its resting place and the term 'duty to act fairly' employed instead.

In the context of appeal and objection procedures the main importance of the common law concept of fairness lies in the requirement that a party be given a fair opportunity to put his case and to answer all significant points adverse to that case.[2] If, for example, an inquiry inspector or the minister proposes to take into account any factual information which he has obtained from one of the parties after the close of an inquiry or which has come into his possession in some other way, fairness demands that he disclose that information and give the parties an opportunity to comment upon the new information.[3]

The concept of natural justice or fairness is not a precise one—what fairness demands in any particular case may depend on the nature of the subject matter and is to be judged in the light of practical realities as to the way in which administrative decisions are reached. However, it may be said that in general the courts will be concerned with the broad question of whether fair procedures have been followed and will not concern themselves with the observance of technicalities appropriate to a private issue decided by a judge;[4] while the courts will, for example, insist on an inquiry being fairly and impartially conducted, they will not insist that formal rules of evidence be applied at an inquiry.[5] As was said in *George v Secretary of State for the Environment*,[6] there is no such thing as a 'technical' breach of natural justice; the court will not grant relief unless 'a reasonable person ... viewing the matter objectively and knowing all the facts which are known to the court, [would] consider that there was a risk that the procedure adopted ... has resulted in injustice or unfairness.'[7] If, for example, the decision-maker receives further representations from one party after the close of an inquiry but gives the other party no opportunity to comment, there is no unfairness if such an opportunity could not possibly have advanced that party's case.[8]

However, the crucial question will always be whether there is an appearance of unfairness and in *Simmons v Secretary of State for the Environment*[9]

20 See for example, *Fairmount Investments Ltd v Secretary of State for the Environment* [1976] 2 All ER 865, [1976] 1 WLR 1255, HL.
1 [1985] AC 374, [1984] 3 All ER 935, HL.
2 It is also a principle of natural justice that there must be no reasonable suspicion of bias on the part of the decision-maker. In *Halifax Building Society v Secretary of State for the Environment* [1983] JPL 816 a decision was quashed because the inquiry inspector appeared hostile to the appellants and seemed reluctant to pay attention to their case. See too *Furmston v Secretary of State for the Environment and Kent County Council* [1983] JPL 49.
3 See, for example. *Hibernian Property Co Ltd v Secretary of State for the Environment* (1973) 27 P&CR 197; and *Fairmount Investments Ltd v Secretary of State for the Environment* [1976] 2 All ER 865, [1976] 1 WLR 1255, HL. There is, however, no obligation to allow the parties to comment on matters of policy—see, for example, *Darlassis v Minister of Education* (1954) 4 P & CR 281; as these cases show 'fact' and 'policy' are not always easily distinguished.
4 See, for example, *Lake District Special Planning Board v Secretary of State for the Environment* (1975) 236 Estates Gazette 417.
5 See p 543 below.
6 (1979) 38 P & CR 609, CA.
7 *Lake District Special Planning Board* (above), *per* Kerr J.
8 See, for example, *George* (above).
9 [1985] JPL 253.

Forbes J quashed a decision of an inspector because the inspector had been seen talking with the chairman of the development control committee after the close of the inquiry. Forbes J concluded that the reasonable man would have been led to the conclusion that something was being done to interfere with the natural course of justice, even though he accepted that the inspector was guilty of no impropriety. So it can only be emphasised that the test varies according to the nature of the unfairness and the particular context.[10]

Measures to improve appeal procedures

In recent times the number of appeals lodged every year under the planning legislation has continued at a high level. In particular, since 1983 there has been a substantial increase each year; from 13,699 planning appeals in 1983 to 18,663 in 1986. Then in 1987 there was set a new record of 22,483. This has not led to an overall increase in the time taken in handling appeals which has in fact decreased since 1976. Nevertheless in response to concern by the Environment Committee's Report on 'Planning: Appeals, Call-In and Major Public Inquiries' the Government stated in their response that 'their principal objective with respect to the planning appeals system is to achieve a sharp reduction of the time taken in normal circumstances to reach a decision in all types of appeal, but without reducing the quality of the decision'.[11]

The number of instances every year in which proposals are initiated by local planning authorities is more limited and, by comparison with appeals, relatively few objections are lodged with the Secretary of State; no corresponding changes have been considered necessary to maintain the efficiency of objection procedures.

In the past the two main means of speeding up the system have been by encouraging written representations and by transferring decision-making to inspectors. While the local planning authority and the appellant have a legal right to a hearing,[12] if they both agree the appeal may be decided on the basis of written submissions. Over the years parties have been increasingly encouraged to opt for such a procedure rather than ask for a public inquiry: in 1984 about 84 per cent of the s 36 appeals were decided through the written representation procedure.

Since 1968 a power has existed for the Secretary of State to transfer the jurisdiction to determine the appeal to the appointed person (the inspector).[13] This means that both in the cases of appeals decided by way of public inquiry and by way of written representations, the inspector does not report to the Secretary of State but makes the decision. Regulations have been made which have transferred all planning application and enforcement notice appeals to inspectors.[14] Appeals made by statutory undertakers and certain appeals relating to listed buildings and conservation areas are still reserved to the Secretary of State.[14a] In addition, the Secretary of State may recover any appeal for his own decision (para 3 of Sch 9). Only 4 to 5 per cent of appeals are recovered by the Secretary of State and in the Department of the

10 See footnote 6 on p 522 as to the purpose of public inquiries.
11 Ibid at p 2.
12 See 36(4).
13 See Sch 9 to the 1971 Act.
14 See Town and Country Planning (Determination of Appeals by Appointed Persons) (Prescribed Classes) Regulation 1981; regulation 3.
14a See reg 4 of the above regulations.

Environment's response to the Fifth Report of the Environment Committee, new guidelines were issued which were expected to reduce this to 2 to 3 per cent. Appeals are now only normally to be recovered in the following cases:

1. Residential development of 150 or more houses.
2. Proposals for development of major importance having more than local significance.
3. Proposals giving rise to significant public controversy.
4. Proposals which raise important or novel issues of development control.
5. Retail developments over 100,000 square feet.
6. Proposals for significant development in the Green Belt.
7. Major proposals involving the winning and working of minerals.
8. Proposals which raise significant legal difficulties.
9. Proposals against which another government department has raised major objections.
10. Cases which can only be decided in conjunction with a case over which inspectors have no jurisdiction (so-called 'linked' cases).

The government's response goes on to state that:

'There may on occasion be other cases which merit recovery because of the particular circumstances. It is expected that the new guidelines will result in the recovery of about 400–450 cases a year, against the background of appeals totalling nearly 20,000 a year. It is reasonable that Ministers and senior officials should be closely concerned with an adequate number of cases each year, not only because of the importance of the cases themselves, but in order to retain knowledge of how the system is working as a whole.'

Where the appeal is transferred to an inspector appointed by the Secretary of State, the inspector has the same powers and duties as the Secretary of State (para 2 of Sch 9), and his decision is treated as that of the Secretary of State (para 3 of Sch 9). It would seem to follow that, like the Secretary of State, while the inspector is bound to have regard to government policies in determining the appeal, he equally must not consider himself bound to apply such policies, (see ch 8, p 205 above). At the same time as trying to ensure more use of the written representations procedures and transferring more appeals to inspectors, the Government is also concerned to reduce the number of appeals and to streamline and speed up the appeal procedures themselves. With regard to the first aim, the Government expects the recent changes to the Use Classes Order and the classes of permitted development to reduce the number of planning applications and consequently the number of appeals.[15] As to the second, the introduction of statutory procedures for written representations and the changes to the Inquiry Procedure Rules are intended to speed up the appeal process.[16] In addition the tighter policy on costs is hoped to deter unnecessary appeals and to reduce delaying tactics.

15 See Government Response to Environment Committee; part 1, para 4.
16 See Town and Country Planning (Appeals) (Written Representations Procedure) Regulations 1987, Town and Country (Inquiry Procedure) Rules 1988, and the Town and Country Planning Appeals (Determination by Inspectors) (Inquiries Procedures) Rules 1988. The new rules for inquiries came into operation on 7 July 1988.

The numbers of full and part-time inspectors are also being increased to cope with the new demand.

B WRITTEN REPRESENTATIONS

The procedure for lodging appeals under ss 36 and 37 of the 1971 Act has already been described (see ch 10)[17] and is the same whether matters are to proceed by written representations or public inquiry. The detailed procedure is now set out in art 26 of the Town and Country Planning General Development Order 1988 and the appeal must be served within the prescribed period[18] on the Secretary of State on a standard form obtainable from the Department of the Environment. The amount of information which must accompany an appeal is now considerable. This is to avoid delays being caused by documents having to be transmitted between the parties later in the process. The following documents must accompany the appeal:

(a) the planning application and the decision if any;
(b) all plans, drawings and documents relating to the application whether or not sent to the authority;
(c) all correspondence with the authority relating to the application;
(d) any notices or certifications provided under ss 26 or 27;
(e) if the appeal relates to an application for approval of details under a planning condition, the documents relating to the original planning application.

An important change, brought into effect in 1987, is that at the same time as notice of appeal is given to the Secretary of State, copies of the notice of appeal and any plans, documents or drawings accompanying the appeal not already sent to the authority must be sent to the local planning authority (art 26 (1) (b) of the GDO). The appeal form asks the appellant to state whether he wishes to proceed by way of written representations. However, until 1987, there were no formal rules governing the written representations procedures; though Government circulars had set out a target time table (see circular 18/86). The lack of statutory powers made it difficult for the Department to ensure that parties kept to such targets. The Housing and Planning Act 1986 inserted a new power in the 1971 Act by which the Secretary of State could make regulations prescribing the procedures to be followed where an appeal was disposed of without an inquiry or a hearing (s 282B). Under this power, the Town and Country Planning (Appeals) (Written Representations Procedure) Regulations 1987 (the 1987 regulations) were made and prescribe time limits for the various stages of the written representations appeal process.

The 1987 regulations apply where the appellant informs the Secretary of State on lodging an appeal that he wishes the appeal to be disposed of on the basis of written representations (reg 3(1)). This would suggest that it is up to the appellant which procedure is used but, in fact, under s 36(4) the local planning authority has the right to insist on a hearing being held. Also the

17 The procedure for lodging an appeal against an enforcement notice is described in ch 12.
18 For appeals under ss 36 and 37 of the 1971 Act the period is six months from the date of the decision or from the expiry of the time allowed for the giving of notice of the local planning authority's decision or within such longer period as the Secretary of State may at any time allow.

Secretary of State may even require an inquiry or hearing where both parties are prepared to proceed without one, if he considers the circumstances warrant a hearing, as for example if there is considerable third party interest. Where it is decided to hold a hearing, the regulations automatically cease to apply (reg 3(3)). It is presumably open to both the appellant and the local planning authority to change their minds and to insist on a hearing having opted for written representations, though this could make them liable for costs, see page 556.

Where the 1987 regulations apply, the aim is that the whole process from appeal to decision letter should take about eleven weeks at the maximum. The main stages are set out below:

Notification by the Secretary of State of the date of receipt
Upon receipt of the notice of appeal, the Secretary of State must forthwith advise both the appellant and the local planning authority of the date of receipt. This date then becomes the 'starting date' from which time runs for various stages in the process (reg 4).

Notice to interested parties by the local planning authority
Third parties now have formal rights in the written representations process. The local planning authority must give written notice to any person who had to be notified or consulted under the Act or an Order or who had made representations at the application state (reg 5). This is wider than the 'section 29(3) parties' who are given rights where an inquiry is held (see p 536) and would include *anyone* who had made representations even if no publicity had been required or their representations had been made out of time. It is not even made clear whether the representations would have had to have been made in writing. Notice, where required, must be given not later than 5 working days after the local planning authority has received notification of the appeal, which would be the date the authority received the copy of the appeal from the appellant. This could be different from the 'starting date'. The notice must make clear that interested parties have the right to make representations within 28 days of the 'starting date'.

Submission of appeals questionnaire by the local planning authority
Not later than 14 days after the 'starting date' the local planning authority must submit a completed appeals questionnaire together with any documents referred to in the questionnaire (unless confidential) to the Secretary of State and send copies to the appellant (reg 6). The information provided through the questionnaire will include the relevant background documents and the planning officer's report where available and so may be sufficient to present the authority's case. If the authority judge this to be sufficient, they can elect at this stage not to submit any further representations (reg 7(2)). This election must be notified to the Secretary of State and the appellant at the time of submitting the questionnaire.

Representations by the parties
Where the local planning authority do not elect to treat the questionnaire stage as their final representations, they may submit representations within 28 days of the starting date (reg 7(3)). The appellant does not, of course, have to respond and, if he decides not to respond, circular 11/87 suggests that the

appellant should notify the Secretary of State as soon as possible. Where he decides to respond, this must be done within 17 days, either of the date the questionnaire was submitted or the date of submission of the representations by the local planning authority, whichever is applicable (reg 7(4)). The date of submission is taken to be the date set out on the documents and not the date received. In both the case of representations by the local planning authority and the appellant, copies must be sent to each other (reg 7(5)).

Any interested party may submit representations to the Secretary of State within 28 days of the 'starting date' and this right is not expressly reserved to those notified under reg 5. Where such representations are passed on to the appellant and the local planning authority, they have seven days in which to respond (reg 7(6)). Regulation 7 does not state that the Secretary of State *must* pass on such representations but he would be under a duty to do so provided they are relevant to the appeal. The regulations do not provide for any further response by the local planning authority to the appellant's representations but circular 11/87 states that if such responses are made within seven days of the appellant's representations they *may* be taken into account if they represent new material (para 13).

Site visit and letter
There is no statutory timetable imposed on the inspector appointed to hear the appeal (or, in the rare case of a recovered appeal being decided by written representations on the Secretary of State himself) but circular 11/87 states that the aim is for a site visit to be held within two weeks of the closing date for representations and that the decision should be issued within two weeks of the site visit (para 15).

Breach of any of the regulations could be grounds for applying to the court for the decision to be quashed but this is unlikely. In this regard, reg 8 gives the Secretary of State power to extend the time limits. Enforcement will, in practice, turn on the powers of the Secretary of State to proceed to decision. This power is set out in reg 9 and distinguishes between two different situations. First, where some representations have been made in time and some have not, the decision may be based only on those made in time. Thus, where the local planning authority had responded in time but not the appellant, the appeal could be determined simply on the grounds of appeal and the local planning authority's response (reg 9(1)). Second, where no written representations have been made in time, the decision can still be made, if it appears to the Secretary of State that he has sufficient material before him to enable him to reach a decision on the merits of the case (reg 9(2)). This distinction would seem to imply that in the first case the Secretary of State can come to a decision on the sole basis of representations made in time, even if he does not have sufficient material before him to make a judgment on the merits. The assumption is presumably that where some representations have been made in time, there will be sufficient material before the Secretary of State. In both cases it must be implicit that written representations made out of time can be ignored. However, the wording of the regulations presents some difficulties. Regulation 7(1) states that 'The notice of appeal and the documents accompanying it shall comprise the appellant's representations in relation to the appeal.' As there must always have been such an appeal for the Secretary of State to come to a decision, this means that there will always have been some written representations made in time. This would make reg 9(2) entirely redundant. It is only if the meaning of 'written representations' in reg 9 is confined to representations made *after* the notice of appeal that the regulation makes sense. Thus reg 9(2) would apply where there had been a notice of appeal but no further exchange of representations in time. Where the appeal was against a deemed refusal (s37) the Secretary of State would only have the appellant's grounds of appeal before him and so would be unable to determine the merits of the case.

However, the above analysis may prove largely academic as, in practice, the Secretary of State (or his inspectors) are unlikely to ignore representations made out of time. The powers under reg 9 will probably only be used where one party has failed to respond at one of the later stages.

Apart from the statutory procedures, the duty to act fairly applies to the written representation procedures. Thus a decision is liable to be quashed by the courts, if the Secretary of State or the inspector takes account of evidence or issues not raised by the parties without giving them an opportunity to comment.[19] Also, the inspector may be under a duty himself to make further investigations by way of a site visit if this would enable him to resolve an issue raised by the parties.[20] There is no express statutory duty for reasons to be given for the decision and s 12 of the Tribunal and Inquiries Act 1971 only applies to local inquiries and hearings (sch 9, para 7(1)).[1] Nevertheless, it has been held that there is a general duty to give reasons and that these reasons must be adequate. So although the decision letter can be short, it must make clear to the parties on appeal the conclusions of the inspector on the principal arguments advanced before him and the reasons for those conclusions.[2] In this regard the principles governing judicial review of decisions made by written representations are generally the same as for decisions made by way of an inquiry or hearing (see ch 20).

The Housing and Planning Act 1986 has provided for costs to be awarded in the cases of appeals decided by way of representations but this has not yet been implemented (1971 Act, s 282A). However, in the case of enforcement notice appeals decided by way of written representations, there has for some time been a power to award costs (1971 Act, s 110).

C PUBLIC INQUIRIES[3]

The public inquiry presents the planning process at its highest profile. It is the institution which, for the public at large, creates the image of planning they know best—the making of a major decision on a controversial development after public and hotly-contested debate. In truth, of course, the reality of most planning inquiries is very different—with lower stakes, less prominence and less controversy.

---

19 *Wontner Smith & Co v Secretary of State for the Environment* [1977] JPL 103; *Ellinas v Department of the Environment and Torbay Borough Council* [1977] JPL 249; and *Lewis Thirkell Ltd v Secretary of State for the Environment* [1978] JPL 844.
20 *Taylor v Secretary of State for Wales and Glyndwr District Council* [1985] JPL 792.
1   But see *Westminster City Council v Secretary of State for the Environment* [1984] JPL 27.
2   *Sir George Grenfell-Baines v Secretary of State for the Environment* [1985] JPL 256.
3   In addition to the works mentioned at note 3 (p 523 above), see Anthony Barker and Mary Couper, 'The Art of Quasi-Judicial Administration: The Planning Appeal and Inquiry Systems in England' (1984) 6 Urban Law and Policy 363.

As already indicated, the main rules governing procedures at most types of inquiry held under the planning legislation are those made under the Tribunals and Inquiries Act 1971 and much of this section is concerned with consideration of these rules and their interpretation by the courts. There are, on the one hand, the Town and Country Planning (Inquiries Procedure) Rules 1988 (the 'Secretary of State Rules') which apply to those inquiries which culminate in the presentation to the Secretary of State of a report on the inquiry. The Secretary of State then decides. These rules apply to all inquiries ordered by the Secretary of State for the purpose of any planning application which the minister has 'called in' for decision by himself rather than by the planning authority (see p 189 above) and to appeals under s 36 which have been recovered by the Secretary of State for decision himself; and to applications or appeals decided by the Secretary of State in respect of listed building consent, conservation area consent and tree preservation orders (r 3 of the Secretary of State Rules). Relatively few inquiries are held under these rules but those that are tend to be the more important ones and those most likely to be the subject of legal challenge. These inquiries are, therefore, considered below in more detail than might seem to be justified by their numbers.[4]

On the other hand there are the Town and Country Planning Appeals (Determination by Inspectors) (Inquiries Procedure) Rules 1988 (the 'Inspector's Rules') which apply to those inquiries which culminate in the making of a final decision not by the Secretary of State but by the inspector himself. The delegated classes are defined in the rules and include, subject to certain exceptions, appeals under ss 36 and 37 of the 1971 Act (ie, appeals against planning authorities' decisions on planning applications or applications for approval of reserved matters and appeals in default of a planning decision), and appeals in relation to listed building consent and conservation area consent, which are decided by inspectors (r 3 of the Inspector's Rules).

The procedures under the two sets of rules are very similar and where the number of the rules is the same only that number is given as a reference. If the numbers are different the Secretary of State Rule is given first and the Inspector's Rule follows in square brackets.

The rules do not now apply to appeals dealt with by a hearing rather than an inquiry or to any appeal dealt with by way of written submissions.

Inquiries relating to enforcement notices have their own rules (see ch 12) and appeals and referred applications arising under the Town and Country Planning (Control of Advertisements) Regulations are not covered by the 1988 rules and separate arrangements are to be made.[5] There are several types of inquiry held under the planning legislation which are not governed by procedural rules.[6] These include, for example, inquiries into objections to revocation and discontinuance orders (see ch 15) and inquiries convened by local planning authorities to hear objections to local plans (see ch 4). In relation to structure plans, the conventional type of public inquiry into objections has been abandoned altogether in favour of an examination in

---

4 Technically the inspector in such cases is the 'appointed person' but in this chapter the term inspector is used and has now been adopted by the Inquiry Rules but not by the Act.
5 In the meantime the old 1974 rules apply (r 21 of the Secretary of State's Rules).
6 Inquiries into objections to compulsory purchase orders promoted under Pt VI of the 1971 Act are governed by the Compulsory Purchase by Public Authorities (Inquiries Procedure) Rules 1976.

public of those strategic issues which the Secretary of State considers ought to be examined (see ch 4).

The conduct of examinations in public and local plan inquiries is governed by codes of practice issued by the Department of the Environment (see ch. 4). In the case of other inquiries where there are no statutory rights, it is likely that the standard procedures will be applied by analogy where appropriate.[7] Where the Secretary of State Rules or the Inspector's Rules apply, they begin to operate from the stage when the local planning authority are notified by the Secretary of State of his intention to hold an inquiry. It is from that time that the rules, augmented by the administrative guidance from the Secretary of State, provide that special procedural mix which characterises the public local inquiry. It is not a completely comprehensive code and much is left to the inspector's discretion. Emphasis in this section is placed inevitably upon those parts of the procedure which are more fully regulated and those, in particular, which have attracted litigation in which decisions consequent upon inquiries have been challenged in the courts. Because challenge to the ultimate legal validity of decisions is frequently founded on procedural error and because inquiries produce such a wealth of publicly-accessible procedural activity, they are a rich vein for aggrieved developers and others to and others to exploit.

Although the courts have on a number of occasions warned against subjecting inquiry reports and decisions to microscopic examinations,[8] partly as a result of the opportunities for review provided by the procedure rules and partly, it seems, as a result of an increased readiness on the part of the judiciary to intervene, the courts have in recent years often been prepared to scrutinise inquiry procedures, reports and decisions fairly closely, exercising what Alder describes[9] as 'a degree of control more detailed than in any other area of judicial review'. This chapter does no more than mention a small proportion of the very large number of decisions on inquiries made by the courts. The effect of the procedure rules and of the courts' decisions in this field has clearly been to reduce the discretion of the decision-maker; the extent to which this has happened and the question whether such a development is necessarily beneficial are matters on which views can differ markedly.

This concern for procedural justice by parties to inquiries and, through them, the courts, coupled with the concern that they share with the Secretary of State for a certain level of speed and efficiency in decision-making, is what produces the central features of the procedural rules. It is they which are supposed to ensure that appropriate persons and bodies have access to an inquiry and that others are, or may be, excluded; that some persons admitted are given a greater role than others; that appropriate issues are brought before the inquiry and tested in public examination whilst others, including much of central government policy, are excluded; that there is a generally adversarial structure but moderated by an inquisitorial role for the inspector; and that the overall style is sufficiently formal to ensure an adequate

7 See *Pollock v Secretary of State for the Environment* [1981] JPL 420, CA and in certain respects the rules of natural justice impose upon the decision-making body obligations similar to those laid down in the Inquires Procedure Rules.
8 See, for recent example, *Wycombe District Council v Secretary of State for the Environment* [1988] JPL 111 at 114 and 115.
9 *Development Control*, p 174.

marshalling of opposing arguments to test the validity of propositions asserted but without the high degree of formality associated with judicial rules of evidence and procedure. The tension between the demands of justice and efficiency through structure and formality on the one hand, and flexibility and informality on the other is nowhere better illustrated than in the study of the inquiry rules.

Circular 10/88 explaining the changes introduced by the 1988 Rules reflected this tension. At para 6 it was stated that 'Many of the changes to the Rules respond to the growing concern about the time taken to decide planning cases which go to local inquiry, particularly those about major development proposals. They also take into account changes since 1974 in inquiry practice and relevant law. The main objective of the new rules is to make the inquiry process, at all stages, as efficient and effective as possible whilst impairing neither the fairness and impartiality of the proceedings nor the ability of participants to make representations which are relevant to the decision'.

We turn now to discussion of the law relating to public inquiries and, in the interests of clarity of presentation but at some cost to analytical coherence, a broadly chronological approach, based on the order of events at an inquiry, is adopted.

1 Pre-inquiry procedures

This is the stage which has been most radically revised by the new Rules. As circular 10/88 points out, effective use of the period before the inquiry opens can make a crucial contribution to the speed and efficiency of the inquiry proceedings themselves. The objectives of the Rules are to ensure the early exchange of information and to identify the principal issues on which the inquiry should concentrate, while organising in advance an efficient and convenient timetable for the proceedings.

Appointment of the inspector and assessor. In the 1971 Act, the inspector is always referred to as the person appointed and used to be so referred to in the rules. However, as 'inspector' is the term which has invariably been used in practice in England and Wales (in Scotland he is called the 'reporter'), the Rules now employ that term. There are, in fact, four categories of inspectors: salaried; consultant and fee paid; Lord Chancellor's Department Panel; and inspectors specially appointed to particular inquiries. Salaried inspectors comprise a full time inspectorate appointed by the Secretary of State, following approval of the Lord Chancellor. The Lord Chancellor's Panel consists of specially qualified persons nominated by the appropriate Secretary of State with the approval of the Lord Chancellor and they are used for large scale proposals for highway planning, energy or specialist developments. Ad hoc inspectors are usually distinguished members of the Planning Bar and are appointed with the approval of the Lord Chancellor for the largest inquiries such as the Sizewell B inquiry. Consultant and fee paid inspectors are used for written representation appeals and do not hold inquiries.

Under r 5 of the Inspector's Rules the Secretary of State must notify the inspector's name to every person entitled to appear at the inquiry (see p 540 below) but where a new inspector is appointed, he may just announce his name and the fact of his appointment at the start of the inquiry. There is no express provision for the identification of the inspector in the case where the Secretary of State himself determines the appeal or application.

It has been the practice for some time to appoint assessors to advise inspectors in cases concerning very technical matters. This practice is now recognised in the 1971 Act which enables an assessor to be appointed to sit with the inspector at the hearing or inquiry and to advise him on matters arising.[10] The assessor's role is entirely advisory and he cannot determine the inspector's recommendations or decision.

Where such an assessor is appointed, the Secretary of State must notify every person entitled to appear at the inquiry of his name and the matter on which he is to advise the inspector (r 9).

Preliminary information. On being notified by the Secretary of State of his intention to cause an inquiry to be held (the date of such written notice is referred to in the rules as the 'relevant date' and determines much of the future timetable) the local planning authority must forthwith inform him and the applicant of the names and addresses of any s 29(3) parties who have made representations to them[11] (r 4(1)). Section 29(3) parties are those parties who are entitled to appear at the inquiry because of their position under s 29 of the 1971 Act and now are defined so as only to include those with an interest in the land and who have made representations within the 21 day period specified in s 27(4). It does not therefore include persons without an interest in land who have made representations in response to publicity[12] (see ch 7 p 184).

Where the Secretary of State has given a direction restricting the grant of permission for the development to which the application or appeal relates or where a government department or local authority or (in the case of a listed building application) the Commission have expressed the view that the application should not be granted, or should be granted only subject to conditions, the local planning authority must inform the Secretary of State or the appropriate department or authority. The Secretary of State or department or authority is then to furnish to the planning authority a written statement of the reasons for the direction or expression of view. Also where representations have been received by persons or bodies consulted under the General Development Order, they must similarly be informed and give reasons (r 4(2) and (3)).

Date and notification of inquiry. It is now required that the Secretary of State should arrange for the inquiry to be opened within a fixed period. In Secretary of State-decided cases the period is not later than 22 weeks after the date of notification to hold the inquiry ('the relevant date') and in inspector-decided cases 20 weeks after that date (r 10). But in the case where a pre-inquiry meeting is held under r 5 of the Secretary of State Rules for major inquiries (see below), it should be held not later than eight weeks from the conclusion of the pre-inquiry meeting. Where the Secretary of State considers

---

10 See Sch 9, para 5(1A) inserted by s 49 of the Housing and Planning Act 1986.
11 The Secretary of State must similarly supply names and addresses of s 29(3) parties who have made representations to him. This would apply in the case of a referred application.
12 A wider definition applies to listed building appeals; see reg 5 of the Town and Country Planning (Listed Buildings and Buildings in Conservation Areas) Regulations 1987 and r 2 of the Secretary of State's Rules.

that it is impracticable to start the inquiry within the specified time, he can extend the date but circular 10/88 expresses the hope that it will be possible and desirable to start the inquiry well before the specified time (para 35).

Twenty-eight days notice should be given of the date, time and place fixed for the holding of the inquiry to every person entitled to appear[13] and the same notice should be given of any variation (r 10(3) [r 10(2)]). In practice, parties are consulted before a date is fixed and it could be a ground for quashing a decision if a date were to be imposed when a party had a good reason for not being able to attend.[14] In this regard it has been announced that each party will now only be permitted one refusal of a date for the inquiry and that once a date has been fixed it will only be changed for exceptional circumstances (see para 39 of circular 10/88). The extent of publicity for an inquiry is in practice to be generally left to the discretion of the local planning authority[15] but the Secretary of State has the power to stipulate requirements in a particular case (r 10(6), [r 10(5)]). Where a local planning authority is required under this power to publish a notice of an inquiry in a newspaper there is a new requirement that this should be done not later than fourteen days before the inquiry. There is also a power for the Secretary of State where the land is under the control of the applicant to require him to put up a site notice (r 10(7), [r 10(6)]).

Service of statements of case. The 1974 rules only required the local planning authority to serve automatically a statement of case before the inquiry started. Now the applicant must serve a statement in every case and any other party who has notified the Secretary of State of a wish to appear at the inquiry may be required to serve a statement of case.[16] The statement of case must be served within a specified period[17] on the Secretary of State, the local planning authority, the applicant and the s 29(3) parties, as appropriate (r 6(1) (3) and (4)).

The 'statement of case' is defined by r 2 as a 'written statement which contains full particulars of the case which a person proposes to put forward

13 See p 540 for those entitled to appear.
14 In *Co-operative Retail Services Ltd v Secretary of State for the Environment* [1980] 1 All ER 449, [1980] 1 WLR 271 the Court of Appeal held that there was no statutory jurisdiction to quash a decision of the Secretary of State to refuse to postpone the start of an inquiry but such a decision could be challenged by way of judicial review; see ch 20. There was, in any event, no evidence that the minister's refusal had resulted in a breach of the rules of natural justice, having regard to the wide discretion of the inspector to adjourn an inquiry if he thought it necessary in the interests of justice—see p 542 below. See too *Ostreicher v Secretary of State for the Environment* [1978] 3 All ER 82, [1978] 1 WLR 810. However, in *R v Secretary of State for the Environment, ex p Mistral Investments* [1984] JPL 516 it was held that in deciding, at the request of the local planning authority, to postpone the holding of a public inquiry, the minister had acted contrary to natural justice in that he had failed to consult the appellants. Also see *Gill & Co v Secretary of State for the Environment* [1978] JPL 373.
15 A failure to inform a party, who had been consulted and who had objected at the application stage, could lead to the decision being quashed as unfair; see *Wilson v Secretary of State for the Environment* [1988] JPL 540.
16 The quid pro quo is that parties who provide a statement of case, when required, are entitled to appear at the inquiry under r 11(1) (h).
17 This varies depending on whether r 5 of the Secretary of State's Rules has been used to require a pre-inquiry meeting (when it is within four weeks of the conclusion of that meeting) and on the party serving the statement, (applicants normally have nine weeks after the relevant date to the local planning authority's six weeks).

at any inquiry and a list of any documents which that person intends to refer to or put in evidence.'[18] The emphasis in r 2(1) that the particulars should be full, shows that it is intended that the statement should be more exhaustive than the old r 6 statement under the 1974 Rules. The department wants inquiries to be surprise free and considers that the more parties know about each other's case at an early stage, the more efficiently will the inquiry run (see para 28 of circular 10/88). There is a further power in r 6(6) enabling the Secretary of State or the inspector to require further information about matters contained in the statement.

For called-in applications going to inquiry the Secretary of State has always been required to serve a statement of the matters which appear to him to be relevant to his consideration of the application. In addition, he now has the discretionary power to do so for appeals (r 6(8)) and the inspector in inspector-decided appeals may also provide such a statement [r 7(1)].[19] Any person serving a statement of case on the local planning authority has also to supply them with a copy and the local planning authority must afford a reasonable opportunity for any person to inspect and, where practical, take copies of all statements and documents; their own statement should specify the time and place at which this opportunity will be afforded (r 6(7) and (9)).

It is not clear what would be the consequences of a failure to comply with the above rules. Rule 14(8) [r 15(8)] allows the inspector to alter or add to a statement during the inquiry and this would suggest that it would be up to the parties to raise any breaches before the inspector.[20] Also, many of the requirements are imposed on persons other than the Secretary of State and in *Performance Cars v Secretary of State for the Environment*[1] it was held that there was no direct sanction for a breach by the local planning authority of r 6 because s 245(4)(b) only related to breaches of the regulations relating to actions of the Secretary of State himself. In *Davies v Secretary of State for Wales*[2] there was a failure to serve a written statement on the appellant but since there was no evidence to show that the failure had caused the appellant substantial prejudice, an application to quash the Secretary of State's decision failed. The question as to the jurisdiction of s 245(4)(b) was not however directly raised.

We would therefore submit that in most cases any breach could be cured during the inquiry and that therefore the crucial question would be whether, as in *Performance Cars*, the inquiry procedure itself was fair.

Pre-inquiry meetings and timetables. Over the last few years it has become customary for inspectors to hold pre-inquiry meetings prior to inquiries

---

18 A local planning authority's statement must also include the terms of any directions and views or representations made by persons or bodies where this information had to be supplied under r 4(2), r 6(2).

19 Except where required to make advance disclosure under r 6, it would seem there is no common law duty for the decision-maker to set out in advance 'policy' issues: see dicta in *H Lavender & Son Ltd v Minister of Housing and Local Government* [1970] 3 All ER 871, [1970] 1 WLR 1231 and *Kent County Council v Secretary of State for the Environment* (1976) 33 P & CR 70.

20 See *Behrman v Secretary of State for the Environment and East Devon District Council* [1979] JPL 677 where Forbes J said that the inspector was not obliged of his own initiative to check that every document was covered by the statement.

1 (1977) 34 P & CR 92, CA.

2 (1976) 33 P & CR 330.

which are expected to last several weeks. In the case of major inquiries these pre-inquiry meetings have lasted several days themselves and have been very important events. Rule 5 of the Secretary of State Rules now provides for special pre-inquiry procedures to apply in the case of major inquiries (though this term is not used) and in particular provides for a pre-inquiry meeting to be held. These procedures are discussed together with the phenomenon of major inquiries at p 560 below.

Rule 5 is intended only to apply to a few exceptional inquiries but inspectors have also been given a formal power to hold a pre-inquiry meeting in other cases than where r 5 applies (r 7). A pre-inquiry meeting may be held where the inspector thinks it desirable and 14 days' notice must be given to those entitled to appear at the inquiry and to any other person whose presence at the meeting appears to the inspector to be desirable.

The Rules do not set out how the pre-inquiry meeting is to be run except that the inspector shall preside at the meeting and shall determine the matters to be discussed and the procedure to be followed[3] (r 5(9)). However, circular 10/88 (Annex 5) contains an extract from a note on the purpose of the pre-inquiry meetings which was attached to the Chief Planning Inspector's Annual Report for 1986/7. This note states that among the matters which may be discussed and resolved at pre-inquiry meetings are the following:

Procedure at inquiry
—Normal sitting hours
—Estimates of duration of the cases (including examination in chief, cross-examination and re-examination) to be provided to allow a programme to be prepared prior to the inquiry;
—Order of presentation of cases—for example, whether parts of the evidence should be dealt with on a topic basis, what the inspector will be looking for in opening and closing submissions;
—Facilities available at venue.

Evidence
—Identification of issues and of areas of uncertainty about which the inspector will need clarification prior to or at the inquiry;
—Nature of the evidence to be submitted;
—Scope for professional witnesses to agree statements of factual material in advance (including site description, planning history) and to narrow areas in dispute;
—Agreement in respect of preparation and exchange of proofs including format (with summary and with technical material as appendices), presentation (with only the summary needing to be read in examination in chief), and timing of exchange of proofs in advance of the inquiry of being submitted;
—Listing and numbering of documents, plans etc.

The above lists reveal that the main purpose of the pre-inquiry meeting is to save time by ensuring an efficient and orderly inquiry. Also, with this aim r 8 enables the inspector to arrange a timetable for the inquiry proceedings which can be varied at any time.

---

3 The inspector is also given a power to require disruptive persons to leave.

2 *Procedure at inquiry*

Appearances at the inquiry. The persons entitled under the rules to appear at, and participate in, an inquiry are: the appellant or applicant; the local planning authority; any local authority, new town or urban development corporation, planning board or National Park committee where the land is situated in their area; parish or community councils who have made representations in accordance with their rights under the GDO; all s 29(3) parties and any one who has served a statement of case when required to under r 6(4);[4] and in the case of a listed building application where the Historic Buildings and Monuments Commission has to be notified, the Commission (r 11).

That is the list of persons entitled to appear at an inquiry. It is a list which ensures that not only the persons most directly concerned (the appellant or applicant and the local planning authority) are involved but also some others who may be regarded as interested 'third parties'. This extension is clearly important as a means of achieving, where necessary, a broad coverage of issues from different perspectives. It ensures a degree of participation in the inquiry process. The statutory list of interested 'third parties' is not, however, comprehensive. It does not open up the inquiry to the public as a whole. This purpose is, however, normally achieved through the exercise of the inspector's discretion. He may permit any other person to appear at the inquiry and it is, in practice, very rare for an inspector to refuse a request to appear. The public inquiry has thus come to be viewed by some as a vehicle for 'public participation' in the planning process. Any person may appear on his own behalf or be represented by counsel, solicitor or any other person (r 11(3)).[5]

If any person entitled to appear at an inquiry fails to do so, the inspector has discretion to proceed with the inquiry[6] (r 14(9), [r 15(9)]).

Representatives of government departments and other authorities at the inquiry. There is a right under r 12(1) for the applicant to require a representative of a government department or other body to attend the inquiry. This applies where directions have been given by the Secretary of State or any local authority or the Commission restricting the grant of planning permission[7] or where views have been expressed in writing by a Minister or government department or local authority restrictive of the application and those views have been included in the local planning authority's statement of case.[8]

Previously a representative of a government department or local authority (attending in pursuance of a directive or adverse view on the proposal) had to

---

4 Where r 5 of the Secretary of State's Rules applies anyone who has served an outline statement in accordance with r 5(6) is entitled to appear.
5 The limitations on how a local authority may be represented have been removed in the new rules.
6 See *Ackerman v Secretary of State for the Environment* [1979] JPL 616 (in the circumstances of the case no breach of natural justice in holding inquiry in absence of a party). See too the comments of Lord Denning MR in *Ostreicher v Secretary of State for the Environment* [1978] 3 All ER 82, [1978] 1 WLR 810, CA.
7 Or, in the case of the Commission, directing how the listed building application is to be determined (r 12(1)(a) and r 4(2)(b)).
8 The same applies where restrictive views of a Minister or Government Department are included in the Secretary of State's statement under r 6(8).

be called as a witness by the local planning authority. This could be awkward where there was a divergence of views and has been dropped. Now the body concerned can be represented in its own right where it is not appropriate for the representative to be called as a witness for the local planning authority. The person attending the inquiry as a representative must state the reasons for the direction or expression of view and give evidence and be cross examined. There are, however, restrictions on cross-examination which is directed at the merits of government policy. This is discussed under cross-examination; see p 544 below.

The procedures. The Planning Inquiries (Attendance of Public) Act 1982 requires that at any planning inquiry[9] oral evidence shall be heard in public and documentary evidence shall be open to public inspection. However, the Secretary of State can direct that evidence shall not be heard or be open to inspection, except by specified persons, where he is satisfied that public disclosure would be contrary to the national interest.

The procedures set out in the rules only provide a broad framework and the most important rule is the one which states that 'Except as otherwise provided in these Rules, the inspector shall determine the procedure at the inquiry' (Rule 14(1), [Rule 15(1)]). Thus, as Lord Denning put it, 'the inspector is master of his own procedure.'[10] The lack of detailed rules is not only in line with the supposed informality of an inquiry but also gives a substantial flexibility to the institution. Thus, although inquiries do tend to follow the adversarial format, they can become inquisitorial or investigatory where necessary.

The rules do provide for the applicant to present his case first and to have the last word, unless the inspector determines otherwise, with the applicant's consent. Other persons are heard in such order as the inspector determines (r 14(2) [r 15(2)]). All persons entitled to appear at the inquiry are now entitled to call evidence but only the applicant, the local planning authority and s 29(3) parties have an entitlement to cross-examine although the inspector may, at his discretion, permit other persons to do so (r 14(3), [r 15(3)]). The giving of evidence and cross-examination are the two main features of the inquiry and raise many issues. These are now considered in turn.

Evidence. Rule 14(3) [r 15(3)] refers to the calling of evidence and usually expert witnesses on policy and technical matters give evidence on behalf of parties. A person who is representing a party can also give evidence but this is unusual and can be confusing. In *Multi Media Productions Ltd v Secretary of State for the Environment*[11] David Widdicombe QC, sitting as a deputy judge, commented 'while there is no rule against someone combining the role of advocate and expert witness at an inquiry, it is generally speaking an undesirable practice. That is why local planning authorities are not represented at inquiries by planning officers. An expert witness should be trying to

---

9 This includes all inquiries set up by the Secretary of State under s 282(1) of the 1971 Act or held by inspectors under para 5 of Sch 9 to the 1971 Act.
10 See *T A Miller Ltd v Minister of Housing and Local Government* [1968] 2 All ER 633, [1968] 1 WLR 992, CA.
11 [1989] JPL 96.

give his time and unbiased professional opinion to assist the inspector. An advocate is trying to argue the best case he can for his client. Someone who combines these conflicting roles must not be surprised if an inspector or a court approaches his evidence with a degree of caution.'

The main evidence of a witness is normally contained in a written proof of evidence. The practice gradually grew up for copies of these proofs to be provided for all the main parties and they were often exchanged in advance. Rule 13 [r 14] now requires that a person entitled to appear at the inquiry who proposes to give evidence by way of a written statement shall send a copy to the inspector either three weeks before the date fixed in the timetable that he is due to give evidence or where there is no timetable three weeks before the date fixed for the inquiry. Copies are to be supplied to the local planning authority and the applicant as relevant. This again reduces the chance of one party being ambushed at the inquiry. These proofs of evidence used to be normally read out in full by the witness but this could waste a great deal of time. The inspector may now require that a summary of the statement be prepared, which is read out instead of the full statement (r 13(1) and (4), [r 14(1) and (4)]. The witness can then be cross-examined on the full statement. Evidence does not have to be restricted to evidence given by a witness appearing at the inquiry. The inspector is now expressly allowed to take into account any written representation or evidence or any other document received by him before or during the inquiry provided he discloses it to the inquiry (r 14(10) [r 15(10)]).[12] There is also a new provision for the inspector to have the power to refuse to permit the giving or production of evidence or the presentation of any other matters which he considers to be irrelevant or repetitious (r 14(4) [r 15(4)]). There used to be the additional provision that the inspector should not require or permit the giving of evidence which would be contrary to the public interest[13] but this does not feature in the new Rules.[14]

The inspector may also allow the planning authority or the appellant or applicant to add to the observations contained in any statement served under the rules or to add to any list of documents which accompanied such a statement 'so far as may be necessary for the purposes of the inquiry' (r 14(8), [r 15(8)])[15] but he must (by adjourning the inquiry if necessary) give every person entitled to appear an adequate opportunity of considering any such fresh matter or documents. In *Performance Cars Ltd v Secretary of State for the Environment*[16] the Court of Appeal held that an extended lunch break did not give the apellants an adequate opportunity to consider documents which had been handed to them by the planning authority just as the inquiry was about to begin. There had therefore been a breach of the procedure rules and of natural justice. The inspector has a general discretion to adjourn the inquiry (r 14(11) [r 15(11)]). This power he can exercise whenever he thinks it

---

12 Compare *B Johnson & Co (Builders) Ltd v Minister of Health* [1947] 2 All ER 395, CA.

13 See *Wordie Property Co Ltd v Secretary of State for Scotland* 1984 SLT 345.

14 This may be because it was considered that an express power was not needed.

15 In *Behrman v Secretary of State for the Environment and East Devon District Council* [1979] JPL 677 the view was expressed that it was not incumbent upon the inspector conducting an inquiry to constantly check every document to see whether it was included in the list; the onus was on the parties themselves to be vigilant.

16 (1977) 34 P & CR 92.

necessary in the interests of justice to any party.[17] In *Gill & Co v Secretary of State for the Environment*[18] the inspector conducting an inquiry was asked to grant an adjournment because of the illness of the main witness for one of the parties. Although the other main party did not oppose the request the inspector refused it. His decision was held to contravene the rules of natural justice. In a case where an adjournment was through the unreasonable behaviour of one of the parties this could lead to an order for costs (see p 556, below).

The inspector has powers to compel the attendance of witnesses and the production of documents and may examine witnesses on oath (1971 Act, s 282(2)). There is nothing to prevent an inspector himself asking questions of parties or witnesses on matters he considers relevant to the inquiry. He may wish to clarify a point or to ensure that any evidence given is properly examined or to bring out matters which might not otherwise be raised. However, the inspector is under no general obligation to seek out material factors or to go routing around to ascertain whether there are any policy documents to which he has not been referred.[19] On occasion he may have to adopt an inquisitorial role in order to safeguard the discretion of the Secretary of State to deal with a planning application as if it had been made to him in first place[20] and there may be cases where the inspector might properly take it upon himself to correct a failure on the part of a planning authority to refer to a relevant policy.[1]

Although the person appointed to conduct an inquiry will generally give a good deal of assistance to a party who is not professionally represented, it is not part of his duty to act as advocate for such a party.[2]

Just as the procedures governing who can give evidence are less rigidly controlled than in a court, so also are the rules of evidence themselves. There is no obligation for evidence to be given on oath and there is no rule against the admission of hearsay evidence. In *TA Miller Ltd v Minister of Housing and Local Government*[3] the Court of Appeal rejected the argument that a letter, which had been written by a person not present at an inquiry into an enforcement notice appeal and which was contradicted by witnesses giving evidence (in this instance on oath) at the inquiry, ought not to have been admitted or relied upon by the inspector who conducted the inquiry because it was hearsay and could not be tested by cross-examination. Lord Denning MR said 'Most of the evidence here was on oath, but that is no reason why hearsay should not be admitted where it can fairly be regarded as reliable. Tribunals are entitled to act on any material which is logically probative, even though it is not evidence in a court of law.'[4] In this case natural justice had been satisfied by giving the appellants a fair opportunity to comment on

---

17 See *Co-operative Retail Services v Secretary of State for the Environment* [1980] 1 All ER 449, [1980] 1 WLR 271, CA.
18 [1978] JPL 373.
19 See *Rhodes v Minister of Housing and Local Government* [1963] 1 All ER 300, [1963] 1 WLR 208; and *London Borough of Greenwich v Secretary of State for the Environment* [1981] JPL 809.
20 See 1971 Act, s 36(3).
1 See *London Borough of Greenwich*, above.
2 See *Snow v Secretary of State for the Environment* (1976) 33 P & CR 81.
3 [1968] 2 All ER 633, [1968] 1 WLR 992; see, too, *Knights Motors v Secretary of State for the Environment* [1984] JPL 584.
4 Ibid at p 302.

the letter and to contradict it. However, in *French Kier Developments Ltd v Secretary of State for the Environment*[5] Willis J said that 'some limit must surely be imposed in fairness to an appellant on the scope of so-called evidence which by no stretch of the imagination can be said to have the slightest evidential value'. Where hearsay evidence is admitted, it is a matter of judgment as to how much weight it should be accorded.[6]

Cross-examination. It has been noted that some parties to an inquiry have a right to cross-examine a witness, while others do so at the discretion of the inspector. Even where parties do not possess an express right to cross-examine, a refusal to allow cross-examination on a particular issue could lead to the decision being quashed by the courts as unfair. In *Nicholson v Secretary of State for Energy*[7] Sir Douglas Frank held that the rules of natural justice conferred on an objector a right to cross-examine witnesses, provided his questions were directed to evidence contrary to his case and were not repetitive, irrelevant or directed to a purpose contrary to the relevant legislation.

However, the inspector has a considerable discretion as to whether to allow a particular line of questioning, even when the party has an express right to cross-examine a witness. He has, in the words of Diplock LJ,[8] 'a wide discretion to exclude irrelevancies and to curb repetition, to control the procedure and to decide how material probative of relevant fact or opinion shall be adduced.' This is now reinforced by r 14 [r 15] which expressly empowers the inspector to refuse to permit cross-examination which he considers irrelevant or repetitious. Repetition should be fairly easy to identify but relevancy is much more difficult. Where a planning officer had given evidence on the considerations which led to the planning authority's decision but was reluctant, when asked in cross-examination, to express his personal opinion, the minister expressed the view that the inspector had acted properly in not pressing the witness to divulge his own views.[9] In *Accountancy Tuition Centre v Secretary of State for the Environment*[10] Sir Douglas Frank, said, however, that such an attitude on the part of a witness was to be deplored for it was not for a witness to decide what questions he should or should not answer.[11]

On the general issue of when it will be improper to disallow cross-examination, the most authoritative pronouncement is to be found in the speech of Lord Diplock in *Bushell v Secretary of State for Environment*[12] where the House of Lords by a majority of four to one upheld an inspector's

---

5 [1977] 1 All ER 296.
6 See *Collis Radio v Secretary of State for the Environment* (1975) 29 P & CR 390.
7 (1978) 76 LGR 693. See however *TA Miller v Minister of Housing and Local Government* [1968] 2 All ER 633, [1968] 1 WLR 992.
8 *Wednesbury Corpn v Minister of Housing and Local Government (No 2)* [1966] 2 QB 275, [1965] 3 All ER 571, CA.
9 See [1968] JPL 708.
10 [1977] JPL 792: see, too, [1979] JPL 257.
11 A Practical Advice Note, 'Planning Officers as Witnesses at Inquries', produced by the Royal Town Planning Institute and published in 'The Planner' of May 1979, deals with the position of a planning officer called as a witness in a case where his professional opinion is not in conformity with the decision of the authority by which he is employed or with the view of a superior officer.
12 [1981] AC 75, [1980] 2 All ER 608.

refusal to allow a Government witness to be questioned on the methodology used in traffic forecasts. Lord Diplock argued that on the question of cross-examination it would be quite fallacious to suppose that in an inquiry of this kind, the only fair way to ascertain matters of fact and expert opinion was by oral testimony of witnesses who were subjected to cross-examination. So refusal by an inspector to allow a party to cross-examine orally at a local inquiry a person who made statements of fact or has expressed expert opinions was not *per se* unfair. He stated:

> 'Whether fairness requires an inspector to permit a person who has made statements on matters of fact or opinion, whether expert or otherwise, to be cross-examined by a party to the inquiry who wishes to dispute a particular statement must depend on all the circumstances. In the instant case, the question arises in connection with expert opinion upon a technical matter. Here the relevant circumstances in considering whether fairness requires that cross-examination should be allowed include the nature of the topic upon which the opinion is expressed, the qualifications of the maker of the statement to deal with that topic, the forensic competence of the proposed cross-examiner, and, most important, the inspector's own views as to whether the likelihood that cross-examination will enable him to make a report which will be more useful to the minister in reaching his decision than it otherwise would be is sufficient to justify any expense and inconvenience to other parties to the inquiry which would be caused by any resulting prolongation of it.'[13]

In *Bushell* Lord Diplock went on to hold that the criteria for calculating traffic need was an essential element of government policy. He held that it was clearly not appropriate for investigation at local inquiries and it was therefore not unfair that cross-examination had not been allowed.

This raises the issue as to what is the proper scope of local inquiries. Rule 12 while providing that government witnesses, attending inquiries to explain the reason for directives and views, shall be subject to cross-examination to the same extent as any other witness, goes on to state that this does not require them 'to answer any question which in the opinion of the inspector is directed to the merits of government policy'.[14]

Given the general purpose of a public inquiry, this is not, in principle, surprising. The Secretary of State is not holding an inquiry to subject his government's policy to scrutiny but in order to enable him or his delegate to decide a local issue of any relevant policy. The place for challenging government policy, it is argued, is in Parliament and not in a public hall in Margate. The same position is maintained when, following an inquiry, the decision on an appeal or application is made on the basis of government policy which has not been mentioned at the inquiry. The views of the parties on the policy are presumed to be irrelevant and no injustice can, therefore, arise from a failure to discuss it at the inquiry. In the majority of small planning inquiries the exclusion from debate of government policy is of little consequence. It is in some large inquiries, however, that, whatever the

13 Ibid at p 97 E to G.
14 This is a change from the 1974 rules which *required* the inspector to disallow such a question even if the representative was prepared to answer it; r 10(4).

constitutional justification for leaving the scrutiny of the policies of ministers to Parliament, the merits of such policies are so central to the issues before the inquiry that they can be ignored only at the expense of public frustration. It may be particularly frustrating for objectors where a very broad view is taken of what actually constitutes government policy. In the *Bushell* case, it was surprising to have the House of Lords hold that the traffic forecasts upon which a proposal to build a road was based were a part of government policy and, therefore, not subject to investigation at a local inquiry.[15]

The recent Court of Appeal decision in *R v Secretary of State for Transport, ex p Gwent County Council*[16] indicates that the courts are prepared to take a more realistic approach. *Gwent* like *Bushell* concerned a scheme proposed by a Minister. Woolf LJ said that 'while the Minister was entitled to have a policy, he had always to be prepared to consider, having regard to special circumstances, departing from that policy. In practice, therefore, from the objectors' point of view, the position was not going to be that different whether the Minister was relying on "a broad" or "a national" or "local policy". In most cases it could be contended that the policy should not be applied in the particular locality'. So, while Woolf LJ was not accepting that the inquiry should investigate the merits of a Government policy in abstract, the fact that Government policy seemed to be applicable to the decision in question did not preclude an investigation of arguments why it should not be applied in the particular case. In doing this Woolf LJ emphasised that the inspector's role was limited to the evaluation of the assertions of the objectors on factual matters and his function was not to advise the Minister as to the weight to give to such assertions if accepted.

Site inspection. A personal visit to the site which is the subject matter of the inquiry will not always be particularly helpful to the inspector but the rules do permit him to make an unaccompanied inspection of the appeal site before, during or after the inquiry without notifying his intention to the parties. Furthermore, he may, and, if so requested by the applicant or by the local planning authority, he must, inspect the site in the company of such parties together with the s 29(3) parties.

The rules now allow for accompanied site inspections during as well as after its close (r 15 and [r 16]). Circular 10/88 points out that in such a case, as with post-inquiry visits, the inspector should refuse to hear evidence or other submissions while it is taking place. It will be legitimate for parties to draw his attention to particular features of the site and its surroundings (see para 50). The date and time of an accompanied visit must be announced during the inquiry but the inspector is not bound to postpone an inspection just because the applicant, the local planning authority or a s 29(3) party is not present.

In so far as the site inspection does no more than assist the inspector to form a clearer understanding of the evidence given at the inquiry or to test the validity of statements made at the inquiry, it can properly be taken into

15 This is to be contrasted with the approach of Lord Denning MR in the Court of Appeal ((1979) 38 P & CR 341) and the dissenting opinion of Lord Edmund Davies in the House of Lords ([1981] AC 75 at 114–115). See also *Kent County Council v Secretary of State for the Environment* (1976) 33 P & CR 70 (ministerial statement in House of Commons as to need for oil refineries a matter of Government policy).
16 [1988] QB 429, [1987] 1 All ER 161.

account without any need to afford the parties an opportunity for comment.[17] If, however, in the course of the site inspection the inspector or appointed person obtains information which was not considered at the inquiry, and there is a real risk that one of the parties might thereby be prejudiced, then, unless the parties are told of the fresh information and given an opportunity to present argument and, if need be, evidence upon the matter, the proceedings may be in breach of the rules of natural justice.[18]

3 *Procedure from close of inquiry to decision*

Up to the stage at which the inquiry itself closes, the procedures in non-delegated and delegated cases run very much in parallel. The objective to that point is the same—to ensure that relevant evidence and arguments are brought to the attention of the inspector in a manner which is both efficient and fair. Thereafter, however, the procedures diverge sharply to reflect the difference in the decision-making process. In the case of a non-delegated appeal or application, attention is focused upon the report of the inquiry—how it is prepared and what it should contain; the possibility of the admission of further evidence thereafter; and the Secretary of State's decision. Delegated cases are, unsurprisingly, procedurally more simple since the step from inquiry to decision by the appointed person is more direct. In what follows, the procedure where the Secretary of State makes the decision is described first.

Secretary of State's cases; the report. Rule 16(1) requires the inspector to make a report in writing to the Secretary of State which shall include his conclusions and his recommendations or his reasons for not making any recommendations.[19] The 1974 rules made a distinction between 'findings of fact' and 'recommendations.'[20] The replacement of 'findings of fact' with 'conclusions' reflects that inspectors make many judgments or conclusions which cannot be described as findings of fact. Whether or not the inspector had come to a finding of fact was very important as the rules provided that if the Secretary of State differed with the inspector on a finding of fact this could result in the decision having to be deferred for further consultation.

17 See *Winchester City Council v Secretary of State for the Environment* (1978) 36 P & CR 455; affd (1979) 39 P & CR 1, CA; and *Coleen Properties v Minister of Housing and Local Government* [1971] 1 All ER 1049, [1971] 1 WLR 433, *per* Sachs LJ.
18 See *Hibernian Property Co Ltd v Secretary of State for the Environment* (1973) 27 P & CR 197 (in which the inspector in the course of the site inspection put to the occupiers of houses which were the subject of the inquiry proceedings questions as to their views on the proposals for the houses); *Fairmount Investments Ltd v Secretary of State for the Environment* [1976] 2 All ER 865, [1976] 1 WLR 1255 (in which the inspector concluded from what he saw on the site inspection that the foundations of the houses which were the subject of the inquiry proceedings were inadequate though no such suggestion had been made at the inquiry); and *Wontner Smith & Co Ltd v Secretary of State for the Environment* [1977] JPL 103.
19 See *Stevens v Minister of Housing and Local Government* (1966) 110 Sol Jo 567, where it was held that the inspector did not err in law in declining to make a recommendation.
20 The Courts had held that the classification by the inspector in his report of a matter as a finding of fact or otherwise was not conclusive; see *Meravale Builders Ltd v Secretary of State for the Environment* (1978) 36 P & CR 87. It was also primarily up to the inspector to decide what issues required findings of fact; see *Continental Sprays Ltd v Minister of Housing and Local Government* (1968) 19 P & CR 774; and *William Boyer & Sons Ltd v Minister of Housing and Local Government* (1968) 20 P&CR 176.

This still applies in case of disagreement on 'matters of fact' but the term 'finding of fact' which proved very elusive to define has now been completely omitted from the rules.

The duty to make a report does not mean that the inspector has to refer to every point or matter raised at the inquiry. He must give a fair account of the main evidence and arguments (including legal argument).[1] Slynn J in *Preston Borough Council v Secretary of State for the Environment*[2] expressed the duty in the following terms. 'Clearly the inspector had discretion to omit material which he considered not to be relevant. He had to analyse and consider and winnow and not merely to record. Again he could put the material in a way which he thought to be right. But at the same time if it was shown that there was something of such importance that really the applicant's or the local authority's case had not been properly put to the Secretary of State, in his judgment the court might in a proper case say that there had been a breach either of the Inquiries Procedure Rules if they applied or the rules of natural justice.'[3]

It is clear that the inspector's conclusions must not be based on some factual issue not raised by the parties or on factual evidence which he has discovered on his own initiative unless he first gives the parties an opportunity to deal with the matter,[4] but equally an inspector cannot be faulted for failing to deal with an issue not put to him at the inquiry.[5]   The inspector is, however, entitled to make use of his own knowledge, experience and common sense and is not bound to accept the evidence of experts or others, even if uncontradicted.[6] He does not, for example, require expert evidence in order to enable him to come to a conclusion on matters of judgment or opinion such as questions of aesthetic taste[7] and he is entitled to make value judgments on technical issues falling within his qualifications and experience.[8] 'It is', said Lord Widgery CJ in *Wholesale Mail Order Supplies Ltd v Secretary of State for the Environment*[9] 'a complete misconception to take the view that matters of professional opinion, in planning in particular,

---

1 See *A B Motor Co of Hull v Minister of Housing and Local Government* (1969) 211 Estates Gazette 289; *Deasy v Minister of Housing and Local Government* (1970) 214 Estates Gazette 415; *Hope v Secretary of State for the Environment* (1975) 31 P & CR 120; *North Surrey Water Co v Secretary of State for the Environment* (1976) 34 P & CR 140; *East Hampshire District Council v Secretary of State for the Environment* [1978] JPL 182; and *Halifax Building Society v Secretary of State for the Environment* [1983] JPL 816.

2 [1978] JPL 548.

3 In special circumstances the court will allow evidence to be filed to show that a particular matter of real importance has been omitted: see *East Hampshire District Council v Secretary of State for the Environment* [1978] JPL 182.

4 See, for example, *Charlton Sand and Ballast Co v Minister of Housing and Local Government* (1964) 190 Estates Gazette 965; *H Sabey & Co Ltd v Secretary of State for the Environment* [1978] 1 All ER 586; and *D E Hudson v Secretary of State for the Environment* [1984] JPL 258.

5 See, for example, *Newbury District Council v Secretary of State for the Environment* [1983] JPL 281; and *Mason v Secretary of State for the Environment* [1984] JPL 332; but see p 554 below.

6 See, for example, *Fairmount Investments Ltd v Secretary of State for the Environment* [1976] 2 All ER 865, [1976] 1 WLR 1255, per Lord Russell of Killowen; and *Kentucky Fried Chicken (GB) Ltd v Secretary of State for the Environment* (1977) 245 Estates Gazette 839.

7 See *Winchester City Council v Secretary of State for the Environment* (1979) 39 P & CR 1, CA.

8 See *Westminster Renslade Ltd v Secretary of State for the Environment* (1983) 48 P & CR 255.

9 (1975) 237 Estates Gazette 185.

require the sort of factual support in evidence which is required in proving the existence of a criminal case.'

In *R v Secretary of State for Transport, ex p Gwent County Council*[10] it was made clear that the inspector does not have to make conclusions on the merits of Government policy. Woolf LJ distinguished between the assertion that increased tolls would damage the local economy and whether, if this was proved, it justified a departure from the standard policy. The former was a proper matter for the inspector to go into but in the case of the latter 'the inspector's opinion was of no more value than of any other member of the public.'

Secretary of State's cases; the assessor's report. Where an assessor has been appointed, he may after the close of the inquiry provide the inspector with a written report. In such a case r 16(3) of the Secretary of State's Rules requires this report to be appended to the inspector's own report and for the inspector to state how far he agrees or disagrees with the assessor, giving his reasons for any disagreement. Otherwise there is no way that a party can know what has passed between the inspector and the assessor. There is, however, no obligation for the assessor to produce a written report and so an assessor's advice may still remain secret, unless disclosed in the inspector's report.

Secretary of State's cases: disagreements between the Secretary of State and his inspector. The Secretary of State has the right and indeed is required to make his own decision and not just rubber stamp his inspector's report. This applies to matters of fact as well as policy and he could also be required to take into account new evidence which has arisen since the inquiry closed which is in the possession of his department.[11] However, both the inquiry rules and the duty to act fairly require that in certain circumstances the Secretary of State must give the parties an opportunity to comment or even to re-open the inquiry. Rule 16(4) covers two separate situations. The first is where the Secretary of State is disposed to disagree with a recommendation[12] of his inspector *because* he differs from him on any matter of fact either mentioned in a conclusion of the inspector or which appears to the Secretary of State to have been material to such a conclusion. In such a case, before coming to a final decision he must notify those persons entitled to appear at the inquiry, of the reasons for the disagreement and afford them an opportunity of making written representations within 21 days of being notified.

The 1974 rules (r 12(2)) imposed this duty where there was a difference on a 'finding of fact'. The new term used; 'any matter of fact', would seem to be substantially narrower as it would appear to exclude conclusions based or derived from matters of fact. The change makes a lot of the old case law redundant but it still may be of some assistance in understanding the present Rule. The courts have always drawn a distinction between findings of fact

---

10 [1988] QB 429, [1987] 1 All ER 161, CA.
11 See *Prest v Secretary of State for Wales* (1983) 81 LGR 193, CA but see *Rea v Minister of Transport* (1981) 48 P & CR 239 which suggests that this is only required where it relates to matters of importance. But see also *Hollis v Secretary of State for the Environment* [1983] JPL 164.
12 A recommendation would include recommendations as to conditions; see *R v Secretary of State for the Environment, ex p Greater London Council* [1986] JPL 32.

and planning judgments or opinions. In *Lord Luke of Pavenham v Minister of Housing and Local Government*,[13] for example, an inquiry report included the statement that the appeal site was defined by a fine-looking wall and formed part of a long-established group of buildings contributing to the attractive character of the area. The Court of Appeal concluded that that was a finding of fact. On the other hand, the report also stated that a well-designed house on the site would not harm the charm of the setting and would not create a precedent. That, the court held, was a mere statement of opinion on the planning merits. The minister was therefore entitled to issue a decision disagreeing with his inspector on the second point without having to give the parties an opportunity to comment.

Then in *Pyrford Properties Ltd v Secretary of State for the Environment*,[14] Sir Douglas Frank suggested that a finding on an existing state of affairs, not being a finding dependent upon aesthetic taste or other subjective opinion, must be a finding of fact, whereas an expression of subjective opinion on the potential consequences of a proposed development would be an expression on planning merits.

The second part of r 16(4) applies where the Secretary of State is disposed to disagree with a recommendation because he has taken into account new evidence or a new matter of fact, not being a matter of Government policy. In such a case, before making his final decision he must not only give the persons who were entitled to appear at the inquiry an opportunity of commenting, but must also reopen the inquiry if requested to by such persons[15] within 21 days of their being notified of the disagreement. Such new evidence or matters of fact would normally come to light after the inquiry closed but it has been held that the Secretary of State can take into account representations made by a party after the inquiry even though those representations could have been made during the inquiry.[16] It may not be easy to say whether material received by the minister constitutes 'new evidence'.[17] In *French Kier Developments Ltd v Secretary of State for the Environment*[18] Willis J held that, where an inspector had disregarded a report which had merely been mentioned at an inquiry, for the Secretary of State to attach any weight to the report amounted to taking 'new evidence' into consideration. It has been held that the confirmation of a structure plan policy by the Secretary of State could amount to new evidence.[19] Though it

---

13 [1968] 1 QB 172, [1967] 2 All ER 1066.

14 (1977) 36 P & CR 28. Also see *Vale Estates v Secretary of State for the Environment* (1971) 69 LGR 543; *Camden London Borough Council* [1975] JPL 602; *Meravale Builders Ltd v Secretary of State for the Environment* (1978) 36 P & CR 87; *J. Sainsbury Ltd v Secretary of State for the Environment* [1978] JPL 379; and *Pollock v Secretary of State for the Environment* [1981] JPL 420, CA.

15 The new rules extend this right to all parties who were entitled to appear, not just s 29(3) parties, as in the 1974 rules.

16 See *Whitecroft plc v Bolton Metropolitan Borough Council* [1984] JPL 875.

17 See, for example, *Hamilton v Roxburgh County Council* 1970 SC 248, [1971] SLT 2. See, too, *Fairmount Investments Ltd v Secretary of State for the Environment* [1976] 2 All ER 865, [1976] 1 WLR 1255; *Bushell v Secretary of State for the Environment* [1981] AC 75, [1980] 2 All ER 608, HL; and *Rea v Minister of Transport* (1982) 48 P & CR 239, CA.

18 [1977] 1 All ER 296.

19 See *R v Bickenhill Parish Council, ex p Secretary of State for the Environment* [1987] JPL 773.

could be argued that this was a matter of Government policy and so excluded from r 16(4).[20]

The term 'new matter of fact' is again narrower than the term 'new issue of fact' used by the 1974 rules. An issue can turn on factual matters and in the *Bickenhill* case[1] Nolan J talked of the confirmation of the structure plan policy as a fact which might give rise to an issue of fact. With regard to the old wording, whether a matter can sensibly and fairly be said to be an 'issue of fact' was said by Willis J in *Camden London Borough Council v Secretary of State for the Environment*,[2] to be very much a matter of impression to be gathered not only from the actual words used but also from the context in which they appear. As stated, matters of 'Government policy' do not have to be disclosed under r 12(3).[3] In this context 'policy' is, as Lord Diplock said in *Bushell v Secretary of State for the Environment*,[4] 'a protean word', and the majority decision of the House of Lords in that case demonstrates how difficult it can be to distinguish between 'fact' and 'policy'.[5] In *Bushell* it was held that particular methods of traffic forecasting employed to determine motorway construction priorities were policy issues. This might be thought to be stretching the word 'policy' to its very limits.[6]

It may be noted that it is only where the Secretary of State is disposed to disagree with a recommendation made by the inspector that the obligations imposed on him by r 16(4) come into operation. If no recommendation has been made,[7] or if the Secretary of State agrees with the inspector's recommendation, the rules do not oblige the minister to give the parties an opportunity to comment on new facts or fresh evidence. If, however, the minister fails to give the parties a chance to comment on such fresh findings or evidence, his action may well be successfully challenged as contrary to natural justice.[8] This is because in parallel with the statutory procedural rules, it seems clear that the principles of natural justice impose on the Secretary of State similar obligations. In *Lithgow v Secretary of State for Scotland*.[9] Lord Dunpark stated that the Secretary of State is not entitled to obtain relevant and material factual information from one of the parties without giving opposing parties an opportunity to answer this. Failure in this respect is so great an infringement of the right of every person with a legal interest to a fair hearing that it invalidates the decision. A breach of natural justice may also occur if the decision-maker takes account of relevant

20 See *Hyndburn Borough Council v Secretary of State for the Environment* [1979] JPL 536.
1 See above.
2 (1975) 235 Estates Gazette 375.
3 This includes the policy of another minister. See for example, *Darlassis v Minister of Education* (1954) 4 P & CR 281; and *Kent County Council v Secretary of State for the Environment* (1976) 33 P & CR 70. Contrast, however, *H Lavender & Son Ltd v Minister of Housing and Local Government* [1970] 3 All ER 871, [1970] 1 WLR 1231.
4 [1981] AC 75, [1980] 2 All ER 608.
5 See too *Lithgow v Secretary of State for Scotland* [1973] SC 1, 1973 SLT 81 (matter of policy that extra cost of alternative route for road outweighed loss of agricultural land).
6 On the exclusion of consideration of the merits of 'government policy' at the inquiry itself, see p 545 above.
7 See *Westminster Bank Ltd v Minister of Housing and Local Government* [1971] AC 508, [1970] 1 All ER 734, *per* Lord Reid.
8 See *Hambledon and Chiddingfold Parish Council v Secretary of State for the Environment* [1976] JPL 502.
9 1973 SC 1, 1973 SLT 81.

information obtained from a source other than one of the parties or bases his decision on some matter which was not in issue at the inquiry.[10] The decision-maker is, however, free to take account of and to attach such weight as he thinks fit to matters of policy, whether or not these have been canvassed at the inquiry and whether or not the parties have had an opportunity to comment.[11]

Bushell would also suggest that the Secretary of State may be able to take into account new evidence which comes from his own department, such as new statistics on traffic, even though such matters cannot be regarded by any stretch of the imagination to be Government policy. Where new evidence is taken into account but an opportunity is given to parties to comment, this will usually be sufficient to satisfy the duty to act fairly and there will be no need to reopen the inquiry.[12] The Secretary of State always has a power to reopen the inquiry and if asked to by one of the parties must exercise this discretion fairly[13] (r 16(5)).

Where r 16 has been broken, it has been held that only the parties to whom duties are owed under that rule can challenge the subsequent decision.[14] Thus in the *Bickenhill*[15] case Nolan J held that the parish council could not claim to be a party aggrieved within the meaning of s 245 because of a procedural failing by the Secretary of State in his obligations to the local planning authority.[16]

Secretary of State's cases: decision and reasons. Rule 17 of the Inquiries Procedure Rules requires the Secretary of State to give notice of his decision, with reasons[17] in writing to all persons entitled to appear at the inquiry who did appear, and to any other party who appeared at the inquiry and asked to be notified of the decision. This rule also provides that any such person who has not received a copy of the inquiry report may obtain one on request.

The courts have repeatedly emphasised that inspectors' reports and the decision letters of the Secretary of State should not be scrutinised as if they were a statute or a contract or a formal document; what has been stigmatised as 'the tooth comb approach'.[18] The basic principle, as first laid down in *Re Poyser and Mills Arbitration*[19] by Megaw J, and since approved by Lord Scarman in *Westminster City Council v Great Portland Estates plc*[20] is that where Parliament provides that reasons be given '... that must be read as meaning that proper, adequate reasons must be given. The reasons that are

10 See, for example, the cases cited in note 18 (p 547 above).
11 See, for example, *Darlassis v Minister of Education* (1954) 4 P & CR 281; and *Bushell v Secretary of State for the Environment* [1981] AC 75, [1980] 2 All ER 608, HL.
12 See *R v Secretary of State for the Environment ex p Greater London Council* [1986] JPL 32.
13 See *R v Secretary of State for the Environment ex p Greater London Council* ibid.
14 *R v Bickenhill Parish Council ex p Secretary of State for the Environment* [1987] JPL 773.
15 See above.
16 The new wording would give a parish council such rights if they had appeared at the inquiry by right because they had asked to be consulted under the GDO; see r 11 and 16.
17 Apart from the rules, s 12 of the Tribunals and Inquiries Act 1971 requires that reasons be given (if asked) for any decision taken after the holding of a statutory inquiry.
18 See Graham Eyre QC in *West Midlands Cooperative Society v Secretary of State for the Environment* [1988] JPL 121.
19 [1964] 2 QB 467, [1963] 1 All ER 612; see also *Givaudan v Minister of Housing and Local Government* [1966] 3 All ER 696, [1967] 1 WLR 250.
20 [1985] AC 661, HL.

set out must be reasons which will not only be intelligible but which deal with the substantial points that have been raised'. Despite the disclaimer, the failure to provide a reasoned decision letter has been the most common ground of challenge and numerous decisions have been quashed by the courts. Decisions have, for example, been quashed on the grounds that the letter conveying the decision did not deal adequately with the main issues;[1] or that it omitted to refer to an important recommendation in the inquiry report;[2] or that it did not make clear whether the minister had had regard to an important consideration;[3] or that it did not make clear the reasons for preferring one view to another,[4] or that it contained contradictory reasons;[5] or that it was simply insufficiently detailed to explain or justify the decision.[6]

The decision letter must make clear any reason for disagreeing with the inspector and since there is more scope for misunderstanding in such a case, 'more comprehensive reasons may be required in such circumstances than where the minister is merely agreeing with the inspector'.[7] The Secretary of State is entitled simply to adopt the inspector's reasoning and recommendations[8] but it is not enough that the reasons can only be arrived at by some complex exercise involving cross-reference from one set of documents to another.[9] However, mere surplusage which does not detract from the rest of the letter will not vitiate the decision.[10] Provided that there is evidence before him to justify such action and provided the parties have had an opportunity to deal with relevant issues, the Secretary of State is entitled to come to a decision in accordance with the recommendation in the inquiry report but for different or additional reasons.[11]

It is primarily for the parties to an inquiry to put forward any issues they wish to be considered. In general, no complaint can be made if the Secretary of State fails to take account of some factor or argument not raised expressly or by implication at the inquiry;[12] the minister is not, for example, bound to consider whether a particular condition can be devised which would overcome a particular planning objection and allow planning permission to be

1 See, for example, *French Kier Developments Ltd v Secretary of State for the Environment and Surrey Health District Council* [1977] JPL 311; and *London Borough of Camden v Secretary of State for the Environment* [1980] JPL 31.

2 See, for example, *Kent Messenger Ltd v Secretary of State for the Environment* (1976) 241 Estates Gazette 25.

3 See, for example, *Ynystawe, Ynyforgan and Glais Gipsy Site Action Group v Secretary of State for Wales* [1981] JPL 874.

4 See, for example, *Seddon Properties Ltd v Secretary of State for the Environment* (1978) 248 Estates Gazette 950.

5 See, for example, *Knights Motors v Secretary of State for the Environment* [1984] JPL 584.

6 See, for example, *Banks Horticultural Products Ltd v Secretary of State for the Environment* (1979) 252 Estates Gazette 811; and *Thornville Properties v Secretary of State for the Environment* [1981] JPL 116.

7 See *London Borough of Greenwich v Secretary of State for the Environment* [1981] JPL 809 and *Rogelan Building Group Ltd v Secretary of State for the Environment* [1981] JPL 506.

8 *London Welsh Association v Secretary of State for the Environment* [1980] JPL 745, CA.

9 See *Sheffield City Council v Secretary of State for the Environment* (1979) 251 Estates Gazette 165, per Drake J.

10 See *French Kier Developments Ltd v Secretary of State for the Environment* [1977] 1 All ER 296, per Willis J.

11 See *Tempo Discount Warehouses v Enfield London Borough* [1979] JPL 97.

12 See, for example, *Chris Fashionware (West End) Ltd v Secretary of State for the Environment* [1980] JPL 678.

granted rather than refused,[13] If, however, a particular issue has been raised at the inquiry the minister will have to consider it;[14] where, for example, a particular condition has been canvassed but the minister considers it unsuitable, he may be under an obligation to consider whether the same object could be achieved by a differently-worded condition.[15] Further, the Secretary of State is presumed to have at his disposal all the information available to his department and may therefore have to call his own attention to any such relevant information.[16]

It appears to be the case that once a decision letter has been issued, any mistake or clerical error it may contain cannot subsequently be corrected.[17] After the issue of the letter the minister is *functus officio*. An obvious silly mistake or clerical error in the letter will not, however, vitiate the decision, so long as the error is not such as to mislead the recipient.[18]

The courts will not automatically quash a decision just because there has been a failure to give adequate or intelligible reasons and the applicant must show that he has suffered substantial prejudice because of the failure.[19] However, normally it will be sufficient to show that a party to the inquiry does not really know what view the Secretary of State took on an important point.[20]

The obligation to provide reasons for a decision may, of course, provide an aggrieved party with ammunition with which to attack the decision. The purpose of the statutory requirements is, said Lord Denning in *Earl of Iveagh v Minister of Housing and Local Government*,[1] 'to enable the parties and the courts to see what matters [the minister] has taken into consideration and what view he has reached on points of fact and law that arise'; the reasons may demonstrate, for example, that an irrelevant consideration was taken into account in arriving at the decision.

Delegated cases: inquiry to decision. Post-inquiry procedure for an appeal delegated for decision to an appointed person is designed to be simpler. There is no separate report on the inquiry. Instead, the inspector normally moves directly to the notification of the parties of his decision and reasons. If, however, he proposes to take into account any new evidence or any new matter of fact, (not being a matter of Government policy) which was not raised at the inquiry and which he considers to be material to his decision, he must first notify the parties and give them an opportunity of making representations or of asking for the re-opening of the inquiry (r 17(2) of the Inspectors' Rules). Also if an assessor makes a written report this must be

13 See *Finlay v Secretary of State for the Environment* [1983] JPL 802. If the minister has it in mind to take such action, the rules of natural justice may require that he give the parties an opportunity to comment—see *Jillings v Secretary of State for the Environment* [1984] JPL 32. See ch 20 p 571.
14 See *Tierney v Secretary of State for the Environment* [1983] JPL 799.
15 See *Robert Hitchins Builders Ltd v Secretary of State for the Environment* [1979] JPL 534, CA.
16 See *Prest v Secretary of State for Wales* (1983) 81 LGR 193; and *Hollis v Secretary of State for the Environment* (1982) 47 P & CR 351.
17 See dicta in *Miller v Weymouth and Melcombe Regis Corpn* (1974) 27 P & CR 468; *Gosling v Secretary of State for the Environment* (1974) 234 Estates Gazette 531; and *Preston Borough Council v Secretary of State for the Environment* [1978] JPL 548.
18 See, for example, *Hope v Secretary of State for the Environment* [1979] JPL 104.
19 See *Bell and Colvill Ltd v Secretary of State for the Environment* [1980] JPL 823.
20 See *Kent Messenger Ltd v Secretary of State for the Environment* [1976] JPL 372.
 1 [1964] 1 QB 395, [1963] 3 All ER 817, CA.

made known under r 17(1) to enable inspection to take place under r 18(2). Like the Secretary of State, he may apply aspects of government policy to his findings and the other 'new evidence' principles and problems also apply.[2] Like the Secretary of State, the inspector must give reasons for his decision (r 18(1) of the Inspectors' Rules), but there have been indications that in a delegated case reasons somewhat less comprehensive than are required in a non-delegated case (above) may suffice.[3] This is because where the Secretary of State makes the decision he has to rely on the inspector's report for the evidence and arguments and so his decision letter has in many cases to deal with these matters in more detail than in the case where there is no report but just the inspector's decision letter.[4] Otherwise the principles governing their nature and extent are broadly similar to those applicable to non-delegated appeals.[5] The decision letter must set out the main issues and the factual basis for the appointed person's conclusions and must be sufficiently detailed to let the parties know what conclusions the appointed person reached on the principal issues of controversy and why he has reached those conclusions.[6]

4 Consequences of breaches of inquiries procedure rules

Many of the rules require steps to be taken within a specified period. The rules provide for the Secretary of State to allow further time for the taking of any step in respect of which such a time limit is laid down. Where time limits are broken, the most likely result is for an order for costs to be made; there are no express sanctions. Breach of the rules could result in the courts quashing the decision but this would only apply where substantial prejudice had been suffered, as it is unlikely that the courts would interpret the rules as going to jurisdiction; see ch 20.

5 Procedure following quashing of decision

The result of a decision being quashed under s 245 is that the Secretary of State can review the whole matter anew.[7] This may lead simply to a rewriting of the decision letter or can result in the inquiry being reopened by the same or a different inspector. The 1988 rules now lay down a special procedure which must be followed where a decision, in respect of which an inquiry has been held, is quashed. This applies to both delegated and non-delegated decisions and ensures that those who were entitled to appear and who did so are given the opportunity to make further comments. A written statement must be sent by the Secretary of State setting out the matters with respect to which further representations are invited within 21 days. Within the same

---

2 See *Lewis Thirkell v Secretary of State for the Environment* [1978] JPL 844.
3 See, for example, *Ellis v Secretary of State for the Environment* (1974) 31 P & CR 130; and *London Borough of Greenwich v Secretary of State for the Environment* [1981] JPL 809.
4 See *DFP (Midlands) Ltd v Secretary of State for the Environment* [1978] JPL 319.
5 See, for example, *London Borough of Greenwich* (above); *Duffy v Secretary of State for the Environment* (1981) 259 Estates Gazette 1081; and *Hope v Secretary of State for the Environment* (1975) 31 P & CR 120.
6 See *Hope* (above); *DFP (Midlands) v Secretary of State for the Environment* [1978] JPL 319; *Bell and Colvill Ltd v Secretary of State for the Environment* [1980] JPL 823; *Hewlett v Secretary of State for the Environment* [1981] JPL 187; and *Enticott and Fullite Ltd v Secretary of State for the Environment* [1981] JPL 759.
7 See *Price Bros (Rode Heath) Ltd v Department of Environment* (1978) 38 P & CR 579, and *Newbury District Council v Secretary of State for the Environment* [1988] JPL 185.

period, parties can ask for the re-opening of the inquiry. The Secretary of State may then at his discretion cause the inquiry to be reopened whether by the same or different inspector, in which case the requirements about notification apply (r 18 [r (19)]).

Such a decision to reopen the inquiry can itself be challenged in the courts. In *R v Secretary of State for the Environment, ex p Fielder Estates (Canvey) Ltd*[8] an inspector had inadvertently closed an inquiry before the day on which he had promised an objector he could give his evidence. The Secretary of State, without consulting the other parties, agreed to the objector's request that a new inquiry with another inspector be held. Roche J quashed this decision on an application for judicial review on the grounds of the failure to consult and because he considered the decision to be irrational. Roche J pointed out that apart from ordering an entirely new inquiry, there were three alternative courses open to the Secretary of State. He could have (a) reopened the inquiry to enable the objector to give his evidence, or (b) directed the objector to send him a written statement of the evidence he had intended to give and, if any new points were raised, allow the applicants an opportunity of meeting those points either by re-opening the inquiry or allowing written representations or (c) asked for the written proof of evidence from the objector and, if no new points were contained in it, ordered the inspector to make his report. Roche J concluded that there was no evidence that the objector would have suffered injustice if the inquiry had been re-opened by the inspector receiving written or oral evidence, while the evidence before him suggested that the course selected was highly probable to cause injustice to the other parties because of the cost or delay. The circumstances of every case are different but the judgment does suggest that the decision to order a totally new inquiry should not be taken lightly and only after extensive consultation of all parties.

6 *Costs*

The Secretary of State is empowered to make orders as to the costs incurred by him in relation to a local inquiry and as to the costs incurred by the parties to the inquiry and as to the parties by whom such costs shall be paid. This is done by applying s 250, sub-ss (2) to (5) of the Local Government Act 1972 to an inquiry held under s 282.[9] The provisions are also applied to inquiries into appeals determined by inspectors.[10]

The power for the Secretary of State to recover his own costs incurred in connection with an inquiry has been widened by s 42 of the Housing and Planning Act 1986. It is now made clear that staff costs and departmental overheads (including costs of other Ministers and Departments) can be recovered as well as the fees of officers involved. It is also provided that he is entitled to costs even where the inquiry does not go ahead. It remains to be seen how these powers will be exercised.

It used to be rare for the Secretary of State to order one party to pay another party's costs but costs are now being increasingly used as a means of improving the speed and efficiency of the appeal process and also as a

8 [1989] JPL 39. Also see *R v Secretary of State for Transport ex p T Ford Ltd* (29 June 1989, unreported).
9 See s 282(2) of the 1971 Act.
10 See 1971 Act, Sch 9, para 5(3).

sanction against unreasonable refusals of planning permission or frivolous appeals.[11] The policy on awards of costs, which is now set out in circular 2/87,[12] has been rewritten and is substantially tougher. There is still an important distinction between planning appeal inquiries and inquiries into compulsory purchase and analogous orders. Broadly speaking, where a person has successfully defended his property against action initiated by a public authority—where, for example, a landowner's objections to a compulsory purchase order are upheld following an inquiry and the order is not confirmed—an award of costs will generally be made. The types of inquiry in which costs will be awarded to successful objectors include inquiries arising out of orders revoking or modifying planning permission, orders requiring discontinuance of an authorised use or the alteration or removal of authorised buildings or works, and compulsory purchase orders. Where an objector is partly successful at such an inquiry—where, for example, he succeeds in having part of his land excluded from a compulsory purchase order—he will be awarded a proportion of his costs.

In other cases costs will normally be awarded only where one party has been guilty of unreasonable behaviour. Even though 'successful', for example, in an appeal against a refusal of planning permission, an appellant will generally not be awarded costs, and indeed an award may be made against a successful party. An award will only be made where the unreasonable conduct has caused the other party to incur expense unnecessarily, either because it should not have been necessary for the case to come before the Secretary of State for decision or because of the manner in which the proceedings at the inquiry were conducted.

In the case of local planning authorities, the circular makes clear that costs will be awarded if applications have been refused without there being complete, precise, specific and relevant reasons or if evidence is not produced to substantiate the reasons for refusal (para 7 of the circular).

Thus, awards may be made if the application is refused solely because it does not conform to the development plan without considering other material considerations or if the refusal is solely based on local opposition or design considerations (paras 8 to 10). Similarly local planning authorities risk having costs awarded against them if the decision goes against previous appeal decisions, judicial authority or official statements of policy (para 11). The imposition of conditions can also lead to the award of costs if the conditions fail to meet the criteria laid down in circular 1/85 (para 13). In the case of enforcement notice appeals, the same principles apply and costs will generally be awarded if an enforcement notice is served where there are no significant planning objections to the alleged breach of control (para 14). Finally, costs can be awarded against planning authorities because of the way in which they handled the processing of the application or the appeal itself (paras 15, 10, 19).

In the case of the appellant, the planning authority may get its costs paid, if the appeal is unreasonable (eg if an appeal decision had recently made clear that the application would not be allowed and there has been no change of circumstances) or if the handling of the appeal is unreasonable and causes

11 The Report of the Chief Planning Inspector for 1986/7 showed that 30% of applications for costs at inquiries are successful.
12 Replacing circular 73/65.

additional expense (e g by introducing a new ground of appeal late in the day) (paras 21 to 23).

Awards of costs either in favour of or against third parties are only made in exceptional circumstances, and will generally only apply in respect to the handling of the appeal (para 25).

Costs can now be awarded by inspectors themselves where the case has been transferred to them for decision.[13] Previously the inspector could only make a recommendation as to costs to the Secretary of State. In such a case, and where the Secretary of State is making the decision, the application for costs should be made to the inspector before the inquiry ends. In this regard circular 2/87 states that 'An application for costs made after the proceedings are completed will be entertained only if the party claiming costs can show good reason for not having done so earlier' (para 27).

Section 250(5) of the Local Government Act 1972 provides that the Secretary of State can make 'orders as to the costs of the parties at the Inquiry.' This wording would indicate that an order can only be made if an inquiry is in fact held and then only in regard to the costs of appearing at the inquiry: this would rule out costs of preparing for an inquiry only to find that the appeal had been withdrawn. The Secretary of State interprets his power 'as enabling him to award to a party the costs necessarily and reasonably incurred in relation to the proceedings before him'. The power does not extend to awards of compensation for indirect costs, e g those resulting from delay. The Secretary of State does not himself determine the amount payable. This is done by a Master of the Supreme Court Taxing Office, if the costs cannot be agreed.

A determination of an application for costs is subject to judicial review[14] and can be challenged on the *Wednesbury* principles.[15] *In R v Secretary of State for the Environment, ex p Reinisch*[16] the Divisional Court rejected the argument that application of the policies on costs set out in a circular constituted an improper fettering of discretion. Further in *Council of the City of Manchester v Secretary of State for the Environment and Mercury Communications Ltd*[17] Kennedy J held that in deciding whether conduct was unreasonable, what matters is the evidence which leads to the relevant decision, not whether the reason given for refusing planning permission was one which no reasonable planning authority could have given. The judge also refused to accept that before an order for costs could be made the local planning authority had to adopt a position which was 'obviously wholly unarguable'. The crucial question instead is whether on the facts the Secretary of State was entitled to conclude that the behaviour of the council was unreasonable.

It has even been held that costs can be awarded because of conduct in parallel proceedings which, if they had been concluded, would have avoided the need for the inquiry. Costs were awarded against Westminster City

13 See para 5(3) of Sch 9 to the 1971 as amended by the Housing and Planning Act 1986, Sch 11 para 8(2).

14 An application under s 245 is probably not applicable, as the determination on costs is probably not a decision 'on an application' or 'or an appeal', see ch 20 p 566.

15 See *R v Secretary of State for the Environment, ex p Wild* [1985] JPL 753; *R v Secretary of State for the Environment and Bray, ex p Havering London Borough Council* [1987] JPL 840.

16 (1971) 70 LGR 126.

17 [1988] JPL 774.

Council for not dealing with a renewed application expeditiously which if granted would have removed the need for the appeal which was the subject of the inquiry.[17a]

D INFORMAL HEARINGS

The applicants and the local planning authority have the right under s 36 to insist on a hearing but they do not have the right to prescribe the type of hearing. Where a hearing is insisted upon, the Secretary of State usually uses his powers under s 282 to cause a local inquiry to be held. However, there is the alternative of an informal hearing. It has been described by the Environment Committee in the following terms: 'The inspector arrives at the hearing fully apprised of all the arguments and can start by summarising the position indicating on which matters he requires more information. In effect, he arrives with an agenda and leads a round table discussion with anything up to a dozen people'.[18] It therefore, has similarities to the 'Examination in Public' used to examine the policies in Structure Plans.

The procedure governing these hearings was rather obscure. It seems that the 1974 rules applied to such hearings but, in practice, many of the rules were not appropriate to them and the appellant and the local planning authority were invited, in agreeing to the procedure set out in a Code of Practice, to waive certain of their entitlements under the Rules. This was not very satisfactory and, with the changes made in the 1988 Rules introducing greater regulation, it was decided that the Rules should not apply to such hearings.[19] Instead, where the appellant and the local planning authority agree the hearings are governed by a new code of practice.[20]

The Environment Committee recommended that an appellant should be able to opt for an informal hearing but this was rejected because of the fear that it might lead to appellants opting for this procedure rather than for written representations,[1] thus increasing the time taken to decide appeals.[2] The new code of practice makes clear that it will be for the Secretary of State to decide, in a case where either the appellant or the local planning authority have expressed their wish to have a hearing, whether to offer the choice between a local inquiry or informal hearing. It is stated that an informal hearing will not be appropriate if many members of the public are likely to be present; if the appeal raises complicated matters of policy; if there are likely to be substantial legal issues raised; or if there is a likelihood that formal cross-examination will be needed to test opposing cases (paras 3 and 4 of the Code).

Both parties have to agree and they can change their minds before the hearing has started. Even once the hearing is in process the inspector can

---

17a See *R v Secretary of State for the Environment, ex p Westminster City Council* [1989] 1 PLR 23.
18 See 'Planning: Appeals, Call-in and Major Public Inquiries', Fifth Report of the House of Commons Environment Committee.
19 See Circular 10/88 para 19.
20 This code is annexed to Circular 10/88 as Annex 2.
 1 See para 43 of the Government's Response to the Fifth Report from the Environment Committee.
 2 It seems that inspectors can decide three written representation cases for every two cases decided by informal hearings.

decide that an inquiry should be held if either party submits that the informal procedure is inappropriate or indeed if it becomes apparent to the inspector himself that the procedure is inappropriate. In such a case a local inquiry will be arranged. The details of the informal procedure are set out in the code.

E MAJOR INQUIRIES

The procedures described in section C above apply to all public inquiries into planning appeals and into planning applications called in for a decision by the Secretary of State, whatever the size or complexity of the proposal in question. However, since the 1960s concern has been expressed about the limitations of the planning inquiry as a mechanism for investigating major proposals.[3]   In part, this concern reflects some dissatisfaction with the wider decision-making process within which the public inquiry operates. This is especially true of certain proposals founded on national policy. Where a promoter supports a proposal by reference to national policy, objectors, not surprisingly, may wish to question the merits of that policy. The general position is that the merits of national policy are not in issue at a public inquiry; they are a matter on which the Government is, in theory, accountable to Parliament. The difficulty arises in cases where there has been little or no Parliamentary discussion of the underlying policy. In such cases, objectors may seek to use the public inquiry as a vehicle for questioning national policy. The disruption of a number of major road inquiries during the 1970s was, in part, symptomatic of this frustration with the wider decision-making process. Consideration of possible solutions to this difficulty are beyond the scope of this book. We mention the difficulty as one explanation for the concern which has been expressed.

From time to time development proposals raising national policy implications will come forward in what might be described as a policy vacuum. In these circumstances it would seem unavoidable that the investigatory process should consider where the national interest lies. Indeed, the Government has accepted that: 'There may well be cases in which a major public inquiry is a perfectly reasonable instrument for inquiring into the policy background as well as the suitability of the particular site or sites'.[4] Also in *R v Secretary of State for Transport, ex p Gwent County Council*[5] Woolf J stated that even in cases of a clearly defined national policy objectors '. . . were perfectly entitled to have investigated all matters on which they relied for saying that the national policy should be departed from within their locality'. It is thus inevitable that such inquiries should be seized upon as an opportunity to criticise and to probe national policies. At the Sizewell B Inquiry,[6] the

---

3 See, for example, G Ganz, *Administrative Procedures*; D Pearce, L Edwards and G Beuret, *Decision-Making for Energy Futures* (Macmillan, 1979); Outer Circle Policy Unit in association with JUSTICE and the Council of Science and Society, *The Big Public Inquiry* (1979); and J Rowan-Robinson, 'The Big Public Inquiry' (1981) 4 Urban Law and Policy 373.

4 See Government's Response to the Fifth Report of the House of Commons Environment Committee, at para 56.

5 [1988] QB 429, [1987] 1 All ER 161, CA.

6 For analysis of the role of Government at the Sizewell B Inquiry see Michael Purdue, Ray Kemp and Tim O'Riordan 'The Government at the Sizewell B Inquiry' 1985 Public Law, 475.

Department of Energy broke new ground by agreeing to allow its policy witness to be questioned on the merits of Government policy, though it is usually accepted that an inspector should refuse to allow such a line of questioning if the Government Department objects.[7]

As the 'major' or 'big' inquiry (the terms tend to be interchangeable) has no statutory existence, definition is difficult. The Department of the Environment in their evidence to the Select Committee suggested that any public inquiry lasting longer than 16 working days was a major public inquiry but as the Committee itself pointed out this is both arbitrary and tautologous as it does not explain *why* certain inquiries take longer than others.[8] More revealing is the statement in the new Code of Practice for major planning inquiries which states that 'The Code is intended for application in cases where the development proposal is of major public interest because of its national or regional implications, or the extent or complexity of the environmental, safety, technical, or scientific issues involved and where for these reasons there are a number of third parties involved as well as the applicant and the local authority'.

It is, however, questionable whether the planning inquiry is well suited to give adequate consideration to matters of alternative sites, alternative strategies and alternative technologies. By the time a proposal is submitted to develop a particular site, plans for the development may be well advanced and the opportunity to persuade the developer to give serious consideration to alternatives may have passed.

Perhaps the most serious criticism of the public inquiry as a mechanism for investigating major proposals is directed at the method of investigation. The Town and Country Planning Association summarised this concern when they commented in the context of the Windscale inquiry[9] that 'the very process of the inquiry might be as important for the future of the nuclear energy debate as the issues under discussion'.[10] Although the inquiry procedure combines features of both an inquisitorial and an adversarial process, the method of investigation is essentially adversarial. Whilst the adversarial process has advantages in terms of the thorough testing of evidence, the inquiry is in effect a confrontation between parties who are likely to be more concerned with defending their position than with determining where the public interest lies. With this type of procedure the initiative as regards seeking out and providing the information for the decision-maker rests largely upon those contributing to, rather than upon the person conducting, the inquiry. With major proposals, inequality between the parties in matters of access to information, expertise and funding may result in an unequal contribution to the inquiry. This will not only be seen as being unfair but may be inefficient if the inspector is not provided with the best available evidence upon which to advise the Minister. However, as the history of the Sizewell B Inquiry showed, the institution of the inquiry can

---

7 See r 12(4) of the 1988 Secretary of State's Rules and *Bushell v Secretary of State for the Environment* [1981] AC 75, [1980] 2 All ER 608, HL.
8 See Committee Report para 135.
9 This was an inquiry held in 1977 under s 35 of the Town and Country Planning Act 1971 into a proposal by British Nuclear Fuels Ltd to construct a thermal oxide reprocessing plant at Windscale in Cumbria.
10 *Town and Country Planning*, May 1978, p 269.

combine an adversarial with an inquisitorial/investigatory approach. At Sizewell B Sir Frank Layfield QC the inspector appointed his own counsel, commissioned research, invited independent witnesses and caused the appointment of technical assessors.[11] However, this approach undoubtedly helped to increase the length and expense of the inquiry which ran for 336 working days from 11 January 1983 to 7 March 1985 (in addition there were three preliminary meetings in 1982 amounting to seven days) and which cost the CEGB at least £15 million. The Sizewell B inquiry was a very special inquiry but the increasing length of major inquiries is of concern to both developers (whose projects are delayed) and to objectors (who cannot afford fully to take part). The underlying problem is that an institution set up to deal with local site-specific problems is being asked to cope with major investigations of policy.

As long ago as 1967 the Government acknowledged that where proposals raised wide or novel issues of more than local significance, 'the ordinary public local inquiry is not satisfactory either as a method of permitting the full issues to be thrashed out or as a basis for a decision which can take into account the whole range of practicable alternatives'.[12] The result was the introduction of a new investigatory procedure, the Planning Inquiry Commission (PIC), provision for which is now contained in ss 47 to 49 of the 1971 Act.

The PIC is intended to cater for planning proposals which raise considerations of national or regional importance or which present unfamiliar technical or scientific aspects and which, in either case, merit a special inquiry. The PIC would operate in two stages. Stage one would involve consideration of the general background to a proposal on the lines of a Royal Commission. Stage two would be a site-specific local inquiry (or inquiries) to look at the details of the proposal and objections to it. The Commission would comprise a panel of between three and five members who would have power to initiate research and consider alternative sites.

The PIC has never been used. The reasons for this are a matter for conjecture;[13] it has been suggested, however, that the procedure would be unacceptable because the first stage of the process would pre-empt the decision on the second stage.[14] In the meantime, there has been no shortage of proposals for alternative procedures for investigating major development proposals.[15]

However, the Government's preference has always been to reshape the conventional model to the new demands rather than to create a completely new institution. This approach is reflected in the new Secretary of State Rules 1988 (see p 532, above). These new rules do not employ the term 'major inquiry' but r 5 is specifically designed for major inquiries. Under r 5 the

---

11 For a critique of the Sizewell B inquiry, see 'Sizewell B: an Anatomy of the Inquiry,' by O'Riordan, Kemp and Purdue, 1988, Macmillan.
12 White Paper, Town and Country Planning Cmnd 3333, 1967.
13 See L. Edwards and J Rowan-Robinson, 'Whatever Happened to the Planning Inquiry Commission?' [1980] JPL 307.
14 See announcement by Mr Peter Shore, then Secretary of State for the Environment, reprinted in [1978] JPL 731. See also 'The Big Public Inquiry' (above).
15 For discussion of some of these see J Rowan-Robinson, 'The Big Public Inquiry' (1981) 4 Urban Law and Policy 373, and O'Riordan, Kemp and Purdue 'Sizewell B: An Anatomy of the Inquiry'; also see recommendations of the House of Commons Environment Committee.

Secretary of State may cause a pre-inquiry meeting to be held if it appears to him to be desirable (r 5(1).) Where this is done, other consequences follow. First, the local planning authority and the applicant must serve on each other and on the Secretary of State an outline statement of case. This outline statement must be served not later than eight weeks from the normal announcement that an inquiry is going to be held (r 5(4)). Other persons who have informed the Secretary of State of their wish to appear at the inquiry may be required to produce an outline statement of case within four weeks (r 5(6)). Second, the Secretary of State must issue a statement of the matters which appear to him to be likely to be relevant to his consideration of the application or appeal. Previously such a statement was only required in cases the Secretary of State had called in an application for his own decision. This statement is not strictly a 'terms of reference' as in law it does not affect the legal duty to consider all 'material considerations', but it will play a key role in delineating the expected scope of the inquiry.

In addition, a non-statutory Code of Practice for major Planning Inquiries has been issued. This code will normally be applied to inquiries to which r 5 has been brought into operation, but elements may apply to other cases where it is considered helpful. This code is set out in Annex 1 to circular 10/88.

The code expands on the procedures set out in r 5 and generally explains the administrative arrangements that are to apply at a major inquiry. Apart from the statutory requirement under r 5 for outline statements and pre-inquiry meetings, a separate inquiry secretariat will be set up which will prepare a register of the participants, breaking them up into classes depending on the extent of the part they propose to play at the inquiry. This register will then be used by the inspector as a guide to the treatment of the participants. The code also provides for the possibility of informal meetings being held to try to get agreement on technical matters. These meetings are not to be used to hear evidence on matters which should appropriately be discussed at the inquiry itself.

An important feature of the code is the extent to which it recognises that at major inquiries the inspector and his assessors have to take on an investigatory role. The procedures on the outline statements and pre-inquiry meeting clearly indicate that the inspector may have to initiate evidence himself by calling expert witnesses. As stated, the Sizewell B Inquiry involved many such investigatory procedures and the Department of the Environment has clearly built on that experience. Another theme is the need, where at all possible, for facts to be agreed between the parties and there is provision for the inspector to draw up a statement of generally agreed facts and matters still in dispute which will be deposited and circulated in the same way as written outline statements.

CHAPTER 20

CHALLENGE OF PLANS, ORDERS AND PLANNING DECISIONS IN THE COURTS

The position regarding recourse to the courts in respect of plans, orders and decisions made under the planning legislation is somewhat complex. The public interest would seem to demand that the validity of plans and the more important types of planning orders and decisions should at some stage become unchallengeable in the courts. Without some cut off point, public or private resources might, for example, be wasted upon development carried out on the strength of a decision subsequently found to have been unlawful. Sections 242–249 of the 1971 Act therefore provide that structure plans, local plans and certain types of planning orders, enforcement notices and actions can be challenged on specified grounds in the High Court within a short period but are not otherwise to be questioned in any legal proceedings whatsoever. The effect of these sections is considered in sections A to C of this chapter.

Although ss 242–249 (above) govern challenge of many of the more important decisions that can be made under the planning legislation, they do not apply to all decisions or actions that may be taken under the legislation; those decisions not covered by the statutory provisions on challenge are subject to the general supervisory jurisdiction of the High Court.

The challenge of such decisions is discussed in section D. Finally, the Act provides in the case of certain decisions that there can be recourse to the magistrates courts; this is covered in section E.

A STATUTORY APPLICATIONS TO QUASH

Section 242 of the 1971 Act states, in effect, that except as provided in the Act the validity of structure plans, local plans and specified types of orders and actions 'shall not be questioned in any legal proceedings whatsoever'. This ouster of the courts' jurisdiction is, however, linked with provisions under which the validity of any such plan, order or action may be challenged in the High Court within a six week period on the grounds laid down in ss 244 and 245 of the 1971 Act. Almost identical provisions are to be found in legislation on compulsory purchase, housing and roads, and several of the cases mentioned in this section arose as a result of action taken under such legislation.

While the grounds on which decisions may be challenged under the 1971 Act have been generously interpreted by the courts, the construction of the provisions setting a time limit upon challenge has generally been strict.

The period of six weeks allowed for challenge in the High Court has often been stigmatised as unduly short. It is even further reduced by the decision of the House of Lords in *Griffiths v Secretary of State for the Environment*,[1] that

1 [1983] 2 AC 51, [1983] 1 All ER 439.

the date actions were taken by the Secretary of State was the time a letter conveying the decision was date stamped and that time ran from that date and not when the decision was received.

Applications to High Court: scope

Structure and local plans, roads orders etc. Under s 244 of the 1971 Act 'any person aggrieved'[2] by a structure plan or local plan, or unitary plan, or by any alteration, repeal or replacement of such a plan, may question its validity in the High Court within six weeks of the publication of the first notice of approval of the plan, alteration, repeal or replacement. Application under s 244 may be made on the grounds that the plan, alteration, repeal or replacement is wholly or to any extent outside the powers of Pt 11 of the 1971 Act or that the requirements of Pt II of the Act or of any regulations made thereunder have not been complied with in relation to the approval or adoption[3] of the plan or its alteration, repeal or replacement.[4] A failure to comply with the non-statutory Codes of Practice for the examination in public of structure plans and for local inquiries (see p 55 and p 68 above) will not on that account alone provide grounds for an application under s 244, though in some circumstances such a failure might involve a breach of the rules of natural justice (in which case the plan might be treated as outside the powers of the Act (below)).

Section 244 also applies (with appropriate modifications) to challenge of the validity of certain roads orders made under the 1971 Act and to orders under s 235 of the 1971 Act relieving statutory undertakers from undertakings which have become impracticable (see s 244(5)).

The wording of s 244 suggests that it is only when a plan has been approved or adopted that its validity can be questioned. Further, s 242(1) provides that, except as provided in s 244, the validity of a structure plan, a local plan or unitary development plan or any alteration, repeal or replacement of any such plan shall not be questioned in any legal proceedings whatsoever.

Further, s 242(1) makes it clear that this prohibition applies both before and after the plan, alteration, repeal or replacement has been approved or adopted. Taken together, these provisions would seem to mean that any challenge of the validity of the procedures leading up to adoption or approval of a plan must be postponed until the plan has actually been approved or adopted, and that procedures leading up to adoption or approval of a plan are not subject to challenge by way of an application for judicial review. However, the statutory provisions only relate to challenge of the validity of a plan or its alteration, repeal or replacement and it would seem that a decision *not to approve or adopt* a plan might in some circumstances be challengeable on common law grounds.[5]

---

2 The meaning of this expression is considered at p 573 below.
3 In *Buckinghamshire County Council v Hall Aggregates (Thames Valley) Ltd and Sand and Gravel Association Ltd* [1985] JPL 634, CA Purchas LJ pointed out that this provision only applies to procedures relating to 'the approval or adoption of the plan' and may not apply to all the earlier procedures required by Pt II of the Act.
4 Decisions on applications to quash structure and local plans are discussed in ch 2 above.
5 See *London Borough of Islington v Secretary of State for the Environment* [1980] JPL 739, (1980) 43 P & CR 300.

It also could be argued that the sections only preclude challenge *before* approval or adoption where the challenge is based on the form or content of the plan and that you could challenge by way of judicial review procedural errors as to plan preparation and consideration (see section D of this chapter).

Other orders and actions. In broadly similar fashion, s 245 of the 1971 Act provides that if any person is aggrieved by any order or action to which the section applies and desires to question the validity of such order or action on the grounds that it is not within the powers of the Act or that any of the 'relevant requirements' have not been complied with, he may, within six weeks from the date on which the order was confirmed or the action taken,[7] make application to the High Court to have the order or action quashed. The expression 'relevant requirements' means any requirements of the 1971 Act or of the Tribunals and Inquiries Act 1971 (or of any enactment replaced thereby) or of any relevant order, regulations or rules made under those statutes (s 245(7)); a failure to comply with the rules relating to inquiry procedures will therefore provide grounds for an application under s 245.

Among the more important orders to which s 245 applies are orders revoking or modifying planning permission, orders discontinuing or modifying authorised uses, tree preservation orders, orders defining areas of special advertisement control and listed building revocation or modification orders. Section 245 also applies, *inter alia*, to the following decisions of the Secretary of State: decisions on planning appeals under s 36 of the 1971 Act, decisions on applications referred to the minister under s 35, decisions relating to applications for consent under tree preservation orders, decisions relating to consents under the advertisement regulations, decisions on appeals against enforcement notices to grant permission or to discharge a condition or limitation, decisions on established use certificates, decisions to confirm or not to confirm purchase notices and decisions on applications for listed building consent referred to the minister (see s 245(3)[8]).

Section 245 therefore applies to many, though not all, of the more important types of order which can be made by the Secretary of State and by local planning authorities under the 1971 Act and to many of the decisions or actions which may be taken by the Secretary of State[9] under the Act. Much local planning authority decision-making is, however, outside the scope of s 245, with the result that it will sometimes be possible to challenge such decisions at common law.

In some cases s 242(3), which sets out the actions to which s 245 applies, speaks of decisions relating to an application, while in other cases it speaks of decisions 'on' particular matters. In *Co-operative Retail Services Ltd v Secretary of State for the Environment*[10] it was held that a decision of the Secretary of State 'on an appeal' meant a decision disposing of the appeal and did not include a decision relating to the adjournment of a public inquiry. It is not clear whether this means that s 245 cannot be used to

---

7 As to the date when action is 'taken' see *Griffiths v Secretary of State for the Environment* [1983] 2 AC 51 (see p 564 above).
8 Applying s 242(2) and (3).
9 The decision of a person appointed by the Secretary of State to determine a planning or enforcement appeal is treated as that of the Secretary of State (1971 Act, Sch 9 para 2(4)).
10 [1980] 1 All ER 449, [1980] 1 WLR 271, CA.

challenge a decision of the Secretary of State declining to accept an appeal. In *Chalgray Ltd v Secretary of State for the Environment*[11] Slynn J accepted that where from the very beginning both the local planning authorities had refused to deal with an appeal then it might well be that s 245 was not applicable. However, he went on to hold that, in the case of an application for approval of details which went beyond the original planning permission, even if the Secretary of State declined to accept jurisdiction the proper course was to dismiss the appeal and this was a decision which could be appealed by way of s 245. Yet in the *Co-operative Retail Services* case, above, Brandon LJ doubted if *Chalgray* was correct and felt that where there was a refusal to consider an appeal, then s 242(4) applies, which indicates that an application for judicial review asking for *mandamus* would be the proper remedy; see below, and in *R v Secretary of State for the Environment, ex p Percy Bilton Industrial Properties Ltd*[12] the Divisional Court granted an order of *mandamus* requiring the Secretary of State to hear an appeal. The reference in s 242(3) to action 'on the part of' the Secretary of State means that action taken by a planning authority (such as a failure to comply with the rules relating to inquiry procedures), even though it occurs in the course of proceedings before the Secretary of State, does not come within the ambit of s 245.[13]

Where, as in the *Co-operative Retail Services* case, the court has no jurisdiction to hear an application under the statute, an application for judicial review may be possible. Section 242(4) of the 1971 Act specifically provides that nothing in s 242 is to affect the exercise of any jurisdiction of any court in respect of any refusal or failure on the part of the Secretary of State to take any such action as is mentioned in s 242(3)(ie, to make a decision of the types mentioned above).

Curiously the wording of s 242(4) seems to limit an application for judicial review to cases where the Secretary of State is failing to carry out his statutory duty and would therefore not cover other errors of law leading up to the final decision.

The statutory grounds of challenge

The plans, orders and decisions to which ss 244 and 245 are applicable may be challenged in the High Court on one or both of two grounds. Though the wording in the two sections differs somewhat, the grounds on which the validity of a plan, order or decision may be attacked under s 244 or s 245 are essentially similar—(1) that the plan, order or decision in question is outside the powers of the Act; and (2) that there has been a failure to comply with a relevant statutory requirement (see s 244(1), (2)(b), and s 245(1), (4)(b)).

The courts have, however, found considerable difficulties in seeking to define different spheres for, or to draw a borderline between, on the one hand, situations in which the order is 'not within the powers of this Act' and,

---

11 (1976) 33 P & CR 10.
12 (1975) 31 P & CR 154.
13 See, for example, *Davies v Secretary of State for Wales* (1976) 33 P & CR 330; and *Performance Cars Ltd v Secretary of State for the Environment* (1977) 34 P & CR 92, CA. Such proceedings may, however, be tainted by failure to comply with the rules of natural justice.

on the other hand, situations in which a 'requirement of this Act has not been complied with'.[14]

Further, in *Miller v Weymouth and Melcombe Regis Corpn*[15] it was held that even if a decision is not within the powers of the Secretary of State, the court retained a discretion and, in the absence of substantial prejudice, would not quash an order.

At first sight the distinction between the two grounds of challenge would seem to be important as the sections state that an application made on the second ground—failure to comply with a statutory requirement—will only succeed if the court is satisfied that the applicant's interests have been substantially prejudiced by the failure (see p 572 below). No such condition needs to be satisfied where a plan, order or decision is attacked on the first ground.

Ground (1) appears to be an attempt to encapsulate in statutory form the common law doctrine of *ultra vires* but in *Smith v East Elloe RDC*[16] a majority of the House of Lords considered (*obiter*) that this ground of challenge should be given a narrow interpretation. Lord Reid would have excluded from the ambit of the statutory provision any misuse of power, whether *bona fide* or *mala fide*. In his view, this ground of challenge included only violation of express statutory requirements. The importance of this view is that, assuming that the statutory provision ousting the court's jurisdiction after six weeks[17] is effective, those defects which are based on common law presumptions, such as breach of natural justice, unreasonableness or acting from improper motives, would not be subject to the court's supervision. In the same case Lords Morton and Somervell expressed the view that challenge on the ground of *mala fides* was excluded. Viscount Simonds and Lord Radcliffe, on the other hand, were inclined to give the provision a wide construction, Lord Radcliffe stating that in his view the words 'is not empowered' were 'apt to include a challenge not only on the ground of *vires* but also on the ground of bad faith or any other ground which would justify the court in setting aside a purported exercise of statutory power'.

Differing views as to the scope of this ground of challenge are also to be found in Scottish decisions. In *Hamilton v Secretary of State for Scotland*[18] Lord Kissen stated that the narrow construction favoured by Lord Reid in the *East Elloe* case was to be preferred; this ground would not, Lord Kissen thought, allow challenge on the ground of failure to observe the rules of natural justice or on grounds of procedural *ultra vires*. Lord Kissen considered that unless one took this narrow view of the first limb of the statutory grounds, the second limb would be superfluous since procedural defects would come under ground (1).[19]

On the other hand, in *Lithgow v Secretary of State for Scotland*[20] Lord Dunpark expressed the view that the phrase 'not within the powers of this

---

14 *Gordondale Investments Ltd v Secretary of State for the Environment* (1971) 23 P & CR 334, CA, per Megaw LJ.
15 (1974) 27 P & CR 468.
16 [1956] AC 736, [1956] 1 All ER 855.
17 See p 579 below.
18 1972 SC 72, 1972 SLT 233. See, too, *Peter Holmes & Son v Secretary of State for Scotland* 1965 SC 1, 1965 SLT 41.
19 However, this appears to ignore the fact that not all procedural defects go to jurisdiction so as to render a decision *ultra vires*.
20 1973 SC 1, 1973 SLT 81.

Act' should receive a broad construction and, though he found that there was no such breach in the case before him, considered the phrase wide enough to allow the court to quash a decision for breach of the rules of natural justice; if, his Lordship said, 'a Minister exercises a statutory power in a manner prohibited by common law, that, in my opinion, is just as much a non-exercise of his statutory powers as the purported exercise of non-existent powers.'[1] As Lord Dunpark pointed out, however, there may be cases where the same facts will 'found two arguments, viz, (i) breach of a statutory requirement and (ii) cumulatively or alternatively, breach of the principles of natural justice' (which would in his view mean that the decision was outside the statutory powers).

As indicated below, it is the broad view of the first ground of challenge which appears to have prevailed. The second ground of challenge embraces those sorts of failure to comply with legislative requirements which do not fall within the first ground and will therefore include defects (such as failure to give reasons for a decision) which may not render a decision *ultra vires* at common law.

The 'Ashbridge formula' and the practice of the courts

In recent times the courts have adopted a broad approach to the scope of the statutory grounds of challenge and have not generally sought to draw fine distinctions between the two grounds. This development owes much to Lord Denning. In *Webb v Minister of Housing and Local Government*[2] he described the judgments in the *East Elloe* case as 'so differing that they give no clear guidance, or at any rate, no guidance that binds us' and in *Ashbridge Investments Ltd v Minister of Housing and Local Government*[3] he said of the statutory grounds of challenge:[4]

'The court can only interfere on the ground that the Minister has gone outside the powers of the Act or that any requirement of the Act has not been complied with. Under this section it seems to me that the court can interfere with the Minister's decision if he has acted on no evidence; or if he has come to a conclusion to which on the evidence he could not reasonably come; or if he has given a wrong interpretation to the words of the statute; or if he has taken into consideration matters which he ought not to have taken into account, or *vice versa*; or has otherwise gone wrong in law. It is identical with the position where the court has power to interfere with the decision of a lower tribunal which has erred in point of law.'

In addition, of course, the statutory grounds of challenge enable the court to quash a decision on account of failure to comply with a statutory requirement.

1 In *Fairmount Investments Ltd v Secretary of State for the Environment* [1976] 2 All ER 865, [1976] 1 WLR 1255 Lord Russell of Killowen expressed the view that breach of the principles of natural justice came within both of the statutory grounds of challenge. See too *Errington v Minister of Health* [1935] 1 KB 249; *Hibernian Property Co Ltd v Secretary of State for the Environment* (1973) 27 P & CR 197; *Hamilton v Roxburgh County Council* 1970 SC 248, 1971 SLT 2; and *George v Secretary of State for the Environment* (1979) 38 P & CR 609.
2 [1965] 2 All ER 193, [1965] 1 WLR 755, CA.
3 [1965] 1 WLR 1320, CA.
4 In this case those contained in the Housing Act 1957.

Lord Denning accepted that the '*Ashbridge* formula' represents an extension of the scope of the statutory provisions.[5] However, in *R v Secretary of State for the Environment, ex p Ostler*[6] he said of his statement in *Ashbridge*: '. . . the Minister did not dispute it. It has been repeatedly followed in this court ever since[7] and never disputed by any Minister. So it is the accepted interpretation.' Assuming that the '*Ashbridge* formula' represents the law, the result is, as Corfield and Carnwath say[8] 'that little, if any, effect is to be given to the actual words of the statutory provision'.

In *Seddon Properties Ltd v Secretary of State for the Environment*[9] Forbes J in a passage which has been frequently used in later cases, gave the following summary of the grounds of challenge:

(1) The Secretary of State must not act perversely. That is, if the court considers that no reasonable person in the position of the Secretary of State, properly directing himself on the relevant material could have reached the conclusion that he did reach, the decision may be overturned. See, for example, *Ashbridge Investments Ltd v Minister of Housing and Local Government*,[10] *per* Lord Denning MR[11] and Harman LJ[12] This is really no more than another example of the principle enshrined in a sentence from the judgment of Lord Greene MR in *Associated Provincial Picture Houses Ltd v Wednesbury Corpn*:[13] 'It is true to say that, if a decision on a competent matter is so unreasonable that no reasonable authority could ever have come to it, then the courts can interfere.'

(2) In reaching his conclusion the Secretary of State must not take into account irrelevant material or fail to take into account that which is relevant: see, for example, again the *Ashbridge Investments* case,[14] *per* Lord Denning MR.[15]

(3) The Secretary of State must abide by the statutory procedures, in particular by the Town and Country Planning (Inquiries Procedure) Rules 1974. These rules require him to give reasons for his decision after a planning inquiry (r 13) [now see r 17 of the 1988 Rules, ch 19], and those reasons must be proper and adequate reasons that are clear and intelligible and deal with the substantial points that have been raised; *Re Poyser and Mills Arbitration*.[16]

---

5   See, for example, *The Discipline of Law* (Butterworths, 1979), pp 106–108.
6   [1977] QB 122, [1976] 3 All ER 90, CA.
7   See, for example, *Re Lamplugh* (1967) 19 P & CR 125; *Coleen Properties v Minister of Housing and Local Government* [1971] 1 All ER 1049, [1971] 1 WLR 433; *Gordondale Investments Ltd v Secretary of State for the Environment* (1971) 23 P & CR 344; *British Dredging (Services) Ltd v Secretary of State for Wales* [1975] 2 All ER 845, [1975] 1 WLR 687; *Eckersley v Secretary of State for the Environment* (1977) 34 P & CR 124; and *Pyrford Properties Ltd v Secretary of State for the Environment* (1977) 36 P & CR 28.
8   *Compulsory Acquisition and Compensation* (Butterworths, 1978), p 55.
9   (1978) 42 P & CR 26.
10 [1965] 3 All ER 371, [1965] 1 WLR 1320, 63 LGR 400, CA.
11 [1965] 1 WLR 1320 at 1326.
12 *Ibid* at p 1328.
13 [1948] 1 KB 223 at 230, [1947] 2 All ER 680, 45 LGR 635, CA.
14 [1965] 1 WLR 1320.
15 *Ibid* at p 1326.
16 [1964] 2 QB 467, [1963] 1 All ER 612.

(4) The Secretary of State in exercising his powers, which include reaching a decision such as that in this case, must not depart from the principles of natural justice: *per* Lord Russell of Killowen in *Fairmount Investments Ltd v Secretary of State for the Environment.*[17]

(5) If the Secretary of State differs from his inspector on a finding of fact or takes into account any new evidence or issue of fact not canvassed at the inquiry, he must, if this involves disagreeing with the inspector's recommendation, notify the parties and give them at least an opportunity of making further representations: rule 12 of the Rules of 1974 [but now see r 16(4) of the 1988 rules].

There are other peripheral principles. If the Secretary of State differs from the inspector on an inference of fact he must have sufficient material to enable him to do so: *per* Lord Denning MR in *Coleen Properties Ltd v Minister of Housing and Local Government.*[18] Otherwise, the courts can interfere in accordance with the first principle stated above. If it is a matter of planning policy, he is free to disagree with the inspector's conclusions or recommendations without bringing into operation r 12: *Lord Luke of Pavenham v Minister of Housing and Local Government,*[19] but, of course, he must make clear what the policy is and its relevance to the issues raised at the inquiry in accordance with the third principle above. If there has been conflicting evidence at the inquiry, it seems to me that he may, if he wishes, prefer one piece of evidence to another, though the material must be there to enable him to do so, he must give reasons for doing so and, if he is disagreeing with a finding of fact by the inspector, he must apply the procedure of r 12. Since the courts will only interfere if he acts beyond his powers (which is the foundation of all the above principles), it is clear that his powers include the determination of the weight to be given to any particular contention; he is entitled to attach what weight he pleases to the various arguments and contentions of the parties; the courts will not entertain a submission that he gave undue weight to one argument or failed to give any weight at all to another. Again, in doing so he must, at any rate if substantial issues are involved, give clear reasons for his decision.

Also, in *Edwin H Bradley & Sons Ltd v Secretary of State for the Environment*[20] Glidewell J said that in the *Ashbridge* case Lord Denning was enunciating 'exactly the same principles' as those formulated by Lord Greene in the *Wednesbury* case.[1] In the latter case Lord Greene set out the principles, on which the courts will exercise their common law powers of supervision over administrative decision-making. It would therefore appear to be the case that the statutory grounds of challenge contained in ss 244 and 245 of the 1971 Act embrace all the grounds on which a public authority's decision may be attacked by way of judicial review. And as regards procedural matters, the statutory grounds of challenge could be wider in that the

17 [1976] 2 All ER 865, [1976] 1 WLR 1255 at 1263, 75 LGR 33, HL.
18 [1971] 1 All ER 1049, [1971] 1 WLR 433 at 438, P & CR 417 CA.
19 [1968] 1 QB 172, [1967] 2 All ER 1066, CA.
20 (1983) 47 P & CR 374.
1 *Associated Provincial Picture Houses Ltd v Wednesbury Corpn* [1948] 1 KB 223, [1947] 2 All ER 680, CA; see p 570 above.

statutory grounds permit the court to quash for breach of some non-mandatory procedural requirements.[2]

Yet even this difference is probably now irrelevant as it seems that all errors of law made by administrative authorities go to jurisdiction,[3] while it seems that the distinction between mandatory and directory procedural rules is increasingly obsolescent.[4]

Substantial prejudice

On the second ground of challenge—failure to comply with a relevant statutory requirement—the court is not entitled to quash for this reason unless it is satisfied that the interests of the applicant have been substantially prejudiced by the failure[5] (see s 244(2)(b) and s 245(4)(b)). The court's general discretion not to quash is considered at p 576 below.

It is not necessary for the applicant to show that the decision would have been different if the statutory requirements had been complied with; 'the loss of a chance of being better off'[6] will be enough to constitute substantial prejudice. If therefore, the defect is more than a mere technicality, the courts will in general readily accept that the applicant has suffered substantial prejudice.[7]

In *Tameside Metropolitan Borough Council v Secretary of State for the Environment*[8] it was held that since the result of allowing a decision of the Secretary of State to stand would be that an eyesore would continue to exist, the planning authority had been substantially prejudiced by a defect in the making of the decision,

In the case of a failure to give adequate reasons as required by the Inquiries Procedure Rules, the courts have held that this amounts to an error of law.[9] Nevertheless, it is clear that a breach of this requirement will not automatically lead to a decision being quashed if no prejudice has been caused to the applicant. Thus in *Bell and Colvill Ltd v Secretary of State for the Environment*[10] Forbes J refused to quash a decision even though the inspector had not made clear why he had rejected a particular argument because in all probability the inspector had thought very little of the argument. In contrast,

---

2 Subject to the qualification that the applicant will have to satisfy the court that he has been substantially prejudiced by the breach; see below.

3 See Lord Diplock in *Re Racal Communications Ltd* [1981] AC 374, [1980] 2 All ER 634, HL.

4 See Woolf LJ in *R v Lambeth London Borough Council, ex p Sharp* [1986] JPL 201.

5 See, for example *Steele v Minister of Housing and Local Government* (1956) 6 P & CR 386; *Gordondale Investments Ltd v Secretary of State for the Environment* (1971) 23 P & CR 334; *Miller v Weymouth and Melcombe Regis Corpn* (1974) 27 P & CR 468; *Camden London Borough Council v Secretary of State for the Environment* (1975) 235 Estates Gazette 375; *Kent County Council v Secretary of State for the Environment* (1976) 33 P & CR 70; *London Borough of Greenwich v Secretary of State for the Environment* [1981] JPL 809; *Schleider v Secretary of State for the Environment* [1983] JPL 383.

6 *Hibernian Property Co Ltd v Secretary of State for the Environment* (1973) 27 P & CR 197, per Browne J.

7 *Darlassis v Minister of Education* (1954) 4 P & CR 281; *Hibernian Property Co. Ltd* (above); *Wilson v Secretary of State for the Environment* [1974] 1 All ER 428, [1973] 1 WLR 1083; and *McMeechan v Secretary of State for the Environment* [1974] JPL 411, CA.

8 [1984] JPL 180.

9 *Re Poyser and Mills Arbitration* [1964] 2QB 467, [1963] 1 All ER 612, and *Givaudan v Minister of Housing and Local Government* [1966] 3 All ER 696, [1967] 1 WLR 250.

10 [1980] JPL 823.

in the Scottish case of *Wordie Property Co Ltd v Secretary of State for Scotland*[11] the Lord President (Lord Emslie) said that a failure on the part of the minister to give proper and adequate reasons for his decision on a planning application could not be other than prejudicial to the applicant. In the same case Lord Cameron said: 'Where an applicant has been deprived of the exercise of a right conferred upon him by Parliament, that fact alone would appear to me *prima facie* to indicate that he has suffered substantial prejudice.' The position may therefore be that a failure to give adequate reasons will lead to the decision being quashed unless the Secretary of State can convince the court that the issue on which the reasons were defective was minimal to the decision as a whole. However, recently in *Simplex G E (Holdings) Ltd v Secretary of State for the Environment*,[12] where it was accepted that the local planning authority had been in breach of the regulations in adopting a local plan without first giving reasons for rejecting a recommendation of the inspector who had held the inquiry, the Court of Appeal upheld the first instance judge's refusal to quash the decision. Staughton LJ stated: 'The council did, in fact, have reasons for not agreeing to the inspector's recommendation that the land should cease to be green belt. That in itself may not be a sufficient reason for exercising the discretion against quashing the relevant part of the plan; otherwise, there would be no point in the provision that reasons must be given. But I cannot see that on the facts of this case Simplex were prejudiced substantially or indeed at all by the failure to give reasons.'

It seems that failure to make early objection to an alleged irregularity may be treated as a factor tending to show that the applicant has not been substantially prejudiced. In *Midlothian District Council v Secretary of State for Scotland*[13] it was held that the planning authority had failed to show that they had been substantially prejudiced, in the course of a public inquiry, by the leading of evidence dealing with matters of which no prior notice had been given; the authority had made no objection at the inquiry, had not sought an opportunity to lead further evidence themselves, and there was in any event, nothing to suggest that further evidence would have made any difference to the decision.

Standing

Only a 'person aggrieved' by a structure plan or local plan or unitary development plan or by the alteration, repeal or replacement of such a plan is entitled to make application to the court under s 244 of the 1971 Act. Under s 245, application to quash any order or decision to which that section applies can be made by (a) a 'person aggrieved' by the order or action in question; or (b) an authority 'directly concerned'[14] with the order or action.

Alongside a liberalisation of the approach towards standing to apply for judicial review of planning decisions, the courts of recent years have been prepared to give a broad meaning to 'person aggrieved'. This is despite an

---

11 1984 SLT 345.
12 [1988] JPL 809.
13 1980 SC 210 (and see comment in 1981 SPLP 17). See, too *Davies v Secretary of State for Wales* [1977] JPL 102; and *George v Secretary of State for the Environment* (1979) 38 P & CR 609, CA.
14 As to the meaning of this expression see s 245(7).

initial decision of the High Court which gave a very restrictive meaning to the term. In *Buxton v Minister of Housing and Local Government*[15] a landowner who had been permitted to appear at a public inquiry into an appeal against a refusal of planning permission in respect of land adjacent to his and who claimed that the minister's decision to grant permission would injure the amenities and diminish the value of his land, was held not to have any right to question the validity of the minister's decision as he was not, for the purposes of the planning legislation, a 'person aggrieved' by the decision. Salmon J considered that in the context of the planning legislation a person is 'aggrieved' by a decision only if his legal rights are infringed in some way.

But in *A-G of Gambia v N'Jie*[16] Lord Denning expressed his disapproval of this narrow interpretation, saying that the words 'person aggrieved' 'are of wide import and should not be subjected to a restrictive interpretation. They do not include, of course, a mere busybody who is interfering in things which do not concern him; but they do include a person who has a genuine grievance because an order has been made which prejudicially affects his interests.' In *Maurice v LCC*[17] the Court of Appeal considered that a householder, the amenities of whose property would have been injuriously affected by the construction of a tall building nearby, was an aggrieved person for the purpose of the London Building Act.

In *Turner v Secretary of State for the Environment*[18] Ackner J refused to follow the decision in *Buxton* and held that members of an amenity society who had given evidence at a public inquiry into a planning application 'called in' by the Secretary of State were 'aggrieved persons' for the purpose of an application to the High Court under the statutory provisions relating to the challenge of planning decisions. In *Bizony v Secretary of State for the Environment*[19] Bridge J was prepared to assume that a 'third party' who had made representations on a planning appeal dealt with on the basis of written representations was an 'aggrieved person'.

It should perhaps be added that in *Buxton* Salmon J expressed the view that: '... anyone given a statutory right to have his representations considered by the Minister impliedly has the right that the Minister in considering those representations, shall act within the powers conferred upon him by the statute and should comply with the relevant requirements.'

In the case of planning application appeals only a limited group of third parties have an express statutory right to have their representations considered by the Secretary of State and to appear at any public inquiry held.[20] These are mainly those persons who have to be notified under s 27 as having legal interests in the land the subject of the application. However, by way of s 29(1) all 'material considerations' must be regarded by the Secretary of State on appeal or a call-in and so anyone who has made representations

---

15 [1961] 1 QB 278, [1960] 3 All ER 408. See, too *Simpson v Edinburgh Corpn* 1960 SC 313, 1961 SLT 17 (see p 591 below).
16 [1961] AC 617, [1961] 2 All ER 504, PC. See too *Arsenal Football Club Ltd v Smith* [1979] AC 1, [1977] 2 All ER 267, HL.
17 [1964] 2 QB 362, [1964] 1 All ER 779.
18 (1973) 28 P & CR 123. See, too the comments of Glidewell J in *Hollis v Secretary of State for the Environment* (1982) 47 P & CR 351.
19 [1976] JPL 306.
20 See ss 36(5) and 35(4) and r 3 of the Inquiries Procedure Rules which defines the so-called 's 29' parties.

which include 'material considerations' is entitled to have these material considerations regarded. So for the purposes of s 245 it is suggested that the phrase will embrace not only persons whose property or legal rights are directly affected by an order or decision to which the section applies but also any person who objected to the order or decision in question, or who took part in a public inquiry or in written representations procedures relating to the order or decision. Further, in *Turner* (above) it was said that 'any person who, in the ordinary sense of the word, is aggrieved by the decision ... should have the right to establish in the courts that the decision is bad in law', and it may be that participation in the decision-making process is not essential before a person who is adversely affected by an order or decision can qualify as an 'aggrieved person'.

Local planning authorities will usually be able to challenge orders and decisions in which they are directly involved, as being the authority which originally made the order or decision to which the proceedings in question relate. However, in the case of local authorities or other public bodies who are simply consulted or who have a power to give directions, they will not be 'the authority directly concerned' (s 245(7)). In most cases they will be able to make application under s 245 as 'persons aggrieved'. However, it is worth noting that in *Greater London Council v Secretary of State for the Environment*[1] Woolf J held that the Greater London Council was not a 'person aggrieved' where a decision was made refusing an appeal but the Greater London Council thought the reasoning was wrong in law. The council had directed that the application should be refused but were worried that the reasoning might be used as a precedent. This suggests that s 245 can only be used to challenge the validity of the actual order or decision and not the reasoning independently of that order or decision. However, Woolf J did indicate that in a proper case on application for judicial review it could be used to challenge the legality of the reasoning of a decision.[2]

As regards challenge of a structure plan or local plan, or unitary development plan or the alteration, repeal or replacement of such a plan, it is suggested that 'aggrieved persons' would include objectors, persons selected to appear at the public examination of a structure plan, persons who appeared at a local plan inquiry, bodies who have to be consulted in the making of a plan, and any person whose property is affected by a plan.[3] Sections 8 and 12 of the 1971 Act require that 'persons who may be expected to desire an opportunity of making representations' about proposed development plan policies be made aware they are entitled to do so. In so far as this class of persons can be ascertained, they must count as 'aggrieved persons'.

Section 244 makes no express provision for challenge of a plan or alteration, etc by a planning authority, and it is not certain that a planning

---

1 [1985] JPL 868.
2 An application was subsequently refused see *R v Secretary of State for the Environment, ex p Greater London Council* (1985) Times, 30 December.
3 See *Edwin H Bradley & Sons Ltd v Secretary of State for the Environment* (1983) 47 P & CR 374; and *Sand and Gravel Association Ltd v Buckinghamshire County Council* [1984] JPL 798. In the former case, the applicants were the owners of land affected by a structure plan, had objected to the plan and had taken part in the plan's public examination, while in the latter case the applicants were an association of mineral operators with interests in land affected by a local plan; in neither case was the applicant's standing questioned. Also see *Rand v Secretary of State for the Environment* [1988] JPL 830.

authority would necessarily qualify as an 'aggrieved person' in relation to action taken by the Secretary of State on the authority's own plan[4] or in relation to a plan made by a different planning authority.

Powers of High Court

On an application under either s 244 or s 245 the High Court may make an interim order suspending the operation of the plan, or the alteration, repeal or replacement of a plan,[5] or of the order or action which is the subject of the application until the final determination of the proceedings[6] (ss 244(2)(a)), 245(4)(a). If satisfied that either of the statutory grounds of challenge has been made out, the court may quash the plan, order or action in question (s 244(2)(b); s 245 (4)(b)).

The courts have taken the view that the word 'may' as used in these provisions is to be construed in a permissive sense, so that even if the statutory conditions for quashing have been satisfied, the court has a discretion not to take such action. In *Peak Park Joint Planning Board v Secretary of State for the Environment and ICI*[7] Sir Douglas Frank said that in general the court's discretion not to quash should be exercised only rarely and in unusual circumstances—only, in effect, where the defect is purely technical or there is no possibility of detriment to the applicant.[8] Where, for example, a factor wrongly taken into account or omitted from consideration was insignificant or did not affect the decision, or an error has operated in the applicant's favour, the court may exercise its discretion not to quash the decision.[9] If, however, there is any doubt as to whether a defect may have affected the decision, that doubt will operate in favour of the applicant.[10] There is clearly a considerable overlap between the issue as to whether the statutory conditions for quashing have been made out and the court's final decision as to whether to grant the remedy. In particular, the judgment as to whether there has been substantial prejudice by a failure to comply with statutory requirements, will obviously be pertinent to the latter decision. This

4 In *Ealing Borough Council v Jones* [1959] 1 QB 384, [1959] 1 All ER 286 a planning authority was held not to be aggrieved by the quashing by the minister of an enforcement notice served by the authority (the legislation was subsequently amended).

5 The operation of a plan, or its alteration, repeal or replacement may be suspended either generally or in so far as it affects any property of the applicant.

6 This interim power does not apply to applications questioning the validity of tree preservation orders, presumably because suspension of such an order might result in the immediate destruction of the trees in question. However, where applicable, a tree preservation order can be suspended in whole or part as a final measure.

7 (1979) 39 P & CR 361.

8 See, too, the judgment of Glidewell J in *Richmond-upon-Thames v London Borough Council Secretary of State for the Environment* [1984] JPL 24 (in the exceptional circumstances of which, however, it was held that quashing was unnecessary).

9 See *Hanks v Minister of Housing and Local Government* [1963] 1 QB 999, [1963] 1 All ER 47; *Miller v Weymouth and Melcombe Regis Corpn* (1974) 27 P & CR 468; *Gosling v Secretary of State for the Environment* (1974) 234 Estates Gazette 531; *Kent County Council v Secretary of State for the Environment* (1976) 33 P & CR 70; *Chichester District Council v Secretary of State for the Environment* [1981] JPL 591; *Property Investment Holdings Ltd v Secretary of State for the Environment* [1984] JPL 587; and in *Glasgow District Council v Secretary of State for Scotland* 1980 SC 150, 1982 SLT 28 it was held that although the reasoning which led the minister to a particular decision was defective, the decision itself was correct and it would therefore be wrong to quash the decision.

10 See *Preston Borough Council v Secretary of State for the Environment* [1978] JPL 548.

overlap is well illustrated by the judgments in the *Simplex*[11] case but as Staughton LJ's judgment makes clear they are distinct issues: if the statutory conditions have not been satisfied, the discretion does not arise to be exercised and, even if substantial prejudice is shown, there could be other reasons for refusing the remedy.

On a number of occasions the courts have stressed that it is only in exceptional circumstances that they will, on a statutory application to quash, admit fresh or extrinsic evidence. They have, however, been prepared to allow such additional evidence (a) to show what material was before the decision-making body; (b) to enable the court to determine whether essential jurisdictional facts were present or essential procedural requirements had been followed; and (c) to establish 'misconduct', such as bias on the part of the decision-maker.[12]

This means that, in practice, the courts are reluctant to look outside the four corners of the inspector's report and the Secretary of State's decision letter or, where the inspector is making the decision, the inspector's decision letter. In *West Midlands Co-operative Society Ltd v Secretary of State for the Environment*[13] Graham Eyre QC, sitting as a deputy judge, argued that even with respect to most grounds of challenge it will be sufficient for the court to confine itself to those documents. Even where it was argued that the decision-maker had failed to take into account material considerations Graham Eyre QC took the view that '... it might be necessary to demonstrate that such matters were as a matter of law, so fundamental or indispensable and, at the very least, of such materiality that in all probability if they could be identified they would have an important influence on the result'.

Evidence is taken by way of affidavit and although there is a power to allow cross-examination, this is very rarely exercised. It seems this is because it might lead to the courts undermining the actual findings of the inspector.[14] There is also an extreme reluctance to allow an inspector to be cross-examined,[15] and in *R v Vincent*[16] Woolf J said that he knew of no instance where an inspector had been cross-examined on any evidence he had filed by way of affidavit.

Effect of quashing

A structure plan, local plan or any alteration, repeal or replacement of any such plan may be quashed in whole or in part and either generally or in so far as it affects the applicant's property (s 244(2)).[17] However, in *Buckingham-*

---

11 [1988] JPL 809, CA.
12 See, for example, *R v Secretary of State for the Environment, ex p Powis* [1981] 1 All ER 788, [1981] 1 WLR 584; *Ashbridge Investments Ltd v Minister of Housing and Local Government* [1965] 1 WLR 1320; *Chichester District Council v Secretary of State for the Environment* [1981] JPL 591; and *Hollis v Secretary of State for the Environment* (1982) 47 P & CR 351.
13 [1988] JPL 121.
14 See also Slynn J in *East Hampshire District Council v Secretary of State for the Environment* [1978] JPL 182.
15 See Lord Denning in *George v Secretary of State for the Environment* (1979) 77 LGR 689, CA.
16 See *Behrman v Secretary of State for the Environment* [1979] JPL 677 and *R v Vincent* [1987] JPL 519.
17 For examples of parts of plans being quashed; see *Westminster County Council v Great Portland Estate* [1985] AC 661; *Fourth Investments Ltd v Bury Metropolitan Borough Council* [1985] JPL 185; and *Barnham v Secretary of State for the Environment* [1985] JPL 861.

shire County Council v Hall Aggregates (Thames Valley) Ltd[18] Purchas LJ warned that quashing part of a plan might be in substance amending the plan by changing the effect of the remaining part. In such a case, the proper order would be to quash the whole of the plan. The manner in which the legislation is phrased appears to mean that it is the plan or other document that is invalidated and not merely the decision to approve or adopt the plan; the result would appear to be that if a plan is quashed the whole plan-making process must begin afresh.

Section 245 of the 1971 Act is silent as to the effect of quashing an order or decision of a kind to which that section applies. So far as orders are concerned, the effect of quashing is that the procedure for making the order will have to begin afresh.[19] The effect of quashing a decision by the Secretary of State will normally be that the matter is remitted to him for further consideration in the light of the court's ruling.[20]

However, in *Kingswood District Council v Secretary of State for the Environment*[1] Graham Eyre QC (sitting as deputy judge) insisted that the Secretary of State had to start again *de novo* with a clean sheet. This meant that '. . . he was under the obligation to have regard to the development plan and other material considerations, and indeed he was obliged by virtue of the statutory provisions to have regard to matters that might be material considerations which had arisen since the date when the matter was originally considered'. Nevertheless, in practice, it will often not be necessary to make a completely fresh start; if, for example, the Secretary of State's decision on a planning appeal is quashed because of a failure to provide adequate reasons, the minister may have to do no more than issue a fresh decision setting out the reasons clearly, or if there has been a failure to consider some relevant matter at a public inquiry it may be unnecessary for the Secretary of State to do more than give the parties an opportunity to comment on that matter. In this regard it may be noted that under the new Inquiry Procedures Rules 1988, the Secretary of State has a discretion to reopen the inquiry.[2]

In dealing with an application under s 245 the court must generally either quash the decision or order *in toto* or leave it standing; there is, in Lord Cameron's words,[3] 'no power to vary or alter or remodel' the order or decision under review. In *British Airports Authority v Secretary of State for Scotland*[4] the First Division of the Court of Session held that having decided that certain conditions attached to grants of planning permission were *ultra*

---

18 [1985] JPL 634, CA.
19 See *Whiteacre Estates (UK) Ltd v Secretary of State for the Environment* [1984] JPL 177 (successful challenge of Secretary of State's decision on purchase notice meant that the notice was itself quashed).
20 See *Hartnell v Minister of Housing and Local Government* [1964] 2 QB 510, *per* Danckwerts LJ; and [1963] 1 WLR 1141, per Sachs J.; *Price Bros (Rode Heath) Ltd v Secretary of State for the Environment* (1978) 38 P & CR 579; and *Rogelan Building Group v Secretary of State for the Environment* [1981] JPL 506.
1 [1988] JPL 248.
2 Rule 18 of the Secretary of State's Rules also provides that where a decision has been quashed, the Secretary of State must inform the persons entitled to appear at the inquiry of the matters which require further representations and give them an opportunity of making such representations or of asking for the inquiry to be reopened.
3 *British Airports Authority v Secretary of State for Scotland* 1979 SC 200, 1979 SLT 197.
4 Above.

vires, the court could not (even if they had wished to do so) simply excise the invalid conditions; the court's only power was to quash the decisions (ie the planning permissions to which the invalid conditions were attached).

However, under s 245 the court has power to quash in part a tree preservation order or an order defining an area of special advertisement control.

'Shall not be questioned'

Under ss 244 and 245 of the 1971 Act an application seeking to challenge the validity of a plan or of an order or action of one of the types specified in the sections must be made before the expiry of a fairly short time limit. In the case of a structure plan or local plan or unitary development plan or any alteration, repeal or replacement of such a plan, application must be made to the High Court within six weeks from the date of publication of the first notice of the approval or adoption of the plan, alteration, repeal or replacement s 244(1). In the case of orders and decisions covered by s 245 application must be made within six weeks from the date when the order was confirmed or the action in question taken (s 245(1)).

Unless challenged in this fashion, the validity of any such plan, order or action 'shall not be questioned in any legal[5] proceedings whatsoever'[6] (s 242(1)).

The shortness of the period allowed for challenge has often been the subject of criticism. In *Smith v East Elloe RDC*[7] for example, Lord Radcliffe described the six week period as 'pitifully inadequate'. Added point is given to that statement by the decision of the House of Lords in *Griffiths v Secretary of State for the Environment*[8] (see above p 565).

In *Smith v East Elloe RDC*[9] the House of Lords held that an 'ouster' clause very similar in its terms to s 242 of the 1971 Act precluded any challenge of a compulsory purchase order outside the six week period even where bad faith in the making of the order was alleged. The majority of their Lordships considered that after the expiry of the six weeks the jurisdiction of the courts was completely ousted.

It is, however, somewhat difficult to reconcile the decision in *Smith* with the later decision of the House of Lords in *Anisminic Ltd v Foreign Compensation Commission*[10] in which it was held that an 'ouster' clause providing that a determination of the Commission should 'not be called into question in any court of law' would not serve to protect a determination made without jurisdiction and which was thus a nullity. In this case Lord Reid said that he could not regard *Smith* as 'a very satisfactory case', there

5 Since s 244(1) only bars challenge in *legal* proceedings, it may not preclude challenge of the *vires* of a development plan's provisions to the Secretary of State—see *Westminster City Council v Secretary of State for the Environment* [1984] JPL 27, *per* Mr David Widdicombe QC, sitting as a deputy High Court judge.
6 Despite dicta in *Hamilton v Roxburgh County Council* 1970 SC 248, 1971 SLT 2 suggesting otherwise, it is clear that the effectiveness of exclusion clauses of this type is not affected by the Tribunals and Inquiries Act 1971—see *Hamilton v Secretary of State for Scotland* 1972 SC 72, 1972 SLT 233; and *Lithgow v Secretary of State for Scotland* 1973 SC 1, 1973 SLT 81.
7 [1956] AC 736, [1956] 1 All ER 855.
8 [1983] 2 AC 51, [1983] 1 All ER 439.
9 [1956] AC 736, [1956] 1 All ER 855.
10 [1969] 2 AC 147, [1969] 1 All ER 208.

having been in that case 'no citation of the authorities on the question whether a clause ousting the jurisdiction of the court applied when nullity was in question'. It is also worthy of note that in *Anisminic* the Court took a very wide view of the circumstances in which a body would be deprived of jurisdiction and its decision therefore rendered a nullity. Lord Reid considered, for example, that a refusal on the part of a decision-making body to consider some matter required to be taken into account, or the taking into account of some irrelevant consideration or a failure in the course of a public inquiry to observe the rules of natural justice would render the body's decision a nullity.

Nevertheless it seems that the courts make a distinction between exclusion clauses which oust the jurisdiction of the courts altogether and exclusion clauses which limit challenge in the courts by fixing a strict time limit in which actions can be brought.

In *R v Secretary of State for the Environment, ex p Ostler*,[11] where it was sought to challenge the validity of a compulsory purchase order outside the six week period. The Court of Appeal followed *Smith* in preference to *Anisminic*, holding that after the expiry of the time limit, challenge in the courts was absolutely prohibited. In *Ostler* the *Anisminic* decision was distinguished on the grounds that the preclusive clause at issue in *Anisminic* sought to oust the courts' jurisdiction completely, whereas in *Ostler* the legislation allowed a six week period for challenge;[12] that *Anisminic* concerned a decision by a 'truly judicial body' whereas in *Ostler* the order was 'very much in the nature of an administrative decision'; that in contrast to the position in *Anisminic*, it was not the minister's jurisdiction to make the order that was sought to be impugned in *Ostler*; and that public policy demanded certainty after the expiry of the six week period. All but the last of these reasons may be thought somewhat unsatisfactory and it is perhaps a matter for regret that by refusing leave to appeal in the *Ostler* case the House of Lords passed up the opportunity to put the law beyond doubt.[13]

In *Westminster City Council v Secretary of State for the Environment*[14] Mr David Widdicombe QC, sitting as a deputy High Court judge, held that after the expiry of the six week period, not only was it too late to challenge the validity of a local plan as such, but it was also too late to question the validity of an individual policy in the plan; after the expiry of the six weeks it was too late to argue in legal proceedings[15] that a particular policy was *ultra vires* and therefore could not properly be applied in determining a planning application. This approach is questionable in that you are not directly challenging the plan itself but are challenging the validity of the determination of the

---

11 [1977] QB 122, [1976] 3 All ER 90. See too *Cartwright v Minister of Housing and Local Government* (1967) 65 LGR 384; *Routh v Reading Corpn* (1970) 217 Estates Gazette 1337, CA; *Hamilton v Secretary of State for Scotland* 1972 SC 72, *Lithgow v Secretary of State for Scotland* 1973 SC 1; *Jeary v Chailey RDC* (1973) 26 P & CR 280; *Martin v Bearsden and Milngavie District Council* 1987 SLT 300.

12 However, in *Anisminic* a majority of the House of Lords had denied the significance of this distinction.

13 [1977] 1 WLR 258. The Parliamentary Commissioner for Administration found 'serious shortcomings' in the way the Department of the Environment had handled the road scheme in question.

14 [1984] JPL 27.

15 The statutory provisions, barring only challenge in 'legal proceedings', may not preclude challenge of *vires* in an appeal to the Secretary of State.

planning application. If that determination is based on immaterial or *ultra vires* considerations, it will be invalid and it should not matter that those considerations are set out in a policy in a development plan which itself cannot now be questioned in the courts.

Until there is a further decision of the House of Lords on the effectiveness of such exclusion or ouster clauses, the issue can never be entirely free from doubt but it seems to us that the wording of the statutory provisions on challenge and the associated ouster clause leaves no room for the operation of the *Anisminic* principle in relation to ss 242 to 245. The statutory provisions allowing for challenge of decisions within six weeks include within their scope decisions which are beyond the powers of the legislation and are in consequence nullities; the natural reading of the associated ouster clause is therefore to include among the decisions to which it refers decisions which are nullities, with the result that after the expiry of the time limit, the court's jurisdiction to interfere with a decision which is a nullity is excluded.[16]

In the most recent decision on the point, *R v Secretary of State for the Environment, ex p Kent*[17] Pill J, without going into the arguments in detail, said that he was unable to distinguish *Ostler* and held that a decision made by the Secretary of State on a s 36 appeal could not be challenged by judicial review outside the six week period either on the ground that the s 27 certificate was bad or because the decision had been made unfairly.

B APPEALS AGAINST DECISIONS ON ENFORCEMENT AND SIMILAR NOTICES

Section 246 provides a means by which the legality of the Secretary of State's determinations of appeals against enforcement and similar notices can be challenged. It applies to enforcement notices, listed building enforcement notices and to orders under s 103 requiring the replacing of trees. Unlike the position with applications to the High Court under ss 244 and 245, s 243 of the 1971 Act does not expressly exclude any other means of questioning the validity of decisions of the Secretary of State on appeals against enforcement notices. So applications for judicial review could possibly be available to challenge the validity of such determinations.[17a] However, strangely, the validity of determinations of inspectors is declared not to be capable of being questioned in any proceedings whatsoever except as provided by s 246; see para 2(3)(a) of Sch 9 to the 1971 Act.[18]

Apart from this last rather obscure provision, in the case of enforcement notices and listed building enforcement notices, the 1971 Act restricts direct legal challenge to the notices themselves. This is done by providing that the

---

16 See too J Alder, 'Time Limit Clauses and Judicial Review—*Smith v East Elloe* Revisited' (1975) 38 MLR 274.

17 [1988] JPL 706. Upheld by the Court of Appeal The Times 12 May 1989.

17a See *R v Secretary of State for the Environment ex p Davidson* The Times 23 June 1989 where the court held it was open to it to consider an application for judical review of a decision of the Secretary of State dismissing an enforcement appeal.

18 In *Thrasyvoulou v Secretary of State for the Environment and Hackney London Borough Council* [1988] QB 809, [1988] 2 All ER 781, Parker LJ on the basis of this provision suggested that this meant you could not reopen the findings of an inspector that there had been no breach of planning control, in an appeal against a subsequent enforcement notice.

validity of such notices shall not be questioned in any proceedings what-soever on any of the grounds on which an appeal could have been made to the Secretary of State (s 243(1)). This ensures that in the vast majority of cases, a person who wishes to challenge an enforcement notice (on legal or other grounds) will, in the first place at least, have to make use of the statutory machinery for appeal to the Secretary of State. The grounds for appeal which are made exclusive to the Secretary of State (set out in s 88(2)) encompass many of the grounds on which the *vires* of an enforcement notice might in the absence of the statutory provisions be open to direct or indirect challenge in the courts (see ch 12).

The result is that judicial intervention is largely focused on the decisions of the Secretary of State and not the decisions of the local planning authorities.

Scope of s 246: decision in proceedings on appeal

The phrase 'decision in proceedings on appeal' is wide enough to encompass more than the final decision determining the appeal. It could cover decisions or rulings leading up to the final decision. In this regard in *Button v Jenkins*[19] the Divisional Court held that a decision by the Secretary of State, refusing to entertain an appeal against an enforcement notice, was a decision by the Secretary of State in proceedings on appeal and could have been challenged by way of s 246. Yet in *Lenlyn Ltd v Secretary of State for the Environment*[20] Hodgson J held that the proper forum for attacking a decision of the Secretary of State not to entertain an appeal was by application for judicial review. Surprisingly, Hodgson J made no reference to the earlier decisions which had equally related to appeals which had been judged to be out of time. Where an enforcement notice is found to be a nullity, it can similarly be argued that the Secretary of State has no jurisdiction to entertain an appeal as there is no notice against which to lodge an appeal. Thus in *Rhymney Valley District Council v Secretary of State for Wales*[1], Nolan J held that where s 246 had been used to attack a decision of an inspector that an enforcement notice was a nullity, this was the wrong procedure and that the appropriate remedy was an application for judicial review. He therefore treated the application under s 246 as if it had been an application for judicial review. This approach seems unduly technical and conflicts with recent House of Lords decisions which emphasise that even *ultra vires* decisions can give rise to legal consequences.[2] Furthermore, in *Dudley Bowers Amusements Enterprises Ltd v Secretary of State for the Environment*[3] David Widdicombe QC (sitting as deputy judge) took the view that s 246 could be used even where it turned out that the enforcement notice was a nullity. As it is the decision that can only be appealed under s 246, strictly s 246 cannot be used to question the validity of an inspector's reasoning if this did not affect the validity of that decision.[4]

19 [1975] 3 All ER 585; followed in *Horsham District Council v Fisher* [1977] JPL 178.
20 [1985] JPL 482.
 1 [1985] JPL 27.
 2 See *Calvin v Carr* [1980] AC 574, [1979] 2 All ER 440, PC; and *London and Clydeside Estates v Aberdeen District Council* [1979] 3 All ER 876, [1980] 1 WLR 182.
 3 [1986] JPL 689.
 4 *Miah v Secretary of State for the Environment* [1986] JPL 756.

The statutory grounds of challenge

Section 246 simply provides for appeal to the High Court on a point of law. This would seem to cover substantially the same grounds as in ss 244 and 245 but in *London Parachuting Ltd v Secretary of State for the Environment*[5] Mann J held that under s 246 there was no power to find facts and that a point could not be raised if that point had neither been put to nor determined by the Secretary of State. This meant that it could not be argued by way of s 246 that the procedures were flawed by a breach of the rules of natural justice, if the inspector or the Secretary of State had not themselves made a decision which had resulted in that unfairness.

An appeal against an enforcement notice results in the Secretary of State or his inspector having to exercise discretion as to whether planning permission should be granted. This exercise of discretion is also challengeable and it therefore follows that an error of law is made if a finding is made without evidence or without taking into account a material consideration. However, in *ELS Wholesale (Wolverhampton) Ltd v Secretary of State for the Environment*[6] May LJ emphasised that the mere weight given to evidence or material considerations did not raise a question of law.

Standing

With respect to enforcement notices (including listed building enforcement notices), s 246 is precise as to who has standing to appeal to the High Court. It is available only to the appellant or the local planning authority[7] or any other person having an interest in the land to which the notice relates. 'Interest in the land' is not defined but would normally be taken to exclude squatters[8] and occupiers of land by virtue of a licence.[9] The provision in the Town and Country Planning Act 1984 which gives persons who occupy the land by virtue of a licence in writing a right to appeal against enforcement notices does not extend to appeals under s 246. So unless such persons have appealed to the Secretary of State, they are excluded from s 246 proceedings. The wording also means that persons who have been served with enforcement notices may be excluded both from appeals to the Secretary of State and to the High Court, as the category of persons who have to be served with notice can include mere occupiers without an interest in land (see ch 12, p 300). More controversially, although the Town and Country Planning (Enforcement Notices and Appeals) Regulations 1981 require occupiers of properties in the locality to be notified of an appeal against an enforcement notice (see reg 7(1)), such persons cannot apply to the High Court under s 246. Further, where the decision is being made by an inspector, any possibility of attacking the decision by way of an application for judicial review is closed off by Sch 9 (see para 2(3)(a)). In the case of orders under s 103 requiring replanting of trees, standing is restricted to the local planning

---

5 [1986] JPL 428. Followed in *Gwillim v Secretary of State for the Environment* [1988] JPL 263.
6 [1987] JPL 844.
7 This includes the Historic Building and Monuments Commission for England in the case of a listed building enforcement notice; s 246(6).
8 See *Scarborough Borough Council v Adams and Adams* (1984) 47 P & CR 133.
9 See *Pennine Raceways Ltd v Kirklees Metropolitan Council* [1983] QB 382, [1982] 3 All ER 628, (1982) 263 Estates Gazette 721.

authority, the appellant and to any other person on whom the order had been served.

Procedures and powers of the High Court

The 1971 Act leaves it to the Rules of the Supreme Court to spell out the detail of the procedures; see Orders 55 and 94. Application is by way of originating motion, notice of which must be served and appeal entered within 28 days; (r 4(2) of Order 55). This is an extremely severe time limit, especially if time runs from the date that the decision is made or sent out rather than the time it is received by the appellant or the local authority. In this respect in *Ringroad Investments Ltd v Secretary of State for the Environment*[10] the majority in the Divisional Court held that they were bound by previous authority[11] to hold that time ran from the date that the decision letter was sent out, even though r 4(4) states that time 'shall be calculated from the date on which notice of the decision was given to the appellant', which might suggest it is the time that it is received that matters. In *Griffiths v Secretary of State for the Environment*[12] the Court of Appeal, although concerned with s 245, considered that the Divisional Court was not bound and felt that the relevant date for the purposes of r 4(4) was the date when the notice was received. Such a view is strictly *obiter* and the point was not discussed in the subsequent decision in the House of Lords. So until the issue is directly before the Court of Appeal, it must be taken that time runs from the date the document recording the decision is sent to the prospective appellant. Even where an appeal under s 246 is clearly out of time, there is power under Order 3 r 5 for the court to extend the time. Thus in *Ringroad Investments Ltd v Secretary of State for the Environment*[13] where appeals were one day out of time an extension of time was granted. On the other hand in *Smith v Secretary of State for the Environment*[14] the Court of Appeal upheld a refusal to extend time for appeal where the only reason for delay was that it was not an easy point of law and the appeal was 27 days out of time. So leave to extend will not be lightly granted. Any appeal is heard and determined by a single judge unless the court directs that the matter shall be heard and determined by a Divisional Court (Order 94, r 12(2A)).

Evidence is normally by way of affadavit, and although there is power to hear fresh evidence to show what material was before the Secretary of State,[15] as with s 245, it would seem that the courts will be reluctant to look beyond the inspector's decision letter or his report and the Secretary of State's decision letter.[16] It has also been held that r 4(4) of Order 55 (which seems to require the appellant to apply to the inspector to supply his written notes of

10 (1979) 40 P & CR 99.
11 See *Minister of Labour v Genner Iron and Steel Co (Wollescote) Ltd* [1967] 3 All ER 278, [1967] 1 WLR 1386.
12 [1983] 2 AC 51, [1983] 2 WLR 172.
13 (1979) 40 P & CR 99.
14 [1988] JPL 358.
15 See r 7(2) of Order 55 and *Green v Minister of Housing and Local Government* [1967] 2 QB 606, [1966] 3 All ER 942 and *Forkhurst v Secretary of State for the Environment* [1982] JPL 448.
16 See Graham Eyre QC in *West Midlands Co-operative Society Ltd v Secretary of State for the Environment* [1988] JPL 12.

the proceedings) only applied where the appellant wished to place before the court all the material that was before the inspector either because the decision letter did not itself contain a record of the evidence or where a ground of appeal was that the inspector's record was so inaccurate that the appellant was entitled to supplement his record.[17]

The powers of the court are limited to remitting the matter to the Secretary of State with the opinion of the court for rehearing and determination by him (Order 94, r 12(5)). In this respect r 12(5) expressly states that even if the court is of the opinion that the decision appealed against was erroneous in point of law 'it shall not set aside or vary that decision'. In addition, the power, contained in r 7(5) of Order 55, for the court to give any decision which could have been made by the Secretary of State is expressly excluded (r 12(6) of Order 94). It has also been held that the court has no power to hold a rehearing of primary facts and must remit the matter back to the Secretary of State to redetermine those primary facts.[18]

However, it has been said that, where the matter is remitted to the Secretary of State, he was in a position to review the whole of the matter and was not restricted to simply correcting the error of the law on the face of the document.[19] An appeal against an enforcement notice empowers the Secretary of State to make several decisions. Not only can he dismiss or uphold the appeal but he can quash or vary the enforcement notice, grant permission, with or without conditions, discharge any condition or limitation and determine the lawful use of the land. It would seem that any of those decisions can be challenged by way of s 246 and a successful challenge to any one decision potentially re-opens any other decisions which have been made on that appeal. This means that it is open to the Secretary of State to review both the appeal against the enforcement notice and the parallel deemed application for planning permission (s 246). So if planning permission had been granted on an appeal against an enforcement notice, this grant could be put in jeopardy by a successful appeal under s 246 even if the grounds of the successful challenge did not directly relate to the grant of permission. In a subsequent decision concerning s 245, Graham Eyre QC went further and said that where the matter was remitted under s 246, the Secretary of State was *obliged* to treat the matter at large.[20] This presumably stems from the fact that s 29 requires the body determining a planning application to have regard to any material consideration. However, if no new material considerations have arisen since the original decision or if the error of law relating to the enforcement notice appeal does not change the planning consideration relating to the deemed planning application, there will be no reason to reconsider the Secretary of State's determination of the application. A decision to grant planning permission or to discharge a condition or limitation under s 88B(1), can also be challenged by way of s 245 (s 242(3)(f)). In *Gill v Secretary of State for the Environment*[1] Glidewell J (as he then was) was of the view that s 245 would be the most appropriate route

---

17 See *Forkhurst v Secretary of State for the Environment,* above and *Weitz v Secretary of State for the Environment* [1983] JPL 811.
18 *Green v Minister of Housing and Local Government* [1967] 2 QB 606, [1966] 3 All ER 942.
19 *Newbury District Council v Secretary of State for the Environment* [1988] JPL 185.
20 *Kingswood District Council v Secretary of State for the Environment* [1988] JPL 248.
  1 [1985] JPL 710.

in most circumstances but he nevertheless held that there was a choice and that s 246 could be used to appeal against a grant of planning permission. In *Gill* this was used by the developer to challenge the validity of a condition attached to the grant of permission. In the case where the deemed application for planning permission is refused, only s 246 is available to appeal against the refusal. If s 245 is used to challenge the grant of planning permission on an enforcement notice appeal, the quashing of the grant of permission will *not* re-open any other decisions made on that appeal. Section 245 can only be used to challenge the grant of permission and not the enforcement notice. However, in *London Borough of Bromley v Secretary of State for the Environment*[2] Lionel Read QC sitting as deputy judge, was prepared to allow an application under s 245 to be amended to include an appeal under s 246 so that an enforcement notice could be remitted back to the Secretary of State for reconsideration. This course was open to the judge because there is no statutory time limit for bringing s 246 proceedings.

C APPEALS AGAINST SECTION 53 DETERMINATIONS

Section 53 of the 1971 Act provides the machinery by means of which any person who proposes to carry out operations on land or to make any change in the use of land can apply for a determination as to whether planning permission would be required (see ch 5). In the case of a decision of the Secretary of State on a s 53 application 'called in' by him or on an appeal from the decision of a local planning authority under s 53, either the person who made the application or the planning authority may, if dissatisfied with the decision in point of law, appeal to the High Court (1971 Act, s 247).[3] The reference in s 247 to a decision 'on an application' or 'on an appeal' suggests that it is only the final determination of the Secretary of State that can be the subject of an appeal.[4]

The reference to points of law presumably means that the court is under the same restrictions as with s 246 and cannot look into points of law not raised before the Secretary of State (see p 583).

D NON-STATUTORY CHALLENGE

Those planning decisions and actions which are not subject to the provisions of the 1971 Act, discussed above, are subject to the general supervisory jurisdiction of the High Court. Most of the important decisions made by the Secretary of State are covered by the above provisions but not all. The provisions do not, for example, apply to decisions relating to the award of expenses incurred in connections with appeals,[5] to decisions relating to costs

---

2 (23 November 1988, unreported).
3 See, for example, *Coleshill and District Investment Co Ltd v Minister of Housing and Local Government* [1969] 2 All ER 525, [1969] 1 WLR 746.
4 Cf *Co-operative Retail Services v Secretary of State for the Environment* [1980] 1 All ER 449, [1980] 1 WLR 271 (p 566 above).
5 See, for example, *R v Secretary of State for the Environment, ex p Reinisch* (1971) 22 P & CR 1022; and *R v Secretary of State for the Environment, ex p Three Rivers District Council* [1983] JPL 730.

incurred in carrying out urgent works on listed buildings,[6] to interlocutory decisions made in the course of certain kinds of appeal[7] or to a refusal or failure on the part of the Secretary of State to take action of the types specified in subsection (3) of s 242 of the 1971 Act.[8]

So far as the actions of local planning authorities are concerned, challenge to the validity of enforcement notices is restricted to a large extent by s 243 of the 1971 Act (see p 581) and an exclusive statutory remedy is provided by s 245 in respect of the types of orders specified in subsection (2) of s 242 of the 1971 Act (see section A of this chapter). These last orders, apart from the case of tree preservation orders, all require the approval or confirmation of the Secretary of State before they take legal effect and so are tantamount to being decisions of the Secretary of State. Much local planning authority decision-making is, however, outside the scope of those provisions of the 1971 Act. Today the predominant means of challenging the legality of such decisions is by way of the application for judicial review and this remedy can be available to challenge the actions of the Secretary of State. It may also still be possible to utilise the private law remedies of damages, declaration and injunction against planning authorities, though, since the House of Lords decision in *O'Reilly v Mackman*,[9] this route may be barred.

Judicial review

The High Court has for long asserted a supervisory jurisdiction over inferior courts, tribunals and other public bodies.[10] These include the public bodies which administer the planning system. Until 1977, this supervision was carried out by resort to two distinct sets of remedies; the prerogative orders of *certiorari, mandamus* and *prohibition* and the private law actions of declaration, injunction and damages. The prerogative orders and the private law remedies substantially overlapped both in jurisdiction and effect but there were important procedural differences which meant that a plaintiff had to carefully weigh up the various advantages and disadvantages of the two sets of remedies. The system was clearly in need of reform to ensure both flexibility and uniformity and in 1977, following various reports by the Law Commission,[11] a new process was introduced by amending the rules of the Supreme Court. Order 53, which had governed applications for the prerogative orders, was amended so that under one application for judicial review, to which a standard procedure applied, it was possible to obtain not only the prerogative orders but also the remedies of declaration, injunction and damages.[12] Further changes were effected in 1980[13] and in 1981 substantially

6 See, for example, *R v Secretary of State for the Environment, ex p Hampshire County Council* (1980) 44 P & CR 343.
7 See, for example, *Co-operative Retail Services Ltd v Secretary of State for the Environment* [1980] 1 All ER 449, [1980] 1 WLR 271.
8 This is made clear by s 242(4); and see, for example, *R v Secretary of State for the Environment, ex p Percy Bilton Industrial Properties Ltd* (1975) 31 P & CR 154; and *R v Secretary of State for the Environment, ex p Newprop* [1983] JPL 386.
9 [1985] 2 AC 237, [1982] 3 All 1124, [1982] 3 WLR 1096.
10 The detailed law relating to judicial review is beyond the scope of this book and resort should be made to specialist textbooks.
11 See Law Commission No 20, Cmnd 4059, Law Commission Working Paper No 40 (1971) and Law Commission Report 'Remedies in Administrative Law', No 73, Cmnd 6407 (1976).
12 See SI 1977 No 1955.
13 See SI 1980 No 2000.

the same changes were put on a statutory basis by s 31 of the Supreme Court Act 1981. Unfortunately, the exact relationship between the new application for judicial review and the existing right to bring private law actions against public bodies was not made clear and the subsequent years have seen the courts exploring how far the first is exclusive of the second.

The scope of judicial review. Neither Order 53 nor s 31 of the Supreme Court Act 1981 defines the kind of matters which are subject to the application for judicial review. It plainly covers all those actions and omissions which were formerly covered by the prerogative orders but it probably goes further and includes 'all activities of a public nature as opposed to a purely private or domestic character.'[14] It is extremely difficult precisely to demarcate the division between public and private law matters especially as the case law is still evolving. The most authoritative and comprehensive definition to date is to be found in Lord Diplock's speech in *Council of Civil Service Unions v Minister for the Civil Service*.[15] There Lord Diplock stated that 'The subject-matter of every judicial review is a decision made by some person (or body of persons) who I will call the 'decision-maker' or else a refusal by him to make a decision'.[16] He then went on to limit the decisions which are subject to judicial review to those which affect some person's private law right or obligations or his legitimate expectations. Diplock also emphasised that 'For a decision to be susceptible to judicial review the decision-maker must be empowered by public law (and not merely, as in arbitration, by agreement between private parties) to make decisions that, if validly made, will lead to administrative action or abstention from action by an authority endowed by law with executive powers ...'. The source of such decision-making power will usually be statutory, but Lord Diplock accepted it could be common law in origin. Thus prerogative powers can be susceptible to judicial review and even powers based on contract if they are sufficiently underpinned by statute.[17]

Applying Lord Diplock's approach to the Town and Country Planning legislation, the many statutory powers and duties contained in the legislation are certainly in principle subject to judicial review. Any objection that only quasi-judicial and not administrative decisions are susceptible to judicial review has long been swept aside. This was made plain, even before the recent reforms by the Divisional Court in the case of *R v Hillingdon London Borough Council, ex p Royco Homes Ltd*[18] where *certiorari* was granted to quash a grant of planning permission and it is now commonplace for an application for judicial review to be used to challenge the validity of grants for planning permission.

As explained earlier, it seems that an exclusion clause, if backed up by an alternative statutory remedy, will be effective to exclude judicial review, at least after the time limit in which to bring the statutory remedy has elapsed. Even if there is no exclusion clause judicial review is essentially at the

---

14 *Per* Woolf J in *R v BBC, ex p Lavelle* [1983] 1 All ER 241, [1983] 1 WLR 23.
15 [1985] AC 374, [1984] 3 All ER 935, HL.
16 At p 1194, para D.
17 See *R v Panel on Take-overs and Mergers, ex p Datafin plc* [1987] QB 815, [1987] 1 All ER 564, CA.
18 [1974] QB 720, [1974] 2 All ER 643.

discretion of the court and it will be refused if there exists a more appropriate alternative remedy.[19]

So in the case of decisions of the Secretary of State on enforcement notice appeals, although there is no direct exclusion of judicial review, an appeal under s 246 is undoubtedly the proper way to challenge the validity of such decisions.[20] In the case of other actions of the Secretary of State judicial review is an appropriate remedy and has been used to challenge the validity of procedural decisions relating to appeals.[1] Decisions of the Secretary of State of State awarding costs on appeals have also been subject to applications for judicial review.[2]

In the case of decisions of local planning authorities, the statutory right of appeal to the Secretary of State may be a reason for refusing an application for judicial review but this will always depend on the particular circumstances. Thus in *R v Hillingdon London Borough Council, ex p Royco Homes Ltd*[3] where the applicant could have appealed to the Secretary of State, Lord Widgery CJ stated that:

'It seems to me that in a very large number of instances it will be found that the statutory system of appeals is more effective and more convenient than an application for *certiorari*, and the principal reason why it may prove itself to be more convenient and more effective is that an appeal to the Secretary of State on all the issues arising between the parties can be disposed of at one hearing. Whether the issue between them is a matter of law or fact or policy or opinion, or a combination of some or all of those, one hearing before the minister has jurisdiction to deal with them all, whereas of course an application for certiorari is limited to cases where the issue is a matter of law and then only when it is a matter of law appearing on the face of the order.'[4]

He, however, went on to allow *certiorari* in the particular circumstances as it was speedier and cheaper than the other methods and was a proper case because 'the decision in question is liable to be upset as a matter of law because on its face it is clearly made without jurisdiction or made in consequence of an error of law'.

Where the applicant for judicial review has no statutory right of appeal, as with the case of neighbours who are challenging the grant of planning

19 See *Pasmore v Oswaldtwistle UDC* [1898] AC 387, HL.
20 Judicial review may be the appropriate remedy where the Secretary of State turns down an appeal under s 88 on the ground that the enforcement notice is a nullity; see *R v Secretary of State for the Environment, ex p Hillingdon London Borough Council* [1986] 1 All ER 810, [1986] 1 WLR 192. Also see *R v Secretary of State for the Environment ex p Davidson* The Times 23 June 1989.
 1 See *Co-operative Retail Services Ltd v Secretary of State for the Environment*, [1980] 1 All ER 449, [1980] 1 WLR 271; *R v Secretary of State for the Environment, ex p Mistral Investments* [1984] JPL 516; and *R v Secretary of State for the Environment, ex p Centre 21* [1985] JPL 865.
 2 See *R v Secretary of State for the Environment and Bray, ex p Havering London District Borough Council* [1987] JPL 840.
 3 [1974] QB 720, [1974] 2 All ER 643.
 4 This last limitation is now doubtful as error of law which is not on the face of the order will still be susceptible to judicial review, as it would seem that all errors of law by administrative authorities go to jurisdiction; see *Re Racal Communications* [1981] AC 374, [1980] 2 All ER 634, HL per Lord Diplock.

permission, judicial review is the only remedy (apart from complaints to the local ombudsman) and this accounts for its growing use and acceptance by the courts as a viable means of challenge.

In most cases judicial review has been used to challenge positive decisions but as Lord Diplock's definition in the GCHQ case indicates, abstention from actions is also susceptible to judicial review. Thus the courts have accepted that the Secretary of State's decisions not to exercise his call-in powers under s 35 can be the subject of an application for judicial review.[5] However, Kerr LJ in the Court of Appeal has emphasised that the room for review was limited because of the unqualified terms of the statutory discretion.[6] A decision by the Secretary of State, in a highways case, not to hold an inquiry has been the subject of a successful application for judicial review[7] and in *R v Stroud District Council, ex p Goodenough*[8] Woolf J held that there had been a failure to consider using statutory powers to repair or compulsorily purchase certain listed buildings.

Where the action has no direct legal consequences, the position is more doubtful but review may nevertheless lie. In *R v Worthing Borough Council, ex p Burch*[9] Mann J quashed an 'opinion' of the Secretary of State for the Environment that he would have granted planning permission for development of Crown Land.[10] The House of Lords decision in *Gillick v West Norfolk and Wisbech Area Health Authority*[11] would also suggest that Government circulars or policy guidance documents might themselves be the subject of review. Certainly *Gillick* was used by Woolf J in *R v Secretary of State for the Environment, ex p Greater London Council*[12] to justify the view that 'the court has jurisdiction to grant declarations without there being any decision yet made by a public body which falls clearly within this passage of Lord Diplock's speech [In the GCHQ case, see above, p 588]'. In that case Woolf J refused to grant a declaration that the inspector's reasoning behind a decision was invalid; the Greater London Council were not able to use s 245 to attack the actual decision since it was in line with their views and so they were not 'a person aggrieved'. The Council, however disagreed with part of the reasoning and did not want it applied in future cases. Woolf J, however, felt that judicial review was not an appropriate remedy as the Greater London Council could oppose any future grants of permission and the reasoning of inspectors did not create a binding precedent.

In conclusion, the scope of judicial review is still being worked out but it provides a flexible and useful remedy in the context of the planning legislation where the statutory provisions for recourse to the courts are either not available or inappropriate.

5 See *R v Secretary of State for the Environment, ex p Newprop* [1983] JPL 386; and *Rhys Williams v Secretary of State for Wales* [1985] JPL 29, CA. Also see Scots decision of *Lakin Ltd v Secretary of State for Scotland* 1988 SLT 780.
6 See *Rhys Williams v Secretary of State for Wales* [1985] JPL 29, at p 33.
7 See *Binney and Anscomb v Secretary of State for the Environment* [1984] JPL 871.
8 (1980) 43 P & CR 59.
9 [1984] JPL 261.
10 See now the procedures set out in the Town and Country Planning Act 1984: described at p 181.
11 [1986] AC 112, [1985] 3 All ER 402.
12 (1985) Times, 30 December.

The procedural rules

Standing. An application for judicial review may be rejected on the grounds that the applicant has not got sufficient interest in the subject matter. In this regard there existed important distinctions between the prerogative orders and the private law remedies. In the case of the private law remedies the courts tended to insist that the applicant show a legal right or at least that he had been caused special damage. Thus in *Gregory v Camden London Borough Council*[13] a neighbour was refused a declaration that a grant of planning permission was invalid on the grounds that the Town and Country Planning legislation did not give any rights to individual members of the public.[14] In contrast with the prerogative orders, although the approach varied between the particular orders, it was normally sufficient for the applicant to show that he had been adversely affected and was thus a 'person aggrieved'.[15]

The new wording of Order 53 and s 31 of the Supreme Court Act 1981 both direct that the court shall not grant leave 'unless it considers that the appellant has a sufficient interest in the matter to which the application relates.' This test of 'sufficient interest' would at first seem to be aimed at the threshold stage of getting leave to proceed with the application but in the House of Lords decision of *IRC v National Federation of Self-Employed and Small Businesses Ltd*[16] it was generally accepted that the test of sufficient interest applies to the full hearing stage and that the test of standing at the threshold stage was very light.[17] However, there remains considerable confusion as to exactly what is meant by 'sufficient interest' and whether the test varies according to what remedy is being requested. With respect to the first question, it seems that it will depend not only on the nature of the particular subject matter; ie does the legislative scheme suggest that individuals have a right to ensure that the law is upheld[18] but also on the seriousness and strength of the particular allegations.[19] As to the second question, while Lord Diplock considered there should be only one approach to standing for all the remedies[20] there is support in the other speeches of the law lords for the view that old differences may re-emerge.[1]

In the specific context of town and country planning, the courts have now accepted that local residents do have 'sufficient interest' to apply for the order of *certiorari* to be used to quash invalid grants of planning permission or listed building consent. In *Covent Garden Community Association Ltd v Greater London Council*[2] Woolf J argued that it was recognised that decisions on planning matters could materially affect residents as they were allowed to

---

13 [1966] 2 All ER 196, [1966] 1 WLR 899.
14 This approach has been taken by the Scots courts; see *Simpson v Edinburgh Corpn* 1960 SC 313 and *Bellway Ltd v Strathclyde Regional Council* 1979 SC 92.
15 See *R. v Hendon RDC, ex p Chorley* [1933] 2 KB 696, but see also *R v Bradford-on-Avon UDC, ex p Boulton* [1964] 2 All ER 696, [1964] 1 WLR 1136.
16 [1982] AC 617, [1981] 2 All ER 93.
17 Lord Diplock, Lord Scarman and to a lesser extent Lord Fraser thought that at the threshold stage it was enough for the plaintiff to show he had an arguable case.
18 per Lord Fraser at p 646D.
19 per Lord Diplock at p 644D.
20 see p 639C
1 *R v Felixstowe Justices, ex p Leigh* [1987] QB 582, [1987] 1 All ER 551 would suggest that the courts may refuse a particular remedy because of the nature of the applicant.
2 [1981] JPL 183.

appear and be heard at public inquiries and their representations were considered in deciding whether to grant permission. He therefore '. . . was quite satisfied that the applicants [the Covent Garden Community Association] had sufficient interest and that it would be out of accord with the general approach to questions of *locus standi* in prerogative proceedings to decide that the applicants had not a right to make the application.' Then in *R v Hammersmith and Fulham Borough Council, ex p People Before Profit Ltd*[3] Comyn J, equating a right to object at public inquiry with standing to apply for judicial review, stated 'In his judgment, a person was entitled to object in a planning matter if he had a legitimate bona fide reason. He did not have to be a ratepayer. He did not have to be a resident. But he was not to be an officious bystander or an officious busybody. He must have what any reasonable person would have said was a legitimate interest in being heard in objection. One could not set down elaborate and comprehensive rules about that because anyone might have a legitimate bona fide interest in places far removed from where they lived. They might be places where people went on holiday, they might be places where people went for sporting events; they might be places which people felt were so much in the national interest that they ought to have been heard about them as a citizen of the country.'[4]

This very wide view of standing in planning gets close to giving a citizen's right to ensure that planning decisions are made validly. Certainly it will be enough for the applicant to be able to show that he will be affected by the decision but it has recently been held that simply interested members of the public do not have standing.[5]

All the above cases concerned applications for judicial review where the applicant was seeking to have the decision quashed by the prerogative order of *certiorari*. It could be that the rules on standing could be different if a declaration or injunction were to be sought by way of judicial review. In the Covent Garden case, Woolf J expressed the view that it was extremely doubtful whether the applicants would have had any *locus standi* to bring legal proceedings in Chancery for a declaration and injunction. He further pointed out that changes in the Order could not alter the substantive law on standing. However, since then the 1981 Act has put the changes on a statutory basis and it would seem sterile and over technical to hold that where a declaration was the appropriate remedy, the test as to standing should be the same as if an action for declaration had been brought separately. In many cases where an applicant has no direct legal rights, it might be more appropriate to grant a declaration than say the prerogative order of *mandamus*.[6] In *Steeples v Derbyshire County Council*[7] Webster J even went as far as to hold that the same rules as to standing applied whether a declaration was sought by way of judicial review under Order 53 or by way of the court's pre-existing power to grant a declaration under Order 15, r 16.

---

3   [1981] JPL 869.
4   Comyn J then went on to rule that where objectors had appeared at the inquiry as an unincorporated association, their later incorporation as a limited company did not take away their right of access to the courts.
5   See *R v Secretary of State for the Environment ex p Rose Theatre Trust No 2* [1989] EGCS 107.
6   See *R v Felixstowe Justices, ex p Leigh* [1987] QB 582, [1987] 1 All ER 551.
7   [1984] 3 All ER 468, [1985] 1 WLR 256.

However, in *Barrs v Bethell*[8] Webster J's approach was repudiated by Warner J and the exclusivity between the two types of remedy imposed by *O'Reilly v Mackman* would suggest that different approaches to declaration should apply depending whether it is being used in a public law or private law context.

Need for arguable case. The fact that leave is required before an application for judicial review goes to a full hearing protects public bodies against frivolous and vexatious litigation. The initial application can be made without the party subject to the application being present but the court may adjourn to allow representation. Rule 3, which specifies that leave is required, does not provide any standard as to when consent is to be given or refused. In this regard in *Re Friends of the Earth*[9] Lord Donaldson MR ruled that 'If *prima facie* there was an arguable case, subject to questions of time and promptitude, leave should be granted. If there was no arguable case leave should not be granted'. The use of the term '*prima facie*' probably relates to the facts and so at this stage it will be presumed that the facts are as alleged and the main question will be whether, given those facts there is an arguable case in law. Otherwise the courts themselves have given no clear guidance as to what is meant by arguable and opinions as to what is or is not arguable can differ.[10] Where leave is refused, a renewed application can be made to the Court of Appeal or if the first application was made on paper, ie no oral hearing, a renewed application can be made to another single judge sitting in open court.[11] It seems at least in civil matters that there is no right of appeal either from a refusal at High Court or Court of Appeal level.[12]

The time limits. Order 53, r 4(1) prescribes that a judicial review application shall be made within three months from the date when grounds for the application first arose. This has been interpreted as the application for leave to apply rather than the substantive application itself. This three month period is not absolute either way. Rule 4(1) also states that the application 'shall be made promptly' and so leave to proceed may be refused, even if the application is made within the three month period, if there is no good reason why it should not have been made earlier. Equally, even if the application is made after three months have elapsed, provision is made for extending the period if the court considers there is good reason. For example in *R v Stratford-on-Avon Borough Council, ex p Jackson*[13] the Court of Appeal, where an application for leave was lodged eight months after the resolution granting planning permission (which was the decision being challenged), concluded that there was 'good reason' for extending the period as the delay had been caused by difficulty in obtaining legal aid.

In addition, s 31(1) of the Supreme Court Act 1981 provides that both leave to apply and relief may be refused if there has been undue delay in the making of the application for judicial review and the court considers that

---

8 [1982] Ch 294, [1982] 1 All ER 106; also *Ashby v Ebdon* [1985] Ch 394, [1984] 3 All ER 869.
9 [1988] JPL 93.
10 See *Re Friends of the Earth*, above, where Kennedy J considered the grounds of the applicable to be 'arguable' but an unanimous of Court of Appeal disagreed.
11 Rule 3(4).
12 See *Re Poh* [1983] 1 All ER 287, [1983] 1 WLR 2, HL.
13 [1985] 3 All ER 769, [1985] 1 WLR 1319.

granting relief would be likely to cause substantial hardship to, or substantially prejudice the rights of any person or would be detrimental to good administration. In the Stratford-on-Avon decision, the court held this provision gave a general discretion and it was not affected by a finding that there was good reason for the delay. So where there has been 'undue delay', either because the application had not been made promptly or within three months, relief can be refused even if there is good cause for the delay.

Evidence. Evidence is submitted in advance of the full hearing by way of affidavits. So normally the full hearing is confined to oral argument on matters of law. However, the new form of Order 53 does expressly provide for both discovery of documents, the administration of interrogatories and the cross-examination of deponents to affidavits (r 8). In all these cases application must be made which should be granted if the justice of the case so requires. Lord Diplock in *O'Reilly v Mackman*[14] therefore claimed that the old disadvantage, which might in the past have resulted in an applicant not being able to seek justice, no longer applied. Yet in practice the courts have the same reluctance to order discovery or cross-examination as they have with regard to the statutory rights of challenge provided by the 1971 Act (see p 577 above).

The grounds of review. In theory there are fundamental differences between judicial review and a right of appeal or review provided by a statute. This is because although the actual remedy of the application for judicial review has now been put on a statutory basis (s 31 of the Supreme Court Act 1981) the grounds of review are not set out in any statute and are essentially a creation of the judiciary. The starting point is the doctrine of *ultra vires* which requires that bodies which exercise powers conferred by Act of Parliament are entitled to act only within the limits express or implied of those powers. The High Court asserts the constitutional right to determine those statutory limits. From this limited constitutional basis the courts have grafted on and evolved principles of procedural fairness and abuse of power which have almost taken on a life of their own. Nevertheless, the courts are constantly aware that they have no right to interfere with the merits of policy decisions. The courts' function is not to re-evaluate the judgments of the relevant authority. Nor should the courts normally become concerned with the reassessment or reinterpretation of the facts upon which an act or decision is based. In contrast, where Parliament confers a right of appeal on a court, it may vest in the court the jurisdiction to correct not only errors of law of all types but errors of fact or to reach a different decision on the basis of a different evaluation of the facts in the matter before it. The court may even be authorised to substitute its own decision for that made initially by the administrative authority.

In the event, as has been seen, the provisions in the 1971 Act only give the courts the power to intervene on what are strictly legal grounds. Further, in practice, there is very little difference between the grounds of review given to the courts by statute and the grounds on which the courts intervene in an application for judicial review. This is because it now seems settled law that, at least with regard to tribunals and administrative authorities, there is a

14 [1983] 2 AC 237, [1982] 3 All ER 1124, HL.

presumption that *all* errors of law go to jurisdiction. In *Re Racal Communications Ltd*[15] Lord Diplock argued that

'Any error of law that could be shown to have been made by them in the course of reaching their decision on matters of fact or of administrative policy would result in their having asked themselves the wrong question with the result that the decision they reached would be a nullity.'

If this statement of the law is correct, the grounds of review of s 245 (the action is not within the powers of this Act') and s 246 ('on a point of law') are substantially no wider or narrower than the normal grounds on which an application for judicial review can be based. This view is strengthened by the fact that it is equally accepted that the order of *certiorari* lies to correct all errors of law on the record and that the 'record' may even be interpreted as including oral evidence.[16] Of course, in the case of decisions and resolutions of local planning authorities, where there does not exist a full 'record' such as an inspector's report or decision letter, it may be difficult for the applicant to unearth the 'error of law'; especially if the courts are reluctant to allow discovery and cross-examination.[17]

On the other hand it may well be that the second ground of s 245; 'that any of the relevant requirements have not been complied with', could be broader than both the grounds for judicial review and s 246. This is because a mere failure to comply with a statutory procedure may not be automatically regarded as an error of law and so will not in itself invalidate the decision or action. The courts in the past have distinguished between statutory procedures which are mandatory, where a failure to comply nullifies the decision, and those which are directory, where failure does not invalidate. So it is possible that a court could intervene under s 245 for a breach of a requirement such as a duty to give reasons, where they could not intervene under an application for judicial review. However, under s 245 the courts can only quash if they are satisfied that the interests of the applicant have been substantially prejudiced while decisions such as *Main v Swansea City Council*[18] and *R v Lambeth London Borough Council, ex p Sharp*[19] show that the courts are increasingly abandoning the mandatory/directory dichotomy with respect to applications for judicial review and instead are focusing on contextual factors such as the existence or lack of substantial prejudice.

In conclusion, the grounds on which the courts can intervene on an application for judicial review are essentially the same as on an application under s 245 and many of the principles set out by Forbes J with regard to s 245 in *Seddon Properties* (see p 570) could equally be referring to an application for judicial review.

15 [1981] AC 374, [1980] 2 All ER 634, HL.
16 See *R v Northumberland Compensation Appeal Tribunal, ex p Shaw* [1952] 1 KB 338, [1952] 1 All ER 122, CA; *R v Crown Court at Knightsbridge, ex p International Sporting Club* [1982] QB 304 [1981] 3 All ER 417, *R v Southampton Justices, ex p Green* [1976] QB 11, [1975] 2 All ER 1073 and *R v Crown Court at Knightsbridge, ex p Aspinall Curzon* (1982) Times, 16 December.
17 But see *R v Lancashire County Council, ex p Huddleston* [1986] 2 All ER 941, CA which suggests courts in future could be more willing to use their powers.
18 (1984) 49 P & CR 26, CA.
19 [1987] JPL 440, CA.

The remedies. The new form that Order 53 takes gives the applicant and the court considerable flexibility. This is because an applicant can claim any permutation of the three prerogative orders of *certiorari, prohibition* and *mandamus* and the private law remedies of declaration, injunction and damages; Order 53 r 2. Thus, where a local planning authority has acted illegally the order of *certiorari* could be used to formally quash the action or alternatively a declaration could be sought that the action was unlawful. The distinction between quashing a decision and declaring it invalid is now more technical than real, since the distinction between jurisdictional and non-jurisdictional errors of law has virtually disappeared. Indeed, it might seem rather futile to go through the exercise of quashing a decision which is in law a nullity. It is nevertheless at least necessary for the court to formally declare it to be a nullity as the courts have held that orders and the like cannot be presumed to be invalid until held to be so by a court of proper jurisdiction.[20] Despite the considerable overlap between *certiorari* and declaration in terms of effect, declaration may be at times the more appropriate remedy. For example, where all that is being sought is the correct interpretation of the meaning of a grant of planning permission, a declaration would clearly be the appropriate remedy.[1] It might also be the more appropriate remedy to test the validity of a statement which did not have any direct legal consequences.[2]

In the case where a local planning authority was threatening to act illegally or to execute an illegal decision, ie send out an invalid grant of permission, *prohibition* would be the appropriate remedy. It has rarely been used in a planning context but it was sought unsuccessfully in *Allen v Corpn of the City of London*[3] to try to restrain the Corporation from determining a planning application in advance of a local public inquiry into a draft local plan. An injunction could be used to achieve the same result.

Mandamus requires a public body to perform a public duty by ordering the body to hear and determine according to law. In *R v Hillingdon London Borough Council, ex p Royco Homes Ltd.*[4] the applicants not only sought *certiorari* to quash the decision imposing the conditions but also an order of *mandamus* to compel the authority to determine the application according to law. The Divisional Court adjourned the application for *mandamus* in order to allow the authority time to reconsider the application, which was then granted without the offending conditions. There is now no need to seek *mandamus* in such circumstances as Order 53 provides that where the court has made an order of *certiorari* quashing a decision the court may, in addition, remit the matter back to the authority with a direction to reconsider it and reach a decision in accordance with the findings of the court; r 9(4). However, *mandamus* has been used to require the Secretary of State to hear an appeal which had been declined for lack of jurisdiction.[5]

---

20 See *Hoffman la–Roche & Co v Secretary of State for Trade and Industry* [1975] AC 295 and Wade's Administrative Law 6th edn. pp 564–643.
1 See for example *Slough Estates v Slough Borough Council (No 2)* [1971] AC 958, [1970] 2 All ER 216.
2 For example, a statement in Government circular; see *R v Worthing Borough Council ex p Burch* [1984] JPL 261, or the reasoning in an inspector's decision; see *R v Secretary of State for the Environment, ex p Greater London Council* (1985) *Times*, 30 December.
3 [1981] JPL 685.
4 [1974] QB 720, [1974] 2 All ER 643.
5 *R v Secretary of State for the Environment, ex p Percy Bilton Industrial Properties Ltd* (1975) 31 P & CR 154.

Mandamus could also be used to compel a local planning authority to comply with statutory procedures. Thus in the Scots decision of *Bovis Homes (Scotland) Ltd v Inverclyde District Council*[6] the Court of Session granted a declaration that the planning authority were bound to determine an application for approval of reserved matters. The applicants could have appealed against the deemed refusal because the time limit had elapsed but the court concluded that they did not have to pursue this statutory remedy. It might be similarly possible to enforce by *mandamus* a local planning authority's duty to give reasons for refusing permission.[7]

Damages can also be sought under an application for judicial review but must be specifically claimed in the application for leave to proceed; Order 53 r 7. It is also only available where there is a right to damages in private law and even then should only be claimed by way of judicial review where the right to damages is subsidiary to or mixed up with a public law matter. Indeed, in *Davy v Spelthorne Borough Council*[8] Lord Wilberforce argued that unless judicial review would lie in its own right, damages could not be given.

This last point emphasises that damages by way of judicial review is not an independent remedy; ie it cannot stand by itself. In the case of declaration and injunction these remedies can only be granted where the court considers it would be just and convenient having regard to the nature of the matters in respect of which relief may be granted by a prerogative order. However, Hodgson J in *R v Bromley London Borough Council, ex p Lambeth London Borough Council*[9] rejected the argument that a declaration could not be awarded on an application for judicial review unless one of the prerogative orders could have been and had, in fact, been claimed in the application. Hodgson J held that it was sufficient that the application was '. . . the sort of thing to which a prerogative order could apply.' The remedies of declaration and injunction are not therefore merely ancillary to the prerogative orders. However, where a declaration, injunction or damages are sought the court may order the proceedings to continue as if they had been begun by writ; Order 53, r 9(5). The wording of r 9(5) suggests that this applies when otherwise the application would have to be refused on the grounds that it is a private law matter and should have been started as a private law action.

Private actions: declarations and injunctions. Neither Order 53 nor s 31 of the Supreme Court Act 1981 expressly provides that the application for judicial review shall be the exclusive procedure available by which the remedies of declaration and injunction may be obtained to protect public law rights. However, in *O'Reilly v Mackman*[10] Lord Diplock, in a speech which was agreed with by the rest of their Lordships, laid down that as a general rule it would be contrary to public policy, and as such an abuse of the process of the court, to permit such public law rights to be protected by way of an ordinary action. This means that today you should not seek a declaration that a grant

6 1982 SLT 473, [1983] JPL 171.
7 Such a duty has been held to be mandatory even though failure does not automatically invalidate the decision; *Brayhead (Ascot) Ltd v Berkshire County Council* [1964] 2 QB 303.
8 [1984] AC 262.
9 (1984) *Times*, 16 June.
10 [1983] 2 AC 237.

of planning permission was invalid as an alternative to an application for judicial review.[11]

However, Lord Diplock accepted that there would be exceptions to this principle and recent decisions of the House of Lords have made inroads into the exclusivity of Order 53. In particular, *Davy v Spelthorne Borough Council*[12] has established that it will not be an abuse of court to bring an ordinary action just because this action indirectly raises public law matters. Most significantly, Lord Wilberforce emphasised that the onus is on the person wishing to have the ordinary action struck out to show not only that the claim in question could have been brought by way of judicial review but that it *should* have been so commenced. Thus, in the context of the Town and Country Planning legislation, it is submitted that it would not be an abuse of court for an owner of land to bring an ordinary action to obtain a declaration as to the meaning of a planning permission or some other decision or order. Problems of interpretation can arise long after it will be too late to seek an application for judicial review and s 53 cannot be used to seek an opinion on the construction of a planning permission.[13] In such a case there would seem to be none of the public policy reasons for holding it to be an abuse, as the public authority is not under attack and it is primarily a private law matter of clarifying the exact rights belonging to a piece of land. It would be different if the applicant was using the action to challenge the validity of actions taken by a local planning authority under a permission.[14] Surprisingly, there would seem to be no recent authority on the matter. In *Wivenhoe Port Ltd v Colchester Borough Council*[15] the Court of Appeal considered an application for a declaration that a grant of permission authorised a building operation. However, the court did not go into the question of the appropriateness of the procedure and there would seem to have been no attempt to strike out the action.[16] Where it is still appropriate to seek declaration by ordinary action rather than by way of judicial review, it would seem to follow that the old rules governing ordinary actions should apply. So, despite Webster J's views in *Steeples v Derbyshire County Council*[17] to have standing the applicant would have to show a legal right or at least special damage.[18]

There would not seem to be much scope for bringing an injunction as an ordinary action to stop local authorities or other public bodies carrying out their functions under the planning legislation.[19] Such actions would almost certainly come within the *O'Reilly v Mackman* principle and be an abuse of process.[20]

---

11 *Pyx Granite Co Ltd v Ministry of Housing and Local Government* [1960] AC 260, [1959] 3 All ER 1, HL provides an example of a declaration being granted in the past.
12 [1984] AC 262, [1983] 3 All ER 278, HL.
13 *East Suffolk County Council v Secretary of State for the Environment* (1972) 70 LGR 595.
14 As in the case of *Irlan Brick Co Ltd v Warrington Borough Council* [1982] JPL 709.
15 [1982] JPL 396, CA.
16 The speeches in *O'Reilly v Mackman* were handed down on 25 November 1982 and the Court of Appeal's judgement was made on 10 May 1983.
17 [1984] 3 All ER 468, [1985] 1 WLR 256.
18 See on this *Barrs v Bethell* [1982] Ch 294, [1982] 1 All ER 106.
19 See *Lever Finance Ltd v Westminster (City) London Borough Council* [1971] 1 QB 222, [1970] 3 All ER 496 for an example of an injunction being granted to restrain an enforcement notice being served.
20 In *Davy v Spelthorne Borough Council* [1984] AC 262, [1983] 3 All ER 278 the application for an injunction to prevent the service of an enforcement notice was struck out.

Damages. An action for damages is almost by definition a private law matter. In *Davy v Spelthorne Borough Council*[1] the House of Lords held that it is not an abuse of process to seek damages by way of an ordinary action just because it would involve consideration of questions of public law. In this case, the applicant claimed damages from the local planning authority on the grounds that he had been negligently advised by them on his rights under the Town and Country Planning Act 1971 and that as a result he had lost his chance of appealing against an enforcement notice. So if the plaintiff had been able to prove negligence the assessment of damages would have involved the court in judging the chances of his appeal succeeding, if it had been made. It was held that such a peripheral public law element did not mean that the applicant ought to have proceeded by way of an application for judicial review. Indeed, Lord Wilberforce considered that the claim could not have been pursued under s 53. It would, however, be different if any right to damages first turned or was dependent on an issue of public law, which involved questioning the validity of the actions of a public authority.[2] In such a case the proper procedure would be first to settle the public law issue directly by an application for judicial review.

Of more practical importance is the question of whether public bodies do owe a duty of care while exercising their functions under the planning legislation. Public bodies are vicariously liable for the torts of their employees carried out in the course of their employment.[3] This means that a local planning authority could be sued in negligence if one of their officials were to be in breach of one of the standard duties of care which apply to all citizens. More problematic is the question of whether the law either imposes a duty of care on local planning authorities as to the way they exercise their various statutory powers,[4] or whether damages can be claimed for breach of their statutory duties. The Court of Appeal's decision in *Strable v Borough Council of Dartford*[5] would indicate that no liability arises in either case. Stephenson LJ giving a judgment, with which Donaldson LJ and Sir David Cairns agreed, stated '... it seemed plain to him. ... that in this field an authority's duties, could not be made the subject of suits by individual property owners who were dissatisfied with its decisions in matters of administrative planning'.[6] Also, while it has been accepted that the duty of care which applies to the exercise of powers under the building legislation should in principle apply to the power of approving plans for development in a planning application,[7] recent House of Lords decisions have substantially restricted the application of the principle in *Anns v London Borough of Merton*.[8] In particular, in *Curran v Northern Ireland Co-ownership Housing*

1 *Ibid.*
2 As in *Cocks v Thanet District Council* [1983] 2 AC 286, [1982] 3 All ER 1135 where the right to damages depended on whether the local authority were correct in holding that the person was voluntarily homeless. Also see *Guevara v Hounslow London Borough Council* (1987) Times, 17 April.
3 *Mersey Docks and Harbour Board v Gibbs* (1886) LR 1 HL 93.
4 On the lines of *Anns v London Borough of Merton* [1978] AC 728, [1977] 2 All ER 492.
5 [1984] JPL 329.
6 In this Stephenson LJ was following the judgment of Judge Wingate Saul in *Evans v LCC* (1960) 12 P & CR 172.
7 *Lyons v F W Booth (Contractors) Ltd and Maidstone Borough Council* (1982) 262 Estates Gazette 981; see also *Ravenseft Properties Ltd v British Gas Corpn* 1981 SPLP 76.
8 [1978] AC 728, [1977] 2 All ER 492.

Association Ltd[9] Lord Bridge laid down important conditions for the application of the principle and in the Privy Council decision of *Yuen Kun Yen v A-G of Hong Kong*[10] the court emphasised that foreseeability of injury was not itself sufficient to found a duty of care and that you require a close and direct relationship between the parties.

Therefore all the indications are that local authorities and other public bodies are not under a duty of care, when exercising their functions as planning authorities.[11]

Further, no right to damages arises because an action of a public body is found to be an invalid.[12] This means that a developer cannot obtain damages even though he may have been caused financial loss by an invalid refusal of planning permission. It would be different if it could be shown that the refusal was malicious or that the authority knew that it was acting invalidly.[13] There is also some authority that a local planning authority could be liable for negligent mis-statements and advice made by its officials. In *Tesco Stores Ltd v Taff-Ely Borough Council*[14] Beldam J seems to have accepted that in principle the council were liable for any loss caused by their Town Clerk negligently issuing a grant of planning permission, when he had no authority to issue such a grant. The judge, however, went on to hold that no damages could be recovered because Tesco knew of the circumstances under which the notice was issued.[15]

Indirect challenge. The courts can rule on the validity of the actions of a public authority indirectly or collaterally; that is the validity may have to be determined in the course of a civil or criminal proceeding. In the context of planning, it is the application of the criminal law which will more often cause such issues. Thus in *R v Jenner*[16] the Court of Appeal ruled that in a criminal prosecution for failure to comply with the terms of a stop notice, the defence could be raised that the stop notice could not prohibit the activities because they had been commenced more than twelve months before the service of the notice. In giving judgment Watkins LJ went out of his way to make clear that the court in so doing would not be holding that the notice itself was invalid but rather holding that the defendant was not guilty of a criminal offence. However, in the case of enforcement notices, the criminal courts will directly rule on the validity of the notices; at least on grounds which are not excluded by s 243.

Support for this approach can be found in Watkins LJ's judgment in *Scarborough Borough Council v Adams*[17] where he held that it was open to persons being prosecuted to argue that an enforcement notice is a nullity or invalid on grounds other than those set out in s 88(2).

---

9 [1987] AC 718, [1987] 2 All ER 13.
10 [1988] AC 175, [1987] 2 All ER 705.
11 For a recent decision in this regard, see *Ryeford Homes Ltd v Sevenoaks District Council* [1989] NLJR 255.
12 *Dunlop v Woollahra Municipal Council* [1982] AC 158, [1981] 1 All ER 1202.
13 See *Bourgoin SA v Ministry of Agriculture* [1986] QB 716, [1985] 3 All ER 585.
14 (1983) 133 NLJ 577.
15 For an account of the case; see C Crawford 'Taff-Ely Revisited—the Negligence Aspect' (1983) 267 EG 579.
16 [1983] 2 All ER 46, [1983] 1 WLR 873.
17 (1983) 47 P & CR 133.

Since *O'Reilly v Mackman*[18] it could, of course, be argued that this was an abuse of process but in *Wandsworth London Borough Council v Winder*[19] the House of Lords unanimously took the view that Order 53 procedure was not intended to curtail or remove a citizen's actionable rights and that, therefore, it could not be an abuse to raise issues relating to such rights as a defence to a civil action even where that resulted in a challenge to the validity of the decision of a public authority. In *Quietlynn Ltd v Plymouth City Council*[20] Webster J argued that where, in proceedings before magistrates, a *bona fide* challenge to the validity of a local authority decision was made, the proceedings should be adjourned to enable an application for judicial review to be made and determined. However, in the later case of *R v Reading Crown Court, ex p Hutchinson*[1] Lloyd LJ disapproved of this approach and stated, 'If the validity of a decision of a local authority is an essential element in the proof of the crime alleged, then I can see no reason why it should not be challenged in the magistrates or Crown Court as the case may be'. Of course, a decision of a magistrates court on the validity of the decision will not have much standing but as Lloyd LJ pointed out in *Hutchinson* an appeal can be made by way of case stated to the Divisional Court who can then make an authoritative ruling. Such an appeal would be just as quick and no more expensive than an application for judicial review.

E APPEALS TO MAGISTRATES AND CROWN COURTS

Very occasionally the 1971 Act provides for a right to appeal to the magistrates' court and then to the Crown Court. Indeed, prior to the Caravan Sites and Control of Development Act 1960, the recipient of an enforcement notice could appeal to the magistrates, but now the only statutory right of appeal is to the Secretary of State; see above p 339. Section 105 gives certain persons a right to appeal against notices as to waste land under s 65 and there is a further right of appeal to the Crown Court under s 106. There is also a provision in s 114 which enables an application to be made to the magistrates' court to obtain an order staying further proceedings on a compulsory purchase order relating to a listed building which is in disrepair. The grounds on which the magistrate can intervene in both cases predominantly turns on matters of fact and this explains their jurisdiction; though in the case of notices under s 65 it might seem simpler to give a right of appeal to the Secretary of State.

18 *Ibid.*
19 [1985] AC 461, [1984] 3 All ER 976.
20 [1988] QB 114, [1987] 3 WLR 189.
 1 [1988] QB 384, [1988] 1 All ER 333.

INDEX